CAPON'S
MARKETING
FRAMEWORK

3rd edition

**AXCESS
CAPON**

www.axcesscapon.com

To access O-codes, go to **www.ocodes.com**

ALSO BY NOEL CAPON

MARKETING

*†‡ *Managing Marketing in the 21st Century* (3rd Edition)

‡ *The Virgin Marketer* (3rd Edition)

* *Marketing for China's Managers: Current and Future Century* (2nd Edition) with Y. Zheng and W. Burgers

* *The Marketing Mavens*

Total Integrated Marketing (with James M. Hulbert)

The Asian Marketing Casebook (with W. Van Honacker)

The Marketing of Financial Services: A Book of Cases

SALES AND ACCOUNT MANAGEMENT

Case Studies in Key, Strategic, and Global Account Management (with C. Senn)

Sales Eats First (with G.S. Tubridy)

Strategic Account Strategy

Managing Global Accounts (with D. Potter and F. Schíndler)

§ *Key Account Management and Planning*

* also published in Chinese

† also published in Spanish

‡ also published in Russian

§ also published in German

CAPON'S MARKETING FRAMEWORK

Noel Capon

Graduate School of Business

Columbia University

New York, NY

Library of Congress Cataloging-in-Publication Data

Capon, Noel
   Capon's Marketing Framework / Noel Capon — 3rd edition
      p. cm.
   Includes index
   ISBN 978-0-9882902-0-4
      1. Capon's—Marketing.   I. Title: Capon's marketing framework.

Editor: Lyn Maize
Copy Editor: Christy Goldfinch
Permissions Editor: Sandra Lord
Book / Cover Design: Anna Botelho

Credits and acknowledgements are a continuation of the copyright page; they are on pages xxi, C1, and C2.

DEDICATION

To Marvela, Elmira,

Alaina, and Noel.

ABOUT THE AUTHOR

 **NOEL CAPON** IS THE R. C. KOPF PROFESSOR of International Marketing and past Chair of the Marketing Division, Graduate School of Business, Columbia University. Educated primarily in Great Britain, Professor Capon earned B.Sc. and Ph.D. degrees in Chemistry from University College, London University. He also received degrees in Business Administration from Manchester (Dip. BA), Harvard (MBA), and Columbia Business School (Ph.D.).

Professor Capon joined the Columbia Business School faculty in 1979. Previously he served on the faculty of, and received tenure from, the University of California – Graduate School of Management, UCLA. He has taught and held faculty positions at Harvard Business School; Australia — Monash University; England — Bradford Management Centre and Manchester Business School; France — INSEAD; Hong Kong — The Hong Kong University of Science and Technology (HKUST); China — China European International Business School (CEIBS — Shanghai); and India — Indian School of Business (ISB — Hyderabad). Professor Capon currently holds the position of Distinguished Visiting Professor at Manchester Business School.

Professor Capon has published more than 60 refereed articles and book chapters, and is editor for sections on Marketing, and Sales Management and Distribution, in the *AMA Management Handbook* (1994). He has published more than 20 books, including *Corporate Strategic Planning*, a major study of the planning practices of major U.S. manufacturing corporations (Columbia University Press 1988); *The Marketing of Financial Services: A Book of Cases* (Prentice-Hall 1992); *Planning the Development of Builders, Leaders, and Managers of Twenty First Century Business* (Kluwer 1996) on the curriculum review process at Columbia Business School; *Why Some Firms Perform Better than Others: Towards a More Integrative Explanation* (Kluwer 1996) on the underpinnings of superior corporate financial performance; *The Asian Marketing Casebook* (Prentice Hall 1999); *Key Account Management and Planning* (Free Press 2001); *Total Integrated Marketing* (Free Press 2003); *The Marketing Mavens* (Crown Business 2007); *Managing Global Accounts* (Wessex 2008); *Strategic Account Strategy* (Wessex 2011); *Sales Eats First* (Wessex 2011); and *Case Studies in Managing Key, Strategic, and Global Customers* (Wessex 2012).

Professor Capon contributes extensively to Columbia Business School's Executive Education. He is the Founding Director of *Managing Strategic Accounts* and the *Global Account Manager Certification* program in conjunction with St. Gallen University (Switzerland). He teaches on Columbia's *Full-time MBA and Executive MBA* (EMBA) programs and its partner program with London Business School. He founded and directed the Advanced Marketing Management Program in conjunction with CEIBS. He also designs, directs, and teaches in numerous custom programs for major corporations globally. In 2001, Professor Capon cofounded The Chief Sales Executive Forum, offering multiple educational opportunities for sales and account management leaders.

Professor Capon's textbooks include *Managing Marketing in the 21st Century* (3rd edition) (Wessex 2012) and *Capon's Marketing Framework* (3rd edition) (Wessex 2013); *The Virgin Marketer* (Wessex 2013) is a companion market planning workbook. Several Student Study Guides are also available. Professor Capon's textbooks are also published in Chinese, Russian, and Spanish.

TABLE OF CONTENTS IN BRIEF

TABLE OF CONTENTS IN DETAIL

PREFACE

In *Capon's Marketing Framework* you will learn about marketing language, logic, strategy, and implementation. To get us off to a good start, we'll begin by providing you the book's positioning.

POSITIONING

As you will learn in Chapter 9, positioning comprises four elements — customer targets, competitor targets, value proposition, and reasons to believe. The positioning for *Capon's Marketing Framework* is:

- **Customer targets.** Marketing instructors who specify texts for undergraduate and graduate marketing courses, and the students who will learn to practice marketing in these courses.

- **Competitor targets.** All textbooks entitled *Marketing Management*, or some close approximation, for use in undergraduate and graduate marketing courses.

- **Value proposition.** *Capon's Marketing Framework* supports instructors in their quest to enhance students' grasp of marketing. Students learn how to successfully address simple and complex marketing problems. They learn *what to do* and *how to do it*, and how to infuse their organizations with a customer-focused view of business. And they pay a fraction of the price of traditional textbooks.

- **Reason to believe.** Professor Capon is among the world's most experienced marketing educators, from one of the world's leading business schools. The author has extensive experience educating students at all levels of business degree programs, as well as senior and mid-level executives in major corporations globally.

PURPOSE

Capon's Marketing Framework is about understanding how to develop market strategy, implement market offers, and manage the marketing process. This is not a book that attempts to describe all there is to know about marketing, but focuses on what the prospective manager needs to know. *Capon's Marketing Framework* differs from other undergraduate and graduate marketing texts. The author takes a position on what he believes is a better or worse course of action for marketers. Marketing is an applied field; the author believes he should provide guidance for good marketing practice.

Furthermore, *Capon's Marketing Framework* focuses on the manager, not just the marketer. For readers committed to a career in marketing (and we hope there are many), this book will form a solid foundation as you study marketing further and deeper. But the vast majority of you will not work in marketing departments, but will instead become senior executives, general managers, CFOs, CEOs, or functional experts who interface with marketing. *Capon's Marketing Framework* is also for you because an understanding and appreciation of marketing is central to virtually every important decision that senior managers make. Because this may be the only marketing course many of you will take, *Capon's Marketing Framework* provides what every general manager and senior executive must know about marketing.

Marketing activity lies at the core of leading and managing a business by providing the focus for interfacing with customers. Marketing is also the source of insight about the market, customers, competitors, and complementers, and the business environment in general. Marketing is concerned with the firm's long-run relationships with customers as well as its short-run sales activity. Marketing must be a major organizational thrust, not just a responsibility assigned to a single functional department. For this reason, *Capon's Marketing Framework* emphasizes the role of marketing in creating value for customers — customer value leads to creating value for other firm stakeholders, including shareholders and employees.

CUSTOMERS: STUDENTS

To better understand how marketing fits into the broader challenge of leading and managing corporations, we address marketing at the firm/business-unit level, as well as in the marketing function. *Capon's Marketing Framework* provides you with a set of concepts and ideas for approaching marketing decisions. The book also gives you a common language for thinking about marketing issues. You will learn to structure and analyze managerial problems in marketing. *Capon's Marketing Framework* prepares you to deal with core marketing issues that future marketers, senior executives, general managers, and CEOs will have to face. The book will also help you think strategically about your firm's markets, products, and services so you can:

- Develop frameworks for approaching simple and complex marketing problems.
- Analyze markets, customers, competitors, your company, and complementers.
- Identify and assess market opportunities and develop market strategy.
- Prepare strategic marketing plans.
- Design implementation programs comprising product, promotion, distribution, and price, aka the *marketing mix*.
- Understand the importance of working across organizational boundaries to align all firm capabilities.
- Assess the success of your marketing initiatives.
- Gain practical experience in addressing marketing issues in a variety of contexts — domestic and international, entrepreneurial startups and established corporations, business (B2B) and consumer (B2C) markets, products and services, and private and public and not-for-profit sectors.

As you work your way through *Capon's Marketing Framework* you will develop a high tolerance for ambiguity — a quality of all successful senior executives, general managers, and CEOs. You will learn that there are no right or wrong answers to marketing problems, just some answers that are better than others. There are no simple — or even complex — formulae in which to plug a set of numbers and find the *right* answer. Rather, you must learn to approach complex and unstructured marketing problems in a creative and measured way. Throughout the book, and at the end of each chapter, are questions and exercises that can help you dig deeper. When appropriate, we urge you to use secondary sources, especially the Internet, to address these issues.

CUSTOMERS: MARKETING FACULTY

For marketing instructors, *Capon's Marketing Framework* provides an opportunity to support your efforts in the classroom by presenting a contemporary perspective on how marketing works within the modern corporation. The book not only offers a firm basis on which to ground your marketing course, but will also challenge your students by including material and ideas not typically covered in marketing texts. Of course, *Capon's Marketing Framework* focuses on how marketing should address customer needs, but it also emphasizes marketing's *bottom line* — shareholder value. By understanding and acting upon the principles and frameworks in this book, students will avoid the many pitfalls of operating in an increasingly complex, competitive, and global environment.

In order to learn how to think appropriately about marketing problems, students must develop skills in marketing problem-solving and analysis. We recommend that your course also use marketing cases and/or simulations in context with this text.[1] Rather than write or include lengthy cases in the text, the Instructor's Manual and website <*www.axcesscapon.com*> provide numerous suggestions for course outlines, cases, and other activities linked to topics in the text. The website also shows ways to approach case analysis.

---

[1] We have had very good experience with Markstrat, www.stratxsimulations.com/.

DIFFERENTIAL ADVANTAGE

Many good marketing textbooks have been published over the years, but they can grow into comprehensive tomes or reference books. Further, they often contain excessive descriptive data and lots of pictures as they move from edition to edition. *Capon's Marketing Framework* has a fresh look and feel for how marketing really works, and offers instructors and students many compelling benefits and values that clearly differentiate this book from others:

1. **More useful and less costly.** When students access *Capon's Marketing Framework*, they pay a fraction of the price of traditional marketing textbooks. Students have three options: printed book, pdf e-book for downloading, and an electronic file to read online — for this option students have a FREE trial, then *pay what you think it's worth*. Quite simply, students who use this book will also be able to afford lunch.

2. **Improving shareholder value.** Business is ever more complex. Students learn the important link between success in delivering value to customers and success in improving shareholder value. This relationship is explicit and shows how world-class marketing decision-making must always consider the impact on shareholders.

3. **Normative focus.** *Capon's Marketing Framework* takes a position on what are appropriate courses of action. Readers should know where the author stands and what he believes. Chapter 1 identifies a set of Marketing Imperatives and a set of Marketing Principles as guides for developing market strategy. The Marketing Imperatives form the basis for the book's macro-organization. Chapter 9 lays out core elements of a market strategy; a strategy that does not include these elements is incomplete.

4. **New ideas relevant to modern marketing environments.** *Capon's Marketing Framework* introduces several genuinely new ideas drawn from personal research and writings and helps students develop critical thinking and problem-solving skills to use them. A textbook should present established procedures, processes, and generalized norms, but such a narrow mandate would perform a disservice to readers. Changes taking place in marketing are dramatic and rapid. They require good problem-solving and analytic skills, as well as sound understanding of principles and practice.

5. **Applying the marketing mix** — as the means of **implementing the firm's market strategy**. For far too long, marketing students have completed their introductory marketing courses believing that marketing equals the marketing mix — product, promotion, distribution, and price. Other critical questions must necessarily precede decisions about marketing-mix elements. For example:

   - What is the essential role of marketing?

   - How does marketing increase shareholder value?

   - How should you segment the market?

   - What is a market strategy? How do you know if your market strategy is complete?

   - Why are brands important? What are key issues for developing a branding strategy?

   Only after these and other questions have been resolved should the firm make marketing-mix decisions.

6. **Balance between B2C and B2B marketing** is critically important. In chapter discussions, sometimes customers are consumers; other times they are organizations. *Capon's Marketing Framework* favors neither one nor the other, but puts significant effort in both B2C and B2B marketing to address key developments in marketing practice.

7. **Branding and marketing metrics** are increasingly important strategic issues for firms — the book devotes full chapters to each.

8. **International, regional, and global marketing.** The world is fast globalizing and firms increasingly seek opportunities outside their domestic markets. They face new and complex issues; hence this chapter focuses exclusively on international, regional, and global marketing.

9. **Public and not-for-profit marketing.** *Capon's Marketing Framework* focuses squarely on marketing challenges facing managers in for-profit businesses. But it will also prove useful for those students interested in not-for-profit and public-sector marketing. First, the vast majority of concepts are readily transferable to these sectors — major differences concern organizational objectives. In the for-profit sector, objectives are unambiguously concerned with profit and shareholder value — in the not-for-profit and public sectors, setting objectives is often a complex undertaking. Second, experience shows that students who develop a firm grounding in for-profit marketing are better prepared for the challenges of not-for-profit and public-sector marketing.

A PEDAGOGICAL FRAMEWORK FOR STUDYING AND LEARNING

The book includes several features to enhance your learning experience:

- **Video Introduction.** The author delivers a short overview of what to expect in the chapter.
- **Learning Objectives.** These highlight the learning you will gain from diligent study of the material in each chapter.
- **Opening Case.** To bring the book to life, each chapter opens with a real-life example of an organization that helps focus the upcoming material.
- **Examples.** The book showcases examples to illustrate specific ideas in each chapter.
- **Key Ideas.** Key ideas are distributed throughout the book and highlighted in the margins for easy reference.
- **Marketing Questions/Marketing Exercises.** To engage you with the text and deepen your understanding, questions/exercises about the material are in the margins.
- **Key Messages.** This section concisely identifies the key learning points in the chapter
- **Videos and Audios.** Many chapters offer video interviews of the author with marketing leaders and audio interviews with the author. Students may access these material via cell phone or personal computer using O-codes and QR codes (below).
- **Questions for Study and Discussion.** Questions to help you reflect on the chapter material and gain deeper insight are gathered at the end of the book.
- **Glossary.** At the end of the book, we gather together and provide an explanation of key marketing terms.

Capon's Marketing Framework is pretty light on pictures, fluff, and entertainment value. This is deliberate, for after all, marketing is a serious business.

ORGANIZATION OF THE BOOK

As laid out in the Table of Contents, *Capon's Marketing Framework* addresses the challenge of managing marketing in five sections and 23 chapters. Briefly:

SECTION I   — MARKETING AND THE FIRM

SECTION II — FUNDAMENTAL INSIGHTS FOR STRATEGIC MARKETING

SECTION III — STRATEGIC MARKETING

SECTION IV — IMPLEMENTING THE MARKET STRATEGY

SECTION V   — SPECIAL MARKETING TOPICS

SECTION 1 — MARKETING AND THE FIRM. This section introduces fundamental concepts in marketing and emphasizes the importance of customers. The section comprises two chapters:

- Chapter 1, *Introduction to Managing Marketing*, provides an introduction to the book. This chapter makes the case for the critical importance of marketing in the modern corporation. The chapter describes two key meanings of marketing — **marketing as a**

philosophy and **six marketing imperatives** that encompass the tasks of strategic marketing. Chapter 1 also introduces four principles that should form the basis for all marketing decision-making — they continue thematically throughout the book.

- Chapter 2, *The Value of Customers*, delves into the notion of customers as critical firm assets. This chapter introduces the concept of customer lifetime value (CLV) and emphasizes the importance of customer retention. The chapter also shows that, in addition to measuring product profitability, the firm should measure customer profitability. The second part of the chapter focuses on actions designed to bind customers closer to the firm, notably customer relationship management (CRM) and customer loyalty programs.

SECTION II — FUNDAMENTAL INSIGHTS FOR STRATEGIC MARKETING. The four chapters in this section focus on securing insight — situation analysis — that lays the foundation for developing market strategy.

- Chapter 3, *Market Insight*, focuses on understanding the market. The chapter framework embraces market structure, market and product evolution, industry forces, and environmental forces.

- Chapter 4, *Customer Insight*, focuses on customers — consumers and organizations. This chapter addresses three main questions: Who are the customers? What do customers need? How do customers buy?

- Chapter 5, *Insight about Competitors, Company, and Complementers*, focuses on those three areas, with an extended section on competitors and a five-step process for gaining insight — identify, describe, evaluate, project, and manage.

- Chapter 6, *Marketing Research*, focuses on marketing research methodologies to gain insight relative to markets, customers, competitors, company, and complementers.

TRANSITION TO STRATEGIC MARKETING. This material shows how planning assumptions form the supporting pillars for strategic marketing and implementation.

SECTION III — STRATEGIC MARKETING. Marketing Imperatives 1, 2, 3 are the *to-dos* of marketing: when and how to apply the four marketing principles. **Strategic marketing** embraces the first three of six imperatives; these imperatives address issues the firm must consider in building the strategic market plan from the foundation of fundamental insights in the situation analysis — Section II.

Marketing Imperative 1 — Determine and Recommend Which Markets to Address

- Chapter 7, *Identifying and Choosing Opportunities*, focuses on growth opportunities. The chapter develops growth strategy frameworks, explores criteria to evaluate growth opportunities, and identifies implementation methods.

Marketing Imperative 2 — Identify and Target Market Segments

- Chapter 8, *Market Segmentation and Targeting*, covers two basic topics: methods of *grouping* customers into market segments, and *targeting* — the process of deciding which segments to address.

Both Imperatives 1 and 2 exemplify the *Principle of Selectivity and Concentration*.

Marketing Imperative 3 — Set Strategic Direction and Positioning

This imperative comprises three separate chapters and advances the concept of market strategy as a fundamental integrating force.

- Chapter 9, *Market Strategy — Integrating Firm Efforts for Marketing Success*, presents critical market strategy components in some depth and shows how they play an integrating role for the marketing mix and other functional programs. In particular, the chapter illustrates applying the *Principles of Differential Advantage, Customer Value, and Integration*.

- Chapter 10, *Managing through the Life Cycle*, uses the product life cycle to focus on the competitive aspects of market strategy. This chapter adopts a scenario approach to develop strategic options for different competitive and life-cycle situations.

- Chapter 11, *Managing Brands*, addresses the management of brands and the increasingly important brand equity concept. Specific issues addressed in this chapter are developing and sustaining a strong brand and managing brand architecture.

SECTION IV — IMPLEMENTING THE MARKET STRATEGY: Marketing Imperatives 4, 5, and 6 focus on implementing the market strategy.

Marketing Imperative 4 — Design the Market Offer
Nine chapters address Imperative 4; they describe the marketing mix and when and how to manage each component in a way that reinforces and implements the market strategy. Appropriately designing the firm's offer is a critical component of the market plan.

Each marketing mix element may bestow value on customers, but our fourfold framework focuses on the major role of each element. Part A — *Providing Customer Value*; Part B — *Communicating Customer Value*; Part C — *Delivering Customer Value*; and Part D — *Getting Paid for Customer Value*.

PART A. PROVIDING CUSTOMER VALUE
Three chapters focus on managing and developing products and services:

- Chapter 12, *Managing the Product Line*, concerns managing product line composition. This chapter leans heavily on strategic portfolio frameworks to complement traditional financial analysis methods. The chapter also addresses complementarity, product line breadth (including trade-offs between product proliferation and simplification), bundling, counterfeiting, evolving the product line, extending product life, product quality, product safety, secondary markets, packaging, and product and packaging disposal.

- Chapter 13, *Managing Services and Customer Service*. Services are important factors in all advanced economies yet they display important differences from physical products. Furthermore, as product quality has improved across the board, customer service has become an increasingly important competitive weapon.

- Chapter 14, *Developing New Products*, discusses success factors for innovative companies and different ways to approach the innovation challenge. This chapter also describes the evolving stage-gate new-product-development process.

PART B. COMMUNICATING CUSTOMER VALUE
Three chapters focus on personal and impersonal communications:

- Chapter 15, *Integrated Marketing Communications*, presents an integrated communications framework for developing communications strategy.

- Chapter 16, *Mass and Digital Communication*, focuses on advertising, direct marketing, publicity and public relations, sales promotion, and the variety of communications opportunities spawned by the Internet and mobile marketing.

- Chapter 17, *Directing and Managing the Field Sales Effort*, deals with personal selling efforts and highlights critical issues in managing the field sales effort. This chapter presents six tasks for developing sales strategy and organization, and addresses contemporary challenges of managing strategic (key) and global accounts.

PART C. DELIVERING CUSTOMER VALUE

- Chapter 18, *Distribution Decisions*, focuses on providing customers with products and services, when and where they want them. The chapter discusses choosing and managing channel relationships, an area of substantial innovation where the Internet is playing a critical role.

PART D. GETTING PAID FOR CUSTOMER VALUE

- Chapter 19, *Critical Underpinnings of Pricing Decisions*, highlights the tremendous revenue and profit implications of pricing decisions. The chapter focuses on critical factors in developing pricing strategy — customer value, costs, competition, and the firm's strategic objectives.

- Chapter 20, *Setting Prices*, shows how to both set actual prices and avoid price reductions. The chapter highlights the pricing toolkit and illustrates various pricing approaches.

Imperatives 3 and 4 draw heavily on the *Principles of Customer Value and Differential Advantage*.

Marketing Imperative 5 — Secure Support from Other Functions

- Chapter 21, *Ensuring the Firm Implements the Market Offer as Planned*, returns to the distinction between marketing as a philosophy and marketing as a function. The chapter highlights successful externally oriented firms and develops a system for making the firm externally oriented and customer-focused so that the various functions support the marketing effort.

Marketing Imperative 6 — Monitor and Control

- Chapter 22, *Monitoring and Controlling Firm Performance and Functioning*, discusses ways of ensuring the firm implements its planned marketing effort and achieves desired results.

Both Imperatives 5 and 6 rest on the *Principle of Integration*.

SECTION V — SPECIAL MARKETING TOPICS

- Chapter 23, *International, Regional, and Global Marketing*, focuses on marketing activity outside the firm's domestic market. This chapter addresses foreign market entry — how to select countries and how to enter. The chapter also addresses alternative international marketing strategies and options for marketing organization.

SUPPLEMENTAL MATERIAL FOR TEACHING AND LEARNING

Capon's Marketing Framework is a standalone book, but several additional materials can help instructors design courses and make the learning experience more meaningful for students. Instructors can access these materials in a protected area at *www.axcesscapon.com*.

- **Instructor's manual:** The manual employs a consistent format, chapter by chapter. Essentially, the manual summarizes critical learning points in each chapter and provides approaches to address *Marketing Questions and Exercises* distributed throughout the text. For the chapter-by-chapter *Questions for Study and Discussion*, the manual offers answers or suggestions for managing class discussion.

- **Test item file:** Prepared by experienced test developer Andrew Yap, this file contains well over 1,000 multiple choice and essay questions for use by instructors in setting tests and examinations. Organized by chapter, this material is available in both Word and Excel (for Blackboard).

- **PowerPoint files:** Each chapter comes with a set of teaching materials in the form of PowerPoint files. Each slide has a *notes* page that suggests how the instructor may use that particular slide for teaching purposes.

- **Case studies:** Two sets of materials are available: a list and short descriptions of many traditional marketing case studies, and a large number of short case studies for FREE pdf download. In both cases, organization is by book chapter. This material also includes two approaches to studying marketing cases — a faculty perspective developed at Columbia Business School and an approach prepared by Mary Cunningham Agee, then a Harvard Business School student, to help fellow students.

Additional study aids for students are accessible from *www.axcesscapon.com*.

- **Student study guide:** The purpose of this publication is to help students in their marketing studies. The guide is structured in the same way as the textbook so that students can easily work back and forth between the two volumes. Available as a printed book and PDF e-book.

- **Electronic flash cards:** Similar in concept to traditional flash cards, electronic flash cards are designed to improve students' marketing expertise.

- **Financial analysis for marketing decisions:** A good understanding of financial analysis is critical for sound marketing decision making. Financial analysis comes in many shapes and forms; students should understand the specific issues that concern marketers. We discuss financial issues throughout *Capon's Marketing Framework*, but do not have space to lay the groundwork. Hence, we have prepared the Marketing Enrichment me01 document that we hope you will find useful. Feel free to download the file and use it as a handy reference. You may access this material with either an O-code or a QR code (next section).

me01

Finally, students have access to two other learning sources via the Internet:

- **Videos.** Each section and chapter has a short introductory video. We note these files with a video icon ▒ and both an O-code and QR code (next section). Videos of the author interviewing marketing experts are at the end of each chapter.

- **Audios.** The author speaks with Dave Basarab about *Marketing Mastery*. We list these files with an audio icon ∩ at the end of appropriate chapters, noted by O-codes and QR codes.

O-CODES AND QR CODES

An innovative feature of the third edition of *Capon's Marketing Framework* is the addition of O-codes and QR codes. The purpose of O-codes and QR codes is to link items in the text to additional material you may find interesting, in an easy way. O-codes and QR codes act as hotlinks in the book's digital versions but, perhaps more importantly, they operate as simple links between the printed version and the Internet. With O-codes, you text a simple code on your mobile phone, or enter that code into a special field at *www.ocodes.com*; with QR codes, you just scan the item with your cell phone, using any QR code scanning app. In either case, you are instantly linked to the content related to that code.

Each O-code you text *from* your phone (or QR code you scan *with* your phone) is automatically saved online for future reference. O-codes are stored in a free account at *www.ocodes.com*, linked to your mobile number. You don't need to create an account before using *Capon's Marketing Framework* O-codes. But if you do create an account (FREE), you may share content by linking to Twitter, Facebook, or Evernote. QR codes are typically saved inside most QR scanning apps; some may also have sharing functionality.

cv01

The O-code phone number for *Capon's Marketing Framework* is 347-609-0751. Add this number to your contact list and simply text any O-code to that number. You can test the link quickly right now by texting the O-code "cv01," or scanning the QR code in the adjacent column. You will link directly to a video introducing *Capon's Marketing Framework*. AxcessCapon does not charge for using O-codes or QR codes; however, your wireless carrier will apply standard text message and data rates. At the time of publication, phone access to O-codes is limited to the U.S. (and some Canadian locations).

Alternatively, you may also test the link using your computer by typing "cv01" into the field on the *www.ocodes.com* home page. No charges apply to computer access.

CHAPTER TEXT. The chapter text contains two item types. Each item has both an O-code and a QR code:

- **Videos.** We identify each video item with a video icon ▶. Each introduction video O-code begins with the letters *cv*; hence, the introductory video for Chapter 12 is `cv1201`. Each end-of-chapter interview video O-code begins with the letter *v*; hence, the first end-of-chapter video for Chapter 16 is `v1602`. You can find the full set of interview videos at O-code `me03`.

- **Audios.** We identify audio files with an audio icon 🎧. Each audio icon begins with the letter *a*. Hence, the first audio file for Chapter 5 is `a501`. The set of audios is available at O-code `me04`.

THE VIRGIN MARKETER

No matter how well-written a textbook, the only way to really learn marketing is by doing it. You simply have to take the ideas, concepts, and frameworks and put them into practice. *The Virgin Marketer* is a companion volume to *Capon's Marketing Framework*. *The Virgin Marketer's* 23 chapters correspond to the 23 chapters in the textbook. Each chapter contains a set of tried-and-true experiential exercises designed to help the user prepare a strategic marketing plan — analyze a marketing situation, develop a market strategy, and design a series of implementation programs.

The best approach is for you to select a product or service as your *marketing case.* Your instructor may assign the case — perhaps a local firm or an entrepreneurial startup. Alternatively, you may select your own product or service. The ideal way to *learn by doing* is to complete each chapter of *The Virgin Marketer* right after you have completed a chapter of this book. Then you use the ideas, concepts, and frameworks while they are fresh in your mind. If you work through your marketing case assiduously, you will finish the book with an operating marketing plan. Strategic marketing plans using *The Virgin Marketer* are available at O-code `me06`.

ACKNOWLEDGEMENTS

Many individuals contributed to *Capon's Marketing Framework* in this and earlier editions. I thank them for their continued support. Here I want to recognize several special groups of people for their roles in bringing this third edition to fruition. Current colleagues include Eva Ascarza, Asim Ansari, Mark Cohen, Jacob Goldenberg, Brett Gordon, Kamel Jedidi, Gita Johar, Eric Johnson, Ran Kivetz, Rajeev Kohli, Leonard Lee, Don Lehmann, Oded Netzer, Michel Pham, Miklos Sarvary, Bernd Schmitt, Scott Shriver, Olivier Toubia, Hitendra Wadhwa, and Keith Wilcox. Former colleagues include Dan Bartels, Rajeev Batra, Jim Bettman, Bill Brandt (deceased), Lee Cooper, John Farley, Paul Farris, Andy Gershoff, Rashi Glazer, Sunil Gupta, Dominique Hanssens, Morris Holbrook, John Howard (deceased), Morgan Jones, Hal Kassarjian, Oded Koenesberg, Aradhna Krishna, Jonathan Levav, Christopher Lovelock (deceased), Rich Lutz, Natalie Mizik, Bill Moore, Massao Nakanishi, Dave Reibstein, Mike Ryan, Abe Shuchman (deceased), Hiro Takeuchi, Bart Weitz, Russ Winer, and Dave Wooten. Former students are too numerous to mention but include faculty leaders George Belch, Hubert Gatignon, Steve Hoch, and Itamar Simonsen. Thanks also to marketing instructors at other business schools including the many adopters of my textbooks; my MBA and EMBA students; and participants in my various educational and consulting engagements with corporations around the world. In various ways, all of you have stimulated and challenged my thinking: I thank you for that. I also thank all members of the Wessex Press production team. I specially recognize my long-time co-author, Mac Hulbert, now Emeritus Professor at Columbia Business School. Mac contributed to previous textbook editions and has been a friend and collaborator for more than 40 years: Mac, many thanks.

We also acknowledge contributions of the business press. To make the third edition of *Capon's Marketing Framework* as relevant as possible, we gleaned many examples, news, and trends from respected online and print business sources like *Bloomberg Businessweek*, *The Economist*, *Financial Times*, *Fortune*, *The New York Times*, and *The Wall Street Journal*. We thank these publications for their contributions. Chapter endnotes contain citations to specific quotations.

CONCLUDING STATEMENT

The extensive experience the author brings to *Capon's Marketing Framework* has infused the book with the very real marketing challenges that face corporations daily around the world. The author writes from the standpoint of a marketing academic with a deep commitment to helping corporations improve their marketing practice and imparting his knowledge and expertise to students at the dawn of their careers.

The material in *Capon's Marketing Framework* will help you to learn about marketing. It will equip you to survive and prosper in your careers as marketers, senior executives, general managers, and CEOs. All those who have helped bring this book to fruition wish you well as you develop your personal intellectual capital.

Capon's Marketing Framework is also a reference for future use. If you become an entrepreneur, this book will help you launch and manage your new business. If you join a firm's marketing department, you will never have enough books on the subject; hopefully this will be one of your favorite reference guides. And, if you find yourself in another function where you work with marketing, you will be equipped to ask your marketing colleagues the right questions.

Good luck!

Noel Capon
R. C. Kopf Professor of International Marketing
Graduate School of Business
Columbia University, New York, New York

ABBREVIATIONS GLOSSARY

To improve readability we avoid spelling out the full names of organizations in examples. Rather, we use the shortened versions or mnemonics by which they are typically known.

Corporations

Advanced Micro Devices	AMD
American Express	AmEx
Barnes & Noble	B&N
Bausch & Lomb	B&L
Black & Decker	B&D
Boston Consulting Group	BCG
Bristol-Myers Squibb	BMS
British Airways	BA
General Electric	GE
General Motors	GM
GlaxoSmithKline	GSK
Hewlett Packard	HP
Home Box Office	HBO
International Business Machines	IBM
International Paper	IP
Johnson & Johnson	J&J
Procter & Gamble	P&G
Texas Instruments	TI
Volkswagen	VW

General Business Terms

Chief executive officer	CEO
Chief financial officer	CFO
Chief marketing officer	CMO
Customer relationship management	CRM
Fast moving consumer goods	FMCG
Personal computer	PC
Research and development	R&D
Senior vice president	SVP

U.S. Government Departments

Consumer Product Safety Commission	CPSC
Environmental Protection Agency	EPA
Federal Communications Commission	FCC
Federal Drug Administration	FDA
Federal Trade Commission	FTC
National Transportation Safety Board	NTSB
Securities and Exchange Commission	SEC

International Organizations

European Union	EU
International Monetary Fund	IMF
United Nations	UN
United Nations Educational, Scientific and Cultural Organization	UNESCO
United States	U S
World Trade Organization	WTO

SECTION I
MARKETING
AND THE FIRM cvs1

To access O-codes, go to www.ocodes.com

Capon's Marketing Framework

SECTION I: MARKETING AND THE FIRM

CHAPTER 1
Introduction to Managing Marketing

CHAPTER 2
The Value of Customers

SECTION II: FUNDAMENTAL INSIGHTS FOR STRATEGIC MARKETING

CHAPTER 3
Market Insight

CHAPTER 4
Customer Insight

CHAPTER 6
Marketing Research

TRANSITION TO STRATEGIC MARKETING

CHAPTER 5
Insight about Competitors, Company, and Complementers

SECTION III: STRATEGIC MARKETING

IMPERATIVE 1
Determine and Recommend Which Markets to Address

CHAPTER 7
Identifying and Choosing Opportunities

IMPERATIVE 2
Identify and Target Market Segments

CHAPTER 8
Market Segmentation and Targeting

IMPERATIVE 3
Set Strategic Direction and Positioning

CHAPTER 9
Market Strategy – Integrating Firm Efforts for Marketing Success

CHAPTER 10
Managing through the Life Cycle

CHAPTER 11
Managing Brands

SECTION IV: IMPLEMENTING THE MARKET STRATEGY

IMPERATIVE 4
Design the Market Offer

PART A: PROVIDING CUSTOMER VALUE

PART B: COMMUNICATING CUSTOMER VALUE

PART C: DELIVERING CUSTOMER VALUE

PART D: GETTING PAID FOR CUSTOMER VALUE

CHAPTER 12
Managing the Product Line

CHAPTER 15
Integrated Marketing Communications

CHAPTER 18
Distribution Decisions

CHAPTER 19
Critical Underpinnings of Pricing Decisions

CHAPTER 13
Managing Services and Customer Service

CHAPTER 16
Mass and Digital Communication

CHAPTER 20
Setting Prices

CHAPTER 14
Developing New Products

CHAPTER 17
Directing and Managing the Field Sales Effort

IMPERATIVE 5
Secure Support from Other Functions

CHAPTER 21
Ensuring the Firm Implements the Market Offer as Planned

IMPERATIVE 6
Monitor and Control

CHAPTER 22
Monitoring and Controlling Firm Functioning and Performance

SECTION V: SPECIAL MARKETING TOPICS

CHAPTER 23
International, Regional, and Global Marketing

CHAPTER I

INTRODUCTION TO MANAGING MARKETING cv101

LEARNING OBJECTIVES

When you have completed this chapter, you will be able to:

- Define the term *marketing*.
- Explain the fundamental business model.
- Articulate why marketing is so important for business organizations.
- Explain how success in attracting, retaining, and growing customers improves shareholder value.
- Articulate how marketing as a philosophy embraces an external orientation.
- Understand how an external orientation differs from various internal orientations.
- Be ready to act on the six marketing imperatives.
- Identify the four marketing principles.
- Understand the book's structure and additional features to enhance learning.

OPENING CASE: STARBUCKS

In 1982, 28-year-old Howard Schultz joined Seattle's specialty coffee emporium, Starbucks Coffee, Tea & Spice and persuaded the owners to transplant Italy's espresso bar concept to downtown Seattle. Starbucks was wildly successful. In 1987, together with local investors, Schultz purchased Starbucks and began a major store expansion. By 2006, Starbucks was the world's leading retailer, roaster, and brand of specialty coffee with 7,950 stores in the U.S. and over 11,000 globally. Starbucks purchases coffee direct from growers, roasts all its coffee, and distributes to its stores. All Starbucks stores are wholly owned, except in foreign countries, where the firm has partnership and licensing agreements with local business people, and in licensed locations in the U.S., such as campus bookstores and airports. All people in company-owned stores work for Starbucks.[1]

For Schultz, Starbucks should be its customers' third place — after home and work. "As a customer, I walk into the store and I'm swept away for a minute, even if I get a coffee to go, because I'm part of this experience that makes me feel better. A missing part of our lives as consumers is that we don't feel valued. So we really take notice when someone touches us and says, 'I appreciate you, I respect you, and I can help you.' … We open five new stores a day, so we have to ensure that there's incredible consistency without having every location seem to be stamped out like a fast-food franchise. That is part of the genius of Starbucks."

Starbucks enhances customers' experience value by focusing on its employees — partners. Schultz observed: "The keys are the culture and values of our company that allow our people to feel the way they do about Starbucks, so that they genuinely want to convey the attributes, the characteristics, the aspirational qualities of what we offer the customer … .We've made a very large investment over the last 20 years in training. We've spent more money every year on training than we do on advertising." Early on, Starbucks did no advertising, preferring to let its clusters of stores fulfill the communications function. Schultz went on: "Starbucks has the lowest attrition of any retail restaurant in North America. We do a cultural, internal audit every year where we go to our people, and we ask them to evaluate our behavior and practices and their trust and confidence in management. And we share those scores with the company."

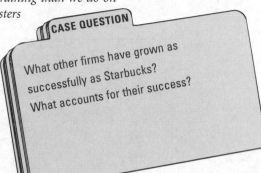

CASE QUESTION

What other firms have grown as successfully as Starbucks? What accounts for their success?

More than 40 million customers monthly frequent Starbucks locations around the world. The most loyal customers visit Starbucks an average of 18 times a month. Starbucks' customer loyalty has brought significant financial success: In 2012, revenues were $13.3 billion; net profits were $1.4 billion, and the share price had tripled from its early 2009 low.

WHAT DOES MARKETING MEAN TODAY?

Marketing plays a critical role in today's business environment, where maximizing **shareholder value** is an increasingly important goal. The essence of marketing focuses on how firms attract, retain, and enhance their relationships with customers. Success in delivering **customer value** leads directly to improving shareholder value and long-run firm prosperity. In *Capon's Marketing Framework*, we explore both the strategic aspects of marketing and the tactical decisions that marketers make every day. But first, we investigate two quite different but related meanings of marketing.

MARKETING AS A PHILOSOPHY embraces the view that marketing is the guiding force or orientation for the entire organization. Firms with a marketing philosophy operate with an external orientation. Such firms focus their attention and resources *outside* the corporation — to acquire, retain, and grow customers — but take careful account of competitors and the broader external environment. By contrast, internally oriented companies focus largely on internal issues like products, services, and processes. *Capon's Marketing Framework* embraces the *marketing-as-philosophy* perspective. The author believes, and has seen in his own career, how powerful and effective a business can be when the entire organization is attuned to the external world. Such agile firms not only sense critical environmental factors but also adapt and change to address them.

KEY IDEA

➤ Marketing is a guiding philosophy for the firm as a whole.

In addition to the philosophical perspective, marketers must possess the tools and decision-making skills to get the marketing job done. Effective marketers implement six marketing imperatives.

MARKETING IMPERATIVES describe the specifics of the marketing job. Executives with marketing and product management titles generally focus on these *must dos* of marketing. We identify two groups:

STRATEGIC MARKETING

- Imperative 1: Determine and recommend which markets to address.
- Imperative 2: Identify and target market segments.
- Imperative 3: Set strategic direction and positioning.

IMPLEMENTING THE MARKET STRATEGY

- Imperative 4: Design the market offer.
- Imperative 5: Secure support from other functions.
- Imperative 6: Monitor and control execution and performance.

As a broader framework when thinking about markets and marketing, marketers must also consider the **four principles** of marketing. These principles should form the basis of marketing decision-making. They act as guidelines for acting on the six imperatives. The four principles are:

- Principle 1: Selectivity and Concentration
- Principle 2: Customer Value
- Principle 3: Differential Advantage
- Principle 4: Integration

Chapter 1's discussion of these issues sets the stage for the entire book.

THE MARKETING JOB

William Rosenberg, Dunkin' Donuts (DD) pioneering entrepreneur, had a very simple philosophy: "The boss is the customer." By implementing Rosenberg's philosophy, DD's franchise operates more than 10,000 outlets in over 30 countries and sells 4 million donuts and 3 million cups of coffee daily.

Target has grown successfully for many years while competitor Kmart has struggled. Target understands and addresses customer needs in a compelling manner — Target has a cool brand, the right product mix, and excellent service. Target illustrates the essence of effective marketing.

Many executives are confused about marketing. It seems so intuitive. Can't anybody be a marketer? Real people at real companies told us that:

- "Marketing is just advertising."
- "Marketing is giving away tee-shirts, products, and concert tickets to potential clients."
- "Marketing's job is to support our sales force."
- "Marketing is what consumers do at the supermarket on a Saturday morning."

These activities relate to the two broader meanings of marketing we just discussed — **marketing as a philosophy,** and marketing as **six imperatives** — but none really captures the true essence of marketing that we highlight in Figure 1.1.

Because of its focus on customers, marketing is the firm's fundamental activity. When marketing delivers *customer value* to satisfy customer needs, the firm *attracts, retains, and grows customers.* If costs are in line, *profits* follow. Profits help the firm *survive* as an independent entity and secure the resources to *grow.* Survival and growth are the critical links between earning profits and enhancing *shareholder value* by increasing stock price. Enhanced shareholder value makes funds available for renewed investment.

Marketing's role includes identifying opportunities, figuring out customer needs, understanding the competition, developing appealing products and services, and communicating value to potential customers. When these tasks are done well, shareholder value increases. Well-known authors Michael Tracy and Fred Wiersema state that "Creating shareholder wealth is not the purpose of the business. It is the reward for creating customer value."[2]

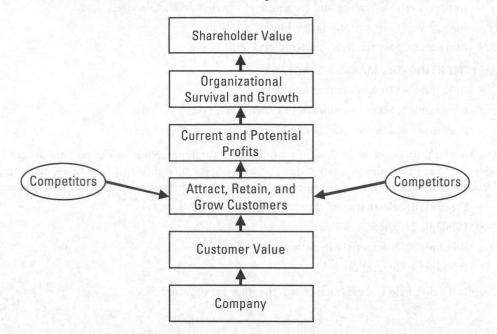

FIGURE 1.1

**THE FUNDAMENTAL
BUSINESS MODEL**

Figure 1.1 also demonstrates the process for achieving the firm's goal of enhancing shareholder value, both for private firms with few shareholders and public firms with many. Growth and long-run profits are the means. Increasing profits in the short run is easy: Just reduce R&D (research and development), cut advertising, and fire half the sales force — but such decisions typically lead to long-run problems. For forward-looking businesses seeking long-run profits, customers are the core assets. Of course, *competitors* seek these same customers. The competitive battle to attract, retain, and grow customers is central to all business activity.

The critical weapon in the battle for customers is straightforward in concept, but may be complex and difficult in execution. Quite simply, the firm must deliver to customers greater value than competitors. Customers reward firms that deliver greater value by purchasing their products and services, today and tomorrow. This **exchange** is the basis of all markets. Customers prefer the value inherent in the firm's products and services to their own money or other resources. The firm prefers the customer's money or other resources to its own products and services.

In sum, when the firm delivers greater customer value than competitors, it should earn profits, survive, grow, and make shareholders very happy. If customers perceive that competitors deliver greater value, ultimately the firm will perish. Just ask one of the more than 100,000 businesses that fail each year in the U.S. Don't just take the author's word for the power of this framework. Lou Gerstner, who led IBM's rejuvenation from its near-death experience, stated, "Everything starts with the customer."[3]

Pre-eminent management theorist, the late Peter Drucker, is generally credited with developing the customer orientation and modern marketing perspective. Drucker stated, "If we want to know what a business is, we have to start with its purpose. There is only one valid definition of any business purpose — *to create a customer*. It is the customer who determines what a business is. For it is the customer, and he alone, who through being willing to pay for a good or service, converts economic resources into wealth, things into goods." Drucker added, "What the business thinks it produces is not of first importance — especially not to the future of the business and its success. What the customer thinks he is buying, what he considers 'value' is decisive … . Because it is [the purpose of a business] to create a customer, [the] business enterprise has two — and only these two — basic functions — marketing and innovation."[4]

Today's customers are more aware and knowledgeable about competitive offers and prices, in part because of the Internet. Airline travelers can easily compare prices on Expedia, Travelocity, Orbitz, or Kayak, and the airlines' own websites. Consumers in advanced affluent societies have ever-increasing numbers of discretionary product and service options and may choose among expensive clothes, an iPad or a European vacation. And more and more intelligent agents may make buying decisions and shop for us.

Marketing encompasses a wide variety of activities the firm undertakes to attract, retain, and grow customers — of course, competitors are trying to do the same thing. If the firm is more successful than its competitors in creating customer value, it will make profits, survive and grow, and enhance shareholder value.

MARKETING AND SHAREHOLDER VALUE

Electronic Accounting Systems (EAS) successfully sold payroll services to firms with 50 to 100 employees. Customers filled in payroll sheets, and EAS arranged courier pickup. But EAS could not serve smaller customers profitably. Former EAS employee Tom Golisano founded Paychex to serve smaller businesses. Paychex's prices were lower than EAS's — partly because customers phoned in payroll information. Paychex also provided a payroll tax return service. Golisano became a billionaire and created significant value for Paychex's shareholders.

Progressive identified a relationship between people's credit history and driving record, then used this insight to profitably insure customers rejected by mainstream insurers — mainly young drivers and those with poor driving records. Progressive is now a leading U.S. insurer and has considerably enhanced shareholder value.

The central focus on shareholder value is deeply rooted in many capitalist countries — particularly the U.S. The **shareholder-value perspective** defines management's job as maximizing returns for the firm's owners — its shareholders. When this perspective dominates, government regulations tend to favor owners. Active shareholder opposition, CEO departures, and sometimes-unfriendly takeover bids, tend to occur when the firm underperforms in shareholder value.

The firm also has other *stakeholders*, like management, labor, or the public at large. In some countries, these stakeholders are more favored than shareholders. Regulation in these countries generally favors managers and protects them from unwelcome mergers and acquisitions. The stakeholder view is particularly popular in Asia, where many firms and politicians are ardent advocates of managerial power.

In recent years, developing global capital markets have favored the shareholder-value perspective. Conservative Japanese electronics giant Panasonic has share-repurchase plans, provides stock options for senior executives, and links managers' salaries to stock market performance. Even in China, stock markets are now firmly established. Increased globalization will inevitably spread the shareholder-value perspective. Enhanced share ownership will give shareholders greater political power — both directly as individual investors and indirectly via third-party investment vehicles like mutual funds.

Traditionally, we find assets on the firm's balance sheet. Balance-sheet assets (current and fixed) include cash, accounts receivable, inventory, land, and plant and equipment — they do not include customers! Balance-sheet assets may be important, but none is absolutely crucial. The only critical asset the firm has to have is paying customers! Customers are the sole source of firm revenues; all firm activities are costs. Balance-sheet assets are assets only because they contribute to attracting, retaining, and growing customers.

But what if balance-sheet assets are not *assets*? What if they are *strategic liabilities*? In the early 1980s, Barnes & Noble became the dominant U.S. bookseller using a bricks-and-mortar strategy. But as the Internet grew, B&N was slow to embrace purchasing books online. Jeff Bezos launched Amazon.com. Amazon is the premier online bookseller and has developed online businesses far beyond books. B&N eventually reacted and now has a decent online book business, but is a distant second to Amazon.

The firm increases shareholder value only if incoming cash flows earn a return on investment at least equal to its **cost of capital** (the weighted average of the firm's cost of equity and cost of debt). When the firm fails to earn its cost of capital, it destroys shareholder value. Unfortunately, managers sometimes forget that the main source of firm cash flows (except new debt and equity) comes from attracting, retaining, and growing customers. Customers provide revenues and cash flow when they believe that the firm's products and services offer better value than competitive alternatives.

MARKETING AS A PHILOSOPHY: EXTERNAL AND INTERNAL ORIENTATIONS

You just learned that the firm enhances shareholder value by attracting, retaining, and growing customers. At a *philosophical* level, then, each employee has some responsibility and marketing is *everybody's* business. At a personal level, because customers are the firm's only revenue source, they also pay everyone's salary! To quote Drucker again, "Marketing is so basic that it cannot be considered a separate function (i.e., a separate skill or work) within the business … it is, first, a central dimension of the entire business. It is the whole business … seen from the customer's point of view. Concern and responsibility for marketing must, therefore, permeate all areas of the enterprise."[5] More recently, David Haines, brand czar of Vodafone, the world's largest cell phone service provider, said, "Marketing is too important to be left to the marketers. It's the obligation of every single individual in the company, whether you're a phone operator, the CEO, or anyone else in the company."[6]

Marketing as a philosophy concerns the firm's entire *orientation*. A firm embracing marketing as a philosophy has an **external orientation**. Other firms focusing on internal business drivers have one of several **internal orientations**.

THE EXTERNAL ORIENTATION

Lou Gerstner described the IBM he inherited as CEO: "[IBM had a] … general disinterest in customer needs, accompanied by a preoccupation with internal politics … a bureaucratic infrastructure that defended turf instead of promoting collaboration, and a management class that presided rather than acted."[7] Gerstner described one of his key strategic decisions: "Drive all we did from the customer back, and turn IBM into a market-driven rather than an internally focused, process-driven enterprise"[8]

The externally oriented firm looks outward to the environment and knows customers are central to its future — Gerstner really understood this aspect of marketing. Marketing is the *point person*[9] — and marketing must gain insight into customers, competitors, and broader environmental factors. The externally oriented firm knows that its current products, services, and processes are the reasons for past and present success. It also knows that as its external environment changes, its products, services, and processes must also change. The externally oriented firm does not fear change — it knows that change is inevitable and that new opportunities are its *lifeblood*. The externally oriented firm invests in new capabilities and competencies to exploit opportunities and create and serve customers.[10]

In difficult economic times, when profits are under pressure, many firms cut spending and investment. The externally oriented firm invests. It may increase its marketing budget, acquire

KEY IDEA

➤ Customers are the sole source of firm revenues; relatedly, all firm activities are costs.

➤ Customers are the firm's core assets, yet they do not appear on the balance sheet.

➤ Some balance-sheet assets act as strategic liabilities.

Marketing Question

Can you identify some firms that work especially hard to enhance shareholder value by focusing on creating customer value? Specifically, what do they do?

weaker rivals, and/or cut prices. In recent recessions, several firms invested in customers and markets and swept past more internally oriented competitors[11]:

- Cisco invested in Asia as competitors were contracting. Within one year Cisco had lead market share in many countries.
- Coca-Cola CEO Muhtar Kent said, "We don't cut marketing in this crisis around the world. We make sure our brands stay healthy and that we exit this tunnel with more market share than when we went in."
- Intel maintained R&D and production spending. Said then Intel CEO Craig Barrett: "You never save your way out of a recession. The only way to get out of a recession stronger than when you went in is to have great new products."[12]
- Kohl's continued new store expansion and old store refurbishing; Sara Lee increased advertising by 25 percent; Starbucks aggressively expanded internationally; Walmart increased capital spending to $10 billion annually.
- Said then Xerox CEO Anne Mulcahy, "Everywhere I went, lenders and investors were demanding I cut R&D spending. But Xerox innovation is sacred … investing in innovation was the best decision I ever made."[13]

CEOs and top managers are generally responsible for establishing an external orientation as the overarching corporate thrust. Leaders of firms like Amazon, Google, P&G, and Starbucks understand this; they really *get it*. Only a CEO like former Wachovia banker John Medlin can dismiss the *tyranny of the quarterly earnings statement* and say, "You've got to expect a down quarter from time to time."[14] Only a CEO like James Burke at Johnson & Johnson can make customer concerns central to the firm. In the 1982 Tylenol cyanide-lacing crisis, J&J immediately withdrew Tylenol capsules until it developed fail-safe packaging. J&J's $250 million write-off demonstrated a long-term investment in customers, and Tylenol quickly returned to market leadership.

Some of the world's most successful companies practice marketing as a philosophy. P&G spends $350 million annually seeking customer and market insight. A senior Pfizer executive asserted: "Our strong belief at Pfizer is that marketing is really an investment, not an expense. Our former CEO, Bill Steers, believed it was important to invest in R&D. He also believed it was equally important to invest in marketing. He said if you are best at both, there's no way you can be beat! … We parallel our R&D spending with a similar investment in research about markets and customers. What separates us from competitors is an assiduous pursuit of information, knowledge, and understanding of our customer."[15]

INTERNAL ORIENTATIONS

In a small and simply organized firm, the sole proprietor (SP) or owner conducts most activities. The SP seeks and serves customers, arranges financing, performs operational functions, and manages the payroll. At a visceral level, the SP knows that customers are critical assets and operates with an external orientation almost by instinct. Can you recall an occasion when your local garage, dry cleaner, hardware store, or other small business treated you personally as an important and valuable asset?

As firms grow, they seek efficiency through specialization and differentiation — operations, sales, product design, finance, legal, technology, and other functions have specific responsibilities. Typically, these organizations develop their own missions, objectives, systems and processes, and business philosophies. Rather than work together to deliver customer value, they may pursue their own agendas, spurred by local customer norms, and management systems that measure, motivate, and reward securing departmental objectives. Nonproductive differentiation that history and internal political rivalries exacerbate may trump a customer focus.

Frequently, internal functions act in mutually inconsistent ways. The sales department tries to increase sales, but operations, working to produce acceptable-quality products at low cost, cuts product varieties; and R&D sees no reason to hurry the new product development process.

Marketing wants to increase advertising spending, but finance reduces budgets to meet financial targets. The individual functions are often important strengths for the firm, but some, like accounting and R&D, are organizationally distant from customers. Focusing too heavily on one function versus another often leads to problems. The common denominator when firms operate in silos (stovepipes) is that delivering customer value often takes a back seat. These firms follow an **internal orientation**.

At internally oriented firms, you often hear the statement, "That's the way we do things around here." Regardless of changes in customer needs, competitor actions, and/or the external environment in general, the firm continues on its current course. Let's look at several internal orientations — operations, sales, finance, and technology:

OPERATIONS ORIENTATION. The firm with an **operations orientation** typically focuses on reducing unit costs. There is nothing wrong with cutting costs — indeed, low costs allow firms to reduce prices and/or earn higher profit margins. But cost reduction that reduces customer value and leads to dissatisfied customers can be a serious problem.

SALES ORIENTATION. Firms with a **sales orientation** focus on short-term sales volume. They place excessive effort in *getting customers to buy what the firm has to offer*, versus the externally oriented alternative of *getting the firm to offer what customers want to buy*.

FINANCE ORIENTATION. The firm with a **finance orientation** focuses too heavily on short-term profits. It tends to avoid expenditures with long-term payoff and mortgage its future by indiscriminately cutting back on R&D, capital investment, marketing research, and/or advertising.

TECHNOLOGY ORIENTATION. A firm with a **technology orientation** focuses on RD&E (research, development, and engineering) and pays little attention to customer value. Panasonic demonstrated a technological orientation. Its engineers believed that lots of buttons and technical gadgets would add technical value to camcorders and increase market share. Unfortunately sales stagnated because customers wanted easy-to-use products and manuals in everyday language.

> *Marketing Exercise*
>
> Interview an executive. Identify examples where functional silos hurt performance — and where different functions worked well together. Why did these different behaviors occur?

See Table 1.1 for characteristics of firms with external and internal orientations.

Dimension	Internal	External
Customer perspective	Transactional	Relational
Focus	Products	Markets
Know-how	Inherent in patents, machinery	Inherent in people, processes
Measurement	Profit, margin, volume	Customer value, satisfaction, retention
Organizational philosophy	Bureaucracy	Adhocracy
Priorities	Efficiency and productivity	Flexibility and responsiveness
Process	Mass production	Mass customization

TABLE 1.1

GENERAL CHARACTERISTICS OF INTERNAL AND EXTERNAL ORIENTATIONS

THE SIX MARKETING IMPERATIVES

The job of putting the marketing philosophy into practice normally falls to people with marketing and/or product-management titles. These people tend to engage in many marketing activities, such as securing data on customers and competitors, developing advertising campaigns, designing direct-mail brochures, meeting with R&D on new products, devising online and mobile strategies, setting prices, and/or preparing persuasive messages for the sales force. Certainly, these activities often enhance the firm's market position, but deciding how to allocate marketers' time and/or other resources requires answers to several questions:

- Which of these activities is critical?
- Do these activities represent the core elements of marketing?
- What critical tasks must the firm perform to truly accomplish its marketing agenda?
- In what order should the firm perform these tasks?

We now discuss the six marketing imperatives — the firm's *must dos* — that are the core elements of *Capon's Marketing Framework*. The first three imperatives focus on **strategic marketing**; the second three imperatives zero in on **implementing the market strategy**.

The Six Marketing Imperatives

Strategic Marketing
- Imperative 1: Determine and recommend which markets to address.
- Imperative 2: Identify and target market segments.
- Imperative 3: Set strategic direction and positioning.

Implementing the Market Strategy
- Imperative 4: Design the market offer.
- Imperative 5: Secure support from other functions.
- Imperative 6: Monitor and control execution and performance.

STRATEGIC MARKETING — IMPERATIVE 1: DETERMINE AND RECOMMEND WHICH MARKETS TO ADDRESS

KEY IDEA

➤ **Imperative 1.** Marketing should identify market opportunities and advise top management on potential strategic actions.

Simply put, the firm must choose those markets where it will compete. To help make these choices, the firm should ask: What businesses are we in? What businesses do we want to be in? Market-choice decisions are typically strategic for the firm, or at least for individual business units. Choosing markets is often more important than choosing technologies and/or products. Given the choice of owning a market or owning a factory, most senior executives would prefer owning a market.

The firm must continually make market-choice decisions. Faster environmental changes open up new market opportunities, but may also lead the firm to exit current markets. Market-choice decisions can totally transform a corporation. Nokia exited its traditional paper-making, rubber-goods, and electric-cable markets as it evolved from a diversified conglomerate to global leadership in wireless communication (but was very slow to introduce smartphones).

The firm must decide where to invest — to compete, or not — in various markets, and decide how much to invest. The firm must answer critical questions about its business and market portfolio:

- In which new businesses and markets shall we invest — people, time, dollars?
- In which current businesses and markets shall we continue to invest?
- How much investment shall we make in these various businesses and markets?
- From which businesses and markets shall we disinvest or withdraw?

Typically, marketing does not make these decisions. Top management has this responsibility, but marketing must provide good advice. For Imperative 1, marketing plays two key roles:

- **Identify opportunities.** Marketing is the only function with explicit responsibility to focus attention outside the firm. Marketing personnel should research the environment to identify potential opportunities and bring these to top management's attention. They should also collect and analyze data that bear on entry decisions. Marketing should be intimately involved with the firm's current markets and businesses and advise on investment and exit decisions.

- **Advise on proposed strategic actions.** Many firm functions develop strategic initiatives. Finance may suggest acquisitions and divestitures; R&D may propose strategic alliances; and the sales force may champion a new distribution system. Marketing has the responsibility to insert itself into these decisions. The firm should fully explore the marketing ramifications of its decisions or disaster may ensue. Most observers believe the AOL/TimeWarner and Quaker/Snapple acquisitions were failures. Perhaps the acquirers would have made superior decisions with better marketing advice!

STRATEGIC MARKETING — IMPERATIVE 2: IDENTIFY AND TARGET MARKET SEGMENTS

In any **B2B** or **B2C** market, customers have a diverse set of needs. A single offer directed at the overall market may satisfy some customers, but typically many customers are dissatisfied. Imperative 2 states that marketing must identify **market segments** — groups of customers with similar needs that value similar benefits, with similar levels of priority.

When the firm does **market segmentation** well, the needs, benefits, and values that define one segment are quite different from the needs, benefits, and values that define other segments. After the firm has identified segments, it must decide which to target.

Note the two elements of Imperative 2: A *creative and analytic* part — identifying market segments; and a *decision-making* part — choosing which segments to target, based on the firm's ability to deliver customer value. Boeing purchased de Havilland Canada (DHC) to address the small, regional segment of the overall aircraft market with the Dash 8. In six years, Boeing lost nearly $1 billion and then sold DHC to Bombardier. Bombardier tripled the Dash 8's market share to 35 percent. Both Boeing and Bombardier did a good job of identifying the small, regional segment, but only Bombardier had the appropriate skills and resources to target this market segment; Boeing did not. This lesson is important — a market segment may be attractive to one firm but unattractive to another.

Market segmentation and targeting is arguably the most critical marketing imperative. Effective segmentation and targeting drive profits.

STRATEGIC MARKETING — IMPERATIVE 3: SET STRATEGIC DIRECTION AND POSITIONING

In Imperative 3, the firm decides how to compete in those market segments it has targeted. For each target segment, marketing must formulate performance objectives. These objectives guide the firm's strategic decisions in the target segments. Second, the firm must decide on its positioning for each segment. It must identify target customers and target competitors, design a more persuasive value proposition than competitors and provide reasons for customers to believe the firm can deliver that value. Together with Imperative 2, positioning completes the critical STP triumvirate — **s**egmentation, **t**argeting, and **p**ositioning.

Typically, individual market segments are at different developmental stages, and hence require different approaches. The appropriate way to address a growing market segment is quite different from a mature or declining segment. In addition, decisions about strategic direction also include questions of branding — how the firm wants customers to view the corporate entity and its products. Top management increasingly views the firm's brands as major corporate assets; hence **branding** issues are among its most important strategic decisions.

Of course, the firm does not make these decisions only once. It faces an ever-changing environmental landscape: Customer needs evolve and competitors enter, exit, and adopt different strategies. The firm's products also evolve as target segments grow, mature, and decline. The firm must continually assess its strategic direction and make necessary course corrections.

IMPLEMENTING THE MARKET STRATEGY — IMPERATIVE 4: DESIGN THE MARKET OFFER

Imperative 4 focuses on design of the **market offer**. The marketing offer is the total benefit package the firm provides customers. Tools for designing the offer are the most well-known part of marketing. If you took a previous marketing course, the professor probably spent significant

KEY IDEA

➤ **Imperative 4.** The firm designs the market offer using the tools of the marketing mix:

• Product

• Promotion

• Distribution (Place)

• Price

time talking about the **marketing mix** (aka the **4Ps**). Marketing mix elements comprise the basic building blocks of the firm's offer to the market:

- **Product.** In general, the product embodies the major benefits the firm offers to satisfy customer needs — these benefits provide value to customers. If the firm offers greater value than its competitors, customer purchases increase. The term *product* typically embraces both physical products and services like airline travel and packaging.

- **Promotion.** Promotion embraces the various ways the firm communicates with customers — informing and persuading them to purchase its products. Promotion includes *mass and digital communications*, like advertising, sales promotions, and social media; and *personal communications*, like the sales force. In addition to informing and persuading, communications may add customer value directly by providing imagery, status, and reassurance.

- **Distribution.** Distribution focuses on how and where customers secure the product. To conform to the 4Ps nomenclature, marketers sometimes refer to *distribution* as **place**.

- **Price.** Price is what customers pay. The firm establishes the feasible price by the equivalent amount of value it offers through its product, promotion, and distribution.

If the firm offers significant benefits and high customer value from its product, communications, and distribution, it can set a high price. But if customer benefits and value are low, price must also be low. If the firm designs good marketing offers, customers purchase its products. When targeting a market segment, the firm can combine marketing-mix elements in an infinite number of ways. Creativity, imagination, innovation, and capability are core ingredients.

IMPLEMENTING THE MARKET STRATEGY — IMPERATIVE 5: SECURE SUPPORT FROM OTHER FUNCTIONS

KEY IDEA

➤ **Imperative 5.** Marketing must keep the firm focused on customer needs, regardless of current feasibility.

➤ Marketing must exercise leadership to encourage cooperation across multiple functions.

Imperatives 1, 2, 3, and 4 concern *where* and *how* questions. Imperatives 1, 2, and 3 focus on *where* the firm will place its resources. Imperative 4 concerns *how* the firm will use its resources to design the market offer. Imperative 5 focuses on how firm functions work together to ensure the firm executes the market offer as designed. Marketing requires two very different types of support:

- **Support for design** — relates to technical, operational, and economic feasibility.
- **Support for implementation** — assumes the design is agreed upon and fixed.

SUPPORT FOR DESIGN. Imperative 4 focuses on designing the market offer that best meets customer needs in a target segment. The firm's ability to deliver the market offer depends on its capabilities and resources. The *best* design for customers may require a product feature the firm cannot make. When the best design is not feasible, marketing must develop extraordinary strength to keep the firm focused on satisfying customer needs — and push specific functions to evolve their capabilities.[16]

SUPPORT FOR IMPLEMENTATION. We often call this support *internal marketing*, or getting *buy-in*. In many firms, marketing designs the offer — but has little authority to implement the design. Marketers must possess the leadership and interpersonal skills to encourage and stimulate cooperation across multiple functions. After all, *the chain is only as strong as its weakest link*. If a key function does not perform, other functions may waste their efforts.

IMPLEMENTING THE MARKET STRATEGY — IMPERATIVE 6: MONITOR AND CONTROL EXECUTION AND PERFORMANCE

It's one thing to plan and implement, but figuring out the firm's performance is quite another. Imperative 6 focuses on *monitor and control* of marketing programs — is the firm achieving its desired results? All things equal, if the firm is successful, it should keep on truckin'; otherwise it should make changes.

Essentially, marketing should continually secure answers to three questions and act accordingly:

- Are the firm's various functions and departments *implementing* the market offer?
- Are the firm's market and financial *performance* reaching planned objectives?
- Based on the current *environment*, are the firm's objectives, strategies, and implementation plans on track, or should it make changes?

IMPLEMENTATION. The firm may have many implementation problems (Imperative 5) like lack of buy-in. But even with excellent buy-in, antiquated or inappropriate management systems create implementation difficulties.

POOR PERFORMANCE. If the firm is not achieving market and/or financial performance objectives, marketing may require more data and further analysis. If environmental change is low, marketing should focus on course corrections by fine-tuning its strategy and/or modifying implementation plans.

ENVIRONMENTAL CHANGE. The firm bases objectives, strategy, and implementation on its best insight into customer needs, competitive offers, and the external environment. A good strategy should accommodate evolutionary changes — more significant change may require new objectives and strategies.

THE FOUR PRINCIPLES OF MARKETING

You just learned that six imperatives are the *must dos* of marketing. Four marketing principles serve as guidelines for implementing these imperatives.

The Four Principles of Marketing

- Principle 1: Selectivity and Concentration
- Principle 2: Customer Value
- Principle 3: Differential Advantage
- Principle 4: Integration

PRINCIPLE 1: SELECTIVITY AND CONCENTRATION

Providing advice on market selection (Imperative 1) and deciding which market segments to target (Imperative 2) are among marketing's primary responsibilities. The basic principle underlying these imperatives is the **Principle of Selectivity and Concentration**.

Two aspects comprise the Selectivity and Concentration principle:

- **Selectivity.** Marketing must carefully choose targets for the firm's efforts.
- **Concentration.** The firm should concentrate its resources against those targets.

This principle is about choosing the firm's battles. It is dangerous to dissipate limited resources over too many alternatives by trying too much. No organization, no matter how large or how successful, has infinite resources. Each must make timely choices. The selectivity element comes into play when marketing recommends which markets to target — Imperative 1, but the best-known manifestation is identifying and targeting market segments — Imperative 2.

As markets become increasingly competitive, hedging bets by allocating small amounts of resources to a broad set of options will certainly fail. For this reason, some experts have relabeled this principle *Concentration and Concession*. Not only must the firm concentrate its resources in chosen segments, it might affirmatively concede other segments to competitors.

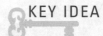

KEY IDEA

➤ **Imperative 6.** Marketing must monitor and control the firm's actions and performance to keep it on track.

Marketing Question

How good a job has Google done in implementing the six Marketing Imperatives?

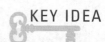

KEY IDEA

➤ **Principle 1: Selectivity and Concentration**

- **Selectivity.** Marketing must carefully choose targets for the firm's efforts.
- **Concentration.** The firm should concentrate its resources against those targets.

PRINCIPLE 2: CUSTOMER VALUE

According to the **Principle of Customer Value**, the firm's marketplace success depends on providing value to customers. This principle is central to marketing's job. Customer insight should drive design and implementation of market offers. Customer value should drive the firm's product and investment decisions — and its performance evaluation. The firm develops, produces, and delivers products and services, but customers perceive value only in the benefits these products and services provide.

Customer value is a moving target. As the environment changes, customers accumulate experience and their needs evolve — the values they seek evolve also. World-class companies continuously invest in marketing research to probe deeply into customer needs, priorities, expectations, and experiences. They feed these results into the product development process to produce greater value for customers.

Cisco continues to be the market-share leader and a major force in technology and networking. Said an important Wall Street analyst, "They [Cisco] don't have the best technology, but they do have the best [customer] relationships."[17] Firms that take their eye off the *customer ball* can get into serious trouble. Sears and Kmart (U.S.), and Sainsbury's and Marks & Spencer (Great Britain), were once powerful and successful retailers. In recent years, each has been in crisis.

PRINCIPLE 3: DIFFERENTIAL ADVANTAGE

The **Principle of Differential Advantage** is closely related to the Principle of Customer Value. Differential advantage is similar to having a *competitive advantage*, a *unique selling proposition (USP)*, or an *edge*. Differential advantage lies at the heart of every successful market strategy. The Principle of Differential Advantage asserts that the firm should offer customers something they value but cannot get elsewhere.

More formally, *a differential advantage is a net benefit or cluster of benefits, offered to a sizable group of customers, which they value and are willing to pay for but cannot get, or believe they cannot get, elsewhere*. To implement this principle, the firm must develop well-designed market offers based on the marketing-mix elements we discussed earlier. If the firm achieves a differential advantage, it should secure improved prices. This principle leads to several implications:

- **Competition.** The principle emphasizes competition. Offering customer value is not enough. To avoid competitive parity, the firm must offer greater value than competitors. The firm must create and re-create its differential advantage to beat competitors.

- **Superiority of differential advantages.** Some differential advantages are better than others. A differential advantage based on proprietary intellectual property (IP), unique product design, or product availability may be more sustainable than one based on communications. A differential advantage based on an organizational process like parts delivery or qualified technicians may be even more sustainable.[18]

- **Eroding differential advantages.** Competition will eventually erode away even the apparently most sustainable differential advantage. Maintaining differential advantage is marketing's most fundamental challenge, and the search for differential advantage must be ongoing. Ideally, the firm should have a hidden differential advantage, ready to trump the competitor's ace!

- **Cannibalizing a differential advantage.** To stay ahead of competition, the firm must be willing to cannibalize its own offers. Many firms will not do so, in part because of strong political constituencies for the status quo. This runs the risk of missing opportunities and passing marketplace initiatives to a competitor.

- **Differential advantage and difference.** A *differential advantage* is not the same as a *difference*. To develop a different market offer may not be difficult. The firm's differences must create benefits that customers recognize, value, and are willing to pay for.

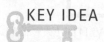

KEY IDEA

➤ **Principle 2: Customer Value**

- The firm earns success by providing value to customers.

- The firm develops, produces, and delivers products and services, but customers perceive value only in the benefits these products and services provide.

Marketing Question

Apple's success has made it one of the world's most admired firms. How do you assess Apple's adherence to the four marketing principles?

KEY IDEA

➤ **Principle 3: Differential Advantage**

- To secure differential advantage, customers must perceive greater value in the firm's offer than in competitor offers.

PRINCIPLE 4: INTEGRATION

Integration is critical to Target's success. "Every one of us, in every functional group, from Stores to Merchandising, from Logistics to Support, identifies with the role as marketing. We're all attempting to build better relationships with our guest [Target's term for customer]. And every decision starts with the guest, so everyone becomes a marketer. We instill that attitude with evangelical passion and great consistency — the evangelizing starts at the top with our Chairman and CEO. Our core brand promise since 1962 has been, 'Expect more, pay less.' We live it — every single function of this company lives it. We search the globe for the best products to serve our guest needs and everyone in the store is hard-wired to meet guest expectations at all times."[19]

The **Principle of Integration** — critical for all marketing efforts — has two dimensions:

- **At the customer.** The firm must carefully integrate and coordinate all design and execution elements it offers to customers. For example, poor advertising can ruin an excellent product; delayed promotional materials can doom a product launch; and improper pricing can cause havoc with sales forecasts.

- **In the firm.** To achieve integration at the customer, the firm must carefully integrate and coordinate all internal activities — this can be difficult. Different functions and/or departments may squabble over priorities or senior management sends ambiguous messages. And individual units focus on defending their *turf* at the expense of delivering customer value.

Firms with an external orientation are more likely to achieve integration because they share the common purpose of serving customers. Sharing responsibility for designing and implementing market offers drives agreement on priorities, and close and cooperative working relationships.

KEY IDEA

➤ **Principle 4: Integration**

- The firm must carefully integrate all elements in the design and execution of its market offer.

- To achieve integration at customers, the firm must coordinate and integrate internal functional activities.

KEY MESSAGES

- Firms that deliver greater customer value than competitors are more successful in attracting, retaining, and growing customers.

- Firms that successfully attract, retain, and grow customers earn profits. They are more likely to survive and grow, and enhance shareholder value.

- Value has two sides. When firms deliver customer value, they attract, retain, and grow customers. When firms attract, retain, and grow customers, they create shareholder value.

- Marketing as a philosophy embraces an external orientation — all organizational members have a responsibility for delivering customer value.

- Six marketing imperatives are *must dos* for the firm.

- Four marketing principles provide the guiding framework within which the firm implements the six marketing imperatives.

VIDEOS AND AUDIOS

Marketing Careers	v102	Ellen	Columbia Business School
Pharmaceutical Marketing	v103	Robert Essner	Wyeth; Columbia Business School
The Role of Marketing	a101		
The Externally Oriented Firm	a102		
Four Marketing Principles	a103		

v102

v103

a101

a102

a103

CHAPTER 2

THE VALUE OF CUSTOMERS

To access O-codes, go to www.ocodes.com

Success is getting the right customers ... and keeping them.

— Charles Cawley, founder of credit card giant MBNA

LEARNING OBJECTIVES

When you have completed this chapter, you will be able to:

- Identify the critical elements that define customer lifetime value.
- Calculate customer profitability and customer lifetime value.
- Recognize the importance of investing in, and retaining, the *right* customers.
- Relate delivering customer value to generating long-term customer loyalty.
- Explain the importance of measuring customer profitability.
- Make tough decisions on dealing with unprofitable current customers.
- Make tough decisions about accepting/rejecting potential customers.
- Establish a customer relationship management (CRM) program.
- Design customer loyalty programs.

OPENING CASE: ROYAL BANK OF CANADA

Toronto-based Royal Bank of Canada (RBC) serves over 14 million personal, business, and public-sector customers via offices in North America and 30 other countries. RBC is Canada's leading bank, with more than 1,700 offices and 5,000 banking machines. What sets RBC apart from competitors is its focus on customer profitability. In RBC's retail business, 17 percent of customers account for 93 percent of profits — an extreme version of the 80/20 rule at 93/17. RBC concentrates on this 17 percent and discourages, or even discards, its least profitable and loss-making customers.

RBC calculates economic profit by customer.[1] Identifying revenue, product profit margins (spreads), and invested capital is easy. RBC tracks labor costs via activity-based costing. RBC monitors costs for back office processing, call centers, and other activities.

RBC's retail bank has nine customer segment managers and many product managers. Each segment and product manager has individual and primary responsibility for strategy and profit and loss (P&L) for their segment/product. This matrix organization encourages collaboration; it works because RBC's culture has always been customer-centric and consensus driven. Also, senior management has clearly signaled that managing for team success is important for career advancement.

RBC'S NEW APPROACH. *RBC traditionally ran mortgage promotions in the spring home-buying season, emphasizing RBC's rates. Competitor banks operated similarly. But Louise Mitchell, RBC's leader for the builders and borrowers segment, pursued a different approach — she targeted the life event of a first home purchase. Mitchell created a value proposition to serve the total needs of first-time home buyers, and add significant value to RBC's shareholders:*

- *First-time home buyers have most of their financial lives ahead of them. Attracting these customers promises long-term banking relationships, with significant growth prospects.*

RBC's product-centric organization could not have executed this promotion; the promotion required coordination among managers responsible for mortgages, savings accounts, financial advice, and marketing. As segment leader, Mitchell was a powerful catalyst. She stated: "Looking through the customer lens," the promotional ideas "jump right out at you."

The result? RBC's first-time-mortgage share grew significantly, particularly in the longest, most profitable (for RBC) terms. Although 2008 was difficult, from 1994 to 2012, RBC earned several increases: revenues — $7.4 billion to $38.2 billion; profits — $1.2 billion to $7.5 billion; share price from less than $10 to more than $60.

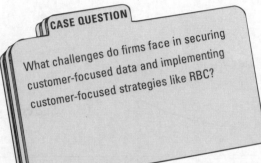

CASE QUESTION

What challenges do firms face in securing customer-focused data and implementing customer-focused strategies like RBC?

Chapter 1 discusses the critical role customers play for the firm's well-being. By attracting, retaining, and growing customers, the firm makes profits today and promises profits tomorrow. Profits allow the firm to survive and grow, and enhance shareholder value. Because of these relationships, customers are the firm's core assets. More precisely, customers are core assets because of two sides of the concept of value. When the firm creates value for customers, it successfully attracts, retains, and grows those customers. By being attracted, retained, and grown, customers create value for the firm and its shareholders.[2] Because retained customers return to buy more products and services, the firm's key goal is to deliver customer value and generate long-term customer loyalty.

This chapter moves beyond the customers-as-assets concept to measuring the value that customers bring to the firm. The critical concept is **customer lifetime value (CLV)** — what the customer is worth. CLV is the discounted future stream of profits the customer generates over the life of its relationship. CLV is the crucial link between the value the firm delivers to customers and the value customers deliver to the firm. Increasing CLV enhances shareholder value. This chapter shows how to use CLV to increase the value customers bring to the firm; both current customers and potential new customers. The chapter also identifies the *right* customers and shows that some customers are undesirable.

Specifically, we address two questions:

- How can we put a monetary value on the firm's current customers and on potential customers it may acquire? This monetary value is CLV.
- How can we use the CLV concept to help the firm enhance shareholder value?

KEY IDEA

➤ When the firm creates value for customers, it successfully attracts, retains, and grows customers.

➤ By being attracted, retained, and grown, customers create value for the firm and its shareholders.

In the second part of this chapter, we examine practical ways in which firms use the CLV concept. Specifically, we address customer relationship management (CRM) and customer loyalty.

CUSTOMER LIFETIME VALUE (CLV)

When customers purchase the firm's products and services, the firm earns revenues; it also accrues costs. If sales revenues are greater than costs, the firm earns profits. The profit earned from an individual customer during a single time period (year) is the **profit margin** — the annual value the customer brings to the firm.[3] Of course, both consumers (B2C) and business partners, distributors, and resellers (B2B) often purchase the firm's products for several successive years. Each year, the firm receives sales revenues, accrues costs, and earns a profit margin. CLV takes into account profit margins the firm earns in each of these years.

Some firm customers this year will not be customers next year. They may defect to competitors, or stop buying the types of products the firm offers. In calculating CLV, we must consider customer *defection* and customer *retention*. **Retention rate** is simply the number of customers at the end of the year, divided by the number of customers at the start of the year. If the firm starts the year with 100 customers and ends the year with 80 of these same customers, its retention rate is 80 percent. Retention is the inverse of defection (churn). In this illustration, the **defection rate** is 20 percent (100 percent minus 80 percent).[4] Understanding CLV allows the firm to better manage its customer base.

CALCULATING CLV

In each year, the firm earns a portion of its CLV. In the first year, it earns CLV (1):

$$\text{CLV (1)} = m \times r/(1 + d)$$

Restating this simple expression in words, CLV (1) is:

- The *profit margin (m)* the firm earns in year 1,
- Multiplied by the *retention rate (r)* — the probability that a customer at the start of the year will still be a customer at the end of the year,
- *Discounted* back to the start of the year, using the term $1/(1+d)$. The **discount rate (d)** is the firm's *cost of capital* — typically provided by the firm's chief financial officer (CFO).

To calculate a customer's total CLV, we simply add up the CLV contributions for each successive year.[5] This is complicated mathematically. We simplify the calculation by assuming that each term — profit margin (m), discount rate (d), and retention rate (r) — is constant year to year.

With these assumptions, CLV equals the profit margin (m) multiplied by a term we call the **margin multiple**.

The margin multiple = $r/(1 + d - r)$, so that:

$$\text{CLV} = m \times r/(1 + d - r)$$

Estimating CLV is quite straightforward using this formula. Table 2.1 makes it easier by providing margin multiple values for different retention rates (r) and discount rates (d).

Suppose the firm earns an annual margin of $500,000, customer retention rate is 70 percent, and the firm's discount rate is 12 percent. From Table 2.1, the margin multiple is 1.67. Hence, CLV = **$500,000 × 1.67 = $835,000**. Of course, we lose some precision with these assumptions but, in most cases, putting us in the right ballpark is sufficient.

Retention Rate (r)	Discount Rate (d)			
	8%	12%	16%	20%
60%	1.25	1.15	1.07	1.00
70%	1.84	1.67	1.52	1.40
80%	2.86	2.50	2.22	2.00
90%	5.00	4.09	3.46	3.00
95%	7.31	5.59	4.52	3.80

TABLE 2.1

THE MARGIN
MULTIPLE =
r/(1+d−r)

Note several things about Table 2.1:

1. The ranges of values for discount rate (d) (8 percent to 20 percent) and retention rate (r) (60 percent to 95 percent) are quite large. They cover most cases for most firms — the margin multiple value spans 1.00 to 7.31.

2. The median value of the margin multiple is around 2.5.

3. Improving retention rate (r) has a greater impact on the margin multiple than reducing discount rate (d):

   a. When retention rate (r) is 90 percent, reducing discount rate (d) from 20 percent to 8 percent improves the margin multiple from 3.00 to 5.00 — 67 percent.

   b. When discount rate (d) is 12 percent, increasing retention rate (r) from 60 percent to 90 percent increases the margin multiple from 1.15 to 4.09 — well over three times! It follows that:

4. All things equal, the firm is better off increasing retention rate (r) than reducing discount rate (d) — cost of capital — by financial engineering. Finance students, please note!

5. Customer retention is a big deal. More on this later.

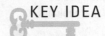

KEY IDEA

➤ Increasing customer retention rate has greater leverage on customer lifetime value than reducing the discount rate.

Example: Lifetime Value of a FedEx Customer

FedEx has identified a market segment — these data apply to FedEx customers in that segment:

Assumptions

- Total FedEx letters shipped per month = 2,285
- Number of FedEx customers = 140
- FedEx profit margin per letter (m) = $8.25
- Discount rate (cost of capital) (d) = 12%
- Annual retention rate (r) = 90%

We assume that these numbers remain constant year to year.

Customer lifetime value calculation:

Number of FedEx letters per customer per annum = 2,285 × 12/140 = 195.8

FedEx profit margin per customer per annum = $8.25 × 195.8 = $1,616

Discount rate (d) = 12%

Retention rate (r) = 90%

From Table 2.1, the **margin multiple** = 4.09

CLV = FedEx profit margin per customer per annum × margin multiple = $1,616 × 4.09 = **$6,609**

Marketing Question

If you were FedEx's CMO, what three options would you consider to increase CLV? Why?

Quite simply, the firm has three, and only three, ways to increase CLV:

- Increase the profit margin (m) the firm earns from customers.
- Increase customer retention rate (r) or reduce customer defection rate.
- Reduce discount rate (d). This is a matter for finance, not for marketing.

INCREASE THE PROFIT MARGIN THE FIRM EARNS FROM CUSTOMERS

The firm has several options for increasing CLV by raising the margins from current customers:

- **Customer selection.** Well-selected current customers provide a base level of profit margin.
- **Customer satisfaction and loyalty.** Well-served customers increase purchases over time. Hence, revenues and profit margins increase.
- **Customization.** Targeted offers to defined segments provide greater customer value.
- **Raise prices.** If customer satisfaction is high, the firm may be able to set higher prices.
- **Reduce operating costs.** As the firm becomes more proficient in serving customers, it reduces operating costs and may reap scale economies with individual customers.

In addition, satisfied customers may help the firm secure revenues from other customers:

- **Learning.** The firm learns by working closely with customers and becomes better able to attract new customers.
- **Network externalities.** In some markets, customers bring value to other customers. The more *sellers* eBay attracts, the more valuable is eBay's service is to its *buyers*. The more *buyers* eBay attracts, the more valuable it is to *sellers*. Television, some printed media, and websites are free, yet their customer traffic has value to advertisers.
- **Positive word of mouth and referrals.** Satisfied customers generate positive word of mouth and provide referrals to potential customers. Lexus secures more new customers from referrals than from any other source.
- **Signals.** Securing a high-profile customer may provide the firm with credibility among other potential customers.

Figure 2.1 shows annual profit margin per customer in the U.S. credit card industry. In year 1, the average credit card issuer loses $80 (from customer acquisition and start-up costs); in year 2, the customer earns the firm $40. Profit margin per customer increases steadily with customer longevity.[6]

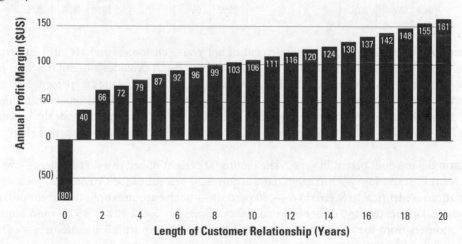

INCREASE CUSTOMER RETENTION RATE — REDUCE CUSTOMER DEFECTION RATE

We just showed that a profit margin (m) increase leads to CLV increase. Of course, profit margin is only relevant if the customer continues to be a customer! The firm continually loses customers and, of course, defection is greater at 80 percent retention rate than 90 percent. Regardless, the number of customers defecting is greatest in the first year — as time goes by, fewer customers defect. Assume the firm acquires 1,000 new customers at the beginning of year 1:

	90% retention	80% retention
Year Start	**1,000** customers	**1,000** customers
Year 1	**900** remain; 100 customers lost	**800** remain; 200 customers lost
Year 2	**810** remain; 90 customers lost	**640** remain; 160 customers lost
Year 3	**729** remain; 81 customers lost	**512** remain; 128 customers lost

These data tell us that customer retention rate has an important impact on customer CLV. Based on an empirical study, a 5 percent increase in customer retention rate enhances CLV by over 50 percent in several U.S. industries.[7]

HOW CUSTOMER RETENTION WORKS

We just saw that customer retention rate is an important CLV driver. We now show how small differences in customer retention lead, over time, to major differences in sales and market share. Figure 2.2 shows three hypothetical scenarios — A, B, and C — each with two firms, Jane's Makeup Emporium and Joe's Beauty Aids, and two time periods, year 1 and year 2. Each scenario shows patterns of customer retention (defection) and customer acquisition. To keep things simple, we assume 1,000 customers in total and that Jane and Joe each start with 500. Our task is to figure out the number of customers that Jane and Joe eventually secure in each scenario, and their steady state market shares.

Scenario A
Year 2

	Jane	Joe
Jane	80%	20%
Joe	20%	80%

Year 1

Scenario B
Year 2

	Jane	Joe
Jane	90%	10%
Joe	20%	80%

Year 1

Scenario C
Year 2

	Jane	Joe
Jane	95%	5%
Joe	20%	80%

Year 1

FIGURE 2.2

ILLUSTRATIVE LONG-RUN MARKET-SHARE SCENARIOS

Scenario A. In year 2, Jane retains 80 percent of her year-1 customers and acquires 20 percent of Joe's. Joe's pattern is identical. This scenario is trivial, but it provides a useful baseline. Jane and Joe essentially swap equal numbers of customers back and forth. Jane's 80 percent retention yields her 400 customers — 500 x 80% = 400 — and she acquires 100 customers from Joe — 500 x 20% = 100. Jane ends up with 500 customers (400 + 100), the same number she had originally. Joe's situation is identical. Jane and Joe each earn 50 percent long-run market share.

Scenario B. Jane does better. In year 2, she retains 90 percent of her year-1 customers — versus 80 percent in scenario A — but again, Jane acquires 20 percent of Joe's customers. Joe's retention pattern is identical to Scenario A — 80 percent — but he acquires only 10 percent of Jane's customers. Jane retains 450 of her original 500 customers — 500 x 90% = 450 — and acquires 100 customers from Joe — 500 x 20% = 100. Jane now ends up with 550 customers — 450 + 100 = 550; Joe has 450 customers.

In year 3, Jane's starting customer base is higher — 550 versus 500 — so she retains 495 customers — 550 x 90% = 495. Joe's starting base is lower — 450 versus 500 — so Jane only acquires 90 of his customers — 450 x 20% = 90. But the combination of acquisition and retention increases Jane's customers from 550 to 585 — 495 + 90. Joe has 415 customers. These numbers converge to a steady state where Jane and Joe have 670 and 330 customers, respectively — 67 percent and 33 percent market shares.

Marketing Question

Suppose a firm's annual revenue growth goal was 15 percent. Consider two situations:

• Customer retention rate = 80 percent

• Customer retention rate = 95 percent

What would the firm's customer acquisition rate have to be in each case? What would be the implications for the firm?

Scenario C. Jane does even better. In year 2, she retains 95 percent of her year-1 customers and again acquires 20 percent of Joe's. Joe's retention pattern is the same as previously — 80 percent — but he acquires only 5 percent of Jane's customers. Using the same process as before, the steady-state customer numbers are 800 for Jane and 200 for Joe — 80 percent and 20 percent market shares respectively — Table 2.2. (You may want to confirm this result for yourself.)

TABLE 2.2

STEADY-STATE
MARKET SHARES[8]

	Steady-State Market Shares	
Jane's Retention Rate	Jane	Joe
80%	50%	50%
90%	67%	33%
95%	80%	20%

To summarize:

- As retention rate increases, steady-state market share increases;
- The higher the retention rate, the greater the impact on market share for a given retention rate increase. For example:
  - When Jane's retention rate is 80 percent, a 10 percent increase — to 90 percent — increases her market share by 17 points — from 50 percent to 67 percent; but,
  - When Jane's retention rate is 90 percent, a 5 percent increase — to 95 percent — increases her market share by 13 points — from 67 percent to 80 percent.

Of course, it may be more expensive to improve retention rate from 90 percent to 95 percent than from 80 percent to 90 percent!

This is a very simple exercise but it demonstrates an important truth — customer retention is a big deal! Relatively small differences in customer retention lead to large differences in long-run market shares.

KEY IDEA

➤ Small increases in customer retention can dramatically improve CLV.

PROFIT MARGINS AND CUSTOMER RETENTION

Table 2.3 combines credit card profit margin data — Figure 2.1, with customer retention data, assuming a 10 percent discount rate. We see the effect of increased profit margin over the length of the customer relationship, based on two different retention rates. Table 2.3 shows:

- When retention rate is 90 percent, total annual profit peaks at $53,460 (year 2), then declines annually. Ten-year discounted profits are **$205,721**.
- When retention rate is 80 percent, total annual profit also peaks in year 2, but at a much lower figure — $42,240. Ten-year discounted profits are **$93,475**.

Hence, the 90 percent to 80 percent retention rate difference leads to a CLV difference of **$112,246** ($205,721 – $93,475).

Marketing Question

Suppose a firm can sustain a 15 percent customer acquisition rate; its goal is to double the customer base. Consider two situations:

- Customer retention rate = 90 percent
- Customer retention rate = 95 percent

In each case, how many years will it take for the firm to reach its goal?

Age of Account	Annual Profit Margin per Customer by Age of Account	90% Retention Rate			80% Retention Rate		
		Number of Customers Remaining	Total Annual Customer Profit Margin by Age of Account	Total Discounted Annual Customer Profit Margin by Age of Account	Number of Customers Remaining	Total Annual Customer Profit Margin by Age of Account	Total Discounted Annual Customer Profit Margin by Age of Account
0	−$80	1000	−$80,000	−$80,000	1000	−$80,000	−$80,000
1	$40	900	$36,000	$32,727	800	$32,000	$29,091
2	$66	810	$53,460	$44,182	640	$42,240	$34,910
3	$72	729	$52,488	$39,435	512	$36,864	$27,696
4	$79	656	$51,824	$35,396	410	$32,390	$22,123
5	$87	590	$51,330	$31,872	328	$28,536	$17,719
6	$92	531	$48,852	$27,576	262	$24,104	$13,606
7	$96	478	$45,888	$23,548	210	$20,160	$10,345
8	$99	430	$42,570	$19,859	168	$16,632	$ 7,759
9	$103	387	$39,861	$16,905	134	$13,802	$ 5,853
10	$106	348	$36,888	$14,221	107	$11,342	$ 4,373
			Total CLV	$205,721		Total CLV	$93,475

TABLE 2.3

PROFITS IN THE U.S. CREDIT CARD INDUSTRY AT DIFFERENT CUSTOMER RETENTION RATES

Marketing Question

What is the source of CLV for: Capital One, Domino's Pizza, Potemkin automobile dealership, and Rolls-Royce aero engines?

ACQUIRING NEW CUSTOMERS

So far, we used CLV to focus on the firm's current customers. We showed that increasing both profit margin and customer retention rate raises CLV. But what about potential future customers? How valuable are they? We can use the same approach to consider potential customers. The biggest difference is that, right now, the firm earns no revenue from these potential customers and, to attract them, it must incur an **acquisition cost (AC)**. Using the same approach as before, we include the cost to acquire these new customers:

$$CLV = m \times r/(1 + d - r) - AC$$

We now have a useful way to think about new customers. All things equal, the firm should acquire a customer if the first term in the CLV expression, $m \times r/(1 + d - r)$, is greater than the acquisition cost (AC). If the acquisition cost were greater, the firm would lose money.

BEING SELECTIVE ABOUT CUSTOMERS

As discussed earlier, much of *Capon's Marketing Framework* focuses on increasing CLV from current customers and acquiring profitable new customers. From Chapter 7 on, we elaborate on the six marketing imperatives that encapsulate approaches for achieving these goals. Here, we identify a broad set of options for addressing current and potential customers — Figure 2.3.

KEY IDEA

➤ The firm should try to acquire customers whose expected CLV is greater than the acquisition cost.

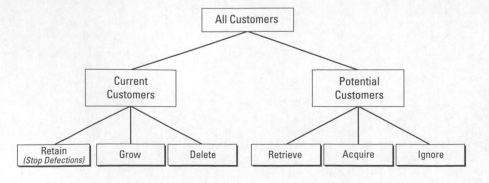

FIGURE 2.3

APPROACHES TO IMPROVING CUSTOMER LIFETIME VALUE

When asked to divide promotional expenses into two buckets — one for retaining current customers and one for attracting new customers — most executives report a focus on attracting new customers. Of course, new customers are critical for firm growth; but the issue is one of balance. Far too often, the firm takes its current customers for granted and spends too little on customer retention! Further, retaining current customers is generally less costly than acquiring new customers. We do not suggest that current customers are more important than new customers. After all, new customers may have greater growth potential. But we do believe the firm should make its customer investment decisions carefully and deliberately.

CURRENT CUSTOMERS

Figure 2.3 shows three firm options for addressing current customers — retain, grow, delete.

RETAIN. The firm's customer base is like a leaky bucket; the firm should plug its holes. By updating products and services to meet evolving customer needs and taking other actions to bind customers more closely, the firm enhances customer satisfaction, increases loyalty, and reduces defections. Satisfied and delighted customers are more likely to continue buying than dissatisfied customers. Wachovia Bank's (now Wells Fargo) customer satisfaction scores improved from 5.5 to 6.5 (1-to-7 scale — Gallup) over a five-year period; annual customer defection declined from 20 percent to 11 percent. In the insurance and mutual fund industries, firms use sophisticated applications to match preferences and try to sell extra products to existing single-product customers. This increased reliance on the firm creates **lock-in**. Some firms implement early warning systems to identify potential defectors:

OfficeMax has a *defection detector.* Said a senior executive: "We have automatic warning signs that apply to all major customers, and then for each one there are also special warning signs that we enter manually. Has the customer gone more than 12 weeks without placing an order? Are orders becoming less frequent? Has the buyer or purchasing manager changed? Has the content or size of the average order decreased? Has the sales rep changed? There may be eight warning signs for a customer, and if five of them go off, that's when our CEO gets on the plane and pays a call to see what's going on and make sure we don't lose a valuable account."[9]

Some firms budget **maintenance expenses** as a retention strategy by offering current customers extra services. Maintenance expenses are not trivial; they reduce the firm's profit margin from current customers. But they are often more cost-effective than having customers defect.

GROW. Satisfied customers may be willing to increase their purchases. The firm may also increase revenues by **cross-selling**. Your cable company provides basic channels for a standard fee, but offers *higher-value* channels like HBO and special sports events for extra fees. Amazon, Groupon, iTunes, and 800Flowers each personalize their communications and cross-sell offers to their customers.

DELETE. Generally, the firm tries to retain and grow current customers so as to increase profit margins. But some customers are not worth having. Most firms have customers that become unprofitable and should seriously consider ending these relationships. We address customer deletion in the next section.

POTENTIAL CUSTOMERS

Potential customers offer an excellent way for the firm to grow. But, as we learned earlier, not all customers are alike. Returning to Figure 2.3, we discuss three broad options for addressing potential customers: retrieve, acquire, ignore.

RETRIEVE. Former customers are a special category because the firm often has more information about them than about other potential customers. The firm knows (or can find out) what

KEY IDEA

➤ The firm's options for addressing current customers are:

- Retain
- Grow
- Delete

they purchased, what they spent, how they make decisions, why they left, and other data that can help the firm serve them again. If the firm understands why customers defect, customer recovery can improve.

ACQUIRE. Most firms devote considerable resources to acquiring profitable new customers. Sometimes the firm seeks customers with similar characteristics to current customers — other times, it wants very different customers. Regardless, the firm should be selective in acquiring only the *right* customers with positive CLV. More on this later.

IGNORE. The firm must decide on desirable customer characteristics and make investments in potential customers that bring positive CLV to the firm. By the same token, it should ignore customers that do not possess these favorable characteristics. Bottom line: The firm must be selective in making investments to secure potential customers.

CUSTOMER PROFITABILITY

Most customers bring value to the firm but some do not. The firm must identify the customers it wants to serve, and develop options for addressing unwelcome customers. To accomplish this task, most firms understand and measure product profitability — revenues minus costs for an individual product or service. Product profit is a key metric for most product managers. Many firms invest heavily in sophisticated accounting systems and data analysis tools that help answer questions like:

- Are our current products profitable?
- Shall we discontinue this old product and, if so, when?
- Shall we introduce a new product?

By contrast, few firms can answer equivalent questions about customers. This failure is especially critical in large global firms with multiple business operations. Profitability data typically reside in individual businesses and geographies whose systems do not always interface with one another. Hence, there is no easy way to extract and integrate sales and profit data for individual customers across businesses and geographies.[10]

The firm's difficulty in measuring enterprise **customer profitability** stands in sharp contrast to treating customers as assets and understanding customer CLV. Product profitability is important, but products and services are only a means to attract, retain, and grow customers. To paraphrase an old management saying: "If you can't measure it, you can't manage it!"

Firms use a variety of methods to gather and assess data relevant to customer activity and profitability. When firms examine revenues, operating costs, and profits by customer, they often find an **80:20 rule**: 80 percent of revenues come from 20 percent of customers. Many firms have installed strategic (or key) account management systems to serve their most important customers.

The converse analogue is the **20:80 rule**: 20 percent of revenues from 80 percent of customers. This rule raises two critical and related questions:

- What does it cost the firm to serve these customers?
- Is it profitable to serve these customers? If not, what action should the firm take?

We should not forget that unprofitable customers may be small or large. Unprofitable small customers typically provide insufficient revenues to offset the costs to serve. By contrast, revenues from large customers may be high, but they require expensive customization and/or service support. They may also bargain down prices below sustainable levels.

The critical firm challenge is to correctly identify the *right* customers. After all, today's unprofitable customers could be tomorrow's big winners. Also, unprofitable large customers may carry

---

Marketing Question

Think of a local business. What approaches does it use to acquire customers? What alternative approaches could it implement?

KEY IDEA

➤ The firm's options for addressing potential customers are:
- Retrieve
- Acquire
- Ignore

KEY IDEA

➤ Measuring product profitability is insufficient; the firm should develop systems for measuring customer profitability.

KEY IDEA

➤ At many firms, 20% of customers provide 80% of revenues.

➤ At these same firms, 80% of customers provide 20% of revenues.

significant overhead allocations; eliminating them lowers overall profits because the overhead remains.[11]

Deciding how to deal with today's unprofitable and least profitable customers is a tricky matter. Creative approaches may increase current profits and/or generate profitable future customers. Figure 2.4 shows how changes in customer classification helped a financial services firm to better isolate customer profitability and improve overall profits.

FIGURE 2.4

CUSTOMER CLASSIFICATION BY A U.S. FINANCIAL SERVICES FIRM

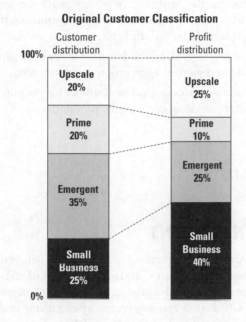

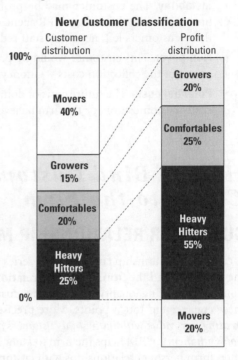

Original Customer Classification

New Customer Classification

KEY IDEA

➤ In general, customers are critical firm assets, but some customers may be liabilities and should be fired.

➤ The firm may have to reject some potential customers because of predicted unprofitability.

CUSTOMER SUITABILITY

Unprofitable customers do not deliver value to the firm. But the firm may cease doing business with a current customer or forgo a potential customer for other reasons:

- **Capacity constraints.** The firm may have insufficient ability — expertise, financial resources, physical capacity — to serve all its customers. When the Sarbanes-Oxley Act vastly increased compliance requirements for large public companies, some accounting firms dropped many smaller clients.[12] Failure to match firm resources to customer needs can lead to dissatisfaction, monetary losses, and harmful word of mouth.[13]

- **Competition.** The customer is a current or potential competitor that could reverse-engineer the firm's product, then launch its own. Hi-tech firms often refuse to sell to competitors; they also stop customers from reselling their products.

- **Evolving strategy.** If the firm shifts direction, drops products, or divests a business, it sheds customers as a byproduct of strategic change.

- **Impact on the firm's reputation.** A firm/customer relationship negatively affects the firm's brand image: Can you find Gucci in Kmart? Or the customer may use the firm's product inappropriately, leading to aggravation, negative word of mouth, and/or financial loss.

- **Impact on the offer.** In many service businesses, fellow customers are integral to the offer. Bad behavior by some customers reduces the value for all customers and can negatively affect employee morale. Rowdy sports fans negatively affect the ambiance in expensive restaurants; college admission departments screen out many applicants. Specific customer profiles the firm should avoid include: *cheats* — like customers who buy products, return them, then re-purchase at returned-merchandise discounts; *thieves* — like pick-

Marketing Question

Which companies do you believe affirmatively seek to fire and/or reject customers? Are they successful in pursuing these activities? What firms inadvertently fire and/or reject *good* customers?

pockets and shoplifters who rob other customers or the firm; *belligerents* — like diners who display insufficient patience in waiting for their meals and verbally abuse waiters; *family feuders* — a subcategory of *belligerents* who fight among themselves; *vandals* — who destroy equipment; and *rule breakers* — like unruly airline passengers who pose a physical danger and affect the service experience for fellow customers. Customers who behave badly also raise firm costs.[14]

- **Instability.** The customer may be profitable but too unstable. People-intensive service businesses like advertising or PR agencies often add employees to serve new customers. If those customers left, necessary staff reductions could be very difficult.

- **Non-payer.** This customer would be profitable if it paid, but it doesn't! Or it eventually pays, but the collection costs — money, human resources, aggravation — are too high.

- **Potential costs.** The future costs of doing business are too high. The customer may require costly customization, or the firm believes future servicing costs will be prohibitive.

How to Bind Customers Closer to the Firm

CUSTOMER RELATIONSHIP MANAGEMENT

A customer relationship comprises the series of over-time interactions or *touch points* between the customer and the firm. **Customer relationship management (CRM)** is a synthesis of relationship marketing, quality management, customer insight, and customer service that manages these engagement touch points. More precisely, CRM is *the ongoing process of identifying and creating new value with individual customers and sharing these benefits over a lifetime of association with them.*[15] CRM helps the firm to *know* its customers better. In B2C, mom-and-pop stores often form personal relationships with customers; CRM helps large firms build and foster relationships with their customers in a systematic way. Strong relationships should drive and sustain customer purchases over a long period of time.

The underlying value of CRM is improving and understanding customer lifetime value (CLV). Customers are the firm's most critical assets, and forming *mutually beneficial relationships* is crucial. CRM systems are successful in firms committed to a true external orientation. Three issues are crucial for success when implementing CRM:

- **Objectives.** The firm must be clear about its objectives. Without good direction and strategy, the firm cannot select from myriad CRM initiatives, costs can easily spiral out of control,[16] and goals are not met.

- **Customer benefits.** The CRM system must provide benefits and values to customers — delightful new products, or high levels of customer service. Many firms focus on value to the firm first, often by cutting costs and giving short shrift to customer value. The CRM system must drive *mutually* beneficial customer relationships.

- **Technology.** Many people think that databases, analytics engines, and other technology are the only components of a CRM system. Of course, technology, databases, and **data-mining** tools often play an important role in gaining customer insight by gathering and analyzing data; but CRM is not only about technology. To repeat, CRM is the holistic approach firms use when forming *mutually beneficial relationships* with customers.

DEVELOPING A CRM SYSTEM

Customer databases for effective CRM systems must be relevant, structured, current, consistent, accurate, accessible, complete, and secure. According to one expert, "To implement CRM, a firm

KEY IDEA

➤ CRM helps the firm form *mutually beneficial relationships* with customers.

➤ Technology has an important role in CRM, but CRM is not about technology.

Marketing Question

CVS/Caremart (CC) is the U.S.'s largest single buyer and dispenser of prescription drugs. What actions could CC take to help reduce national healthcare costs?

must have an integrated database available at every customer touch point and analyze that data well. ... [CRM] allows companies to automate the way they interact with their customers and to communicate with relevant, timely messages."[17] A large firm's database contains longitudinal (over time) data on millions of customers. Adding state-of-the-art *data-mining* technology in the context of a *test-and-learn* culture secures and manipulates these data to yield marketing insight. Capital One's expertise has shaken up the credit card industry, and Harrah's (casinos and hotels) has achieved marked success with timely and relevant multi-channel customer communication. Communications with customers are more personal, yet the firm can still mass-customize its offers. Direct marketer Fingerhut maintains 100 pages of data per customer, mostly about buying habits. Customer data is equally important for firms with few customers, like your local dry cleaner or garage, where paper and pencil may be just the right technology.

The firm must identify each customer. In some service industries, customer databases are fundamental to formal relationships, like bank accounts, insurance policies, and telephone service. But these firms often collect and store data by account or policy number, rather than by customer. Hence, the best customers — those who buy multiple services — escape attention.

Identifying customers that purchase from an intermediary like a retailer or distributor can be difficult. Indirect methods of gathering these data include customer-get-customer campaigns, customer value cards, factory warranties, loyalty cards, mail inserts, social media, special events, syndicated questionnaires, telephone help lines, third-party lifestyle databases, and websites — supplemented by data from marketing information firms. Many firms invest heavily in customer databases. Types of data include[18]:

- **Customer characteristics.** Demographic data independent of the firm: B2C — name, gender, age, and address. B2B — sales revenues, number of employees, age of organization, and industry.

- **Customer contact history.** From phone calls for product information and customer service requests — B2C, to data on deliveries, sales calls, and technical service calls — B2B.

- **Customer purchase history.** What was purchased, when, by what method — cash or credit — through what intermediary (if any), at what price, and with what price discounts. Data should include delivery method and the firm's profit margin on each purchase.

- **Customer response data to firm decisions.** Captures perceptions, preferences, and actions relative to marketing-mix variables like sales promotions, direct marketing, and price changes.

- **Customer value to the firm.** Relevant data for assessing customer lifetime value (CLV).

The database should be sufficiently flexible to follow individuals and track life changes. In B2C, consumers move and change jobs, marital status, names, and family size; their needs also change. In B2B, decision-makers and influencers change jobs within firms and change firms; firms themselves also have changing needs.

Every customer response, contact, and purchase deserves an entry. But the firm should not limit itself to data on its own customer relationships; it should also seek data on its customers' relationships with its competitors. An equipment provider should know the age and equipment types installed at the customer by *all* providers. A financial services firm should collect data on its customers' relationships with other suppliers. These data may be available direct from customers or from third-party data providers.

A well-developed customer database is valuable to the firm and others. Often, a corporate-level database that integrates all customer information with many levels of line of business access and granularity make the best sense. Other controls, like security, privacy, and restrictions on data use are also critical concerns for the firm.

ASSESSING THE VALUE OF CUSTOMERS AND DESIGNING FIRM ACTIONS

The firm implementing CRM well acts with significantly greater focus. It estimates profitability and CLV by customer, anticipates key customer events, and initiates action. A B2C firm might send consumers vacation ideas; a B2B firm might alert customers that ordering seasonal stock can add value. The more comprehensive the customer database, and the more creative the firm, the more valuable will be its initiatives. It can offer new products and services and give greater customer service to its more valuable and loyal customers. However, in making offers, the firm must be concerned about the **communications tipping point**, the level after which its communications create customer resentment. Amazon spends significant effort to identify its tipping point.

High-value, high-loyalty customers are very important, yet some firms offer better service to low-value customers. Express checkout lanes in supermarkets reward customers who make fewer purchases. The Fairway supermarket on New York's Upper West Side and Central Market stores in Texas strive to cut waiting time for all customers.

Loyalty programs are central to many CRM systems. Well-designed programs play a major role in retaining customers. All loyalty programs have a similar structure; encouraging customers to earn rewards by purchasing goods and services. Some designs are simple, like *buy-many-get-one-free* programs at car washes or JCPenney's *baker's dozen*: "Buy 12 panties, earn the 13th free." Other programs, like those from airlines, hotels, and credit cards, drive loyalty through complex, multi-tiered incentives.

KEY MESSAGES

- Customer lifetime value (CLV) is the critical link between delivering value to customers and creating value for the firm and its shareholders.
- The firm improves CLV by increasing profit margin (m) and customer retention rate (r), and decreasing discount rate (d).
- Increasing customer retention rate (r) has greater leverage on CLV than decreasing discount rate (d).
- The firm has three broad options for addressing current customers — retain, grow, and delete.
- The firm has three broad options for addressing potential customers — retrieve, acquire, and ignore.
- The firm should strive to understand the reasons for customer retention and defection and act accordingly.
- Some of the firm's current customers are probably unprofitable — but a fraction of these may present future opportunities.
- The firm may forgo a customer relationship for reasons other than poor profitability.
- A well-designed customer relationship management (CRM) system deepen the firm's knowledge about its customers.
- Understanding customer value to the firm and customer loyalty allows the firm to design effective loyalty programs.

VIDEOS AND AUDIOS

Loyalty Programs   v202 📺   Ran Kivetz   Columbia Business School

v202

SECTION II

FUNDAMENTAL INSIGHTS FOR STRATEGIC MARKETING cvs2 📽

To access O-codes, go to **www.ocodes.com**

FUNDAMENTAL INSIGHTS FOR STRATEGIC MARKETING comprises four chapters, Chapter 3 through Chapter 6. These chapters focus on the data, knowledge, and insights the firm must secure to make effective marketing decisions. Data are facts about a particular topic, like a customer's demographic characteristics, and purchasing data. Knowledge is the meaning the firm gains from combining data as in a customer profile. Insight results from further knowledge combinations that provide ideas for action, like linking a customer profile to an R&D project. The firm needs data and knowledge, but should also strive for insight.

To build a strong foundation for developing market strategy, the firm must secure insight in several core areas — market; customers; competitors, company, and complementers — we call these the M4Cs. The insight is the *situation analysis* for the market plan.

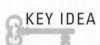

KEY IDEA

➤ The firm must secure insight in three broad areas:

- Market
- Customers
- Competitors, the company, and complementers

— the M4Cs.

- **Market.** Good market insight helps the firm decide what parts of the market to address. The firm must understand market demand, today's participants and the pressures they face, and how each may evolve over time — Chapter 3.

- **Customers.** The firm tries to satisfy customer needs via market offers. The firm must identify customers, and gain insight into their needs and the processes they use to make purchase decisions — Chapter 4.

- **Competitors, company, and complementers.** Both the firm and competitors seek to attract, retain, and grow customers. As the firm secures *competitive* insight, it also learns about its own *company* capabilities and how to win in the market. We also discuss firm *complementers* — organizations that help the firm achieve its objectives — Chapter 5.

Chapter 6 addresses approaches to securing insight via *marketing research*. Following Chapter 6, we show how to use insight from the situation analysis to construct assumptions that form the foundation of the market plan.

Capon's Marketing Framework

SECTION I: MARKETING AND THE FIRM

CHAPTER 1
Introduction to Managing Marketing

CHAPTER 2
The Value of Customers

SECTION II: FUNDAMENTAL INSIGHTS FOR STRATEGIC MARKETING

CHAPTER 3
Market Insight

CHAPTER 4
Customer Insight

CHAPTER 5
Insight about Competitors, Company, and Complementers

CHAPTER 6
Marketing Research

TRANSITION TO STRATEGIC MARKETING

SECTION III: STRATEGIC MARKETING

IMPERATIVE 1
Determine and Recommend Which Markets to Address

CHAPTER 7
Identifying and Choosing Opportunities

IMPERATIVE 2
Identify and Target Market Segments

CHAPTER 8
Market Segmentation and Targeting

IMPERATIVE 3
Set Strategic Direction and Positioning

CHAPTER 9
Market Strategy – Integrating Firm Efforts for Marketing Success

CHAPTER 10
Managing through the Life Cycle

CHAPTER 11
Managing Brands

SECTION IV: IMPLEMENTING THE MARKET STRATEGY

IMPERATIVE 4
Design the Market Offer

PART A: PROVIDING CUSTOMER VALUE

PART B: COMMUNICATING CUSTOMER VALUE

PART C: DELIVERING CUSTOMER VALUE

PART D: GETTING PAID FOR CUSTOMER VALUE

CHAPTER 12
Managing the Product Line

CHAPTER 15
Integrated Marketing Communications

CHAPTER 18
Distribution Decisions

CHAPTER 19
Critical Underpinnings of Pricing Decisions

CHAPTER 13
Managing Services and Customer Service

CHAPTER 16
Mass and Digital Communication

CHAPTER 20
Setting Prices

CHAPTER 14
Developing New Products

CHAPTER 17
Directing and Managing the Field Sales Effort

IMPERATIVE 5
Secure Support from Other Functions

CHAPTER 21
Ensuring the Firm Implements the Market Offer as Planned

IMPERATIVE 6
Monitor and Control

CHAPTER 22
Monitoring and Controlling Firm Functioning and Performance

SECTION V: SPECIAL MARKETING TOPICS

CHAPTER 23
International, Regional, and Global Marketing

CHAPTER 3
MARKET INSIGHT

Why am I a great player? Because I go to where the puck will be.

— Wayne Gretzky

LEARNING OBJECTIVES

When you have completed this chapter, you will be able to:

- Analyze and understand market structure.
- Understand alternative ways of thinking about products that firms offer.
- Distinguish among product class, product form, product line, and product item.
- Forecast market and product evolution using a life-cycle framework.
- Summarize industry forces exerting pressure on the firm.
- Recognize major environmental forces affecting the firm and industry.
- Show how industry and environmental forces interact.

OPENING CASE: NETFLIX

Since the mid-1970s, when Sony introduced Betamax technology, watching videos at home, typically on TV, has become a major sociocultural trend. VHS eclipsed Betamax, and consumers used videotape recorders/players to record and play back TV programs, and play movies secured from retailers. Initially, most retailers were small local stores, but many went out of business in the 1990s as Blockbuster became dominant, in part because of larger inventories.

When DVDs replaced VHS tapes, California entrepreneur Reed Hastings founded Netflix, an online DVD-rental service, www.netflix.com. Netflix subscribers create a list of videos they want to rent, selecting from more than 100,000 movies and TV programs. DVDs arrive by U.S. Mail in distinctive red envelopes. When a subscriber returns a DVD in a prepaid envelope, Netflix sends another. There are no due dates, no late fees, and no shipping fees. Netflix analyzes subscriber choices and recommendations; subscribers may search by actor, critic, customer recommendation, decade, director, genre, new releases, studio, and title. Subscribers may request movies not yet released on video: Netflix sends them out as available. More than 50,000 Netflix titles are in distribution every day.

For its DVD offerings, Netflix maintains about 60 warehouses in major metropolitan areas. Employees pick up returning DVD envelopes from post offices in the early morning. By mid-afternoon, Netflix has sorted returned DVDs and delivered ordered DVDs to post offices. Subscribers living within 50 miles of a warehouse typically receive delivery in one business day. Netflix ships roughly 2 million DVDs daily. Netflix faces competition from bricks-and-mortar video stores, notably Blockbuster (filed for bankruptcy in 2010). Redbox and Blockbuster also offer standalone kiosks containing relatively few popular DVDs in super-markets, drugstores, and fast-food restaurants for $1 overnight.

In 2007, Netflix started streaming movies and TV episodes for viewing on various devices. Netflix offers several subscriber plans. Customers may select DVD-only, streaming-only, or combination DVD/streaming plans. A critical competitive area is the ability to secure rights to recently released movies from movie studios, and length of the movie-house-only window (traditionally averaging 120 days). Netflix has also diversified into content production. Netflix has more than 30 million members in 40 countries; revenues exceed $3.5 billion. Originally priced at around $15, in mid 2011 Netflix's share price reached $298 but trades at around half that value (2013).

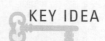

CASE QUESTION

What environmental changes enabled Netflix to successfully innovate in the home video market? How do you assess Netflix's decision to offer streaming videos? Why did Netflix stock price drop so significantly?

In 2010, Nokia was global market-share leader in cell phones — 450 million sold. But Nokia faced fierce price compe-tition from Asian producers for basic cell phones; also, Nokia's market share of smartphones dropped considerably as Apple's iPhone and Android phones (Google software) gained strength. In 2011, Nokia's stock price dropped 80 percent from a 2008 high. Significant events in 2011 were: Google acquired Motorola Mobility; Nokia abandoned its smart-phone operating systems, agreeing to base future models on Microsoft's Windows Phone 7.

Defining the market is a fundamental but tricky marketing challenge. If the firm defines the market too narrowly, it risks being blindsided by competitors. (Netscape's Navigator web browser lost most of its 90 percent usage share to upstart Internet Explorer.) If the firm defines the market too broadly, it will not allocate its resources effectively. The firm must also understand the market's evolutionary patterns and the forces that drive this process. Because most forces are external in nature, the firm that embraces an external orientation, with customers and competi-tors in mind, generally understands its markets better than firms with internal orientations.

Figure 3.1 shows the four aspects of **market insight** this chapter covers. Each aspect provides a different window on the market and lays a foundation for developing the market strategy. Together they help the firm anticipate market change and identify and size new opportunities:

- **Market structure.** We define the market and show that effective market partitioning helps the firm identify opportunities and gain differential advantage. The chapter shows how different product classes and product forms serve customer needs, and we explore factors affecting market size.

- **Market and product evolution.** Markets evolve. Sometimes evolutionary patterns are predictable, like the market for geriatric healthcare — secured from age-distribution demographics. Other markets are unpredictable, like demand for home-rebuilding prod-ucts in hurricane-prone areas. Products also evolve as customers refine their needs and competitors compete for sales. Technological evolution can also drive market evolution. We use a life-cycle framework to show how markets and products evolve.

- **Industry forces.** Industry forces include various competitive and supply-chain pressures. The *five forces* we identify impinge directly on the firm.

- **Environmental forces.** These broad-scale environmental forces impact both the firm and other industry participants. We use the PESTLE framework — political, economic, socio-cultural, technological, legal/regulatory, and environmental (physical) to gain insight.

KEY IDEA

➤ Market insight com-prises four separate aspects:

- Market structure
- Market and product evolution
- Industry forces
- Environmental forces

FIGURE 3.1

CRITICAL BUILDING
BLOCKS FOR SECURING
MARKET INSIGHT

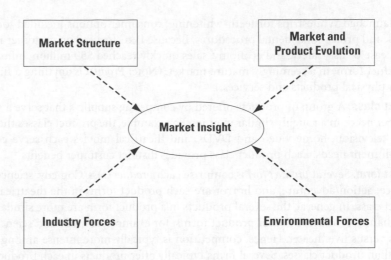

KEY IDEA

➤ When firms secure
good market insight,
they do a better job of
identifying and sizing
opportunities and
gaining differential
advantage.

*Marketing
Question*

Select a firm/product with
which you are familiar.
Define the market at different levels. How much more
broadly could you go and
still maintain a focus?

The firm must keep two things squarely in mind when seeking insight in these four aspects:

- **State of nature.** The firm must understand the current state of nature. For example: What competitors does the firm face today? How many baby boomers are in its target market?

- **Trends.** The firm must also identify trends. For example: What additional direct competitors will it face in two years? How will demographic changes affect the market?

Good market insight can put the firm ahead and provide significant competitive advantage. Post September 11, 2001, Alcoa predicted significant demand for secure cockpit doors on passenger aircraft and won a commanding share of the retrofit market.

MARKET STRUCTURE

We use three separate concepts to describe **market structure**: the market; products and/or services serving the market; and the firm's products. We also discuss factors affecting market size.

THE MARKET

KEY IDEA

➤ Markets comprise
people and organiza-
tions that require goods
and services to satisfy
their needs, and are
willing and able to pay.

Markets comprise customers — people and organizations — who require products and services to satisfy their needs. Basic customer needs like food, clothing, and shelter are enduring; many offerings satisfy these needs. Other needs, like entertainment, tend to be more transitory. Of course, to be in the market, customers must also possess sufficient purchasing power — and interest — to buy what firms are offering.

The concept of a *market* is slippery because we can identify a market at several different levels. The transportation market is the basic need to move people and things from point A to point B. In turn, the transportation market comprises several more narrowly defined markets — ground, air, and water transportation. Even more narrowly, we can define the automobile market and, more narrowly still, the market for particular types of automobiles like SUVs and hybrids.

In defining a market, it's best to start broad, and then focus in as necessary. A broad approach ensures against **marketing myopia**,[1] the risk of defining a market too narrowly because of biases or insufficient data. A broad definition provides greater scope in searching for opportunity.[2]

PRODUCTS SERVING THE MARKET

Both the firm and competitors provide products and services to the market. A useful categorization of product offerings is **product class**, **product form**, **product line**, and **product item**.[3] These distinctions help the firm identify opportunities and/or emerging competitors.

When P&G launched Whitestrips for teeth-whitening, consumer options included toothpaste, bleaches, gels, and professional dental procedures. Because P&G focused on customer needs for convenience, ease of use, safety, and economy, sales quickly reached $50 million annually with this new product form, in a seemingly mature market. (Note: *Product* is anything a firm offers for sale, both physical products and services.)

- **Product class.** A group of products offered by competing suppliers that serve a subset of customer needs in a roughly similar manner. For example, the product classes theater, live music, television, home video and DVDs, and theatrical movies each serve consumer entertainment needs. Each product class provides distinct customer benefits.
- **Product form.** Several *product forms* comprise each *product class*. Comedy, science fiction, romance, action/adventure, and horror are each product forms in the theatrical movies product class. In general, the several products in a product form are more similar to each other than to products in other product forms; for example, comedy and science-fiction movies versus live theater. Hence, competition is typically more intense among product forms than product classes. Several firms typically offer products in each product form.

Product classes and product forms provide a useful framework for thinking about markets, but things are not always straightforward. Competitive changes and technological evolution often blur product-class and product-form boundaries. In the entertainment market, Netflix changed movie-rental dynamics by introducing online ordering and home delivery; streaming video is causing another market change. Several years ago, many consumers purchased cash management, life insurance, property and casualty insurance, and investments from different firms. Deregulation led to a single *financial services* market offering *one-stop* shopping. Similarly, engineering plastics now compete with metal in many applications. Previously, your automobile's oil pan and fuel tank were made of metal; today, they are probably made of plastic.

THE FIRM'S PRODUCTS

Product classes and product forms embrace products from all competitors. One firm may offer products in multiple product classes; another may specialize in just one or two product forms. IBM offers products in many (but not all) product forms in the information systems product class; Acer offers only PCs (IBM no longer offers PCs). When we consider individual firms, we speak of product lines and product items.

- **Product line.** A group of related products that a single firm offers.
- **Product item.** A subset of the product line. A product item is uniquely identified, like having a specific size and color.

FACTORS AFFECTING MARKET SIZE

Current and potential market sizes are important data for evaluating the firm's opportunities. Before entering a market, the firm should know the numbers of current and potential customers and their purchasing power. The firm should consider factors like population size, population mix, geographic population shifts, income and income distribution, and age distribution.[4]

POPULATION SIZE. World population exceeds 7 billion. Increasing by 200,000 people daily, by 2030, population will exceed 8 billion. Population is unevenly distributed across nations: highs — China, 1.3 billion; India, 1.2 billion: lows — Nauru, 9,000; Tuvalu 10,000.

Population growth rates also differ markedly across nations and are falling globally. In many developed nations, annual growth rates are less than 1 percent, and some are negative, leading to population declines. Important drivers are social norms promoting education, work opportunities for women, and greater access to birth control. Conversely, in many less-developed countries, particularly in Latin America, population growth is well over 2 percent. Population control programs are successful in some countries like Bangladesh; China enforces a one-child policy. In some African countries, birth rates are high, but AIDS is taking a heavy toll.

KEY IDEA

➤ We can view any market as comprising several different areas.
➤ The firm avoids *marketing myopia* by using a broad market definition.

Marketing Question

Suppose you had been a senior marketing executive at Kodak in the mid-1990s; how would you have defined Kodak's market? How would you change this definition today?

KEY IDEA

➤ A useful way of categorizing products in a market is:

Market level:
- Product class
- Product form

Firm level:
- Product line
- Product item

POPULATION MIX. In many developed countries, immigration drives population-mix changes. Of the world's 200 million immigrants (foreign-born residents), the U.S. leads with 35 million. Other countries with large immigrant populations are Russia (13 million); Germany and Ukraine (7 million); France, India, and Canada (6 million); and Saudi Arabia (5 million). Most labor migration, legal and illegal, is from less-developed countries to more-developed countries. Frequently, provider and receiver countries are geographically close like Mexico and the U.S., and Turkey and Germany. Reduced mobility barriers in the European Union (EU) increase population shifts; the long-standing pattern of Asian workers in Middle Eastern countries continues apace.[5]

> Goya Foods, the largest Hispanic family-owned U.S. food firm (fourth-largest Hispanic firm overall), has revenues exceeding $1 billion. In many grocery stores, Goya has its own shop within a shop. Goya offers a broad range of imported products including Spanish olive oil, seasonings like Mexican chiles, and Caribbean fruit juices.

Marketing Question

What industries and businesses are affected by population shifts?

GEOGRAPHIC POPULATION SHIFTS. Generally, as national income grows, people leave rural areas for urban areas. Then urban areas become overcrowded — Mumbai (India) 14 million and Sao Paulo (Brazil) 11 million. China predicts 500 million people will move from rural to urban areas by 2050. In developed countries, a more recent trend is *exurban* growth — return to rural communities. Desire for less crowding, a slower life pace, and advances in information technology are enabling this trend. In contrast, some affluent empty-nester baby boomers are returning to regenerate city centers. Population shifts often follow the sun. In the U.S., the Northeast is losing population to the Southeast and Southwest. From 1990 to 2010, the U.S. population grew by 9.7 percent, but several states grew much faster — Nevada (35 percent), Arizona (25 percent), Utah (24 percent), Idaho (21 percent), and Texas (21 percent).

INCOME AND INCOME DISTRIBUTION. For many years, the U.S. was the world's richest country in per capita income, but Qatar, Luxembourg, Singapore, Norway, and the UAE now surpass the U.S. Several countries are close behind but most are far less wealthy. In many poor countries, small elite minorities enjoy most national wealth.

Population, income, and income distribution influence the size of many markets. Economic development and demographic changes are shifting opportunities from traditional markets to emerging markets. Especially important are the BRICI countries — Brazil, Russia, India, China, and Indonesia. Firms like CitiCorp, ExxonMobil, GE, Nestlé, and P&G continue to develop global organizations to tap this potential. Additionally, emerging market countries are generating their own multinationals like Brazil (Embraer), China (Haier, Huawei, Lenovo), and India (Tata Motors, Wipro).

KEY IDEA

➤ Critical variables affecting market size include:

• Population size
• Population mix
• Geographic population shifts
• Income and income distribution
• Age distribution

AGE DISTRIBUTION. Table 3.1 shows increasing median ages in selected developed and developing countries. Major drivers are decreasing birth rates and family size and increasing life expectancy. These shifts have enormous implications for B2C marketers. In developed countries, large numbers of retirement-age consumers (baby boomers) are active, have significant discretionary income, and are more sophisticated buyers — cruises and assisted-living facilities are growth markets. By contrast, countries with median ages in the mid-20s — Mexico, Brazil, Indonesia — offer opportunities for Coke, Pepsi, McDonald's, KFC, and other marketers whose products appeal to a younger demographic.

TABLE 3.1

MEDIAN AGES IN SELECTED COUNTRIES[6]

Country	Median Age, 2000	Projected Median Age, 2040
Japan	41.3	54.2
Spain	37.4	52.3
Australia	35.2	43.3
U.S.	35.2	39.0
Brazil	25.4	38.8
Indonesia	24.6	37.4
Mexico	22.9	38.7
Niger	15.1	17.8

Other important market-size drivers include marriage, marrying age, divorce and remarriage, same-sex marriage, infant and adult mortality, and work force composition. These variables often help the firm make good market-size predictions — birth rates and infant mortality influence demand for products like diapers and car seats.

MARKET AND PRODUCT EVOLUTION

Life cycles are the most common way to describe the evolution of markets and products — product classes, product forms, product lines, and product items. Figure 3.2 shows a classic S-shaped curve depicting the sales trajectory. A good understanding of life cycles helps the firm predict future market conditions and develop robust strategies. Typically, we partition life cycles into five stages (phases) — introduction, early growth, late growth, maturity, and decline.

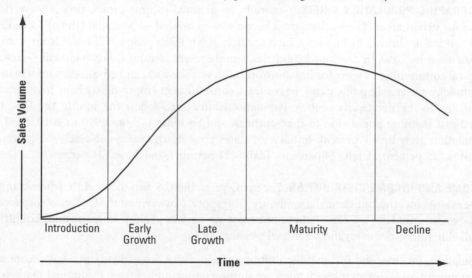

FIGURE 3.2

THE CLASSIC LIFE CYCLE

THE FAMILY OF LIFE CYCLES

The several life cycles fall into a simple hierarchy based on longevity and demand. *Market life cycles* last longest — generally, the firm has little impact on market life cycles. *Product-class* and *product-form* life cycles are each shorter than the market life cycle. Understanding these two life cycles is helpful in developing a market strategy.

Product-line and product-item life cycles are critical for product and **brand managers** as they significantly influence product line and product item performance. Firm actions greatly impact these life cycles; they are shorter than product-class and product-form life cycles and come in many different shapes. But because they provide little insight into competitor activity, they are not very helpful for drawing strategic implications.

PRODUCT-FORM LIFE CYCLES

The firm gains the greatest insight into market and product evolution by examining product forms. Although product classes compete with one another, competition both within and across product forms is typically more intense. For example, although desktop PCs compete with laptops, the various brands of laptop PCs compete more fiercely with one another. Although actual life-cycle curves often depart from the idealized shape in Figure 3.2, across product forms, life-cycle stages follow one from another in a remarkably consistent fashion. Hence, product-form life cycles can provide important strategic insights.

Marketing Question

How would an analysis of population, income, and income distribution help PepsiCo defeat Coca-Cola in developing countries?

KEY IDEA

➤ The product life cycle comprises several stages:

• Introduction
• Early growth
• Late growth
• Maturity
• Decline

As Figure 3.2 shows, we typically categorize product-form life cycles into five stages:

• **Introduction**. Sales volume is initially low.
• **Early growth**. Sales volume grows at an increasing rate.
• **Late growth**. Sales volume grows, but at a decreasing rate.
• **Maturity**. Sales volume grows at about the same rate as GNP.
• **Decline**. Sales volume eventually declines.

STAGE 1: INTRODUCTION. Product introduction frequently follows many years of R&D and reflects the first market entry/entries by leading firms. Honda launched the first gasoline/ electric hybrid car in 1999, but modern-day research started in the mid-1970s! Uncertainty characterizes introduction. The firm explores questions like: Will the product perform adequately? What is the best technology? What segments should we target? What is the optimal market strategy? Will customer demand be sufficient? What specific benefits do customers require? Which competitors will enter? When? What resources will be necessary? What are our chances of success? Products currently in introduction include implantable ID chips for humans and RFID (radio frequency identification) chips for identifying products.

In the introduction stage, suppliers struggle to build profitable volume. Typically, the firm offers a single product design, but prices may not cover total costs. Managers expect that unit costs will fall as sales increase and ultimately the firm will earn profits. Introduction requires significant educational effort. Firms use advertising and/or personal selling to show product value to customers and distributors. But production problems, product failures, and/or an inability to expand capacity may cause delays.[7] Sometimes the first product version has low quality and performs poorly, yet may possess the seeds of an important breakthrough. BlackBerrys, iPads, smartphones, and other hand-held electronic devices are now widely popular, but their success was built in part on the Apple Newton, the failed pioneer (launched 1993/withdrawn 1998). The introduction stage may last many years, but fierce competition, increased innovation, and customer willingness to try new products are shortening this stage.

STAGE 2: EARLY GROWTH. Many products do not reach early growth, but the survivors' sales revenues grow at an increasing rate. Hybrid cars and tablet computers are in early growth — cellular phones with built-in cameras have moved from early growth to late growth. Increasing sales and high profit margins attract other entrants. New players often bring capacity, resources, and a loyal customer base to fuel market growth. As competitors struggle for market position, new distribution channels open up, and promotional effort remains high. Previously, advertising and promotion emphasized generating primary demand — buy a hybrid car. Now the focus shifts to differentiation and selective demand based on features, functionality, and customer perceptions — buy a Ford Fusion hybrid. Firms secure production and marketing efficiencies, and price becomes a competitive weapon. Many firms increase sales and work at managing costs. Caution: The firm's sales may increase, but market share *decreases* if competitors grow faster!

STAGE 3: LATE GROWTH. By late growth, the many uncertainties from introduction and early growth are largely resolved. Sales continue to increase, but the growth rate slows. Strong competitors initiate tough actions to maintain historic growth patterns and force weaker entrants to withdraw. Firms differentiate products by introducing and promoting design and packaging variations. The distribution infrastructure is usually well developed but outlets are more selective about brands and product items. Price is a major competitive weapon, squeezing distributor margins. Purchase terms like credit, warranties, and customer service become more favorable to purchasers.

STAGE 4: MATURITY. Slow-growth or flat year-to-year sales characterize maturity. Most sales are to repeat and loyal users. Examples include most everyday products like detergents and kitchen appliances. Because competitive situations vary widely, the firm must secure deep market insight. Some markets are concentrated, others are fragmented:

• **Concentrated markets.** For economists, a concentrated market is an *oligopoly*. A few major players enjoy most sales; niche firms make the rest. Market leaders often enjoy

KEY IDEA

➤ Markets and products generally evolve in a consistent manner.

➤ The life-cycle framework is useful for describing market and product evolution.

entry barriers like economies of scale, brand preference, and/or distribution-channel dominance. Market positions achieved by early maturity often survive for many years, like IBM — mainframe computers, GE — steam turbine generators, and Gillette — shaving products.

Many firms pursue product differentiation approaches, but competitors may quickly offer *me-too* products. Increasingly, firms focus on value-added services, packaging, distribution, and branding and promotion. They streamline operations and distribution to reduce costs, then price competitively. Leaders get in trouble when they fail to innovate new products and processes and do not reduce costs.

- **Fragmented markets.** No firm has a large market share. Fragmentation generally occurs because of some combination of low entry barriers, high exit barriers, regulation, diverse market needs, and high transportation costs. Examples include personal services like dentistry, education, and home plumbing and electrical contracting.

STAGE 5: DECLINE. Maturity may last many years, but eventually sales turn down. Products in decline include carbon paper, chemical-film cameras, and videotapes. Sometimes decline is slow — payphones; but it may also be precipitous — vinyl records. When decline is swift, over-capacity often leads to fierce price competition. Managing costs is a high priority — firms prune product lines and reduce inventory and marketing expenses. Strong firms may increase sales as weaker competitors exit. Firms often raise prices to cover costs as sales drop, but sales decline further, in a vicious cycle. Marketing efforts should target remaining customers. Firms with good cost management and a core of loyal price-insensitive buyers can be quite profitable.

The product-form life cycle is a useful framework, but two points are important:

- **Life-cycle shape.** A product's sales trajectory depends on several factors — underlying customer demand, product quality and consistency, and overall resource commitment by participating firms. In general, life cycles are shortening.[8]
- **Profit curves.** Profit curves do not mirror sales curves. On average, profit margins are greatest in early growth — then drop in late growth and maturity. But gross profit may be greater later in the cycle — lower profit margins, but higher volume.

INDUSTRY FORCES

The **five-forces model** in Figure 3.3 identifies the several industry forces firms face — current direct competitors, new direct entrants, indirect competitors, suppliers, and buyers.[9] Some forces affect the firm specifically; others may impact the entire industry, like fuel prices for airlines. Strong industry forces may drive profitability downwards, as in the airline and paper industries. The firm must develop a good understanding of these forces and their implications.

KEY IDEA

➤ Product-form life-cycle stages have consistent characteristics across products and services.

Marketing Question

Think about the firm/product you selected earlier (p. 35). What factors help determine market size — population, income distribution, and/or age distribution? What other factors will help determine market size in three to five years?

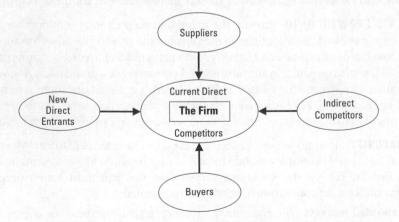

FIGURE 3.3

INDUSTRY FORCES — THE FIVE-FORCES MODEL

CURRENT DIRECT COMPETITORS

A firm's **current direct competitors** offer customers similar benefits with similar products, technology, and/or business models. Current direct competitors are the competitive *status quo*, the traditional rivalry between established players. In the automobile industry, Ford, GM, and Toyota have been direct rivals for decades; U.S. domestic banking rivals include Bank of America, Citicorp, and JPMorgan Chase; Panasonic, Philips, Samsung, and Sony compete in consumer electronics; and Airbus and Boeing in large commercial aircraft. Typically, managers in rival firms know their traditional competitors well. They observe their actions and performance, their successes and failures. They have good insight into strengths and weaknesses and likely strategic moves. They may even have worked for them!

Current direct competitors may be traditional or may have been created via acquisitions, divestitures, leveraged buyouts, and/or mergers that continually change the competitive landscape.

* **Traditional direct competitors** fight according to *established rules of the game*. In mature markets, one firm rarely gains advantage quickly; rather, an improved position typically results from long-run sustained effort. Establishing competitive advantage is difficult. Firms sometimes *cross the line* by working with competitors: Hoffman-La Roche and BASF paid $725 million to settle U.S. Justice Department charges of collusion in maintaining high global prices for vitamins.

   Globalization and industry concentration affect direct competition in many markets. Consolidation leads to global oligopoly — a few firms share the global market. In large commercial aircraft, only Boeing and Airbus remain. In passenger tires, Bridgestone, Continental, Goodyear, and Michelin together enjoy over 80 percent global market share.

* **Acquisitions and divestitures.** Suppose one of your competitors or an outside firm acquires a second competitor — an independent firm or a divestiture. Your competitor has changed: Objectives, strategy, action programs, and resources will most likely all be different.

* **Mergers.** In a merger, two entities combine as *equal* partners to create a stronger firm. By pooling strengths and mitigating weaknesses, the new entity is often a tougher competitor with capabilities that outstrip either former firm. Mergers between Chase Manhattan and J.P. Morgan, then between JP Morgan Chase and Bank One, created JPMorgan Chase, a much tougher competitor for Citicorp and Bank of America. Of course, many mergers may not succeed; for example, the highly criticized Sears/Kmart combination.

* **Leveraged buyouts (LBOs).** Sometimes firms rationalize their portfolios and *spin off* business units; typically, these LBOs incur heavy debt as the price for independence. Lacking corporate resources, the now-independent unit may struggle. But it may also focus on debt reduction and become a more nimble and tough competitor. Firestone spun off its Accuride division offering rims and wheels for truck manufacturers. Free from Firestone's budget constraints, neglect, and low status, Accuride pre-emptively added production capacity, lowered prices, and offered better terms. In less than two years, Accuride doubled market share and increased profits 66 percent.[10]

NEW DIRECT ENTRANTS

New direct entrants are defined as companies offering products and services similar to the firm, but previously they did not compete. Nintendo and Sega dominated electronic games; Sony's PlayStation and Microsoft's Xbox were new direct entrants. Entry barriers significantly affect market entry. Regardless, new direct entrants may emerge from many sources:

* **Firm employees.** In some industries, firm employees pose a significant competitive threat. They may develop new business ideas and/or technologies the firm will not fund and leave to pursue them. Several former Fairchild Semiconductor employees founded Intel. Potential competition from employees is greatest when the firm's core asset is intellectual capital as in advertising, consulting, and financial services. Credit Suisse First Boston

hired Deutsche Bank's entire 132-person technology group. When *the firm's major assets arrive at 9 a.m. and leave at 5 p.m.*, retaining them is crucial.

- **Geographic expansion.** New direct entrants are often profitable, well-capitalized firms from a different geography. They have solid strengths and cost advantages but may lack market knowledge and customer relationships. They may use superior cost positions to support low price strategies and aggressively seek market share. Many Asian firms entered U.S. and European markets to devastating effect: Panasonic, Samsung, and Sony in consumer electronics; Canon in high-speed copying; Nissan and Toyota in automobiles; and LG and Samsung in cell phones.

- **Networks.** A network is a group of firms and/or individuals that collaborate using their combined talents and resources. Networks are very flexible and change composition as requirements evolve.[11] *Capon's Marketing Framework* competes with traditional textbooks, but a network made it possible. Critical components were an author; reviewers; developmental, copy, and permissions editors; book, cover, and website designers; test-bank, caselet, and instructors' manual developers; video technicians; credit card processors; and for the printed version, a prepublication service provider, printer, fulfillment house, wholesaler, bricks-and-mortar and online retailers, and package delivery services.

- **New sales and distribution channels.** Firms that develop new distribution channels can pose significant challenges to traditional players. Direct marketers L.L. Bean and Lands' End are tough competitors for department stores. Amazon competes with traditional distribution via the Internet. And pyramid sales forces like Amway in consumer goods and Primerica in life insurance are tough competitors.[12] Strong firms that add channels also heighten competition. Avon became more competitive with cosmetics firms by adding department store distribution to traditional door-to-door Avon Ladies.

- **Startup entry.** A startup is unencumbered by the *status quo*; flexibility and talent can make startups potent competitors. By contrast, the incumbent firm may have old facilities, old technology, old processes, and/or an established organization and personnel set in their ways. Successful airline startups include jetBlue (U.S.) and easyJet and Ryanair (Europe).

- **Strategic alliances.** Some firms will not assume the risks and costs of new market entry. They may lack critical assets like capital, skills, technology, or market access. When two firms pool resources, the **strategic alliance** may be stronger than either firm separately. Many U.S. and European firms enter Asian markets with local partners. Of course, many partnerships fail — partner objectives diverge, and/or one partner fails to provide agreed resources.

INDIRECT COMPETITORS

Indirect competitors and the firm offer customers similar *benefits/values*, but provide them in significantly different ways. These *functional substitutes* often appear as different product forms or product classes. Xerox copiers manage information — they compete with computers, fax machines, video conferencing, and the Internet. Indirect competitors may redefine the industry by using different distribution methods, suppliers, technologies, and/or business models. Netflix customers pay monthly subscription fees and receive their selections by mail and/or streaming video (Opening Case); Redbox offers vastly fewer DVDs from vending machines in supermarkets, drug stores, and fast-food restaurants — $1 overnight. More broadly, cruise lines compete with automobile and clothing manufacturers — each seeking discretionary consumer income. Movie theaters compete with cable TV, online and retail video rental, restaurants, sporting events, and other entertainment.

Indirect competitors often attack from different industry sectors; incumbents sometimes ignore them. International Paper's market share in paper cups increased, but sales declined as plastic replaced paper. Sometimes regulations prohibit responding to indirect competitors. For many years, U.S. commercial banks could not offer money-market and mutual funds to compete with Fidelity and Vanguard. Changes in the law removed this restriction.

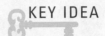

KEY IDEA

➤ The firm may face competition from new direct entrants:
- Firm employees
- Geographic expansion
- Networks
- New sales and distribution channels
- Startup entry
- Strategic alliances

Marketing Question

Think about the firm/product you selected earlier (p. 35). Identify:
- Current direct competitors
- Potential new direct entrants
- Indirect competitors
- Suppliers
- Buyers

In the next few years:
- What changes do you expect in current direct competitors?
- What positive and negative implications for the firm may occur from acquisitions, mergers, and leveraged buyouts?
- How should relationships with the firm's suppliers and buyers affect its strategy?

SUPPLIERS

Suppliers provide the firm's inputs. Typically, pressure on the firm increases as supplier importance increases — like providing a critical input or a large percentage of purchases. Periodically, Apple faces pressure from music labels unhappy with iTunes' sales terms. Extreme pressure can send firms into bankruptcy: Business-class-only airlines Eos, MAXjet, and Silverjet each failed when fuel prices rose.[13] Pressure may also arise if the supplier brand is attractive to firm customers: PC buyers value the Intel brand; PC manufacturers feel pressure from Intel and Intel earns high profit margins. Pressure is strongest when the supplier is a monopoly like local telephone firms, government services, and railroads; the firm may also have to accept poor service and/or delivery. Sometimes multiple suppliers form *cartels*, like oil (OPEC) and diamonds (De Beers), to manage production volumes and hence prices.

Of course, a supplier's most important job is to supply! Supplier failure to honor commitments can play havoc with the firm's operations. Nissan cut its steel supplier base from five to two — Nippon Steel and JFE. When these firms could not meet its needs, Nissan had to close plants and slash automobile output by tens of thousands.

The most severe supplier threat is **forward integration** — the supplier becomes a direct competitor by conducting operations that the firm currently performs.[14] Boeing suppliers gained expertise that could benefit Boeing's competitors. Many firms in less-developed countries are outsourced manufacturers for U.S. and European firms; but they also develop the skills for future forward integration. Indian diamond jewelry makers now sell branded products that compete with former customers. Some firms work hard to inhibit such forward integration: One firm relabeled and repainted supplier components to disguise their origin; another designed its products to be incompatible with component suppliers.[15]

KEY IDEA

➤ The most significant threats from suppliers and buyers are, respectively:

• Forward integration
• Backward integration

BUYERS

Buyers purchase the firm's products. A firm with many small customers faces little buyer pressure, but a small number of large customers can exert tremendous pressure. Buyer pressure typically increases as its market share increases. The firm's margins shrink when powerful customers demand price discounts and expensive services. De Beers sets the price for diamonds; suppliers can take it or leave it! Walmart demands, and receives, many supplier concessions, and leading automobile firms secure large concessions from parts suppliers. The most severe buyer threat is **backward integration** — the buyer becomes a new direct competitor by conducting operations the firm currently performs.

ENVIRONMENTAL FORCES[16]

Environmental forces affect the firm and other industry participants. Figure 3.4 shows how these **PESTLE** forces — *political, economic, sociocultural, technological, legal/regulatory* and *environmental (physical)* — and industry forces relate to one another. Some PESTLE forces affect individual businesses. Other forces like the World Trade Organization (WTO) (political), exchange rate movements (economic), and the Internet (technological) impact the entire firm.

Forward-thinking firms seek out leading indicators of environmental trends. Many firms are now developing *green* products that appeal to environmentally-concerned customers. Germany leads in environmental legislation and related political activism; California spawns many youth-oriented trends; African-American male teenagers are a leading fashion influence; and research at universities like Cambridge, Columbia, MIT, and Stanford often leads the way in biotechnology, computers, medicine, and telecommunications.

KEY IDEA

➤ The firm faces a broad set of environmental forces — PESTLE:

• Political
• Economic
• Sociocultural
• Technological
• Legal/regulatory
• Environmental (physical)

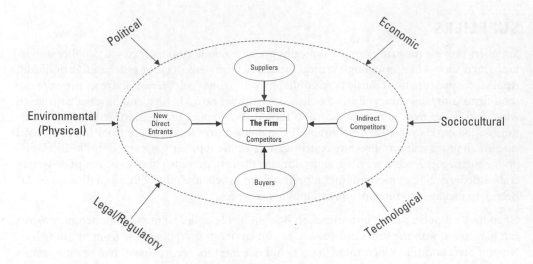

FIGURE 3.4

**THE PESTLE MODEL —
ENVIRONMENTAL
FORCES ACTING
ON THE INDUSTRY**

POLITICAL

Governments set the frameworks for regulators to develop the rules for business. Separate government departments at different levels (federal, state, local) are also often large purchasers, in part to make investments for the public good, and sometimes are sellers — like the U.S. Postal Service. Governments set the frameworks for regulators to develop the rules for business. Typically, governments intervene in economies via fiscal and monetary policy to pursue political ends and enhance consumer welfare by creating a *level playing field*. In recent years, many national governments realized that regulations designed to protect consumers locked in competitive structures, restricted competitive entry, and stifled innovation contrary to intended results.

Firms and/or trade associations try to influence political actions by contributing to political campaigns and hiring lobbyists to influence legislation and the rule-making process.

ECONOMIC

The country's economic well-being influences market demand. High inflation, high and rising interest rates, falling share prices, and a depreciating currency point to an unhealthy economy. But some measures can be ambiguous. High inflation rates are generally a negative indicator; but very low and below zero inflation rates, like in 1990s Japan, are also negative. High savings rates are generally positive, but too high rates lower consumption. Because *expectations* influence spending patterns, evaluating direction and rate of change are critical. China's GDP is quite low, but GDP growth is high, and China is now a major market.

SOCIOCULTURAL

Culture is "the distinctive customs, achievements, products, outlook, etc., of a society or group; the way of life of a society or group."[17] Culture is learned early in life, largely by influence from family, schools, and religious institutions. Cultural norms are resistant to change but do evolve. Generally, people do not notice culture in their everyday lives, but recognize cultural values by comparison with different cultures. What is normal in one culture may seem odd in another. Most cultures give gifts, but meanings can differ widely. Chinese associate white, blue, and black gifts with funerals; sharp objects like knives and scissors symbolize cutting off a friendship.

CULTURAL GROUPS. A cultural group may inhabit a nation-state, like Brazil or Iran; a geographic region within a nation, like the South or Midwest in the U.S.; or a multinational region, like

*Marketing
Question*

Nestlé Prepared Foods (NPF) identified several trends — increasing time pressure on dual-income households, sharpening decline in culinary skills, growth of empty-nester households, increasing belief that good food equals good health, and growing concern with obesity. How would you advise NPF?

Latin America or Southeast Asia. A cultural group may also comprise a people, regardless of geographic location, like the Armenian, Jewish, and Kurdish diasporas.

A cultural group may comprise different subcultures, each reflecting both group culture and sub-cultural elements. Three important U.S. subcultures are Baby Boomers, Generation X, and Generation Y; each represents a different marketing opportunity.[18] Religious and social-issue groups may also play a critical role by pressuring firms to behave in ways they view as appropriate: Religious and family groups boycotted Ford for sponsoring gay rights parades.

LOCALIZATION AND GLOBALIZATION. An important contemporary cultural issue is the tension between localization and globalization. Enhanced travel, improved communications and transportation, the Internet, and globally available television and movies are ready lubricants. Indeed, Levi's jeans and Marlboro cigarettes benefited from scores of cowboy movies distributed around the world. But many individuals and groups resist globalization in general, and U.S. and Western influence in particular. Protesters routinely disrupt WTO meetings; the Iraq war spurred global boycotts of U.S. products, and U.S. consumers have boycotted French products. Global and local trends have a profound impact on firms and the products they produce and sell.

TECHNOLOGICAL

Since World War II, technological innovation has produced many products and services we now take for granted. A partial list: color television, dry copiers, synthetic and optical fibers, cell phones, computers, integrated circuits, microwave ovens, passenger jet aircraft, communication satellites, ATMs, virtually all plastics, and antibiotic drugs. These innovations changed individual, household, and organizational life; re-structured industries; and drove economic growth.

Today, the pace of technological change continues to accelerate. In the 20 years between 1970 and 1990, six product classes in consumer electronics achieved mass acceptance — video recorders, video cameras, videogame consoles, CD players, telephone answering machines, and cordless telephones. Since the mid-1990s, widely adopted products include personal computers, personal digital assistants (PDAs), digital cameras, DVD players, MP3 players, and digital video recorders (DVRs). The Internet (boxed insert p. 46) has changed the way entire industries compete and offers previously unimaginable customer benefits. eBay affects the way many people buy and sell products — half a million U.S. residents make their living selling products on eBay. In South Korea, most households are connected to the Internet at one gigabyte per second, *200 times faster* than the average U.S. connection.

Some technological innovations are industry-specific; others affect the entire economy. Moore's law states that transistor density on computer chips and microprocessor speed double every 18 to 24 months; improving price/performance ratios are transforming industry and commerce. Access to computers and cell phones continues to increase, and computing power infuses increasing numbers of products. Automobiles, aircraft, surgical equipment, and elevators already use computer technology to operate more efficiently, predictably, and safely.

KEY IDEA

➤ Technological innovation can be:

• Sustaining — improving performance of established products

• Disruptive — offering new value propositions

Technological change can be either sustaining or disruptive[19]:

- **Sustaining technologies** are often incremental. They improve performance for *current* products on dimensions that *existing* customers value. Examples include *cordless* vacuum cleaners, *power* drills, and *mobile* telephones versus *land-line* products.

- **Disruptive technologies** bring new and very different value propositions. They change customer behavior by finding new applications and initially a few new-to-the-market customers. Included are PCs versus typewriters, digital music downloads to iPods and other devices versus store-bought CDs. Disruptive technologies spawn products that threaten and change entire industries. For existing customers, early product versions are typically inferior — like the first digital cameras — more expensive and complicated than chemical-film cameras. But as cost-benefit ratios improve, the disruptive technology surpasses the old technology. When disruptive technology becomes mainstream it threatens old technology firms that do not adapt. Examples: digital cameras and discount brokerages that significantly affected market leaders such as Kodak and Merrill Lynch, respectively, and changed the face of these industries.

Generally, current suppliers invest in sustaining technologies to serve the needs of current customers; new entrants introduce disruptive technologies that initially satisfy new and different customers. In the disk-drive industry, current disk-drive suppliers pioneered 14-inch Winchester and 2.5-inch drives — sustaining innovations for mainframe and laptop computers, respectively. By contrast, 8.5-, 5.25-, 3.5-, and 1.8-inch drives were disruptive technologies. Initially, each innovation satisfied the needs of different customers, respectively, manufacturers of mini-computers, desktop PCs, laptops, and portable heart-monitoring devices.

The Internet

The Internet is a *killer app.*[20] Like movable type, the telephone, and the automobile, the Internet has changed the way society works and functions. The automobile changed the way people live, shop, work, and spend leisure time — the Internet is doing the same.

The Internet is an efficient distribution channel, interactive communications tool, marketplace, and information system. Firms communicate with customers and suppliers in new ways; increasing interconnectedness, open standards, and new protocols will further ease information flow. The type and quantity of data the firm collects, stores, and distributes is also changing. Many retailers transmit cash register data direct to suppliers. Inventory costs have fallen as the ratio of goods shipped to goods in inventory has dropped from 1:2 (1970) to 1:1.2 (2010). Firms can also collect and manage data about current and potential customers, and take action in real time.

The Internet reduces transactions costs; Table 3.2 shows the dramatic impact on personal financial services. When insurance buyers and sellers meet on the Internet, they eliminate agents and brokers — and their fees. Internet purchases are common for financial instruments, airline travel, and hotel reservations.

TABLE 3.2

AVERAGE COST PER TRANSACTION IN RETAIL BANKING[21]

Mode	Cost / Transaction
Branch teller	$2.50
Telephone	$1.00
ATM	$0.40
Voice response	$0.24
Internet	$0.10

Lead generation and advertising for small businesses is shifting from the Yellow Pages to real-time, adaptable, adjustable text ads spread across thousands of web pages. No longer must consumers' "fingers do the walking." Google Adwords and Facebook ensure that contextually appropriate ads reach target customers.

Sellers reach more buyers on the Internet; buyers access more suppliers. eBay benefits from this *network effect*. As more sellers post products on eBay, eBay's buyers receive greater value. As more buyers purchase on eBay, eBay's sellers receive greater value!

B2B exchanges are popular. Firms like GE post requirements; pre-approved suppliers bid in a *reverse auction*. (Note: In reverse auctions, prices go down, not up, as in traditional English auctions.) Some firms form B2B-exchange alliances with competitors to develop reverse auctions. DaimlerChrysler, Ford, and GM formed the Covisint exchange (since sold).

Perhaps the Internet's greatest impact will be in industries where products can be digitized. Recorded music has seen significant turmoil, including widespread piracy — iTunes has brought some stability. Movies and other videos may enter a turbulent phase as transmission capacity increases. Many Internet sites provide content — Google and Yahoo! — news, and interaction via chat rooms and bulletin boards, with suppliers, vendors, and customers.

Interactivity and accessibility of online content has upended the media industry. User-generated content and meta-data created by communities are watchwords for the next generation of Internet media firms. YouTube, Blogger, Wikipedia, and others have based their success on user-generated journals, videos, and other data. The firm's emerging role will be editor or gatekeeper, sorting out what's good and adapting as necessary.

Perhaps the most important recent trends are the growth of Facebook, LinkedIn, Twitter, and others, and the Internet's interface with mobile devices like cell phones and tablet computers. The emerging managerial role is to be fully aware of the various developments and to take advantage of emerging firm opportunities.

LEGAL/REGULATORY

The legal framework (LF) establishes the rules for business. LF aims to protect societal interests, regulate market power, hinder collusion, and stop deceptive practices. LFs differ across countries, but generally govern mergers and acquisitions, capital movements, consumer protection, and employment conditions. In the aftermath of the 2008–2009 economic crisis, the U.S. placed heavy restriction on the financial sector via Dodd-Frank legislation.

The U.S. and Britain have well-developed systems based on statute and case law; the Napoleonic Code generally forms the LF in continental Europe. By contrast, poorly developed systems of commercial law in Russia and China cause major problems for foreign firms. In China, product copying and illegal use of brand names is rampant, despite China's WTO membership.

Individuals, firms, and governments use LFs to advance their interests. Individuals file lawsuits about poorly designed or manufactured products. Firms sue suppliers, customers, and competitors, and governments bring lawsuits. The U.S. government sued Microsoft for antitrust violations; New York Attorneys General Elliot Spitzer and Andrew Cuomo sued many financial service firms and their senior executives. Typically, legislation drives regulation. Powerful regulatory bodies, like the EPA, FCC, FDA, FTC, and NTSB in the U.S. and their equivalents in other countries, enact rules embodying legislation.

ENVIRONMENTAL (PHYSICAL)

Natural and man-made forces coexist in an uneasy equilibrium. Humans have little or no control over natural phenomena like asteroids hitting the earth, earthquakes, erupting volcanoes, hurricanes and tornadoes, monsoons, tsunamis, and everyday weather patterns. In 2010 and 2011, volcanic ash from Iceland and Chile, respectively, upset European air travel for several days and devastated the Bariloche, Argentina, tourist industry. Forces like Hurricane Sandy in the U.S., Japan's tsunami, and Thailand's floods (2011) highlight the fragility of increasingly decentralized yet tightly integrated global supply chains — production of many products and commerce suffered from these events in many parts of the world. By contrast, human action is driving rainforest and wetland destruction, global warming,[22] pollution, raw material shortages, retreating coastlines, and the shrinking ozone layer.

Firms face increasing pressure from governments, environmentalists, single-issue advocacy groups, and the public at large to provide increased transparency and assume greater environmental responsibility for their products, packaging, and production systems. Some firms are aggressively enacting *green* strategies. HP recycles 70,000 tons annually (about 10 percent of sales).

KEY IDEA

➤ Environmental forces are constantly in flux; they also interact with each other.

INTERACTIONS AMONG PESTLE FORCES

Figure 3.5 shows the PESTLE forces acting on the industry as interconnected; examples are legion. The Internet (technological) has major implications for sociocultural and political forces, especially in countries with little political freedom. In South Korea, huge government investment in broadband infrastructure (political) is spurring domestic innovation (technological). In Germany, recycling has vital economic, environmental (physical), and political dimensions. As environmental change and turbulence grow, interconnectedness among PESTLE forces will increase.

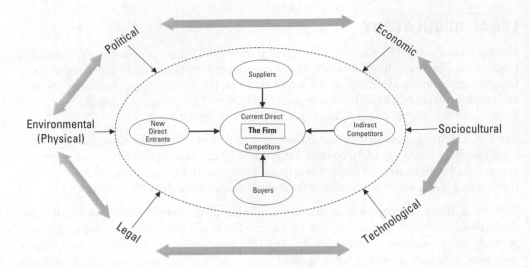

FIGURE 3.5

THE AUGMENTED INDUSTRY ENVIRONMENT

KEY MESSAGES

To gain market insight, the firm should focus on four broad areas — market structure, market and product evolution, industry forces, and environmental forces:

Market Structure:

- The *market* comprises customers requiring goods and services to satisfy their needs.
- The firm should define the market at several levels.
- *Product class* and *product form* refer to products that all suppliers offer. Product class is a broader level of aggregation than product form.
- Firms offer *product items* to the market — a *product line* comprises multiple product items.
- Fundamental drivers of market size are population and purchasing power.

Market and Product Evolution:

- The life-cycle framework is a good way to think about market and product evolution.
- The length of life cycles is in the order: market > product class > product form.
- Life cycles have several stages: introduction, early growth, late growth, maturity, and decline — each with distinguishing characteristics.
- Profit-margin life cycles do not mirror sales life cycles.

Industry Forces:

- The *five-forces model* is a useful way of examining pressures on the firm.
- The five forces are *current direct competitors*, *new direct entrants*, *indirect competitors*, *suppliers*, and *buyers*. Each force affects the firm in a different way.

Environmental Forces:

- Environmental forces impact both the firm and other industry players.
- Environmental forces are *political, economic, sociocultural, technological, legal/regulatory,* and *environmental (physical)* — PESTLE.
- The PESTLE forces are in a continuous state of flux and are increasingly interconnected.

VIDEOS AND AUDIOS

Market Insight   a301

a301

CHAPTER 4

CUSTOMER INSIGHT cv401

To access O-codes, go to **www.ocodes.com**

LEARNING OBJECTIVES

When you have completed this chapter, you will be able to:

- Define and describe customer insight.
- Identify customers, and distinguish between macro and micro customers and between direct and indirect customers.
- Identify the various roles people play in the purchase-decision process.
- Use several frameworks to understand customer value.
- Analyze critical stages in the purchase-decision process.
- Highlight how customers choose among purchase alternatives.
- Classify customer purchasing processes to help develop market strategies.
- Understand the key influences on consumer (B2C) and organizational (B2B) purchases.

OPENING CASE: IKEA

IKEA is the world's most successful global retailer. All IKEA stores operate under a franchise from IKEA Systems B.V. The first IKEA store opened in Almhult, Sweden, in 1958. IKEA's vision is "to create a better everyday life for many people." IKEA is not just another furniture retailer; franchising supports IKEA's vision by easing market expansion. IKEA provides designers with customer insight for fashioning many different types of value.

In 2012, revenues for the 320 IKEA stores in more than 40 countries exceeded €25 billion. Targeting middle-class customers, IKEA offers a broad range of affordable, IKEA-designed, contemporary home-furnishing products. IKEA's immense product line spans 20 different categories including bathroom, beds and mattresses, bookcase and storage, pet products, lighting, TV and media solutions, tables and chairs, and work areas. Many IKEA stores also offer food products.

IKEA strives for low costs via a focus on design and function; high volumes push down costs and prices even further. To reduce transportation costs, IKEA ships in flat packs. Customers purchase products in the store, pick them up at the warehouse, then drive home. Customers do simple assembly, with an IKEA-provided wrench and instructions. IKEA's mantra, "You do your part. We do our part. Together we save money," supports its low-price approach.

By close attention to customer needs, IKEA has become a home furnishings icon. IKEA distributes millions of catalogs, printed in multiple languages, free to households in its primary market areas around the world. IKEA stores have more than 700 million annual visitors.

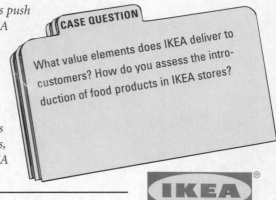

IKEA strives to deliver great customer value. Customers are the firm's core assets. When the firm does a good job of delivering customer value, it attracts, retains, and grows customers, makes profits today and tomorrow, survives and grows, and enhances shareholder value. To succeed in the customer-value challenge, the firm must develop good **customer insight**, based on deep customer understanding. This chapter focuses on how successful firms secure customer insight.

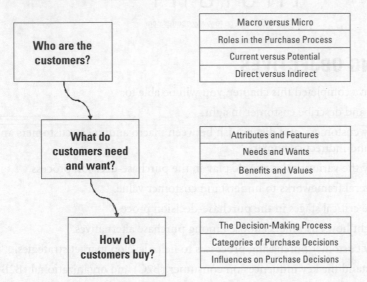

FIGURE 4.1

CUSTOMER INSIGHT

To deliver value to customers, the firm must answer the three questions in Figure 4.1:

- **Who are the customers?** So far, we have used the term *customer* fairly loosely. Now we focus by considering direct and indirect customers, and current and potential customers. The firm must also know who is involved in the purchase decision, and the various roles individuals play in the **decision-making unit (DMU)**.

- **What do customers need and want?** Understanding customer needs is critical for delivering benefits and values. Securing customer insight may require in-depth customer research and a deep understanding of customer value.

- **How do customers buy?** The firm must know the intricacies of the customer **decision-making process (DMP)**, and the various influencing factors. We consider consumer (B2C) and organizational (B2B) purchase decisions separately.

KEY IDEA

➤ To secure customer insight, the firm must correctly *identify* customers.

FIGURE 4.2

IDENTIFYING CUSTOMERS

KEY IDEA

➤ • Macro-level customers are organizations.
 • Micro-level customers are individuals.

KEY IDEA

➤ Organizations do not make decisions; people in organizations make decisions.

WHO ARE THE CUSTOMERS?

Identifying customers is the crucial first step in securing **customer insight**. This is not a trivial matter. The most obvious response to the *who* question is: The customer pays for goods and services. Right? This answer is often wrong and is almost always inadequate. Figure 4.2 shows the firm must cast a wide net for customers. We prefer this definition:

A customer is any person or organization, in the channel of distribution or decision (excluding competitors), whose actions can affect the purchase of the firm's products and services.

This definition is purposely broad because identifying customers is often like a detective's job. Many individuals may be involved in decisions to purchase the firm's products and services. The definition reflects the fact that:

- Both organizations — **macro level** — and individuals — **micro level** — are customers.
- **Customer** roles in purchase decisions include influencers and decision-makers.
- The firm should consider both **current customers** and **potential customers**.
- **Direct customers** pay the firm for products and services, but **indirect customers** — customers of direct customers (and of other indirect customers) — frequently influence purchases.
- Some *two-sided markets* comprise customers that *pay* for products, and customers that receive *free* products. Sellers pay auction houses, buyers receive service free; advertisers pay TV stations, consumers watch TV programs free.

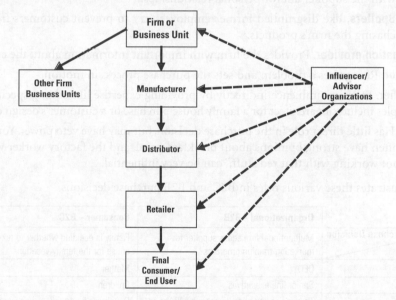

MACRO-LEVEL CUSTOMERS AND MICRO-LEVEL CUSTOMERS

To gain customer insight, the firm must understand how various customer types fit into the buying process. **Macro-level customers** are the organizational units — manufacturers, wholesalers, retailers, government entities (B2B), and families (B2C) that purchase products and services. **Micro-level customers** are individuals within the macro-level customer that influence purchase or have decision-making authority. Let us be very clear: Organizations do not make decisions; people in organizations make decisions. When micro-level customers jointly make a purchase decision, they act as a **decision-making unit (DMU)**.[1]

ROLES IN THE PURCHASE DECISION

Both macro-level and micro-level customers play several different roles in purchase decisions. *Macro-level customers* like distributors and retailers *purchase* the firm's products; they also *sell*, *deliver*, *store*, and/or *service* them. Customers like governments, standards bodies, and consulting firms may *influence* other *macro-level customers* to buy the firm's products.

Micro-level customers play similar roles in both B2C and B2B purchase decisions:

- **Buyer.** Has formal power to execute the purchase, like company purchasing agents.

- **Coach.** Helps the firm navigate the customer's organization and advises how to address influencers and decision-makers.

- **Decision-maker.** Has the formal power to make the purchase decision.

- **Gatekeeper.** Has the power to impede access to decision-makers and influencers. Secretaries, administrative assistants, and purchasing agents often play this role.

- **Information provider.** Provides the firm with important information about the customer.

- **Influencer.** The decision-maker values the influencer's opinion. In family purchases, the influencer may be a friend, colleague, spouse, child, or grandparent. Organizational influencers include operations, engineering, marketing, and/or general management. Two special types of influencer are champions/sponsors and spoilers.

    - **Champions/Sponsors** promote the firm's interests, based on positive experiences with the supplier and/or personal relationships.

    - **Spoilers**, like disgruntled former employees, try to prevent customers from purchasing the firm's products.

- **Information provider.** Provides the firm with important information about the customer.

- **Initiator.** Recognizes a problem and sets the purchase process in motion.

- **Specifier.** Exercises influence indirectly by providing expertise like setting specifications. Examples include an architect for a family house purchase or a customer's design engineer.

- **User.** Has little direct role in the purchase decision, but may have veto power. Young children often have strong opinions about breakfast cereal, and the factory worker who says, "I'm not working with that red stuff," can be very influential.

Table 4.1 illustrates these various roles in B2C and B2B purchase decisions.

Purchase Decision Roles	Organizational - B2B	Consumer – B2C
	Multinational firm seeks supplier for marketing training programs	Family is deciding whether to take a cruise for the family vacation
Decision-maker	CEO	Mother
Influencer	Senior line executives	Children
Spoiler	Two senior line executives with MBAs from Harvard and Wharton	Daughter's boyfriend — has summer job at a Caribbean resort
Champion	Senior executives committed to Columbia Business School	Second cousin (works for cruise line)
Specifier	Junior human resource (HR) personnel who develop the program	Grandmother (has some basic requirements that must be met)
Gatekeeper	Senior HR personnel	Live-in housekeeper
Buyer	Purchasing officer	Father
Information Provider	Bricker's — good source on executive education	Travel agent
User	Middle managers	Mother, father, children, grandparents

TABLE 4.1

ILLUSTRATION OF ROLES IN B2B AND B2C PURCHASE DECISIONS

KEY IDEA

➤ The firm must pay attention to both:
  • Current customers
  • Potential customers

CURRENT CUSTOMERS AND POTENTIAL CUSTOMERS

Current customers provide revenues and profits today. Chapter 2 highlighted the role of customer retention for future revenues and profits. But the firm must also identify potential customers. Alcoa works with universities to train students in metalworking design, and McKinsey happily places its consultants at senior positions in client firms.

DIRECT CUSTOMERS AND INDIRECT CUSTOMERS

Marketing Question

Banks are persistent in soliciting students for credit cards. Why? How could they be more effective?

Typically, the firm's direct customers exchange money for products and services. Many indirect customers buy the firm's products from these direct customers or from other indirect customers. Sometimes direct customers are distributors or retailers, or end users that buy and use the firm's finished products. In other cases, direct customers transform the firm's product before their own product reaches their customers.

The direct-versus-indirect customer distinction is very important. The firm has a business relationship with direct customers but *may not know* its indirect customers, and hence have little insight into the benefits and values they seek. Until **customer relationship management (CRM)** technology became widely available, FMCG firms like P&G typically could not identify their indirect customers — consumers purchasing their products. Today, FMCG firms learn via contests, promotions, and websites. Stouffer's encourages website registration to learn about recipes and menu items; correspondingly, Stouffer's gains better insight into consumer needs.

KEY IDEA

➤ *Indirect* customers may be more important than *direct* customers — they are often final users and ultimately drive product demand.

To reinforce the importance of indirect customers, consider what a senior UPS executive told us: "As a company we are very focused, not just on our customers and what we do that helps them, but on what we do that helps their customer. We're always looking through our customer to their customer. We continually ask ourselves … how does our technology, our products/services and opportunities transcend our customer's relationship with their customers."[2]

KEY IDEA

➤ To *attract, retain,* and *grow* customers, the firm must:
  • Develop offers of value to satisfy customer needs
  • Communicate the value of those offers to customers

WHAT DO CUSTOMERS NEED AND WANT?

The firm attracts, retains, and grows customers by delivering value to satisfy their needs. **Customer value** equates to the value in the firm's offer less the customer's monetary, time, effort, and emotional costs. Two sorts of firm action are crucial:

  • Make offers of value to satisfy customers' needs.
  • Communicate the value of those offers to customers.[3]

The Opening Case shows that IKEA provides both customer value and communicates customer value. If the firm offers value, but customers don't know about it, they will not purchase. If the firm communicates its offer extensively, but customers don't perceive value (like GM advertising the Hummer as gasoline prices rise), they will not purchase. We discuss customer needs, how they relate to product attributes/features, and the benefits and values that customers receive.

RECOGNIZED NEEDS VERSUS LATENT NEEDS

Marketing Question

What product did a firm target to you that did not satisfy your needs? What needs did the product not satisfy? Why do you think this occurred?

Sometimes customers understand their needs — **recognized needs**; sometimes they don't — **latent needs**. Recognized needs may be expressed or non-expressed:

  • **Expressed needs.** Customers often ask for advice on how to satisfy their needs.
  • **Non-expressed needs.** Customers sometimes do not express their needs, like teenage girls contemplating condom purchases.

Customers are not consciously aware of *latent needs*. These needs may surface as technological innovation raises awareness and customers require benefits/values they could not previously express. A few years ago, few consumers could have articulated a need for cell phones. But widespread availability surfaced a latent need of wanting to stay in constant contact.

ATTRIBUTES AND FEATURES VERSUS BENEFITS AND VALUES

Many firms define their products and services in terms of **attributes** and **features**. Think about television advertising touting *new and improved*. Now read very carefully. Customers *do not care about your products and services* — they are not interested in the attributes and features. Customers *do care* about satisfying *their needs* and the *benefits and values* your products and services provide. You must communicate them clearly. Let us be very clear about these terms:

- **Attributes and features.** Design elements or functions the firm builds into its products and services — typically of great concern to design engineers.
- **Benefits.** Something the product or service delivers that satisfies customer needs.
- **Values.** Something the product or service provides that has broader scope than benefits.

Most firms sell products and services that in turn provide benefits and values. Recently, some firms have begun selling benefits and values directly to customers. IBM's *on-demand computing* customers do not pay for hardware and software; they only pay for the computing power they use. Similarly, some airlines pay for airplane engines per hour of operating life.

HIERARCHIES OF NEEDS, FEATURES, BENEFITS, AND VALUES

Psychologists have studied individual needs extensively. We explore a popular need framework developed by psychologist Abraham Maslow that marketers often use. Maslow's ideas form the basis of the feature/benefit/value ladder.

MASLOW'S HIERARCHY OF NEEDS. Maslow's classic framework identifies five major groups of needs: *physiological, safety and security, social, ego,* and *self-actualization* — ordered low to high.[4] Generally, we expect individuals to satisfy lower-level *physiological*, and safety and security needs before higher-level needs like *ego* and *self-actualization*.

Products like groceries, clothing, and housing satisfy lower-level *physiological* needs; sports equipment and educational services satisfy higher-level *social, ego,* and *self-actualization* needs. But firms can design market offers (products, advertising and promotion, distribution, and price) for groceries, clothing, and housing that also satisfy higher-level *social* and *ego* needs. Examples, respectively: organic food, designer fashions, and neighborhood location. Satisfying both *higher-level* needs and *lower-level* needs should provide greater customer value than satisfying *lower-level* needs alone. A woman is more likely to buy hair shampoo she believes will make her attractive (*ego* need) than if it just cleans her hair (*physiological* need). Table 4.2 applies Maslow's framework to two purchasing decisions.

Product / Need	Folgers Coffee	Krispy Kreme Donuts
Self-Actualization (self-fulfillment)	Savoring	Be part of a cultural phenomenon
Ego (prestige, success, self-respect)	Confidence, achievement	Be in vogue (especially among Gen-Xers)
Social (love, affection, friendship, belonging)	Togetherness, freshness, taste	Eating donuts is a group experience that creates a sense of *togetherness*
Safety & Security (protection, order, security)	Easy on the stomach, no jitters	Safe, easy for kids to eat — and no mess
Physiological (food, drink, air, shelter, sex)	Satisfies thirst, keeps you alert, keeps you warm	Satisfies hunger and the sweet tooth

KEY IDEA

➤ Customer needs are *recognized* or *latent*. Recognized needs may be *expressed* or *non-expressed*.

KEY IDEA

➤ Maslow's approach places a person's needs in an ordered hierarchy.

TABLE 4.2

USING MASLOW'S HIERARCHY OF NEEDS TO GAIN INSIGHT INTO TWO CONSUMER PURCHASES

LADDERING FEATURES, BENEFITS, AND VALUES. Many marketers meld Maslow's hierarchical approach to individual needs with the feature/benefit/value distinction to form a **feature/benefit/value ladder**. Figure 4.3 demonstrates the ladder's three main characteristics:

- **Focuses attention on customer value.** Firms typically design attributes/features into their products and services. The feature/benefit/value ladder forces a translation into benefits and values for customers. B&D's drills deliver many benefits and values.

- **Provides alternatives for communicating with customers.** The variety of benefits and values broadens the firm's options for communicating with customers. The best communications depend on factors like stage of market development and competitive threats. Potential B&D communications like *drill speed and bit hardness, makes holes easily*, and *supports do-it-yourself activity* are quite different from each other.

- **Broadens the view of competition.** When the firm focuses on attributes/features, its scope is direct competitors; a focus on customer benefits and values broadens this scope. With an attributes/features focus, B&D's competitors are electric drill manufacturers. Focusing on Benefit A — makes holes easily — introduces competitors like explosives, nails, lasers, water drills, and woodpeckers (!). Higher-level benefits broaden competitive scope even further.

FIGURE 4.3

FEATURE/BENEFIT/VALUE LADDERS FOR BLACK & DECKER DRILLS AND NIVEA SKIN CREAM

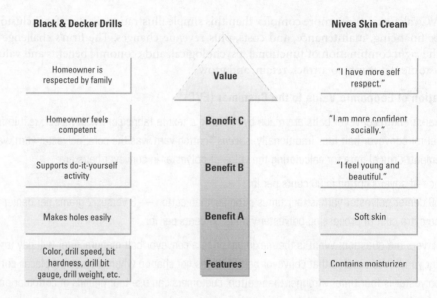

In general, customers using the firm's products and services focus on the benefits and values they provide. Resellers like distributors, retailers, and wholesalers are more interested in economic benefits like profit margins, net profit, and return on investment. Different customer types seek different benefits and values, so the firm should develop several feature/benefit/value ladders.

FUNCTIONAL, PSYCHOLOGICAL, AND ECONOMIC BENEFITS AND VALUES

Customers base their purchase decisions on a need hierarchy. The firm must translate the attributes/features of its offer into a hierarchy of benefits and values that align with these needs. But we must go one step further to explore three types of benefits and values.

FUNCTIONAL BENEFITS AND VALUES. Firms design products and services to provide functional benefits and values that satisfy customer needs. Food products satisfy hunger needs; disc brakes stop automobiles. Sometimes customers and firms discover functional benefits serendipitously: Customers found that Avon's Skin So Soft moisturizer was effective as a mosquito repellent; Pfizer developed *Viagra* to address heart disease but discovered it could treat erectile dysfunction.

PSYCHOLOGICAL BENEFITS AND VALUES. Psychological values typically satisfy status, affiliation, reassurance, risk, and security needs. Firms often offer psychological and functional benefits together. Fine-dining restaurants provide high-quality food and ambience (functional) and also prestige (psychological). An automobile may provide fast acceleration, efficiency, and comfort (functional), but also status (psychological). Generally, psychological values transcend functional benefits and appear higher up the feature/benefit/value ladder.[5]

ECONOMIC BENEFITS AND VALUES. Economic benefits and values concern financial aspects like price and credit terms. Price is often the primary purchase driver, especially in tough economies when customers trade off functional and psychological benefits to secure low prices. Walmart, purchasing clubs, dollar stores, discount airlines, and generic drug producers provide economic benefits via lower prices. In B2B markets, price is often critical, but sometimes firms deliver cost-cutting economic benefits at *higher prices* by providing greater functional benefits. GE strengthens customer relationships by helping customers improve operational effectiveness.

Economic value for the customer (EVC) is the competitive product's price, plus the net added value (positive differentiation value less negative differentiation value) from the firm's product. The boxed insert shows the EVC calculation for a polyester product used in making conveyor belts.[6]

Many EVC calculations are more complex than this simple illustration. Factors for inclusion are customer financing, maintenance, and costs, plus revenue changes. The firm's challenge is to deliver the *right* combination of functional, psychological, and economic benefits and values to those customers it wants to attract, retain, and grow.

Illustration of Economic Value to the Customer (EVC)

Industrial-strength conveyor belts are made by covering a textile fabric core with rubber; textile fiber strength is crucial for conveyor belt life. Traditionally, *sevens** cotton yarn was the core; polyester yarn was a potential replacement. Critical data for calculating the value of polyester in conveyor belts are:

- Price of sevens cotton is 90 cents per lb.
- 750 denier polyester yarn is four times stronger than cotton — 8 versus 2 grams per denier (g.p.d.)
- The extra cost of processing polyester yarn is 30 cents per lb.

EVC answers the question: What is the maximum price a conveyor belt manufacturer will pay for polyester yarn? (We assume that conveyor belt life does not change when polyester replaces cotton.) Since polyester is four times stronger than cotton, customers can use four pounds of cotton or one pound of polyester.

- Cotton: sevens cotton yarn @ 90 cents per lb. — reference value
- Polyester equivalence: 1 lb. of 750 denier polyester yarn or 4 lbs. of sevens cotton = $3.60 — reference value plus positive differentiation value
- Extra cost to process polyester yarn = 30 cents per lb. — negative differentiation value
- Net polyester equivalence = $3.60 less $0.30 = $3.30 — total economic value[7]

In sum, based on the economic value analysis, conveyor belt manufacturers should be indifferent between:

a. Sevens cotton @ 90 cents per lb., and
b. 750 denier polyester @ $3.30 per lb.

Hence, the maximum polyester price is $3.30 per lb. At any price above $3.30 per lb., conveyor belt manufacturers would be better off sticking with cotton.

*Sevens cotton is the standard type of cotton yarn used in industrial applications.

> ### *Marketing Question*
>
> Think about one of your favorite products. What *functional* benefits does it provide? What *psychological* benefits does it provide? Be creative!

> ### *Marketing Question*
>
> The three major overnight shipping firms offer various benefits and values. Do you agree with these category assignments, based on their slogans?
>
> **Functional Provider:**
> UPS – "Moving at the speed of business" and "See what Brown can do for you."
>
> **Psychological Provider:**
> FedEx – "Be absolutely sure" (that is, don't get fired).
>
> **Economic Provider:**
> United States Postal Service (USPS) – "We deliver." USPS's prices are lower than UPS and FedEx.

CHARACTERISTICS OF BENEFITS AND VALUES

ACTUAL VALUE VERSUS POTENTIAL VALUE. The critical value the firm offers may lie not in the product itself, but in the customer's ability to secure additional value, if and when needed. The AmEx Platinum Card's Concierge program locates hard-to-find items, delivers gifts, provides secretarial services in remote areas, and offers secure reservations in upscale restaurants. Most cardholders rarely use these services, but their availability has high value.

FUTURE VALUE. Generally, customers purchase products and services for benefits and values they expect to receive directly. But they may also purchase today for expected future benefits and values. When a B2B customer purchases from a technology firm, a key factor may be benefits inherent in the supplier relationship like preferential access to *beta* (pre-release) versions of future technology. Dell buys most of its computer chips from Intel (versus AMD) in part because Intel gives Dell early insight into new technologies.

PRESENCE VALUE. The firm may provide considerable customer value just by being a supplier, so long as its products are acceptable and prices are reasonable. When a customer has one strong and one weak supplier, the weak supplier's presence keeps the strong supplier *honest* and inhibits the exercise of monopoly power. For many years, Airbus played this role versus Boeing in passenger aircraft; AMD plays this role versus Intel in computer chips.

SCARCITY VALUE. Some firms like fashion retailer Zara deliberately make small product volumes to provide scarcity value. Beanie Babies notoriously limited production runs then ruthlessly retired prized stuffed animals; many Harley-Davidson models have long wait times due to scarcity.

VALUE FOR WHOM. Consumers typically make purchases for themselves, friends, colleagues, family members, or a group like the family. A B2B purchase may satisfy either organizational or individual needs. To ensure that the organization receives the value, firms like Walmart go to great lengths to prohibit purchasing agents from receiving any individual benefits, like gifts, lunch, tips, or other items from suppliers.

WHEN CUSTOMERS RECOGNIZE VALUE. Sometimes customers have good data about the benefits and values a product provides; other times they are uncertain and cannot assess value until long after purchase. **Search, use,** and **credence** benefits capture this uncertainty and may offer important insight:

- **Search benefits** — significant product and service data from the firm and/or independent sources like *Consumer Reports*. Customers may even inspect and try products, like test-driving a car.
- **Use benefits** — relatively little data on customer value before purchase, like many services. Value is revealed when the product or service is consumed, like a concert performance, or an expensive restaurant meal.
- **Credence benefits** — impossible to assess value until long after purchase. Examples include an investment's economic benefits or health benefits from some medical procedures.

BEYOND CUSTOMER BENEFITS AND VALUES – CUSTOMER EXPERIENCES

In addition to explaining why customers buy, recent consumer behavior research focuses on consumption and needs for **experiences** — states, conditions, or events that consciously affect buying behavior. A single event can create many different experiences. A New York City ballet aficionado experiences a touring Bolshoi performance differently from someone seeing his first ballet. Also, the experience may have more value than the product. Consider coffee. Many cafes sell coffee for around $1 per cup. Starbucks' coffee is several dollars per cup but it also offers a personal and memorable experience.

Five modes of customer experience are[8]:

- **Sense.** Creates sensory experiences through sight, smell, sound, taste, and touch.
- **Feel.** Appeals to inner feelings and emotions. Attempts to create affective experiences, ranging from mildly positive to strong emotions of joy and pride.
- **Think.** Appeals to the intellect. Creates problem-solving experiences that engage creatively.
- **Act.** Enriches by showing alternative ways of doing things, alternative lifestyles and interactions.
- **Relate.** Contains aspects of sense, feel, think, and act, but reaches beyond individual personal, private feelings to something outside his/her private state.

This framework offers a methodical way of determining those experiences the firm wants customers to associate with its products.

HOW DO CUSTOMERS BUY?

The purchase **decision-making process (DMP)** ranges from relatively simple — buying a mid-morning snack — to highly complex — the U.S. government purchasing a new fighter jet. The DMP can be as quick as an impulse purchase or take months or even years.[9] Marketers must understand how customers move through the process and identify options for influence.

PURCHASE-DECISION STAGES

Figure 4.4 shows the DMP as a robust purchase model with five stages. Each DMP may involve multiple feedback loops both within and among stages. The customer may identify a need or problem early on and then elaborate on that need as she secures information and evaluates alternatives. Some purchases are *planned*; others are *unplanned* (made spontaneously during a shopping trip or in response to an online offer).

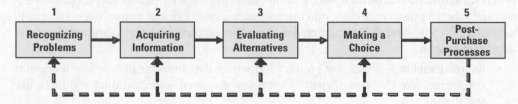

STAGE 1 – RECOGNIZING PROBLEMS. Some customer needs are critical to system functioning: food and drink for individuals, and raw materials and capital equipment for firms. Other needs are discretionary. The customer may recognize a need independently, or a potential supplier may point it out.

STAGE 2 – ACQUIRING INFORMATION. After recognizing a problem, customers generally seek information to help identify:

- The *feature* set — attributes/features that may satisfy the need.
- Criteria for evaluating satisfactory performance by the attributes/features.
- The *awareness* set — alternatives that may satisfy the need.
- The degree to which each alternative meets the attribute/feature criteria.

Customers can acquire information *externally* and *internally*. External information: from *personal sources* like colleagues, family, friends, and salespeople and from *impersonal sources* like advertising, the press, or online reviews. The degree of external search relates to current knowledge, involvement in the purchase. Internal information comes from the customer's own perceptual information store, including memory.

KEY IDEA

➤ The firm should try to understand customers' evaluation processes.

KEY IDEA

➤ Membership in the customer's consideration set is crucial for the firm.

Marketing Question

Describe your DMP for choosing the current educational institution you are attending. Identify the various stages. How did you approach each stage?

KEY IDEA

➤ Customers often deviate from rationality in making purchase decisions.

Marketing Question

Do you always act rationally in your purchase decisions? Identify situations where you have behaved less than rationally.

Marketing Exercise

Based on your deviations from rationality in the previous question, suggest marketing actions a firm could take with one of the products you purchase.

STAGES 3 AND 4 – EVALUATING ALTERNATIVES AND MAKING A CHOICE. Customers evaluate alternatives based on information they acquire in Stage 2. Frequently, customers exclude several alternatives in the *awareness set* with little evaluation, by forming a short list — *consideration set*, based on the purchase criteria. Customer choices from the consideration set may be rational, or may deviate from rationality. By understanding the customer evaluation process, the firm can influence the purchase decision in its favor. We examine one rational approach, and others that deviate from rationality:

A. Rational approach. This approach implies the customer:

- Identifies attributes/features that deliver the required benefits and values.
- Decides on the relative importance of these benefits and values.
- Forms a belief about how well the attributes/features of each alternative deliver these benefits and values.

The firm can take several actions to improve the value it offers customers:

- Improve perceived performance on important attributes.
- Add new valued attributes, especially important ones.
- Show customers that it performs better than competitors on important attributes.
- Show that the attributes where it performs really well are highly important.

Some attributes may be baseline requirements, or *antes*; only alternatives scoring sufficiently well enter the consideration set. Safety is often an *ante* for airline travel; customers do not trade off schedule or frequent-flier miles for safety.

B. Deviations from rationality. *Behavioral decision theory* and *behavioral economics* researchers have identified many purchase processes that seem *irrational* in both B2C and B2B markets; customers seem to base their choices on irrelevant factors.

Research shows several factors that affect deviations from rationality in purchasing decisions[10]:

- **Compromise** effect. Customers tend to avoid extreme price/value options in favor of intermediates. Given the choice between two microwave ovens, low price — $109.99 and medium price — $179.99, forty-three percent chose the medium-price oven. When customers chose among three ovens, the original two ovens plus a high-price oven — $199.99, they chose the $179.99 more than 60 percent of the time.[11] How many drink-size choices do you have at McDonald's or Starbucks?

- **How customers evaluate the alternatives.** Many factors affect how people evaluate alternatives, even just focusing attention on an alternative. Suppose a waiter offers the diner a choice between yogurt and fruit salad, then says, "How much more or less attractive to you is yogurt?" The probability of choosing yogurt increases![12]

- **When customers evaluate the alternatives.** Time of purchase may be rational — we buy Coke and Pepsi when it's hot and we are thirsty. But researchers found eBay prices for weekend purchases were 2 percent higher than during the week.

STAGE 5 – POST-PURCHASE PROCESSES. Customers typically engage in several post-purchase processes. These can affect future purchases — for customers and others they influence[13]:

- **Use.** For some products the firm may only be concerned with sales; for others, like credit cards, use is important. Use is particularly critical in pharmaceuticals; compliance failure causes 125,000 U.S. deaths annually.

- **Dissonance reduction.** If the product/service does not meet expectations, customers may reduce dissonance by seeking information and/or recalibrating product performance. Most dissonance reduction occurs when customers expend significant time and/or money to acquire the product.

- **Communications with customers/potential customers.** Word of mouth has always been an important post-purchase process; many firms hire people to stimulate customer-to-customer communication. Social media has increased the importance of word of mouth, and made it crucial to track. Anti-firm websites like *chase-sucks.com* and *walmart-blows.com* or random *tweets* can be a significant issue for firms.

- **Comparison with others.** Consumers modify consumption when they learn that neighbors' behavior is more socially acceptable. Electricity consumption decreases when utilities tell customers that neighbors with similar-size homes are more frugal.

- **Product and packaging disposal.** Environmental advocates are paying increasing attention to disposal. Many jurisdictions require customers to separate garbage into different categories. In France and Germany, firms must recover packaging and used products! HP and Kodak encourage returning used printer cartridges and disposable cameras, respectively.

- **Repurchase.** Repurchase drives CLV. All things equal, high customer satisfaction increases customer loyalty and repurchase.

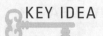

INFLUENCES ON CONSUMER PURCHASE PROCESSES

We explore several influences on consumer purchase processes. Deep understanding of *environmental* and *individual* factors can help the firm be proactive in developing strategy. Figure 4.5 shows **environmental influences** ranging from broad to narrow: culture, social class, other people, family, and the situation.

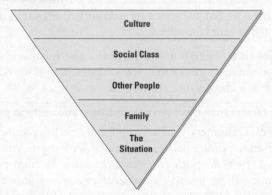

FIGURE 4.5

ENVIRONMENTAL INFLUENCES ON CONSUMERS' PURCHASING DECISIONS

CULTURE. Consumer purchasing behavior and product preferences are conditioned by cultural and subcultural norms. The firm must be careful not to violate these norms, especially abroad.[14] In the West, the female head of household traditionally does the weekly shopping; in rural Bangladesh, men do the shopping. Indonesians smoke more than 200 billion cigarettes annually, but only 10 percent are the standard *white* variety; 90 percent are *kreteks*, a clove cigarette that adds chocolate, cinnamon, coffee, licorice, and pineapple to tobacco.[15] In the U.S., business-casual dress policies have affected fiber, garment, detergent, and washing machine manufacturers.

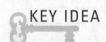

Cosmopolitan, the sex-oriented women's magazine, appears in almost 50 countries. Local editions consider cultural sensitivities and legal realities. Indian editions have no articles on sexual positions, sex is never explicitly mentioned in China, and Swedish society is so open that sex receives little attention. In Hong Kong, most models are local Asian celebrities, but in the PRC, most models are Western.

Cemex, the Mexican cement producer, tapped into *tandas*, a traditional community savings scheme. In Cemex's *Patrimonio Hoy* program, groups of 70 persons contribute about 120 pesos per week for 70 weeks. Each week, the program selects a *winner* who receives sufficient materials to build an extra room onto his or her home. Cemex also provides technical building assistance. Cemex's cement consumption by do-it-yourself homebuilders tripled.[16]

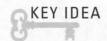

SOCIAL CLASS. All societies have hierarchically ordered groupings or social classes. Wealth and income are key discriminators, but occupation, residential location, and education also matter. Sometimes individuals migrate across classes. Values and interests, and purchases like clothing and leisure activities, are often similar within a social class.

OTHER PEOPLE. Other people and groups influence consumers. Individuals have frequent face-to-face contact with **primary reference groups** — family members and organizational work groups. **Secondary reference groups** include club and church members and professional organizations. **Aspirational groups** are those a person would like to join for reasons like prestige. People with expertise are particularly influential if they belong to attractive reference groups. Soccer player David Beckham is influential with many teenagers; he has significant expertise and style and belongs to an aspirational reference group — professional soccer players.

FAMILY. The *nuclear family* (father, mother, children) and/or *extended family* (grandparents, aunts, uncles, cousins, in-laws) may exert considerable influence. The relative nuclear family versus extended family influence is culturally determined. Nuclear family influence predominates in the West; extended family influence is very important in many Asian countries.

SITUATION. Consumers face situational influences daily — presentations and displays, and time constraints. *Purchase location aesthetics* are also important. People purchase real estate on vacation while enjoying free meals and other perks. U.S. college students purchase and consume more alcohol at football games, parties, and spring break than other times.

Important individual factors are cognitive and economic resources, technological competence, time, physical and mental health, should/want conflicts, life-cycle stage, and lifestyle.

INFLUENCES ON ORGANIZATIONAL PURCHASE PROCESSES

Organizational buying generally concerns larger sums of money than consumer purchases, is often more protracted and complex, engages more people, and may involve company politics. Processes and/or rules often govern organizational purchasing or *procurement* and interfacing with suppliers.[17]

CHANGES IN THE PROCUREMENT PROCESS

Important changes include:

BROADER SCOPE OF PROCUREMENT RESPONSIBILITIES. Historically, purchasing departments focused on buying factory inputs. Today, procurement is often also responsible for spending categories like auto rental, consulting services, and travel.

CENTRALIZATION. Technological advances in telecommunications, computers, and the Internet provide corporate buyers with greater leverage. They can secure complete, accurate, and timely purchasing data on individual suppliers from the firm's decentralized units and track purchasing performance against benchmark databases.

GLOBALIZATION. The centralizing trend just discussed is expanding globally as multinational firms broaden supplier searches. They want global contracts and are increasingly ready to switch suppliers as price differentials appear and disappear.

INTERNET. Using *reverse auctions*, Internet-based B2B exchanges significantly affect the purchase of standard products. Buyers have better (and cheaper) access to information to drive out market inefficiencies and price differentials.

PROCUREMENT EXPERTISE. Skilled procurement staffs introduce new strategies like **strategic sourcing** to reduce costs, improve quality, and increase efficiency. To become a *preferred supplier*, the firm must complete an extensive *request for information* (RFI); only then can it respond to a detailed *request for proposal* (RFP). Long-standing relationships mean little as procurement personnel gain deep insight into supplier cost structures and aggressively negotiate prices.

EVOLUTION IN BUYER-SELLER RELATIONSHIPS

Some firms evolve relationships with selected customers from vendor to quality supplier, and even to partner.

VENDOR. Customer and supplier operate at *arm's-length* in this traditional adversarial relationship. Contracts are typically short-term with frequent re-bidding. Price is critical; buyers switch suppliers for small price differentials and/or better delivery. Salespeople meet with purchasing agents who restrict the information they provide suppliers to maintain negotiating positions.

QUALITY SUPPLIER. Both supplier and customer believe they receive value — like high-quality final products — from a close long-term relationship. Each firm plans for continuous quality improvement. The supplier secures advantage by providing greater value than competitors.

PARTNER. Both firms share (or jointly develop) future strategies, technologies, and resources, and focus on the entire value chain. The customer bases critical buying decisions on value versus price. Each firm is deeply involved in the other's product-development cycles. Routine and sensitive information flows freely, as the supplier learns about/solves important customer problems.

INCREASED CORPORATE ATTENTION TO PROCUREMENT

At many firms, the *procurement spend/company-revenue ratio* has increased dramatically. Traditional *purchasing* is evolving from an unimportant managerial backwater into highly strategic *procurement*. Several factors are responsible:

BRANDING. The rising importance of branding allows many firms to resell products made by others. The author is writing this book on a MacBook Pro; Apple did not manufacture the computer, carrying case, or power cord, but the complete package arrived ready to use.

ORGANIZATIONAL DOWNSIZING. Many firms are downsizing by replacing labor with capital. Equipment, raw material, and supply expenses have increased, relative to other costs.

OUTSOURCING. Outsourcing allows firms to reduce balance-sheet assets and fixed costs while increasing productivity, functional expertise, and flexibility. Many major firms outsource data centers and other business processes to IBM, HP, and Accenture. Others outsource software development, human resource and accounting functions, and call centers to India.

REDUCING THE NUMBER OF SUPPLIERS

Traditional purchasing departments sent specifications to many potential suppliers and then chose on criteria like price and delivery. Because streamlined supply-chain systems improve efficiency and effectiveness in converting raw materials to finished products, many firms are forging closer relationships with fewer suppliers.

KEY MESSAGES

To attract, retain, and grow customers, the firm gains deep customer insight by answering three critical questions:

Who are the customers? The firm should explore several issues:

- Macro-level customers — organizations; and micro-level customers — individuals.
- The many different roles individuals play in the purchase process.
- Current customers and potential customers.
- Direct customers that exchange money for the firm's products and services, and indirect customers that receive value from the firm's products and services through intermediaries.

What do customers need and want? The firm satisfies customer needs by making value offers. The firm should gain customer insight into:

- Recognized needs customers express — expressed needs; latent needs customers do not express — non-expressed needs.
- Who receives the firm's value — the customer organization or an individual in the organization.
- Attributes and features comprising the firm's product; benefits and values the firm offers to customers.
- Hierarchies of needs, attributes/features, benefits, and values.
- Different types of value, including functional, psychological, and economic.
- Customer experiences that transcend customer benefits and values — customer experiences.

How do customers buy? The firm gains insight from the customer's purchase-decision process:

- The process comprises five stages — recognizing problems, acquiring information, evaluating alternatives, making a choice, and engaging in post-purchase processes.
- The dominant way customers evaluate alternatives is the linear-compensatory approach.
- Customers may deviate from rationality in their purchase decisions.
- We can usefully categorize purchase decisions into three types: routinized-response behavior, limited problem-solving, and extended problem-solving.
- Environmental factors that influence consumer purchase decisions include culture, social class, other people, family, and the situation.
- Individual influences like various types of resources, life-cycle stage, lifestyle, physical and mental health, and should/want conflicts influence the consumer purchase decision.
- Key factors influencing organizational purchase decisions are changes in the procurement process, evolution in buyer-seller relationships, increased corporate attention to procurement, and reducing the number of suppliers.

VIDEOS AND AUDIOS

Procurement at Merck	v402	Howard Richman	Merck
Customer Insight	a401		

v402

a401

CHAPTER 5

INSIGHT ABOUT COMPETITORS, COMPANY, AND COMPLEMENTERS cv501

To access O-codes, go to **www.ocodes.com**

LEARNING OBJECTIVES

When you have completed this chapter you will be able to:

- Articulate the importance of gaining *competitor* insight.
- Identify the firm's current (today) competitors and potential (tomorrow) competitors.
- Identify the firm's direct and indirect competitors.
- Describe competitors' capabilities and difficulties.
- Evaluate competitors by identifying their strategic options.
- Project competitors' objectives and future actions.
- Manage competitors' behavior.
- Assess the firm's competitive position.
- Understand the various sources and types of complementarity.

OPENING CASE: BOEING AND AIRBUS

Boeing and Airbus — headquartered in Chicago and Toulouse, France, respectively — compete intensely in the large passenger jet aircraft market. Boeing (founded 1916) launched modern jet-aircraft in 1958 and has close to 25,000 in service; Airbus started in 1972 and has more than 5,000 planes flying. Boeing has been market leader since the 1930s, but recently Airbus has challenged its position. In 2003, for the first time, Airbus delivered more aircraft than Boeing; Airbus has also secured more aircraft orders. Although Airbus is winning on annual plane sales, Boeing earns up to 55 percent of aircraft value because its 747 dominates the wide-body market with 1,500 built.[1]

Airbus' high-passenger capacity A380 threatens Boeing's position in wide-body jets, but Boeing's 787 fuel-efficient Dreamliner is expected to compete strongly in shorter-haul markets. There is no love lost between Boeing and Airbus. Rival executives commonly denigrate each other's products, and the firms have a long-standing dispute over government subsidies.

Airbus was formed in the 1960s as a consortium of European aviation firms to compete with the U.S. In 2001, this loose alliance evolved into the European Aeronautic Defence and Space Company (EADS) when three Continental European firms merged. EADS (80 percent) and BAE Systems (formerly British Aerospace) (20 percent) owned the new Airbus. From the start, conflicts between its French and German shareholders troubled EADS. In 2006, British BAE Systems sold its 20 percent ownership and EADS CEO Noël Forgead and Airbus CEO Gustav Humbert resigned amid allegations of insider trading.

During the past several years, Boeing (2012 revenues $82 billion; 70,000 employees) has retired several McDonnell Douglas (acquired 1997) aircraft, along with the Boeing 757. Boeing now offers the following models:

- Boeing 737: twin-engine narrow-body, 85–215 passengers, short-medium range, 1966*
- Boeing 747: quad-engine large wide-body, 85–524 passengers, long haul, 1969*
- Boeing 767: twin-engine small narrow-body, 180–375 passengers, short-medium range, 1981*
- Boeing 777: twin-engine medium wide-body, 330–550 passengers, long haul, 1996*

Boeing's newest aircraft is the twin-engine medium wide-body 787 — Dreamliner — seating 210–330 passengers. Boeing claims the Dreamliner is 20 percent more fuel efficient than comparable planes. Fuel savings come from engine (GE and Rolls-Royce) and aerodynamic improvements, greater use of lighter-weight composites, and advanced systems. But supply-chain problems delayed the Dreamliner's introduction by several years, and battery problems later stalled deliveries. In early 2009, Boeing had more than 800 firm orders.

Airbus (2012 revenues € 37 billion, 63,000 employees) offers several passenger models:

- Airbus A320: twin-engine single aisle, seating 180 passengers, short-medium range, 1987*
- Airbus A318 (shortened A320): twin-engine twin aisle, seating 107 passengers, 2002*
- Airbus A319 (shortened A320): twin-engine single aisle, seating 145 passengers, 1995*
- Airbus A321 (stretched A320): twin-engine single aisle, seating 220 passengers, long haul, 1993*
- Airbus A330: twin-engine twin aisle, seating 253–440 passengers, 1992*
- Airbus A340: quad-engine twin aisle, seating 261–440 passengers, long haul, 1991*

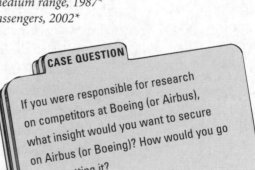

CASE QUESTION

If you were responsible for research on competitors at Boeing (or Airbus), what insight would you want to secure on Airbus (or Boeing)? How would you go about getting it?

Airbus' newest aircraft is the A380, a quad-engine twin-aisle plane seating 555–840 passengers, the world's largest passenger aircraft. It also planned the A350, derived from the A330, a twin-engine twin-aisle plane seating 250–350 passengers designed to compete with Boeing's Dreamliner.

*first flight

In Chapter 5, we build on the five-forces model from Chapter 3 to discuss the firm's competitive challenges. We *identify* specific competitors and present a process for gaining competitor insight. **Competitive insight** is securing deep understanding of competitors to provide a unique strategic perspective.

Ultimately, we would like to know what competitors *cannot do*; what competitors *will not do*; and what will *put competitors at a disadvantage if they do*. Specifically, we develop a competitive insight framework by exploring how to *identify* competitors; *describe* competitors — capabilities and difficulties (strengths and weaknesses); *evaluate* competitors — strategic options; *project* competitor actions — figure out what they will do; and *manage* competitors — influence their behavior to benefit the firm. As the firm gains insight into competitors, it also gains insight into itself — *company insight.* We also explore complementers: organizations that can help the firm achieve its objectives — *complementer insight.*

Competitors

DEVELOPING COMPETITIVE INSIGHT

Competitive intensity is increasing across the board in virtually all industries. Any executive will tell you that increased competition is a global phenomenon. Competition is especially tough where: industries are deregulating, rapid changes are occurring in product and/or process technology, state-owned enterprises are privatizing, and governments are reducing or removing tariffs, quotas, and other competitive barriers. Competition is also challenging in industries where regulatory restrictions are increasing, like financial services and pharmaceuticals. The firm must work harder and smarter to attain in-depth competitive insight and build that insight into strategic marketing decision-making. Only then will the firm develop the differential advantage it requires to attract, retain, and grow customers.

Many firms put too little emphasis on gaining competitive insight. They may claim lack of time or resources, or simply be myopic, perhaps paralyzed by *groupthink,*[2] and not understand the competitive threat. Good competitor insight reduces decision-making uncertainty. The fundamental marketing job is to attract, retain, and grow customers, but other guys are trying to do the same thing! The firm should always know who competitors are today and who they will be tomorrow: what they are doing now and what they may do in the future. This chapter shows that developing good competitive insight has major firm value.

Gaining sound competitive insight is not easy, but most major firms like IBM, Xerox, and Citibank deploy significant effort. Firms often face internal challenges in securing and acting on competitive insight. The firm gets into trouble when it:

- Bases insight on out-of-date data from tired sources.
- Claims the cost of securing good competitive data is too high.
- Does not commit necessary resources.
- Fails to go beyond basic description of competitors.
- Focuses on current competitors but ignores potential competitors.
- Gains good insight but does not take action.

Figure 5.1 shows a five-step framework for gaining competitor insight. Steps 1 and 2, *identifying* and *describing* competitors, are critical but insufficient; unfortunately, many firms stop right here. Identifying and describing competitors are the foundation for *evaluating* — step 3; *projecting* — step 4; and *managing* — step 5. To gain superior competitor insight, the firm must excel at each step and be very clear about what it does and does not know.

Marketing Question

As a Starbucks competitive analyst, what information would help you complete the competitive insight framework in Figure 5.1?

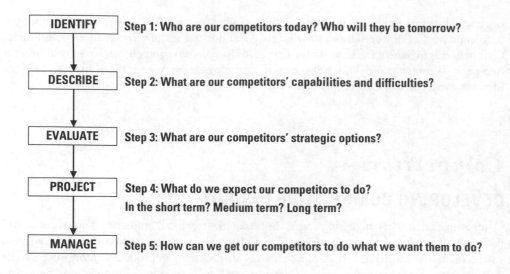

IDENTIFY	Step 1: Who are our competitors today? Who will they be tomorrow?
DESCRIBE	Step 2: What are our competitors' capabilities and difficulties?
EVALUATE	Step 3: What are our competitors' strategic options?
PROJECT	Step 4: What do we expect our competitors to do? In the short term? Medium term? Long term?
MANAGE	Step 5: How can we get our competitors to do what we want them to do?

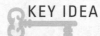

FIGURE 5.1

A FRAMEWORK FOR GAINING COMPETITIVE INSIGHT

🔑 **KEY IDEA**

➤ Critical elements for gaining competitive insight are:
  • Identify
  • Describe
  • Evaluate
  • Project
  • Manage

IDENTIFYING COMPETITORS

A **competitor** is any organization whose products and services provide similar or superior benefits and values to the same customers the firm seeks to attract, retain, and grow. Of course, by making purchases, customers decide who competes with whom. Today the firm faces **current competitors**; tomorrow it may face **potential competitors**. Chapter 5 argues for a broad view of competitors, just as Chapter 4 argues for a broad view of customers. Many firms view competition too narrowly, focusing only on firms like themselves. For years, Hollywood did not realize that television was a competitor; paper cup manufacturers did not address competition from plastic cups, only other paper goods suppliers. When the firm views competition too narrowly, it fails to identify many medium- and long-term threats. The firm should consider three key areas:

  • Structure of competition
  • Competitive dynamics
  • The firm as competitor

🔑 **KEY IDEA**

➤ Competitive insight is securing a sufficiently deep understanding of competitors to provide a unique perspective.

➤ Competitive insight is crucial for attracting, retaining, and growing customers.

➤ The firm must act on competitive insight in its own decision-making.

THE STRUCTURE OF COMPETITION

Figure 5.2 reprises the *five-forces model* — Chapter 3. Three of the five forces represent competition: *current direct competitors*, *new direct entrants*, and *indirect competitors*. The two other forces are *suppliers* and *buyers*. We learned earlier that extreme forms of supplier and buyer pressure are, respectively, *forward* and *backward integration*; by undertaking operations the firm currently conducts, they become *direct competitors*. We simplify the *five-forces* approach and develop two identifying dimensions that help evaluate competitors and gain deep insight.

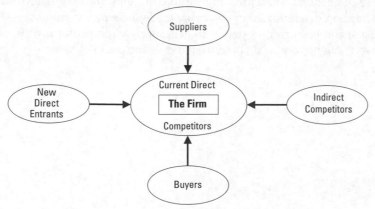

FIGURE 5.2

STRUCTURE OF COMPETITION

DIRECT VERSUS INDIRECT COMPETITORS. Direct competitors target similar customers to the firm by offering similar benefits and values with similar products, technology, and/or business models. **Indirect competitors** target the same customers with similar benefits and values, but have *different* products, technology, and/or business models.

CURRENT VERSUS POTENTIAL COMPETITORS. Today the firm faces **current competitors**; those it may face tomorrow are **potential competitors** — some may not even be around today.

The Figure 5.3 framework identifies four types of competitive threat. It helps the firm decide which are most serious and where it should deploy resources:

- **Current direct competitors, cell A.** The competitive *status quo* — the traditional rivalry between established firms.
- **Current indirect competitors, cell B.** More difficult to identify than cell A competitors. They act differently and develop customer benefits and values differently.
- **Potential direct competitors, cell C.** Behave like Cell A competitors, but may emerge from a different industry or geography.
- **Potential indirect competitors, cell D.** The most difficult competitors to identify. They do not compete today, and it is unclear when and where they will emerge.

FIGURE 5.3

**A FRAMEWORK
FOR IDENTIFYING
COMPETITIVE THREATS**

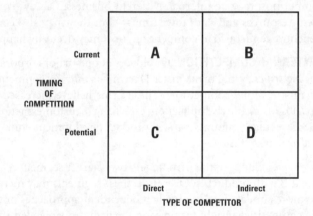

COMPETITIVE DYNAMICS

We can extend Figure 5.3 to show competitive evolution. Dramatic change may occur: New competitors may enter or local/regional competitors may become national/multinational. Figure 5.4 shows various paths competitors can take. These paths may help the firm forecast the competitive threat transitions. We identify eight transitions:

- **Transition I.** From *potential direct* competitor (C) to *current* direct competitor (A)
- **Transition II.** From *potential indirect* competitor (D) to *current* indirect competitor (B)
- **Transition III.** From *potential direct* competitor (C) to *withdrawal* — no longer a threat
- **Transition IV.** From *potential indirect* competitor (D) to *withdrawal* — no longer a threat
- **Transition V.** From *current direct* competitor (A) to *withdrawal* — no longer a threat
- **Transition VI.** From *current indirect* competitor (B) to *withdrawal* — no longer a threat
- **Transition VII.** From *current direct* competitor (A) to *current indirect* competitor (B). The direct competitor has developed some new approach to satisfy customer needs.
- **Transition VIII.** From *current indirect* competitor (B) to *current direct* competitor (A). The indirect competitor has decided to compete on an *apples-to-apples* basis.

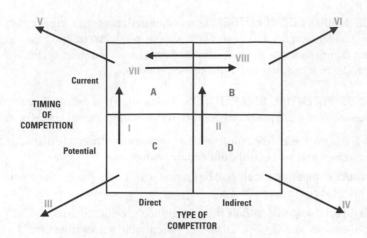

FIGURE 5.4

A FRAMEWORK
FOR TRACKING
COMPETITIVE
THREATS

THE FIRM AS A COMPETITOR

Our unstated assumption is that all competitors are other firms. But for product and brand managers, the toughest competition may be internal. Different businesses always compete for financial, human, and system resources and sales force time — but they may also compete for customers. The firm may encourage **intra-firm** competition, or it may occur by happenstance.

DELIBERATELY INDUCED INTERNAL COMPETITION. Employees at one major corporation refer to its business units as *warring tribes*. Some firms foster Darwinian *internal* competition so as to improve effectiveness against *external* competitors. These firms believe increased competitiveness more than compensates for resource duplication, especially if customers tend to switch products and/ or brands. P&G regularly mounts parallel product development efforts to innovate better products and get to market faster.

Internal competition often evolves. Suppose the firm targets two market segments — segment A with product I, and segment B with product II. Over time, these segments may merge, and/or the firm's products become more similar. Two originally independent approaches now become competitive. In step 1 of the competitive insight framework, the firm probably identifies several external competitors. In steps 2 through 5, the firm should focus on the most serious competitive threats and develop deep competitive insight about them.

DESCRIBING COMPETITORS

Describing competitors concerns four key areas:

- What *competitor data* should the firm collect?
- What *sources* of competitor data are available?
- What *processes* should the firm use for competitive data-gathering?
- What *frameworks* can the firm use to describe competitors?

Jackson and Walker (disguised names) are strategically important chemical subsidiaries of major U.S. multinationals operating in Asia/Pacific. Jackson has 60 percent market share and is highly profitable; Walker has 20 percent market share and is barely breaking even. Jackson learns that Walker's president is retiring. Information on the new president is: male; early 40s; chemical engineer by training; 20+ years with Walker's parent; joined Walker's parent after graduate school; known as a turnaround manager; has just successfully completed a smaller turnaround; known as a *margin-raiser*.

CONTINUES ON NEXT PAGE

Jackson's analysis and action: Jackson decided that, within reason, it wanted Walker to be successful — a successful competitor would take predictable actions; an unsuccessful competitor could be a *wild card*. Jackson knew that Walker would not leave the market and also knew the new president's *margin-raiser* reputation.

Jackson raised prices modestly. Because of its 60 percent market share, Jackson would significantly increase profits if Walker followed suit. When Walker's president arrived, he also raised prices. Walker became moderately profitable. Jackson invested some of its increased profits in additional services to strengthen its position.

Jackson based its action on good competitor insight. By learning about Walker's new president, Jackson developed an innovative strategy that allowed it to *win*.

COLLECTING COMPETITOR DATA

Marketing Exercise

Suppose you were brand manager for leading U.S. bottled-water firm Poland Spring. Identify a direct or indirect competitor. On a single sheet of paper, sketch out a data-gathering plan. For each data item, note why you want to collect it.

To describe competitors effectively, the firm must decide what it wants to know, based on the sort of decisions it has to make. We consider **level of data** and **type of data**.

LEVEL OF DATA. The firm should consider several organizational levels like corporate, business unit, market, and market segment. A competitive data profile on GE by a home appliance firm might include answers to several types of question. To illustrate:

- **Corporate.** How does GE allocate resources across its major businesses like financial services, healthcare, home appliances, and jet engines? What are its acquisition and divestiture plans? What effort is GE placing on innovation versus increasing efficiency?
- **Business unit.** How does GE allocate resources across its home appliance portfolio: refrigerators, dishwashers, washers and driers, and ranges?
- **Market.** What is GE's strategy in the refrigerator market? How does GE segment the market? Where is GE focusing its effort, by segment? What is GE's R&D in refrigerators? What is GE's capacity and capacity utilization for refrigerator production?
- **Market segment.** For segments where the firm competes with GE: What brand(s) does GE offer? How does GE position these brands? What are GE's models? What are GE's prices? What are GE's credit terms? How do retailers display GE's products? What is GE's promotional emphasis: advertising, sales force, direct mail? Is GE active on the Internet? What is GE's core message? How do target customers evaluate GE's offers? What is GE's refrigerator profitability by segment?

Responsibility for competitor data-gathering typically varies by data type and level. At corporate and the business units, a competitive intelligence group often has direct access to industry analysts and consulting firms. Product and market managers are generally responsible for market and market-segment data. Responsible persons should develop their own data networks. Because the types of data vary by level, appropriate data-gathering approaches, analysis methods, and methodologies vary widely.

TYPE OF DATA. The firm should collect both quantitative and qualitative data. *Quantitative* data includes measures like market share and profitability: SEC filings often provide these data for public companies; business data services supply profiles for private firms. *Qualitative* data include competitor manager expertise, commitment to various businesses, and anticipated strategic moves. The Internet offers many ways to obtain qualitative data. The data Jackson compiled on Walker's new president are in the qualitative category.

Competitive data-gathering should not focus solely on marketing issues. Information about products and services is crucial, but the firm should also seek data on costing systems, financial strength, logistics, operations, R&D, speed of action, and business philosophy (including willingness to innovate and take risks). In his early days in oil and gas, T. Boone Pickens learned about a rival's drilling activity by having a spotter watch the drilling floor with binoculars from

KEY IDEA

➤ The firm should seek competitive data at several levels:

- Corporate
- Business
- Market
- Market segment

These data may be:

- Primary
- Secondary

half a mile away. By counting the number of joints connecting the 30-foot lengths of drill pipe, Pickens knew the depth of the competitor's wells.[3] Xerox purchases competitive products from dealers and assesses both customer value and manufacturing cost. The firm should always be on the lookout for illegally acting competitors. Patent and trademark violations, predatory pricing, price fixing, and misleading advertising should be matters of concern.

SOURCES OF COMPETITIVE DATA

The firm probably already has some competitive data internally; it needs a process to make these data available to the analyst. The firm should also seek competitor data externally. For both internal and external data, there are two approaches.

- **Secondary data** are available in various reports, publications, and the Internet; the firm must collect, sort, and give them meaning, based on the questions it wants answered.
- **Primary data** require a focused acquisition effort like customer interviews and surveys. For important data, the analyst should seek multiple sources, filter for reliability, and cross-validate. Table 5.1 lists data sources for various competitive issues.

Generic Modes of Competition	Sample Internal Sources	Sample External Sources
Availability	• Distribution and logistics personnel • Sales force reports	• Customer satisfaction surveys • Third-party (industry analysts) studies • Distributor access
Features	• Sales, marketing, engineering personnel • Internal analyses and trials	• Trade publication product reviews • Competitor literature, consultants • Competitor websites
Functionality	• Competitor supplier analysis • Product comparison studies • Reverse engineering	• Customer reports • Specialist trade reports/industry observers

General information	• Senior firm executives	• The Internet, including
		  • Competitor websites
		  • Rumor sites, e.g., www.gawker.com
		  • Complaint sites, e.g., www.PayPalsucks.com
		  • Blogs and forums
		• Investment bankers/industry analysts
		• Media (local, national)
		• Annual reports, SEC filings, 10Ks
		• Suppliers

Image and reputation	• Marketing, sales, and advertising personnel • Tracking studies	• Customer perceptions, third-party studies • Competitor advertising, promotion, and public relations
Product line	• Sales, marketing, engineering personnel • Industry studies	• Competitor product catalogs • Trade shows • Trade associations, press, consultants • Regulatory and patent filings
Price	• Marketing, sales, and service personnel • Sales force reports	• Competitor price lists • Interviews with end customers
Selling and relationships	• Sales force reports • Managerial assessments	• Interviews with customers and channel members
Service	• Service personnel comparisons • Comparative studies	• Customer, third-party assessments • Mystery shopper reports

TABLE 5.1

SAMPLE INTERNAL AND EXTERNAL DATA SOURCES[4]

Marketing Question

Returning from an industry conference, the attractive young woman took her seat on the plane. The middle-aged man in the next seat glanced at her reading material, noting they had both attended the same conference. He introduced himself as marketing VP of a major pharmaceutical firm. She introduced herself as a product manager for its chief competitor. Trying to impress, the VP discussed, at length, his firm's marketing plans. The young woman listened attentively!

Did the young woman behave ethically? Would your answer change if she had not indicated her employment status? What do you think of the VP's behavior?

KEY IDEA

➤ The firm can secure timely and relevant competitive information from many internal and external sources.

KEY IDEA

➤ The firm should develop formal processes to secure timely and relevant competitive information.

KEY IDEA

➤ The firm should not use unethical or illegal processes to collect competitor data.

➤ Leaky organizations help the firm secure competitive data.

➤ Good counter-intelligence procedures prevent proprietary data from leaking to competitors.

INTERNAL PROCESSES FOR SECURING COMPETITIVE DATA

Many competitive data-gathering efforts fail because of poor processes — too few sources, failure to cross-validate, and/or short-term focused when the firm needs a longer-term view. Competitive data-gathering options differ by focus and required resources:

- **Competing.** Sometimes the best way to learn about competitors is just to observe them. By operating in the marketplace day-by-day, an observant firm can gain significant competitive insight.

- **Competitive intelligence department (CID).** The CID is responsible for collecting, analyzing, and distributing competitive information. The CID can be highly focused, but is expensive.

- **Competitive intelligence system.** The firm builds a culture where all employees are responsible for competitive intelligence. They come across competitive data daily; the critical step is to share these data with a competitor intelligence group. Group members check, sort, and digest the data they receive, then send it to those who need it. This approach is relatively inexpensive, but is relatively unfocused.

- **Formal development of strategic plans.** When the firm has few major competitors, it can develop strategic plans as though it were the competitor. This highly-focused approach is usually only practical for one or two competitors. Boeing may use it (and the following) for Airbus, and AMD for Intel, and vice versa.

- **Gaming with multifunctional teams.** In these *war games*, executive teams play one of two roles: the firm or the competitor. Each team develops and presents its strategy approach and action plans; the *firm* and the *competitor* then develop counter-strategies and action plans. Conducted at one- or two-day offsite meetings, this process often generates important insights.

- **Review of business lost and business gained.** When the firm wins or loses a sale it should find out why it won or lost. In well-managed firms, this process is standard operating procedure. Typically, customers are willing to share this sort of information.

- **Shadow system.** Individual executives or teams *shadow* specific competitors, either as a full- or part-time job. When shadowing is an extra responsibility, it can be an effective way of focusing attention on specific competitors, at relatively low cost.

Students and executives are often concerned about the ethics and legality of competitor data-gathering. Our position is clear: There are many ethical and legal approaches to securing competitor data; the firm should not use unethical or illegal methods like bribery, covert recording, knowingly jeopardizing someone's job, misrepresentation, or placing *moles* at competitors. A widespread perception of industrial espionage by foreign governments led the U.S. Congress to pass the 1996 Economic Espionage Act making the theft or misappropriation of trade secrets a federal crime.

Some methods are not illegal but they may be unethical, like setting up job interviews to trawl for competitor data when no jobs are available. Other unethical approaches include searching through competitors' garbage placed on the street.

Firms can secure good competitive data without breaking any rules — most organizations are *leaky*. When the firm's competitive data-gathering efforts fail, the reason is usually insufficient resources and/or unfocused efforts. But, if competitors are leaky, your firm may also be leaky! Counter-intelligence is vital. The firm should take affirmative steps to protect its data:

- Classify information according to the degree of secrecy warranted.

- Execute employee **noncompete agreements** to prohibit former employees from working for competitors for a defined time period.

- Train employees on the danger of loose tongues, especially when attending industry meetings and social events. Teach them to be good listeners — ears open and mouths shut!

- Use **nondisclosure agreements (NDAs)** to prohibit revealing information to third parties. NDAs are standard for consultants and others working on a contract basis.

FRAMEWORKS TO DESCRIBE COMPETITORS

To gain insight, the firm must organize competitive data into a useful framework. Good competitive insight often results from a *differential diagnosis* of the firm versus competitors. We use four basic building blocks: *competitor's organization, strengths and vulnerabilities, firm in the environment*, and *mind-set*. These analytic guidelines help the firm understand the competitor's *current strategy and performance*. The firm also gains insight into the competitor's future strategy.[6] The firm should adapt the framework for the level of competitive insight it seeks — corporate, business unit, market, or market segment.

COMPETITOR'S ORGANIZATION. How the organization functions:

- **Culture.** The behaviors, norms, beliefs, and values that together describe what the competitor stands for and how its members operate and behave.
- **Infrastructure.** The line organization — basic responsibilities and reporting relationships.
- **Processes.** Accounting, information, control and reward systems, and processes.

STRENGTHS AND VULNERABILITIES.[7] Assets, capabilities, competences (and failings):

- **Assets.** Financial, human, knowledge, organizational, perceptual, physical, and political assets that embrace the competitor's brand equity and customer loyalty — proprietary and non-proprietary. The firm should also evaluate competitor liabilities, emotional commitments or *blind spots* that sometimes compromise hard-headed business judgments.
- **Capabilities and competencies.** Activities the competitor does well, including *local* expertise and broad-scale abilities, and areas where it does poorly. Specific product-related abilities are: conceive and design, finance, produce, manage, and market. The competitor's approach to risk and speed of action may also be a competence — or not!

FIRM IN THE ENVIRONMENT. Embraces relationships with other organizations:

- **Value chain.** Major work activities the competitor conducts and how they connect to external entities like suppliers and customers. The firm asks four core questions:
  - Where does the competitor have a cost advantage?
  - Where is the competitor at a cost disadvantage?
  - Where does the competitor have a value advantage?
  - Where is the competitor at a value disadvantage?
- **Alliances and special relationships. Alliances** are formal economic relationships between the competitor and other entities (partners) — customers, distributors, and suppliers. **Special relationships** are informal and may embrace government agencies, political parties, and public interest groups — as well as suppliers and customers.
- **Networks.** Interconnected sets of alliances and relationships. Each fulfills a unique role. Rather than compete with a single competitor, the firm may compete with a network.

MIND-SET. How the competitor thinks and the bases for its decisions. What are its *assumptions*? What does the competitor take for granted, or as a *given*? Assumptions are the outcomes of analysts' judgments, inferred from competitive data.

CURRENT STRATEGY AND PERFORMANCE. How the competitor behaves and its results:

- **Market strategy.** The firm observes competitor actions and infers its objectives, segment choices, and strategies.[8]
- **Other major resource commitments.** The competitor may build new factories, expand existing plants, and/or spend extensively on a particular type of R&D. The competitor may also display different levels of commitment to various businesses.

KEY IDEA

➤ The firm should use a rigorous framework to organize competitor data-gathering.

- **Performance.** Most performance measures are market-oriented or financially based. Market measures include market share and customer satisfaction. Financial measures range from product-line profitability, operating margin (profit), to stock price performance.

Won't the firm using this framework collect a tremendous amount of information, and won't it be overwhelming? Right! Describing competitors is not for the faint-hearted. When the task seems too great, remember that competitors are trying to attract, retain, and grow the same customers as you. If they are successful, they will survive and grow, and your firm will not. And you will be out of a job. The best way to appreciate this framework is to use it. We suggest you answer the Marketing Question (p. 74).

PUTTING IT ALL TOGETHER

Sometimes the firm gains competitive insight directly from the data it collects. Other times it must integrate several data items. The firm can secure data on the competitor's advertising, distribution, product, price, service, and other factors — but it does not *see* what was behind these actions. The firm must make inferences from these data. Table 5.2 illustrates making inferences from *indicator* data.

TABLE 5.2

DRAWING INFERENCES FROM COMPETITOR DATA[9]

Indicators	Inferences
Hired new customer service manager	Competitor going to upgrade service quality
Reorganized customer support and service (CSS)	Initial confirmation of alerting signal
CSS now reports to VP of marketing (versus sales)	Signals increased importance of service
Initiating new training programs for sales force	Enhancing service for all key customer segments
Emphasizes customer service in advertising	Service valuable to attract, retain, and grow customers
CEO comments: "Customers expect quality in services as well as in the product."	Service is becoming part of the competitor's mind-set — will be institutionalized
Customer to our salesperson: "ABC is now doing things for us they never did before."	Confirms competitor is institutionalizing and leveraging service

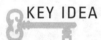

KEY IDEA

➤ Organizations do not make decisions — *people* in organizations make decisions.

Finally, competitors *do not make* decisions: People working for competitors make decisions. The firm should identify competitors' decision-makers and influencers. The Jackson example (p. 70) shows that career backgrounds, successes, and failures provide good competitor insight.

EVALUATING COMPETITORS

The reason for evaluating competitors is to generate their strategic options. Knowing these options allows the firm to project competitor actions. Identifying competitors (step 1) and describing competitors (step 2) are fine, but these are just the building blocks of competitive insight. The firm can only justify competitive intelligence efforts if they provide insight into competitors' future actions. **Competitor assessment analysis** helps answer three competitive evaluation questions:

- What options does the competitor have to be successful?
- What would the competitor have to do to pursue each option?
- Is the competitor capable? (Does it have the resources to implement a particular option?)

COMPETITOR ASSESSMENT ANALYSIS

This powerful tool focuses on an individual competitor or group of similar competitors in a market or market segment and maps customer perspectives into required resources. The firm and competitors satisfy customer needs by delivering benefits and values. But they must possess resources to deliver these benefits and values. The competitor assessment analysis (CAA) allows the firm to identify where it has a *differential advantage* and where competitors have *differential advantages*. Recall from Chapter 1: A *differential advantage is a net benefit or cluster of benefits, offered to a sizable group of customers, which they value and are willing to pay for but cannot get, or believe they cannot get, elsewhere.* Identifying differential advantage has five stages. Table 5.3 illustrates CAA for one competitor in a market segment.

Customer Requirements: Needs, Benefits, Values **A**	Customer Importance Rank **B**	**Necessary Capabilities / Resources C**				
		Efficient Manufacturing	**Good Distribution**	**Just-in-Time Delivery**	**Well-Funded R&D**	**Access to Low-Cost Materials**
Easy product availability	1	* YN	* YYY			
Low prices	2	* YN				* YYN
Low inventories	3			* N		
Access to cutting-edge technology	4				* YYN	
Etc.						

TABLE 5.3

ILLUSTRATION OF A COMPETITOR ASSESSMENT ANALYSIS

- **Stage 1 – Identify customer requirements in terms of needs, benefits, and values.** Brainstorm and/or use marketing research.
- **Stage 2 – Rank in order of importance.** Reduce Stage 1 items to a manageable number, typically six to 10. Rank items in order of importance to customers — columns A and B.
- **Stage 3 – Determine necessary capabilities/resources.** Any firm would require these capabilities/resources to satisfy customer requirements in column A. Needs/benefits or values map directly into capabilities/resources. To satisfy the most important item, *easy product availability*, requires *efficient manufacturing* and *good distribution*. To offer *low prices* requires *efficient manufacturing* and *access to low-cost materials*. Enter capabilities/resources in row C.
- **Stage 4 – Identify the matches.** Place an asterisk (*) in each matrix cell where a customer need/benefit or value — column A, intersects with a firm capability/resource — row C. Typically, the result is a sparse matrix; for any particular customer need/benefit or value, some capabilities/resources are irrelevant. For customer requirement *easy product availability — just-in-time delivery, well-funded R&D*, and *access to low-cost materials* are not decisive. Of course, sometimes a capability/resource addresses more than one customer need/benefit or value.
- **Stage 5 – Examine the matches.** Ask up to three questions of each asterisked matrix cell. Asking a subsequent question depends on the answer to a previous question:
  a. **Relevance.** Does the firm have the capabilities/resources necessary to address the customer need/benefit or value? If yes, enter **Y**; if no, enter **N**, and stop.
  b. **Superiority.** For each cell where you entered **Y**: Are firm capabilities/resources superior to the competitor? If yes, enter **Y**; if no, enter **N**, and stop.
  c. **Sustainability.** For each cell where you entered **YY**: Would it be difficult for the competitor to match the firm's capabilities/resources? If yes, enter **Y**; if no, enter **N**.

The meaning of the entries is:

- **YYY.** The firm has a sustainable *differential advantage*. The firm's capabilities/resources match customer needs/benefits or values; they are superior to the competitor; it would be difficult for the competitor to catch up.

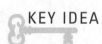

- **YYN.** Firm capabilities/resources match customer needs/benefits or values; the firm has an advantage, but the competitor could match the firm relatively easily.
- **YN.** Firm capabilities/resources match customer needs/benefits or values, but are no better than the competitor.
- **N.** The firm has a significant weakness or gap. The competitor completing a similar analysis would likely show a **YYY** and have its own differential advantage.

Returning to Table 5.3, we explore competitor options by examining several cells:

- **YYY** – *easy product availability/good distribution.* The firm has a differential advantage in the customers' most important requirement. If the competitor is serious about this market segment, it would expend significant resources to improve its distribution.
- **YYN** – *low prices/access to low-cost materials; access to cutting-edge technology/well-funded R&D.* The firm leads the competitor in the customer's second and fourth most important areas. The competitor may invest in procurement and/or increase its R&D budget.
- **YN** – *easy product availability/efficient manufacturing; low prices/efficient manufacturing.* The firm and competitor perform equally well in the customer's most and second most important areas. The competitor may work on improving manufacturing efficiency.
- **N** – *low inventories/just-in-time delivery.* The competitor dominates. It will probably focus customer communications on *low inventories* to make sure it stays ahead.

Now that the firm views the market segment from the competitor perspective, it can project those options the competitor will pursue. It should repeat the analysis for another competitor.

PROJECTING COMPETITORS' ACTIONS

The evaluation step generates a set of options for the competitor; the firm must assess which option the competitor will choose. Will it continue its current strategy? Or make a strategic change — short term, medium term, or long term? What specific change(s) will the competitor make? To start: what is the competitor trying to achieve? Specific questions include:

- What are the competitor's objectives in the market? Understanding objectives can help predict resource allocations.
- What market segments will the competitor address? How will it try to achieve its objectives — price leadership, operational excellence, product leadership, distribution strength, or what? What customer behavior is the competitor seeking to address?
- What is the competitor's staying power? Is it committed for the long run, or will it withdraw if the going gets tough? Of course, sometimes withdrawal is not in the firm's best interest, as a competitor's divested unit may become a stronger and more difficult competitor.

Scenarios are a particularly effective way of evaluating competitor options; they help the firm understand and predict competitor action.[10] The scenario for a plausible option is a descriptive narrative of how the future may evolve; the firm should develop a scenario for each option. Based on various conditions and assumptions, the firm can compare and contrast the scenarios to gain insight into possible competitor actions. The firm projects competitor behavior by selecting the most probable action from the alternative scenarios. Three major types of scenarios are:

- **Emergent scenarios.** Start with the current strategy and consider what might emerge.
- **Unconstrained scenarios.** Based on open-ended *what-if* questions that suggest possible end states.
- **Constrained scenarios.** *What-if* scenarios that ask how the competitor may act under different market and/or industry conditions.

Effective scenarios have several important attributes:

- **Articulated plot and logic.** The *story* comprises a set of events and a coherent logic.
- **Internally consistent logic.** The *story* hangs together.
- **Specific time frame.** The *story* specifies a time element for key events, actions, and results.
- **Decision/action-oriented.** The firm can derive and demonstrate implications for its current and future decisions.

As the firm builds scenarios, it must incorporate:

- **An end state.** An outcome at some specific future point.
- **A plot.** What the competitor must do to get to the end state.
- **Driving forces.** The circumstances, conditions, events, and trends that shape or drive the story described in a particular plot.
- **Logics.** The evidence and rationale for the end state and plot.

This description of scenarios and their attributes is fairly abstract, so we show an illustration. Our fictional firm is a yogurt manufacturer — Sunshine. Sunshine's major competitor — Moonglow — is contemplating a low-price market entry. We start by elaborating Moonglow's *projected strategy alternative* — low-price entry. This option, together with *supporting logics for Moonglow* and *supporting logics for Moonglow's environment*, allows us to *identify consequences for Moonglow*. These *consequences* lead directly to *implications for Sunshine*.

MOONGLOW'S PROJECTED STRATEGY ALTERNATIVE. Key elements in the strategy are:

- Add a low-price product line aimed at customers for generic products.
- Use a different brand name.
- Maintain a high service level and use the same superior national distribution.
- Price similarly to low-end competitors and position against rivals' low-end products.
- Gain financial break-even in one year and 10 percent low-end market share in three years.

SUPPORTING LOGICS FOR MOONGLOW.

- Moonglow must extend its product line to gain scope economies and pre-empt competition.
- Moonglow can acquire a supply of products from well-established vendors.
- Moonglow has demonstrated a capacity for building the required alliances.
- The entry fits Moonglow's apparent core assumptions that distinct market segments exist.
- The entry would leverage Moonglow's extensive marketing and sales capabilities.
- Moonglow's organizational culture — to be *the best in the industry* — supports the entry.

SUPPORTING LOGICS FOR MOONGLOW'S ENVIRONMENT.

- Growth rates in Moonglow's current segments do not support its announced revenue targets.
- Low-end segments have higher growth rates.
- The channels are demanding broad product coverage from suppliers.
- Successful competitors at the low end may be contemplating adding higher-end products.
- New vendors are specializing in providing products to branded competitors.
- The projected strategy could succeed if Moonglow can quickly establish a brand name, with a superior image, at a comparatively low price and with strong channel support.

CONSEQUENCES FOR MOONGLOW. Moonglow will have to:

- Determine product content.
- Secure vendors.
- Create marketing programs.
- Develop products.
- Establish its own manufacturing.
- Build trade relationships for the new product line.
- Organize its sales force.

In addition:

- Moonglow could gain significant early market penetration.
- Moonglow will face significant issues on how best to differentiate its product line, build brand name image, and leverage distribution channels.
- Moonglow will need to monitor each execution step.

IMPLICATIONS FOR SUNSHINE. Moonglow's new market entry:

- Would pose a direct threat to Sunshine's current market strategy.
- Would radically change current market assumptions.
- May eliminate potential sources of supply.
- May jeopardize potential alliance partners.
- Similar products would address the same customers through the same channels.
- Sunshine's existing capabilities may be insufficient to sustain sales growth.
- Sunshine will need to introduce new options.
- Sunshine may need to introduce a new product line more quickly than planned.

Note how this scenario fulfills the conditions we outlined. The scenario has an *articulated plot and logic*, an *internally consistent logic*, a *specific time frame*, and is *decision/action-oriented*. Of course, this is just one possible scenario Sunshine might develop for Moonglow. To predict what Moonglow will actually do, Sunshine must develop a scenario for each of Moonglow's plausible options. Sunshine then selects what it believes is Moonglow's most likely course of action and positions accordingly.

MANAGING COMPETITORS

Identifying competitor options and projecting competitor strategies put the firm in good position. But shaping (managing) competitor actions is even better! Before trying to get competitors to behave in beneficial ways, the firm must answer two questions:

- What actions does the firm want its competitor(s) to take?
- What actions does the firm prefer that its competitor(s) not take?

Ecolab and Diversey (disguised names) were leading suppliers of cleaning chemicals to U.S. hospitals, office buildings, restaurants, and schools. Ecolab *encouraged* Diversey to focus on smaller independent customers by raising prices modestly; Diversey *took the bait* and its gross margins improved. By contrast, Ecolab targeted large chain customers and won business with aggressive pricing. But Ecolab had thrown Diversey a *curveball*; higher gross margins did not offset increased costs-to-serve and Diversey lost money. By focusing on large customers, Ecolab reduced its costs-to-serve and profits improved.

In general, the firm may affect competitor behavior by **signaling**.[11] Firm signals may be pre-emptive — like stating what the firm will do so as to encourage competitors to act in favorable ways; *tit-for-tat* — to prohibit competitor gains; or *warning* — pre-announcing a response to possible competitor action.

The Company

The firm does not need separate analytic frameworks for self-assessment. By developing good competitor insight, the firm secures good **company insight** as a by-product. Two approaches help the firm gain self-insight — *company description* and *company assessment analysis*.

KEY IDEA

➤ The firm projects future competitor actions by identifying the most likely scenario from a set of alternative scenarios.

KEY IDEA

➤ The firm may be able to *manage* competitors by sending signals.

➤ The major signals available to the firm are:
- Pre-emptive
- Tit-for-tat
- Warning

➤ The firm may also send competitors misleading information.

COMPANY DESCRIPTION

The four building blocks are *the firm's organization, strengths and vulnerabilities, firm in the environment* and *mind-set* — just as previously used for describing competitors (p. 74). These elements help show how the firm settled on its *current strategy* and achieved its *current performance*. To apply this framework, simply substitute *the firm* wherever *competitor* appears.

COMPANY ASSESSMENT ANALYSIS

Competitor assessment analysis (CAA) (pp. 75–76) identifies where the firm *possesses* a differential advantage, and where it might place resources to *secure* future differential advantage. We reproduce the analytic findings but now interpret them from the firm's perspective. We take Table 5.3 is the starting point:

- **YYY** — *easy product availability/good distribution.* The firm has a differential advantage in the customers' most important requirement. The firm should maintain its position by making deliberate investments to continually enhance its distribution system.

- **YYN** — *low prices/access to low-cost materials; access to cutting-edge technology/well-funded R&D.* The firm leads the competitor in the customer's second and fourth most important areas. It should keep a close eye on the competitor and make the necessary investments to maintain its leadership position.

- **YN** — *easy product availability/efficient manufacturing; low prices/efficient manufacturing.* The firm has a significant vulnerability in the customer's second most important area. The firm and its competitor are equal, but effective investment would put the competitor ahead. The firm cannot afford this to happen.

- **N** — *low inventories/just-in-time delivery.* The competitor dominates; no doubt it emphasizes its good performance with customers. The firm may find it difficult to achieve parity, but this is the customers' third most important area.

Company description and company assessment analysis give the firm invaluable insight into its own position versus competitors. For *company description*, the firm must gather a significant amount of data. For *company assessment analysis*, it simply reinterprets the CAA from the firm's perspective.

Complementers

A **complementer** is any organization whose actions affect the firm's sales[12]; of course, we exclude purchasers. Both independent organizations and competitors can be complementers.

INDEPENDENT ORGANIZATIONS AS COMPLEMENTERS

When independent organizations develop mutually beneficial strategies, they frustrate competitors and help each other generate sales. IBM has a complementer relationship with software firm SAP. IBM and SAP cross-license and develop software to integrate each other's products; SAP also trains IBM service engineers on SAP products. SAP generates 25 percent of sales from its IBM relationship; SAP helps IBM sell several million dollars' worth of hardware annually.

Microsoft, Nintendo, and Sony successfully persuaded complementers to develop games for their consols. Likewise, Apple's iPhone has well over 125,000 complementary applications and accessories produced by thousands of developers; but the iPhone (and iPad) put tremendous pressure on its primary wireless complementer — AT&T's data network. In home laundry, design changes in washers and driers have major implications for detergent manufacturers;

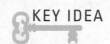

KEY IDEA

➤ Competitor assessment analysis (CAA) is a valuable tool for gaining company insight.

KEY IDEA

➤ Independent organizations, including customers and suppliers, can be complementers for the firm.

fabric designs have important implications for both appliance and detergent manufacturers. P&G and major appliance manufacturers work together to address new customer needs and align innovations across various industry sectors. Complementary relationships often drive major industry changes — rising oil prices have major implications for automobiles; indeed, electric utilities may switch to electric car fleets to spur market development.

CUSTOMERS AS COMPLEMENTERS. Customers act as complementers when they enhance the firm's offer. Comfort (disguised name) specializes in fraud detection systems based on statistical models. Customers supply data to Comfort's data consortium. Comfort uses this data to improve its detection systems.

SUPPLIERS AS COMPLEMENTERS. Suppliers often complement the firm's actions to increase sales. Car makers expect suppliers to conduct R&D to improve automobile performance. McDonald's expects suppliers to contribute ideas and concepts to help grow McDonald's business — to be a *McPartner*, a supplier must do more than just deliver products!

COMPETITORS AS COMPLEMENTERS

As a general rule, competitors are the firm's nemesis. They try to attract, retain, and grow the same customers as the firm. But competitors can also act as complementers, without getting into antitrust problems. We distinguish among strong, weak, and unwelcome complementarity.

STRONG COMPLEMENTARITY: MARKETPLACE (FRONT-OFFICE). Sometimes competitors work together to better satisfy customer needs, like agreeing on technological standards. Verizon and other telephone firms agreed on standards for ultra-fast fiber optic lines that reduced costs, sped introduction, and helped each firm compete with cable companies. Without this type of cooperation, customers are often uncertain about which technology will succeed; they withhold purchases and the market develops more slowly.

A firm with new technology making a direct market entry essentially has two choices — go it alone or offer its technology to competitors. If the firm acts alone, it must shoulder the entire market development effort. When it decides on **cooperation**, the market develops faster, but the firm must accept a diminished position. This decision involves difficult trade-offs.

> Sony was first to enter consumer videotape with Betamax. Sony failed, in part because JVC provided its VHS format to competitors. JVC's licensees helped expand acceptance, and Sony ultimately withdrew. By contrast, all major electronic firms adopted the DVD-replacing Blu-ray format championed by Sony.

STRONG COMPLEMENTARITY (BACK OFFICE). Competitors may *compete* fiercely in the market, but their back offices *collaborate* extensively. **Back-office cooperation** in non-customer-facing activities reduces costs and improves efficiency for all firms. Examples include:

- General Mills, Columbo yogurt, and Land O'Lakes butter share delivery trucks.
- Italian tile manufacturers jointly purchase freight to reduce international shipping costs.
- Major airlines collaborate in interline arrangements to move luggage among airlines.[13]
- Retail brokerage houses work closely with competitors to clear trades.
- U.S. paper makers routinely swap products at list price to save freight costs.

WEAK COMPLEMENTARITY. Marketplace and back-office complementarity generally require formal agreements. Other types of complementarity are weaker but may contribute positively:

- **Cost reduction.** When several competitors have common suppliers, one competitor's actions may affect the others. Dell and HP compete in PCs, but if either firm's sales expand total volume, joint purchases of computer chips increase. Chip suppliers achieve scale economies that reduce costs — ultimately, chip prices decline for all PC producers.

KEY IDEA

➤ Competitors can complement the firm in the marketplace (front office) or back office.

➤ Competitors may be *strong* or *weak* complementers.

- **Greater customer value.** A firm's product may provide greater customer benefit when combined with a rival's product. Complementary drug regimens — *drug cocktails* — are an increasing trend; they dominate AIDS treatment. BMS initially introduced blood-thinning product Plavix as a competitor to aspirin; today BMS positions Plavix and aspirin as complementers.

- **Increasing demand.** Competitors engage in joint advertising and other promotions so all firms benefit. Many shopping malls draw consumers from large distances; all stores gain.

- **Keep the firm sharp.** Tough competition keeps a firm on its toes. Some firms deliberately seek out tough competitors. One German engineering firm always launches new products in Japan.

- **Market development.** Competitor market development actions may assist the firm. Monsanto's success with genetically modified seeds has helped competitor DuPont.

- **Political action.** Competitors join trade associations to lobby governments for favorable decisions.

UNWELCOME COMPLEMENTARITY. Sometimes firms do not want their products associated with other firms — unwelcome complementers. Automobile and aircraft manufacturers fight fiercely against unauthorized parts manufacturers; they believe these parts degrade their products. Callaway Golf was very successful with its oversized Big Bertha golf clubs. Spalding advertised that its Top-Flite/Club System C balls improved play with Big Bertha clubs. Callaway sued Spalding for trademark infringement, false advertising, and unfair competition; the case was settled out of court. Callaway later launched its line of Callaway Rule 35 premium golf balls!

Marketing Question

What organizations are complementers for NBC (U.S. television network)?

KEY IDEA

➤ A firm's complementary product activities may be unwelcome by competitors.

KEY MESSAGES

- The firm must gain deep competitor insight in pursuit of differential advantage.

- A structured competitor insight process asks several questions:
  - **Identify.** Who are the firm's competitors:
    - Current competitors — today?
    - Direct competitors?
    - Potential competitors — tomorrow?
    - Indirect competitors?
  - **Describe.** What are the competitors' capabilities and difficulties?
  - **Evaluate.** What are the competitors' strategic options?
  - **Project.** What do we expect the competitors to do?
  - **Manage.** How can we get the competitors to do what we want them to do?

- Answering these questions is not a simple matter but, for each question, several approaches help improve competitor insight.

- The firm must know itself —company insight — but this is a simpler task.

- The firm must understand its complementary relationships. Complementers can help the firm achieve its objectives.

- Both independent organizations and competitors can be complementers, each in different ways.

VIDEOS AND AUDIOS

Competitor Insight   a501 🎧

a501

CHAPTER 6

MARKETING

RESEARCH cv601 🖳

To access O-codes, go to www.ocodes.com

LEARNING OBJECTIVES

When you have completed this chapter, you will be able to:

- Translate your marketing problems and issues into actionable research questions.
- Think systematically about the marketing research process.
- Become familiar with the language and terminology of marketing research.
- Interact productively with specialist marketing researchers.
- Appreciate the potential importance of Big Data.
- Use marketing research data to obtain greater customer insight.[1]
- Identify new marketing research techniques to help secure differential advantage.
- Assess market and sales potential, and make market and sales forecasts.
- Understand the category development index (CDI) and brand development index (BDI).
- Become a sophisticated user (and client) of marketing research.
- Recognize the limitations and drawbacks of marketing research.

OPENING CASE: THOMSON FINANCIAL

Thomson Financial (TF) provides information and decision analysis tools for the financial market and has evolved steadily in recent years via organic development and acquisition.[2] TF continually redefines offerings to keep pace with evolving market needs. TF focuses on helping organizations inform and build front-end customer strategy (FECS) by developing unique ways to gather, interpret, and disseminate customer insight. TF has a large customer base and many competitors; insight gleaned from customer experiences play a key role in differentiation and strategy development.

Warren Breakstone, TF's COO for global sales, marketing, and services, realized the importance of measuring overall customer experience at all service touch points — sales, account management, training, and help-desk support. Breakstone launched an annual global benchmarking satisfaction study, together with intermittent check-ups on clients that recently used training or help-desk services. Breakstone said, "The most important result was a deeper understanding of customer satisfaction drivers; that helped priority-setting and framed resource allocation decisions. We began to understand the complex interplay between product satisfaction and customer services."

Breakstone said that customers might be very satisfied with a particular aspect of help-desk support. But that might not be a strong driver of customer satisfaction or increase the likelihood of referrals (an important customer-loyalty measure). Teasing out key customer-satisfaction drivers allowed TF to focus on actions generating the greatest impact. One high-end customer subgroup greatly valued TF's financial-modeling consulting service. TF doubled its modeling investment, and consulting services became more successful.

For Breakstone, gaining customer insight is more than executing quantitative benchmarking studies. "The key is to incorporate an understanding of how the data impacts ongoing decisions. Customer satisfaction measures have allowed us to challenge assumptions and make more fact-based decisions. We introduce more data into our discussions of what we should do differently going forward. We are dedicated to linking customer research to our day-to-day decisions." Breakstone said that many firms do not have this discipline; research reports lie dormant, and customer insights are never explored.

Kim Collins, marketing SVP for TF's Corporate Services, builds client insight via structured monthly pulse surveys measuring customer satisfaction with TF training and support functions. Collins said, "I believe that true insight is gleaned from comprehensive, detailed, and continual measurement of customer experiences with products and services at every touch point with customers. Insight is the intelligence we gather when we stop to listen to clients. Only then do we begin to understand the impact, positive or negative, we're having on customer workflow."

Collins' online surveys are briefer than the annual benchmarking studies — only five to 10 questions — but they deliver important data for trend analysis. They also alert Corporate Services to potential problems with customers' experiences. TF's rapid response mitigates dissatisfaction, but also reminds customers that TF is listening to their concerns and cares about their experiences. By involving cross-functional teams in the pulse initiative, customer insights infiltrate important functional areas.

Gaining customer insight is crucial for Thomson Financial. TF gains short-term and long-term insight, then applies this insight to its decision-making processes.

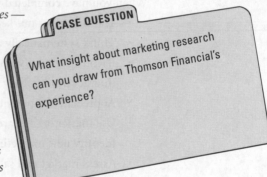

CASE QUESTION

What insight about marketing research can you draw from Thomson Financial's experience?

I think one of the big dangers in today's marketing is that you get these big volumes of stuff, data, which mean nothing. In fact, I hate marketing research, but I love actionable customer insight. You have to work a bit harder. You have to apply your brain to really think through what questions you want to ask people. I think the issue is really thinking through what action you're going to take as a result of your study, rather than just producing a 150-page report that isn't actionable. What's important is research to take action, rather than research just to prove a point. We're not into that.

—David Haines, former Director of Global Branding, Vodafone[3]

Marketing research is any process of data collection, analysis, and interpretation the firm adopts to improve the quality of its marketing efforts. The firm may conduct marketing research on actual and potential customers, but also on customer influencers like legislators and regulators. Sometimes marketing research focuses on behavior. Other times the concern is with mental states like awareness, perceptions, attitudes, and intentions — at any and all stages in the customer experience. Marketing research also subsumes activities like gathering competitive intelligence — Chapter 5, and measuring marketing effectiveness. The related term *market research* has a narrower focus — specifically gathering data about current and potential markets.

Chapter 6 is not designed to make you a marketing research expert. There are many fine books and courses to guide you toward that goal. But we do believe that astute marketers must become *intelligent customers* of marketing research. You need to know where marketing research can be helpful and where it cannot. You must learn what sorts of questions to ask your marketing research suppliers and how to interpret their answers. This chapter also addresses specific and very important topics for marketers: assessing market and sales potential and making sound marketing and sales forecasts.

THE MARKETING RESEARCH PROCESS

Bristol-Myers Squibb's (BMS) marketing research mission is "to ensure the superior use of information and analysis to objectively identify opportunities, frame and validate strategic options, monitor results, provide insights, and build cumulative knowledge."[4] BMS believes that superior customer understanding will provide critical insights for integrating into its decision-making processes. By championing industry-leading techniques, BMS' understanding and anticipation of market evolution provides critical insight into strategic issues. Insights from marketing research allow BMS to create leading programs, earn superior marketing and financial results, and develop and retain top business leaders. These lofty goals provide a window into the importance of timely and effective marketing research in developing the firm's future.

The purpose of marketing research is simply to help the firm make better marketing decisions. The **marketing research process** should follow a basic problem-solving approach. After all, without problems, marketing research would be unnecessary. A critical element of success rests on the relationship between the manager and the researcher. Marketing research is a support function helping the firm make better decisions, but never forget: The manager is ultimately responsible for interpretation, and the decision and its outcomes.

Responsibility for marketing research often extends beyond the marketing research department, single manager, or business unit. A former senior executive at Target shared its approach to securing significant growth: "We identified trends with a dedicated trend group that travels the world to find new trends in everything from apparel to home décor to food, and we used a tool called the trend curve to segment the life cycle of trends. This helped us determine when it will be hot, so we can get it into our stores at the right time for our guests. But we also involved the rest of the company. When anyone is traveling abroad, the expectation is that they will carve out time to go and understand what is happening in London, Berlin, Antwerp, Prague, Tokyo, or wherever they were. We wanted to know, what's emerging? What is the cool restaurant? What are the teenagers wearing? What are the young artists showing? Target had an excellent trend department, but we also had people in every area of the company who have carved out the niche of being trend czars, because everyone has that role to play. We expected everyone to cultivate an eye."[5]

To ensure that marketing research is tightly aligned with marketing decision-making, the marketing research process must follow a consistent methodology. Key elements are in Figure 6.1.

DEFINE THE BUSINESS ISSUE

As a manager, you have primary responsibility for defining the business issue. Of course, marketing researchers (internal department or outsourced supplier) may encourage you to think more deeply about your concerns. Sometimes the *presenting* (immediate) problem may actually be a symptom. You may believe that poor sales performance is due to lazy salespeople, but marketing research may suggest other potential causes like untrained first-line sales managers or unsatisfactory products. A Total Quality Management (TQM) methodology, illustrated in Table 6.1, asks *five whys* as it seeks the root cause of an issue. Of course, you may already have sufficient data to solve the problem. If not, you should state your issue as clearly, completely, and simply as possible, then call in the marketing researchers.

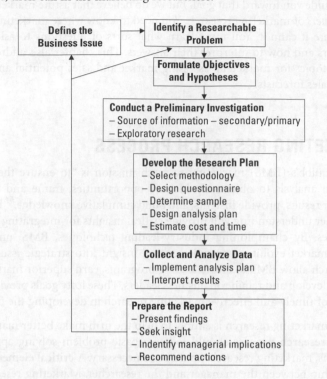

FIGURE 6.1

THE MARKETING RESEARCH PROCESS

Round	Apparent Business Issue (Symptom)	Question (Cause)
1	Our sales performance isn't up to par.	Why?
2	Salespeople aren't putting in enough effort.	Why?
3	It's hard to persuade customers to buy our products.	Why?
4	Our products don't really satisfy their needs.	Why?
5	Our product design process is deficient on customer insight.	Why?

TABLE 6.1

AN ILLUSTRATION OF DEFINING THE BUSINESS ISSUE

IDENTIFY A RESEARCHABLE PROBLEM

Marketing research may be unable to solve all your problems, but a good marketing researcher will help you frame the issues and problems so that research can be useful. (Sometimes managers expect too much, and exploratory research is necessary to frame the problem; a consulting firm's outside perspective may also be useful.) Good marketing research can highlight the facts, point you in the right direction, and help you reduce uncertainty. But there is always a time cost of executing marketing research — forgone revenues and/or competitor action. You should always weigh the value of reducing uncertainty against these costs, and collaborate with your researchers to define a researchable problem.

FORMULATE OBJECTIVES AND HYPOTHESES

Together with the marketing researchers, you should agree on the research objectives and hypotheses you will test. (You may revise the hypotheses after exploratory research.) Objectives and hypotheses are usually related, but hypotheses are always more specific. Suppose your objective is to identify a market opportunity for a new product. Specific hypotheses may relate to positioning alternatives, price points, and brand name. You should be very clear about what insight you are looking for. Examples include:

- **What:**
  - What do consumers think about our product versus competitor products?
  - What specifically do they think are the key benefits and values we offer?
  - What benefits and values should we highlight in our communications?
- **Why:**
  - Why do some consumers switch brands?
  - Why are some consumers fiercely brand loyal?
- **How and how much:**
  - How frequently do consumers purchase our product?
  - How do consumers prefer to buy?
  - How much do consumers purchase on each purchase occasion?
  - How much do consumers consume on each use occasion?
- **Who:**
  - Who makes the purchase decision for these products?
  - Who influences the purchase decision?
  - Who consumes these products?
- **When:**
  - When do consumers make the decision to purchase these products?
  - When do consumers purchase these products?
  - When do consumers consume these products?

Different research questions may require different methodologies like exploratory or causal research for *why* questions and qualitative research for *how*, *what*, *who*, and *when* questions.

CONDUCT A PRELIMINARY INVESTIGATION

Before conducting *primary* research directly with respondents, you should always evaluate *secondary* data. Secondary data (existing sources) may be inside the firm, but are often outside. (We discuss distinctions between primary and secondary data, and qualitative and quantitative data, later in the chapter.) Secondary data may provide partial (or even complete) answers to your research questions more quickly and less expensively than primary data. In other cases, you may commence primary research by talking informally to colleagues — someone may have previously addressed a problem like yours in a former job or company. You may also conduct an exploratory *qualitative* study to secure preliminary insight. By these means, you may be able to narrow the scope of your enquiry by identifying gaps between the data you need to meet your research objectives and the data you already have. Typically, this information gap is the basis for larger-scale and more *quantifiable* research, where costs really mount. Skipping the preliminary stage can lead to heavy expenditures without commensurate insight.

DEVELOP THE RESEARCH PLAN

As your research blueprint, the more detailed research plan should include data-collection methodologies, embracing developing data-collection instruments like questionnaires. The research plan should also contain a sampling plan identifying who will provide data. Quite simply, you want to make sure you get the right data from the right people at the right time. You should also specify the analytic methods you anticipate using, including time and cost estimates, both for management approval and negotiating contracts with outside suppliers. Experienced firms apply a similar discipline to internal research projects and suppliers.

COLLECT AND ANALYZE DATA

With a research plan in place, you are now ready to begin your research. Make sure you use the *right* method, not just one that's easy. If you plan to collect survey data:

- Make sure your subjects are representative of the target population.
- Pay careful attention to response rates.
- Implement procedures for dealing with non-responders.
- Be concerned with data integrity.
- Make sure data collectors act honestly.

No matter how carefully you plan your analysis, additional follow-up analyses may seem appropriate, but they add time and expense. Carefully weigh anticipated value versus the scope of your research plan.

The marketing manager and marketing researcher should collaborate in interpreting the results. Marketing researchers should serve as experts on questionnaire design, sampling methods, analytic techniques, and interpreting statistically significant results. But marketing managers are responsible for restricting researcher interpretations to these issues; after all, marketing researchers may lack insight into the problem context. Marketing managers have ultimate decision-making responsibility and should not encourage researchers to make recommendations beyond their expertise.

PREPARE THE REPORT

As a marketing manager, you will often review marketing research reports that others prepare. They present findings, but your goal and responsibility is always to seek insight. Many firms are rich in data and information, but lack knowledge and have little insight.

Accurate inferences drawn from raw data or processed information constitute knowledge. Many firms devote considerable effort to codifying knowledge and making it widely available (often with varying access); some firms even appoint *knowledge czars* (chief knowledge officers). Insight is different from knowledge. You develop insight by combining different knowledge elements, or using knowledge to create new meaning. Fred Smith's (FedEx) insight was that freight forwarders using passenger airlines could not provide reliable overnight package delivery. Steve Jobs and Steve Wozniak had customer-focused insights that founded the PC industry. Jeff Bezos (Amazon) and Reed Hastings (Netflix) had insights that disrupted industries and led to great success.

Good reports make assumptions transparent, clearly present the findings, and develop managerial implications. You may propose further research to clarify incompletely answered questions, but marketing research can only reduce uncertainty, never eliminate it entirely. A good report proposes alternative courses of action and makes specific recommendations; after all, the goal of any research project should be some change in practice. Changes may range from minor course corrections to major innovations. If the report recommends no changes, at best you validated a current direction; at worst, you asked the wrong questions! Beware of research that is mere ritual, or managers who ignore results.

Marketing Question

It's the first day at your new job and your boss calls you into her office. "I want you to design a marketing research study to determine the reasons for customer loyalty." Prepare a response for your boss.

BIG DATA

In recent years, driven largely by growth in the Internet and social media, the availability and quantity of digital data has mushroomed; hence, the term we hear so much about — **Big Data**.[6]

From a marketing perspective, the firm's challenge is to secure meaning and insight from Big Data to make better decisions. The firm succeeds by identifying relevant data and applying appropriate analytic methods to gain insight.

Three trends (3Vs) are driving marketers to use Big Data[7]:

- **Volume.** Data quantity is fast growing — 2.5 exabytes* of data are created daily, doubling every 40 months.
- **Velocity.** Data are increasingly available very quickly; hence, the firm can take action in real time.
- **Variety.** Data sources and data types continue to multiply.

A simple example concerning book retailers illustrates the opportunities open to marketers:

> Traditional retail booksellers typically have little data on individual customers. At best, an effective loyalty program provides data on member purchases and facilitates generalized promotional offers. By contrast, today's online booksellers have individual-level data on books purchased. These retailers also have data on books viewed, samples downloaded, and website navigation. And they can assess the influence of promotions, reviews, and page layouts on purchase decisions. Online retailers can make and automate informed recommendations to individuals, personalize promotional offers, and even enhance the service experience. By examining similarities across individuals and groups, online retailers can more accurately forecast future sales, and continually update customer insight.[8]

The good news for marketers is the increased volume, velocity, and variety of data. The bad news is that many data sources are unstructured and unwieldy, and originate and/or are stored in multiple locations. Note that this data characterization may be equally true for firm-level data — spread across various functions, businesses, and geographies — as for external data.

The payoff for creating value from Big Data analytics is huge, and particularly so if the firm can *connect the dots* among multiple data sources. For example, using location data from mobile devices, and purchase data from clickstreams, the firm can identify and contact the *right* customers, at the *right* time, in the *right* place. Traditionally, Sears housed data for its Sears, Craftsman, and Lands' End brands in different databases and data warehouses. As a result, comprehensive cross-brand promotions were difficult, time-consuming, and costly to prepare. By synchronizing these data and viewing them in one place, Sears was able to identify opportunities and design better promotions (more timely, granular, and personalized). Sears also reduced development time for a comprehensive set of promotions from 8 weeks to less than one week.

Marketing researchers seek meaning from data via **data mining**. Data mining uses powerful statistical methods and algorithms to search databases to identify patterns. One increasingly popular data-mining approach for brand managers is **sentiment analysis**. By *mining* vast amounts of user-generated content on social media, the firm learns how current and potential customers perceive its brands. The firm can track changes and develop new approaches to improve emotional connections with customers.

---

*1 exabyte = 1 billion gigabytes

CONTINUES ON NEXT PAGE

Using Big Data and advanced analytics, the marketing research goal is to isolate the *signal* in the vast amount of *noise* in the data so as to make *predictive* (forward-looking) judgments. Of course, the firm must ensure that the relationships it finds are meaningful and replicable, and clearly distinguish between correlational and causal relationships.

Perhaps the best metaphor for understanding Big Data is a river (data) fed by many tributaries (data types); the surrounding topography allows new tributaries to form from time to time (new data types).[9] The marketing researcher fishes in the river, trying to hook one of the tasty fish (insight) that live out of sight. Only fishing skill (good methodology) and perseverance can ensure catching a fish rather than an old boot!

CRITICAL DISTINCTIONS IN MARKETING RESEARCH

As a marketing manager, you will be responsible for directing marketing researchers and the marketing research process. Here we make some critical distinctions that can help you devise marketing research plans.

PRIMARY AND SECONDARY RESEARCH

Best practice dictates assessing available secondary data, then filling information *gaps* with primary data.

SECONDARY RESEARCH. Some person or organization has already collected secondary data for another purpose. Three basic types of secondary data are:

- **Company data.** Comprises routinely generated data from transactions with customers and suppliers; information from internal databases on capacity, costs, and production; customer lists; customer purchases and payment history; delivery, maintenance, and servicing reports; salesperson call reports; and previously completed marketing research reports. Company data also includes data collected by customers or partners, like bar code **scanner data** and RFID tracking data.

- **Public data.** Includes information about competitors, customers, and suppliers; industry trends; and technologies. Sources include competitor annual reports; competitor and public domain websites; general business and industry-specific media and books; government and trade associations; government and published academic research; websites (like dnb.com, Dialog.com, LexisNexis.com); legal and government filings; supplier white papers; trade show literature; and presentations. Public data also include semi-public data like syndicated research reports from firms like Nielsen and IRI, and reports from industry and financial analysts. Locating data is often a challenge, but subscription databases and Internet search engines have eased this task.

- **Technical analysis.** Includes objective, repeatable descriptions of products and services or production capacity collected by internal engineers or developers. Examples include benchmarking product design and reverse engineering competitor products to estimate manufacturing costs and supply-chain processes.

PRIMARY RESEARCH. As noted earlier, **primary research** is typically more expensive than secondary research. The firm usually collects primary data for a specific purpose, often to close gaps between data required to make decisions and secondary research data. Primary data sources depend on the research problem but may include previous, current, and/or potential customers, especially people in various purchase and consumption roles; industry experts and trade association personnel; and distribution channel members like agents, brokers,

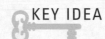

KEY IDEA

➤ *Secondary* marketing research uses data relevant to your research that some person or organization has already collected for another purpose.

➤ *Primary* marketing research requires that you collect new data.

Marketing Question

Suppose you need to know the sales for a product class or product form that interests you. What secondary sources will provide these data?

distributors, retailers, and wholesalers. Sometimes the firm lowers primary data costs by joining a syndicate/consortium whose members seek data from similar respondents.

All primary research requires a stimulus, frequently a question the researcher wants answered. Sometimes the firm provides specific stimuli like advertising or positioning concepts, attribute lists or product profiles, advertising or sales messages, or competitive materials/products.

QUALITATIVE AND QUANTITATIVE RESEARCH

Two major approaches to marketing research are *qualitative* and *quantitative*:

QUALITATIVE RESEARCH. Qualitative research (QualR) is typically not concerned with numbers. QualR is generally flexible and versatile, but is rarely conclusive and does not project to a larger population. Firms often conduct QualR to pursue interesting questions, uncover customer needs, identify buyer behavior, gain a better understanding of business issues and the *language* people use, develop ideas, and help define and prioritize marketing research problems. QualR can help assess how customers *feel* about products and suppliers. Small-scale exploratory primary QualR often precedes large-scale quantitative data collection.

A particular issue in QualR is the difference between self-reported responses and data on actual behavior. Both can be valuable, but the researcher should always be skeptical about self-reports. Just because a respondent says, "I did X" or "I will do X" does not mean the respondent actually did, or will do, X. Respondents may purposely mislead researchers, but mismatches between self-reports and actual behavior are often due to poor memory, bias, and/or unclear questions. Researchers should seek convergence; the Kimberly-Clark example is instructive:

> Focus groups provided Kimberly-Clark (KC) with little insight into why Huggies baby wipes were losing sales. It introduced a new observational technique, a camera mounted on a pair of glasses that consumers wore at home. In focus groups, mothers talked about changing babies on a diaper table. From the cameras, researchers saw that mothers changed babies on many surfaces, often in awkward positions, and struggled with containers requiring two hands. KC redesigned packages for wipes, shampoo, and lotions so that mothers could easily dispense them with one hand.

QUANTITATIVE RESEARCH. Quantitative research (QuanR) uses numerical data and mathematical analyses, often from large representative samples. Marketing researchers use QuanR to test hypotheses formulated earlier in the research process. Some analyses are quite simple; others are highly complex. The researcher should ask three types of question when considering QuanR:

- **Internal validity.** Do these data measure what I want to be measuring?
- **Reliability.** If I repeat data collection, will I get the same results?
- **External validity.** Will the results I secure generalize to other populations?

Sometimes drawing the line between QualR and QuanR is difficult, as some forms of qualitative data are amenable to quantitative analysis. Researchers are always pursuing new forms of quantitative analysis, but qualitative data gathering is also evolving. Firms striving for increased customer insight are driving these innovations.

Figure 6.2 shows how primary and secondary research can be either qualitative or quantitative. Generally, quantitative approaches to primary research data yield more insight than qualitative approaches. But with secondary research, the firm can often gain significant insight from the large amounts of qualitative data that are often available.

KEY IDEA

➤ *Qualitative* research is not concerned with numbers.

➤ *Quantitative* research focuses on quantitative analysis.

	Primary	Secondary
Qualitative	Small-group discussions with customers about product alternatives	Review of advertising campaigns from various product suppliers
Quantitative	Large-scale sample survey of customers about product alternatives; test hypotheses by quantitative methods	Secure independent research reports on customers' views of product alternatives; conduct quantitative analyses

FIGURE 6.2

ILLUSTRATION OF RESEARCH TYPES

SECURING QUALITATIVE RESEARCH DATA

Now let's look at a few of the more popular primary data-gathering methods for securing insight into customers' needs and motivations.

FOCUS GROUPS

Single location **focus groups** are one of the most popular qualitative data collection methods. Typically, focus groups comprise eight to 12 members (often paid for participation and selected for their interest, knowledge, and/or experience with the topic) moderated by a skilled facilitator. The facilitator asks carefully scripted probing questions, maintains good participant interaction, and tries to ensure comparable contribution per member. Focus groups have the advantage that one member's ideas can spark responses in another. Potential problems include strong individuals dominating the discussion, less than honest responses, psychologically defensive behavior, yea-saying (unreflective agreement), and a conservative bias in favor of the known versus the unknown. The requirement of a central location can also limit participation and skew results if the firm takes insufficient care with member selection. Managers and researchers often receive immediate feedback by watching focus group discussions through one-way glass. Typically, researchers record and transcribe focus group discussions. Effective focus groups require significant skill. Telephone and video-conference focus groups are newer alternatives. They reduce problems of dominating participants and travel costs, but limit the degree of participant interaction.

ONE-ON-ONE INTERVIEWS (OOOs)

One-on-one interviews (OOOs) combine direct and indirect questions asked of individuals to probe needs and underlying purchase motivations. Mostly, researchers conduct OOOs in person — in the respondent's home or office, in a public place like a shopping mall, or on the telephone. OOOs avoid the various biases sometimes found in focus groups and can address more sensitive topics, but are generally more expensive and time-consuming. OOOs cannot build on ideas from others, but dialog can be more open and skilled interviewers secure significant insight.

INTERNET: BLOGS, FORUMS, SOCIAL NETWORKS, TWITTER, WIKIS, YOUTUBE

One specific feature of the online world is that customers are increasingly willing to post complimentary and/or critical comments about products, brands, and firms. By offering its own forum, the firm may receive valuable customer feedback. The firm must also be vigilant about

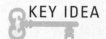

other online postings; many bloggers develop significant followings and become very influential. Data-mining services capture consumer ratings on independent sites, and count and analyze web conversations for specific phrases about products, brands, and firms; hence, they quantify essentially qualitative data. Firms learn about performance perceptions, where to improve, and ideas for new product features and services. Of course, because posters are often anonymous, marketing researchers must carefully weigh the validity of these types of qualitative data.

PROJECTIVE TECHNIQUES

Researchers use projective techniques (aka motivation research) mainly to uncover latent customer needs. Developed by psychologists, projective techniques have a long history in marketing:

• **Constructing a collage.** The respondent collects pictures from newspapers and magazines that express his feeling about the topic.

• **Imagery.** The respondent draws a picture showing her interacting with the product, then interprets the picture.

• **Role-playing.** Respondents pretend they are a brand's friend and write it a letter, or they explain why a neighbor/work colleague may like/dislike a particular product. Role-playing and storytelling (below) avoid arousing the respondent's subconscious defenses.

• **Sentence completion.** The respondent completes an incomplete sentence.

• **Storytelling.** The respondent receives a picture/description of a situation relevant to the topic. The respondent makes up a story about one or more characters in the stimulus.

• **Word associations.** The researcher supplies a stimulus word. The respondent offers the first word that comes to mind. Applications include image studies and branding research.

OBSERVATION

Yogi Berra said, "You can see a lot just by looking."[10]

The firm gains insight just by observing. Broadly speaking, there are two categories — planned and unplanned:

PLANNED OBSERVATION. The firm does not ask questions, but secures insight by watching (sometimes using one-way mirrors) and recording behavior (often by video) in naturalistic settings. The researcher assesses subjects' behavior, including emotional responses, body language, and person-to-person interactions. Observation is a reliable technique provided the researcher uses correct methods. Although difficult to code, observational data are objective, accurate, and unbiased by researcher intervention:

Ralph Lauren observed mothers and daughters leaving a Lauren store in Connecticut — mothers with shopping bags, daughters without. Lauren developed *Rugby* to address the 14-to-29 demographic. Ritz-Carlton's *Mystique* system catalogs and shares employees' observations about guests among its 60 hotels. When a guest checks in to a Ritz-Carlton hotel, employees act on these observations to provide extra service.

UNPLANNED OBSERVATION. Individuals may gain significant insight about markets, customers, and/or competitors without planning to do so. Simple observation may trigger an idea with tremendous payoff:

Former Virginia governor Gerald Baliles said: "When I was in China, I was struck by how often I encountered chicken feet in the soups, foods, and markets. When I got back, my people called the poultry industry to find out what they do with chicken feet. They were chopped off on the assembly lines and discarded. Today Virginia ships 40 tons a month of chicken feet to the Far East."

ETHNOGRAPHIC RESEARCH

Derived from anthropology, **ethnographic research** is an observational method where researchers spend *a day in the life of (DILO)* their customers,[11] corresponding to the anthropologist *living with the tribe*. Observers gain insight into their subjects' culture and belief systems, uncover needs, and understand how customers integrate products into their daily lives. Intel's cultural anthropologists examine the interface of technology and humanity; when Tom Katzen was responsible for marketing Levi's jeans to teenagers, he spent Saturday mornings in ticket lines at San Francisco's Fillmore Auditorium, observing the way teenagers customized their blue jeans. Many firms employ *cool hunters* to observe people's behavior and clothing in natural settings like inner-city basketball courts and fashionable nightclubs, and to hang out on social networking sites like Facebook.

Before Toyota designed the Lexus LS 400 specifically for the U.S., the chief engineer and his team lived for several months in Southern California's upscale Laguna Hills. They visited many upscale metropolitan areas around the U.S. — Coral Gables, Miami; north Lake Shore Drive, Chicago; and Westchester County, New York. They learned how luxury car owners drive, treat their cars, and deal with valet parking. They learned the role cars played in these people's lives and product and service expectations. The Lexus has been an unqualified success.

> ### Marketing Question
>
> Go to your local supermarket and observe consumer behavior in the cereal aisle. What can you learn? What hypotheses can you develop that you could test by quantitative methods?

SECURING QUANTITATIVE RESEARCH DATA

Alternative ways of securing data for quantitative analysis are:

SURVEYS

Sample **surveys** of the target population are the most common way to secure primary data for quantitative analysis. Selecting a sample reflecting the underlying population is critical. So is assessing the required sample size for estimating parameter(s) of interest at the desired accuracy level. Detailed discussion of both topics is beyond the scope of this chapter, but as a rule, there are critical trade-offs between cost, flexibility, and time. The firm can reduce costs by joining a marketing research firm's omnibus survey.

Questionnaire design is critical to survey success and should involve both the marketing researcher and marketing manager. Development can be relatively unstructured and qualitative, but producing the final questionnaire requires much thought. The questionnaire should avoid biases from yea-saying and question order. Questions should not be vague, ambiguous, complex, difficult to answer, or easily misinterpreted. Good questionnaire design typically includes both open-ended and closed-ended questions. Questionnaires should always be pretested. Table 6.2 identifies several standard approaches to asking questions.

Approach	Example	Comments
Rank ordering	Put "1" for the brand you would most likely buy; "2" for the next most likely brand, etc., until you have ordered all brands: Dell, HP, Lenovo, Macintosh, VAIO	Rotate brand order. Secures ordinal measures (below).[12]
Constant sum	Allocate 100 points among these benefits so that the more important benefits get the most points.	Secures ratio measures (below).
Paired comparison	Circle the brand in each pair that you would most likely buy: Dell or HP Dell or Macintosh Lenovo or VAIO	Comparisons limited by respondent fatigue.[13] Secures interval measures (below).

TABLE 6.2

SELECTED STANDARD APPROACHES TO ASKING QUESTIONS

CONTINUES ON NEXT PAGE

TABLE 6.2

CONTINUED

Approach	Example						Comments
Likert-type scales	Agree or disagree: Dell computers are easy to maintain:						Be careful of positivity bias. Use positively/negatively worded items. Use multiple items for reliability.
	1 Strongly agree	2 Agree	3 Neutral	4 Disagree	5 Strongly disagree		
Semantic differential scales	Rate (focal object) on these scales by circling the number that best reflects your opinion.						Use 7–12 sets of bipolar adjectives. Factor analyze to secure the underlying meaning.
	Dumb 1 2 3 4 5 6 7 8 9 10 Smart						
	Weak 1 2 3 4 5 6 7 8 9 10 Strong						
	Bad 1 2 3 4 5 6 7 8 9 10 Good						
	Soft 1 2 3 4 5 6 7 8 9 10 Hard						
	Easy 1 2 3 4 5 6 7 8 9 10 Difficult						
	Fast 1 2 3 4 5 6 7 8 9 10 Slow						

KEY IDEA

➤ When designing a process to collect survey data, the firm must make several important trade-offs among, primarily:

• Cost
• Time
• Flexibility

PANELS

For many marketing research projects, securing survey data from different respondent samples is fine. But sometimes the firm wants to follow up on individual responses. In a **tracking (longitudinal) study**, the firm forms a **panel** of individuals who agree to provide responses periodically. Maintaining a panel is challenging, but judicious member replacement can keep a panel going almost indefinitely.[14] Panel data allows the firm to *keep its pulse* on customers, conduct more sophisticated analysis, and better identify causal relationships. Because panels are expensive to maintain and administer, firms like Nielsen and IRI form and manage panels. These panels provide a sense of data independence and several user firms share the costs. Online marketing research firms like Greenfield Online and Harris Interactive maintain large panels from which firms can select sub-populations for specific surveys. Combining self-reported panel data with actual use data may provide significant insight.

OBJECTIVE SALES DATA

The firm's sales reporting system can provide valuable quantitative data. But sales data to end-user customers may be difficult to secure when products move through distribution channels. In supermarkets, the widespread use of barcodes and retail scanners makes it easy to collect and store sales data by **sku** (**stock-keeping unit**). IRI and Nielsen each secure scanner data from several thousand supermarkets in many urban markets; they aggregate and sell these data to manufacturers. Collection and use of automatically collected sales data is likely to increase. By remotely monitoring vending machine sales, a firm can better schedule deliveries, adjust product mix, price dynamically, and make personalized offers for purchasing by cell phone. Internet firms collect sales data directly by individual and, together with search data from *cookies*, develop buyer profiles for making purchase recommendations. EZ Pass systems automatically measure use of road services.

KEY IDEA

➤ Approaches to securing quantitative research data include:

• Surveys
• Panels
• Objective sales data
• Behavioral measurement
• Experiments
• Prediction markets

BEHAVIORAL MEASUREMENT

Increasingly, firms use technology for marketing research. *Infrared sensors*, *video cameras*, and *digital voice recorders* monitor supermarket aisle-traffic patterns; *checkout scanners* measure consumer purchases. Electronic metering systems capture radio listenership and TV viewing by channel; GPS-enabled *cell phones* identify consumer locations. Some researchers provide subjects with *digital cameras*; others use *galvanometers* to measure consumers' physiological changes to stimuli. *Tachistoscopes* measure recognition speed by projecting images like package designs for short time-periods, and advertising researchers often use *eye-movement* devices.

EXPERIMENTS

Experiments allow researchers to definitively establish causal relationships like A → B. The researcher manipulates independent variables like advertising and price, and measures results (dependent variables) like awareness and sales. Superior experimental designs include a control group. Because many non-manipulated and unmeasured variables can affect results, researchers typically use random assignment for experimental and control groups. Experiments range between limited-scale laboratory studies and large field experiments. The critical trade-off is typically between cost and researchers' ability to draw conclusions.

What most firms fail to realize is that day-to-day business life can function as a *natural experiment*. Rather than manipulate independent variables, the firm can use the *natural* variability in its decisions to seek relationships with results. Costs of data storage and analysis are fast reducing and some firms evolve their actions in real time. Leading firms are becoming learning organizations by treating their entire set of marketing actions as data in natural experiments.[15]

> ### *Marketing Question*
>
> How would you design an experiment to measure the impact of advertising spending and price on sales of your product? (Choose your own product.)

PREDICTION MARKETS

In prediction markets, buyers and sellers trade assets whose cash value is tied to a particular event. Dating to the mid-1990s, public prediction markets have successfully predicted Oscar nominations and various economic events. Lloyds TSB assesses new product ideas. In its *TagTrade* market, Best Buy employees trade imaginary stocks for new service packages and sales forecasts. In many cases, prediction markets secure better results than experts.[16]

ANALYZING QUANTITATIVE RESEARCH DATA

Quantitative research data are amenable to a broad variety of statistical analyses. If the underlying assumptions are valid, quantitative methods can have significant predictive power and be very helpful to the firm in making marketing decisions. But quantitative data analysis is a huge topic that we do not address in this chapter. Many fine marketing research textbooks are available for interested students.

MARKET AND SALES POTENTIALS, MARKET AND SALES FORECASTS

Yogi Berra said, "It's tough to make predictions, especially about the future."[17]

Chapters 3, 4, 5, and now Chapter 6 have armed you with many approaches, concepts, ideas, and options for designing and conducting marketing research studies. You have a solid base of knowledge for securing greater insight into markets, customers, competitors, and complementers. These insights will enable you to build more powerful market strategies and implementation plans, as you prepare to deliver customer value and secure differential advantage.

However, one item we have deferred from securing market insight — Chapter 3 — is predicting market size and firm sales. These predictions are critical for many reasons — identifying attractiveness of a market opportunity, production planning, and budgeting the firm's financial, human, and other resources.

> ### KEY IDEA
>
> ➤ In assessing the market, the firm should project:
> - Market potential
> - Market forecast
>
> ➤ In assessing firm possibilities, the firm should project:
> - Sales potential
> - Sales forecast

Two related concepts — **potentials** and **forecasts** — are important for understanding market demand and firm performance. Unfortunately, many managers are confused about these terms. Potentials and forecasts are quite different, but each has important quantitative aspects. *Potential* embraces having a *capability or future state*:

- **Market potential** — what market sales could become.
- **Sales potential** — what the firm's sales could become.

By contrast, *forecast* concerns *expectations*:

- **Forecast market size** — expected market sales in a given time period.
- **Sales forecast** — the firm's expected sales in a given time period.

We explore ways to assess potentials and forecasts, and conclude Chapter 6 by discussing *category development index (CDI)* and *brand development index (BDI)*.

ASSESSING MARKET POTENTIAL

Market potential is the *maximum market-level sales,* from all suppliers, that the firm believes could occur in a future time period. Since all markets go through life cycles, the firm wants to have some idea of market sales at various life-cycle stages. Market potential is an upper bound to actual sales, based on a set of assumptions about future market conditions. Market potential is especially important when contemplating entry in a new market.

To assess market potential, the firm should estimate the number of likely customers and the amounts they are likely to buy. Of course, the identity of likely customers may change as the life cycle evolves; propensity to buy evolves also. The three steps are:

- **Identify likely market segments.** Most markets comprise several segments. The firm must understand these segments, even though some may not buy at each time period.
- **Estimate numbers of customers in each segment.** The firm estimates the number of customers likely to buy in the time period for which it seeks market potential.
- **Estimate the number of products to be purchased.** The firm estimates the number of products customers in each segment are likely to buy for the relevant time period.

Table 6.3 shows typical market potential calculations for a new consumer product — for three years, six years, and 10 years after launch. In this illustration, we assume three market segments.

TABLE 6.3

MARKET POTENTIAL CALCULATIONS

Time Period	Market Segments	Total Number of Customers in Each Segment (millions) A	Percent Likely to Buy (%) B	Expected Number of Customers Likely to Buy C = A × B (millions)	Number of Units Those Purchasing are Likely to Buy D	Segment Potential Calculation E = C × D (million units)	Market Potential (million units): Sum of Es
3 years after launch	Seg. 1	10	50%	5	5	25	
	Seg. 2	6	20%	1.2	2	2.4	**27.4**
	Seg. 3	8	0%	0	0	0	
6 years after launch	Seg. 1	11	70%	7.7	6	46.2	
	Seg. 2	6	40%	2.4	4	9.6	**58.6**
	Seg. 3	7	10%	0.7	4	2.8	
10 years after launch	Seg. 1	12	70%	8.4	7	58.8	
	Seg. 2	6	50%	3.0	6	18	**93**
	Seg. 3	6	30%	1.8	9	16.2	

Several interesting points within this table are:

- The firm believes the numbers of customers in each segment will change over time. Segment 1 increases, segment 2 stays the same, and segment 3 decreases.
- The percentage of customers likely to buy also evolves. Segment 1 increases, then stays constant; segment 2 increases continuously; segment 3 is zero initially, then increases.
- For each segment, the firm predicts only a fraction of customers will purchase.
- The amount purchased increases for each segment, quite dramatically for segment 3.
- For each time period, market potential is the sum of individual segment potentials.

The firm can estimate *market potential revenues* by multiplying *potential units* by the estimated price in each time period.

ASSESSING SALES POTENTIAL

Sales potential is the maximum sales the firm could achieve in a given time period. Of course, sales potential is conditioned on assumptions about market potential, the firm's likely efforts, and future market conditions like number and strength of competitors.

The firm can calculate sales potential directly from market potential by assessing potential market share. The firm's potential share depends both on the resources it could commit to the market and the actions it believes competitors will take. If the firm contemplates increasing resources over time (and/or believes that competitors will reduce commitments) estimated potential market share should also increase. Table 6.4 shows illustrative sales potential calculations based on market potential estimates from Table 6.3.

Time Period	Market Potential (million units) A	Firm's Potential Market Share (%) B	Sales Potential (million units) C = A × B
3 years after launch	27.4	10%	2.74
6 years after launch	58.6	20%	11.72
10 years after launch	93	30%	27.9

FORECASTING MARKET SIZE

Market forecasts often focus on the short run, like the upcoming year, where the firm can assess market conditions with a fair degree of accuracy. To forecast market size, the firm may focus either on the overall market or on individual segments that it later aggregates. Generally, a segmented approach provides better forecasts (if data are available). Three broad approaches to assessing market size are:

JUDGMENTAL METHODS. These are the simplest methods for forecasting market size:

- **Executive judgment.** The responsible manager has deep familiarity with the product class, competitive offers, customer needs and satisfaction levels, current market size, and many environmental factors. She makes her own intuitive judgments.
- **Delphi method.** A valuable approach when several people have opinions about the market. Each person makes a market forecast and specifies the rationale. Each person then receives all forecasts and rationales, and revises their forecast. Forecasts often converge after a couple of rounds, but may require several rounds.

KEY IDEA

➤ Market potential is the maximum sales the firm expects in the market in a given time period from all suppliers.
➤ Market forecast is the expected market size.
➤ Sales potential is the maximum sales the firm could achieve in a given time period.
➤ Sales forecast is the firm's expected sales.

TABLE 6.4

SALES POTENTIAL CALCULATION

Marketing Exercise

Form a group of five or six students. Each person in the group forecasts the Dow Jones average (or some other event) for the last day of class and provides a rationale. Team members exchange forecasts and rationales and repeat the process one or more times. On the last day of class, compare the forecast with the actual Dow Jones average.

TIME-BASED METHODS. These methods use past sales to predict future sales directly:

- **Judgmental extrapolation.** A special case of executive judgment using history to predict the percentage change from the previous year. The basis could be the most recent year-to-year change, a simple average of the previous two (three, four, five) years' changes, or a weighted average of previous years' changes, with greater weight to more recent years.

- **Linear extrapolation.** Two-variable regression analysis estimates year-by-year change in sales. Forecast sales for next year are last year sales plus an increment (or decrement) based on prior year sales. The forecaster calculates the extrapolation increment mathematically, but must decide how many prior years to use.

- **Moving average.** The manager uses sales data from previous years to calculate an average; this average is the forecast. For each successive year, the manager drops the earliest sales datum and adds in the most recent datum. Hence, sales from several years ago do not weigh too heavily in the forecast. Once again, the manager must judge how many years to include.

- **Exponential smoothing (ES).** Rather than making the forecast based only on actual sales data from previous years, exponential smoothing uses both actual sales from last year and last year's forecast sales. ES calculates a smoothing parameter, "a," from previous sales data:

$$\text{Forecast sales}_{t+1} = a \times \text{actual sales}_t + (1 - a) \times \text{forecast sales}_t$$

The value of "a" depends on the relative weight given to the prior year's actual sales versus the prior year's forecast sales; "a" ranges from zero to one. If historic sales were fairly constant, forecast sales weigh quite heavily, and "a" is on the low side. If sales change substantially year by year, as in a growth market, "a" may be close to 1.

KEY IDEA

➤ Time-based methods for forecasting are:
- Judgmental extrapolation
- Linear extrapolation
- Moving average
- Exponential smoothing

Table 6.5 shows how to use these methods to forecast global market size for consumer durable A. Column 2 shows actual sales; columns to the right show market size forecasts using judgmental extrapolation, linear extrapolation, moving average, and exponential smoothing. In each case, the first forecasts are for 2000. Forecasts by judgmental extrapolation are based on the actual percentage change in sales for the most recent year. For the other methods, forecasts are based on the previous five years' sales. For example, the forecasts for year 6 are based on data for years 1, 2, 3, 4, and 5; forecasts for year 9 are based on years 4, 5, 6, 7, and 8. We can make several inferences:

- Actual sales increase markedly in year 9 and subsequent years; deviations are mostly greater for later years for all forecasting methods.

- Because actual sales growth is high in later years, simple judgmental extrapolation does best. Other methods are handicapped, to a greater or lesser extent, by sales from earlier years. This finding is especially marked for the five-year moving average. (Moving-average forecasts with fewer years [not reported] do better.)

- For all years, the exponential smoothing forecast is the previous year's actual sales. Sales increased significantly and the smoothing constant, a, is equal to 1.

TABLE 6.5

PREDICTING GLOBAL MARKET SIZES FOR CONSUMER DURABLE A (000s)

Year	Actual Sales	Judgmental Extrapolation		Linear Extrapolation		Moving Average		Exponential Smoothing	
		Forecast Sales	Deviation from Actual Sales	Forecast Sales	Deviation from Actual Sales	Forecast Sales	Deviation from Actual Sales	Forecast Sales	Deviation from Actual Sales
1	8,791	—	—	—	—	—	—	—	—
2	11,148	—	—	—	—	—	—	—	—
3	14,043	—	—	—	—	—	—	—	—
4	15,482	—	—	—	—	—	—	—	—
5	19,858	—	—	—	—	—	—	—	—

CONTINUES ON NEXT PAGE

Year	Actual Sales	Judgmental Extrapolation		Linear Extrapolation		Moving Average		Exponential Smoothing	
		Forecast Sales	Deviation from Actual Sales	Forecast Sales	Deviation from Actual Sales	Forecast Sales	Deviation from Actual Sales	Forecast Sales	Deviation from Actual Sales
6	26,352	25,470	(882)	21,805	(4,547)	13,864	(12,488)	19,858	(6,494)
7	27,968	34,970	7,002	28,224	256	17,377	(10,591)	26,352	(1,616)
8	30,799	29,683	(1,116)	32,357	1,558	20,741	(10,058)	27,968	(2,831)
9	39,365	33,917	(5,448)	35,715	(3,650)	24,092	(15,273)	30,799	(8,566)
10	48,926	50,313	1,387	41,907	(7,019)	28,868	(20,058)	39,365	(9,561)
11	65,271	60,809	(4,462)	51,646	(13,625)	34,682	(30,589)	48,926	(16,345)
12	82,314	87,076	4,762	70,286	(12,028)	42,466	(39,848)	65,271	(17,043)

TABLE 6.5

CONTINUED

CAUSAL-FACTOR METHODS. The most common causal-factor method for predicting market size is *multiple regression analysis*.[18] The researcher selects several independent (predictor) variables that she believes could be related to market size, the dependent (criterion) variable. She uses historical data to determine the relationships, if any, between these predictor variables and market size. She then uses these relationships to predict future sales.

MAKING THE SALES FORECAST

The sales forecast is the firm's expected sales in a future time period, often the upcoming year. The sales forecast is central to many day-by-day operations. Of course, *actual* factors can cause *actual* firm sales to be quite different from *forecast* sales. Many firms use three broad approaches to sales forecasting: *top-down*, *bottom-up*, and *synthetic*.

TOP-DOWN SALES FORECASTING. Top-down sales forecasts follow directly from analyses of market potential, market-size (or individual market segment) forecasts, and the firm's market share estimates — typically contained in the marketing plan. Calculations are relatively simple but the marketer must understand market subtleties and nuances:

Sales forecast = forecast market size × forecast market share

BOTTOM-UP SALES FORECASTING. Bottom-up forecasts embrace the granularity (and reality) of sales by customer that is absent in top-down forecasts — salespeople can personally discuss customer requirements. The firm aggregates forecasts from individual salespeople to develop the bottom-up sales forecast. (In some firms, the sales forecast derives from a sales pipeline system — Chapter 17.) The downside of bottom-up forecasting is that salespeople may *lowball* estimates if the firm uses these forecasts to set sales quotas that affect take-home pay.

SYNTHETIC SALES FORECASTS. Synthetic sales forecasts combine the best features of top-down and bottom-up forecasting. The top-down forecast derives from the market planning process; the sales department independently prepares a bottom-up forecast. If these numbers are similar, the task is over. In most cases, the top-down sales forecast is higher, and sales managers and individual salespeople must re-examine their forecasts customer by customer to see where increases are possible. These reworked forecasts are the building blocks for a revised bottom-up sales forecast. Simultaneously, marketing reworks the top-down forecast. Hopefully, the revised forecasts agree. If not, senior management typically decides the forecast by executive decision, and sales managers apportions increases to individual salespeople.

KEY IDEA

➤ Many firms develop synthetic sales forecasts using a combination of *top-down* and *bottom-up* approaches.

KEY IDEA

➤ Important practical approaches for assessing market and sales potentials are:

• Category development index (CDI)

• Brand development index (BDI)

CATEGORY AND BRAND DEVELOPMENT INDICES

The **category development index (CDI)** and **brand development index (BDI)** are useful devices for assessing market and sales, potentials and forecasts. Each index relies on dividing the market into separate areas; CDI and BDI measure category and brand strengths in those areas. FMCG firms typically base CDIs and BDIs on geography:

• CDI — the percentage of category sales divided by the percentage of U.S. population, converted to a percentage.

• BDI — the percentage of brand sales divided by the percentage of U.S. population, converted to a percentage.

We covered a lot of ground in this chapter, but in many ways we have only scratched the surface of marketing research. We hope your key take-away is that marketing research can be very helpful in securing insight the firm requires to successfully execute the six marketing imperatives. But you should also realize that marketing research is no panacea. The manager and researcher must make many decisions before investing in a particular study. We have given you a glimpse of some of the available options.

KEY MESSAGES

• Marketing research results should be actionable.

• Good marketing research can give the firm a differential advantage.

• Marketing researchers should provide analysis and insight; marketing managers make decisions.

• Marketing research studies should follow a rigorous process.

• Marketing researchers make critical distinctions between primary and secondary research, and qualitative and quantitative research.

• Both qualitative and quantitative research use several methodologies. Qualitative research is increasingly more popular.

• The various techniques for collecting survey data have advantages and disadvantages.

• Several methods are available for assessing market and sales potentials, and making market and sales forecasts.

VIDEOS AND AUDIOS

| The Future of Marketing Research | v602 | Oded Netzer | Columbia Business School |
| Securing Insight | v603 | Spencer Pingel | Colgate-Palmolive |

v602

v603

TRANSITION TO
STRATEGIC MARKETING

CHAPTERS 3 THROUGH 6 FOCUS ON SECURING market, customer, competitor, company, and complementer insight. Some insight is fairly broad — like factors driving market growth or anticipated technological change; other insight is much narrower — like identifying new competitor entry or a specific competence the firm may secure. Regardless, the material in these chapters forms the basis for the *situation analysis* — the foundation for the market plan, leading to *Strategic Marketing* — Section III; and *Implementing the Market Strategy* — Section IV.

The best way to build a solid superstructure is to transition from *insight* in the situation analysis to *assumptions* about the future. Planning assumptions help the firm identify forces for change and outline expected business conditions; they are critical supporting elements for both strategic and operational market plans. Drawing from the various insight elements, marketers should identify candidate planning assumptions, like:

1. Consumers will not accept price increases greater than 1 percent annually.
2. New textile fibers will gain greater than 10 percent market share by 20XY+1.

To complete the process, the marketer should identify implications for the firm of each key assumption, then turn these assumptions into "We believe…" statements. Examples are:

- We believe consumers will not accept price increases greater than 1 percent annually.
- We believe new textile fibers will gain greater than 10 percent market share by 20XY+1.

A useful metaphor for illustrating the role of planning assumptions in the market plan is the *bridge* — Figure T.1. The bridge represents market strategy and implementation, taking the firm from *today* towards *tomorrow*. The bridge is built on pillars — *planning assumptions* — supported by a foundation — *situation analysis*. If the pillars are weak and/or the foundation is insecure, when the water rises the bridge will collapse and wash down the river. Correspondingly, a weak situation analysis and/or ill-developed planning assumptions will lead to failure. Section II teaches how to develop insight to construct a solid foundation of situation analysis; planning assumptions transition from that foundation into critical support for market strategy and implementation.

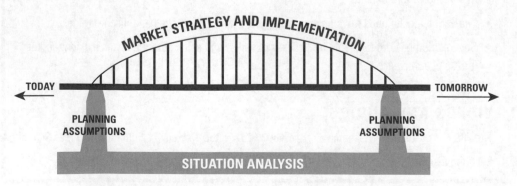

FIGURE T.1

PLANNING ASSUMPTIONS: THE BRIDGE METAPHOR

SECTION III

STRATEGIC
MARKETING cvs3

To access O-codes, go to www.ocodes.com

SECTION III — STRATEGIC MARKETING — COMPRISES FIVE CHAPTERS, Chapter 7 through Chapter 11. These chapters focus on the firm's critical strategic marketing decisions. The section embraces the first three Marketing Imperatives: Imperative 1 — Determine and Recommend Which Markets to Address; Imperative 2 — Identify and Target Market Segments; and Imperative 3 — Set Strategic Direction and Positioning.

Chapter 7, Identifying and Choosing Opportunities, addresses Imperative I. This chapter develops approaches for making market-choice decision — what markets to address and what markets not to address. Chapter 7 also offers various approaches for implementing the firm's market choices.

Chapter 8, Market Segmentation and Targeting, addresses Imperative 2. This chapter follows logically from market-choice decisions. Having selected markets, the firm must decide what parts of those markets to address. We shall see that the firm must engage in two processes: form market segments and then decide which of those segments to target for effort.

Chapters 9, 10, and 11 together address Imperative 3. Chapter 9, Market Strategy: Integrating the Firm's Efforts for Marketing Success, lays out the critical components of a market strategy; market strategies that omit any of these components are incomplete. The purpose of Chapter 10, Managing through the Life Cycle, is to help firms develop preemptive strategies by examining alternative scenarios based on life-cycle stage and competitive position. Finally, Chapter 11, Managing Brands, discusses the value of brands, key branding concepts, and approaches to building and maintaining strong brands.

Capon's Marketing Framework

SECTION I: MARKETING AND THE FIRM

CHAPTER 1
Introduction to Managing Marketing

CHAPTER 2
The Value of Customers

SECTION II: FUNDAMENTAL INSIGHTS FOR STRATEGIC MARKETING

CHAPTER 3
Market Insight

CHAPTER 4
Customer Insight

CHAPTER 5
Insight about Competitors, Company, and Complementers

CHAPTER 6
Marketing Research

TRANSITION TO STRATEGIC MARKETING

SECTION III: STRATEGIC MARKETING

IMPERATIVE 1
Determine and Recommend Which Markets to Address

CHAPTER 7
Identifying and Choosing Opportunities

IMPERATIVE 2
Identify and Target Market Segments

CHAPTER 8
Market Segmentation and Targeting

IMPERATIVE 3
Set Strategic Direction and Positioning

CHAPTER 9
Market Strategy – Integrating Firm Efforts for Marketing Success

CHAPTER 10
Managing through the Life Cycle

CHAPTER 11
Managing Brands

SECTION IV: IMPLEMENTING THE MARKET STRATEGY

IMPERATIVE 4
Design the Market Offer

PART A: PROVIDING CUSTOMER VALUE

PART B: COMMUNICATING CUSTOMER VALUE

PART C: DELIVERING CUSTOMER VALUE

PART D: GETTING PAID FOR CUSTOMER VALUE

CHAPTER 12
Managing the Product Line

CHAPTER 15
Integrated Marketing Communications

CHAPTER 18
Distribution Decisions

CHAPTER 19
Critical Underpinnings of Pricing Decisions

CHAPTER 13
Managing Services and Customer Service

CHAPTER 16
Mass and Digital Communication

CHAPTER 20
Setting Prices

CHAPTER 14
Developing New Products

CHAPTER 17
Directing and Managing the Field Sales Effort

IMPERATIVE 5
Secure Support from Other Functions

CHAPTER 21
Ensuring the Firm Implements the Market Offer as Planned

IMPERATIVE 6
Monitor and Control

CHAPTER 22
Monitoring and Controlling Firm Functioning and Performance

SECTION V: SPECIAL MARKETING TOPICS

CHAPTER 23
International, Regional, and Global Marketing

IMPERATIVE 1

Determine and Recommend Which Markets to Address

CHAPTER 7

IDENTIFYING AND CHOOSING OPPORTUNITIES

I am going to wait for the next big thing.

— Steve Jobs[1]

LEARNING OBJECTIVES

When you have completed this chapter, you will be able to:

- Understand marketing's role in identifying new opportunities.
- Ensure the firm makes its strategic decisions with marketing input.
- Determine the fundamental elements that comprise a strategy for growth.
- Develop criteria for evaluating individual opportunities.
- Assess alternative ways to implement a strategy for growth.

OPENING CASE: ZIPCAR

Established nationwide firms in car-rental include Advantage, Alamo, Avis, Budget, Dollar, Enterprise, Hertz, National, and Thrifty. Hertz, Avis, and National mainly compete on location and service, especially in airports. Advantage, Alamo, Budget, Dollar, and Thrifty compete on price. Enterprise became the leading car-rental firm overall by offering replacement cars for owners whose cars were being repaired. Surely the car-rental market is saturated? Not according to Zipcar, a car-sharing firm.

Car-sharing started in Germany in the 1980s, but Zipcar was first in the U.S. Car-rental firms traditionally offered minimum one-day rentals to customers with good driving and credit records and meet

age requirements. By contrast, Zipcar is a membership organization — customers pay an annual $50 membership fee and rent by the hour. The more than 50 cities with car-sharing service include Atlanta, Baltimore, Boston, Chicago, Gainesville, Los Angeles, New York, Philadelphia, Pittsburgh, Portland, San Diego, San Francisco, Seattle, Washington D.C., and Vancouver. In 2010, Zipcar entered Europe by acquiring London-based Streetcar.

Zipcar members share cars; each Zipcar has a home location in a pay garage, street, or other designated location. Members can book 30 makes and models including hybrids, Smart cars, sedans, pickup trucks, SUVs, minivans, and sports cars online or by phone. They open the car with an access card (similar to a credit card), return the car to the same location, and check out with the card. Fees are around $10 per hour including gas and insurance; Zipcar also offers monthly arrangements for specified hours (like 6 p.m. to midnight, Monday to Friday) and daily commuting. Zipcar's small staff monitors cars via wireless and computer technologies. Some cities, hoping to ease congestion, provide free or subsidized parking.

City dwellers use Zipcars evenings and weekends; important customer groups for daily use are business and government. Portland uses car-sharing for its motor pool fleet, aiming to reduce annual operating, maintenance, and fuel costs by 25 percent and cut capital outlays. Discussing its business membership, mainly for hybrids, Starbucks' spokespeople said, "We need our partners [employees] to be able to take short trips to meetings and for other business purposes." And, "The Zipcar program and hybrid offering is a win-win for the environment and Starbucks. We reduce the number of vehicles ... and offer environmentally friendly, hassle-free mobility for our partners."

Zipcar also partners with university parking and transportation departments to offer car-sharing to students, faculty, and staff. Because many students are 18–20 and ineligible for car rentals, Zipcar has an under–21 program that offers special deals. In 2011, Zipcar agreed to use Ford cars at campus locations; Ford subsidizes student Zipcar membership and rental fees. Zipcar has 10,000 vehicles and 650,000 members and 80 percent market share; Hertz with Connect by Hertz, Enterprise, and U-Haul offer car sharing in some urban locations.

> **CASE QUESTION**
>
> Do you think Zipcar will be successful in the long run? Why or why not? Do you think Connect by Hertz or Enterprise's WeCar will be successful? Why or why not? How should these market changes affect Zipcar's long-run strategy?

In Chapters 3 through 6, we learned to develop *insight* into the M4Cs — markets, customers, competitors, company, and complementers; and then made the transition to form *planning assumptions.* Now we shift direction to make *decisions* and focus on the six marketing imperatives. Marketing's first, and arguably most important, imperative is to influence firm decisions about which markets to address. *Market-choice decisions* are typically strategic for the firm or business unit. CEOs or general managers usually decide which opportunities are the most attractive, but marketing plays a critical role.

Growth is critical for injecting vigor into the firm, providing resources and rewards, keeping management on its toes, and retaining talent. Marketing should identify growth opportunities by systematically screening many alternatives. These opportunities may be in the firm's core business, in adjacencies close to the core, or further afield. In consumer truck rental, U-Haul was barely breaking even with an older truck fleet, higher maintenance costs, and lower prices than competition. But when No. 2 Ryder exited, U-Haul prospered by tapping an adjacent *profit pool* — accessories like boxes, insurance, trailer rental, and storage space.[2] Examples of successfully identifying opportunities in unrelated areas — *white spaces* — where customer needs were unsatisfied include Zipcar — automobile rental; Cirque du Soleil — neither traditional circus nor theater; NetJets — partial ownership of corporate jets; Starbucks; and Viagra.[3]

Marketing should play a key role in developing screening criteria for individual opportunities and helping make the business case for firm investments. Marketing should assess market

> **Marketing Question**
>
> Can you identify examples of firms that have successfully entered *white spaces*?

potential, validate market size and growth, evaluate likely competitive challenges, and examine individual opportunity alignment with strategic initiatives. Marketing may act as internal entrepreneur, mobilizing resources like market development, R&D, strategic alliances, and acquisitions for developing opportunities.

Some opportunities may be unprofitable in the short run but offer significant long-run potential. Some opportunities surface in good times; others result directly from adverse economic circumstances. Regardless, opportunities may originate in many places. R&D develops new technologies and/or product ideas it believes have market viability. Sales and engineering may propose strategic alliances or buying, selling, or licensing technology. When opportunities have marketing implications, marketing should be part of the discussion. The firm should make go/no-go decisions with the best available marketing insight — including voice-of-the-customer input. Unfortunately, in many firms, finance drives acquisition and divestiture decisions with little or no marketing input.

Figure 7.1 presents a systematic three-stage approach for developing, selecting, and implementing opportunities:

1. **Strategy for growth**: Provides guidance and analysis to generate opportunities.
2. **Screening criteria**: Used to evaluate and select individual opportunities.
3. **Implementation**: Specific actions the firm may take to achieve its objectives.

KEY IDEA

➤ A comprehensive approach for securing higher growth comprises:

• **Strategy for growth**
• Screening criteria
• Implementation

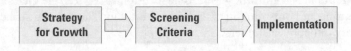

FIGURE 7.1

A COMPREHENSIVE APPROACH FOR SECURING HIGHER GROWTH

STRATEGY FOR GROWTH

Some pizza restaurant chains are highly profitable, but IBM does not make pizzas. Smartphones (like the iPhone) are fast growing and profitable, but Walmart does not produce them. Downloading music from the Internet is big business, but Carnival Cruise Lines does not offer this service. Each opportunity seems attractive, but these firms did not invest. Why not?

The reason is simple. Each of these firms has a **strategy for growth**; their strategies did not surface these options. A strategy for growth uses a set of frameworks to help the firm evaluate current businesses, decide which businesses *to be in*, and which businesses *not to be in*. Figure 7.2 shows that firms can generate attractive opportunities using four components: **vision**, **mission**, **growth path**, and **timing of entry**.

FIGURE 7.2

COMPONENTS OF A STRATEGY FOR GROWTH

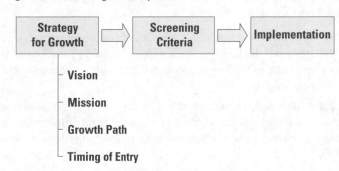

KEY IDEA

➤ A strategy for growth has four components:

• Vision
• Mission
• Growth path
• Timing of entry

VISION

Vision is a description of the firm's ideal future state — an impressionistic picture of what the future should be.[4] *Corporate vision* concerns the firm as a whole; *business-unit vision* focuses on an individual business. Good visions set a broad direction — they should inspire employees for the long run. A good vision is not too broad, nor too specific nor easily achievable.[5]

Visions

Ford Motor Company – circa 1920s – "A car in every garage."

Microsoft – 1980s and 1990s – "A personal computer on every desk"; 2000s – "To enable people and businesses throughout the world to realize their full potential"

These examples show the power of a good vision. Ford's vision led to the Model T, the production-line system, and continual price reductions. Ford's share of the U.S. automobile market reached over 50 percent by the mid-1920s. Microsoft had one vision for much of the 1980s and 1990s; when this became outmoded, Microsoft created a new, broader vision.

Marketing should make sure the vision is outward-looking. Without marketing input, vision can easily be too inwardly focused on what the firm does well. Of course, firm actions must support the vision — simply stating a goal doesn't mean you will achieve it. One CEO publicly announced his firm's vision: "to become our customers' most preferred supplier across all purchasing categories." This statement raised customer expectations far beyond the firm's ability to deliver, ultimately creating customer dissatisfaction. British Airways (BA) CEO made a similar mistake, publicly committing to "excellent customer service." He then single-mindedly pursued cost-cutting and outsourcing that alienated BA staff. The ensuing strike stranded tens of thousands very unhappy customers.

Developing a vision is one thing; having employees actively embrace the vision is another. When senior executives and consultants construct the firm's vision in isolation, employee buy-in may be minimal. When the firm involves employees, vision takes longer to develop. But broad participation and input lead to better visions. At Aramark, the large Philadelphia-based services firm, more than 8,500 employees participated directly in developing the new vision.

MISSION

The firm creates a vision to provide a lofty aspirational view of its overall direction. **Mission** guides the firm's search for market opportunities more directly.[6] A well-developed mission keeps the firm focused in a limited arena where success is likely. Mission avoids dispersing firm energy and resources in multiple directions. An ideal mission codifies opportunity areas where the firm does well or aspires to do well. A firm with several business units should develop missions at both the corporate and business-unit levels; the corporate mission should encompass individual business missions.

ARTICULATING THE MISSION. Mission states what the firm/business unit *will do*; by what it omits, mission also states what the firm/business unit *will not do*! (What business shall we be in? What business shall we *not* be in?) Three internal resource (IR) dimensions and two externally focused (EF) dimensions are critical:

- **IR — Core ingredient or natural resource.** The firm maximizes value from a core ingredient or natural resource. *We are a forest products company* implies the firm could make and sell products based on many technologies to many markets, so long as they were made from wood.

- **IR — Product/service.** This firm's mission focuses on a product/service. *We are an automobile firm* directs the firm to make cars that may use various fuels — alcohol, diesel, ethanol, gasoline, hydrogen, or natural gas, based on several technologies — electro-mechanical, fuel cell, gas-turbine, internal-combustion, hybrid, or steam.

KEY IDEA

➤ *Vision* is the description of an ideal future state for a firm or business unit. Vision sets a broad direction for the firm. When developed with employee participation, a vision can inspire the entire organization for the long run.

Marketing Question

How do you evaluate the following visions? Are they too broad? Are they too narrow? Are they inspiring?

- IBM (1990s) – "To lead big companies into the brave new networked world, IBM will devise their technology strategies, build and run their systems, and ultimately become the architect and repository for corporate computing, tying together not just companies, but entire industries."

- Merck – "We are in the business of preserving and improving human life."

KEY IDEA

➤ The firm's *mission* should guide its search for opportunity.

➤ Five approaches to developing mission are:

Internally focused:
- Core ingredient or natural resource
- Product or service
- Technology

Externally focused:
- Customer needs
- Market or market segment

Marketing Question

Based on your knowledge and/or online research, write one-sentence missions for AXA, Citigroup, Comcast, Disney, ExxonMobil, Facebook, Ford, GE, Groupon, Hitachi, IP, Morgan Stanley, Novartis, Siemens, Toyota, Twitter, Verizon, Yahoo!, and/or Xerox.

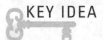

KEY IDEA

➤ The firm's mission can use a single approach or combine approaches.

➤ The firm should pro-actively revise its mission.

- **IR — Technology.** The firm focuses on a core technology. *We are an electronics firm* directs the search for opportunities to electronics, using any raw material and selling products into any market, so long as the core technology were electronics.
- **EF — Customer needs.** This mission directs the firm to serve customers having a specific set of needs, with any product, using any technology. *We satisfy people's transportation needs* could embrace making bicycles, automobiles, trucks, helicopters, or airplanes.[7]
- **EF — Market/market segment.** A firm with this type of mission could make many products, using various raw materials and technologies targeted at a single segment. FMCG firms like P&G and Unilever offer many household and personal-care products to consumers.

The firm/business unit can choose among these dimensions to develop missions, or may combine dimensions. Courtyard by Marriott's mission — *To provide economy and quality-minded frequent business travelers with a premier lodging facility, which is consistently perceived as clean, comfortable, well maintained, and attractive, staffed by friendly, attentive, and efficient people* — combines product/service and market/market segment.

EVOLVING THE MISSION. Typically, successful firms evolve their missions. If opportunities are scarce with the current mission, or a target of opportunity appears, the firm should consider *broadening* the mission, but be cautious about the modified direction. Cannondale successfully expanded its mission from high-end bicycles to embrace dirt bikes and all-terrain vehicles, but Cisco's B2C entry with the Flip video camera was a failure.

Some firms *narrow* missions by dropping products, divesting businesses, or breaking up into two or more businesses. DuPont exited oil and textile fibers; Corning divested healthcare services and consumer products. Other firms *return to the core business* (*stick to the knitting*): Under CEO Art Laffley, P&G grew from its core — laundry products, baby diapers, feminine care, and hair care; built on strengths to enter new beauty and personal care categories; and expanded in developing markets. Some firms like Guinness — the Irish brewer — narrow product scope but place major effort on *expanding* geographic scope.

GROWTH PATH

Mission provides a broad approach to identifying potential opportunities; **growth path** is more focused. Growth path is specifically concerned with the trade-off between expected financial return and risk. The firm should consider three factors:

- Revenue and profit potential of opportunities relative to the required investment
- Core competencies from its portfolio of businesses, technologies, products, and markets
- Assessment of risk

The firm's expected financial returns, competencies, and risks from the opportunities it pursues coexist in a dynamic relationship. By investing in one opportunity, the firm may develop new competencies. These enhanced competencies may, in turn, make previously unattractive opportunities attractive. Expected financial returns and risks also change.

Figure 7.3 shows that the growth-path matrix uses two dimensions — *market* and *product/technology* — to analyze opportunities. We trisect each dimension — *existing*, *related*, and *new* — to develop nine matrix cells — A through I. Each cell represents a different type of opportunity. For ease of exposition, we combine individual cells to develop four broad approaches to growth: *market penetration*, *product growth*, *market growth*, and *product and market diversification*.

	Existing	Related	New (to firm)
New	**Market Growth 2:** Market Expansion (G)	**Business Expansion:** Concentric Products (H)	**Conglomeration** (I)
Related	**Market Growth 1:** Market Extension (D)	**Business Extension** (E)	**Business Expansion:** Concentric Markets (F)
Existing	**Market Penetration** (A)	**Product Growth 1:** Product Extension (B)	**Product Growth 2:** Product Expansion (C)

Market (vertical axis)

Product/Technology

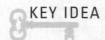

FIGURE 7.3

THE GROWTH-PATH MATRIX

KEY IDEA

➤ The four fundamental *growth-path* directions are:

• Market penetration
• Product growth
• Market growth
• Product and market diversification

These four growth directions comprise nine individual growth paths.

MARKET PENETRATION (CELL A). Most firms spend significant resources pursuing market-penetration strategies. The firm focuses effort on existing (or slightly modified) products in existing markets. The firm bases growth on core competencies, and has minimal *knowledge* risk. Of course, the firm may face significant risk from competitors.

PRODUCT GROWTH (CELLS B AND C). The firm brings new products to existing markets. A ski resort that adds ice-skating, downhill sledding, snowmobiling, and tubing pursues a product-growth strategy. *Product growth 1 (product extension — cell B)* and *product growth 2 (product expansion — cell C)* differ in the degree of product newness. Product extensions relate to current products; product expansions are unrelated and hence more risky. For a bank skilled in making corporate loans, lock-box services are a product extension. Complex derivatives, requiring significant new technical expertise, are a product expansion.

MARKET GROWTH (CELLS D AND G). The firm sells existing products to new markets via market development. *Market growth 1 (market extension — cell D)* and *market growth 2 (market expansion — cell G)* differ in degree of market newness. For the bank skilled in corporate loans, loans to public and/or nonprofit enterprises is a market extension. Loans to individuals is a market expansion. Generally, market expansions are more risky than market extensions.

Geographic expansion is a popular market growth option.

PRODUCT AND MARKET DIVERSIFICATION (CELLS E, F, H, AND I). A critical characteristic of *market penetration, product growth,* and *market growth* is that at least one of the two growth dimensions is *existing.* For product and market diversification, both *market and product/technology* change to either *related* or *new.* Opportunities are more risky, and the business as a whole shifts direction.

Business extension (cell E) requires moderate change for both *market* and *product/technology.* Nike made a product extension when it added athletic apparel to its core footwear line. By contrast, adding sporty street apparel was a business extension — *related* product to *related* market. *Business expansion* requires new products and related markets *(concentric markets — cell F),* or new markets and related products *(concentric products — cell H).* Risk is greatest in *conglomeration (cell I) —* new products and new markets. Conglomeration by internal development is generally more risky than by acquisition, but many conglomerate acquisitions also fail. Quaker purchased Snapple from Triarc for $1.7 billion but made significant errors in distribution and promotion. Three years later, Triarc repurchased Snapple for $300 million. Another conglomeration failure:

Under CEO Jean Paul Messier, a French water utility firm renamed itself Vivendi and began acquiring entertainment, media, and communications firms. Vivendi purchased the Seagram Company to secure Universal Studios and bought USA Networks' entertainment assets — it also began divesting water companies. When Vivendi faced bankruptcy, the board fired Messier and started selling assets. Vivendi exited water, and now focuses on media and telecommunications.

CHOOSING THE *RIGHT* GROWTH PATH. To identify and separate worthwhile opportunities from others typically requires significant marketing research and analysis. The firm should identify the scope of the opportunity, competition, and assess its ability to deliver the necessary customer value to secure differential advantage. More generally, the firm should evaluate its ability to be successful in various growth paths. For example, the firm may perform well with *market growth* but poorly with *product and market diversification*. If so, the firm should probably favor *market-growth* opportunities and set a higher bar for *product and market diversifications*.

As a starting point for developing decision rules about new opportunities, the firm should conduct a retrospective growth-path analysis. It could go back, say, five years and classify each pursued opportunity into one of the nine cells, then assess success or failure. The firm may discover some areas where it generally performs well and others where it performs poorly.

TIMING OF ENTRY

Along with identifying the *right* growth path, when to seize an opportunity — **timing of entry** — is also crucial. Chapter 3 discusses five product life-cycle stages — *introduction, early growth, late growth, maturity,* and *decline.* Early stages have high uncertainty in both products and markets, but uncertainty decreases as the life cycle evolves. Correspondingly, competitive pressures typically increase. Figure 7.4 explores links between the first four life-cycle stages and specific strategic options for timing of market entry — *pioneer, follow-the-leader, segmenter,* and *me-too.*[8]

Marketing Question

Pick a country other than your own. Which firms from that country earn revenues from countries in more than three continents? What other diversification directions have these firms taken?

FIGURE 7.4

TIMING OF MARKET ENTRY

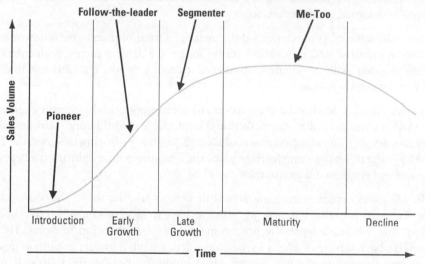

PIONEER. *Pioneers* blaze trails and create new markets via consistent and extensive R&D. Pioneers accept risk and understand that failure often accompanies success. Pioneers possess the R&D skills and internal processes to consistently develop new products/services, and the marketing capabilities to open up new markets. Pioneers have sufficient resources to support heavy R&D expenditures and fund market development; sometimes market-entry costs exceed R&D spending. Firms that commonly pioneer new products include Apple, DuPont, IBM, Intel, 3M, Sony, major pharmaceutical firms (like GSK, Novartis, and Pfizer), and biotech firms. Pioneers are not always successful, even when they bring products to market. Apple pioneered personal digital assistants (PDA) with the Newton, but Palm became market leader. Regardless, Apple also pioneered paid-music downloads (iTunes, iPod), smartphones (iPhone), and tablet computers (iPad).

FOLLOW-THE-LEADER. *Follow-the-leader* firms enter rapidly growing markets on the heels of pioneers. Pioneers make large research investments to develop innovative new products/ services; follow-the-leader firms focus on development. In what is sometimes called the used-apple policy, the *follower* lets the pioneer take the first bite. If the apple is fine, the follower enters; if not, it passes.[9] Follow-the-leader firms are happy for pioneers to invest heavily in R&D and market development — followers pursue the pioneer quickly with developmental R&D. Market insight is critical; followers should enter as soon as possible after a successful pioneer. A successful follow-the-leader should have:

- Vision of serving a mass market
- Good competitive intelligence to develop products/services as soon as possible
- Good developmental engineers to leverage/enhance the pioneer's successful research
- Proactive patent lawyers to identify weak spots in pioneer patents
- Financial strength and commitment to outspend the pioneer
- Ability to differentiate offers and deliver superior customer value.
- Will and persistence to succeed[10]

Many industry leaders like FedEx (air package delivery), Gillette (razors), Google (search), Intel (microprocessors), Microsoft (operating system software, browsers, and search), Pampers (disposable diapers), and Xerox (copiers) entered their markets as follow-the-leader firms.[11] Ford and Nissan both introduced hybrid cars many years after Toyota.

SEGMENTER. *Segmenters* enter established markets in late growth by adding value for specific segments. Segmenter strategies can be very effective in maturing markets. As customers gain knowledge and experience, their preferences typically become more specific. Using insightful marketing research, segmenters identify the unique needs of specific customer groups, then offer specially designed products/services.

Segmenter skill sets and competencies differ markedly from pioneers and follow-the-leaders. Technological expertise and innovation are no longer the driving forces. Segmenters require marketing research skills to identify unsatisfied customer needs, but also the flexibility to address narrow market niches.

Medical device maker Medtronic used successful segmentation and platform engineering to capture market share in cardiac pacemakers and implantable defibrillators.[12] Airbus and Boeing use modular design to produce commercial aircraft families — Boeing designed the 707, 727, 737, and 757 aircraft on the same fuselage platform. The automobile industry is a heavy user of these design and engineering approaches:

ME-TOO. *Me-too-ers* enter mature markets with limited product lines. They base low-price/low-cost strategies on value engineering, efficient high-volume production (often in low-cost countries), low overhead, aggressive procurement, and great attention to detail. They spend little on R&D, have similar products to market leaders, are often leaders in process innovation, and have very focused marketing. Generic drug producers, notably Teva (Israel), are *poster children* for this strategy, although technological copying difficulties may cause problems. Me-too-ers can wreak havoc in segmented markets where firms compete with value-added offers. Many Chinese firms pursue this approach.

CHOOSING THE *RIGHT* TIMING-OF-ENTRY STRATEGY. Similar to growth-path decisions, the firm should identify which *timing-of-entry* strategy best fits its capabilities, then match this strategy to market opportunities. Of course, as markets evolve, the firm must also evolve its capabilities.

SCREENING CRITERIA: EVALUATING OPPORTUNITIES

We showed how growth strategy helps the firm identify opportunities; but which specific opportunities should the firm pursue? Figure 7.5 shows five **screening criteria** — *objectives*, *compatibility (fit)*, *core competence*, and *synergy* — that help the firm evaluate opportunities and decide where to invest.

KEY IDEA

➤ The four *timing-of-entry* options are:

- Pioneer
- Follow-the-leader
- Segmenter
- Me-too

These options correspond, respectively, to entry in various stages of the product life cycle:

- Introduction
- Early growth
- Late growth
- Maturity

➤ The firm must match capabilities to timing-of-entry strategy. Capabilities must evolve as markets evolve.

KEY IDEA

➤ A comprehensive approach for securing higher growth comprises:

- Strategy for growth
- **Screening criteria**
- Implementation

FIGURE 7.5

SCREENING CRITERIA

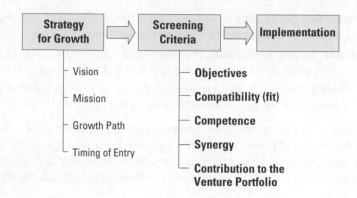

KEY IDEA

➤ The firm should consider five perspectives when evaluating opportunities:

• Objectives
• Compatibility (fit)
• Core competence
• Synergy
• Contribution to the venture portfolio

🔑 **KEY IDEA**

➤ In setting *objectives*, the firm should strike a balance between:

• Revenue and profit growth
• Risk
• Timing
• Stability
• Flexibility

....

OBJECTIVES

The crucial first criterion for an investment opportunity is to satisfy firm objectives. Revenue and profit growth are critical for creating shareholder value, but unmitigated growth can be a real problem. The firm must temper growth ambitions with concern for risk, timing, stability, and flexibility.

REVENUE AND PROFIT GROWTH. To assess revenue and profit potential, the firm should consider both financial and non-financial measures. Standard financial measures include timing of cash flows, payback, return on investment (ROI), profit margin, net present value (NPV), and internal rate of return (IRR).[13] Leading indicators of profit performance embrace market size, expected market growth rate, market potential, forces driving market growth, number/strength of competitors, and market share forecasts; these factors influence revenue, cost, and profit forecasts.

Sometimes firms reject new opportunities because forecast performance is inferior to *historic* performance with some existing product(s). This comparison is incorrect. The firm should compare *forecast* market share, revenues, and profits from the new opportunity versus *forecast* market share, revenues, and profits without it. Despite a significant lead in expensive laser printers, HP added inexpensive inkjet printers (lower margins) to avoid losing market share.

RISK. The firm must weigh forecast revenues and profits against the risk and required investment. The firm should consider the opportunity's return-risk profile and the impact that each opportunity has on other opportunities. Generally, potential return and risk are correlated, but some opportunities offer good returns at low risk.[14]

TIMING. In addition to financial return and risk, the firm must consider the timing of contribution to profits. A moderate return opportunity that delivers profits in the medium term may be more attractive than a higher return opportunity promising profits much later.

STABILITY. Suppose the firm must choose between two opportunities: A — high growth, significant profit variability; B — lower growth, low profit variability. The firm may prefer the lower growth, low variability — higher *stability* — option. Schneider Electric Mexico focuses on markets it can serve through existing distributors. Schneider believes these revenues are more stable than revenues from potentially more profitable large electricity generation projects requiring major investments.

FLEXIBILITY. All firms face increasing environmental change and complexity. No matter how good the firm's forecasting, it may be blindsided by unexpected events. *Insurance policies* give the firm *flexibility* to deal with changed circumstances:

• **Acquisition.** Intel, Microsoft, and Cisco acquire firms with positions in adjacent markets.
• **Joint technology agreements.** Oil companies often form partnerships for oil-drilling platforms and operations, like Texaco and Shell in the Gulf of Mexico.

- **Partial ownership.** Major drug companies frequently take this approach with biotechnology firms. BMS purchased shares in cancer-drug developer ImClone.
- **Research and development (R&D).** The firm hedges its bets by investing in competing fields. Car companies invest in hybrid, electric, and fuel cell technologies.
- **Venture capital.** The firm provides venture capital to startup companies but retains options to increase ownership. Cisco is a leader in this approach.

Originally a textile power-loom producer, Toyota morphed into automobiles. Today its investments include prefabricated houses, resort development, helicopter operations and surveying, airport management, advertising agency, consulting, horticulture, golf course operations, and a professional soccer team. Some, but not all, have synergies with its automobile business.

COMPATIBILITY (FIT)

Can the firm be successful in the opportunity? The firm should examine three core types of compatibility (fit): product-market fit, product-company fit, and company-market fit.

PRODUCT-MARKET FIT. Is the product appropriate for the market? Restated: Does the product satisfy customer needs in target market segments better than its competitors? Firms most often assess *product-market fit* through ongoing marketing research and market-testing. Timing is particularly important in assessing product-market fit as the firm and environment evolve.

PRODUCT-COMPANY FIT. Does the firm possess the financial, human, and other abilities/resources to succeed? Can the firm successfully upgrade its efforts as the market evolves? Sometimes a firm has great product-market fit but lacks distribution strength to reach customers. Independent inventors often have this problem — product-market fit is great, but product-company fit is poor.

COMPANY-MARKET FIT. Can the firm compete effectively in the market? Does it have sufficient customer insight, reputation, resources, and skills to defeat competitors? Product-market fit and product-company fit may both be fine, but poor *company-market fit* may lead to a reject decision. Geographic expansion offers many examples. Suppose a foreign market is attractive for the firm's product — good product-market fit, and the firm is skilled at producing, promoting, and distributing the product in its home market — good company-product fit. Little experience in the foreign market — poor company-market fit — may lead to opportunity rejection.

CORE COMPETENCE

Core competences are knowledge, skills, and other capabilities/resources the firm possesses.[15] The *core-competence* criterion is straightforward: Does the firm *bring anything to the party*? Can the firm *take anything from the party*? More formally: Does this opportunity leverage the firm's core competencies or allow it to develop new ones? If the answer is *no* to both questions, the firm should probably reject the opportunity. But one *yes* may be sufficient to continue.

Generally, the firm is better off pursuing opportunities that use its core competences. The firm can more easily gain differential advantage, like Coca-Cola introducing a new sports drink or Toyota launching a new automobile. Two Boston entrepreneurs developed a competence in buying common Internet domain names like beer.com, creditcards.com, and chocolate.com, developing sites, then selling. But core competence is not the only criterion — the opportunity must satisfy other criteria. Further, an opportunity may be attractive *even if the firm has little competence* — if it can *secure* competence by investing. Intel abandoned its core competence in memory chips, but gained competence in microprocessor technology and manufacturing. When Jeff Bezos left New York for Seattle in his secondhand car, he had little competence for building Amazon, but it became the leading online retailer.

Marketing Question

Can you identify three examples of successful product-market fit? Can you identify three examples of failed product-market fit? What are the risks of unsuccessful product-market fit?

KEY IDEA

➤ The three important types of *compatibility (fit)* are:

- Product-market fit
- Product-company fit
- Company-market fit

KEY IDEA

➤ Core competence comprises the firm's knowledge, skills, and capabilities.

SYNERGY

Synergy explores how an opportunity relates to existing firm capabilities/resources.[16] *Positive synergy* reflects the notion that 2+2 can be greater than 4! Synergy kicks in when the firm uses existing resources for an opportunity. If the firm sells a new product through existing distributors, like P&G or Unilever adding new products for supermarkets, it gains distribution synergy. If the firm makes the product in existing facilities, it gains manufacturing synergy. The firm should not decline an opportunity for lack of positive synergy — but positive synergy can enhance profits.

When 2+2 is less than 4, *negative synergy* is at work; pursuing a new opportunity may erode revenues and profits from existing products. Allergy-relief prescription drug Claritin was a major profit-maker for Schering Plough (SP); SP launched an over-the-counter version to reach the larger market for non-prescription allergy relief medicines. Prescription Claritin sales dropped more than 40 percent.

KEY IDEA

➤ Synergy expresses the idea that 2 + 2 = 5.

CONTRIBUTION TO THE VENTURE PORTFOLIO

In addition to considering opportunities individually, the firm should consider all opportunities as elements in its **venture portfolio**. A firm with good cash flow but few growth businesses may invest heavily on longer-term, higher-risk options. A firm with little cash may focus on short-term, low/moderate-risk opportunities. Generally, conservatively managed firms invest in low-risk opportunities that pay off quickly. Aggressive firms accept greater risk for potentially higher returns that pay off in the long term. Potential return and risk are typically correlated, but some opportunities may offer good returns at low risk.

IMPLEMENTING GROWTH STRATEGIES

P&G funded a new group, Corporate New Ventures, with $250 million seed money. Using *My Idea*, a corporate collaboration network, P&G employees funnel ideas to an innovation panel. Accepted projects tap into P&G's entire global resource base. Within two years, P&G launched 58 new products. Swiffer, the successful new cleaning product, was launched in 10 months — half the normal time.

Figure 7.6 shows several options for implementing the firm's growth strategy.[17]

INTERNAL DEVELOPMENT

Many firms put significant effort into *internal development* of new products/services. Internal development is appropriate in all cells of the growth-path matrix and for all timing-of-entry options. Some evidence suggests a strong positive correlation between R&D spending and corporate profitability.[18] Internal development is not just for technologists and engineers; marketing can play a major role in directing R&D efforts by infusing external insight at all developmental stages.

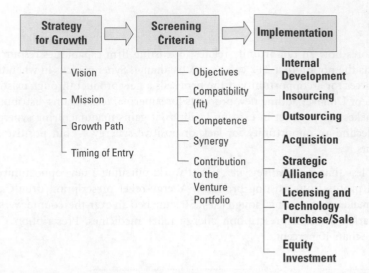

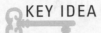

FIGURE 7.6

IMPLEMENTING
GROWTH STRATEGIES

KEY IDEA

➤ A comprehensive
approach for
securing higher
growth comprises:

• Strategy for growth
• Screening criteria
• **Implementation**

KEY IDEA

➤ Options for implement-
ing a growth strategy
include:

• Internal development
• Insourcing
• Outsourcing
• Acquisition
• Strategic alliance
• Licensing and
technology
purchase/sale
• Equity investment

Advantages of internal development over alternative growth modes are:

• **Control.** The firm has control over the entire development process. The firm purchases (or leases) required resources and makes all decisions about suppliers and distributors.

• **Cost.** Internal development is typically less expensive than securing new products by acquisition and other means.

Disadvantages of internal development are:

• **Expertise.** The firm must successfully direct the R&D effort, or the resulting products may require commercialization skills the firm does not possess.

• **Resources.** Some resources may be unavailable, or too expensive to develop/ acquire.

• **Time.** Market windows are increasingly short; internal development takes time.

INSOURCING

The firm captures more added value in the supply chain by undertaking additional activities in developing, producing, marketing, distributing, and promoting. The firm can expand upstream by conducting supplier activities — *backward integration*, or downstream by conducting customer activities — *forward integration*. Adjacencies (activities closely related to core competences) are prime insourcing candidates and may help develop new core competences.

OUTSOURCING

Outsourcing is the opposite of insourcing — the firm engages other firms to undertake activities it previously conducted in-house. With outsourcing, the firm can better focus resources on delivering customer value and securing differential advantage. Firms outsource a wide range of activities like managing information systems and technology infrastructure, accounts payable, benefits management and payroll, and procurement.

A common contemporary outsourcing aspect is *offshoring* — contracting with non-U.S-based firms. A common area is customer service operations. We're sure many readers have called a help desk and spoken with someone in India, Malaysia, or the Philippines. Cost reduction typically drives offshoring, but partners in different time zones can also provide scalable, flexible staffing. Quality control is important, especially when customer care is involved.

ACQUISITION

We learned earlier that the firm can use **acquisitions** — individual business units or entire firms, to gain competences that provide customer value and secure differential advantage. Generally, growth by acquisition has a speed advantage — the firm gains immediate access to new products and/or markets. The firm also gains supporting infrastructure — human resources, operational capabilities, and systems and processes. Firms that grow extensively by acquisition include Cisco, GE, J&J, Microsoft, and Oracle. Former IBM CEO Lou Gerstner said:

> *IBM made 90 acquisitions during my tenure. The most successful were those that fit neatly into an organic growth plan. IBM's purchase of Informix is a great example. We were neck-and-neck with Oracle in the database business, and Informix, another database company, had lost its momentum and market leadership. We didn't need to buy Informix to get into the database business or to shore up a weak position. However, we did acquire a set of customers more quickly and more efficiently than we could have following a go-it-alone strategy.*[19]

But acquisitions are no panacea. Acquiring successful firms/business units can be expensive; marrying the cultures of acquired and acquiring firms/businesses may also be difficult. The important question is whether or not an acquisition adds value. Value creation depends on the specific acquisition, but we can usefully distinguish between two very different types:

MAJOR ACQUISITIONS. These multi-million-dollar acquisitions often make the headlines: Alcan's acquisition of Pechiney (aluminum) and BHP's acquisition of Alcan; AOL/Time Warner; Delta Airlines/Northwest, United Airlines/ Continental, and Boston Scientific's bidding war with J&J for Guidant. But bigger is not always better; many business leaders and scholars have spoken out against these types of acquisitions. They assert that CEO hubris often drives $100 million-plus acquisitions.[20] Academic studies suggest that 70 percent of acquisitions are dilutive for the acquiring firm's shareholders, and that *in the heat of the chase* acquirers typically overpay.[21]

SMALL *FILL-IN* ACQUISITIONS. Small *fill-in* acquisitions complement an existing strategy. Amazon was unsuccessful in selling footwear online, so it acquired Zappos.com (leading online footwear retailer). IBM's experience exemplifies this type of acquisition. Research suggests that modest acquisitions are the most successful, as they are easier to implement, and acquirers may get good deals.[22]

STRATEGIC ALLIANCE

Generally, *strategic alliances* address poor product-company fit and/or poor company-market fit without the capital investment and risks inherent in acquisitions. A good alliance partner complements firm strengths and/or compensates for firm weakness; the combined entity is stronger than either firm acting alone. Prototypical alliances are between small, innovative firms and well-established firms with strong marketing, good customer reputations, and deep pockets.

Strategic alliances can be an attractive way to secure needed resources. But like acquisitions, strategic alliances are no panacea; many fail due to changed objectives by one or more partners, incompatible organizational cultures, insufficient resources, lack of planning, and/or managerial attention.[23] What appears attractive in theory can be difficult to execute in practice.

LICENSING AND TECHNOLOGY PURCHASE/SALE

Licensing and technology purchase are alternative ways to access technology developed by others. In licensing, the licensor owns the technology; the licensee typically pays a minimum royalty (fixed payment regardless of use) plus an earned royalty rate based on volume (units/dollars) or profits. Technology purchasers typically pay a fixed price to own the technology. In both cases, the acquiring firm avoids the risks and expenses of R&D, but may pay a high price to secure successful new technology. Forest Laboratories licenses, develops, and sells drugs developed by small pharmaceutical firms.

EQUITY INVESTMENT

Many firms augment internal development efforts by making *equity investments* — taking partial ownership in startups. Sometimes firms form or *incubate* startups by spinning off their own successful product development efforts. Typically, the firm retains the ability to increase its equity position later.

KEY MESSAGES

Marketing's first imperative is to determine and recommend which markets to address. A marketing perspective should infuse critical strategic decisions — marketing should focus on two areas:

- Identify potential opportunities.
- Provide marketing input for other strategic actions the firm is contemplating.

A systematic approach to developing, selecting, and implementing opportunities has four elements:

- Strategy for growth — frameworks to help the firm decide which businesses to be in/not in:
  - Vision — description of an ideal future state for the firm/business unit.
  - Mission — directly guides the firm's search for opportunity.
  - Growth path — a focused approach to identifying opportunities, trades off return and risk.
  - Timing of entry — market-entry options related to stage of the product life cycle.

- Screening criteria — a method for evaluating individual opportunities. Key considerations:
  - Objectives — including growth, risk, timing, stability, and flexibility.
  - Compatibility (fit) — product-market fit, product-company fit, company-market fit.
  - Core competence — using special capabilities to achieve differential advantage.
  - Synergy — 2 + 2 = 5.
  - Contribution to the venture portfolio.

- Implementation — specific actions to implement the firm's growth strategy:
  - Internal development — new products and services developed via firm efforts.
  - Insourcing — capturing greater value-added, either upstream or downstream.
  - Outsourcing — engaging other firms to conduct needed activities.
  - Acquisition — purchasing an entire firm or business unit.
  - Strategic alliance — an agreement with a partner firm to jointly exploit an opportunity.
  - Licensing and technology purchase — options to access technology developed by others.
  - Equity investment — taking ownership positions in startups.

VIDEOS AND AUDIOS

Marketing Imperative 1   a701 🎧

a701

IMPERATIVE 2

Identify and Target
Market Segments

CHAPTER 8

MARKET
SEGMENTATION
AND TARGETING cv801

To access Q-codes, go to www.ocodes.com

LEARNING OBJECTIVES

When you have completed this chapter, you will be able to:

- Deconstruct a market into readily distinguishable customer groups.
- Recognize differences between market segments and customer segments.
- Select a market segmentation scheme to better understand market opportunities.
- Understand needs and preferences common to customers in each market segment.
- Develop criteria for constructing *good* market segments.
- Assess identifying characteristics for market segments.
- Address several complex issues in developing and engaging market segments.
- Decide which segments to target for marketing effort.
- Understand how different size firms should approach market segmentation.

OPENING CASE: MARRIOTT HOTELS, RESORTS, AND SUITES

In 1985, Marriott Hotels, Resorts, and Suites was a domestic (U.S.) mid- to large-size hotel chain, managing 67,034 rooms at 160 properties. Marriott decided to enhance traveler value by segmenting the market, then targeting selected segments each with a different brand. Then as now, Marriott was the flagship brand. Each new brand supports Marriott's overall brand identity — a commitment to superior customer service — and trains employees to have a passion for service. Employees:

- *Do whatever it takes to take care of customers.*
- *Pay extraordinary attention to detail.*
- *Take pride in their physical surroundings.*
- *Use their creativity to find new ways to meet the needs of customers.*

Marriott believes all customers require a base service level but that customers differ in their willingness to pay for different levels of comfort and luxury. Management also knows that many customers stay a few nights, but a growing number, like business people on assignment, require accommodations for several weeks. Recognizing the varying needs of hotel customers, Marriott was the first major hotel chain to base its strategy on market segmentation. Marriott grew new brands organically, but implemented its strategy in part by acquisition.

Marriott's flagship brand continues to target customers needing fine restaurants, meeting rooms, athletic facilities, and other upscale amenities. But Marriott added several additional brands addressing different segments:

- **Courtyard** — *a moderately priced hotel providing some amenities, like an exercise room and a restaurant for breakfast for business travelers.*

- **Edition Hotels** — *a personal, intimate, individualized, and unique lodging experience.*

- **ExecuStay** — *furnished apartments for stays of 30 days or more.*

- **Fairfield Inn & Suites** — *an inexpensively priced, high quality hotel easily accessible by car, on or near the U.S. main interstate highway system.*

- **Renaissance Hotels** — *an international hotel with upscale amenities.*

- **Residence Inn** — *an extended-stay hotel for job relocation, job assignment, and government contracting.*

- **Ritz-Carlton** — *the ultimate in luxury hotels in urban centers.*

- **SpringHill Suites** — *an all-suites hotel at an upper-moderate price.*

- **TownePlace Suites** — *similar to Residence Inn, but lower priced.*

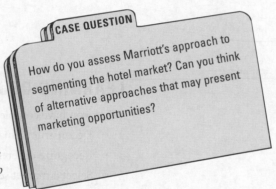

CASE QUESTION

How do you assess Marriott's approach to segmenting the hotel market? Can you think of alternative approaches that may present marketing opportunities?

Each Marriott brand has a distinct personality and style. Marriott works hard to communicate the essence and strength of each brand so that target customers know what to expect. There is some customer crossover, but each brand focuses on a defined market segment. Internal competition is small.

Marriott has achieved extraordinary results from its segmentation and targeting strategy. The Courtyard brand manages more rooms than the entire firm managed in 1985. Total number of rooms managed has increased to more than 600,000 rooms at 3,800 properties.

Market segments and market segmentation are fundamental marketing concepts. Customers in a market either have a variety of different needs, or have similar needs with different priorities. Either way, the firm's job is to place customers in groups so that each group is relatively homogeneous in its needs profile.

A specifically designed market offer satisfies one market segment; a different market segment requires a different market offer. To design and produce effective market offers, the firm must understand each segment's need profile. A firm intent on serving a large market like snack foods must make several market offers, at least one per market segment, to meet varying customer preferences. Typically, a single offer, like potato chips, fails to satisfy the many diverse customers who purchase *snack foods*.

Because customers have different need profiles, marketers must complete three separate, but related, strategic marketing tasks:

1. **Identify market segments.** Figure out the best way to group customers based on market, customer, competitor, and complementer insight — Chapters 3, 4, and 5, using approaches from Chapter 6.

2. **Target market segments.** Resources are always scarce. The firm must decide which segments to target for effort; rarely can a firm address all market segments.

 **KEY IDEA**

➤ Critical strategic marketing decisions are:

- Identify market segments
- Target market segments
- Develop market segment strategy

Note an important distinction between these tasks. *Identifying* market segments is creative and analytic. *Targeting* market segments requires a strategic decision — the firm applies resources to some market segments and ignores others. Identifying and targeting the *right* market segments is a crucial strategic marketing task.

3. **Develop market segment strategy.** The firm develops a market segment strategy, including a positioning statement, for each target segment — Chapter 9. Typically, the firm's *market strategy* combines several *market segment strategies*.

Section 4 — Chapters 12 through 22 — focuses on implementing the market strategy.

THE MARKET SEGMENTATION PROCESS

Most National car rental customers are corporate executives — most Alamo customers are leisure travelers. National and Alamo's parent company combined their operations — airport counters, buses, rental agents, and automobiles. Dual Alamo/National logos were ubiquitous. Customers had difficulty distinguishing the brands. Complaints doubled, especially from National's customers, who paid 10 to 20 percent more than Alamo's customers.

Market segmentation is a conceptual and analytic process critical for developing and implementing effective market strategies. In the market-segmentation process, the firm groups actual and potential customers in a market into various **market segments**. The firm then chooses which segments to **target** for effort. The firm must *position* itself in each target segment (segmentation, targeting, positioning [STP]) and develop a *market segment strategy*. When the segment strategy is set, the firm designs a suitable market offer.

Figure 8.1 describes the process of designing and implementing market offers for each target segment. By executing the process well, the firm:

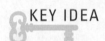

KEY IDEA

➤ Market segmentation is a conceptual and analytic process. Market segmentation is critical for developing and implementing an effective market strategy.

- Secures better insight into the market, customers, competitors, company, and complementers — in particular, customer needs — and forms stronger planning assumptions.
- Develops a clearer focus on market strategy by targeting specific customer groups.
- Identifies opportunities to customize for target segments.
- Designs better offers comprising product, promotion, distribution, and price.
- Secures superior differential advantage and greater customer satisfaction and loyalty.
- Uses resources more efficiently and earns higher profitability.

FIGURE 8.1

SEGMENTATION, TARGETING, AND POSITIONING

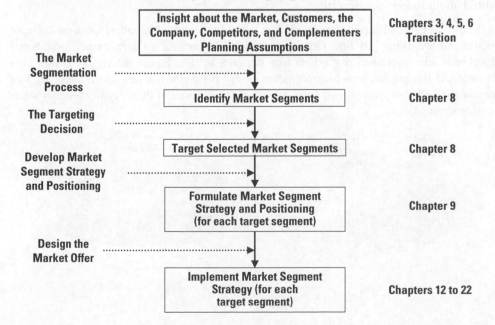

The fundamental premise underlying market segmentation is: In any broadly defined market, customer need profiles are heterogeneous (different). Customers have different needs and/or different priorities of needs. They seek different benefits and values based on these differing need profiles. The segmentation task is to divide the market into several discrete groups of customers, each with relatively homogeneous (similar) need profiles. These customer need profiles differ from segment to segment, so an individual customer falls into one, but only one segment.[1] Alamo/National's parent (previous boxed insert) does not seem to understand that its market comprises two quite different segments.

Market segmentation is often a compromise. At one extreme, the firm develops one strategy, one positioning, and one offer for the entire market — mass marketing. This one-size-fits-all approach is the most efficient, lowest-cost way to address a broad market. But customer need profiles are typically heterogeneous, so many customers would be unsatisfied. At the other extreme, the firm develops a unique or specialized offer for each customer. Such customization ensures a good match between customer needs and the firm's market offer. But firms rarely earn sufficient revenues to offset development and implementation costs. Market segmentation operates between these extremes. The firm identifies homogeneous groups of customers — market segments — with similar need profiles: The firm targets one or more segments, and develops specific strategies, positionings, and offers to satisfy the needs of customers in those segments.

LEVELS OF SEGMENTATION

Segmentation forms smaller, more discrete groups out of a whole. The firm chooses a broad market to address — Marketing Imperative 1 — then identifies several market segments. Within any single market segment, the firm may segment further, forming **customer segments**. Some practitioners define the first-level grouping as market segmentation, and the finer-grained, second-level segmentation as customer segmentation.

We reinforce this idea with a simple example. Suppose half of the students in your class prefer *hot tea*, and half prefer *iced tea*. Figure 8.2 (left) shows a tea supplier that does not understand this segmentation and so offers the best *average* product — *warm tea*. Without alternatives, students wanting tea will purchase *warm tea*. They may desire *hot tea* or *iced tea*, but at least *warm tea* is tea!

Suppose a new supplier understands the segmentation. The supplier offers *hot tea* — the *hot-tea* students switch from *warm tea*. If a third supplier enters with *iced tea*, the *iced-tea* students also switch. The *warm-tea* supplier quickly loses customers because its competitors are more insightful about market segmentation.

How should the original supplier respond? The *hot-tea* and *iced-tea* suppliers focus on different segments and are doing just fine. One response is to segment at an even deeper level. Some students may like *sweetened tea*; others like *unsweetened* tea. Figure 8.2 (right) shows how to deconstruct the market into four segments — *hot sweetened tea*, *hot unsweetened tea*, *iced sweetened tea*, and *iced unsweetened tea*. A focus on one or more of these segments better satisfies customer needs.

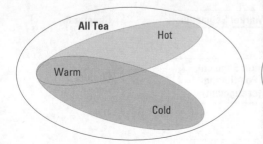
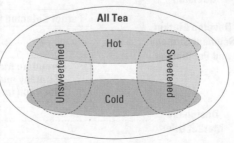

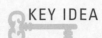

KEY IDEA

➤ The market segmentation process identifies groups of customers. When segmentation is done well, customers within a segment have similar need profiles. Customers in different segments have different need profiles.

Marketing Question

What firms demonstrate the *warm-tea* syndrome — address markets generally, even though customer groups have different need profiles?

FIGURE 8.2

BENEFITS OF FINER-GRAINED SEGMENTATION: A TEA MARKET EXAMPLE

DEVELOPING MARKET SEGMENTS

The firm can approach the market segmentation process from two directions: **customer needs** first or **candidate descriptor (segmentation) variables** first. The firm can also use *qualitative* or *quantitative* approaches.

CUSTOMER NEEDS FIRST. The firm identifies differing customer need profiles, then uses these profiles to form groups. Customers within each group have relatively homogeneous (similar) need profiles, but the various groups have heterogeneous (different) profiles. The firm's second task is to select descriptor (segmentation) variables that identify these groups.

AT&T's data system organization identified three market segments based on complexity of customer communications needs:

- Tier 1 segment — needs satisfied by common *off-the-shelf* products.

- Tier 2 segment — needs satisfied by *off-the-shelf* products plus some options.

- Tier 3 segment — requires tailored solutions.

AT&T's three segments seem sensible — each segment's needs differ from the other segments. AT&T's challenge is to identify distinguishing customer characteristics in each segment. Tier 1: What characteristics define customers that want *off-the-shelf* products? Are these small companies or large companies? Do they compete in specific industries? Are they located in specific geographic areas?

CANDIDATE DESCRIPTOR (SEGMENTATION) VARIABLES FIRST. The firm uses candidate descriptor variables to construct customer groups. Then it searches for homogeneous (similar) need profiles within each group, and heterogeneous (different) need profiles across groups. If the firm cannot find *good* need profiles — similarity within groups and differences across groups, it tries again with different descriptors.

Geography and demography are popular categories of descriptor (segmentation) variables. MTV frequently uses country or geography when tailoring customer offers: MTV operates 38 separate nationally focused channels like MTV Romania and MTV Indonesia. In the Philippines, local hamburger chain Jollibee (69 percent market share) outsells McDonald's (16 percent) by using national origin and demographics to better meet Filipinos' needs. Jollibee's stores in Asia and California target customers of Filipino descent.

Forming groups using geographic and demographic variables is relatively easy, but they may not be *good* market segments. Behavioral and socio-psychological variables are often more effective. Figure 8.3 shows a pharmaceutical firm's attempt to segment the physician market using two variables. Each variable has two levels: *approach to treatment* — aggressive or conservative; *type of data* — relies on scientific evidence or relies on clinical experience. The firm formed four segments: *risk taker, hard headed, path finder,* and *tortoise*. The firm could easily identify physicians characterizing each segment; this approach and was far more effective than classifying by geography or demography.

The main problem of starting with candidate descriptor (segmentation) variables is that customer groups may not have distinct need profiles — descriptor variables do not produce segments at all. The marketer must repeat the process with other descriptor variable(s). The physician example shows that behavioral and/or socio-psychological variables may be more effective than geographic and demographic variables in forming *good* market segments. But assigning customers to market segments formed from behavioral and/or socio-psychological variables may be difficult. Generally, segmentation approaches that start with customer needs are preferable.

KEY IDEA

➤ The best approach for forming market segments is to group customers based on need profiles. The firm should then use descriptor (segmentation) variables to identify different segments.

KEY IDEA

➤ Four categories of candidate descriptor (segmentation) variables can define market segments:
- Geographic
- Demographic
- Behavioral
- Socio-psychological

Approach to Treatment

	Aggressive	Conservative
Relies on scientific evidence	*Risk Taker*	*Hard Headed*
Relies on clinical experience	*Path Finder*	*Tortoise*

Type of Data

FIGURE 8.3

EXAMPLE OF TWO-VARIABLE SEGMENTATION OF PHYSICIANS

METHODOLOGICAL APPROACHES TO FORMING SEGMENTS

Methodological approaches to forming market segments fall into two main categories:

QUALITATIVE. The segmentation task is highly judgmental, requiring significant conceptual skill. The firm's raw material is creative insight, typically gained from marketing research, and/or customer relationship management (CRM) systems.

QUANTITATIVE (DATA CRUNCHING). Large-scale market segmentation studies use extensive customer survey data and sophisticated multivariate statistical techniques. Cluster analysis approaches include the following steps:

- Develop many statements (variables) about customer needs.
- Develop a set of questions (variables) that identify customers.
- Administer statements and questions to a random sample of current and potential customers.
- Analyze customer need responses by cluster analysis. Choose the number of clusters (segments) that form the *best* groupings of customer needs.
- Examine each customer cluster (segment) for identifying characteristics.

Mobil used a similar process to segment the gasoline market.[2]

> *Marketing Question*
>
> How would you segment the market for dog food? Two possible approaches are:
>
> 1. Descriptors of dogs.
> 2. Need profiles of dog owners.
>
> Which approach is easier? Which approach provides greater insight into the dog food market?

> *Marketing Question*
>
> Many observers believe electric vehicles will gain a significant share of the automobile market. How would you segment the market for electric vehicles? What are the implications of your segmentation scheme for product design?

Before the Exxon merger, Mobil's profits were under severe pressure — gasoline prices were low, and Mobil was not the low-cost producer. Mobil conducted a large-scale segmentation study and identified the five segments of gasoline buyers — Table 8.1.

These five segments satisfied the criteria for *good* segments. Mobil decided to target three segments — Road Warriors, True Blues, and Generation F3. IT took the following actions:

- Upgrade convenience stores so they would become *destination* convenience stores.
- Speed up refueling by introducing the Mobil Speed Pass, based on new technology.
- Introduce widespread customer-service training for its employees.
- Develop a direct marketing program to recognize and encourage customer loyalty.

Through market segmentation, Mobil improved market share and profits in a highly competitive mature market. When Exxon and Mobil merged, ExxonMobil adopted Mobil's pioneering approach.

TABLE 8.1

MARKET SEGMENTS
OF GASOLINE BUYERS

Segment	Size (% of all buyers)	Description
Road Warriors	16	Generally higher-income, middle-aged men; drive 25,000 to 50,000 miles per year; buy premium gas with a credit card; purchase sandwiches and drinks from the convenience store, sometimes use the car wash.
True Blues	16	Usually men and women with moderate to high incomes; brand loyal and sometimes gas station loyal; frequently buy premium gasoline and pay cash.
Generation F3 — Food, Fuel, Fast	27	Upwardly mobile men and women; half under 25; constantly on the go; drive a lot and snack heavily from the convenience store.
Homebodies	21	Usually housewives shuttling children around during the day; use whatever gasoline station is in town or along their travel routes.
Price Shoppers	20	Generally neither loyal to a brand nor a gas station; rarely buy premium; frequently on tight budgets; historically Mobil's target customers.

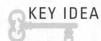

KEY IDEA

➤ The market segmentation process may combine creativity and sophisticated data analysis.

Marketing Question

When the magazine *Mirabella* ceased publication, *The New York Times* noted that *Mirabella* was aimed at "women who are no longer 24 years old, who care passionately about literary criticism and serious articles about, say, contemporary philosophers — and equally as passionately about where to buy those just adorable hot-pink leather pants."[3] Where did *Mirabella* fail in its segment criteria?

KEY IDEA

➤ Criteria for *good* segments:
- Differentiated
- Identifiable
- Accessible
- Appropriate size
- Measurable
- Stable

The fundamental segmentation task is to link each segment's need profile to appropriate descriptor (segmentation) variables. If segmentation is done well, each segment has a well-defined need profile and is easily described by descriptor variables. Frequently, the firm makes several successive attempts to segment a market. Each attempt uses customer need profiles and candidate descriptor variables; they converge somewhere in the middle.

MARKET SEGMENTS

We just discussed developing market segments, but was the market segmentation process successful? **Good segments** are those the firm could target for marketing effort with a reasonable chance of success. So far, we focused on two important segmentation criteria:

- **Differentiated:** Customers in different segments have different need profiles. Accordingly, they should respond differently to market offers.

- **Identifiable:** The firm can identify customers by using descriptor (segmentation) variables and hence reach them with market offers.

Good market segments satisfy four additional criteria:

- **Accessible:** The firm can reach the segment via communications and distribution channels using appropriate and cost-effective approaches.

- **Appropriate size:** Different firms like different size segments. Generally, large firms want large segments to justify their efforts and costs. By contrast, small firms like small segments so they can avoid large and powerful competitors.

- **Measurable:** The firm can measure important characteristics like size and growth.

- **Stable:** Customers stay in the segment for a reasonable period of time.

Marketers must remember that market segments are not *real, correct, incorrect,* or *unchanging.* Customers do not have market segment membership stamped on their foreheads! Market segments derive from appropriate data collection and analysis and creative insight. They help firms direct resources to those parts of the market where success is likely.

KEY QUESTIONS ABOUT MARKET SEGMENTS

Managers often raise questions regarding their own approaches to market segments and the market segmentation process. Here are the most common:

HOW MANY MARKET SEGMENTS ARE ENOUGH? How should the firm trade off enhancing customer satisfaction by defining large numbers of market segments, and seeking cost efficiency via few segments? Walmart faces this problem: Walmart's low-cost, low-price business model has brought great success; its current challenge is addressing segments defined by local needs without incurring significant cost penalties.[4] The core options are:

- **Large number of segments.** As the firm identifies increased numbers of segments, the similarity of customer need profiles within each segment increases. Hence the firm can earn high customer satisfaction by targeting specialized groups. But product development, marketing costs, and other resource requirements are high and economies of scale are few. Also, managing many segments is a complex challenge.
- **Small number of segments.** When the firm develops fewer segments, customer needs are less granular and more diffuse. Customer satisfaction from addressing individual segments is necessarily lower, but costs are also lower and segment management is less difficult.

Firms experienced in market segmentation typically opt for a relatively small number of segments, often between five and eight. They may develop more discrete segments during the segmentation process, but include a rationalizing step to a smaller number.

In some industries, firms target several fine-grained segments via a **modularity** approach. Modularity speaks to product design, using individual components in multiple products to serve multiple segments. Chapter 3 showed that Boeing and Airbus each use modular design, parts standardization, and advanced information technology in airplane manufacture. The Boeing 727, 737, and 757 serve different customer needs, yet some fuselage sections are identical, inherited from the 707.

Technological advances increase design and production flexibility. Computer-aided design (CAD) speeds development; computer-aided manufacturing (CAM) reduces set-up times. CAD/CAM innovations make product variations less expensive and allow customer personalization without the typical cost of making *one-offs*. Amazon.com is an excellent example of using information technology to personalize the user experience and reduce the cost of variety. Amazon uses **recommendation systems**, based on historic purchasing patterns, to advise customers of products meeting their preferences; they also remind customers of birthdays and other events that may trigger purchases.

CAN AN INDIVIDUAL CUSTOMER BE A MARKET SEGMENT? Firms that address B2B markets, or sell consumer goods through large retail chains, often focus their efforts on individual customers — **segments-of-one**. The firm treats an individual **strategic (key) account** as a market segment in its own right.

Historically, in B2C markets, individual artisans like custom tailors offered personally designed *bespoke* products to individuals, typically at high prices. Today, firms can integrate personally designed products with flexible mass production techniques — **mass customization** — and gain two advantages.[5] More precisely tailored products enhance customer satisfaction and loyalty, and the firm reduces finished-goods inventory throughout production and distribution.

Panasonic retailers measure consumers for bicycles, just as tailors measure for suits. The retailer transmits measurements to the factory; custom-made bicycles are available in a few days. Similarly, Levi Strauss and Lands' End offer custom-made pants through Internet-based systems. Optical retailers like LensCrafters deliver individually fashioned spectacles within a few hours. At Callaway's *performance centers*, golfers receive computer analyses of their golf swing and place orders for clubs cut to a precise length and bent to a specific angle. Renault's goal is to build and deliver cars within 15 days of receiving a customer order.

Many Internet firms personalize products using *choiceboard* models.[6] Dell customers design their own PCs; Mattel customers design their own Barbie dolls. Hallmark sends personal e-mail reminders for birthdays and other anniversaries so customers can send cards that arrive on time.

DO MARKET SEGMENTS EVOLVE? We emphasized that market segmentation is critical to developing market strategy. If two firms are equally accomplished in designing market offers, the

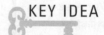

KEY IDEA

➤ B2B firms often treat major customers as individual market segments. In B2C markets, many firms practice mass customization.

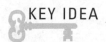

KEY IDEA

➤ As customer need profiles evolve, the firm must continually evolve its segmentation.

firm with better market segmentation will win. This firm's offers will be more precisely tailored to customer needs than those of competitors.

But customer need profiles are constantly evolving, so the firm's segmentation must also evolve, based on good market, customer, competitor, and complementer insight. When markets are young, early entrants are often successful providing basic functional benefits. Then, as the product life cycle evolves, competitors enter and basic functional benefits become the *cost of entry*. The firm achieves differential advantage by identifying customers with finer-grained needs and delivering appropriate benefits and values. Cell phones are a good example. Early in the product life cycle, the most important benefit was phone portability. Later, that benefit became less important in customer decision-making, and the need profiles of some market segments focused on additional functional benefits like e-mail, text messaging, and taking photos. Other segments focused on design and fashion statements.

HOW DO CUSTOMER LIFE CYCLES AFFECT MARKET SEGMENTS? Generally, promoting and selling products to current customers is less expensive than focusing on new customers. Firms increasingly recognize the lifetime value of current customers (CLV) and continually refocus their efforts to increase long-term customer loyalty. B2B customers may continue indefinitely, but individual human consumers follow a predictable life cycle. B2C firms have two polar options:

- **Focus on a fixed age group.** The firm targets an age-defined segment, continually adding new consumers as current customers age and leave the market. Magazines often favor this approach — *Teen People, Time for Kids, Sports Illustrated for Kids,* and *Seventeen.*

- **Retain consumers as they age.** The firm evolves its offer to match changing customer need profiles and reaps the benefits of customer loyalty. But eventually, consumers stop buying. Ford and GM abandoned Mercury and Oldsmobile respectively.

DOES A *SEGMENT* OF CUSTOMERS DIFFER FROM A *GROUP* OF CUSTOMERS? We take a hard line on the definition of segments. Within a segment, customers have similar need profiles; these profiles differ from customers in other segments. By contrast, the firm can form groups in many ways: by degree of use, propensity to buy innovative products, and customer loyalty. Groups may be very important for understanding buyer behavior, but they may not be segments.

To illustrate, many firms group customers by level of use — heavy, medium, and light users. This grouping is often very useful for allocating marketing effort; generally, firms place more effort on heavy users than on light users. But the heavy user group is *not* a segment; customers may be heavy users for very different reasons. Consider frequent users of car rental: Two very different segments are traveling business people who want cars during the week, and city dwellers who want to leave town on the weekends; each segment has different needs. McDonald's has a heavy-user group, but those customers fall into quite separate segments: families with young children, and single males in blue-collar jobs. In general, the firm should develop groups *before* segments.

CAN WE DEVELOP SEGMENTS BASED ON JUST OUR CURRENT CUSTOMERS? Most firms segment the entire market, both current and potential customers. But when the firm has many current customers, it may use customer relationship management (CRM) approaches — Chapter 2 — to place purchase transactions in a **data warehouse**. The firm can then use **data-mining** techniques to identify groups based on purchasing patterns and tailor offers to individual customers based on those patterns.[7]

Tesco (British supermarket) offers a good example of data mining in action. Tesco's loyalty card pays quarterly rebates based on cumulative customer purchases. Tesco has 16 million card users; 10 million consumers use their cards weekly. Tesco analyzes data from more than 600 million shopping baskets annually and places customers into roughly 40,000 groups. Tesco tailors rewards and incentives to consumers in these groups via 36 million personalized mailings annually.[8]

TARGETING MARKET SEGMENTS

The firm never has sufficient resources and/or abilities to address all segments in a market; hence, it must decide where to target its efforts. Some segments receive greater effort and resources; some segments receive little or no effort. By effective targeting, the firm better addresses customer needs and minimizes direct competition. When making targeting decisions, the firm should be conscious of the Principle of Selectivity and Concentration — Chapter 1.

- Marketing must carefully choose targets for firm efforts.
- The firm should concentrate resources against those targets.

The Principle of Selectivity and Concentration governs both Marketing Imperative 1 and Marketing Imperative 2, but there is a difference. For Marketing Imperative 1, Determine and Recommend Which Markets to Address, marketing's role is *advisory*, helping the firm decide. For Marketing Imperative 2, Identify and Target Market Segments, marketing has a *decision-making* role. When the firm has chosen its markets, marketing has the explicit responsibility to identify and target segments.

Whole Foods (WF) is a good example of successful segmentation and targeting in the competitive supermarket industry. WF targets the health-conscious segment with supermarket-style natural food stores, offering one-stop shopping and educational materials on its environmental practices. WF has grown from a single store (1980) to an $11 billion, 340-store chain with 73,000 employees; average sales per square foot are close to twice that of regular supermarkets.

International document and package delivery firm DHL used successive approaches to targeting. Initially, DHL formed three segments based on customer needs:

- **Ad hoc** — small irregular shippers or occasional buyers
- **Regular** — high-volume shippers not requiring supply-chain solutions
- **Advantage** — shippers that need and want a supply-chain solution

The *advantage* segment offered DHL high revenue and profit potential and good partnership candidates. DHL also targeted the advantage segment because it could provide supply-chain solutions. DHL also selected 10 industry segments where it could offer industry-specific knowledge and solutions. Finally, DHL selected specific firms in those industries for selling effort.

Different approaches can help the firm decide which segments to target.

THE MULTIFACTOR MATRIX APPROACH TO TARGETING (STRATEGIC POSITION ANALYSIS)

The **multifactor matrix** (*strategic position analysis*) helps the firm decide which market segments to target. For each candidate segment, the firm must answer two questions:

- How attractive is this segment? (Later, we discuss what makes a segment attractive.)
- Does the firm have the business strengths to win in this segment?

Figure 8.4 shows the conclusion of the analysis — a **market segment attractiveness** versus **business strengths** matrix. We trisect each axis — *high, medium, low* — and label the nine cells A through I. We illustrate by considering three cells:

- Cell C — high market attractiveness, high business strengths: A segment with these characteristics is a no-brainer; the firm should target this segment.
- Cell G — low market attractiveness, low business strengths: A segment with these characteristics is also a no-brainer, but the decision is very different; do not waste resources.
- Cell E — medium market attractiveness, medium business strengths: This decision is more difficult; the segment is somewhat attractive and the firm has some strengths.

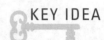

KEY IDEA

➤ For each target market segment, the firm should develop a unique offer precisely tailored to the need profile of customers in that segment.

Marketing Question

In recent years, newsstand sales and subscriptions declined for many news magazines — *Bloomberg Businessweek, Fortune,* and *Time;* and *Newsweek* and *U.S. News & World Report* have ceased print production — but *The Economist* has had significant increases. Why is *The Economist* successful? What market segment(s) does it target?

FIGURE 8.4

THE MULTIFACTOR MATRIX (STRATEGIC POSITION ANALYSIS) — MARKET SEGMENT ATTRACTIVENESS VERSUS BUSINESS STRENGTHS

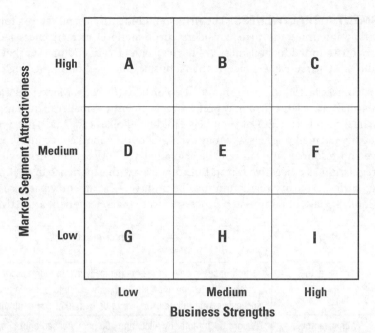

More generally, the firm should seriously consider targeting market segments that fall in the top right corner — B, C, F — but avoid the bottom left corner — D, G, H. Segments in the diagonal cells — A, E, I — are more questionable; each has both positive and negative features.

We just discussed the conclusion of the analysis — the multifactor matrix. Now, we show (a) how to develop the matrix, and (b) how to make the most effective segment-targeting decisions. First, we identify two sets of criteria:

- **Market segment attractiveness.** Factors that make a market segment attractive to the firm.
- **Business strengths.** What any competitor would need to be successful in the segment.

Factors that make market segments attractive differ from firm to firm; business strengths needed to win differ from market segment to market segment. Table 8.2 identifies general factors to start an evaluation; actual factors are specific to the firm and candidate segments.

TABLE 8.2

TARGETING MARKET SEGMENTS: TYPICAL CRITERIA FOR ASSESSING SEGMENT ATTRACTIVENESS AND BUSINESS STRENGTHS NEEDED TO WIN

Market Segment Attractiveness	Business Strengths
Ability to use available resources	Brand value
Barriers to entry	Distribution facilities
Barriers to exit	Financial leverage
Customer service valued	Government relations
Degree of vertical integration	Liquidity
Likely competitor actions	Market segment share
Market segment growth rate	Marketing skills
Market segment potential	Modernity of plant and equipment
Market segment size	Production capacity
Potential profit margins	Profitability record
Regulatory constraints	Raw materials position
Social factors	Sales force
Technological change	Service levels
	Technological expertise

MARKET SEGMENT ATTRACTIVENESS. The firm should identify useful factors for evaluating many segments. Sometimes the firm considers corporate-level attractiveness factors; other times, it focuses on an individual business. A business with growth and market share objectives typically has different attractiveness factors than a business focused on improving cash flow.

For each attractiveness factor, the firm should also consider *direction*. Market segment size is a factor for many analysts. A large firm may prefer large segments; a smaller firm may prefer small segments. Michael Steinbeis, CEO of Steinbeis Holding, global leader in battery labels, said: "We want to be big in small markets. We may even pull out if a market becomes too large and, due to our size and resources, we can only be a small player."[9] Also, many firms view excessive government regulation as a negative factor. But for a firm with experience in dealing with regulatory bureaucracies, extensive regulation may be positive — as an entry barrier for potential competitors. Table 8.3 lays out a five-step process to score market segment attractiveness.

KEY IDEA

➤ In deciding which segments to target, the firm should ask two questions:
  • How attractive is this segment?
  • Does the firm have the business strengths to win?

Step Number	Step	Description
1	Identify factors	The firm seeks several factors (typically five to eight) according to the statement: "Given our history, objectives, culture, management style, successes, and failures, we like to be in market segments that offer ..."
2	Weight factors	Weight each factor by allocating 100 points based on its importance to the firm. Factor weights sum to 100.
3	Rate market segments	Rate each market segment according to how well it performs on each factor (1 = poor; 10 = excellent).
4	Develop factor scores	For each segment, form individual factor scores by multiplying the results of step 2 and step 3 for each factor. Factor score = Weighting × Rating.
5	Develop the market segment attractiveness score	Sum individual factor scores.

TABLE 8:3

SCORING THE ATTRACTIVENESS OF A MARKET SEGMENT

Marketing Exercise

Choose a firm that is a potential employer and a market segment that may be appropriate for that firm. Complete a market segment attractiveness analysis.

The firm completes Steps 1 and 2 once. These results are constant for all segments the firm is evaluating for which it has similar objectives. At Step 3, the analysis shifts to individual market segments. At Step 5, the firm develops a market segment attractiveness score — from 100 to 1,000. More attractive segments earn higher scores. Table 8.4 shows how Robinson (fictional firm, plastics manufacturer) evaluated the plastic accessories segment — the segment scored 595 in attractiveness.

Factor	Robinson's Weighting	Plastic Accessories Segment Rating (1 to 10 scale)	Factor Score (weighting × rating)
Ability to build new strengths	10	6	60
Easy customer access	15	9	135
High market growth	20	7	140
Large potential size	20	5	100
Little regulation	10	8	80
Use excess resources	10	2	20
Weak competition	15	4	60
Total	100		**595**

TABLE 8.4

ASSESSING THE ATTRACTIVENESS OF THE PLASTIC ACCESSORIES MARKET SEGMENT TO ROBINSON

BUSINESS STRENGTHS. Required business strengths are specific to each market segment being evaluated. First, the firm must identify those strengths (capabilities/resources) *any* competitor would require to be successful. Second, it must assess the firm's possession of those strengths. Table 8.5 lays out a five-step process to score the firm's business strengths for a market segment.

TABLE 8.5

SCORING THE
FIRM'S BUSINESS
STRENGTHS

Step Number	Step	Description
1	Identify factors	For each segment, the firm selects several factors (typically five to eight) according to the statement: "To be successful in this market segment, any competitor must possess the following strengths ..."
2	Weight factors	Weight each factor by allocating 100 points based on its importance for being successful in the segment. Factor weights sum to 100.
3	Rate the firm	Rate the firm according to its possession of these strengths (1 = poor; 10 = excellent)
4	Develop factor scores	For each factor, form individual factor scores by multiplying the results of step 2 and step 3 for each factor. Factor score = Weighting × Rating.
5	Develop the business strengths score	Sum the individual factor scores.

Steps 1 and 2 focus on the necessary strengths for being successful in the market segment. At Step 3, the analysis shifts to evaluating the degree to which the firm possesses these strengths. At Step 5, the firm develops a business strengths score — from 100 to 1,000. Higher scores demonstrate greater strengths for competing in the segment. Table 8.6 shows how Robinson assessed its strengths in the plastic accessories segment — it scored 645 on business strengths.

TABLE 8.6

ASSESSING ROBINSON'S
BUSINESS STRENGTHS
IN THE PLASTIC
ACCESSORIES
MARKET SEGMENT

Factor	Plastic Accessories Segment Weighting	Robinson's Rating (1 to 10 scale)	Factor Score (weighting × rating)
Deep pockets	10	9	90
Fast-moving organization	5	3	15
Good R&D	25	7	175
High-quality service	15	6	90
In-place distribution	20	5	100
Low-cost operations	10	4	40
Well-trained sales force	15	9	135
Total	100		**645**

Marketing Question

Review the Robinson example in Table 8.6. How could Robinson secure a better business strengths score?

The market segment attractiveness/business strengths analysis is a one-time snapshot; both market segments and the firm evolve. Segment attractiveness factors, importance weightings, and/or the assessment of individual segments will change. Similarly, business strength factors, importance weightings, and assessment of the firm will also change. This analysis is not a *one-time deal*; the firm should update periodically.

WHICH MARKET SEGMENTS TO TARGET? The multifactor matrix produces two index numbers per market segment: *attractiveness* and *business strengths*. In the Robinson example, index numbers are 595 and 645 respectively — the "X" point in Figure 8.5. The *cut points* — 400 and 700 — discriminate low, medium, and high.

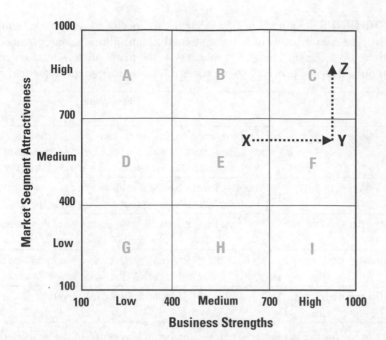

FIGURE 8.5

ROBINSON'S
ASSESSMENT
OF THE PLASTIC
ACCESSORIES
MARKET SEGMENT

The "X" position is not immutably fixed; we must assess whether the plastics accessories segment can shift from cell E to cells B, C, or F. Robinson has two movement options — horizontal and vertical:

- **Horizontal:** To move from X to Y, Robinson must improve business strengths. Returning to Table 8.6, *Good R&D* (25) and *In-place distribution* (20) are most important; Robinson scored 7 and 5 respectively. Astute investment, acquisition, or forming an alliance may improve business strengths.

- **Vertical:** To move vertically — from Y to Z — is more subtle. Robinson should secure deeper market insight and refine its definition of this segment.

KEY IDEA

➤ A firm can improve market segment position by investing in those business strengths that determine success.

➤ A firm may identify more attractive market segments by refining its segmentation approach.

TARGETING MARKET SEGMENTS AND COMPANY SIZE

Large firms generally have greater resources than small firms, so a large firm that segments and targets well is difficult to beat. The Opening Case showed how hotel-industry leader Marriott targets several market segments with various brands. Marriott's performance is exemplary in its industry. Whirlpool is another large firm that targets multiple segments — in both developed and less-developed countries. In the latter, Whirlpool targets low-income customers with its Ideale washing machine; it makes minor design changes to appeal to local tastes. In Brazil, Ideale is white, has a transparent acrylic lid, and sits on four legs. In China, Ideale is light blue and gray, has a foldable top, and a heavy-duty cycle for *grease removal*. In India, Ideale is green, blue, and white; is on casters for easy rolling; and has a delicate *sari* cycle.

Market segmentation and targeting can even the odds for smaller firms. Many large firms cannot achieve specialized focus on market segments — internal constituencies disagree about segment targets and decision-making is often protracted. Large firms may also spread themselves too thin over many segments, allowing smaller, more-focused, competitors to gain advantage. Southwest Airlines and jetBlue pressure airline majors like American, Delta, and United; and easyJet and Ryanair are winning in Europe.

Sometimes smaller firms win when larger firms ignore, reduce service to, or withdraw from less attractive (for them) market segments. In passenger aircraft, Bombardier Aerospace (Canada) and Embraer (Brazil) profitably produce *short-hop* planes designed to travel between main hubs and smaller regional airports. They avoid stiff competition from large plane builders Boeing and Airbus.

Small firms with limited resources enjoy focus advantages of targeting few segments and building strong customer relationships, almost by default. They don't *choose* to target fewer segments: they just don't have the resources to target more. But successful small firms must understand their success is due to focus. When a small firm does not understand this reality it may expand into segments dominated by resource-rich competitors, like *www.Positively-You.com*:

Virtual bookstore *www.Positively-You.com* focused on self-help and motivational books and became profitable in six months! *New York Times* columnist Thomas Friedman wrote a highly complimentary op-ed piece, and website traffic increased dramatically. Positively-You expanded to compete more directly with Amazon.com — the result was a disaster, and within one year the store was out of business. Said owner Lyle Bowlin, "We were doing well as a small niche player, but when we decided to go after Amazon, we lost our way."[10]

Smaller firms face three other problems:

- **Demand shortage.** Of necessity, small firms target few market segments. If demand drops, other segments cannot cushion the impact. Industry-wide recessions wreak havoc with specialized firms.
- **High costs.** Narrow focus implies high costs that cannot be offset by high prices.
- **Too successful.** The small firm is *too* successful and attracts the attention of major players. Startup Guiltless Gourmet (GG) grew its line of baked low-fat tortilla chips into a $23 million enterprise. When snacks giant Frito Lay entered, GG's revenues fell precipitously.

KEY IDEA

➤ Large firms and small firms each have advantages in targeting market segments. Missteps can cause each to lose a strong position.

KEY MESSAGES

- Market segmentation is fundamental to developing the market strategy. The firm has three separate, but related, strategic-level tasks:
    - Conduct a market segmentation process to identify market segments.
    - Decide which of the identified market segments to target for effort.
    - Develop a market segment strategy and positioning for each target segment.

    We discussed items 1 and 2 in this chapter; we take up item 3 in Chapter 9.

- Segmentation is a process for deconstructing the market into customer groups.

- Customers in a market segment have homogeneous (similar) need profiles; customers in other market segments have heterogeneous (different) need profiles.

- The firm can approach the segmentation process in two different ways:
    - Identifying groups of customers that differ in need profiles.
    - Using candidate descriptor (segmentation) variables to form groups, then seeing if need profiles differ.

- The firm should avoid ineffective ways of segmenting markets.

- Useful segments must satisfy six separate criteria: differentiated, identifiable, accessible, appropriate size, measurable, and stable.

- The segmentation process is creative and analytic, requiring good market, customer, competitor, and complementer insight. By contrast, targeting requires the firm to make decisions.

- The *multifactor matrix* is a useful approach for making targeting decisions.

- Large firms generally succeed by targeting multiple segments; small firms succeed by targeting few segments.

VIDEOS AND AUDIOS

Market Segmentation and Targeting	v802 🎥	Ron Boire	Toys R Us
Marketing Imperative 2	a801 🎧		

v802

a801

IMPERATIVE 3

*Set Strategic Direction
and Positioning*

CHAPTER 9

MARKET STRATEGY— INTEGRATING FIRM EFFORTS FOR MARKETING SUCCESS cv901

To access O-codes, go to www.ocodes.com

LEARNING OBJECTIVES

When you have completed this chapter, you will be able to:

- Articulate the purpose and functions of market and market-segment strategies.
- Provide direction to the firm and/or business unit.
- Know how to achieve differential advantage.
- Guide the effective allocation of scarce resources.
- Achieve cross-functional integration.
- Lay out the elements of a market-segment strategy.
- Select a strategic focus and design a positioning statement.
- Identify effective and ineffective market and market-segment strategies.
- Develop and manage market strategies targeted at multiple segments.

OPENING CASE: MAYO CLINIC

Mayo Clinic is the best known and most powerful healthcare brand in the world. Since the late 1880s, Mayo Clinic has delivered superb medical care to patients, provided value to many con-

135

stituencies, and wielded differential advantage over competitors. Mayo Clinic's history continues to define its differential advantage over other direct healthcare providers, even when every major hospital and medical institution has professional marketing and public relations staffs.

Mayo Clinic's market strategy has always had two core operating principles. First: "The best interest of the patient is the only interest to be considered." Second: "Two heads are better than one, and three are even better." Focused on these principles, Mayo Clinic has 53,000 employees serving more than one million patients annually from the U.S. and around the world — at three clinic and hospital centers in Rochester, Minnesota; Jacksonville, Florida; and Scottsdale and Phoenix, Arizona. Mayo Clinic also maintains offices in Canada, Mexico, and the United Arab Emirates (UAE) to facilitate appointments, and provide hotel and visa assistance.

Mayo Clinic's brand awareness is extraordinary. The chair of Mayo Clinic's marketing division said, "Our research shows that in the U.S. we register over 1.8 billion consumer impressions a year — 90 percent of the population is aware of Mayo Clinic, 33 percent know someone who has been a Mayo Clinic patient, and 18 percent would make us their first choice for a serious health need if there were no financial barriers. Patients from all 50 U.S. states as well as from 150 countries typically visit each of our three clinics every year."[1]

Part of Mayo Clinic's success results from its alignment of mission and organization. All caregivers serve as consultants to one another and function as members of multiple-patient care teams. All employes receive salary checks from the same account, signed by the same person. Mayo Clinic's collaborative model extends to patients' referring physicians.

Mayo Clinic receives extensive public relations coverage when celebrities like entertainers, professional athletes, and government and business leaders visit for care. In small U.S. towns, word of mouth about someone's good experience at Mayo Clinic often leads to a local feature story in the newspaper, TV, or radio, and is frequently picked up by regional and national news services.

At a time of managed care and restricted provider lists, Mayo Clinic's tiny share of a huge market makes it attractive to many insurers. Research shows the greatest benefit from the Mayo brand is peace of mind — knowing it's there if you need it. Midwest U.S. consumers, in particular, find great value in insurance products that include Mayo Clinic.

Mayo Clinic grounds its market strategy in delivering customer value and securing differential advantage. Although a non-profit organization, Mayo Clinic's enormous financial success funds leading-edge research and hospital facilities, a medical school, high staff-per-patient ratio, and a roster of world-class physicians and researchers. All these constituents count on customer willingness to pay and to face the inconvenience of traveling to a Mayo Clinic for treatment.

CASE QUESTION

What are the critical elements in Mayo Clinic's market strategy?

Chapter 7 discussed Imperative 1, Determine and Recommend Which Markets to Address. Chapter 8 discussed Imperative 2: Identify and Target Market Segments, addressing two separate, but related, strategic-level tasks. First, we learned how to conduct the *market segmentation process* and identify *market segments*. Second, we showed how the firm should decide which segments to *target* for marketing effort.

Chapter 9 is the first of three chapters that discuss separate aspects of Imperative 3: Set Strategic Direction and Positioning. Here we focus on developing **market strategy**, arguably one of marketing's most important roles and responsibilities. As we learned in earlier chapters, the market strategy goal is very simple — *to attract, retain, and grow customers, in the face of competitors trying to do the same thing*. The market strategy declares what the firm *will do* and what it *will not do*. Externally, a well-developed strategy reflects the common theme and emphasis of the firm's approach to the market. Internally, it coordinates the actions of many departments and people. An effective market strategy is crucial for success.[2]

KEY IDEA

➤ The goal of market and market-segment strategies is very simple — *to attract, retain, and grow customers in the face of competitors trying to do the same thing.*

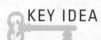

KEY IDEA

➤ The market strategy is the firm's game plan for addressing the market. The market strategy states:

- What the firm is trying to achieve
- What the firm will do
- What the firm will not do

The firm partitions each chosen market into several market segments; then decides which segment(s) to target for effort. If the firm's segmentation is effective, customers in each segment have homogeneous (similar) need profiles. But across segments, these profiles are heterogeneous (different). The extent and type of competition also varies by segment. Because of these differences, the firm must develop a separate strategy for each target segment; positioning is the heart of the *market-segment* strategy. The *market strategy* comprises one or more *market-segment* strategies.

THE PURPOSE OF MARKET AND MARKET-SEGMENT STRATEGIES

Imagine an NFL team going through the football season without a strategy. What are its chances of reaching the Super Bowl? Very slim — luck only goes so far. The team would lack direction and focus and be unable to leverage its strengths. The team would not deploy players effectively, and they would not coordinate with one another. In short, the team would not develop a differential advantage against opponents. ***The same is true in business. To be successful, a firm must have a clear market strategy to "win" in the marketplace.***

KEY IDEA

➤ The market strategy requires decisions about:

- Results
- Resources
- Actions

Strategy is one of the most abused and most misunderstood terms in business, yet important in any manager's vocabulary. The market strategy builds on planning assumptions formed from market, customer, competitor, company, and complementer insight. The market strategy is the firm's game plan for the market, pointing the way to firm actions. The market strategy specifies what the firm is trying to achieve, which market segments it will target for effort, and how it will position itself in those segments. The firm must make three types of decisions:

- **Results.** What the firm wants to achieve from addressing the market.
- **Resources.** Broadly, how the firm will deploy its resources to achieve these results.
- **Actions.** What specific actions the firm intends to take to be successful.

Well-developed market-segment and market strategies fulfill four purposes for the firm: Provide strategic direction in the market, show how to secure differential advantage, guide the effective allocation of scarce resources, and achieve cross-functional and cross-business integration.

KEY IDEA

➤ Well-developed market and market-segment strategies fulfill four purposes for the firm:

- Provide strategic direction in the market
- Show how to secure differential advantage
- Guide the effective allocation of scarce resources
- Achieve cross-functional integration

PROVIDING STRATEGIC DIRECTION IN THE MARKET

Market and market-segment strategies provide strategic direction on how to attract, retain, and grow customers, in the face of competitors trying to do the same thing. We expect markets, customer needs, and competitive challenges to evolve and become more complex. The market strategy must guide the firm in the changing environment. Achieving this purpose is more difficult, yet more essential, the greater the complexity and change the firm faces.

SECURING DIFFERENTIAL ADVANTAGE

Well-developed market-segment and market strategies must clarify why customers should buy from the firm rather than competitors. They also show how the firm will gain differential advantage. Recall from earlier chapters that a *differential advantage is a net benefit or cluster of benefits, offered to a sizable group of customers, which they value and are willing to pay for, but cannot get, or believe they cannot get, elsewhere.* Table 9.1 describes criteria for evaluating *good* market-segment and market strategies. The firm should reject any market-segment or market strategy that cannot withstand probable competitor responses.[3] The firm should also develop contingency plans, or *what if* responses, to possible competitor actions. Contingency planning leads to strategies that secure differential advantage, and helps the firm act pre-emptively — before competitors.

Criteria	Strategy Description
Cannot do	The firm takes actions competitors cannot duplicate — typically, they lack a key resource or competence.
Will not do	The firm's competitors could match the strategy, but are unlikely to do so. The firm needs significant competitive insight to make this judgment.
Will be relatively disadvantaged if they do	The firm believes the competitor will duplicate its strategic moves — but believes the firm will receive a disproportionate benefit.
Will be benefited by	The firm believes its actions will be advantageous both to itself and its competitors.

TABLE 9.1

SECURING DIFFERENTIAL ADVANTAGE

GUIDING THE EFFECTIVE ALLOCATION OF SCARCE RESOURCES

All firms have limited resources like capital, plant capacity, sales force time, and technological capability. These limitations apply at each organizational level and functional area. Faced with these constraints, the firm must allocate resources to secure differential advantage. The firm must make two types of allocations. *Externally*, the firm allocates resources among target market segments, selecting the resources for securing differential advantage by segment. *Internally*, the firm allocates resources among activities like product development, advertising, and selling.

ACHIEVING CROSS-FUNCTIONAL INTEGRATION

Achieving integration across different parts of the firm and/or business unit is critical, yet often elusive. The market strategy must coordinate the actions of various parts of the firm, so they all pull together to secure differential advantage. Without effective integration, significant internal conflict can arise.

Market-strategy owners must develop support throughout the firm. The various functions and/or business units likely have different opinions about the market strategy: The sales department wants to increase sales and operations wants to reduce costs, in part because that it what they are paid to do. But actions that seem reasonable from the perspective of a specific function may be inappropriate when market considerations are paramount. Well-managed contention is healthy, for it surfaces different perspectives on key issues. But all parties must focus on external issues and take a holistic view on how the firm can win.

ELEMENTS OF THE MARKET-SEGMENT STRATEGY

A market is best viewed as a set of market segments. To be successful, the firm should target specific segments with strategies that create differential advantage. Generally, firms perform well when they focus on a few segments versus the market as a whole. Hertz, Alamo, and Enterprise are major players in car rental, but each focuses on a specific segment: Hertz — business travelers with speed and convenience; Alamo — vacation travelers with low prices; and Enterprise — local convenience to drivers whose cars are being repaired.

Because of market segment differences, the basic market-strategy unit is the market-segment strategy. A market strategy frequently combines several interrelated market-segment strategies. Figure 9.1 shows the four pillars of a market segment strategy are:

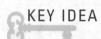
KEY IDEA

➤ An effective market strategy helps the firm allocate resources.

• *Externally* — the firm allocates resources to target market segments so as to secure differential advantage.

• *Internally* — the firm allocates resources across internal activities.

FIGURE 9.1

**ELEMENTS OF THE
MARKET-SEGMENT
STRATEGY**

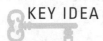 **KEY IDEA**

➤ Inter-functional conflict is endemic. Formulating the market strategy should resolve this conflict and achieve cross-functional integration.

Marketing Question

In rural areas of emerging countries, the farmer uses a yoke on his team of oxen. Is *yoke* a good metaphor for the market strategy?

Marketing Question

The market strategy is not visible, but we can *reverse engineer* a strategy by observing firm actions. Suppose you compete with McDonald's. What implementation programs can you identify? Then ask these questions: What core segment does McDonald's address? How do you assess McDonald's performance objectives? What is McDonald's strategic focus? What is McDonald's positioning? Is McDonald's positioning *good* for the future?

Performance objectives, *strategic focus*, and *positioning* are conceptual devices requiring creativity. Product and brand managers or marketing and business directors typically develop these elements based on planning assumptions formed from market, customer, competitor, company, and complementer insight. *Implementation programs* are more tangible. The firm secures integrated implementation by clearly articulating and gaining commitment to performance objectives, strategic focus, and positioning.

PERFORMANCE OBJECTIVES

If you don't know where you're going, any road will get you there.

— Lewis Carroll, *Alice in Wonderland*

Before the firm figures out what it will do, it must know where it's headed. **Performance objectives** articulate the firm's goals for the market segment. Two components state clearly and simply what the firm is trying to achieve: strategic objectives and operational objectives.

STRATEGIC OBJECTIVES

Strategic objectives establish the type of results the firm requires; they are qualitative and directional. Strategic objectives are not concerned with numbers, but declare, in general terms, how the firm will measure its success. Many people confuse strategic objectives with mission statements — Chapter 7. The difference is clear: Mission states where the firm will seek market opportunities; strategic objectives state the types of results the firm seeks.

The three broad categories of strategic objectives are growth and market share, profitability, and cash flow. Each strategic objective is attractive, but they often conflict. Many firms set growth and market share as key strategic objectives, but have to spend on fixed assets, working capital, and marketing expenses. These expenditures negatively affect short-term cash flow and profitability.[4]

Because these strategic objective categories typically conflict, the firm must make trade-offs. The firm must set explicit priorities — primary and secondary — for various stages of the market or product life cycle. The firm must resist the tendency to demand increased growth, market share, profit, *and* cash flow, all at the same time. The conditions for achieving on all dimensions simultaneously are very rare.

Figure 9.2 is a classic illustration of how strategic objectives evolve in a product life-cycle framework. In the introduction and early growth stages, firms often set priorities on growth and/or market share. These objectives shift to profit in late growth and for much of the maturity stage. Late in the maturity stage, especially if decline is imminent, cash flow predominates; hence the term *cash cow*. These guidelines are not cast-iron prescriptions for selecting primary strategic objectives, but simply show many firms' behavior, assuming results reflect original objectives (on average).

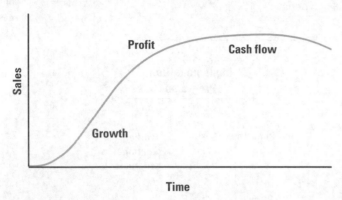

KEY IDEA

➤ Priorities for strategic objectives evolve during product life-cycle stages.

FIGURE 9.2

EVOLUTION OF STRATEGIC OBJECTIVES

OPERATIONAL OBJECTIVES

Strategic objectives are qualitative and directional, but *operational objectives* are quantitative and time-bound. Operational objectives provide the numbers and time frame to attach to strategic objectives. What types of numbers? Operational objectives answer the following questions: How much is required, and by when? Operational objectives should specify how much growth, market share, profit, and/or cash flow the firm should earn during a specific time frame.

The firm uses operational objectives to evaluate performance. Operational objectives should be **SMART** — **s**pecific, **m**easurable, **a**chievable, **r**ealistic, and **t**imely. Operational objectives should also be challenging, but not out of reach and demotivating. During the market-segment-strategy development process, the firm should continually revisit its operational objectives in the context of budgetary implications.

KEY IDEA

➤ The firm must make trade-offs among the three categories of strategic objectives:
• Growth and market share
• Profitability
• Cash flow

KEY IDEA

➤ Operational objectives provide the numbers to attach to the strategic objectives; they specify how much is needed and by when.

SETTING PERFORMANCE OBJECTIVES

Sometimes managers fail to distinguish between strategic and operational objectives. Far too often, they state objectives in terms of profits, "Our profit target for 20XY is $45 million." In principle, setting a $45 million target is not wrong, but the problem is in not asking (yet alone answering) two basic questions. *How will achieving this profit objective affect the firm's overall objectives?* and *How shall we get there?*

Improving short-term profits is not that difficult. Just cut spending on new products, advertising, sales promotion, and salaries; raise prices; and tighten credit terms. The firm will quickly increase profits, but in time will lose market share and profitability. To avoid such results, the firm must articulate the trade-offs among the various strategic objectives and secure agreement from all functional areas. Only then should the firm insert numbers to form the operational objectives.

Generally, strategic and operational objectives should not change during the operating period. But if significant environmental change occurs, or the planning assumptions underlying market forecasts change substantially, then the forecasts and performance objectives should change also.

KEY IDEA

➤ Managers should explicitly discuss trade-offs and expectations among strategic objectives before setting operational objectives.

STRATEGIC FOCUS

Once the firm has established performance objectives for its target market segment, it must decide where to allocate resources. The **strategic focus** does exactly that — Figure 9.1, p. 139. Figure 9.3 illustrates the firm's options using a **means/ends tree** to outline, assess, and choose among various alternatives for improving profits and return on investment (ROI).[5] The tree has two main branches: Branch A — *increase unit sales volume*; Branch B — *improve margins and investment returns*. The firm must select among the branches and sub-branches to create a focus that best helps achieve its strategic and operational performance objectives.

FIGURE 9.3

STRATEGIC FOCUS–
A TREE OF
ALTERNATIVES

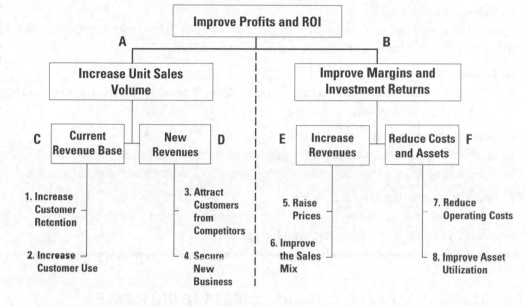

KEY IDEA
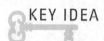

➤ The four ways to increase unit sales are:

- Increase customer retention
- Increase customer use
- Attract customers from competitors
- Secure new business

INCREASE UNIT SALES VOLUME (BRANCH A)

Branch A has two sub-branches, C and D, for increasing unit sales volume. Each sub-branch provides two alternatives. In sub-branch C, the firm enhances current revenues by *increasing customer retention* and *increasing customer use*. In sub-branch D, the firm secures new revenues by *attracting customers from competitors* and *securing new business* by identifying opportunities.

Examples of Increasing Unit Sales Volume — keyed to Figure 9.3

C1. Increase customer retention

To consumers who financed a new GM automobile, GM offered identical financing for a second new car purchased within the financing period.

C2. Increase customer use

Verizon cross-sells long distance, Internet access, and television services. Similarly, cable TV firms sell telephone service and Internet access. Often these firms make bundled offers.

D3. Attract customers from competitors

DirecTV explicitly targets the customers of cable TV firms; natural gas retailers target heating oil customers.

D4. Secure new business

Drug companies make *ask-your-physician* appeals, targeting *non-users* to generate interest, leading to trial. Examples include Plavix — blood thinner; Viagra — erectile dysfunction; and Wellbutrin — anxiety disorder.

IMPROVE MARGINS AND INVESTMENT RETURNS (BRANCH B)

Branch B has two sub-branches, E and F, for improving margins and investment returns, holding unit sales constant. In sub-branch E, the firm increases revenues by *raising prices* and *improving the sales mix* — selling more of its higher-profit products and less of its lower-profit products. In sub-branch F, the firm lowers costs and assets by *reducing operating costs* and *improving asset utilization* like reducing accounts receivable and inventory.

Examples of Improving Margins and Investment Returns — keyed to Figure 9.3

E5. Raise prices

Firms with monopoly-like positions often use this approach — cable TV firms and their suppliers like ESPN and Disney; also, seasonal products like amusement parks and airline travel.

E6. Improve the sales mix

Many B2B firms add services or offer additional features, trying to persuade customers to trade up to more expensive offers with higher profit margins.

F7. Reduce operating costs

Many firms reduce costs by downsizing (firing workers), re-engineering processes, and outsourcing internal operations. Other approaches include cutting back on advertising, and other promotional and selling expenses.

F8. Improve asset utilization

Dell's make-to-order manufacturing system minimizes inventory investment. Also, by receiving payment before making the product, Dell operates with **negative working capital**.

> ### *Marketing Question*
>
> Your firm wants to gain customers from competitors. How will you approach *win-back*? How will this differ from gaining new customers by *switching*?

CHOOSING A STRATEGIC FOCUS: INCREASE UNIT SALES VOLUME OR IMPROVE MARGINS AND INVESTMENT RETURNS?

Question: How should the firm trade off alternatives in Branch A with alternatives in Branch B? After all, many are in conflict. Targeting competitor customers may be a viable option for increasing unit sales, but it won't be successful if the firm simultaneously cuts advertising and selling expenses!

Answer: The firm's choice of alternative(s) should closely parallel its primary strategic objective. For growth, the firm should focus on Branch A alternatives; but for increasing cash flow, it should focus on Branch B. If the primary strategic objective is improving profits, the firm should mix and match — select alternatives from both Branches A and B. What is very clear: The firm cannot pursue too many alternatives simultaneously without losing focus, and violating the Principle of Selectivity and Concentration.

 KEY IDEA

➤ The four ways to improve margins and investment returns are:
- Raise prices
- Improve the sales mix
- Reduce operating costs
- Improve asset utilization

POSITIONING

For many marketers and marketing faculty, **positioning** is the heart of the market-segment strategy — Figure 9.1, p. 139. The firm seeks to create a unique and favorable image for the firm's product in customers' minds. Clarity is key; confusion is positioning's enemy.

We must emphasize the critical distinction between *targeting* a market segment and *positioning* in a market segment. Chapter 8 discussed targeting market segments; Chapter 9 assumes the firm has made the targeting decision. Now we focus on developing a strategy to compete successfully in the target segment. Positioning requires four key decisions *within* the segment:

- Select customer targets.
- Frame competitor targets.

- Design the value proposition.
- Articulate reasons to believe.

We discuss these decisions sequentially but they are highly interrelated. Typically, the firm goes back and forth among these decisions until they form a coherent whole. Figure 9.4 breaks down the process by identifying considerations in selecting customer targets, framing competitor targets, and designing the value proposition.

FIGURE 9.4

THE ELEMENTS OF POSITIONING

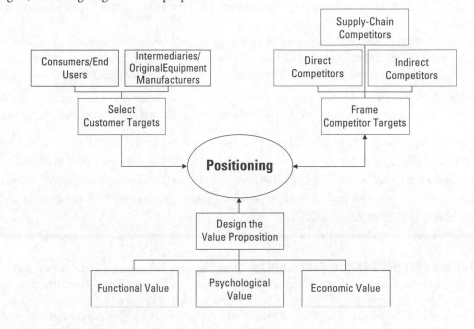

KEY IDEA

➤ The core elements of positioning are:

- Select customer targets
- Frame competitor targets
- Design the value proposition
- Articulate reasons to believe

SELECTING CUSTOMER TARGETS

Customer targets are where the firm places the bulk of its marketing efforts. Unless you target the right customers, your chances of success are slim. Three issues are important:

- **Choosing the distribution system.** The firm must identify the appropriate distribution system — possibly comprising multiple levels — so its products reach end-user customers.
- **Targeting levels within the distribution system.** The firm must decide which level(s) in the distribution system should receive the most marketing effort.
- **Targeting specific person types/roles.** The firm must identify what specific person types/roles it should target for effort at the chosen distribution levels.

CHOOSING THE DISTRIBUTION SYSTEM. The firm's products (components, raw materials, or services) may reach end-user customers in many different ways — direct or via third-party organizations.[6] Examples for tangible products include:

KEY IDEA

➤ Critical issues in selecting customer targets are:

- Choosing the distribution system
- Targeting levels within the distribution system
- Targeting specific person types/roles

- A component manufacturer sells products to finished-goods manufacturers.
- A component manufacturer sells products to sub-assembly manufacturers; in turn, they sell their products to finished-goods manufacturers.
- Products produced by finished-goods manufacturers pass through distributors, wholesalers, and/or retailers before reaching end-user customers.

Many industries have well-established distribution systems whereby products travel *downstream* from level to level, ultimately reaching end-user customers. But the firm may develop innovative channels to gain differential advantage. Today, many firms avoid distributors, wholesalers, and retailers (and their margins) by targeting consumers directly via the Internet.

TARGETING LEVELS WITHIN THE DISTRIBUTION SYSTEM. With limited resources, the firm must decide which distribution levels to target for effort. Broad options are *push* and *pull* — Chapter 15:

- **Push strategy.** The firm places most marketing effort *upstream* on direct customers like manufacturers and distributors. A firm selling finished consumer products focuses on retailers; a raw material/component producer focuses on finished-goods manufacturers. The firm expects these customers (and/or their customers) to promote its products to end users.

- **Pull strategy.** The firm places most marketing effort *downstream* on indirect customers — consumers/end users. FMCG firms focus on consumers; raw material/component manufacturers focus on end-user customers — like the *intel inside* campaign.

Typically, the firm cannot apply equal effort at all potential customer targets. The firm should designate primary and secondary targets. Mattel shows the importance of customer targeting:

> Mattel introduced *Barbie* at the 1959 Toy Fair — retail buyer response was negative. Essentially, they told Ruth Handler, Mattel founder and Barbie's originator: "Little girls want baby dolls; they want to pretend to be mommies." Motivational researcher Ernest Dichter advised Handler to launch Barbie with TV advertising. When girls saw TV ads for Barbie, they — and their mothers — stampeded the stores.[7] By targeting the final consumer, Mattel achieved global market leadership in the toy industry.

TARGETING SPECIFIC PERSON TYPES/ROLES. Once the firm has selected distribution level, it must decide which specific influencers and/or decision-makers to target. Typically the firm wants to change or reinforce behavior and/or mental states like knowledge, attitudes, and purchase intentions. Recall: Organizations do not make decisions — people in organizations make decisions! For a firm targeting households, potential individual targets are husband, wife, children, grandparents, uncles, and aunts. China's one-child policy leads toy firms to target doting grandparents; in the U.S., firms target children directly. Tweens (eight to 12 years) are an increasingly important segment.

B2B firms also make individual-level targeting decisions. A firm selling raw materials to manufacturers may target operations managers, design engineers, marketing and sales executives, purchasing agents, and/or general managers. Relatedly, a well-known floor-covering firm markets heavily to retailers, but focuses on retail salespeople by providing spiffs (cash incentives).

Creativity is important in customer targeting. The firm should consider:

- **Reachability.** Target customers should be easy to reach — but gaining access may be difficult. In B2B, procurement personnel often block access to individual customers like designers, engineers, operations personnel, sales and marketing managers, and senior executives.

- **Obvious versus creative targets.** Some customers are easy to identify and reach, but targeting them can be ineffective because they are obvious — they may also be competitors' customer targets! Deep customer insight, creativity, and a contrarian position can pay great dividends.[8] FedEx's early success came from targeting executives and their secretaries rather than shipping managers, the traditional decision-makers.

- **Influentials.** Customer targets may not be decision-makers, but they should influence the buying decision. Neglecting important influentials can be fatal.

- **Personally benefits but does not pay.** The ideal customer target has significant influence and personally benefits from the purchase, but does not pay. Examples include:
  - Children influencing parental decisions.
  - Doctors writing prescriptions.
  - Executives whose firms pay travel expenses.
  - Politicians and regulators serving their constituents — they spend taxpayers' money.

KEY IDEA

➤ The firm competes for customer targets — decision-makers and/or influencers.

Targeting these customers can raise ethical issues. Many people object to children's advertising; others object to targeting government lobbyists.

FRAMING COMPETITOR TARGETS

The firm decides which competitors to compete against. **Competitor targets** can be current and/or potential competitors, direct and/or indirect competitors, and/or supply-chain competitors. Choice of competitor target depends on firm strength in the market segment.

The firm can place competitors into one of two categories — competitors to avoid and competitors the firm is quite happy (and chooses) to face. This partition helps the firm design its value proposition (next section). Competitive targeting shapes customer perceptions of the firm's offer and helps the firm refine its claims. Table 9.2's positioning alternatives suggest four competitor framings for 7-Up.

TABLE 9.2

FRAMING COMPETITOR TARGETS

Claim	Type	Market Opportunities	Customer Implications
"7-Up tastes better than Sprite"	Comparison with direct competitor	One lemon-lime soda substitutes for another	Compare us
"7-Up, the best-tasting lemon-lime soda"	Product form superiority	The whole lemon-lime product form	The best choice when drinking lemon-lime
"7-Up, the uncola"	Out of product form	The cola product form	The alternative to cola. "We're different"
"7-Up, the real thing, the only one," etc.	Implied or claimed uniqueness	All beverages?	There's no other drink quite like it

SUBTLETY IN COMPETITOR TARGETING. The most effective competitor targeting may not be obvious. Who benefits from designating major accounting firms as the Big 3? — Number 3! The Big 3's competitor target is number 4. Visa advertises that many restaurants globally accept its card, but relatively few accept AmEx. Visa wants customers to believe AmEx is a direct competitor. But Visa's real competitor target is MasterCard.

 **KEY IDEA**

➤ The firm's competitive target can be:

• Current or potential
• Direct or indirect
• Supply chain

➤ Sometimes the targeted competitor is not immediately obvious.

DESIGNING THE VALUE PROPOSITION

A well-designed **value proposition** provides a convincing answer to a deceptively simple question: "Why should target customers prefer the firm's offer to those of competitors?" *Positioning is the heart of the strategy* — the *value proposition* is the heart of positioning. The firm bases its value proposition on functional, psychological, and economic value and related benefits it offers customers. The value proposition defines how the firm gains customers and beats competitors. Related terms are *key buying incentive*, *differentiated core benefit*, *core strategy*, and *unique selling proposition*, but *value proposition* best captures the concept.

Examples of Clear and Effective Value Propositions

• Apple's Macintosh computers — *It just works*
• *Cosmopolitan* — Fun, fearless, female
• Federal Express (now FedEx) delivers on time — *When it absolutely, positively has to get there overnight*
• HSBC — Global reach, local understanding
• iPod — Take your music with you
• Kate Spade — Curious, charming, clever
• Telephone calls made with Sprint are very clear — *You can hear a pin drop*
• Victoria's Secret — Sexy, sophisticated, glamorous, feminine, forever young
• Walmart — Always low prices — *Always*

The firm should base its value proposition on the Principles of Customer Value and Differential Advantage — Chapter 1:

- Focus on satisfying important customer needs,
- Attempt to meet these needs better than competitors and, where possible,
- Offer customer benefits and values that are difficult for competitors to imitate.

In particular, the value proposition should follow the BUSCH system — **b**elievable, **u**nique, **s**ustainable, **c**ompelling, and **h**onest.[9] The value proposition plays two separate but related roles: *externally* as the firm's major competitive weapon for attractive, retaining, and growing customers; *internally* for defining the firm's implementation task.

ARTICULATING REASONS TO BELIEVE

Declaring the firm's intentions in the *value proposition* is one thing; convincing target customers that the firm will deliver on its promises is quite another. The **reasons-to-believe** statement is an essential component of positioning as it supports the firm's value proposition with compelling facts to make its claims believable — like scientific evidence, independent testing data, testimonials, proven firm competencies and/or prior performance, and/or factual information on product attributes. Examples of possible *reasons-to-believe* statements include:

- Cisco — technical expertise in routers and many successful installations worldwide.
- Citibank — vast network of branches around the world.
- CommerceOne — a convenience bank: hours 7 a.m. to 7 p.m., 7 days a week.
- J&J — Tylenol. Clinical evidence of superior pain relief.
- P&G — detergents. P&G's long experience in detergents and a huge commitment to R&D.

DEVELOPING POSITIONING STATEMENTS

Positioning is not what you do to a product — positioning is what you do to the mind of the prospect.[10]

The capstone of the positioning process is a compelling positioning statement: Positioning is vital for guiding and coordinating the firm's marketing efforts. But developing the positioning statement is complex, difficult, and time-consuming. Many people may be involved. A senior Unilever marketing executive alleged that it often takes longer to develop product positioning than to develop the product! When P&G introduced *Whitestrips* (teeth whitener), it delayed expensive TV ads and store testing. Rather, it refined Whitestrips positioning and assessed consumer interest while undertaking a six-month online advertising and sales campaign.

Positioning must clearly distinguish the firm's offer from competitor offers.[11] Positioning should:

Convince	[customer target]
In the context of other alternatives	[competitor target]
That they will receive these benefits and values	[value proposition]
Because we have these capabilities/features	[reasons to believe]

Table 9.3 shows a positioning statement for Cemex (Mexican multinational cement producer). Note the value proposition differs by customer target.

Marketing Question.

Google is the market leader in Internet search; Microsoft's search entry is Bing. How would you advise Microsoft to increase market share? How would you advise Google to resist Microsoft's efforts?

KEY IDEA

➤ The value proposition is the firm's major competitive weapon for *attracting, retaining,* and *growing* customers; it also defines the firm's implementation focus.

➤ The firm must develop a value proposition for each target customer type.

KEY IDEA

➤ "Positioning is not what you do to a product: Positioning is what you do to the mind of the prospect."

TABLE 9.3

EXAMPLE: POSITIONING STATEMENT FOR CEMEX[12]

Task	Focus	Positioning Item
Convince	Builders and contractors; site managers and project investors	Customer Target
In the context of other alternatives	Traditional cement producers	Competitor Target
That they will receive these benefits	Site managers: Consistent delivery within 30 minutes of Cemex receiving an order — versus the three-hour standard Project investors: Additional revenues from early project completion	Value Proposition
Because we have these capabilities	A global positioning satellite system on each truck. Computer software that combines truck positions with plant output and customer orders to calculate optimal destinations. The ability to redirect trucks en route.[13]	Reasons to Believe

TABLE 9.3

EXAMPLE: POSITIONING STATEMENT FOR CEMEX[12]

Marketing Question

Select your favorite (or least favorite) politician. In his/her most recent political campaign, what segments did s/he target? How did the positioning — customer target, competitive target, value proposition, reasons to believe — differ from segment to segment? How did segment strategies mutually interface?

Marketing Question

Sales of erectile dysfunction drugs — Viagra, Levitra, and Cialis — approximate $5 billion annually. Viagra and Cialis each have about 40 percent market share. How are the three drugs positioned? How, if at all, have their positionings evolved? What recommendations would you make for each drug? How does patent expiration factor into your recommendations?

Positioning statements should be **d**istinct, **c**ompelling, **a**uthentic, **p**ersuasive, and **s**ustainable (DCAPS). Creativity can be crucial. Guinness Stout traditionally served a limited market of older men and women. Guinness repositioned Guinness Stout as a friendly beverage for younger consumers. Guinness also leveraged brand heritage by offering the *Guinness* experience at more than 2,000 Irish pubs worldwide. Sales increased dramatically.

Positioning is especially important for new products. Unilever and P&G *get it*, but many firms launch new products with ineffective positioning. Positioning statements are not advertising messages, but DCAPS positioning provides excellent guidance for creative personnel at advertising agencies.

IMPLEMENTATION PROGRAMS

Strategic focus and positioning specify the firm's approach to achieve performance objectives. **Implementation programs** — Figure 9.1, p. 139 — describe specific actions the firm must take to execute its approach. Any good market or market-segment strategy must seriously address both the marketing mix and other functional programs.

IMPLEMENTING THE MARKETING MIX

Chapters 12 through 20 focus on individual marketing-mix elements. These elements must support the value proposition, and must also support other marketing-mix elements. Table 9.4 shows how the Steubenware marketing-mix elements support one another for high-quality glass crystal in the gift segment. We assume that the value proposition revolves around psychological value, assurance that recipients will love Steubenware gifts for their high quality, scarcity, and image.

TABLE 9.4

MARKETING MIX FOR STEUBENWARE IN THE GIFT SEGMENT

Marketing-Mix Element	Steubenware's Implementations
Product	Extremely high quality — Steuben destroys products with imperfections
Service	High-quality pre- and post-sale service
Advertising	High-quality shelter magazines like *Good Housekeeping*
Sales promotion	Brochure material and display racks are high quality
Selling strategy	Focuses on product quality
Distribution	Few retail outlets, but high quality — specialty and upscale department stores
Price	High price — reflecting high image

ALIGNING CROSS-FUNCTIONAL SUPPORT

Even though marketing may *own* the market strategy, competition is so intense that the entire firm must work together as a competitive weapon by aligning all functional areas to support the value proposition. A leading U.S. business magazine was in crisis when competition challenged its 50-year market dominance. The firm pulled together a cross-functional team to develop and implement a new market strategy. This approach successfully reinforced the magazine's leadership and produced its best-ever financial result!

If one or more functional areas cannot provide support, the firm must revisit the value proposition. This analysis is critical. Going forward without full support commits the cardinal marketing sin — making promises to customers the firm cannot keep. Customers do not care which individual or department is at fault. They want, and expect, the benefits and values the firm promised. They rightly believe the firm should fix the problem.

MANAGING MULTI-SEGMENT STRATEGIES

This chapter shows how to construct a strategy — performance objectives, strategic focus, positioning, and implementation programs — for addressing a target market segment. But the firm often targets several segments simultaneously; hence it must develop several market-segment strategies. Each segment strategy requires its own performance objectives, strategic focus, positioning, and implementation programs. The firm must ensure that each segment strategy is distinct. Pottery Barn Kids' positioning is distinct from Pottery Barn — but Pottery Barn is not well distinguished from its down-market chain, West Elm. When the firm targets multiple segments, it faces three possible implementation situations:

- **Independence.** Individual segment strategies and implementation programs are unrelated.
- **Positive synergies.** The firm enjoys positive **synergies** from implementation programs across segments. The firm may secure cost efficiencies from using the same sales force, distribution channels, and/or sharing brand equity.
- **Negative synergies.** The firm suffers negative synergy from implementation programs across segments. Multiple products confuse the sales force; brand extensions confuse customers. Almaden is a strong brand of popularly priced wine, but a $100 Almeden bottle would probably not do well!

The firm's individual market-segment strategies and implementation programs must together form a coherent market strategy. Because of increasing complexity in customer need profiles, multiple-segment issues are especially intriguing and challenging.

KEY IDEA

➤ The firm implements market segment strategy via:
- Marketing mix
- Other functional programs

Marketing Question

What is the iPhone's value proposition? What is its marketing mix? Do the marketing-mix elements support the value proposition and one another?

KEY IDEA

➤ Marketing-mix programs should support the value proposition, and all elements should support one another.

KEY IDEA

➤ Together, individual market segment strategies must form a coherent market strategy.

➤ Market segment strategies must be individually distinct, yet the firm should seek positive synergies in implementation programs.

KEY MESSAGES

The market strategy has four key purposes:

- Providing strategic direction in the market.
- Securing differential advantage.
- Guiding the effective allocation of scarce resources.
- Achieving cross-functional integration.

The market-segment strategy has four key elements; each element has several constituent parts:

- **Performance objectives**: Results the firm hopes to achieve:
  - **Strategic objectives** — qualitative and directional. Strategic objectives typically fall into one of three categories: growth and market share, profitability, and cash flow.
  - **Operational objectives** — quantitative and time-bound. How much and by when.

- **Strategic focus**: The broad direction of the strategy. Has two main branches — *increase unit sales volume* and *improve margins and investment returns*.
  - **Increase unit sales volume** has two branches:
    - **Current revenue base** — *increase customer retention* and/or *customer use*.
    - **Secure new revenues** — *attract customers from competitors* and/or *new business*.
  - **Improve margins and investment returns** also has two branches:
    - **Increase revenues** — *raise prices* and/or *improve the sales mix*.
    - **Reduce costs and assets** — *reduce operating costs* and/or *improve asset utilization*.

- **Positioning**: How target customers should view the firm's offer. Requires four key decisions:
  - **Select customer targets** — choose the distribution system, level(s) to target, and the specific person types/roles.
  - **Frame competitor targets** — competitors the firm decides to go up against.
  - **Design the value proposition** — why customers should prefer the firm's offer.
  - **Articulate reasons to believe** — supporting evidence for the value proposition.

- **Implementation programs**: Actions the firm must take to execute the strategy. Two types:
  - **Marketing mix**: Externally — product, service, promotion, distribution, and price.
  - **Supporting functional programs**: Internally — integrate functional areas to work together.

If the firm targets multiple market segments, each segment strategy must be distinct. The firm should seek positive synergy among its implementation programs.

VIDEOS AND AUDIOS

Marketing Imperative 3 — Market Strategy   a901 🎧
Marketing Imperative 4   a902 🎧

a901

a902

IMPERATIVE 3

Set Strategic Direction and Positioning

CHAPTER 10

MANAGING THROUGH THE LIFE CYCLE cv1001

To access O-codes, go to **www.ocodes.com**

There are risks and costs to a program of action. But they are far less than the long-range risks and costs of inaction.

— John F. Kennedy

LEARNING OBJECTIVES

When you have completed this chapter, you will be able to:

- Appreciate the critical importance of pre-emption in developing competitive strategy.
- Use the product life-cycle framework to generate several plausible scenarios.
- Identify and assess business characteristics and strategic considerations for each scenario.
- Generate strategic options for each scenario.
- Recognize effective life-cycle strategies.

OPENING CASE: RYANAIR

Ryanair upset the life cycle for European air travel when it entered the Ireland-England market in 1985 with flights from Waterford (southeast Ireland) to London's Gatwick Airport. In 1986, Ryanair challenged the government-owned British Airways and Aer Lingus duopoly on the Dublin-London route with flights to London's Luton Airport. Ryanair's initial £99 roundtrip price was less than half the £209 duopoly price. In 1986, Ryanair alone carried 82,000 passengers versus route totals of 500,000 annually for the previous several years. Observers believed Ryanair passengers came from three sources: British Airways and Aer Lingus passengers; new air-travel passengers from the 750,000 annually who made the nine-hour trip by rail and ferry for fares as low as £55; and passengers who previously didn't travel because of high airline prices and/or the inconvenience of rail and ferry.

In the late 1980s, Ryanair added jet aircraft and rapidly expanded its route network to 15 destinations: from Dublin to other British cities and continental Europe, and from London (Luton) to different parts of Ireland. Ryanair offered conventional airline services including business-class travel and a frequent-flyer club. But intense price competition and new capacity from British Airways and Aer Lingus led to significant accumulated losses and a forced restructuring. Ryanair then adopted Southwest Airlines' model to become Europe's first low-fare airline, offering a single class of service, using a single type of aircraft configured with the maximum number of seats, and high-frequency schedules. Ryanair switched from London (Luton) to Stansted Airport — its new terminal had a direct rail link to London's Liverpool Street station. Dublin Airport became the origin of most Irish flights. Ryanair was profitable by 1991.

NEW AIRPORT SECURITY PROCEDURES

PUT FUN BACK INTO FLYING

To support its low-price strategy, Ryanair obsessively cut costs: Ryanair eliminated free drinks and meals; high-capacity utilization pushed down overhead costs. Airport destinations were a significant distance from the advertised cities; Ryanair promised economic growth and employment benefits to negotiate lower landing fees and other costs, and secure local marketing support. Ryanair revamped its route structure so that typical flights were one hour or less, and organized its hubs to reduce maintenance costs and turn-around times.

By 2005, Ryanair was Europe's largest airline, carrying 31 million passengers mostly via online booking. To celebrate its 20th birthday, and continuing its practice of airline-seat sales, Ryanair offered 100,000 seats at 99 pence. In 2012, Ryanair flew 300 Boeing 737-800 aircraft on 1,100 routes through 41 bases serving more than 175 destinations, including three in North Africa. Ryanair carried 70 million passengers, earned more than €3 billion revenues, and made €400 million profits.

CASE QUESTION

The Ireland-Britain market seemed to be in maturity when Ryanair entered. Ryanair's actions shifted the life cycle into a period of dynamic growth. How do you explain this transformation? What other examples of this phenomenon can you identify?

Chapter 10 is the second of three chapters discussing separate facets of Imperative 3: Set Strategic Direction and Positioning. Chapter 9 showed how to develop market segment strategy and market strategy. Earlier in the book, Chapter 3 showed how the **life-cycle framework** can help the firm generate useful market insights. In this chapter, we revisit the life-cycle framework to help the firm make more effective decisions in competitive markets.

By anticipating competitor actions — and sometimes their timing — the firm can develop **pre-emptive** strategies. A pre-emptive strategy means acting before your competitors, perhaps targeting an emerging segment or introducing a new product. Ryanair is a good example of pre-emptive action. Acting pre-emptively often involves risks, and failure may be visible and costly. But the costs of not acting may be significant, particularly for established players. These **opportunity costs** are the market share gains and increased profits the firm did not earn. Opportunity costs are insidious; they do not appear on the firm's income statement, but they may be more significant than costs that do.

Consider Apple and the iPod — many observers counseled caution. They said to Apple: "You are a computer company; you have no experience in digital music. Napster has closed, and downloading music via the Internet faces immense uncertainty. Sony owns portable music players with the Walkman; this is their turf, and they will fight you fiercely." Many would have heeded these arguments, but not Steve Jobs. The iPod launch was an enormous success and even helped Apple sell more Macintosh computers. Think of the opportunity costs Apple would have incurred by not launching the iPod, or the iPhone, or the iPad.

KEY IDEA

➤ Firms failing to act pre-emptively may face significant opportunity costs.

By not acting, the firm opens up potential entry windows for competitors. Firms often hesitate because *going out on a limb* is visible and risky. Neither Aer Lingus nor British Airways acted effectively in the face of Ryanair's disruptive change in air travel. Market-leading firms should view pre-emption as an insurance policy — when change is swift, the costs of inaction escalate rapidly. Firms that will not pay *insurance premiums* should prepare for market share losses.

The life-cycle framework offers a good way to design insurance policies. Understanding how life cycles and competitive strategies evolve is valuable for forecasting and anticipating likely scenarios. With these scenarios, the firm is better equipped to generate good competitive strategic options.

DEVELOPING COMPETITIVE STRATEGIC OPTIONS

The firm generates **strategic options** by developing scenarios that let it anticipate future competitor actions. The main building block is the classic life cycle — introduction, early growth, late growth, maturity, and decline — typically at the product-form level. The *life-cycle approach* is very powerful because market conditions tend to be similar at the same life-cycle stage across many products and technologies. Each scenario has a limited number of strategic options. These options are valuable input into formulating firm strategy, but creativity is always important. The firm should avoid becoming too predictable, even when it is market leader. This chapter discusses how to generate strategic options from nine scenarios — Figure 10.1.

FIGURE 10.1

LIFE-CYCLE SCENARIOS

Marketing Question

Can you identify firms and products corresponding to the nine scenarios in Figure 10.1?

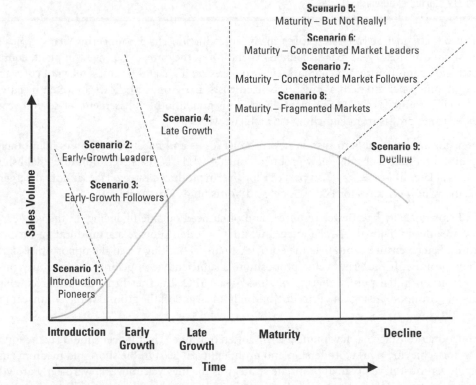

🗝 KEY IDEA

➤ Nine scenarios based on
  • Product life cycle
  • Competitive position

  are the basic building blocks for developing competitive strategic options.

➤ Life cycles are shortening for many products.

Although the scenarios and strategic options are valid for many product life cycles, generally life cycles are shortening. Implications are:

• When life cycles were longer, firms could enter a market, fail, redevelop products, and re-enter with a reasonable chance of success. Today, re-entry windows are closing.

• Shortening life cycles reduce the time — in early growth — to earn the highest unit margins.

• Good strategic thinking early in the life cycle is more important than ever.

- Faster cycles require proactive management of strategy over the life cycle; evolutionary approaches may be too slow.

Identifying scenarios and developing strategic options is more important than ever. This chapter is designed specifically to improve students' ability to formulate strategic options and design good competitive strategies.

Building Product Life-Cycle Scenarios

Let's walk through the nine product life-cycle-based scenarios in Figure 10.1. Each scenario description begins with a brief introduction; then we focus on creating and analyzing alternative objectives and strategies.[1] But we must be very clear about one thing: We cannot tell you what strategy to follow for a given scenario, because your best strategy depends in part on competitor actions. Instead, we give you some strategic options to think about.

SCENARIO 1: INTRODUCTION STAGE: PIONEERS

> Gillette spent $1 billion on developing and initially marketing the Mach3 razor. First-year marketing spending was $300 million for a simultaneous launch in 19 countries. Gillette's corporate profits dropped in the launch year due to Mach3's startup expenses.

Most products do not generate profits in the introduction stage. Pioneering firms typically incur significant R&D and market launch expenditures; they must also invest in plant, equipment, and systems before launch. Marketing expenses are high, and revenues may not cover the firm's ongoing operating costs, much less fixed costs. Early on, cash flows are often negative. Kevin Plank, founder of *Under Armour*, lived in his grandmother's basement for several years before earning profits from launching new athletic wear.

Some firms are better able to sustain new product losses and negative cash flows than others. Large firms typically subsidize new product launches with cash earned from more established products at later life-cycle stages, as part of a long-term product strategy. Tide laundry detergent funds many new ventures for P&G; Google AdWords funds Google initiatives.

Small firms typically have fewer resources and often need outside financing. In the very early stages, wealthy individuals — aka **angel investors** — often provide startup funding for new ventures. Later, **venture capitalists** may provide financial backing when the opportunity starts to show promise. If the firm's value proposition is sufficiently compelling, the firm may raise funds from an initial public offering of stock — an **IPO**. Internet firms like Amazon, eBay, Facebook, Groupon, Instagram, Priceline, and Yahoo! all got off the ground with venture capital and/or IPOs.

The introduction stage has few **pioneer** firms, often only one. The pioneer should lay the foundation for achieving market leadership and profitability, at least in the short and medium run. The pioneer must develop an appropriate strategy as the life cycle moves toward early growth. The pioneer must demonstrate value to target customers and reduce any market uncertainty that the product is just a *short-term wonder* — it may even work with competitors to agree on technological standards (viz., VHS and Blu-ray technologies). The pioneer must also build a marketing organization and distribution infrastructure.

A particularly effective way of slowing/forestalling competitive entry is to create (or exploit) **entry barriers** — government-imposed, product-specific, and firm-driven.[2]

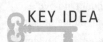

GOVERNMENT-IMPOSED BARRIERS

Patents are the most common government-imposed barrier. Patents provide owners with legal monopolies for several years. Firms can petition the courts to enforce these patent monopolies via patent infringement lawsuits, effectively creating long-term barriers for competitors, like Apple's suits against Samsung in smartphones. Even the filing of patents that are not ultimately approved can act as a short-term barrier. Pharmaceutical companies are especially frequent users of patent barriers. Other government impediments include trade barriers, preferential tax treatment, and outright subsidies. Sometimes the pioneer benefits from a barrier or barrier structure already in place; other times, it may lobby the government for a specific benefit. Sun, Netscape, and Novell all encouraged the U.S. government to take action against Microsoft, slowing its entry into various markets.

PRODUCT-SPECIFIC BARRIERS

Product-specific barriers relate directly to the product and include access to capital, raw materials, human resources, and a minimum scale of operations. Sometimes these barriers relate to the product itself so the firm can exploit them; other times, the firm can actively raise barriers. Of course, product and/or process innovations cause product-specific barriers to diminish over time. In previous decades, consumers sent film rolls to central laboratories for processing; then storefront mini-labs made the process much more convenient; today, consumers print their own images from digital cameras.

FIRM-DRIVEN BARRIERS

The firm can build *low-cost* barriers via **penetration pricing**. The firm may also develop and exploit **first-mover advantages**[3]:

LOW-COST BARRIERS AND PENETRATION PRICING. With penetration pricing (PP), the firm plans on low profit margins for a substantial time period, aka *buying* market share. PP is risky and takes significant resolve. PP requires substantial resources as the firm continually reduces costs and prices, builds capacity, and grows quickly. If successful, low prices built on low costs and experience curve advantages are a significant entry barrier. Figure 10.2 shows the relationship between price and unit cost for a PP strategy.

FIGURE 10.2

PRICE AND UNIT COST TRAJECTORIES FOR PENETRATION PRICING AND SKIM PRICING

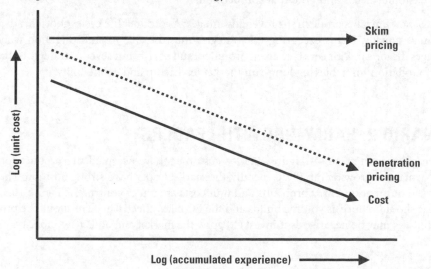

The most advantageous conditions for PP are price-sensitive markets with few government- or product-specific entry barriers. The classic example was Henry Ford's goal to put a Model T in every American garage. Ford invented the assembly line, dramatically lowering production costs; reduced prices continuously; and by the mid-1920s, exceeded 50 percent market share.

PP is particularly attractive if customer **switching costs** are high and the after-market for complementary products is significant. Firms selling durable goods and consumables — razors and razor blades, printers and toner — frequently price durables low and consumables high. PP works only if demand for the basic product remains strong; PP fails when customers demand variation.

The Experience Curve

The cost curve in Figure 10.2 is a classic **experience curve** (EC). As accumulated volume (experience) in making, promoting, and distributing a product increases, costs can be made to decline in a predictable manner. The EC is a straight-line relationship when we plot log (unit cost) against log (accumulated experience). Cost reductions result from tough decisions to take advantage of organizational learning, economies of scale, advances in process technology, product redesign, and enlightened cost management. The EC has an important influence on many marketing decisions, especially pricing.

FIRST-MOVER ADVANTAGE. The pioneer may earn advantages because it was first. The pioneer may be able to sustain technological advantage by improving products and/or developing new applications.

If the pioneer's products are high-quality, it may earn a leading reputation among consumers and distributors. Early market entry also gives the pioneer superior market knowledge. But the pioneer must judiciously turn these advantages into buyer switching costs, or a fast follower will surpass it. One key for sustaining first-mover advantage is to build a strong brand, establishing the *standard* against which customers judge subsequent entries.[4]

Whereas a successful penetration strategy delivers continued price reductions, a firm with first-mover advantages may maintain high prices — **price skimming** (PS). As Figure 10.2 shows, PS keeps prices high, even as the firm reduces costs and earns high profits.[5] PS works if government and/or product-specific entry barriers are high, customer willingness to try is strong, and customers are relatively price-insensitive. The pharmaceutical industry is a good example; patents protect firms from competition, and products deliver significant health benefits. PS strategies fail when entry barriers are low and/or customers are price-sensitive. PS also fails if the firm ignores customer needs and potential competition.

Generally, new entrants erode first-mover advantages: As product life cycles shorten, advantages erode more quickly. Firms executing PS strategies must be able to shift direction when their advantages disappear. Pioneers face an environment full of risk, but several strategic options can lay the foundation for achieving long-run market leadership and profitability.

SCENARIO 2: EARLY-GROWTH LEADERS

By the early-growth stage — Figure 10.3 — customers have accepted the product form and market demand is growing rapidly. Generally, the market leader has a strong position. The leader has worked out market-entry problems and unit costs are under control. As Figure 10.3 shows, unit costs should reduce as volume builds and the EC takes effect. The firm should be profitable, but cash flows may be negative as it invests to grow the market and adds new capacity.

KEY IDEA

➤ When the firm executes a low-price penetration strategy, it must accept low profit margins for a substantial time period. Continual cost reductions are essential to sustain low prices.

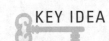

KEY IDEA

➤ A *pioneer* can sustain first-mover advantages by producing high-quality products. The firm earns a leading reputation and sets the stage for creating a strong brand.

FIGURE 10.3

**EARLY-GROWTH-STAGE
SCENARIOS**

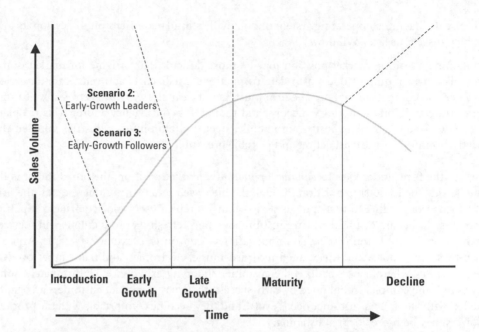

*Marketing
Question*

The iPod and iTunes have
gained large shares of the
digital music and music
download markets. What
barriers did Apple erect for
potential followers?

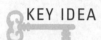KEY IDEA

➤ By the early-growth
stage, customers
accept the product,
and the market leader
should be profitable.

The leader has four strategic options — two each based on *continuing* and *surrendering* leadership:

- Continue to be leader — enhance position.
- Continue to be leader — maintain position.
- Surrender leadership — retreat to a market segment or segments.
- Surrender leadership — exit the market.

CONTINUE TO BE LEADER: ENHANCE POSITION

The firm leverages its success to seek market dominance. The firm grows and broadens the market by continuously investing in R&D to produce new products, extensive advertising, and personal selling. The firm increases production capacity ahead of market demand and aggressively reduces costs. As competitors enter, firm communications shift from market development to emphasizing superiority over competitors. Regarding the U.S. cell phone market, a senior marketing executive at Nokia told us, "While Motorola and Ericsson were still selling American consumers on switching to digital, we were already selling the superior features and performance of Nokia digital phones to separate customer segments."[6] Leaders may also block competitors by entering emerging market segments, new geographic areas, and new distribution channels.

*Marketing
Question*

In the Opening Case in
Chapter 7, we examined
the car-sharing firm Zipcar.
Zipcar has successfully
navigated introduction and
now faces the early-growth
stage. Using the framework
in this chapter, and whatever
data you can secure, suggest
a growth strategy for Zipcar.

CONTINUE TO BE LEADER: MAINTAIN POSITION

The firm may prefer a more conservative approach and merely try to maintain market position. The firm may enjoy monopoly-like status and be concerned about potential political, legal, and regulatory difficulties, like Microsoft has faced. Alternatively, customers may demand additional sources of supply and/or strong competitors may enter, making it clear they intend to stay. Sometimes technological standards drive this option. Multiple standards cause uncertainty, prospective customers postpone purchase, and the market develops more slowly. The firm may elect to work with competitors on a single standard rather than go it alone. The early consumer-video, HDTV, and wireless technology markets are all good examples. In consumer video, Sony's early Betamax entry had limited success but VHS quickly surpassed Beta when several producers settled on a single standard and shared the market development effort. Apple's early refusal to license its Macintosh operating system undoubtedly stimulated Microsoft to develop its own graphical-user interface (Windows).

Maintaining a leading market position may be more difficult than striving for market dominance. The firm requires good up-to-date competitive intelligence, and must carefully select customer and competitor targets. The firm must have a clear strategy, sufficient resolve to stick to the strategy despite temporary hiccups, and thoughtful contingency and/or scenario planning. Historically, U.S. firms in the automobile, steel, and aluminum industries pursued this objective to mitigate antitrust action and possible breakup.

Whether the firm undertakes to *enhance* or *maintain* market position, the broad thrust is the same: to ride the leadership position through the life cycle to maturity. Along the way, the firm shifts focus from selling to first-time users, to selling to repeat users and acquiring competitor customers. To be successful, the firm must broaden and refresh its product line, add services, and build its brand by enhancing communications. Amazon is a textbook example: Amazon began by selling books, and then added recorded music, electronics, and many other product category *stores*, where it personalizes the customer shopping experience. Unfortunately, some leaders become complacent; blinded by early success, they may even treat customers arrogantly (like J&J with stents). As customer needs evolve and they become comfortable with the product, followers may be more adept at listening.

SURRENDER LEADERSHIP: RETREAT TO A MARKET SEGMENT OR SEGMENTS

Unlike market-share loss from competitive pressure, the firm makes a deliberate choice to surrender leadership. The firm may lack resources for fully developing the market and/or funding an ongoing stream of new products. Or a financially stronger competitor sets a market-leadership goal, and the firm knows it cannot win a head-to-head battle. The firm decides to target one or more market segments as a specialized competitor, believing that *discretion is the better part of valor*.

Sometimes, the follower initiates a penetration strategy by building economies of scale and cutting prices. The firm must identify less-price-sensitive segments where it can add value and overcome its cost disadvantage. The firm requires good market research capabilities to identify market segments and the organizational flexibility to address them. Apple, HP, and IBM have all felt this sort of pressure at various times.

SURRENDER LEADERSHIP: EXIT THE MARKET

Leaving a market after being the pioneering leader can seem defeatist, but may be prudent. Throughout the life cycle, as customer needs and markets evolve, the firm should continually assess the value of its market position, based on the projected stream of discounted profits. If this projected value is less than the current sale value, the firm should consider exiting, especially if the product is not central to its mission.

The firm's products may be strategically significant for a potential acquirer, fit well with its current products, and hence be of immense value. The acquirer may also have the resources to invest and drive product growth, like eBay's Skype purchase (widely considered a failure; since divested and acquired by Microsoft). Biotech and other technology firms often face the *sell* decision by inventing products they are ill-equipped to commercialize. Successful innovators are often better off selling to firms with strong marketing expertise. Colgate's liquid soap and P&G's Crest SpinBrush were both secured from small firms that elected to sell.

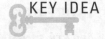

KEY IDEA

➤ *Early-growth leaders* have four quite different options:

• Continue to be leader — enhance position
• Continue to be leader — maintain position
• Surrender leadership — retreat to a market segment or segments
• Surrender leadership — exit the market

Marketing Question

Suppose you have the following information about a market:

• Market growth rate — 15 percent annually
• Leader's market share — 40 percent
• Follower's market share — 10 percent
• Leader's growth rate — 15 percent annually.

Question: How fast must the follower grow annually to overtake the leader in six years?

Answer: 45 percent.

SCENARIO 3: EARLY-GROWTH FOLLOWERS

Some firms prefer to be **followers**, entering markets in the early-growth stage. By pursuing a *wait-and-see* strategy, they can better assess market potential. Followers leverage past successes and learn from the leader's mistakes. But early on, the follower trails the market leader. The follower has lower sales, higher unit costs, and less experience than the leader. Unless the leader is price skimming, followers are often unprofitable, and cash flow is probably also negative.

Followers in early growth have similar strategic options to the leader. But because they start from inferior positions, choosing among them has a different cadence. The options are:

- Seek market leadership.
- Settle for second place.
- Focus on gaining leadership in a market segment or segments.
- Exit the market.

SEEK MARKET LEADERSHIP

The follower can pursue leadership by **imitating** or **leapfrogging** the market leader. In each case, the follower needs good competitive intelligence and entry as soon as possible:

IMITATION. Imitation means what it says. The follower copies the leader but executes more effectively. Successful imitators spend heavily to play *catch-up* on product development and outspend the leader in promotion. If possible, the follower leverages an existing marketing or distribution infrastructure and clearly highlights its differentiated value. The follower should not confuse imitation with price cutting. Early in the PC life cycle, suppliers offered many designs that earned price premiums, but price competition accelerated as the industry standardized. In search, follower Google eclipsed Overture (formerly GoTo) with a well-executed imitation strategy, and Facebook raced ahead of Myspace in social media. Low price was not a factor in either case.

LEAPFROG. The follower improves on the leader. The follower offers enhanced value by developing innovative and superior products, and/or it enters emerging market segments before the leader. Generally, the leapfrogger avoids head-to-head price competition; it may spend more heavily on R&D than the leader, while marketing spending is also high. In video games, Nintendo and Sega leapfrogged first-mover Atari's original video game. Later, Sony Playstation leapfrogged both Nintendo and Sega by offering 3-D graphics and enhanced digital soundtracks. Playstation 3 and Microsoft's Xbox target a different segment — late teens and early 20-somethings — than Nintendo's young teenager target. But Nintendo leapfrogged both Sony and Microsoft by introducing the Wii.

Effective leapfroggers often do an excellent job of anticipating emerging customer needs. They spot segment opportunities before leaders, quickly offering new values and securing differential advantage. The most successful followers *change the rules.*[7]

For either *imitation* or *leapfrog*, followers must make long-run commitments. Because they must play catch-up, resource requirements can be enormous. Sometimes pioneers make it easy for followers by neither improving products nor investing sufficiently in promotion and distribution, and by keeping prices high.

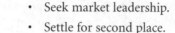
SETTLE FOR SECOND PLACE

Former GE CEO Jack Welch famously mandated that GE be number *one* or *two* in each of its markets. A follower needs substantial resources to become market leader, so settling for second place may be a reasonable and profitable option. Several situations argue for this alternative.

Perhaps the leader is content with current market share and does not seek to increase it; customers may demand a second supplier; multiple competitors may help simplify product standards; and/or the political/legal/regulatory environment may be favorable.

FOCUS ON A MARKET SEGMENT OR SEGMENTS

This option may be attractive if the follower has fewer resources than the leader and other followers, and if the segment (or segments) is attractive. When drugs go off patent, pharmaceutical firms often withdraw marketing support, but add services for a narrow physician segment. In Britain, BMS earns sales and profits from anti-cancer drug Taxol, long after patent expiration. BMS provides kits to prepare the drug for patients and replaces these free of charge if patients miss their appointments.

EXIT THE MARKET

If the business sale value is greater than the projected discounted profit stream, the firm should consider exiting the market. Because the product is in early growth, it may have high value for a potential acquirer eager to enter the product's market (market segment).

SCENARIO 4: LATE-GROWTH STAGE

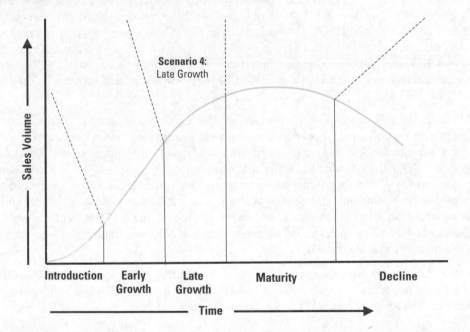

By late growth — Figure 10.4 — the firm receives minimal value from early market leadership or being a fast follower. Although the customer benefits and values that drove purchase in introduction and early growth are still important, they may not enter customer choice decisions. More likely, these elements have become *qualifiers* or *antes*, rather than *determining*. The firm must focus on identifying and offering customers determining benefits and values. Early in the passenger air travel market, safety was critical. Today, most travelers believe major airlines, flying similar airplanes, are equally safe: Safety is an *ante*. Determining benefits and values are frequent-flyer miles, time convenience, and availability of a direct flight.

The firm requires considerable marketing research skills to conduct market segmentation studies, to determine which segment(s) to target, to decide how to satisfy customer needs in the

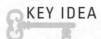

target segment(s), and to monitor evolving segments for new opportunities. Successful firms address target segments with *rifle shot marketing*, and then build defensible positions against competitors. Even small segments may offer good profit potential. Many local and regional retailers successfully compete against national chains. Think about your own town: What examples can you identify? Whole Foods successfully targets a market segment prepared to pay more for higher-quality groceries.

The critical success factor for both leaders and followers boils down to commitment. There are really two broad strategic options — target many segments or settle for a more limited position by targeting just a few. The firm's decision should be based on clear insight about markets and market segments and a rigorous assessment of its ability to serve them successfully.

FIGURE 10.5

MATURITY-STAGE SCENARIOS

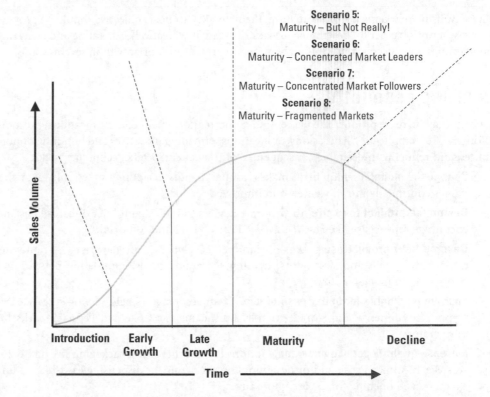

SCENARIO 5: GROWTH IN A MATURE MARKET

Before the firm examines strategic options in maturity — Figure 10.5 — it must affirm that the life cycle really is in *maturity*. Perhaps there are possibilities for market growth. To make the point succinctly, some authors assert, "There is no such thing as a mature business, there are only mature managers!"[8] When assessing if the life cycle is in maturity, the firm must analyze barriers to growth:

BEHAVIORAL BARRIERS. Requiring significant behavioral change by customers is often a barrier. *Techies* were early users of PCs and their difficult-to-use operating systems like CPM and MS-DOS. The mass market developed only when Apple, and then Microsoft, launched *easy-to-use* intuitive options. Customer behavior changes can also rejuvenate markets. Bicycles were old-fashioned by the late 1970s, but sales increased dramatically when exercising became fashionable in the 1980s.

ECONOMIC BARRIERS. Economic barriers are often linked to technology. When its Roundup herbicide lost patent protection in the Philippines, Monsanto cut prices to compete with cheaper generics. Monsanto discovered it had vastly underestimated price elasticity[9]; sales grew dramatically when many farmers could afford Roundup.

GOVERNMENT-IMPOSED BARRIERS. When the government removes regulations, competitors often enter, and growth explodes. The U.S. government opened bandwidths to commercial use and wireless-based products expanded rapidly. Deregulation of air transportation spawned rapid growth in airfreight and passenger air travel.

TECHNOLOGICAL BARRIERS. Innovation may obliterate technological barriers to growth. AT&T's transistor technology rejuvenated radios. Improved microprocessors made PCs portable and much cheaper. Inline skates revived the almost-dead roller-skating industry.

Generally, if the market is not *really* mature, the firm's key strategic objective should be growth. The most serious barrier to growth may be lack of creativity. Creatively generating and analyzing opportunities and approaching seemingly mature markets can spur growth in several ways.

INCREASE PRODUCT USE

The firm may increase product use via reminder and reinforcement communications; promoting different use applications, occasions, or locations; providing incentives and bundling opportunities; and reducing undesirable consequences of frequency. Specific techniques include:

- **Change the model.** Fashion firms make seasonal changes in clothing styles; software companies continually introduce new and improved versions.
- **Design the product to expire.** Incorporate devices to indicate product discard dates and encourage repurchase like *best-if-used-by* dates on beer and soft drinks.
- **Develop new product uses.** Arm & Hammer developed many new uses — removing refrigerator smells and sink odors, treating swimming pools, eliminating perspiration odor, and sanitizing laundry.
- **Improve packaging for better ease of use.** Examples include single-serving cereals, easy-to-pour condiments, and storage-friendly bulk items like Coke and Pepsi 12-packs for refrigerators
- **Increase quantity per use occasion.** Options include increasing packaging size, like a 20- versus a 12-ounce Pepsi; and/or designing the packaging for dispensing ease, like adding a larger-sized opening for Tabasco hot sauce.
- **Make the product easier to use.** Consumers do not have to clean or disinfect disposable contact lenses. Pharmaceutical firms often redesign injectable drugs as tablets, time-release capsules, and long-lived patches to ease patient burdens and encourage use.

IMPROVE THE PRODUCT/SERVICE

Firms should expect sales to slow if products do not satisfy customer needs. The remedy is simple: *Improve the offer!* Sometimes even apparently minor changes can increase sales significantly. Clorox introduced a lemon-fresh version of Pine-Sol household floor and wall cleaner — sales grew by 25 percent. Clorox added a squirt of floral scent or a twist of lemon to Clorox bleach and gained 1 percent market share.

Because product quality has improved significantly in many industries, and gaining product-based advantage is difficult, many firms use services to rejuvenate their brands. IBM based its recent success on a shift from hardware and software to providing services. You've seen the commercials. Today, IBM operates information technology systems and platforms for thousands of major firms like DuPont and Merck.[10]

KEY IDEA

➤ Creative ways to drive growth in the maturity stage:
- Increase product use
- Improve the product/ service
- Improve physical distribution
- Reduce price
- Reposition the brand
- Enter new markets

KEY IDEA

➤ Markets that seem
mature may have
growth potential wait-
ing to be unlocked via
creative approaches.

IMPROVE PHYSICAL DISTRIBUTION

Sophisticated package delivery and tracking systems helped grow electronic commerce. Off the Alaskan coast, Bill Webber e-mails pictures of caught salmon to chefs, packs chosen items in insulated bubble-wrap liners for shipping boxes, then ships by FedEx. The premium-priced fish arrive at restaurants 48 hours after leaving the water.

REDUCE PRICE

This chapter's Opening Case shows how Ryanair transformed a seemingly mature airline market into growth with a low-price strategy. Southwest Airlines previously had similar success in the U.S. The author is trying to transform the marketing textbook market.

REPOSITION THE BRAND

The firm offers the same product but with new benefits/values for new customers. In a classic example, Honda repositioned motorcycles from a product made for *longhaired guys* and *the police officers chasing them* to *a family activity*.

ENTER NEW MARKETS

Many firms define new markets by geography — in particular, emerging markets like the BRICI countries (Brazil, Russia, India, China, Indonesia) with millions of low-income customers. To supply sufficiently low-priced products, firms must modify traditional practices.

KEY IDEA

➤ Market leaders in
concentrated mature
markets should have:

• Low costs
• Decent profits
• Positive cash flows

SCENARIO 6: LEADERS IN CONCENTRATED MATURE MARKETS

Generally, **concentrated markets** support a few substantial competitors whose aggregate market share often exceeds 60 percent; several small players may target market niches. Profit margins should be high for low-cost leaders; investment should be relatively low (because growth is low); and cash flow should be strongly positive.

The market leader has two strategic options:

• Maintain leadership over the long run.
• Harvest the business.[11]

MAINTAIN LEADERSHIP OVER THE LONG RUN

The core decision for maintaining market leadership is choosing the *right* investment level. Generally, we advocate *cautious* investment. With the *right* investment, in the *right* areas, the firm may reap profits for many years. *Overinvestment* to gain market share from entrenched competitors often wastes resources. Pressures for overinvestment are:

• Few alternative opportunities
• Internally focused funding criteria
• Political power of mature-product champions

Increasing short-run profits is not difficult; the trick is finding the right investment level to sustain profits in the medium- and long run. Reasons for underinvestment are:

• Fear of cannibalization

- Inertia
- Limited view of competition
- Misunderstanding the challenger's strategy

Of course, complacency and arrogance can accentuate any or all of these errors, and past success can blind the firm to evolving market realities. Generally, the firm can maintain leadership via incremental product improvements; it should also invest in marketing activities that build and sustain brand equity and demonstrate competitive superiority. When a clinical trial showed that Lipitor (cholesterol-lowering drug) reduced heart attack risk by 16 percent, Pfizer widely advertised the result; Lipitor achieved over 40 percent market share.

The firm should speed up product development and invest in process technology for more efficient lower-cost operations. Process technology change can severely affect market leaders that do not adapt. Traditional integrated steel firms like U.S. Steel and Bethlehem Steel were competitively disadvantaged versus Nucor and others with electric arc mini-mills. The firm should also consider *variating* fixed costs — reducing fixed costs and increasing variable costs. Then, if sales slip, costs also reduce. The firm should tightly manage working capital by reducing accounts receivable and inventory and lengthening accounts payable.

New product innovation should also concern market leaders. Products based on new technology can destroy leadership positions — compact discs versus vinyl records; e-mail versus fax. Kodak could not make the transition from chemical film to digital imaging successfully and filed for bankruptcy. An external orientation is the best protection against this sort of market erosion. Distribution can also be challenging. Early in the life cycle, the firm may have developed a distribution system to reach end-user customers. But as some end users grow in size and expertise, they demand direct distribution to secure lower prices by cutting out distributor margins.

HARVEST

The firm is market leader, but a **harvest** strategy may be more important than maintaining sales and market share. Reasons include:

- Change in the firm's strategy.
- Desire to avoid specific competitors.
- Government regulations impose restrictions.
- Investment requirements become too high.
- New technology makes the product obsolete.

Once the firm decides to harvest, the critical question is *fast* or *slow*? Fast harvesting — divest the product and gain immediate cash. Slow harvesting — the firm should focus on three issues:

- Cut costs by simplifying the product line and reducing support.
- Minimize further investment in the product.
- Raise prices.

The more aggressive the firm's actions, the more quickly it will exit the market.

SCENARIO 7: FOLLOWERS IN CONCENTRATED MATURE MARKETS

Followers have smaller market shares than the leader; they probably also have higher costs, lower profits, and are weaker financially. But leaders can lose position by poor decisions, and followers may attain leadership by inspired management. Airbus caught up with Boeing in large

KEY IDEA

➤ *Market leaders* in concentrated mature markets have two major options:

- Long-run leadership
- Harvesting: May be *fast* or *slow*

KEY IDEA

➤ Followers in concentrated mature markets typically have higher costs, lower profits, and less financial strength than market leaders. But they may rejuvenate to become a major threat.

jet aircraft (Chapter 5 Opening Case); Southwest Airlines is now the leading domestic U.S. airline. Most firms have products that fit scenario 7; hence, this scenario has broad applicability. The follower has three basic strategic options, each with several sub-options.

IMPROVE MARKET POSITION

Careful and creative market segmentation, kenneling, and direct attack are three primary alternatives to grow and, perhaps, ultimately dethrone the market leader:

MARKET SEGMENTATION. Options for segmentation typically appear in early growth and become numerous in late growth and maturity. Creative segmentation is the dominant option for counteracting the market leader's advantages.

Firms often identify and target market segments by adding benefits to satisfy customers' ever more fine-grained needs, often at higher prices. But in maturity, there is often one segment that just wants basic product benefits, *getting back to basics* — at a low price.

KENNELING. Kenneling is a metaphor for bringing several *dog* (seemingly worthless) products together. A follower may acquire several unprofitable (or marginally profitable) low-market-share products, and then execute a *roll-up* into a single offer. By rationalizing operations, distribution, and/or marketing, the follower may become a strong competitor. This approach is common in B2B markets.

DIRECT ATTACK. If the leader has been lazy, underinvested, set prices too high, and/or served customers poorly, direct attack may be the follower's best option. Good market intelligence helps find the leader's weak spots, so the follower can invest to exploit them. In financial information, new-entrant Bloomberg went head-to-head against Dow Jones and Reuters; pre-installed software in custom-made terminals let subscribers do their own financial analyses. Now Bloomberg and Thomson-Reuters share the terminal market. Similarly, Bratz dolls were the most successful direct attack on Mattel's Barbie.

In industries as diverse as credit cards and pharmaceuticals, market leaders have lost share to new entrants offering better products and/or lower prices. Firefox offers greater virus security and faster inter-website speed.

KEEP ON TRUCKIN'

This adage describes maintaining or rationalizing the firm's current position:

MAINTAIN POSITION. Holding market share roughly constant over the long run can be viable if the firm has a profitable market position and strengths in one or more segments.

RATIONALIZE POSITION. If profits are marginal or negative, rationalizing operations may be the way to go. The firm should examine all aspects of operations, distribution, and sales with *a fine-tooth comb*, and make tough cost-cutting decisions.

EXIT

Followers should choose *exit* if profitability is unlikely and/or the product's future is doubtful, perhaps due to negative brand image or slowing market demand. Choices are **divest** or **liquidate**:

DIVEST. By finding a buyer for which the product is a good fit, the firm can secure cash quickly.

LIQUIDATE. If no buyers appear, the only reasonable action may be liquidation — closing down and selling assets.

SCENARIO 8: FRAGMENTED MATURE MARKETS

Fragmented markets have many players, but no firm is dominant. Hence, leader/follower distinctions have little relevance. An important objective is increasing market share. Two strategic options for restructuring or repositioning offers are acquisition, and standardization and branding:

- Acquisition
- Standardization and branding

ACQUISITION

Acquisition is similar to kenneling — p. 165; it can be very successful when geography drives fragmentation. A global firm may acquire many national companies to secure greater market share. AXA, the French insurance giant, built strong regional positions in the fragmented global insurance industry by acquisition.

STANDARDIZATION AND BRANDING

In fragmented industries, many players typically offer a wide range of products/services. Standardization is a way to reduce variation and improve consistency across various suppliers; branding assures customers that each provider supplies the same value. Sometimes firms use *franchising* to attract small, independently owned players — Chapter 18. Franchisees maintain independence, but take advantage of the franchisor's brand and other services. Examples include Century 21 — real estate; and Holiday Inn — hospitality.

SCENARIO 9: MARKETS IN DECLINE

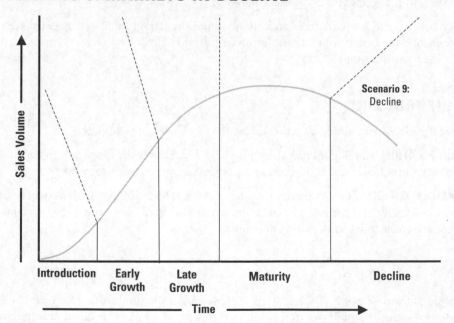

Figure 10.6 identifies the decline scenario. "So now you've graduated; we're delighted that you've joined us. We're going to throw you in the deep end. You will be in charge of our *Franklin* product where sales have been declining for the past few years." How would you like this assignment? Most new managers would not be happy, yet firms can make good profits from declining products. Indeed, ROI can be quite high; the firm has probably depreciated its capital equipment so investment is low.[12]

KEY IDEA

➤ In mature fragmented markets, no firm has a large market share.

KEY IDEA

➤ Major options in fragmented markets are:
- Acquisition
- Standardization and branding

FIGURE 10.6

DECLINE-STAGE SCENARIOS

We learned earlier that the pioneer has little competition early in the life cycle. But as the market grows, competitors typically enter. In the decline stage of the life cycle, the reverse occurs — new entry is unlikely and competitors exit. Good examples are videotape recorders, many canned foods, public telephones, full-service travel agents, and *sake* in Japan. Two dimensions are important in analyzing declining markets: market hospitality and firm business strengths.

MARKET HOSPITALITY. A declining market is **inhospitable** if:

- Decline is rapid and/or uncertain.
- The market is commodity-based; there are no price-insensitive segments.
- Competitors:
  - are viable and credible.
  - are evenly balanced and view the market as strategically important.
  - have high fixed costs and are very sensitive to sales declines.
- Customer switching costs are low.
- Bankruptcy laws allow failing competitors to return with lower costs, like U.S. airlines.
- Competitor exit barriers are high — for example, they cannot easily redeploy assets.
- Competitors are emotionally committed to their products.
- The product is part of a vertically integrated supply system.
- The government or the community pressures (or subsidizes) some firms to remain.

Characteristics of **hospitable** markets tend to be the opposite of these conditions.

BUSINESS STRENGTHS. Firms with good **business strengths** should have low costs, good raw material contracts, and/or be able to keep productive assets running without major investment. If, in addition, the market is hospitable, pursuing actions toward leadership may be a viable option. The firm should:

- Publicly recognize the decline — but also demonstrate its commitment.
- Market aggressively by adding new products, increasing advertising and promotion, and/or cutting prices — the newspaper industry is a good example.
- Consider reducing production capacity like several U.S. domestic airlines.
- Consider encouraging competitors to exit by offering long-term supply contracts for their customers. Buying competitors' assets may also be an option.

Generally, when the firm has poor business strengths it should harvest or divest. It should also exit from inhospitable markets unless it can dominate one or more price-insensitive segments.

LEVERAGE THE BRAND

Notwithstanding market decline, and in addition to the above options, the firm may be able to leverage a strong brand in other markets. By diversifying away from its original business, the firm may yet survive and grow. Faced with a decline in cigarette smoking, Zippo, makers of the iconic lighter, introduced life-style products like camping supplies, casual clothing, fragrances, and watches. But this path may be quite difficult; Zippo discontinued earlier entries into tape measures, key holders, and belt buckles.

KEY IDEA

➤ Firms can make considerable profits in declining markets.

KEY IDEA

➤ In a declining market, the firm's options depend on market hospitality and its business strengths.

Marketing Question

Suppose you were a full-service travel agent. What actions would you take to ensure your survival?

KEY IDEA

➤ The firm may be able to leverage a declining brand into new markets.

KEY MESSAGES

Pre-emption is an important dimension of strategy-making; acting before competitors can put the firm in good competitive position. Using the product life-cycle framework, we constructed nine scenarios for developing pre-emptive strategies:

- Introduction
- Early-Growth Leaders
- Early-Growth Followers
- Late Growth
- Maturity – But Not Really
- Maturity – Concentrated Market Leaders
- Maturity – Concentrated Market Followers
- Maturity – Fragmented Markets
- Decline

These scenarios can help the firm think through its strategy by anticipating, and striving to influence, change. For each scenario, we developed a family of strategic options. Notwithstanding the value of identifying these options, the best competitive strategies are often contrarian. When the firm surprises competitors, it can gain significantly.

VIDEOS AND AUDIOS

Managing through the Life Cycle   v1002 🎥   Ron Boire   Toys R Us

v1002

IMPERATIVE 3

*Set Strategic Direction
and Positioning*

CHAPTER 11

MANAGING

BRANDS cv1101

To access O-codes, go to **www.ocodes.com**

If this business were to be split up, I would be glad to take the

brands, trademarks, and goodwill, and you could have all the

bricks and mortar and I would fare better than you.

— John Stuart, then Chairman of Quaker Oats[1]

LEARNING OBJECTIVES

When you have completed this chapter, you will be able to:
- Understand the nature of brands and the values they provide for buyers and sellers.
- Comprehend the changing role of brands and branding.
- Distinguish between customer brand equity and firm brand equity.
- Measure the monetary value of customer brand equity and firm brand equity.
- Build and sustain a strong brand.
- Construct the firm's brand architecture.
- Make decisions about multi-branding versus umbrella branding, brand broadening, and brand migration.
- Address branding issues for strategic alliances.
- Revitalize struggling brands.

OPENING CASE: SAP

In the first decade of the 21st century, SAP doubled the value of the SAP brand and moved signifi-cantly up the global rankings. How did SAP achieve such success?

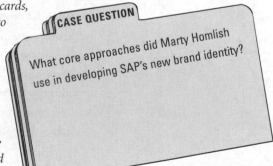

In 2000, SAP was the world's largest enterprise systems software firm and third-largest independent software supplier overall.[2] SAP had 12,500 customers and 25,000 software installations in more than 50 countries, mainly with large global firms. SAP's culture was technologically driven and based its success on innovative product development; marketing and branding were not significant. Marketing was decentralized at the national level and multiple advertising agencies produced local campaigns. SAP's branding tagline changed frequently in the previous decade: "We Can Change Your Business Perspective"; "A Better Return on Information"; "The City of 'e'"; "The Time of New Management"; and "You Can, It Does". SAP had one global website, 30 local country sites, many subsidiary sites, and more than 9,000 web pages without a common theme. SAP's brand identity was weak and unclear, and CEO Hasso Plattner concluded its messaging was sprawling, inconsistent, and confusing.

Plattner broke several taboos by bringing in Martin Homlish from Sony Electronics as SAP's new Global Chief Marketing Officer — hiring from outside SAP, outside the software industry, and outside Germany. Homlish's challenge was to transform SAP's marketing and to reposition the SAP brand to have broader, sustainable appeal. Said Homlish, "I saw SAP as a marketer's dream ... great products, strong history of innovation, and a loyal customer base. All we had to do was transform marketing." Homlish faced three core challenges: communicate the brand consistently, align the organization, and create a brand flexible enough to support challenging business objectives in a dynamic industry.

Homlish was particularly concerned about the rapid swings in SAP's messaging. He sought a brand identity that could evolve over time. Meeting with customers, Homlish said, "I found a common theme. SAP was considered a mission-critical part of almost every great company." SAP's brand identity became: SAP turns businesses into best-run businesses. *The tagline to convey the new identity was,* "The Best-Run Businesses Run SAP."

Homlish redesigned SAP's brand architecture: SAP became the masterbrand; product brands like my SAP CRM were sub-brands. SAP aligned national websites with the global site. Changes to the global site then triggered changes to local sites using state-of-the-art web content management applications. SAP placed all global advertising with Ogilvy & Mather and reinforced its new brand identity with simple headlines that complemented the tagline: "Lufthansa runs SAP" and "Adidas runs SAP." Large posters in airports around the world helped globalize the SAP brand.

SAP Global Marketing developed a series of tools to align regional marketing. Homlish installed a branding culture by involving local field offices as co-developers of global messaging. He addressed Kick-Off meetings to field organizations in the North America, Europe, Middle East, and Africa (EMEA) regions. SAP Global Marketing created country champions *to roll out each campaign and gain internal support. Said Homlish, "When I arrived at SAP and would ask questions about our company and our products, I would get a lot of jargon ... SAP-anese — it confused me and our customers." SAP Global Marketing distributed pocket-sized brand cards, stating core positioning, attributes, and personality of brands, worldwide to all employees. SAP Global Marketing also selected brand ambassadors to champion the brand locally.*

CASE QUESTION

What core approaches did Marty Homlish use in developing SAP's new brand identity?

Homlish's actions led SAP — 240,000 customers in 180 countries — to powerful results. According to BusinessWeek's (BW) annual brand rankings, from 2000 to 2012, SAP's brand value more than doubled to $15.6 billion. In 2012, BW ranked SAP at number 25, above established brands like Ford, Sony, Volkswagen, and Xerox. SAP's revenues and profits grew from $5.1 billion and $796 million, respectively (1999), to $16.7 billion and $2.4 billion in 2012.

Chapter 11 is the third of three chapters discussing separate facets of Imperative 3: Set Strategic Direction and Positioning. Chapter 9 discussed developing strategy for market segments and

markets; in Chapter 10, we focused on pre-emption and used the life-cycle framework to develop scenarios for generating competitive strategic options. In this chapter, we focus on branding and managing brands. As with previous topics, deep insight into markets, customers, competitors, company, and complementers is critical for making good branding decisions.

In recent years, branding has shifted from being a relatively low-level tactical issue concerned with naming products/services to being a critical driver of contemporary marketing practice. Today, the value of many firm brands far outstrips the value of their tangible assets. Accountants and financiers are re-examining the nature of brands as they rethink basic assumptions about the value of the firm. Brands also have value for customers, and branding is now a major decision area for both senior managers and marketing executives alike.

WHAT IS A BRAND?

Brands are different from products. A leading marketer once said, "A product is something that is made in a factory; a brand is something that is bought by a customer. A competitor can copy a product; a brand is unique. A product can be quickly outdated; a successful brand is timeless."[3]

Throughout history, sellers have branded their goods and services. Medieval goldsmiths and silversmiths branded their products. The branding iron was an essential tool for U.S. ranchers; if a rancher had a reputation for high quality cattle, his brand secured higher prices at market. The traditional definition follows logically: A brand is a "name, term, sign, symbol or design (or letter, number, or character), or a combination of them intended to identify the goods and services of one seller or group of sellers and to differentiate them from the competition."[4] Brands are a part of everyday life for firms and customers — logos, names, package designs, symbols, and trademarks are on everything we drive, drink, wear, and eat.

The most often used *signifier* is brand name, but other signifiers can be as (or more) important. Target stores are associated with the color red and UPS with brown; the *Financial Times* and fiberglass insulation from Dow Corning (U.S.) and ACI (Australia) are pink. We all recognize Absolut and Coca-Cola brands by the *visual* signifiers of their bottles.

Today, brands have meaning far beyond these outward manifestations. By offering customers value via its brands, the firm secures value for its shareholders. The brand has become a symbol around which the firm and its customers construct a relationship. We define a **brand** as: *A collection of perceptions and associations that customers hold about a product, a service, or a company. This collection embodies values that create meaning for customers that represent a promise of the experience customers expect when they have contact with the brand.*[5] Important implications are:

- The primary meaning of any brand is carried in customer minds. Great brands are really owned by customers, not by firms.
- The brand makes an implicit or explicit promise of a customer experience.[6] This promise provides value to customers over and above the product/service. By providing this additional value, the firm earns value for shareholders.

- Figure 11.1 shows that the term *brand* applies widely to an individual product, a product line, or a group of product lines:

  - **Individual product.** An individual product such as Aveo (Chevrolet), Camry (Toyota), Fiesta (Ford), Leaf (Nissan), Town & Country (Chrysler), or MX-5 Miata (Mazda).

  - **Product line.** A group of closely related products serving a similar function. The Ragu **family or masterbrand** embraces several types of sauces — Cheese, Chunky Garden Style, Light, Old World Style, Pizza, and Robust Blend Hearty.

  - **Group of product lines.** A group of product lines fulfilling many different functions. These **monolithic** brands are often *corporate brands* — Carrefour, Citigroup, GE, Google, IBM, Marks & Spencer, Microsoft, Nike, and Yamaha.

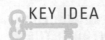

KEY IDEA

➤ The firm may brand products at different levels of aggregation.

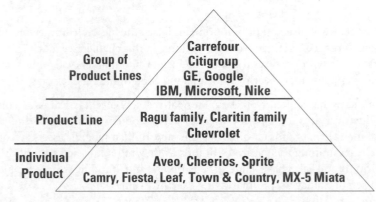

FIGURE 11.1

LEVELS OF BRANDING

Sometimes a brand's meaning evolves. In the U.S., Honda's original association was motorcycles — today, Honda's associations include automobiles and lawnmowers. Some brands, like Virgin, move away from their origins and become quite abstract:

Virgin — Evolution of a Brand

The original brand associations for Virgin were tied to publishing rock-and-roll records. Expansion into record stores broadened Virgin's brand associations, but Virgin sold its record business and diversified into many product classes — Virgin Atlantic (airlines), Virgin Books, Virgin Bridal Shops, Virgin Cars (retail distribution), Virgin Direct (financial services), Virgin Electronics, Virgin Limousines, Virgin Megastores (retail distribution), Virgin Mobile (cellular phone service), Virgin Sound and Vision (educational computer software), Virgin Vacations, and Radio Free Virgin. More recently, Virgin announced its entry into space travel — Virgin Galactic.

The Virgin brand is now uncoupled from its origins, yet still articulates its original abstract values. Virgin's brand identity is a higher-order sense of fun-loving, hip, irreverent, anti-establishment *underdogness*. Virgin's ongoing battles with British Airways and CEO Sir Richard Branson's personal activities — including attempts at around-the-world balloon flights — strongly support the brand identity. Some observers criticize Virgin's extensions as random and capricious but Branson's response is quite direct: "Branding is everything. I think it's also wise to diversify; this enables you to have a contingency plan when the economy is going through a rough patch."[7]

Sometimes firms use multiple brands, like Toyota Corolla or the American Express Personal Card. The firm earns value from the monolithic brand, Toyota and American Express, and additional value from individual product brands. Other features of brands include:

- Anything can be branded — a product; service; town, city, or country; even yourself!

- Brands can provide psychological value like safety and security — ADT, Volvo; and winning attitude — Wheaties, Nike.

- Brands may become generic — synonymous with the product class. U.S. examples include Aspirin, Band-Aid, Google, and Kleenex; in Britain — Biro and Hoover.

Marketing Exercise

Select a brand. How did you learn about it? Write down all your associations. For each brand association, assess the extent to which it is *strong* versus *weak*, *favorable* versus *unfavorable*, and *unique* versus *common*.

Marketing Exercise

Find a working friend or relative, and give the Brand Coffee Machine Test. Stand at the coffee machine and ask, "What does your product or company brand stand for?" Then press the *fill* button or lever. If the person cannot give a good answer by the time your cup fills, the brand fails. The organization cannot expect customers to understand the brand's meaning if employees do not.[9]

TABLE 11.1

BRAND PERSONALITY[10]

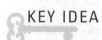

KEY IDEA

➤ *Brand identity* comprises associations the firm *wants* people to hold.

➤ *Brand image* comprises associations people *actually* hold.

- Customer judgments and expectations about brands drive purchase decisions.
- Customers often form communities to demonstrate commitment to brands, like Harley-Davidson riders and Macintosh users.[8]

The firm must choose a **brand identity** for each of its brands — associations like personal, lifestyle, or type of customer it *wants* people to hold. The firm must also decide how, if at all, the various brand identities should relate to each other. By contrast, **brand image** comprises the actual associations customers hold about the brand. The firm should audit brand image on a regular basis.

BRAND ASSOCIATIONS

The firm should strive for **brand associations** that reinforce the desired brand identity and align these associations with brand image. Brand associations are thoughts the customer generates when faced with a stimulus like brand name, logo, message, or spokesperson. **Brand personality** captures the idea of enduring and distinct human or emotional characteristics associated with a brand — Table 11.1.

Dimensions	Descriptors	Examples
Competence	Intelligent — technical, corporate, serious Reliable — hardworking, secure, efficient, trustworthy, careful, credible Successful — leader, confident, influential	*The Wall Street Journal*
Excitement	Daring — trendy, exciting, off-beat, flashy, provocative Imaginative — unique, humorous, surprising, artistic, fun Spirited — cool, young, lively, outgoing, adventurous Up-to-date — independent, contemporary, innovative, aggressive	MTV, Mountain Dew
Ruggedness	Outdoors — masculine, Western, active, athletic Tough — rugged, strong, no-nonsense	L.L. Bean
Sincerity	Cheerful — sentimental, friendly, warm, happy Down-to-earth — family-oriented, small-town, conventional, blue collar, all American Honest — sincere, real, ethical, thoughtful, caring Wholesome — original, genuine, ageless, classic, old-fashioned	Hallmark cards, Skippy peanut butter
Sophistication	Charming — feminine, smooth, sexy, gentle Upper class — glamorous, good-looking, pretentious, sophisticated	Chanel, Dior

Effective brand associations are:

- **Strong.** Personally relevant for customers and presented consistently over time.
- **Favorable.** Desired by customers and successfully delivered by the brand.
- **Unique.** Perceived by customers as unique, different from other brands.

Generally, the firm uses implementation tools like communications, distribution outlet, and product design and quality to achieve alignment between brand identity and brand image. Sometimes brand associations (positive and negative) are outside the firm's control. Many people associate Levi's (jeans) and Marlboro (cigarettes) with U.S. cowboy movies. These associations are generally positive; in contrast, widespread opposition to U.S. policies (Iraq war) has affected some brands negatively. To avoid negative associations, McDonald's focuses on local ownership, local suppliers, distinct store designs, and unique menu items — like the *McArabia*, a chicken sandwich on Arabian-style bread.

BRANDING IS NOT JUST FOR CONSUMERS ...

Many people assume that branding is just for B2C marketing. Not so![11] Branding is also very important in B2B markets, especially for firms with many customers like SAP — Opening Case. Specific industries include banking, capital goods, computing, consulting, office equipment, and shipping; individual firms for which branding is critical are Brother, Canon, Caterpillar, DuPont, FedEx, GE, IBM, Intel, Microsoft, Office Depot, Oracle, Sun, TNT, and Xerox — Figure 11.2.

FIGURE 11.2

BRANDING IS NOT JUST FOR CONSUMERS!

B2C and B2B branding use different languages: B2C firms focus on brand image or associations; B2B firms talk about building relationships, and customer confidence. B2B firms want customers to view them as experienced, risk-free, and trustworthy suppliers. Oftentimes, branding is more important than technology — a well-managed brand outlasts many technology changes.

... AND IS NOT JUST ABOUT ADVERTISING

Another common misunderstanding is that branding should focus only on consumers or end-user customers and that advertising is the only approach. Not so! Reaching a broad audience with its communications is as important for corporate brands as for many product brands. Communications targets extend beyond current and potential customers and include:

- Alliance partners
- Intermediaries
- Other government bodies
- Regulators
- Bondholders
- Investment analysts
- Owners/shareholders
- Suppliers
- Employees
- Media
- Prospective employees

In addition to traditional advertising, the firm can build and reinforce brand identity via other communication forms like brochures, direct mail and e-mail, participation in social-media groups, managerial actions like speeches and broadcasts (Twitter, blogs, and other digital communications), products and packaging, promotions, publicity and public relations, stationery, physical facilities, telephone interactions, and websites. The CEO can have a major impact on a firm's brand by becoming the *face and feel* of the company; good examples are Richard Branson — Virgin; Tim Cook — Apple; Mark Cuban — Dallas Mavericks; and Warren Buffett — Berkshire Hathaway.

Firm employees are an increasingly important branding audience and communications channel. Eli Lilly (pharmaceuticals), Verizon (telecommunications), and many other leading firms conduct extensive branding programs to ensure that employees internalize and represent the firm's brand identity properly. Regularly and periodically, these firms measure how employees perceive company brands. Internal branding is especially important for business services and consulting firms, and B2C firms like retailers, where employees regularly interface with customers. Regarding social media, most firms carefully select employees who can *evangelize* and represent the brand in *tweets*, chat rooms, and online communities. The firm should also conduct branding audits of constituencies like suppliers and affiliates.

BRAND EQUITY AND THE VALUE OF BRANDS

By effectively developing and implementing market strategy, the firm creates brand value. The firm may also use brand value to develop and implement market strategy. Excellent branding operates as a virtuous circle, continually employing and enhancing the firm's equity in its brands.

KEY IDEA

➤ Brand personality comprises five important dimensions:

- Competence
- Excitement
- Ruggedness
- Sincerity
- Sophistication

KEY IDEA

➤ The brand/production relationship may take several different forms.

KEY IDEA

➤ Customers may secure significant value from a brand — *before* and *after* purchase.

KEY IDEA

➤ Brand equity reflects the trust established between the brand owner and its customers.

Brand equity captures the idea that brands deliver value, over and above actual products/services. The most widely accepted definition of brand equity is "a set of brand assets and liabilities linked to a brand, its name, and symbol that add to (or subtract from) the value provided by a product or service to a firm and/or that firm's customers."[12] From this definition we see that brand value accrues to both the *firm* and its *customers*. It follows that there are two types of brand equity: *customer brand equity (CBE)* — the value customers receive; and *firm brand equity (FBE)* — the value firms receive.

CUSTOMER BRAND EQUITY

The brand provides customers two types of value: *pre-purchase equity* and *post-purchase equity*.

PRE-PURCHASE EQUITY — what customers *believe* before purchase — reduces customer search costs and purchase risks. In overnight package delivery, many business customers believe FedEx offers great *functional* value — packages arrive on time. Many airline passengers believe jetBlue and Southwest Airlines (U.S.), and easyJet and Ryanair (Europe) offer superior *economic* value. Others believe the American Express Platinum card, Air Jordan and Air Max sneakers, and fashion items from Armani, Dior, Prada, and Versace provide *psychological* values like status and prestige. The classic pre-purchase CBE example is: "You never get fired for buying IBM."

POST-PURCHASE EQUITY enhances the customer's consumption experience. After purchase, brands provide *functional* value — doing the job they were designed to do — and *economic* value — like low cost of ownership. They also provide *psychological* value — like feelings of security from insurance and the assurance of continued *functional* value. Post-purchase psychological value (like status and prestige) can have long-lasting effects, especially if ownership and use are transparent and communicated to others.

Sometimes high CBE focuses on a specific product class. Tide *detergent* typically engenders positive customer values, but consumers would probably view Tide *toothpaste* or Tide *cookies* negatively. Other brands provide customer value across several product classes; examples include corporate brands like *Virgin*, and movie brands like *Star Wars* and *Harry Potter* that earn significant revenues from a wide variety of accessory products in addition to the movies. CBE, either pre- or post-purchase, is generally greater when:

- Comparing alternative products is difficult.
- Customers do not realize value until some time after purchase.
- Customers are inexperienced or unfamiliar with the product class.
- Product quality from some suppliers is variable.
- The product is socially visible.
- There is mental flexibility in portraying the brand.

FIRM BRAND EQUITY

FBE results from customer responses to firm actions and links directly to CBE. High brand awareness, positive attitudes, high perceived quality, positive word of mouth, intention to purchase, purchase, brand loyalty, positive brand image and associations, and satisfaction all enhance FBE. CBE and FBE reflect the trust between the brand and its customers. A former Sony chairman opined: "Our biggest asset is four letters, S-o-n-y. It's not so much our buildings or our engineers or our factories, but our name."[13] Former American Express, RJR Nabisco, and IBM CEO Lou Gerstner had a similar philosophy:

> Shelly Lazarus, CEO of Ogilvy & Mather Worldwide, said: "I learned a big lesson from Lou. Once you've set a strategy, you never ever violate it. Nobody ever got a free card, a discounted card, or bundled pricing. Lou would say, 'This is a violation of the brand, and we're not doing it.'"[14]

High FBE has many positives. Firms with high FBE:

- Can set higher prices and earn better profit margins.
- More easily introduce similarly branded items in different product classes and markets.
- Use cross-selling to encourage existing customers to purchase in different product classes.
- Generate leverage in distribution channels by securing more and better shelf space and more favorable transaction terms.
- Raise entry barriers for competitors.
- Exploit licensing opportunities.

Generally, CBE and FBE build slowly, but new brands sometimes gain strength relatively quickly — eBay, Google, Leapfrog, Red Bull, Ryanair, and Yahoo! Nonetheless, CBE, and hence FBE, are fragile and can dissipate quickly if the firm mis-steps. Many firms unwittingly cause brand equity declines by product proliferation, price-cutting, offering discounts and promotions, using inferior components, squeezing suppliers or channel partners, and simple neglect.[15] Tommy Hilfiger's sales went from red hot to stalled when product proliferation and out-of-control distribution (more than 10,000 department stores and discount outlets) diluted brand value.

Managerial mishaps can also wreak havoc with FBE. Examples include product recalls by Dow Corning (breast implants) and Merck (*Vioxx*) and product failures by Firestone (*Ford Explorer* tires) and Toyota (unplanned acceleration). Brand equity is fragile, but some brands have greater **brand resilience** than others. In 1982, J&J withdrew Tylenol capsules in the face of a cyanide-poisoning scare (six people died; unsolved); sales plummeted to zero. J&J's timely and caring response led to a quick Tylenol rebound when it introduced more secure packaging and ramped up distribution and promotion. Planning for damage control and crisis management is increasingly important.

MONETIZING BRAND EQUITY

We just explored the value the brand brings to customers — customer brand equity (CBE); and to the firm — firm brand equity (FBE). Now we focus on the monetary value of brands.

CUSTOMER BRAND EQUITY

Customers receive value from a *generic* product; typically, they receive greater value from a *branded* product. The difference in value — brand less generic — equals CBE. The **dollar-metric** method assesses the monetary value of CBE. The firm asks a customer how much extra she would pay for the branded product versus an unbranded product; this amount is CBE's monetary value. Actually, this figure is *potential* CBE — the customer only receives brand equity after purchase. If the price is higher than she is willing to pay, there is no CBE. The firm can also assess the *marginal* CBE of one brand versus another: How much extra will the customer pay for her favored brand?

FIRM BRAND EQUITY

FBE relates directly to the brand's current and future ability to attract paying customers and increase shareholder value.[16] Valuation components are:

- **Revenue.** The price difference between the branded product and an identical generic product, multiplied by the branded product's forecast excess sales volume.
- **Cost.** The costs of supporting the brand.

KEY IDEA

➤ Brand equity generally builds up slowly over time.

KEY IDEA

➤ A brand can quickly lose value if not managed properly.

Marketing Question

Some individuals build brands; others reap the fruits of successful brand building; still others attempt to recover brand equity following well-publicized missteps. What can you learn about branding from Paris Hilton, Michael Jordan, Sarah Palin, Martha Stewart, Maria Sharapova, Donald Trump, and Tiger Woods? Feel free to substitute your own selections.

BASIC APPROACH. FBE's monetary value is the sum of the year-by-year differences between revenues and costs, discounted to the present.[17] Unfortunately, this straightforward approach has two inherent problems:

- An unbranded equivalent to the branded product may not exist.
- The approach ignores potential for brand broadening (leveraging) — using the brand to enter a new product form/product class. Brand value is unconstrained by current products, product lines, or customers. Many brands have customer-attracting properties over and above the product (set of products) to which they are currently attached. The brand *Pan Am*, unattached to an aircraft or airline, sold for several million dollars.

MARKET VALUE METHOD. The market provides the best FBE measure; this approach works well for publicly traded corporate brands. FBE equals market value less book value, plus non-brand intangibles like human resources, know-how, and patents. When Ford purchased Jaguar for $2.5 billion, its book value was $0.4 billion. Observers viewed the $2.1 billion difference (2.5 less 0.4) as Jaguar's brand equity. When market value does not exist, as for most product brands, the firm must use internal methods.

INTERNAL METHODS. Two internal methods for assessing FBE are:

- **Replacement cost.** The firm multiplies the anticipated brand-replacement cost by the probability of success.[18]
- **Cash flow.** These approaches are intuitively more appealing, but estimating future cash flows is difficult. Interbrand (brand consultant) uses a proprietary method to estimate FBE based on future cash flows.

Calculating the *marginal* FBE of one brand versus another is probably easier than calculating an absolute value. New United Motor Manufacturing Inc. (NUMMI) (GM/Toyota joint venture) manufactured two virtually identical cars — Geo Prizm (GM) and Corolla (Toyota). Corolla had a premium price and depreciated more slowly. Figure 11.3 shows Corolla's 120,000 (200,000 – 80,000) annual unit volume benefit and $400 ($11,100 – $10,700) price benefit.

KEY IDEA

➤ Internal approaches for calculating firm brand equity are:

- Replacement cost
- Cash flow methods

....

FIGURE 11.3

THE MONETARY VALUE OF FIRM BRAND EQUITY — AUTOMOBILE EXAMPLE

KEY IDEA

➤ The firm earns a contribution to FBE only when a customer purchases the brand.

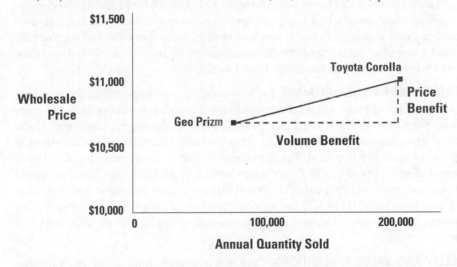

BUILDING AND SUSTAINING A STRONG BRAND

An important goal of developing and implementing market strategy is to build and sustain a strong brand. Strong brands induce positive responses from customers. In turn, these positive responses enhance brand strength and are a powerful influence on the firm's market strategy.

BUILDING A STRONG BRAND

Strong brands have value for both the firm and its customers. The firm builds a strong brand by making good decisions during the branding process — Figure 11.4.

Brand Identity

↓

Brand Awareness

↓

Brand Associations and Brand Image

↓

Brand Quality and
Value Perceptions

↓

Brand Loyalty

↓

Brand Broadening

FIGURE 11.4

**BUILDING A
STRONG BRAND**[19]

BRAND IDENTITY. Brand identity is what the firm wants the brand to mean. Said Eli Lilly CEO Sidney Taurel, "Our brand is our identity. It is who we are in the eyes of our customers ... shareholders, prospective employees, suppliers, and the communities where we operate."[20]

Brand identity is the blueprint for many marketing decisions; indeed, brand identity defines the limits on product quality, service, promotion, distribution, and price. Executing on brand identity is critical to customers forming the desired associations and brand image (below).

BRAND AWARENESS. Typically, the firm must invest significantly to achieve **brand awareness** at target customers. When the brand is first entrant in a new product form, the pioneer must educate potential customers about the product form, as well as about the brand. Gojo educated consumers, medical professionals, and retailers about its new type of hand-washing liquid — Purell. Launching a new corporate brand is also very costly. Lucent spent $50 million to create corporate brand awareness. But a brand may stay in memory for many years — Datsun, Esso, Master Charge — even after retirement by the brand owner.

BRAND ASSOCIATIONS AND BRAND IMAGE. Brand associations are the meanings the brand has for individual customers — *brand image* is the overall sum of brand associations. Each and every marketing implementation decision the firm takes has a role in developing customers' brand associations and hence brand image — product design, service, communications, distribution outlet, and price. Consistency is critical: The firm should strive for congruence between brand image and brand identity. Brand equity always suffers when brand identity and brand image are mismatched. Suppose the basis for a product's brand identity is high prestige — yet customers form brand image from inferior product and service quality, poor advertising execution, downscale distribution, and low price. Customer response would most likely be negative, and FBE would suffer.

BRAND QUALITY AND VALUE PERCEPTIONS. Consistency in communications and customer **brand experiences** are crucial for developing positive brand quality and value perceptions.

A specific problem for value perceptions is cutting prices and/or offering short-term price promotions. Sales may spike in the short run but cause long-term brand damage as customers hold off buying until the next promotion. Vlasic discounted pickle prices so far that despite volume increases, margin declines eventually forced it into bankruptcy. Clorox faced a similar problem, but reduced discounting and increased television advertising led to higher long-run revenues and profits.

Many global 100 firms have *brand police* or a *brand czar* to oversee branding consistency. These executives make sure the brand name, logos and symbols, and all messaging — including advertising, brochures, websites, and social media — retain consistency. Brand czars provide specific guidance on colors, font size, graphics, signs, stationery, uniforms, vehicles, and words; they also ensure conformity to consistent standards. We saw this consistency in the SAP Opening Case.

BRAND LOYALTY. Consistency in brand quality and value perceptions lead to **brand loyalty**. Brand loyalty inspires positive word of mouth, referrals, and repeat purchase. Vertical marketers (own retail outlets) like Starbucks (coffee) and Ben & Jerry's (ice cream) know the importance of consistency. They build *brand coherence* through personnel and the design and decor of retail facilities. By contrast, most car firms have difficulty providing brand-enhancing experiences in independently owned dealerships. A serious problem for hotel management firms like Hilton, Holiday Inn, and Sheraton is *off-message* execution by individual franchised hotels; inconsistency in the customer experience affects loyalty to the entire chain.

The firm earns high brand loyalty by:

•   Selecting the *right* brand identity for target customers and consistently executing on that identity.

•   Ensuring that firm employees and third-party organizations (like advertising agencies) are motivated to deliver on the brand identity.

•   Continuously measuring customer satisfaction with the brand and making the necessary course corrections. (Following section: Sustaining a Strong Brand.)

BRAND BROADENING. Repeat purchase, customer loyalty, and favorable word-of-mouth should follow successful brand identity development and execution. The firm may broaden (leverage) a strong brand to other product forms (and classes).

SUSTAINING A STRONG BRAND

The key to sustaining a strong brand for the long run is continual assessment of *brand health*. Many firms measure brand managers on short-term revenues, profits, and/or market share. This practice is rather like examining the firm's income statement but neglecting its balance sheet. **Brand health checks** use metrics indicating FBE changes.

Typical brand health checks use a *balanced-scorecard* approach — Chapter 22. Four popular types of measures — Table 11.2 — and sources are:

•   **Purchasing and sales** — firm accounting and CRM systems and industry-focused research suppliers.

•   **Perceptual** — survey research.

•   **Marketing support** — firm accounting and business intelligence systems and industry-focused suppliers.

•   **Profitability** — firm accounting system.

Brand-health checks are not one-time events. Brand-health checks should occur regularly — quarterly or bi-annually. The firm should compare current brand health to historic trends and benchmark competing brands.[21] Results from brand health checks should lead to appropriate changes in market strategy and execution.

Type of Measure	Measure	Description of Measure
Purchasing and sales	Market breadth	Number and type of customers purchasing the brand
	Market depth	Extent of repeat purchase
	Market share	Brand sales as a percentage of total market sales (units and/or dollars)
Perceptual	Awareness	Degree of brand awareness
	Brand image	Brand associations, congruence with brand identity
	Quality	Perception of brand quality (from blind tests)
	Uniqueness	Extent of differentiation from competition
	Value	Extent to which the brand provides good value for money
Marketing support	Advertising	Market share/advertising share
		Advertising/total marketing spend
	Distribution	Extent of distribution coverage in target outlets
		For retail goods, quality of display, especially key accounts
	Relative price	Price compared to competitive brands
Profitability	Profit	Gross margin earned from the brand
		Economic value added (EVA) of the brand

TABLE 11.2

REPRESENTATIVE SELECTION OF BRAND HEALTH CHECK MEASURES

MANAGING BRAND ARCHITECTURE

Many firms maintain a brand *portfolio* — multiple brands, each with its own brand identity. The LVMH (global luxury goods leader) corporate brand offers *Louis Vuitton* tan and brown monogrammed bags for several hundred dollars, *Murakami* bags at $1,000, and *Suhali* goatskin bags averaging $2,000. The firm's **brand architecture** — its organizing structure for multiple brands — is an important decision area.

Because firm brands have a major impact on shareholder value, branding decisions should have high priority. The firm should carefully consider what to brand, brand identities, and desired brand associations. The firm should also carefully plan brand additions (internally developed and secured by acquisition) and deletions. The firm must also consider interrelationships among the corporate brand, product class brands, and individual product brands. The firms' brand portfolio should evolve as markets evolve. Anheuser-Busch changed its portfolio as customers switched to different beers, from low-end to higher-end, and from fuller to lighter.

MULTI-BRANDING VERSUS UMBRELLA BRANDING

In **multi-branding** — aka *House of Brands* strategy — the firm uses multiple brands for its various products.[22] The firm seeks target-customer loyalty to individual brands, but not necessarily to the parent-company brand. Do you know the corporate owner of Aguila, Coors, Cristal, Foster's, Hamm's, Henry Weinhard, Icehouse, Keystone, Leinenkugel, Miller, Milwaukee's Best, Mickey's, Molson, Olde English 800, and Tyskie?*

By contrast, a firm using **umbrella branding** emphasizes a monolithic brand for several products (or product lines). Consumers know Yamaha for electronic musical instruments (keyboards and guitars), traditional musical instruments (pianos), home audio products, computer peripherals, motorcycles, and even Grand Prix engines.

KEY IDEA

➤ The firm should carefully manage evolution of the brand portfolio.

➤ Firms adjust brand portfolios in response to shifting customer trends, competitor action, and mergers and acquisitions.

Marketing Question

How do you assess the branding strategy for your college, school, or university? Does your institution pursue a multi-branding strategy or an umbrella branding strategy? How could your college, school, or university improve its branding?

KEY IDEA

➤ Both *multi-branding* and *umbrella branding* enjoy pros and cons.

* South Africa's SABMiller.

BRAND BROADENING (LEVERAGING)

Brand broadening (leveraging) occurs when the firm undertakes a *brand extension* — attaching an existing brand to a different product (form/class) to address a new opportunity — like Harley-Davidson restaurants and Coca-Cola clothing. Brand leveraging reduces launch costs and/or increases profits for small investments.[23] A new product with a leveraged brand gains automatic brand awareness. Before leveraging, the firm must consider potential opportunities and obstacles, and several branding issues.

OPPORTUNITIES AND OBSTACLES. The firm must address the following sorts of questions:

- Is there sufficient demand for the new venture?
- Is the firm sufficiently strong to succeed in the face of competition?
- Can the firm access the new market through current distribution channels?
- Is the firm capable of satisfying potential demand?
- Does the firm have access to raw materials and other production inputs?
- Does the firm possess other competencies necessary for success?

BRANDING ISSUES. These concern brand associations held by customers and their fit with the extension:

- Do customers perceive a fit between the original product form (class) and the new product form (class) in terms of product features and concepts?
- What are customer brand image and associations for the core product? Will these associations *transfer* to the new product?
- What is the reverse relationship? How will customer associations for the new product *back transfer* to brand associations for the core product?
- How does the corporate and/or monolithic brand relate to these associations?

Once the firm has addressed opportunities, obstacles, and several issues, the brand must meet two baseline conditions for an extension to be viable:

- The brand must have strong positive associations.
- Brand associations and the product extension should not be incongruous. How do you rate the likely success for *Tide* candies? *Mercedes-Benz* orange juice? *Victoria's Secret* soup?

Brand extensions tend to fail when:

- Associations between the brand and the extension are not obvious.
- The brand has a unique image and associations that do not transfer.
- The new product form (class) has a dominant competitor.
- The positioning is confusing and/or inconsistent.
- The extension's quality does not match customer expectations for the brand.

Brand dilution is a potentially serious issue: The brand extension fails, FBE reduces, and overall sales fall. Trouble![24]

BRAND MIGRATION

We noted earlier that firms sometimes retire individual brands. Perhaps the target market/segment has contracted, competition may be severe, and/or brand identity may no longer fit with evolving customer needs. Sometimes brand support is expensive, and/or a brand may have lost value because of managerial neglect, a lost internal battle for resources, and/or harvesting for profits and cash. Other times, the firm may decide to refocus efforts on fewer, stronger brands and/or seek economies of scale in marketing. Federated Department Stores retired

Marketing Question

Using well-known brands, suggest some brand extensions. Why do you think they would succeed? Suggest brand extensions you think would not succeed. Why?

Marketing Question

In 1984, Bulgari sold Bulgari brand luxury products in five Bulgari stores. By 2003, Bulgari had 180 stores; 600 outlets also sold Bulgari watches, and 14,000 outlets sold Bulgari perfumes. Bulgari formed Bulgari Hotels and Resorts in a joint venture with Marriott. Do you think Bulgari hotels will succeed? Why or why not? Do you think Bulgari's acquisition by LVMH will affect its hotel venture?

Abraham & Strauss, L.S. Ayers, Bon Marché, Bullocks, Burdines, Famous-Barr, Filene's, Foley's, Goldsmith's, Hecht's, Jordan Marsh, Kaufmann's, Lazarus, I. Magnin, Marshall Field's, Meier & Frank, Rich's, Robinsons-May, Stern's, Strawbridge's, and The Jones Store in favor of Macy's.

Sometimes the firm secures brands via acquisition and then retires them. Citicorp retired Schroder Salomon Smith Barney; Morgan Stanley retired Dean Witter. Also, the firm may be contractually obligated to stop using the brand. B&D acquired GE's small appliance (housewares) business but could use the GE brand for only five years. In these cases, the challenge is to retain the brand equity being retired by transferring it to another brand.

Vodafone, the world's largest cell-phone-service provider, previously comprised many strong domestic brands. Vodafone migrated these brands to *Vodafone* (Vo - voice, da - data, fone - phone). Said Vodafone's global-branding director, "Vodafone uses a dual branding strategy designed to give all constituents — employees, customers, and trade partners — a period of time so people can intellectually *get it*. In Germany we did *D2/Vodafone*, then *Vodafone/D2*, and then we just dropped the *D2* to become *Vodafone*.[25]

KEY IDEA

➤ The firm conserves brand equity by effective brand migration.

STRATEGIC ALLIANCES

Strategic alliances can extend the firm's brand into new market segments. Alliances can range from informal or contractual working relationships to new entities structured as legal joint ventures. Most alliances focus on competency — one firm's strengths compensate for the other firm's weaknesses, and vice versa. Strategic alliances have important **co-branding** implications when the co-branding partner can transfer positive customer attitudes. Co-branding between customers and suppliers is increasingly common; many PC manufacturers co-brand with Intel.

When firms co-brand with themselves they must ensure that brand associations are appropriate for the product and target segment. In Asia, Holiday Inn closely associates its parent brand with Crowne Plaza hotels; Crowne Plaza is an **endorsed brand**. By contrast, in the U.S., Crowne Plaza is a **standalone brand**; Holiday Inn associations negatively affect Crowne Plaza's brand image.

KEY IDEA

➤ The firm can enhance brand equity with effective strategic alliances.

KEY IDEA

➤ Three ways to reposition a brand are:
• Target new market segment(s)
• Change brand associations
• Alter the competitive target

➤ Continuous innovation pre-empts the need to revitalize a brand.

AGING AND DEFUNCT BRANDS

Some aging brands have loyal customers and survive for many years. But these are exceptions. The marketing landscape is littered with the corpses of once-valuable and famous brands. As markets evolve, weakly positioned brands may not be economically viable. Chapter 10 identifies a second option for improving sales in mature markets — *repositioning the brand*.

Brand reintroduction and/or brand revitalization is the key objective for *repositioning*. Key options are:

- **Target new market segment(s).** Colgate-Palmolive, Avon, and *Reader's Digest* each increased sales by targeting new geographic segments outside the U.S. To its surprise, Sears found that core U.S. customers were *not* male hardware buyers, but 25-to-50-year-old women with children. Sears successfully repositioned by refocusing promotion and expanding clothing and cosmetics products.

- **Change brand associations.** Successful examples are Honda's classic motorcycling repositioning from *long-haired guys and the police officers chasing them* to *a family activity* — "you meet the nicest people on a Honda" (Chapter 10). Britain's Labor government changed the country's associations from backward-looking and tradition-based to future-oriented youthfulness, excitement, and opportunity.

- **Alter the competitive target.** Bacardi successfully repositioned its light rum to compete against vodka and scotch whisky, rather than other rums.

The firm can avoid the necessity for revitalization by continually innovating, adding new products, and keeping the brand vital and relevant.

Marketing Question

Founded during the California Gold Rush, Levi Strauss' denim (de Nîmes) jeans became an American icon. In 1996, Levi's sales were $7.1 billion, mostly in mid-market outlets like JCPenney and Sears. Annual sales are now $4 billion–$5 billion, and most manufacturing is offshore. What advice would you give Levi Strauss' top management?

KEY MESSAGES

- The nature of brands has changed from signifiers of goods and services to symbols for constructing relationships between the firm and customers.

- A positive relationship between the brand and customers can significantly enhance shareholder value.

- The firm can brand individual products, product lines, and/or product groups.

- The firm should choose a brand identity and supporting associations.

- Brand image represents the associations customers hold about the brand. The firm should strive to achieve alignment between brand image and brand identity.

- Some important items about brands and branding are:
  - Branding is important in both B2C and B2B.
  - Branding is much more than advertising.
  - Customers are only one of several audiences for brand messages.
  - For product brands, we cannot assume that the brand owner is also the manufacturer.

- Customer brand equity (CBE) and firm brand equity (FBE) are two distinct constructs. Each can be monetized.

- To build a strong brand, the firm must execute a process through which it establishes brand identity, creates brand awareness, forms brand associations and brand image, develops consistent brand quality and value perceptions, builds brand loyalty and, possibly, leverages brand strength to new products/services.

- To sustain a strong brand, the firm should regularly measure brand health and act on results.

- To secure the best results from branding efforts, the firm should make serious decisions about various facets of brand architecture.

VIDEOS AND AUDIOS

Branding	v1102 🎥	Schmitt	Columbia Business School
Brand Management	v1103 🎥	Barton Warner	Bayer HealthCare
Marketing Imperative 3 — Branding	a1101 🎧		

v1102

v1103

a1101

SECTION IV

IMPLEMENTING THE MARKET STRATEGY cvs4

To access O-codes, go to **www.ocodes.com**

SECTION IV — IMPLEMENTING THE MARKET STRATEGY — COMPRISES 11 CHAPTERS, Chapter 12 through Chapter 22. The section embraces the second three Marketing Imperatives: Imperative 4 — Design the Market Offer; Imperative 5 — Secure Support from Other Functions; and Imperative 6 — Monitor and Control.

The largest group of chapters — Chapters 12 through 20 — address Imperative 4. We organize the material on designing the market offer into four parts.

Part A, *Providing Customer Value*, comprises three chapters. Chapter 12, Managing the Product Line, considers the firm's products as elements in a product portfolio, each with specific roles, together with several product-related issues. Chapter 13, Managing Services and Customer Service, focuses on product/service differences and highlights the importance of customer service. Chapter 14, Developing New Products, introduces the stage/gate process for developing new products.

Part B, *Communicating Customer Value*, also comprises three chapters. Chapter 15, Integrated Marketing Communications, frames an integrated communications strategy. Chapter 16, Mass and Digital Communications, focuses on advertising and other non-personal communications approaches. Chapter 17, Directing and Managing the Field Sales Effort, discusses six core tasks for developing and implementing the sales strategy.

Part C, *Delivering Customer Value*, comprises a single chapter. Chapter 18, Distribution Decisions, focuses on how the firm's products reach end-user customers.

Part D, *Getting Paid for Customer Value*, comprises two chapters: Chapter 19, Critical Underpinnings of Pricing Decisions, and Chapter 20, Setting Prices.

Imperatives 5 and 6 each merit a single chapter. Chapter 21, Ensuring the Firm Implements the Market Offer as Planned, addresses Imperative 5 and focuses on building an externally oriented firm. Chapter 22, Monitoring and Controlling Firm Functioning and Performance, considers Imperative 6 and shows how to maintain the firm's planned trajectory.

Capon's Marketing Framework

SECTION I: MARKETING AND THE FIRM

CHAPTER 1
Introduction to Managing Marketing

CHAPTER 2
The Value of Customers

SECTION II: FUNDAMENTAL INSIGHTS FOR STRATEGIC MARKETING

CHAPTER 3
Market Insight

CHAPTER 4
Customer Insight

CHAPTER 5
Insight about Competitors, Company, and Complementers

CHAPTER 6
Marketing Research

TRANSITION TO STRATEGIC MARKETING

SECTION III: STRATEGIC MARKETING

IMPERATIVE 1
Determine and Recommend Which Markets to Address

CHAPTER 7
Identifying and Choosing Opportunities

IMPERATIVE 2
Identify and Target Market Segments

CHAPTER 8
Market Segmentation and Targeting

IMPERATIVE 3
Set Strategic Direction and Positioning

CHAPTER 9
Market Strategy – Integrating Firm Efforts for Marketing Success

CHAPTER 10
Managing through the Life Cycle

CHAPTER 11
Managing Brands

SECTION IV: IMPLEMENTING THE MARKET STRATEGY

IMPERATIVE 4
Design the Market Offer

PART A: PROVIDING CUSTOMER VALUE	PART B: COMMUNICATING CUSTOMER VALUE	PART C: DELIVERING CUSTOMER VALUE	PART D: GETTING PAID FOR CUSTOMER VALUE
CHAPTER 12 Managing the Product Line	**CHAPTER 15** Integrated Marketing Communications	**CHAPTER 18** Distribution Decisions	**CHAPTER 19** Critical Underpinnings of Pricing Decisions
CHAPTER 13 Managing Services and Customer Service	**CHAPTER 16** Mass and Digital Communication		**CHAPTER 20** Setting Prices
CHAPTER 14 Developing New Products	**CHAPTER 17** Directing and Managing the Field Sales Effort		

IMPERATIVE 5
Secure Support from Other Functions

CHAPTER 21
Ensuring the Firm Implements the Market Offer as Planned

IMPERATIVE 6
Monitor and Control

CHAPTER 22
Monitoring and Controlling Firm Functioning and Performance

SECTION V: SPECIAL MARKETING TOPICS

CHAPTER 23
International, Regional, and Global Marketing

IMPERATIVE 4
Design the Market Offer

PART A – PROVIDING CUSTOMER VALUE

CHAPTER 12

MANAGING THE
PRODUCT LINE cv1201

To access O-codes, go to www.ocodes.com

LEARNING OBJECTIVES

When you have completed this chapter, you will be able to:

- Understand the importance of managing the product line as a portfolio.
- Apply alternative approaches to managing the product portfolio.
- Manage key interrelationships among products.
- Address the pressures for product proliferation and product-line simplification.
- Manage both diverse and complementary product lines.
- Deal with important product issues like bundling, counterfeiting, evolving the product line, extending product life, product quality, and secondary market products.
- Anticipate concerns about product safety, packaging, and disposal of products and packaging.

OPENING CASE: SWIFFER

Introduced by P&G in 1999, the Swiffer Sweeper (SS) was not just a new product; it was the first in a new product class — a line of products for cleaning surfaces. The Swiffer product line now comprises several different cleaning products for a variety of surfaces. The Swiffer design includes both hardware *and* disposables. *The hardware is a pole and attachment that grips the disposable, typically a dry or wet cloth. The choice of disposable depends on the surface being cleaned; regardless, the consumer discards the cloth after cleaning. P&G provides refills in various scents: SS dry cloths — 16-count refills, in unscented, Lavender Vanilla & Comfort, or Sweet Citrus & Zest; wet cloths — 24-count refills, in Open Window Fresh, Lavender Vanilla & Comfort, or Sweet Citrus & Zest. Some products are available as starter kits.*

Swiffer comprises the following products: Swiffer Sweeper, Swiffer SweeperVac, Swiffer Dusters, Swiffer X-Large, Swiffer Sweeper Professional, SwifferWetJet, *and* Swiffer Dust & Shine.

Most Swiffer products have differently designed hardware and disposables, but P&G has a consistent business model. The hardware has a low price and generates little profit; P&G makes its money on refills. The premium-priced Swiffer line is part of P&G's Household Care business, roughly 50 percent of total firm revenues. P&G now has 26 billion-dollar brands. Swiffer is one of 16 brands with revenue between $500 million and $1 billion with the potential to become a billion-dollar brand.

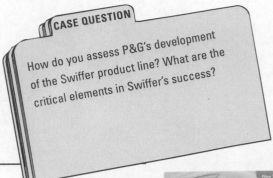

CASE QUESTION

How do you assess P&G's development of the Swiffer product line? What are the critical elements in Swiffer's success?

Chapter 12 is the first of three chapters in Part A of Imperative 4 — *Design the Market Offer*. Part A focuses on *Providing Customer Value*. Chapter 12 addresses *Managing the Product Line*.

Products and services are central to the firm's marketing mix. Since decisions about products and services cross functional lines, they have a broader impact on firm operations than other marketing-mix variables like promotion, distribution, customer service, and pricing. Firms also face difficult issues allocating limited resources across product portfolios. Optimal product-line breadth is a critical issue; product proliferation and product-line simplification can each have dramatic effects on shareholder value. Introducing new products — Chapter 14 — is critical. Product safety can embroil the firm in legal and ethical problems; increased societal expectations regarding health (like fast food and obesity) and environmental concerns (like pesticides and packaging and product disposal) highlight the importance of product decisions.

THE PRODUCT PORTFOLIO CONCEPT

The firm's **product portfolio** is a collection of products.[1] Large firms offer thousands of products, often grouped by business unit (GE example). Corporate leaders allocate resources among business units. Business-unit heads make resource allocations among products based on their assessments of potential growth and profitability.[2]

The firm does *not* optimize overall profits by maximizing short-run profits from each individual product. Rather, the firm should use a **portfolio approach** to product management, balancing objectives and resource allocations across all products. For example, the firm's new products require investment in R&D, plant and equipment, and promotional activities; these products consume cash. The firm typically believes that securing market position is more important than earning profits, at least in the short run when the market is growing. By contrast, when growth slows and investment requirements diminish, established products become more profitable and generate cash. The firm uses this cash to develop and support new and younger products. The cycle continues.

The firm optimizes shareholder value when the **product portfolio** is *balanced*; an **imbalanced** portfolio puts shareholder interests at risk. Imbalances occur when the firm funds too many new products and creates shortages of cash and other resources. Imbalances also occur when the firm has too many old products; good short-term financial results may mask a failure to invest sufficiently in the future. Securing the *right* balance of successful new products and profitable established products is important for enhancing shareholder value.

The key to a successful product strategy is setting objectives and allocating resources based on each product's role in the portfolio. The firm should manage some products to achieve growth objectives, and other products to maximize profits or cash flow. The firm's challenge is to allocate the *right* financial and human resources such that each product achieves its objectives. Of course, within the firm, the various products compete for scarce resources. This chapter shows portfolio analysis methods used by many firms to make these difficult resource allocation decisions. But first we describe traditional financial analysis methods for making these decisions.

KEY IDEA

➤ The firm's products have important resource-related interrelationships.

➤ The firm does not optimize its overall profits by maximizing profits from individual products. It must consider the entire product portfolio.

➤ Firms with imbalanced portfolios are vulnerable to acquisition.

Marketing Question

How would you convince a skeptical finance vice president that she should enhance her approach to investment assessment with portfolio analysis?

Marketing Question

Suppose the products in your business unit span the range from introduction to decline. Corporate has sent a finance VP to assess your business unit and to *help you*! What would you be most con-cerned about?

Marketing Question

Suppose you were GE's marketing manager for refrigerators. How would you address assumptions underlying your financial analysis, like target market share, technological change, future competitive structure, competitor strategies, and the role of government?

FINANCIAL ANALYSIS METHODS

Superior financial performance is critical for delivering increased shareholder value. Hence, a **financial analysis perspective** for assessing potential financial return from products is both important and proper. Approaches include[3]:

- **Return on investment (ROI).** ROI calculations project future accounting data. They com-pare the product's forecast rate of return with a target (**hurdle**) rate. If the forecast rate exceeds the target rate and resources are available, the firm invests.[4]

- **Payback.** Payback is the forecast time to pay back the investment. In general, shorter pay-backs are better than longer paybacks. Payback's problem is ignoring profits earned after the payback period.

Neither *ROI* nor *payback* distinguishes among time periods. They treat financial flows similarly regardless of when they occur. Because of this defect, most firms use approaches that account for the time value of money:

- **Net present value (NPV)** and **internal rate of return (IRR)**. NPV and IRR are the most common financial analysis methods for assessing investment opportunities. Discount fac-tors account for the time value of money. Both methods use actual cash flows rather than financial and cost accounting data. They assess cash inflows (like sales revenues) when earned and cash outflows (like costs and investments) when paid out.[5]

  - NPV uses a predetermined discount factor, typically the firm's cost of capital. The firm calculates NPV for various opportunities, then ranks by monetary value.

  - For **IRR**, the firm calculates the discount rate that equalizes cash inflows and cash out-flows. IRR typically ranks opportunities whose IRR exceeds the hurdle rate.

More recently, firms use *economic profit* or *economic value added (EVA)*. EVA equals the firm's annual profit less an explicit charge for capital.[6] A summary of approaches:

Financial Analysis Approaches

1. **Forecast Return on Investment (%) (ROI)** — (Sales Revenues less Costs)/Investment = Profits/Investment (based on forecast accounting data).

2. **Payback (years, months)** — time to pay back the initial investment.

3. **Net Present Value (NPV)** — the dollar value of an opportunity. Discounts all cash outflows and inflows by a predetermined factor, typically the firm's cost of capital.

4. **Internal Rate of Return (IRR)** — the discount rate that equalizes cash inflows and cash outflows.

5. **Economic Profit** — the opportunity's annual profit less an explicit charge for capital.

Today, many firms modify/augment financial analysis by examining the assumptions underlying financial projections, and requiring managers to think more deeply about them. Typically, precise answers are not possible, but the process leads to a more externally oriented approach — like portfolio analysis — for allocating resources.

PORTFOLIO ANALYSIS

Portfolio analysis (PA) is central to many firms' strategic planning processes. PA is best viewed as an *additional* tool for allocating resources, not as an *alternative* to FA. PA is a systematic, organized, and easily communicable way of assembling, assessing, and integrating important information about products and markets with the goal of constructing a balanced portfolio. PA helps the firm set strategic direction, establish investment priorities, and allocate resources.[7] The firm can use portfolio analysis to evaluate both businesses and products.

PA has dramatically affected many firms' resource allocation processes; PA includes factors traditional financial analysis ignores. Table 12.1 illustrates several differences between FA and PA.[8] Using FA and PA together leads to better investment decisions than either approach alone.

Variable	Financial Analysis	Portfolio Analysis
General approach	Financial- and budget-oriented	Market- and competitive-oriented
Investment decision focus	Technologies/facilities	Products/markets/customers/applications
Key concerns	Derived profit and cash flow numbers	Market and competitive factors underlying the financial numbers
Tools	Capital budgeting	Growth-share and multifactor matrices
Typical measures	ROI, payback, NPV, IRR, EVA	Market — size, growth, competitive strength

TABLE 12.1

FINANCIAL AND PORTFOLIO ANALYSIS — INVESTMENT DECISIONS AND STRATEGIC DIRECTIONS

Two important PA methods are the **growth-share matrix** and the **multifactor matrix**.

THE GROWTH-SHARE MATRIX. The Boston Consulting Group (BCG) developed the original PA. As the name implies, core dimensions are growth and share: *forecast long-run market growth* and *relative market share*.[9] Figure 12.1 shows each dimension bisected to produce a four-cell classification. Matrix entries represent products (or businesses). Typically, each circle's size is proportional to sales revenues or invested assets.

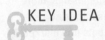

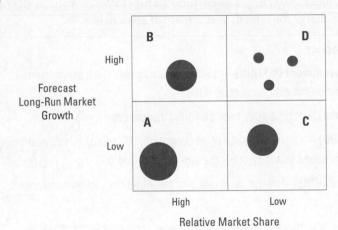

FIGURE 12.1

AN ILLUSTRATIVE GROWTH-SHARE MATRIX

The growth-share matrix places heavy emphasis on the financial characteristics of products in each cell. High-share products are typically more profitable than low-share products. Growth products typically require significant investment in fixed assets, working capital, and market development. Figure 12.2 describes conventional labels and classic strategic recommendations for products in each cell.

The firm should consider the generalized recommendations from Figure 12.3 carefully, because they are widely advocated and applied. The best way to view the growth-share matrix is as a device for raising and discussing *what-if* or contingency questions.

THE MULTIFACTOR MATRIX. The growth-share matrix spawned many other portfolio approaches, some public and some proprietary. The most popular is the **multifactor matrix**, aka GE/McKinsey screen.[10] The multifactor matrix redefines the growth-share axes: *Long-run*

FIGURE 12.2

PRODUCT CHARACTERISTICS IN THE GROWTH-SHARE MATRIX

KEY IDEA

➤ Product labels derived from the growth-share matrix are:

- Cash cows
- Stars
- Dogs
- Problem children

Marketing Question

Suppose 20 percent of all products are in *high-growth* markets and 80 percent are in *low-growth* markets; and that 10 percent of all products are market leaders. What percentage of products are Cash Cows? Dogs? Stars? Problem Children? What does your result imply for the challenges you will face as an executive?

Marketing Question

Identify all Disney businesses — like amusement parks, movies, retail stores, and character licensing — and place them in a growth-share matrix. (You may have to guess a bit.) Which businesses are Cash Cows? Dogs? Stars? Problem Children? How do you think Disney should allocate resources? What additional factors should Disney consider in examining new wholly owned or alliance opportunities?

Cash Cows. Low Market Growth/High Market Share (Cell A)

Classic characteristics of cash cows are:

- Low costs. From experience curve effects — Chapter 10.
- Premium prices. As market leader, cash cows may command premium prices.
- Low reinvestment. Low-growth, mature products require relatively low investment.

Cash cows should be highly profitable and are often the firm's primary internal cash source. Examples include Microsoft Office, IBM mainframes, and P&G Tide detergent. If the firm successfully holds market share, it can *milk* a cash cow and generate cash for many years. Environmental changes like regulatory shifts, patent expiration, innovative competitors, or new technology threaten cash cows by changing demand patterns. Then the firm may *harvest* the product to increase short-term cash flow — raising prices, reducing or eliminating services, and/or cutting promotional support.

Firms with cash cows can make two types of errors. First, they *over-milk* their cash cows and cash flow *dries up*. Starved of investment, the product trails in technology and loses cost leadership and market position.[11] U.S. and European car and steel firms are good examples. In a second scenario, the firm over-invests, reducing financial return and leaving little cash for other opportunities.

Stars. High Market Growth, High Market Share (Cell B)

Stars are relatively rare; few products enjoy dominant positions in high-growth markets. Stars are often profitable in accounting terms, but use significant cash because their growth requires substantial investment. Groupon and Twitter are good examples. Despite the firm's best efforts, market growth eventually slows. If the firm invests appropriately and retains good market share, profits and cash flow improve, and the star transforms into a *cash cow*. The major error firms make with stars is to cut back investment too early. The star loses dominance and transforms into a *dog* — cell C.

Dogs. Low Market Growth, Low Market Share (Cell C)

Dogs is a pejorative term for products with unfavorable characteristics:

- High costs relative to the leader; dogs do not enjoy the same economy-of-scale or experience curve advantages.
- Prices may be lower than the market leader.

Dogs are often unprofitable or earn only low profits; they are also often the focus of top management attention. Better-positioned dogs often generate positive cash flow but may still be a drag on firm resources. Dogs are the most numerous of all products in any economy. Examples include Lenovo's personal computers and CBS and Fox in U.S. broadcast television. Firms with dogs should consider:

- Developing new segmentation approaches that strengthen their positions.
- Refreshing products with additional value from new features.
- Maximizing short-run cash flows by liquidating or divesting. IBM sold its *barely profitable* PC business to Lenovo.
- Implement a *kennel* strategy (Chapter 10) by acquiring similar products to achieve viable scale.

Problem Children (aka Lottery Tickets, Question Marks, Wildcats). High Market Growth, Low Market Share (Cell D)

Problem children combine the uncertainties of high-growth markets with non-dominant market shares. Examples include iRiver, RCA, and M-Pio MP3 players; each has less than 10 percent market share versus well over 50 percent for Apple's iPod. Problem children that grow with the market consume substantial investment capital. Such investment may be risky, as growth does not guarantee future profits. Growing with the market moves the problem-child from cell D to cell C. Hence the key choice for problem children is often *double or quit*!

- *Double*. Large strategic investments can move the product to market leadership. Sony successfully overtook Nintendo in video games with high spending in product development and promotion. By contrast, Philips' CD-Interactive (CDI), a user-friendly interactive CD system launched when CD-ROM was in its infancy, was quickly overtaken. A less risky approach seeks dominance in a defensible market segment(s).
- *Quit*. Exit, immediately or gradually. The product may command a good price from an aggressive follower. Small biotech firms often sell their new drugs to big pharma.

market growth becomes *market attractiveness; relative market share* becomes *business strengths.* The user identifies several factors to measure each dimension.

Figure 12.3 illustrates the multifactor matrix.[12] The most attractive cell, C, is empty but the firm has some small entries in two other attractive cells, B and F; it should probably invest in these products. The large entries in cells A and E are questionable; the firm should examine them carefully. Finally, the firm should make the tough decision — retain or remove — about the poorly positioned large cell G product:

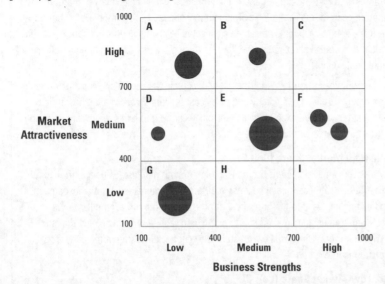

FIGURE 12.3

AN ILLUSTRATIVE MULTIFACTOR MATRIX

THE GROWTH-SHARE AND MULTIFACTOR MATRICES. Each method helps the firm make resource allocations, in part by visual display. Table 12.2 shows advantages and disadvantages.

Comparison Criteria	Growth-Share Matrix	Multifactor Matrix
Ability to manipulate entries	Difficult	Easy
Accommodates new businesses	Not well	Yes
Application across firm	Single set of criteria	Multiple sets of criteria
Appropriate for fragmented markets	No	Yes
Communicability	Easy	More difficult
Criteria	Limited but unambiguous	Unlimited but disputable
Explicit consideration of risk	No	Yes, if required
Grouping tendency of entries	Low market growth/low market share (bottom right)	High/high, high/medium, medium/high, medium/medium (top right)
Implementability	Easy	More difficult
Measures	Basically objective	Highly subjective
Realism	May be limited	May have more
Sensitivity to basic assumptions	Yes	Yes
Sensitivity to market definition	Yes	Yes
Underlying focus	Cash flow	ROI

TABLE 12.2

COMPARISON OF THE PORTFOLIO APPROACHES

 KEY IDEA

➤ The firm can use the multifactor matrix for resource allocation among products.

➤ The growth-share and multifactor matrices have advantages and disadvantages that impact the viability of strategic recommendations they generate.

The *growth-share matrix* has only two criteria: long-run market growth and RMS. Once managers agree on market definition, the firm can measure these objectively. Reasonable people may disagree about forecast market growth, but RMS is relatively simple to measure. Hence, managers have limited ability to manipulate entries for their favorite products. But having just two criteria can also be a weakness; forecast long-run market growth and RMS may not capture all relevant issues. By contrast, the *multifactor matrix* addresses the realism issue by using several criteria, and so embraces many factors that the growth-share matrix omits. But reasonable managers may disagree about the criteria, and weightings and ratings are often highly subjective. Hence, political and organizational power issues can enter the analysis.

OTHER IMPORTANT PRODUCT INTERRELATIONSHIPS

Products compete for resources; they may also be interrelated in other strategic ways.

INTERRELATIONSHIPS AT THE CUSTOMER

Some products are directly complementary, like razors and razor blades, printers and toner, satellite dishes and program content, and hardware and disposables (as with Swiffer — Opening Case). When each product needs the other, the firm can be successful by placing either or both in its portfolio. If the firm offers both products, like HP printers and toner, pricing becomes particularly crucial.

POSITIVE COMPLEMENTARITY. In many markets, customers who buy one type of product are more likely to buy a related product — **positive complementarity**. Michelin sells passenger tires and the *Michelin Guide* book. The *Michelin Guide* encourages car travel; when travel increases, tire wear is greater and tire sales rise. Positive attributes associated with the *Michelin Guide* also carry over to Michelin tires, and vice versa. Verizon knows that traditional local wire based telephone service is declining, so it offers customers long-distance, DSL, and wireless services. Satisfied customers for Apple's iPod are favorably disposed to buy Macintosh computers. Sometimes a complementary product is closely related to an initial purchase. Positive complementarity occurs when customers trade up to higher-quality, higher-profit products. GM's historic strategy traded customers up from Chevrolet to Pontiac, Buick, Oldsmobile, and Cadillac.

NEGATIVE COMPLEMENTARITY. Customer dissatisfaction with one product can negatively affect sales of another. Before passage of the Sarbanes-Oxley Act, investment banks knew that critical equity research reports negatively affected their ability to sell investment banking services. Professional services and accounting firms knew that company audits exposing financial problems might cut off lucrative consulting contracts. Arthur Andersen failed to acknowledge and address Enron's irregular accounting because it feared such negative complementarity.

INTERRELATIONSHIPS AT THE FIRM

Sometimes firm products have important internal interrelationships with each other.

STRATEGIC ROLES. Different products may have separate yet mutually reinforcing strategic roles. The Swatch Group (TSG) markets watch brands in five price ranges:

- Prestige and Luxury range: Breguet, Blancpain, Glashütte Original, Jaquet Droz, Léon Hatot, Omega
- High range: Longines, Rado, Union Glashütte
- Middle range: Tissot, Calvin Klein, Balmain, Certina, Mido, Hamilton
- Basic range: Swatch, Flik Flak
- Private label: Endura

Each range targets a different market segment and has a different strategic role. TSG earns most profit from products in the top two ranges and less from the middle range. Basic range and private-label products are profitable, but act as **firewalls**. They stop competitors offering low-price watches, thus protecting TSG's middle-, high-, and prestige- and luxury-range products.[13]

MULTIPLE BUSINESS UNITS. Interrelationship issues occur with products from different business units when they address (or could address) the same market. The firm has three options:

- **Develop separate missions.** Products from different business units have different missions — Chapter 7. The firm does not *squander* resources by having multiple business units address a single market opportunity.

- **Intra-firm collaboration.** The firm develops processes for separate business units to work together. At J&J, corporate account managers integrated products from several units to form a single offering for operating rooms: Ethicon — sutures and topical products to stop bleeding; Ethicon Endo Surgery — cutters, staplers, and electro-surgery devices; Codman — surgical instruments and shunts to relieve pressure on the brain; Dupuy — orthopedic implants; and Cordis — peripheral stents.

- **Intra-firm competition.** This Darwinian approach allows products from different business units to pursue overlapping missions. As long as one business unit seizes the opportunity, the firm accepts efficiency losses in product development and promotion.

PRODUCT LINE BREADTH: PROLIFERATION VERSUS SIMPLIFICATION

Firms often face conflicting pressures for product line size: pressures for *broadening* and pressures for *narrowing*. The firm must trade off these pressures.

PRODUCT PROLIFERATION

Variety in customer needs often drives **product proliferation** as firms add products to fill product-line gaps. Time Inc. traditionally published male-oriented magazines, like *Time*, *Sports Illustrated*, *Money*, and *Fortune*. Time sought growth by targeting new audiences like women, children, teenagers, and minorities, and broadened its product line to include *Entertainment Weekly*, *In Style*, *People*, *People en Español*, *Teen People*, *Parenting*, *Sports Illustrated for Kids*, *Sunset*, *Baby Talk*, and *Martha Stewart Living*.

Sometimes firms tap different customer needs by offering products in different versions or variations. Common version differentiators are[14]:

- **Access and functionality.** Some firms offer differing versions of information or media products for different audiences based on: user interface — simple for casual users, complex for serious users; speed of operation — slow for casual users, fast for professional users; and access to features or functionality.

- **Product performance.** Some firms, like plastics producers, make high-quality products for high prices and *degraded* products for price-sensitive customers. Production economics makes this approach more viable than manufacturing lower-value versions directly.

- **Time availability.** Package delivery firms like FedEx and UPS offer next-day delivery before 10 A.M., after 10 A.M., and second-day delivery. Publishers initially offer hardcover books and sell paperback copies later. Hollywood launches movies in theaters, then releases them later on DVD or as Internet downloads.

Firms seeking market dominance in FMCG frequently offer multiple products to maximize display space. They also offer **firewall products** to defend profitable products and deter competitive entry. P&G maintains market leadership in laundry detergents by offering six brands, embracing 53 versions and 122 skus.

When product proliferation is excessive, costs spiral out of control and the firm loses market position. Motorola lost global leadership in cell phones in part because of a large product line. Fifteen teams of 20 people each supported 128 separate phone types, often with little parts commonality. Purchasing, manufacturing, administrative, and marketing costs were very high.

The difference between product proliferation and market segmentation confuses many students. *Product proliferation* refers to product variety. *Market segmentation* explores differences in customer needs. Generally, product variations do not target different market segments; they just offer variety. Customers for cereals, fasteners, jams and jellies, salad dressings, spices, and even water (flavors, vitamins) demand a wide choice assortment. Sometimes firms provide variety through packaging, like Tylenol in caplet, cool caplet, EZ tab, geltab, and liquid versions.

SIMPLIFYING THE PRODUCT LINE

The late Peter Drucker famously posed the question, "If you weren't already in your business, would you enter it today?" If the answer is no, the firm must answer a second question: "What are you going to do about it?" One answer is to slim down its brand and product portfolios. Unilever reduced its brand portfolio to 400 global and regional brands (from 1,600) — approximately 90 percent of its then $27 billion revenues — and exited the U.S. detergent market. Unilever then sold, reduced support for, and/or consolidated its remaining national and local brands into stronger brands. Firms typically streamline product lines due to pressure from increased competition. In B2C, distribution-channel consolidation and store brand growth are important factors.

The firm may reap significant benefits from simplifying the product line, but should make product deletion decisions carefully. When firms eliminate high-volume *loss-making* products, they often discover that these products were carrying a large share of overhead. The remaining products must assume this overhead; their costs increase and overall profits fall!

OTHER PRODUCT-LINE ISSUES

Now we examine several other issues for managing the product line:

BUNDLING

The firm can sell products as single *unbundled* items; it may also combine products or products and services as *bundled* offers. Sometimes firms bundle attractive products with less-attractive products to increase overall sales and profits. Performing arts organizations often sell series subscriptions that combine popular and less-popular events. B2B firms often bundle products with service support. In *mixed bundling*, the firm sells products both unbundled and bundled.

Bundling and unbundling decisions are difficult. If the firm shifts from bundling to unbundling, customers may reject less-attractive items. But continued bundling risks losing sales to more focused competitors. Major airlines emphasize round-trips — bundled; but often lose sales to discounters offering low-price one-way fares — unbundled. Weak competition allows the firm to bundle for longer, but it should develop contingency plans for unbundling.

COUNTERFEITING

Illegal product copying and brand piracy are increasingly prevalent globally. The best protection is continual vigilance regarding trademark, copyright, and design patents. The firm should work with local law enforcement, but problems multiply when counterfeiters operate internationally.[15]

EVOLVING THE PRODUCT LINE

The firm must address several key issues in evolving the product line.

EXTENDING PRODUCT LIFE. Firms often try to extend product life. We show the typical practice of pharmaceutical firms when their patents expire. Firms in other industries apply variations of these approaches:

- Add additional services to support customers.
- Combine the drug with another drug having a complementary effect.
- Develop new dosage formulations.
- Devise a different method of drug delivery — like patch versus pill.
- Get FDA approval for other *indications* — that is, additional disease states.
- Persuade more physicians to prescribe the product and educate pharmacists.
- Switch the drug from prescription to over-the-counter.

IMPROVING THE PRODUCT MIX. Firms can increase profits by introducing higher-margin products, possibly by replacing lower-margin products. Gillette pursued this strategy for many years with successively more expensive razor systems. Nissan and Toyota entered the U.S. market with low-price cars and then moved upmarket, eventually introducing the Infiniti and Lexus, respectively.

PRODUCT CANNIBALIZATION. To pre-empt (or stave off) competitive threats and/or address new market segments, firms often introduce lower margin products that may **cannibalize** sales of higher-margin products. When contemplating cannibalization, the firm should consider three important issues:

- **Balancing effects.** A new product entry may cannibalize existing product sales and cause an immediate profit reduction. But the firm should enjoy incremental value from improved market share and brand presence.
- **Fear of lower profits.** When the firm introduces a new low-price (lower-profit) product, customers may switch from the original high-price (high-profit) product to the new entry, reducing overall firm profits. Fear of this scenario may generate internal pressures against a new entry and immobilize the firm.
- **How to decide.** Many firms make product entry decisions by comparing their most recent history with forecast results after introducing the new product. This practice is incorrect. The firm should always compare *forecast* profits *with* the new product to *forecast* profits *without* the new product. In many markets, some customers want low-priced products. If they cannot buy from the firm, they will buy from competitors.

PRODUCT REPLACEMENT. When the firm secures differential advantage with a better product, competitors often imitate and reduce price. The best approach is to replace the older product with an innovative successor. Ideally, the firm introduces a higher-value replacement shortly before the competitor's launch. Successful pre-emption weakens competitor resolve to compete against the incumbent. Good competitive intelligence and appropriate timing is critical for managing the replacement cycle.

LIMITATIONS ON PRODUCT AVAILABILITY. Some firms deliberately under-produce so as to create customer value via scarcity. This practice is common in sneakers where Adidas, Converse, Diesel, Nike, and Vans each offer limited editions.

PRODUCT QUALITY

Product quality is very important to customers and is necessary for any serious competitor. *BusinessWeek* showed that the share price of Baldridge winners, the well-known U.S. quality award, consistently outperformed the S&P 500 index by a factor of 3:1.

Marketing Question

Think about firms where you have worked or those you have read about. Can you identify examples of ill-advised product eliminations?

KEY IDEA

➤ Product managers should address several product-line issues:

- Extending product life
- Improving the product mix
- Product cannibalization
- Product replacement
- Limitations on product availability

KEY IDEA

➤ Product quality and product safety have critical marketing implications.

PRODUCT SAFETY

In many jurisdictions, regulatory bodies like the FDA and CPSC (U.S.) enforce laws protecting consumers from product hazards. Regardless, producers have a special responsibility to ensure their products do not harm customers. Unfortunately, some firms do not behave properly. Chinese firms added toxic melamine (protein powder) to animal feed. How the firm responds to product safety issues can be a key differentiating factor.

SECONDARY MARKET PRODUCTS

Owners of durable products like automobiles often resell in the **secondary market**. For customers purchasing new cars, the forecast resale price is often an important product attribute. Automobile firms often try to enhance resale prices by certifying previously owned vehicles.

PACKAGING

Packaging is important for guaranteeing product integrity in storage and distribution. But packaging can also communicate information, represent a significant brand statement (like the hourglass Coke bottle), and/or provide convenience benefits.

DISPOSAL: PRODUCTS AND PACKAGING

Traditionally, customers were responsible for disposing of packaging and used products. But governments, particularly in Europe, have passed environmentally friendly laws focused on disposal. To address disposal issues, cost concerns, and the potential impact on brand image, many firms promote recycling. Some firms make new products with parts from discarded products. Good examples include auto parts, car batteries, computers, and toner cartridges. *Remanufacturing* is a $50 billion industry — some firms build remanufacturing into their product development processes.

KEY MESSAGES

Managing the firm's product line is a major challenge. The firm must make decisions in four areas:

- **The product portfolio.**

    - The firm should construct a balanced portfolio where some products generate growth and market share, some products earn profits, and some deliver cash flow.
    - The firm's key challenge is allocating resources across the portfolio. Financial analysis methods have advantages and disadvantages. The firm should supplement financial analysis with portfolio analysis, using the growth-share and/or multifactor matrix.

- **Other product interrelationships.** The firm's products may be interrelated at the customer — the firm should seek positive complementarity and avoid negative complementarity. Products may also be interrelated at the firm, playing different strategic roles.

- **Product-line breadth: proliferation versus simplification.** The firm faces conflicting pressures for *product proliferation* and *product simplification.* Variety in customer needs drives proliferation, and many firms offer similar versions of the same product. The reader should not confuse product proliferation with market segmentation. Industry consolidation often drives simplification, but the firm should make product deletion decisions carefully, using well-thought-through criteria.

- **Other product-line issues.** The firm should address many other product management issues, including bundling; counterfeiting; evolving the product line; product quality; product safety; secondary market products; packaging; and disposal of products and packaging.

VIDEOS AND AUDIOS

| Luxury Goods | v1202 🎥 | Ketty Maisonrouge | Columbia Business School |

v1202

IMPERATIVE 4

Design the Market Offer

PART A – PROVIDING CUSTOMER VALUE

CHAPTER 13

MANAGING SERVICES AND CUSTOMER SERVICE cv1301

To access O-codes, go to **www.ocodes.com**

LEARNING OBJECTIVES

When you have completed this chapter, you will be able to:

- Distinguish among products, services, and customer service.
- Understand why services are becoming increasingly important to firms and customers.
- Identify critical dimensions across which products differ from services.
- Discriminate among different types of services.
- Diagnose quality-related problems and opportunities in service delivery.
- Specify key dimensions of customer service.
- Appreciate the strategic role of customer service.

OPENING CASE: CELEBRITY CRUISES

Celebrity Cruises (11 ships) is a subsidiary of Royal Caribbean Cruises Ltd., positioned upscale of Holland America and Carnival Cruise lines. At 91,000 tons, Celebrity Constellation is a member of the Millennium class with a 940-person crew and capacity for 2,450 passengers. The Constellation *serves mostly U.S. guests in the Caribbean, the Americas, and Europe.*

In addition to the Master, key officers are Chief Engineer, Staff Captain, and Hotel Director. The Hotel Director is responsible for the entire guest experience, from embarkation to disembarkation. He described how Celebrity optimizes every guest's experience: "Celebrity has made sure that the ship's design and craftsmanship are first rate — from the guest staterooms to all public areas like the Celebrity Theater, San Marco restaurant, and the pools.

"Many guest options are continuously available. We have over a dozen restaurants, cafés, and bars. There's a show every night in the Celebrity Theater — our own Celebrity Singers and Dancers do four shows a week, but we also have comedians and a capella singers. There's a library, casino, Internet café, swimming pools, whirlpools, a shopping arcade, and a fully equipped gym and schedule of classes. On the day at sea from Aruba to San Juan, we have an art auction, bingo, karaoke, shuffleboard, bridge, ping-pong, and many other activities. Then there are special children's programs. We provide guests with many options — they can partake of them or not — and we change them from time to time, based on feedback.

"The crew is the most important factor in delivering the guest experience; we call them Celebrity Family Members (CFMs). We think of ourselves as a family and believe very strongly that happy employees lead to happy guests. We carefully select the entire staff. Agents in many countries around the world source CFMs from the many applications they receive. Celebrity Constellation has CFMs from 58 different countries. That makes for a more interesting guest experience.

"All CFMs are on contracts, ranging from eight months for waiters to four months for officers, with two months off. Fleet-wide, staff retention is 60 to 70 percent. Our on-board training and development manager puts a lot of effort into training, especially the first week of a contract, to set clear expectations. There's a lot of management by walking around and a systematic staff-appraisal system. The CFMs work hard for long hours — that's partly the reason for the two-month break between contracts. Each month we give the Shining Star award for outstanding service. We select five CFMs from a host of nominations — the winners earn cash and other prizes.

"If we provide a great guest experience, we get customer loyalty. On this cruise, about 800 of our 2,000 guests are repeaters from Celebrity cruises. On European cruises, the loyalty rate is often more than 50 percent. We have three levels of the Captain's Club customer loyalty program: Classic — 1 to 5 cruises; Select — 6 to 10 cruises; and Elite — 11 + cruises. Each level offers rewards like stateroom upgrades, interaction with the captain and senior officers, preferential treatment for embarkation and disembarkation, and restaurant seating. Guests can book future cruises on board, and we keep in touch after the cruise.

"We use a comprehensive formal system for guest evaluations, including CFM performance — both scaled and open-ended responses — at the end of each cruise. They go to the head office in Miami, and we get the results in a couple of days. These are very important — they are the raw material for appraising our crew and making changes in the guest experience."

Used with permission of Celebrity Cruises Inc.

CASE QUESTION

What special human resource issues does cruise line management face? How do these issues differ from managing a passenger airline?

Some firms produce and sell *tangible* products like cars, computers, kitchen equipment, and TVs. Much of *Capon's Marketing Framework* focuses on these firms and their approach to markets. But many other firms produce and sell *intangible* services like beauty treatments, information technology services, retail distribution, tax preparation, and transportation. But the product/service distinction is often fuzzy, as many products also have service components. Car companies offer financing, insurance, and warranties; Sony provides delivery, extended warranties, and installation. Further, technology advances allow some products to morph into services as customers purchase the benefits and values the product delivers as a service, rather than the product itself. They may lease (service), rather than buy, an automobile (product); or hire IBM or EDS to support and manage their information systems (service), rather than buy hardware and software (product) directly.

Because they are intangible, services can pose a real managerial challenge. Yet well-designed and well-delivered services create customer satisfaction and loyalty, differential advantage, high profits, and positive word of mouth. *Customer service* is a special type of service, a key way for the firm to augment its **core product** or **core service** by providing experiences to differentiate it from competitors. Samsung and many other firms sell electronic products, but offer customer service in the form of online and phone support.

PRODUCTS, SERVICES, AND CUSTOMER SERVICE

The distinction between *products* and *services* remains one of marketing's great confusions. Some people use the term *product* to describe any core offering — including both *physical products* and *services*. We use this convenient shorthand throughout much of the book. Regardless, in Chapter 13, we separate a tangible **physical product**, one that can be touched and perhaps kicked or sat upon, from a service. A **service** is *any act or performance that one party can offer another that is essentially intangible and does not result in the ownership of anything.* Or, *"anything that cannot be dropped on your foot!"*[1] Most services concern people — education, medical treatment, restaurants, theater, and transportation; products — car repair, house cleaning, real estate, and retail distribution; or information — business, financial, and legal services, and marketing research.

As we learned in Chapter 4, *essentially, customers do not want your products or services; they want the benefits and values your products and services provide!* Sometimes customers receive benefits and values from a physical product like a car, clothing, food, house, or washing machine. Other times, they receive benefits and values from a service like a haircut, Internet provider, medical procedure, sporting event, or travel. Either way, to *attract*, *retain*, and *grow* customers, the firm must develop offers of value to satisfy customer needs. Relatedly, increasing numbers of firms promote the benefits and values their products provide as services, rather than the products themselves. Rolls-Royce offers *TotalCare*, a program where customers pay a fee *per hour of flight* — a service.

The firm can enhance the benefits and value inherent in its product or service by adding **customer service** like delivery, information, repair, sales support, technical support, and warranties. Honda offers the Accord as a core physical product, but also provides customer service before, during, and after purchase. FedEx core service is overnight package delivery, but it surrounds the core with billing statements, documentation, information, logistical advice, order-taking, package-tracking, pickup, and supplies. Finally, a core service for one firm can be customer service for another. Delivery may be *customer service* for your local pizza parlor, but for a chain that only delivers pizza, delivery is part of its *core service*.

GROWTH IN THE SERVICE SECTOR

The service sector of advanced economies has grown dramatically in recent years, making product, service, and customer-service distinctions increasingly important. Services account for upward of 70 percent of total employment and GDP in developed countries.[2] Many service firms now populate the *Fortune* 500, and social enterprises like government and non-profit organizations (NGOs) almost exclusively offer services. Prime examples are education, garbage collection, health and human services, and policing. Rising incomes, age-related demographic shifts, and technology are all driving services growth. Other important private-sector growth factors are:

- **Customer behavior changes.** Customers preference for purchasing is decreasing. Many consumers prefer to avoid ownership responsibilities; firms want to remove investments from balance sheets to increase return-on-investment (ROI). Correspondingly, financial services like credit, leasing, and rental services are growing.

- **Deregulation.** Deregulation in service industries like electricity, financial services, natural gas, telecommunications, and transportation eases market entry; entrants with innovative strategies fuel growth.

- **Franchising.** **Franchising** is the backbone of the hospitality, restaurant, and tax preparation industries; leading brands include Hilton, McDonald's, and H&R Block respectively. But businesses like closet installation, commercial property restoration, onsite computer and electronics repairs, and window-cleaning are also growing via franchising.

- **Globalization.** Innovations in technology and communications make products and services accessible to global markets. Firms conduct business across the world using many derivative service strategies to meet the diverse needs of new customers.

- **Leveraging core competence.** Some firms find that in-house activities are valuable to other firms, so they repackage and sell them as services. Florida Light and Power, winner of Japan's prestigious Deming quality award, offers quality workshops; Xerox also consults on quality management. Disney offers executive programs in leadership and customer service. SAS trains flight crews from other airlines, maintains planes, and helps Swedish firms prepare employees for relocation.[3]

- **Outsourcing.** Many firms narrow their missions and downsize to focus on core competencies; hence, they **outsource** activities and processes previously performed internally, and often secure better value/cost ratios. Examples include call-center customer-service support, financial transactions, HR functions (benefits, payroll), legal advice, security, technology, telephony, and manufacturing. Outsourcing provides suppliers with service opportunities and potentially higher profit margins than physical products. EDS, IBM, and Unisys design, install, and operate customers' computer and information systems; and firms like Accenture manage various transactional and transformational business processes.

- **Technology.** Technological advances allow firms to connect with customers on increasingly individualized bases, and deliver ongoing and complementary services.

CHARACTERISTICS OF SERVICES

Physical products differ from services in several important ways:

INTANGIBILITY

Services focusing on *people* generally require the customer's physical presence or interactivity; services focusing on *products and information* generally do not. The location for services like factory maintenance, gardening, and house cleaning is generally fixed. Customers can consume other services in various places like seeing a movie in a theater, at home, or on the phone; and receive medical services at a doctor's office, hospital, at home, or perhaps virtually.

Although some services like restaurant meals and in-store product purchases are more tangible than others, the core experience is still intangible. In general, *intangibility* makes customer evaluation of services more subjective than for physical goods. Hence, tangible service elements often play an important role in forming expectations for, and evaluation of, the service experience. Service tangibles include facilities, equipment, and personnel. Some firms provide additional tangibility via service guarantees.

SERVICE FACILITIES. Consideration for where the firm delivers the service:

- **Exterior.** Includes the location, outside view, and signage. These tangible elements provide information about the interior where the firm provides the service; the exterior either attracts customers to, or detracts from, the service experience.

- **Interior.** Has two dimensions:
  - **Offstage.** Out of customer sight.
  - **Onstage.** Where customers experience deeds, efforts, and performance.

Marketing Question

Think about the last time you purchased a cell phone. During the purchase, how important to you was the product? How important was the associated service?

Was there a service guarantee? Did the guarantee meet the noted criteria? Did the provider communicate the guarantee well? What could the provider have done better? Have you received a guarantee for any other purchase?

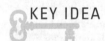

KEY IDEA

➤ *Moments of truth* are opportunities for customer satisfaction or dissatisfaction.

KEY IDEA

➤ For services, production and consumption are inseparable.

SERVICE EQUIPMENT. Generally, services require a tangible physical product: air travel — airplane; iTunes — iPod or phone; haircut — scissors and a mirror. **Service equipment** quality often influences the service experience. Many passengers choose airlines with new planes (Singapore Airlines, jetBlue) versus those with older fleets.

SERVICE PERSONNEL. Some work offstage; others work onstage. Airline mechanics and baggage handlers generally work offstage; ticket agents and flight attendants are onstage. The customer experience depends on how well all **service personnel** perform their functions. Because appearance, demeanor, and manner of onstage personnel offer important quality cues, many service personnel wear uniforms. Bringing offstage personnel onstage can enhance the customer experience. David Letterman frequently brings crew members onstage for his late-night TV talk show. Airline pilots make frequent announcements and often converse with deplaning passengers.

Customers have many interactions with onstage service personnel. Jan Carlzon (former SAS airline president) used the phrase **moment of truth** to emphasize their importance. At each *moment of truth*, customers can be satisfied or dissatisfied.[4] Customers make judgments based on their own interactions, and the interactions of service personnel with other customers. Managing customer/service-personnel interactions across all engagement channels is a major firm challenge. Disney's elaborate training and management program carefully controls employee response behavior so that each customer has a *magical* and consistent experience. Even more difficult is managing customer interactions with distributor and franchisee employees.

Another serious concern for service firms like advertising agencies, beauty salons, and those offering business and professional services is the relative strength of employee versus firm relationships with customers. When the service person-to-customer relationship is strong, employees may resign and take customers with them — Chapter 5. Better company communications can strengthen firm-customer bonds.

SERVICE GUARANTEES. Guarantees about the service experience provide tangible value should the firm fail to keep its promises. Good **service guarantees** are unconditional, painless to invoke, and easy and quick to collect.[5] Cort Furniture Rental guarantees on-time delivery and pickup, showroom-quality products, upgraded replacement if substitution is necessary, exchange of any item within two days, and a total refund if any problem cannot be fixed. The service agreement should be simple to understand and communicate, and meaningfully related to the service it guarantees. Good guarantees work because customers have positive experiences with the guarantee. They should also motivate employees to improve service quality by working hard to avoid customers invoking the guarantee.

INSEPARABILITY

Many firms manufacture, sell, ship, and store physical goods. These firms deal with demand and supply fluctuations and imperfect forecasting via inventory controls. For service businesses, provider and customer are inexorably linked, making production and consumption are innately *inseparable*. Because firms cannot inventory services, demand forecasting is critical. Crowded restaurants, long ski-lift lines, and standing-room-only on public transportation all result from excess demand. To address supply/demand imbalances the firm must modify supply and/or demand; hence, data mining and predictive analytics are becoming important tools.

MODIFY SUPPLY. The firm can address short-run demand fluctuations by *increasing* (stretching) capacity like working longer hours, outsourcing, renting or sharing extra facilities and equipment, and adding full-time or part-time workers. The critical challenge is maintaining service quality: An upscale hair salon should not hire temporary stylists unless their skills meet the salon's standards. The firm can *decrease* supply by scheduling employee training, maintenance, and renovations.

MODIFY DEMAND. The firm should analyze demand patterns, answering questions like:

- Does service demand follow a regular, predictable cycle? If so, is the cycle length daily, weekly, monthly, or annual?
- What causes these fluctuations — climate, paydays, school vacations, or work schedules?
- Are there random demand fluctuations — births, crime, weather, or economic conditions?
- Can we disaggregate use patterns by market segments or profitability?

Based on the answers, the firm must decide which segments to target — then increase/decrease demand as necessary. To *increase* demand, the firm may improve service offerings, provide better time and place convenience, communicate more effectively with potential customers, and/or reduce prices. To *decrease* demand — **demarketing** — the firm can offer customers incentives to switch to lower demand periods or reduce marketing activities like cutting advertising/promotion spending and service availability, and increasing price.[6]

KEY IDEA

➤ The firm cannot inventory services. The firm must address excess supply (demand) by decreasing (increasing) supply or increasing (decreasing) demand.

VARIABILITY

Lack of consistency follows directly from human involvement in service delivery. Firms address variability in product manufacturing using quality tools, but these are more difficult for services. Nonetheless, approaches like **Six Sigma**, a data-driven methodology that eliminates defects in any process, can be effective for securing consistency in service systems.

HUMAN CAPITAL. Employee selection and training are critical for improving employee performance and reducing service variability. Treating employees appropriately is also important. Virgin puts employees ahead of customers under the philosophy that "happy employees mean happy customers." Virgin believes that poorly treated employees will not deliver high customer satisfaction.

KEY IDEA

➤ Reducing variability is more difficult for services than for products.

Sometimes service variability is positive; service providers enhance satisfaction by tailoring actions to individual customers and responding to their needs in real time. To secure such behavior, reward systems and empowerment should encourage employees *to go the extra mile* to serve customers, not penalize them for innovating or for breaking rules to provide a better customer experience. Ritz Carlton allows every employee up to $2,000 to remedy customer service issues on the spot — no questions asked. Many firms identify and applaud company heroes who deliver exceptional service.

SUBSTITUTE CAPITAL FOR LABOR. The firm can remove human variability via automation like using dispensing machines for cash, drinks, sandwiches, and subway cards. Cost reduction objectives often drive these innovations, but they reduce variability nonetheless. The downside: Machines break down and customers may desire human contact. Some bank customers prefer human tellers to ATMs, and many people object to quasi-personal communication (voice-recognition systems) in call centers; they want human interaction. Do you?

KEY IDEA

➤ Service variability can be positive when service providers tailor behavior for individual customers.
➤ The firm can reduce human variability via automation.

PERISHABILITY

Perishability is tightly linked to inseparability and the inability to inventory services, but focuses on situations where supply is committed but demand is not. In one situation, demand is apparently sufficient but unpaid, like patients missing doctors' appointments — reminder systems attempt to address this problem. In another, demand is variable or insufficient; the firm may offer lower prices — like last-minute booths in New York and London theater districts, and StubHub for sporting events.

KEY IDEA

➤ Because they cannot be inventoried, services are perishable.

DIVISIBILITY

We view most products as single entities: An automobile is a single unit, not a collection of components like an engine, seats, transmission, and wheels. *Divisibility* is a key service characteristic with many core and surrounding services comprise a sequence of activities conducted over time. Consider the many activities impacting your impression of your marketing course, from registration to final grade.

LACK OF ACQUISITION

People acquire and frequently own products, but not services. They *experience* the physical manifestation of services like a smoother-running car, a dashing haircut, or an auction *win* on eBay. But typically the service is, at best, a set of associations in memory. Yet a service experience can be highly salient, and related associations very influential. Positive associations drive repurchase and positive word of mouth. Negative associations lead customers to avoid the service provider and dissuade others.

ROLE OF CUSTOMERS

Firms rarely refuse to sell products to customers because of the effect on other customers. But customers experience many services in group settings, so customer-customer interaction is a critical issue for many service firms. The drunken airline passenger, the sleeping student in a finance class, and the baseball fan behind home plate shouting out pitches — each affects other customers' experiences. The firm must not unthinkingly believe *the customer is always right*. Some organizations have systems for rejecting customers — like college admission departments, nightclub bouncers, and restaurant maitre d's.

SERVICE QUALITY

In general, high customer satisfaction drives customer loyalty, repurchase, and positive word of mouth, and enhances shareholder value.[7] The converse is also true. Figure 13.1 shows the **SERVQUAL** model: Customer satisfaction relates to service quality via **expectations disconfirmation** — Gap 5 is the *difference* between perceived quality and expected quality[8]:

- **Customer satisfaction.** Perceived service is *better* than expected service.
- **Customer dissatisfaction.** Perceived service is *worse* than expected service:

> Two computer hardware firms (disguised) competed fiercely. Firm **A** promised service visits within four hours of a request; firm **B** promised eight hours. **A** averaged five and a half hours; **B** averaged seven hours. **A**'s service performance was better, but **B**'s satisfaction ratings were higher!

Gap 5 depends on four other gaps:

- **Gap 1.** The firm does not understand the customer's service expectations.
- **Gap 2.** Service quality specifications do not reflect firm beliefs about service expectations.
- **Gap 3.** Service delivery performance does not meet service specifications.
- **Gap 4.** External communications about service quality do not reflect service performance.

SERVQUAL identifies a dilemma. The firm may increase short-run sales by advertising high service quality, but if *perceived* quality is lower than *expected* quality customers will be dissatisfied. Yet, if the firm under-promises on service quality, sales may be low. Also, rising customer expectations make it increasingly difficult to deliver greater-than-expected service.

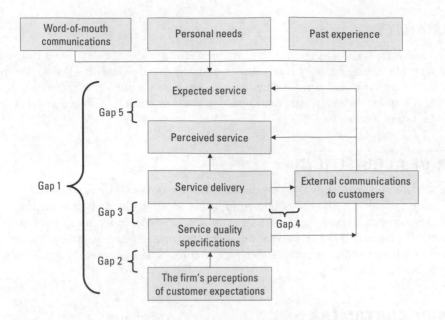

FIGURE 13.1

THE SERVQUAL MODEL FOR DIAGNOSING SERVICE QUALITY

> *Marketing Question*
>
> Think about your favorite coffee shop. How do you perceive service quality? Evaluate tangibles, reliability, responsiveness, assurance, and empathy.

MEASURING AND MANAGING SERVICE QUALITY

In SERVQUAL, five key variables influence perceived service quality:

- **Tangibles.** Appearance of communication materials, equipment, personnel, and physical facilities.
- **Reliability.** Ability to perform the promised service accurately and dependably.
- **Responsiveness.** Willingness to help customers and provide prompt service.
- **Assurance.** Employee courtesy, knowledge, and ability to convey confidence and trust.
- **Empathy.** Provision of caring, individualized attention to customers.

Table 13.1 shows the 22-item SERVQUAL scale. Respondents provide service quality expectations data QE; and service perceptions data for providers — QP.[9] The provider's total SERVQUAL score comprises QP minus QE differences, summed over all 22 items. Subscale scores for tangibles, reliability, responsiveness, assurance, and empathy provide finer-grained data and offer action recommendations. Figure 13.2 plots hypothetical scores for one provider: *Reliability* and *empathy* are fine, but the firm may be overemphasizing *empathy*. The firm should focus on *assurance* — high expectations but low perceived performance, and *tangibles.* The provider should also keep an eye on *responsiveness.*

KEY IDEA

➤ SERVQUAL's subscale scores —

- Tangibles
- Reliability
- Responsiveness
- Assurance
- Empathy

— provide actionable items for improving service performance.

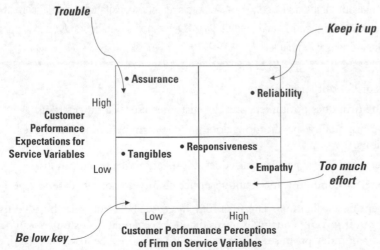

FIGURE 13.2

CUSTOMER EXPECTATIONS AND PERFORMANCE PERCEPTION ON FIVE SERVICE DIMENSIONS

....
TABLE 13.1

THE SERVQUAL SCALE

SERVQUAL Dimensions	SERVQUAL Expectations Item, QE	SERVQUAL Perception item, QP
Tangibles	1. Excellent_____companies will have modern-looking equipment.	XYZ has modern-looking equipment.
	2. The physical facilities at excellent _____ companies will be visually appealing.	XYZ's physical facilities are visually appealing.
	3. Employees at excellent _____ companies will be neat-appearing.	XYZ's employees are neat-appearing.
	4. Material associated with the service (such as pamphlets or statements) will be visually appealing in an excellent _____ company.	Material associated with the service (such as pamphlets or statements) are visually appealing at XYZ.
Reliability	5. When excellent _____ companies promise to do something by a certain time, they will do so.	When XYZ promises to do something by a certain time, it does so.
	6. When a customer has a problem, excellent _____ companies will show a sincere interest in solving it.	When you have a problem, XYZ shows a sincere interest in solving it.
	7. Excellent _____ companies will perform the service right the first time.	XYZ performs the service right the first time.
	8. Excellent _____ companies will provide their services at the time they promise to do so.	XYZ provides its services at the time it promises to do so,
	9. Excellent _____ companies will insist on error-free records.	XYZ insists on error-free records.
Responsiveness	10. Employees in excellent _____ companies will tell customers exactly when services will be performed.	Employees in XYZ tell you exactly when services will be performed.
	11. Employees in excellent _____ companies will give prompt service to customers.	Employees in XYZ give you prompt service.
	12. Employees in excellent _____ companies will always be willing to help customers.	Employees in XYZ are always willing to help you.
	13. Employees in excellent _____ companies will never be too busy to respond to customers' requests.	Employees in XYZ are never too busy to respond to your requests.
Assurance	14. The behavior of employees in excellent _____ companies will instill confidence in customers.	The behavior of employees in XYZ instills confidence in you.
	15. Customers of excellent _____ companies will feel safe in their transactions.	You feel safe in your transactions with XYZ.
	16. Employees in excellent _____ companies will be consistently courteous with customers.	Employees in XYZ are consistently courteous with you.
	17. Employees in excellent _____ companies will have the knowledge to answer customers' questions.	Employees in XYZ have the knowledge to answer your questions.
Empathy	18. Excellent _____ companies will give customers individual attention.	XYZ gives you individual attention.
	19. Excellent _____ companies will have operating hours convenient to all their customers.	XYZ has operating hours convenient to all its customers.
	20. Excellent _____ companies will have employees who give customers personal attention.	XYZ has employees who give you personal attention.
	21. Excellent _____ companies will have the customer's best interests at heart.	XYZ has your best interests at heart.
	22. The employees of excellent _____ companies will understand the specific needs of their customers.	Employees of XYZ understand your specific needs.

a. All questions answered on a 1-to-7 scale: 1 = Strongly disagree, 7 = Strongly agree.

b. The blank line in the Expectations items is for the particular industry, sub-industry, or department being studied.

c. XYZ in the Perception items stands for the company being studied.

ISSUES IN IMPROVING SERVICE QUALITY

To improve service quality, the firm should consider several issues:

- **Customer co-production.** Some firms improve service quality via customer participation in service delivery. Examples include self-service restaurants and self-checkout super-markets. Previously, FedEx customers tracked packages by phoning customer service representatives; today they track packages via the Internet. Customers enjoy better service and FedEx cuts costs. Nirvana! Some firms promote co-production via differential pricing like airlines, whose online prices are often lower than telephone reservations.

- **Improving the offer.** The firm enhances service quality by adding customer service. FMCG firms provide retailers with *plan-o-grams* (layouts) for arranging shelf space. Private banks offer money management seminars for children of high-net-worth clients. Additional customer service is particularly important in mature markets.

  Sometimes firms improve quality by removing services! Popular and profitable Southwest Airlines (SWA) uses secondary airfields, on-board ticketing, and non-assigned seats; and has no interline baggage transfer with other airlines. By reducing costs, SWA offers low fares; high-frequency flights, good on-time performance, and a fun experience that lead customers to rate service quality high.

- **Maintaining the service environment.** The output from some services negatively affects the physical environment: dirty plates and glasses in restaurants, dirty towels in health clubs, and hair on the barber's floor. Quickly restoring the environment improves service quality.

- **Service performance and information.** Customers want high service quality, but they also want to know when they will receive the service. London's Heathrow Express provides passengers with accurate estimates of train arrivals and departures — on the platform and on the train. In many cities, clocks advise motorists and pedestrians when traffic lights will change.

- **Service quality failures and service recovery.** Despite the firm's best efforts, service errors do occur. To minimize customer defection, the firm should deal swiftly with service failure and aggressively manage service recovery. Done well, formerly unhappy customers become loyal, even advocates. The firm should address failure by upgrading products, services, and/or customer service. Overall, few aggrieved customers complain — they just defect. But complaints are an opportunity to learn customer *pain points*.[10] Firms should make complaining easier but should follow up swiftly and aggressively:

Increasingly, customers complain in public, especially on the Internet. They post stories on bulletin boards, Twitter, and YouTube, or set up attack websites: AOL, The Gap, JPMorgan Chase, McDonald's, Microsoft, and United Airlines have all been targets. How the firm manages its reputation within the digital realm is an increasingly critical issue. Some firms employ web watchers to monitor complaints and answer questions. Many firms sponsor *user groups* on Facebook or LinkedIn; or host YouTube channels to help manage perceptions.

CUSTOMER SERVICE

At the start of this chapter, we showed that core services differ from customer services. *Customer service* is any act, performance, or information that enhances the firm's core product or service. Customer service is critical for **customer relationship management (CRM)** — Chapter 2 — and can be as important as the core product. IBM did not dominate mainframes because of superior technology or lower prices. IBM's differential advantage was customer service: "You never get fired for buying IBM."

KEY IDEA

➤ High satisfaction no longer guarantees high customer retention. Firms must delight customers.

KEY IDEA

➤ All firms experience service failures; how the firm addresses them is key.

KEY IDEA

➤ A drive for service efficiency can lead to inflexible systems that cannot deal with idiosyncratic customer behavior.

KEY IDEA

➤ Few aggrieved customers *complain* — they just *defect.* The firm should make complaining easier, then follow up swiftly and aggressively.

KEY IDEA

➤ Customer service can be more central to customer decision-making than the core product or service.

GE Power Systems (GEPS) focused on improving customer service when electric utility deregulation spawned severe price pressure. GEPS reduced replacement time for old or damaged parts from 12 to six weeks, and advised U.S. customers on doing business in Europe and Asia. GEPS provided maintenance staff for equipment upgrades and moved one-third of its engineers from new product development to new service development.

TYPES OF CUSTOMER SERVICE

Figure 13.3 shows the **flower of customer service**, embracing eight dimensions for augmenting the core product/service. We illustrate the information dimension[11]:

FIGURE 13.3

THE FLOWER OF CUSTOMER SERVICE

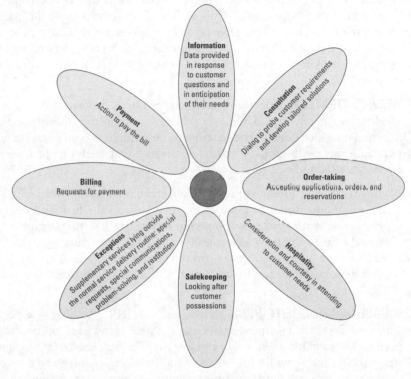

Marketing Question

Recall when you last purchased an expensive product or service online or from a bricks & mortar store. Where did the provider do well — billing, consultation, exceptions, hospitality, information, order-taking, payment, or safekeeping? Where could it improve?

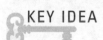 **KEY IDEA**

➤ Customer service differs in relationship to purchase:
• Before
• During
• After

We can also classify customer service by phase of the purchase process. Each phase has different customer requirements where different customer services are appropriate[12]:

• **Pre-purchase.** Assist customers preparing for purchase, including help identifying needs. Also, promotional activities providing information about products and purchase locations.

• **During purchase.** Includes help with selection, customization agreements, financing, personal selling, product assortments, product trial, and quality assurance.

At The Musician's Planet, customers can try out a guitar and make a demo tape. At REI (Seattle), consumers can attempt a 64-foot climbing wall, examine a water pump in an indoor river, or test a Gore-Tex jacket in a rainstorm. Some clothing stores use advanced imaging technology to portray dresses with different styles and fabrics. Levi Strauss' imaging machine takes precise customer measurements for custom jeans.

• **Post-purchase.** Most marketing activity occurs pre- and during purchase; most customer service occurs after purchase. Post-purchase service (PPS) helps customers pay for, transport, receive, install, use, return and exchange, repair, service, and dispose of products.[13] PPS addresses problems and complaints and includes remanufacturing, spare parts availability, technical service, toll-free service telephone numbers, training, warranties, and websites. The firm may provide some PPS (for some customers) at no charge, but with astute segmentation and pricing, PPS can be very profitable.[14] PPS can also act as an early-warning system for detecting quality problems; hence, PPS raises repurchase rates, enhances cross-selling, and increases customer retention.

DELIVERING EXCEPTIONAL CUSTOMER SERVICE

The firm has several levers for delivering outstanding customer service:

TOP MANAGEMENT SUPPORT AND INVOLVEMENT. Top managers should over-communicate that serving customers well is crucial — they should build a culture where all employees emphasize customer service. It's one thing to *talk the talk*, but top managers should also *walk the walk* by *getting their hands dirty* interacting with customers. In B2C firms, they might spend a day or so a month in customer service, like senior Toyota executives when introducing the Lexus. They should identify and reward customer service *heroes* and publicly acknowledge their successes. In B2B firms, top managers should support strategic account managers by serving as *Executive Sponsors* for strategic customers — Chapter 17. CEO Steve Ballmer is Microsoft's *Executive Sponsor* for Walmart.

CUSTOMER SERVICE STRATEGY. In developing its market strategy, the firm identifies customer *product- or service-based needs*, then develops a value proposition to satisfy those needs — Chapter 9. In formulating a **customer service strategy**, the firm focuses on customer *needs for customer service*. Customers with similar product- or service-based needs may have very different customer service needs, and vice versa.

Standard marketing research techniques provide insight about customer service needs. At retail, mystery shopping programs examine customer experiences with the firm and competitors. Generally, the firm should strive to surpass competitor service levels. Setting customer expectations slightly below the firm's ability to deliver leads to positive expectations disconfirmations. Because it can be expensive to provide, some firms offer customer service at varying levels. All customers receive a basic customer service backbone; additional service depends on customer importance.[15]

HUMAN RESOURCE MANAGEMENT (HRM). Human resource (HR) planning — especially for onstage personnel — is integral to superior customer service.[16] Many *front-line* positions, particularly in retail and hospitality, are low skill and low pay. The firm should develop good HR policies and apply them rigorously. Traditional recruiting, selecting, training and development, appraisal, recognition, reward, and retention tools are important to ensure a good employee/firm fit.

High personnel costs lead many firms to outsource customer service call-centers to India, Kenya, Malaysia, and the Philippines. Although well-educated and English-speaking, candidates typically require training in products/services and in speaking with a U.S. accent. Costs often drive outsourcing decisions, but the firm must balance cost reductions with cultural fit and service quality.

SERVICE INFRASTRUCTURE. The firm must design the appropriate infrastructure, including technology and human resources, to support the customer service strategy. Some customer services, like repairs, depend heavily on people; others, like web-based reservation systems, depend on technology. Paradoxically, many highly people-intensive service systems, like airline passenger and baggage check-in, require the most sophisticated technology investments.

Customer interfaces are crucial. Most customers want simple interfaces and a single customer service representative; customers dislike being passed around. Many firms generate customer dissatisfaction by creating specialists (for cost reasons) and making one-stop calls impossible. Other firms outsource customer service to third-party providers. The author purchased an HDTV and related accessories from BestBuy. The store experience was excellent and an automated phone call provided installation information. But then the customer service experience

KEY IDEA

➤ Customer service has eight *flower-of-service* dimensions:

- Billing
- Consultation
- Exceptions
- Hospitality
- Information
- Order-taking
- Payment
- Safekeeping

KEY IDEA

➤ Customers requiring *similar* products and services may have *differing* customer service needs, and vice versa.

KEY IDEA

➤ Human resource planning for customer service employees requires special attention to:

- Recruiting
- Selecting
- Training and development
- Appraisal
- Recognition
- Reward
- Retention

KEY IDEA

➤ Critical elements in delivering exceptional customer service are:

- Top management support and involvement
- Customer service strategy
- Human resource management
- Service infrastructure
- Measuring customer service quality

KEY IDEA

➤ Customer service infrastructure combines the technological and human resources necessary to deliver high-level customer service.

KEY IDEA

➤ Customer defection rate is a more valuable performance measure than customer satisfaction. The firm should identify and measure critical elements driving customer satisfaction.

fell apart: a half-hour spent on the telephone waiting to speak to a human — a third-party installer. And of course, we're sharing the experience with *you*.

Many firms use web-based technological solutions to reduce personnel costs. Well-designed systems — like some airline and hotel reservations — guide customers seamlessly; they improve customer service, provide intimacy and connectivity to the firm, *and* reduce costs. Poorly designed systems can be intensely annoying and highly dissatisfying.

Reporting relationships and customer service interfaces with other firm functions are important infrastructure issues. Xerox customers interfaced with sales, service, and business operations. Commissioned salespeople strove to place machines, but were difficult to find when customers required information or wanted to switch to better-suited products. Customer service had to clean up many problems created by the sales force. Xerox eventually teamed up sales, service, and business operations to share responsibility in sales districts, and harmonized reward systems.[17]

MEASURING CUSTOMER SERVICE QUALITY. *If you can't measure it, you can't manage it.* Customer satisfaction is a good measure, but across-the-board quality improvements have made it less useful. Customer defection rate is better.[18] Identifying defectors is easy when customers must terminate a formal relationship like banking, insurance, and telephone service, but difficult when individual customer records do not exist.

Analyzing the causes of defection provides valuable information for improving service delivery. The firm should identify and regularly measure critical elements of customer service against performance standards. Differences between standards and actual performance should form the basis for modifying customer service. The firm should also design employee-reward programs based on performance against standards.

KEY MESSAGES

- Sometimes the firm's core offering is a service — sometimes a physical product.
- Customer service complements either a core product or a core service.
- Some products are transitioning to services as customers purchase the benefits that physical products deliver, rather than purchase the products.
- Several characteristics distinguish services — core services and customer service — from physical products. Each has important marketing implications:
  - Intangibility
  - Variability
  - Divisibility
  - Role of customers
  - Inseparability
  - Perishability
  - Lack of acquisition
- SERVQUAL is an important diagnostic tool for understanding and improving services.
- High service quality generally leads to greater customer satisfaction, but greater competition and increased quality are weakening the customer satisfaction/loyalty relationship.
- The firm can deliver customer service pre-, during, and post-purchase.
- Well-designed and well-delivered customer service allow the firm to reap significant benefits from repurchase and positive word of mouth.

IMPERATIVE 4

Design the Market Offer

....

PART A – PROVIDING CUSTOMER VALUE

CHAPTER 14

DEVELOPING

NEW PRODUCTS cv1401

To access O-codes, go to **www.ocodes.com**

The best way to predict the future is to invent it.

— Alan Kay, Xerox PARC scientist, 1971

LEARNING OBJECTIVES

When you have completed this chapter, you will be able to:

- Distinguish among different types of innovation for developing and marketing new products.
- Identify critical success factors for consistent innovation.
- Understand and explain the relationship between marketing and innovation.
- Contrast the different ways firms approach the innovation challenge.
- Explain how innovative firms develop successful new products.
- Understand the marketing significance of being an innovative firm.
- Implement the stage-gate, new product development process.
- Understand the factors driving successful new product adoption.
- Classify product adopters into various categories by speed of adoption.

OPENING CASE: THOMSON FINANCIAL — BOARDLINK

Thomson Financial (TF) provides information and decision tools for the financial market. TF successfully launched BoardLink, a product that facilitates information flow between firms and their boards of directors.[1]

The process that led to BoardLink began when TF acquired CCBN and formed Thomson Corporate Executive Services (TCES). Greg Radner, CCBN's marketing head, was responsible for identifying CCBN's next generation products. Radner leveraged CCBN's traditional customer touch points like sales and service calls to understand the challenges clients were facing. These informal customer discussions identified a common pain point — providing board members with information they needed for board meetings in a timely manner.

Radner and CCBN's sales and support teams conducted in-depth informal customer discussions. They generated solution ideas and tested them with potential customers. Radner's new product development team took detailed notes of every customer conversation and shared these data with every team member. Radner asserted the core underpinning of his new product development effort was securing a deep understanding of customer needs.

Business school graduate Jeron Paul joined Radner and CCBN's clients in developing the concept. Concept development quickly morphed into concept validation as potential customers became excited at the prospect of solving a significant problem. BoardLink also generated significant internal excitement because of the potential for organic growth.

Radner quickly built a 15-person product development team spanning technology, sales, quality assurance, and product developers in the U.S. and Bangalore, India. Radner and Paul also worked with market research professionals from Client Insight LLC (CI), a market research firm specializing in financial markets. CI implemented a three-phase marketing research plan that included: (1) a real-time concept test with a small sample of board members in several industries, (2) a more quantitative, concept test with a large sample of potential customers; and, once the prototype was developed, (3) a usability study to understand potential users' ability to execute common tasks. Throughout development, Radner ensured that each team member heard every potential customer voice as they gave feedback and interacted with the evolving prototype. Hence, internal pushback to design and user interface changes was minimal.

TF successfully launched BoardLink. Within a few months, BoardLink was the solution of choice for board members in 12 organizations. Between 75 percent and 85 percent of the 100-plus board members who signed up to access BoardLink were regular users.

Radner said BoardLink's success was due to two key factors: First, the strong focus on product usability throughout the development process ensured that customers could easily make BoardLink part of their workflow. Second, Thomson launched BoardLink at an acceptable price. TCES focuses on product improvement. Said Radner, "Our customers are telling us what our next thing will be, and we're listening."

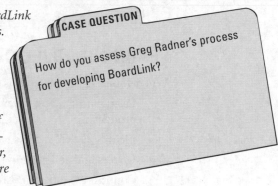

CASE QUESTION

How do you assess Greg Radner's process for developing BoardLink?

Today, many firms are dissecting and improving internal systems and processes and culture to increase innovation capabilities, and sharpening external searches for new products. New technologies and development processes improve new product success rates and help firms reduce time to market. Both business and academia now pay great attention to managing innovation and developing new products as a critical way to achieve differential advantage.

THOMSON
THOMSON BOARDLINK™

KEY IDEA

➤ Successful new products enhance shareholder value.

WHERE AND HOW INNOVATION OCCURS

Marketing Exercise

Select two modern-day successful entrepreneurs. Use the Internet and your analytic skills to assess why each has been successful.

If we are to achieve results never before accomplished, we must employ methods never before attempted.

— Sir Francis Bacon

The late Peter Drucker asserted that marketing was one of the firm's two basic functions, but:

> ... *Marketing alone does not make a business enterprise. The second function of a business, therefore, is innovation. In the organization of the business enterprise, innovation can no more be considered a separate function than marketing. It is not confined to engineering or research, but extends across all parts of the business. Innovation can be defined as the task of endowing human and material resources with new and greater wealth-producing capacity.*[2]

> 3M and DuPont are product innovators; L.L. Bean, Virgin, and Nordstrom are customer service innovators; Apple is a technology and retail innovator.

KEY IDEA

➤ *Sustaining* innovations improve products and processes on existing performance dimensions.

➤ *Disruptive* innovations offer new and very different value propositions.

➤ Leading firms often invest in sustaining versus disruptive innovations.

Chapter 14 focuses on new product innovation and its impact on developing and managing the firm's products. In general, successful innovation provides better, cheaper, and/or faster benefits and values to customers. Chapter 3 introduced the ideas of *sustaining* and *disruptive* technologies. Sustaining technologies spawn innovations that improve established products on performance dimensions valued by major customers. Innovations driven by disruptive technologies offer new and very different value propositions. Initially, these innovations may underperform existing products or processes, but a few fringe customers recognize value. Later, as cost-benefit ratios improve, disruptive technologies surpass the old technology and broaden their appeal. Researchers believe that leading firms often miss *disruptive innovations* because they are committed to an existing way of doing business via *cultural lock-in*.[3]

Serving existing customers is fine in the short run, but creating new customers is essential for the long run. Many firms focus on existing customers by investing in *sustaining innovations*, but they ignore *disruptive innovations* where entrenched interests may place roadblocks. Because *sustaining* and *disruptive* innovations are so different, when firms pursue both, they should do so in separate organizational units.[4]

WHAT FOSTERS PRODUCT INNOVATION

Firms vary widely in their abilities to develop innovative new products. A Columbia Business School study classified less than one-third of a *Fortune* 500 sample as *product innovators*, but these firms earned the best returns on capital. Three factors were most important for success:

- **Market selection.** High-growth markets stimulate innovation.
- **Organization.** Formal structures to foster R&D efforts; supportive cultures.
- **R&D.** Significant and consistent R&D spending, especially applied versus fundamental.

Funding and business objectives are critical innovation issues. Unfortunately, some firms' business units focus too narrowly on short-term profits; hence investments to create disruptive innovations and/or new businesses are insufficient.

Marketing Question

Your CEO has asked why General Mills and P&G are successful innovators. What will you tell her? Use your competitive insight skills.

NEW PRODUCT DEVELOPMENT

Approaches to innovation and new product development are deeply embedded in the firm's culture. If innovation performance is unsatisfactory, the firm's culture may have to change.

New product success is critical for the many firms that introduce thousands of new products annually. These firms often set aggressive product-development targets like: 30 percent annual revenues from products launched in the previous four years. Reckitt Benckiser earns 35–40 percent revenues from products launched in the previous three years. Some firms benchmark product development processes to identify global best practices, then make appropriate changes in their own processes. Other firms encourage broad employee experimentation by allowing unapproved *skunkworks* projects. W.L Gore (Gore-Tex) nurtures many small projects, often started by employees who convince peers their ideas have merit.

One widespread problem is that product developers are sometimes indifferent to the potential marketability of their discoveries. The firm can address this issue by using market-oriented criteria in the development process. At BASF, scientists write marketing plans for products they expect to develop. At GE, scientists regularly meet with marketing and business-unit executives to ensure their projects are linked to the businesses.

Four approaches to new product development, each with its own financial return, risk, and time characteristics, are:

- **Basic technology research.** Typically aimed at disruptive innovations. Examples: DNA mapping, finding new chemical entities for pharmaceuticals, advanced analytics, and electrical super-conductivity.
- **Applied technology research.** Uses basic technology to develop new products. Example: pharmaceutical research adapting new chemical entities to treat medical conditions.
- **Market-focused development.** Focuses on marketable products, often by improving ease of use or developing complementary products. Example: pharmaceutical firms developing new delivery methods like pills, patches, or injections.
- **Market tinkering.** Makes minor modifications to current products. Examples: new dessert flavors or different scents for a floor cleaner.

When approaching new product development, marketers should think carefully about several areas: problem focus, market knowledge, firm competence, complementer products, and effectiveness measures.

The Stage-Gate Process for New Product Development

The **stage-gate process** is a systematic way of generating, then pruning, a large number of ideas into a small number of products the firm successfully launches. Figure 14.1 shows a *gate* after each *stage* where the firm must make a go/no-go decision.

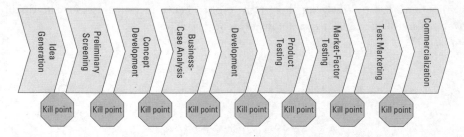

KEY IDEA

➤ Critical factors for successful new product development are:

- Market selection
- Organization
- R&D

KEY IDEA

➤ Product development trade-offs include:

- Time
- Risk
- Financial return

KEY IDEA

➤ Four new product development approaches are:

- Basic technology research
- Applied technology research
- Market-focused development
- Market tinkering

Marketing Question

Using the four approaches to new product development, how would you classify Apple's iPod, a new MP3 player from Sony, the BlackBerry, Coke Zero, Starbucks Frappuccino, *The Apprentice*, *The Apprentice: Martha Stewart*? Why?

FIGURE 14.1

THE STAGE-GATE NEW PRODUCT DEVELOPMENT PROCESS

TABLE 14.1

TYPES OF CRITERIA FOR MOVING FROM ONE STAGE TO ANOTHER IN THE STAGE-GATE PROCESS

Table 14.1 shows the criteria firms typically use to move product through the various gates (stages). Resource commitments increase dramatically as a project moves from idea to new product launch. Dismissing an idea is inexpensive, but the costs of a failed launch are substantial. Each *gate* is a place to stop, a **kill point**. The firm should clearly specify criteria for each *gate*; only projects that meet the criteria pass though the *gate* and enter the following *stage*. Since each subsequent stage typically involves greater investment and risk, projects should not pass kill points lightly.

Stage in the Process	Typical Criteria
Idea generation	Provides incremental customer value; makes sense as a potential product
Preliminary screening	Technologically feasible; likely market need; fits with firm strategy
Concept development	Well-defined product concept; continues to meet previous criteria
Business-case analysis	Fits firm strategy; coherent business plan; forecasts meet market and financial goals
Development	Fulfills concept definition
Product testing	Performs as planned in business-case analysis
Market-factor testing	Customer attitudes and purchasing as anticipated in business-case analysis
Test marketing	Positive customer response; revenues, market position, and profitability as anticipated
Commercialization	Revenues, market position, and profitability as anticipated

IDEA GENERATION

It takes a large number of high-quality ideas to create a new product development portfolio that drives long-term growth. Customers are often a good source of new product ideas, but the firm should use any possible idea source — see the Hyatt boxed insert. The firm should document and assess the most promising ideas. Typically, the firm quickly discards many ideas, but discarded ideas may help generate others with greater promise.

> In 1957, Jay Pritzker waited for a flight at Los Angeles International Airport. He noticed that Fat Eddie's coffee shop, in Hyatt Von Dehn's hotel, was unusually busy and the hotel had no vacancies. Pritzker bet that executives would want to stay in quality hotels near large airports. He wrote out a $2.2 million offer for the hotel on a napkin. In 2012, Global Hyatt Corporation owned, operated, managed, or franchised 365 hotels and resorts in 45 countries.

NUMBER OF IDEAS

Firms that generate only a few marginal-quality ideas have few new product successes. Successful firms eliminate many ideas during the development process. Hence, they must identify a large number of ideas to find the one idea that produces a successful product. In many studies, the average ratio of new product ideas to successful products is about 100:1; in agricultural chemicals the ratio is 10,000:1.

SCOPE OF SEARCH

Focused search within the firm's mission — Chapter 7 — typically generates better ideas than unfocused search.[5] As the firm's mission evolves, so should its scope of search.

> Most ski resorts focus resources on ski hills. But skiers and snowboarders spend only 20 percent of their time on the hill; the rest is spent in restaurants, après-ski bars, and shops. Vail Resorts (Colorado) understands; Vail manages six hotels, 72 restaurants, 40 shops, and more than 13,000 condominiums, in addition to its ski slopes.

NEW IDEA SOURCES

The firm should secure ideas from many sources, both inside and outside the organization. The firm must resist the *not-invented-here* (NIH) syndrome that denigrates ideas from outside sources. P&G embraces a *reapplied-with-pride* (RWP) approach. Sources are:

INTERNAL GENERATION. R&D is often a major idea source. Success rates depend on factors like budget and type of people hired, and motivations. Kellogg's Institute for Food and Nutrition Research invests heavily in food laboratories and restaurant-quality kitchens. Researchers are diverse in education and training (from 22 countries). They are also very productive; in one month they generated 65 new product concepts and 94 new packaging ideas — more than 15 percent of revenues derive from center projects. Manufacturing and operations also generate new product ideas. Many firms conduct employee competitions and even offer employees seed capital to pursue their own ideas.

CUSTOMERS. Many innovations start with customers. Kraft used insight from customer focus groups to launch new variations of Oreo cookies. Sometimes firm employees spend time with customers to observe their likes, dislikes, difficulties, and *pain points* with current products and processes. LEGO works with 44 LEGO ambassadors from 27 countries seeking advice on new products. (Over one million people annually attend LEGO conventions.) LEGO also secures feedback from its social media community (Mindstorm) early in the development process. Cisco, GE, PepsiCo, and others conduct customer-idea competitions: Staples generated 8,300 ideas in one contest; BMW prototyped several suggestions from more than 1,000 customers who used its idea tool-kit during one year. 3M secures inventions from lead users, completes development, and markets the products.[6]

COMPETITORS. Some firms just copy competitor products; others identify improvement options; and still others seek opportunities via product-line gaps.

INDEPENDENT INVENTORS. These persons can be a vital source of ideas. Inventors and outside firms now provide 35 percent of P&G's new product ideas. Examples of products successfully developed and marketed by independent inventors include: Cuisinart (food mixer), dental implants, Kitty Litter, Matchbox toys, SuperSoaker watergun, and Velcro. Of course, independent inventors founded Apple, Facebook, Googles, HP, Nike, and many other well-known successful firms.

REGULATIONS. Regulations often cause market inefficiencies that stimulate ideas to build businesses. Leased lines, satellites, and voice-over-Internet protocol (VOIP) each helped circumvent local monopolies for international telephone calls.

SERENDIPITY. New product ideas sometimes arise unexpectedly. Pfizer was testing sildenafil citrate for angina when it discovered the unexpected side effect of treating erectile dysfunction. Pfizer developed Viagra.

IDEA LIBRARIES. Ideas have their own right time. The environment changes and ideas with no value at time A may have great value at time B. AT&T's video telephone failed, but reappeared

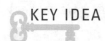

KEY IDEA

➤ New product development stages are:
- Idea generation
- Preliminary screening
- Concept development
- Business-case analysis
- Development
- Product testing
- Market-factor testing
- Test marketing
- Commercialization

Marketing Exercise

Four Wharton graduates founded Warby Parker (WP), an online eyewear retailer. WP operates through a mail-order, home-trial program. Get together with a few classmates; can you generate some new product ideas on which to found a business?

many years later as video conferencing and Skype. Firms should develop **idea libraries** that they search periodically and systematically.

NEW IDEA PROCESSES

The two main approaches for generating new product ideas are **structured** and **unstructured thinking**.

Structured Thinking for Generating New Product Ideas[7]

- **Attribute listing.** Write down all product attributes: For a ballpoint pen, these might include casing material and color, ink quality and color, point width, weight, and price. Construct a table with attributes as column heads. Identify attribute variations, focusing on ways to improve.

- **Morphological analysis.** Builds on attribute listing. Combine items in each column to develop new and interesting new product ideas.

Unstructured Thinking for Generating New Product Ideas

- **Brainstorming.** Focus on a problem and seek radical solutions. Brainstorming helps participants break everyday patterns and find new ways to look for solutions. Ideas should be as broad and odd as possible. Because judgment and analysis stunt idea generation, brainstorming prohibits discussion and/or evaluation until the idea flow is exhausted. Individual brainstorming tends to produce a wider range of ideas; group brainstorming tends to be more effective because of the experience and creativity of all members.

- **Mind mapping.** Write the problem in the center of a page and draw a circle around it. Write associations with the problem in circles elsewhere on the page and draw links to the problem. Each *association* is the focus for another linked set of associations. Seek a solution by examining local clusters of associations.

- **Provocation.** Uses a stupid untrue statement to shock participants from established patterns. A *provocation* in the ballpoint pen example might be: "Ballpoint pens cannot write."

- **Random input.** Used to regenerate brainstorming sessions. The facilitator selects a random noun from book titles, a prepared word list, or a random picture to help generate ideas. In the ballpoint pen example, random words might be cars, trees, factories, or carpets.

- *Six Thinking Hats.* Each of six different-colored real or imaginary *hats* represents a different nature of thought. *Green* — creative ideas; *red* — emotions, by expressing feelings about an idea or process; *white* — analytic; *black* — pessimistic; *yellow* — optimistic; *blue* — procedural.[8]

Marketing Question

Select one of the *unstructured thinking* processes. Work with some fellow students to generate ideas to keep people cool in summer.

PRELIMINARY SCREENING

The goal of **preliminary screening** is to create a balanced portfolio of high-potential new product ideas. For most firms, a balanced portfolio includes ideas ranging from low-return/low-risk to high-return/high-risk, with revenue generation in both the short and long run. Screening decisions for high-risk, high-return, long-time-to-revenue ideas are quite difficult. Figure 14.2 shows a balanced portfolio on return and risk.

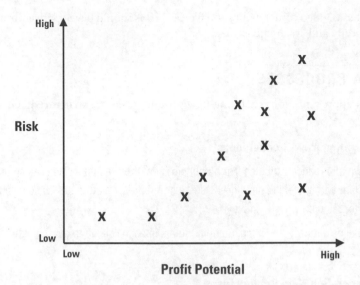

FIGURE 14.2

**RISK AND RETURN IN
NEW PRODUCT IDEAS —
A BALANCED PORTFOLIO**

KEY IDEA

➤ Preliminary screening
seeks a balanced port-
folio of new product
ideas by varying
screening criteria
across idea types.

*Marketing
Question*

Collect the ideas you
developed for one of the
Marketing Questions, p. 219.
Develop a set of screening
criteria and select the most
promising idea.

Preliminary screening typically involves securing opinions from knowledgeable marketing and/or technical personnel, customers, and even suppliers. The exact mix depends on the idea. Preliminary screening is the first stage for eliminating new product ideas.

Because return and risk profiles differ markedly among ideas, the firm should use several sets of criteria. For example, criteria for ideas leading to new-to-the-world products should differ from those for additions to existing product lines. A useful way to assess new ideas is the *spider web* diagram — Figure 14.3. Each 10-point-scale spoke represents a screening criterion; poor scores are near the center, good scores near the periphery. The firm has assessed an idea on eight criteria; it scores relatively well on several criteria, but poorly on two.

FIGURE 14.3

**ASSESSING NEW
PRODUCT IDEAS**

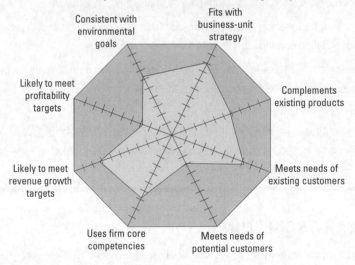

CONCEPT DEVELOPMENT

The **product concept** (**concept definition**) describes the product idea. Good concepts detail deliverable customer benefits. FMCG firms take pains to express new product ideas as robust product concepts. The process is highly iterative. Some examples (status) are:

- Breath fresheners for dogs (successful new product)
- Inexpensive four-passenger business jet (under development at Honda and GE)
- Diet baby foods (not under development)

- Global positioning satellite (GPS) locator for children (launched and doing well)
- Rechargeable laptop using energy from typing on the keyboard (not under development)
- SUV Smart car (under development by Smart for the U.S. market)

Criteria for approval should be similar to preliminary screening. Understanding customer needs, particularly unmet needs, is very helpful in crafting and testing concept definitions.

Product concepts must appeal to customers and should guide development teams. Firms get in trouble when concepts drift during development. Pontiac's concept for the Aztek was a small, youth-oriented sport utility. But to launch the car quickly and economically, Pontiac used GM's minivan frame. Aztec's appearance received mixed reviews and its $22,000–$27,000 price was too high for the youth market; Aztec sold poorly.

Marketing Question

Develop a Concept Definition for the successfully screened idea in the Marketing Question, p. 219.

BUSINESS-CASE ANALYSIS

Business-case analysis (BCA) sits between *concept approval* and *development*. BCA assesses the concept's financial viability and considers various risk factors. Projects must meet minimum financial targets to move forward. The heart of BCA is a draft marketing plan; the firm lays out its market strategy, given successful development. The firm must think through market segmentation, choose target segments, and prepare positioning — including a value proposition for securing differential advantage.

Four considerations underlie forecast financial performance:

- **Sales revenues.** As discussed; these forecasts can be highly uncertain.
- **Cost of goods sold (COGS).** All ongoing costs to make and sell the product. **Gross profit** equals sales revenues less COGS. The firm may incur losses in the launch phase.
- **Investment costs.** Include all costs to develop the product, plus fixed investment for factories and equipment. The firm incurs many of these costs before it earns any revenues.
- **Discounting.** The firm must discount all future cash flows to the present.

KEY IDEA

➤ Business-case analysis assesses the financial viability of a product concept.

➤ Forecasting sales revenues is the most difficult step.

DEVELOPMENT

A successful business-case analysis sets the stage for **development**. Development typically occurs deep in the firm. Design, engineering, and R&D focus initially on product design and functional performance, but the firm must also involve other groups. Input from manufacturing and service helps ensure the product can be made and serviced efficiently.[9] Development also benefits from customer involvement.

Development by multifunctional teams, including *voice of the customer*, helps avoid time-consuming back-and-forth interactions that slow linear, sequential processes. Achieving consensus may be difficult, but teams often produce better products. Caution: Using teams may lead to loss of specialist expertise. Functional experts can become organizationally disconnected from their specialties. Requiring clear written reports, intensive problem-solving meetings, good direct supervision, and standard work procedures can mitigate these problems.[10]

Marketing Question

Many drivers use cars as on-the-road offices. Show how you would design any mid-size model for office use. Would this change if the car were also the family vehicle?

Motorola charged engineer Ron Jellico with creating the thinnest cell phone ever. Jellico's engineering team (ultimately 20 strong) met daily at 4 p.m. for one-hour meetings (often lasting until 7 p.m.). The team flouted Motorola's development rules by keeping the project secret, even from close colleagues, and using materials and processes never before tried. Engineers made breakthroughs like putting the antenna in the mouthpiece and the battery alongside the circuit board. Originally planned as a niche product, the RAZR sold more than 20 million units in the first year.

PRODUCT DESIGN

As product quality improves, design becomes increasingly important for customer satisfaction. During development, the firm must make performance trade-offs among product attributes, but it should always keep the value proposition squarely in mind. The firm must also address negative side effects, possibly with creative design approaches.

Product Design at Sony

A senior Sony Electronics executive said: "The most exciting thing about Sony to me is when you're in a line-up review and they're showing you a product and you get this 28-year-old product planner and this 30-year-old designer and they walk into a room and they pull back a piece of cloth and they show you a product that you've been working together on for a year and you go 'Oh my God, it's perfect.' And when you get into those moments, you know, it's about the passion that Sony has for great products. This is a passionate organization that really believes in creating the best possible product that you can create, and the designers, product planners and senior marketers just love what they're doing.

"There's this one designer in Tokyo. He's in his 30s now, but when you see this guy! He's going to walk into the room and you're going to think, 'Oh my God, a street person has escaped and he's loose in the building.' And his pants are four sizes too big and his clothes just hang on and he looks like he hasn't slept in a week ... Most products you'll look at and you'll say, 'OK, I could give you 20 comments on how to improve the design.' But when he pulls back the drape, you're not going to have anything to say. On this one occasion I was in Tokyo and he showed us a CD player, and the stuff was perfect. It was just perfect. That line of CD players sold six million units in the U.S. alone. And we didn't have to touch it. So that's the strength of Sony, people like that ... somebody with passion designed that thing."[11]

Development is typically the most time-consuming stage in new product development. Faster development helps gain first-mover advantage and enhance revenues. Continuous development on a 24/7 cycle is one option. At Bechtel and other firms, development teams in London, U.S., and Japan take over from each other as the day ends/begins. At Toyota, competitive teams work in parallel toward the same goal. Still other firms form collaborative relationships with customers and independent individuals/organizations.

> *Marketing Exercise*
>
> Identify three examples of superb design. Bring visuals or the actual product to class.

NEW PRODUCT DEVELOPMENT PORTFOLIO

For most firms, the new product development portfolio is a critical element in the entire venture portfolio, along with insourcing, outsourcing, acquisition, strategic alliance, licensing and technology purchase, and equity investment — Chapter 7. Regardless, the new product development portfolio is especially critical because of the ongoing large quantity of firm resources involved. Further, environmental change; strategy evolution; development successes, failures, advances, and retreats; and new entries from successful business case analyses require the firm to update the portfolio periodically. Successful new product firms display top management commitment selective top management involvement, and multiple efforts. Specifically, four goals are important:

- **Portfolio value.** The firm should consider forecast profits, risk, timing, and required resources.
- **Portfolio balance.** Ensure projects are appropriately dispersed among high/low risk, short/long term; across various product forms, markets, and technologies; and across types of development efforts — basic technology research, applied technology research, market-focused development, and market tinkering.

- **Strategic alignment.** The product innovation strategy should be directly linked to the business strategy via resource allocation into *strategic buckets.*
- **Right number of projects.** Resources are limited. Too many projects and the entire product development process slows leading to missed deadlines including product launches. The firm should rank projects and make tough decision to cull projects that don't make the cut.

PRODUCT TESTING

The firm should test new products for aesthetic, ergonomic, functional, and use characteristics. There is no single test or type of test. Rather, development follows a series of *develop → test → develop* feedback loops until the product is ready for market-factor testing.

The two major types of product test are:

- **Alpha tests — in-company.** For most new products, firm employees provide critical feedback. Several **alpha tests** may run simultaneously; alpha tests often lead to further development.
- **Beta tests — with customers. Beta tests** typically follow successful alpha tests. But firms sometimes conduct beta tests on product features before they finish development. The firm may also conduct several beta tests as development is concluding. Beta tests give customers an early look at developing/soon-to-be-introduced new products.

Speedy testing has many advantages, but inadequate testing can cause major problems. During a moose-avoidance test in a sharp turn at 38 mph, a Swedish journalist tipped over Daimler-Benz's (DB) first subcompact (Mercedes A-Class). DB had invested $1.5 billion in the car; DB spent $171 million to solve the problem.

MARKET-FACTOR TESTING

The product is only one element in the firm's market offer. First-rate products fail if the firm poorly designs and/or implements the rest of the marketing mix. Conversely, the firm may be successful with marginal products if other marketing-mix elements are superior. The firm should evaluate implementation elements like advertising and distribution via **market-factor testing**. Generally, the firm tests other market factors when product development is complete, but sometimes market-factor and product testing occur in parallel. The firm can test using simulated environments or virtually on the Internet.

TEST MARKETING

Test marketing simulates actual market conditions. Typically, the firm selects two geographic areas with similar market and customer profiles, considering issues like seasonality. The firm implements the full market launch program in one geography; the other geography acts as a control to isolate product launch results. Global firms often speed time to commercialization by test marketing simultaneously in several countries. For any test market, measurement is crucial and includes:

- **Input measures** — advertising, training, sales effort
- **Intermediate measures** — customer awareness, interest
- **Output measures** — sales, profits, customer satisfaction

KEY IDEA

➤ Multi-functional teams and customer involvement aid the development process.

➤ Design is an increasingly important part of the development process.

KEY IDEA

➤ The firm should conduct *in-company alpha tests* throughout development. The firm should conduct *customer beta tests* in later phases.

➤ Failure to test products sufficiently can have serious marketing and financial consequences.

KEY IDEA

➤ Product testing is insufficient — the firm should test the entire market offer.

KEY IDEA

➤ Market-factor testing includes simulated environments and virtual testing.

Marketing Question

Have you ever been part of a test market in your local grocery store or retail outlet? Did you try the product? Did the firm launch it successfully, or was it killed?

FMCG firms collect point-of-sales data from supermarket scanners. Consumer panels and/or independent surveys provide intermediate measures and customer satisfaction.

Test marketing has pros and cons:

- Pros — saves launch costs; fine-tunes launch; may provide unexpected insight
- Cons — expense and time costs; alerts competitors; excessive attention is non-replicable at launch

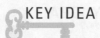

COMMERCIALIZATION

Successful completion of the stage-gate process results in a product ready for launch and **commercialization**. The firm assigns resources to construct facilities and expend marketing effort. The launch strategy must consider issues like forecast sales, time to bring facilities on line, production and inventory requirements, adherence to planned launch date, competitive lead time, expected competitive response, patent or trade secret protection, and available resources.

All marketing-mix elements are important for launch. Regarding communications, B2C firms often use celebrity spokespersons and advertising to promote new products. They also use *product placement*, working with directors and producers so that actors use products in movies and TV shows. B2B firms focus on good distribution and support programs, including getting key opinion leaders to use new products.

Traditionally, firms launched new products domestically, then later in foreign markets. Today, many firms launch in multiple national markets simultaneously, especially information products where copying is a problem.

No one likes commercial failure, but the best companies learn from commercialization mistakes. Corning failed with a DNA chip designed to print all 28,000 human genes onto slides for research, but identified the drug-discovery market and now sells Epic for testing potential drugs. British Airways' flat beds upstaged Virgin's new reclined sleeper seats, but Virgin used its learning to develop a *leapfrog* innovation, the *upper-class suite*, that helped improve business-class market share.

PRODUCT ADOPTION

The goal of commercialization efforts is customer product adoption. But not all customers adopt at the same time. As part of product planning, the firm should anticipate five categories of customer adoption behavior[12]:

- **Innovators** (2.5 percent) — *Explorers.*[13] The first to adopt the innovation but are only a small part of the population. Typically, other customers do not emulate these *venturesome* risk-takers.
- **Early adopters** (13.5 percent) — *Visionaries.* Follow the innovators. Are more *respected* in their communities and are opinion leaders for others.
- **Early majority** (34 percent) — *Pragmatists.* Motivated by current problems and make decisions *deliberately*; influenced by early adopters.
- **Late majority** (34 percent) — *Conservatives.* A *skeptical* group that adopts only when half the population has adopted. Tend to be price sensitive.
- **Laggards** (16 percent) — *Critics.* These *traditionalists* are suspicious of change, averse to novelty, and adopt only when adoption and use are widespread.

Identifying potential customers by **adoption category** for a new product innovation is a critical marketing challenge. In B2C, early adopters tend to be better educated, socio-economically advantaged, and younger. Avon maintains a database on innovators and early adopters for cosmetics and targets them for new product launches. But innovators and early adopters for one product may be early or late majority for another. Figure 14.4 shows that a product innovation must cross the **chasm** from early adopters to early majority and the mainstream market to be successful.[14] Many new products fail to cross the chasm; for others, it takes a long time.

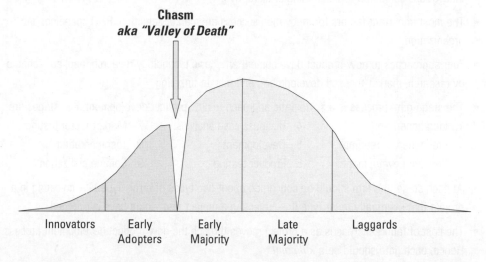

Chasm
aka "Valley of Death"

Innovators   Early Adopters   Early Majority   Late Majority   Laggards

The **ACCORD** acronym summarizes several factors affecting speed of adoption and commercial success. Consider the successful introduction of EZ Pass on toll roads and bridges. The EZ Pass device attaches to a vehicle windshield. An electronic signal at the tollbooth recognizes the device, allows passage, and deducts payment from an account linked to a credit card. The account automatically replenishes when the balance falls to a pre-set level:

- **Advantage.** Saves time at tollbooth; automatic bill payment more convenient than cash.
- **Compatibility.** Driver behavior largely unchanged; initiating the credit card account is trivial.
- **Complexity.** Learning minimal: driver attaches the device; drives through the tollbooth.
- **Observability** (Communicability). Benefits easy to understand and communicate.
- **Risk.** Little risk to trying the EZ Pass system — no upfront payment.
- **Divisibility** (Reversibility). Driver can easily switch back to cash.

KEY MESSAGES

- Successful new products are a major factor in creating shareholder wealth.

- Innovations can be either sustaining or disruptive.

- The most important factors for innovation success are market selection, R&D spending, and organization.

- Four approaches to new product development are: basic technology research, applied technology research, market-focused development, and market tinkering.

- The stage-gate process is a systematic approach to new product development. Key stages are:
  1. Idea generation
  2. Preliminary screening
  3. Concept development
  4. Business-case analysis
  5. Development
  6. Product testing
  7. Market-factor testing
  8. Test marketing
  9. Commercialization

- At each stage, the firm should be concerned about two types of error: Type I — investing in a project that eventually fails; Type II — rejecting a project that would have succeeded.

- The cost of failure increases as a project moves through the new product development process. Hence, each gate should be a *kill point*.

- New product success depends on *crossing the chasm* from early adopters to early majority.

- The speed of adoption for a successful project depends on the ACCORD factors. (Do you know what they are?)

VIDEOS AND AUDIOS

| Innovation | v1402 📹 | William Duggan | Columbia Business School |
| Creativity | v1403 📹 | Jacob Goldenberg | Hebrew University/Columbia Business School |

v1402

v1403

IMPERATIVE 4
Design the Market Offer

PART B – COMMUNICATING CUSTOMER VALUE

CHAPTER 15

INTEGRATED MARKETING COMMUNICATIONS cv1501

To access O-codes, go to **www.ocodes.com**

LEARNING OBJECTIVES

When you have completed this chapter, you will be able to:

- Articulate the causes of miscommunication problems.
- Enumerate the various communications tools the firm can use.
- Integrate communications tools into a communications strategy.
- Distinguish between *push*, *pull*, and combination *push/pull* communication strategies.
- Set communications objectives.

OPENING CASE: CALIFORNIA CHEESE

California's dairy industry faced a significant problem that would likely become more severe — milk surpluses caused by increasing milk productivity. The California Milk Advisory Board (CMAB) evaluated several options and selected cheese as its flagship product for California dairy production. To meet its challenge, CMAB implemented a three-part strategy:

- **Certification mark.** *The mark (seal) showed California with a rising sun and rolling plains on a golden, cheese-colored background: "Real California Cheese" was at the periphery. CMAB had this mark placed on as many cheese packages as possible; in all advertising, coupons, and promotional literature; and on restaurant menus and table tents.*
- **Advertising campaign.** *CMAB implemented the Real California Cheese campaign, "California cheese is great cheese," in newspapers, magazines, outdoors, and on radio and TV. The primary target was women aged 25-54, married with children, income slightly above the national average. The advertising tone and manner tried to create an emotional bond of fondness and affection for California cheese. The advertising used human, intelligent, and humorous messages; but no superiority claim.*

- **Promotional campaign.** *CMAB used in-store cross-promotions with instantly redeemable coupons, product sampling, and self-liquidating offers, like high-quality coffee table books about cheese. Cross-promotional partners were products frequently consumed with cheese, like bread, crackers, and wine.*

After 10 years, CMAB introduced "It's the cheese" — making the exaggerated claim that people came to California for the cheese. Several years later, CMAB introduced "Happy Cows," with the tagline, "Great cheese comes from Happy Cows. Happy Cows come from California." The advertisements showed cows talking, enjoying, and thinking like people about California's best-known features — sunny skies, earthquakes (portrayed positively), and beautiful scenery. More recently, the loquacious cows implored consumers to make California milk and cheese part of their family.

CMAB used spot TV advertising in markets outside California where Real California Cheese had a major presence, supplemented by outdoor, bus and bus-shelter, and radio advertising. Later, when Real California Cheese was sold in many major U.S. markets, CMAB introduced national advertising including during the Super Bowl.

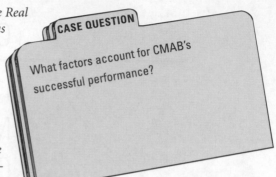

CASE QUESTION

What factors account for CMAB's successful performance?

California cheese achieved spectacular awareness levels. Three out of four Californians reported seeing the Real California Cheese seal where they shopped and 95 percent purchased Real California Cheese. Sales increased 600 percent over a 20-year period beginning in the mid-1980s. Cheese production increased dramatically: from 280 million to 1,990 billion pounds.

We've all heard the popular saying: "If we build a better mousetrap, customers will come." Rubbish! Customers will not *come* unless they know about the mousetrap; that's the purpose of communication. To be successful, the firm must communicate the offer's benefits and value to target customers. Many communications tools and techniques are available for the firm. In this chapter, we consider several broad categories:

- **Personal communications** — face-to-face personal selling, telemarketing/telesales, and service;

- **Mass communications** — traditional advertising, direct marketing, packaging, publicity & public relations, sales promotion (including product placement and trade shows); and

- **Digital communications** — online advertising and public relations, websites, **blogs** and microblogs (like Twitter), quasi-personal communication, and mobile marketing.

Traditionally, firms also planned for some **word-of-mouth** communications to enhance the value of their messages. Social networking and digital media has changed the paradigm; creating greater communications options between and among customers. For marketing professionals, the vast array of communications options is both a blessing and a curse. *Blessing:* The firm has many more communications alternatives. *Curse:* Coordinating multiple messages to multiple targets while producing a coherent, consistent, and integrated whole can be very difficult.

Integrated marketing communications captures the idea of coordinating various communications and promotional messages with the *right* communication tools and techniques, delivered to the *right* audiences at the *right* times. This chapter reviews communications strategies and tactics for reaching target audiences and achieving firm objectives.

THE COMMUNICATIONS PROCESS

An integrated communications program is critical for successfully implementing the firm's market strategy and achieving its objectives. But it's not easy to do. Before we get into the marketing aspects of integrated communication, let's revisit the principles of communication. Figure 15.1 shows the basis for any **communication process**. The *sender* sends a *message* to a *receiver*; the *receiver* receives the message. The dotted line shows that, in some communication processes, the *receiver* also communicates with the *sender*. Ideally, the receiver receives the message the sender *intended* to send. If this does not occur, there is **miscommunication** — typically not a good outcome, particularly for marketers. Three main sources of miscommunication are:

• **Encoding error.** Typically, some person or organizational entity decides on the intended message, but this message is not sent properly. Perhaps the advertising agency misinterprets the product's positioning and does not craft an appropriate message. Or salesforce training is ineffective, and they don't communicate the *right* message.

• **Distortion.** The firm sends the intended message, but communication is distorted; hence, the receiver does not receive the sent message. Consumers receive similar print and TV advertisements differently, like a TV advertisement running on *The Daily Show* versus an identical message on *60 Minutes*. Or the salesperson's accent may affect the received message.

• **Decoding error.** Communications targets may receive the same message differently because of selective attention, perception, and/or retention, related to individual perception, memory, and/or belief systems. Hence, the message is misperceived and/or misunderstood.

A critical marketing challenge is understanding and minimizing the causes of miscommunication.

FIGURE 15.1

THE COMMUNICATIONS PROCESS

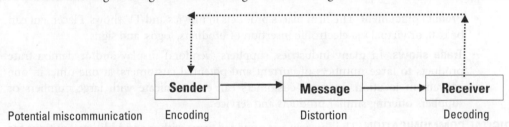

Potential miscommunication   Encoding   Distortion   Decoding

COMMUNICATIONS TOOLS

Communications tools are the ways marketers interface with target audiences. The two traditional categories the firm drives are **personal communication** and **mass communication**. In this chapter, we embrace two additional categories — **digital communication** and **word-of-mouth communication (WOM)**, and their impact on today's integrated communications strategies.

PERSONAL COMMUNICATION. Interpersonal (often *face-to-face*) communication occurs among individuals or groups. Most personal communication in marketing occurs when salespeople and other firm representatives, like technical- and customer-service personnel, interact with customers individually or as team members. In many firms, **telemarketing/telesales** people supplement or replace field salespeople. Some firms script personal communications, but most often interpersonal communication evolves spontaneously during the interaction.

MASS COMMUNICATION. The most pervasive forms of marketing communication occur without interpersonal contact between sender and receiver, particularly in B2C marketing.[1]

Typically, the firm has greater control over message content in mass communication than in personal communication. Various types of mass communication include:

- **Advertising.** The firm pays for communications directed at a mass audience. Advertising embraces different modes, typically visual and audio, deployed via many types of media. *Visual-static media* refers to printed matter, including billboards, brochures, magazines, newspapers, point-of-purchase displays, signage, and trade journals. *Visual-dynamic media* includes television, movies, and online advertising. *Audio* includes radio and newer communications types like podcasts.[2]

- **Direct marketing.** This category includes all paid and sponsored company communications directed at individuals. Most direct marketing is printed *direct* mail, but modern versions include targeted audio/video messages and direct e-mail.

- **Packaging.** Packaging's main value is to protect the product. But packaging is also a communications vehicle, delivering information and visual appeal.

- **Publicity & public relations (P&PR).** Publicity is communication for which the firm does not pay directly. Typically, the firm provides or *places* information like a photograph, press release, story, or video with a third-party transmitter. The transmitter, like an industry analyst, magazine, or news organization, incorporates the material in its own communications. Public relations (PR) embraces publicity but is broader; PR includes other ways of gaining favorable responses for the firm. Typical PR activities include sponsoring events, giving speeches, participating in community activities, donating money to charity, and other public-facing activities.

- **Sales promotion (SP).** SP communications provide extra value for customers; firms often design SP to induce immediate sales. Consumer promotions include contests, coupons, games, point-of-purchase materials, premiums, rebates, and samples. Special forms of SP are:

  - **Product placement.** The firm places products in movies and TV shows. Placement can be real, or virtual via electronic insertion of products, logos, and signs.

  - **Trade shows.** In many industries, suppliers (vendors) display and/or demonstrate products to large numbers of current and potential customers, at one time, in one convenient location. In turn, customers can communicate with large numbers of suppliers offering similar products and services.

DIGITAL COMMUNICATION. The Internet has provided firms with many additional options for communicating with customers. Some methods are electronic analogues of traditional communication tools like various types of advertising on third-party websites and direct marketing via e-mail.

Other methods are specific to the medium, like firm websites, blogs and microblogs, social media, quasi-personal communications, and mobile marketing. Traditional and digital communications can also be linked via technologies like O-codes and QR codes for print media (used in *Capon's Marketing Framework*) and ads (TV, digital, mobile) containing web URLs, Facebook pages, and Twitter hashtags. In contrast to many types of communications, at firm websites and social media groups, customers frequently self-select the communications they receive. Some websites are morphing into **quasi-personal communication (QPC)**, embracing interaction and feedback without human involvement, usually via artificial intelligence. Customers talk on the telephone to computer servers via voice recognition software. QPC allows firms and customers to communicate on a one-on-one basis.[3]

Further, the Internet is shifting from a computer-only medium onto TV sets (and TV programs onto computers), and to cell phones and tablet computers — mobile marketing.

WORD-OF-MOUTH (WOM) COMMUNICATION. Communication among customers and potential customers can impact many purchase elements like brand choice, distribution channel, and timing. Communications about a firm or product can be positive or negative, depending on the customer experience. Because customers typically have no commercial interest in the firm or product, they often have higher credibility than paid communicators. Generally, firms have little control over **WOM** but increasingly they orchestrate **buzz-marketing**, **guerilla-marketing**, and **viral-marketing** campaigns to encourage positive communications.[4] Some firms tap into established groups to take advantage of *social networking*. Cheerleaders are often popular students in high school: Hence, both P&G and PepsiCo provide information and samples to organizations that promote high school cheerleading camps and competitions.

DEVELOPING THE COMMUNICATIONS STRATEGY

Table 15.1 depicts critical questions for developing communications strategy.

Basic Questions	Subsidiary Questions
1. Who are our communications targets?	Specifically, with what entities shall we communicate?
2. What are our communications objectives?	How do communications objectives vary by communications target?
3. What key message do we want to get across?	How should our message vary across communications targets?
4. What communications tools shall we use?	What combination of personal, mass, digital, and WOM communications is appropriate?
5. What communications budget shall we set?	How shall we apportion the communications budget among the different communications tools?
6. When is the *right* time to communicate?	What is the appropriate timing for the various targeted messages, considering seasonality and other factors?

COMMUNICATIONS TARGETS

The firm has two major types of communication targets: *directly related* to firm offers and *not directly related* to such offers. Some targets are decision-makers; others are influencers.

DIRECTLY RELATED COMMUNICATIONS TARGETS. The firm should be most concerned with reaching customers specified in the positioning statement of its market strategy — Chapter 9. These include current and potential customers, direct and indirect customers, and third-party specifiers and advisors. Once identified, the firm can decide which communications strategies are most appropriate — **push** or **pull** — Figure 15.2:

- **Push strategy.** This type of communications focuses on *direct* customers. In the Figure 15.2 illustration (left), the subcomponent manufacturer (SM) places efforts on component manufacturers (CM). The SM expects CMs to communicate with finished-goods manufacturers and other indirect customers further down the channel. Many B2B firms use *push* communications strategies, most effectively delivered by the sales force. The firm expects direct customers to communicate with indirect customers further down the channel.
- **Pull strategy.** These communications focus on *indirect* customers further down the channel, like final consumers or other end-user customers — Figure 15.2 (right). By encouraging these customers to request and purchase finished goods, the firm generates *pull* and drives its own sales.

Most firms use *either* push or pull strategies, but resource-rich firms often use a combination. FMCG firms like P&G and Unilever rely heavily on *pull*-based advertising directed at consumers. But they also execute major *push* efforts targeted at retailers.

Regulations influence communications targets in some industries. The FDA previously banned direct-to-consumer prescription-drug advertising but has relaxed this prohibition in recent years (many countries still ban the practice); pull strategies now encourage patients to "ask your doctor." The firm may also attempt to *signal* competitors — Chapter 5.

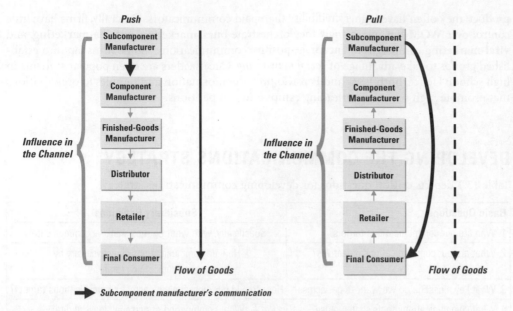

Marketing may also have various internal communications targets. Sometimes there is a disconnect between sales and marketing. A critical marketing challenge is ensuring that salespeople *buy in* and use the *right* communications when addressing customers. Marketing may also communicate with all employees so they internalize the firm's brand identity — Chapter 11.

NOT DIRECTLY RELATED COMMUNICATIONS TARGETS. Many firms have communications targets *not directly related* to products. Capital markets are a special case; firms or their agents (like investment banks) target investors to secure debt and equity financing. Although *not directly related* to firm products, communications to these targets can have a serious impact on customers. Help-wanted advertisements for highly trained personnel may indicate technological leadership and that firm products are worth buying.

COMMUNICATIONS OBJECTIVES

Typically, long-run marketing communications objectives are to increase sales units and/or revenues, and repeat purchase of firm products. Other requirements may be securing awareness, knowledge, liking, and/or trial. When we consider objectives for *directly related* customer targets, major considerations are type of target and the firm's market strategy.

COMMUNICATIONS TARGET. Table 15.2 shows possible communications objectives for different customer types:

Type of Customer	Communication Objectives for Customers
Component manufacturer	– Learn how to assemble firm subcomponents into customer components – Purchase subcomponents for use in components – Inventory sufficient components to satisfy finished-goods manufacturers
Third-party advisor	– Recommend firm subcomponents to component manufacturers
Finished-goods manufacturer	– Agree to purchase components for finished products – Agree to place subcomponent brand on finished product
Distributor	– Train salespeople to communicate benefits and sell finished products to retailers
Retailer	– Agree to budget co-op advertising funds for finished products
Consumer	– Become aware, understand, like, try, and continue to purchase finished products

FIGURE 15.2

COMMUNICATIONS TARGETS IN PUSH AND PULL STRATEGIES

KEY IDEA

➤ Most firms use one of two communications strategies:
- Push
- Pull

Resource-rich firms often use combination *push/pull* strategies.

KEY IDEA

➤ Firms have many communications targets other than customers.

KEY IDEA

➤ Core considerations for the communications strategy are:
- Communications targets
- Communications objectives
- Communications messages
- Communications tools
- Budgeting and timing

TABLE 15.2

ILLUSTRATIVE COMMUNICATION OBJECTIVES FOR A SUBCOMPONENT MANUFACTURER

Marketing Question

Develop a communications plan for your favorite local restaurant. How does your plan improve on the restaurant's current actions?

Marketing Question

Using the Table 15.2 framework, identify target customers and short- and long-term communications objectives for a firm making global position satellite (GPS) systems for pleasure boats.

Marketing Question

Identify a firm(s) that relies heavily on a *pull* strategy. Is the firm successful? If so, why? If not, why not?

Marketing Question

What are the benefits and challenges of using a *pull* strategy?

Communications objectives for competitors and complementers are very different from firm objectives for customers. Typically, the firm tries to influence competitor and complementer actions so customers perceive firm offers more favorably.

THE FIRM'S MARKET STRATEGY. The firm identifies customer targets in the positioning statement of the market strategy — Chapter 9. These targets are also the firm's communication targets. The firm must align communications objectives with selected alternatives in the *strategic focus* to increase unit sales volume:

- Increase customer retention (reduce defection).
- Increase customer use.
- Attract customers from competitors.
- Secure new business.

Communications objectives depend on the age and type of the firm's business and market conditions. In new markets, the firm must necessarily focus on identifying, qualifying, communicating, and selling to *non-users*. Conversely, if the firm is well-placed in a mature market, its objectives probably focus more on retaining *current customers*.

COMMUNICATIONS MESSAGES

Constructing the appropriate message for a customer target is central to developing the communications strategy. The core underlying principle is that message design should reflect the value proposition (positioning element) in the firm's market strategy. If the firm has multiple customer targets, each with different value propositions, then the firm must design multiple messages.

COMMUNICATIONS TOOLS

Communications objectives and messages drive firm choice of communication tools. Suppose the communications objective is to build awareness for a new product among a broad consumer group; common sense tells us that advertising is probably more effective than sending salespeople door-to-door. But if the objective is selling sophisticated capital goods to large industrial companies, personal selling would likely be more productive in delivering messages and answering customer questions. Table 15.3 helps firms match communication tools to communications objectives and target customers. In the illustration, a wholesaler is trying to distribute and sell a new product. The wholesaler decides to:

- *Identify* potential retailers via direct marketing.
- *Qualify* retailers by telemarketing.
- *Sell* to qualified retailers via personal selling and its website.
- *Provide* retailers with ongoing sales and service via a sales and service team.

TABLE 15.3

MATCHING COMMUNICATIONS TARGETS, OBJECTIVES, AND TOOLS

Communication Tools	Communications Targets and Objectives			
	Identify potential retailers	Qualify retailers	Sell to qualified retailers	Provide retailers with ongoing sales and service
Personal selling			****	
Telemarketing/telesales		****		
Individual service personnel				
Sales and service teams				****
Advertising				
Direct marketing	****			

CONTINUES ON NEXT PAGE

	Communications Targets and Objectives			
Communication Tools	Identify potential retailers	Qualify retailers	Sell to qualified retailers	Provide retailers with ongoing sales and service
Publicity & public relations				
Sales promotion				
Online advertising and public relations				
Website			****	
Blogs and microblogs				
Social media				
Mobile marketing				

TABLE 15.3

CONTINUED

The wholesaler chooses *not* to use advertising, publicity & public relations, sales promotion, individual service personnel, or digital approaches other than its website. The wholesaler should develop a similar chart for each customer target.

BUDGETING AND TIMING

The budgeting and timing of firm communications efforts are critical for determining the most effective communications strategy. Both budgeting and timing relate directly to communications objectives and selected communication tools. Chapter 16 discusses budgeting in greater detail in an advertising context. Timing issues are especially critical in developing and executing *multi-point* integrated communications campaigns.

INTEGRATING COMMUNICATIONS EFFORTS

By now, you should have a good understanding of the communications process, know the key questions for developing a communications strategy, and be familiar with communications tools. The firm's core challenge is to develop an effective **integrated marketing communications** program to maximize the impact of its strategy and achieve objectives. Figure 15.3 shows four types of integration for which the firm should strive:

A. Communications for all targets in a single market segment.

B. Communications with other marketing implementation variables — product, service, distribution, price.

C. Communications for all targets in several market segments.

D. Communications for all targets — market segments, markets, businesses, corporate.

Marketing Exercise

Design a social media strategy for the Chevy Volt.

KEY IDEA

➤ Communications objectives and timelines drive the choice of communication tools.

Marketing Question

Can you identify a firm that confused customers by sending discrepant messages?

KEY IDEA

➤ Communications integration occurs at several levels.

➤ Integration ensures maximum communications impact to achieve firm objectives.

FIGURE 15.3

**COORDINATING AND
INTEGRATING
COMMUNICATIONS**

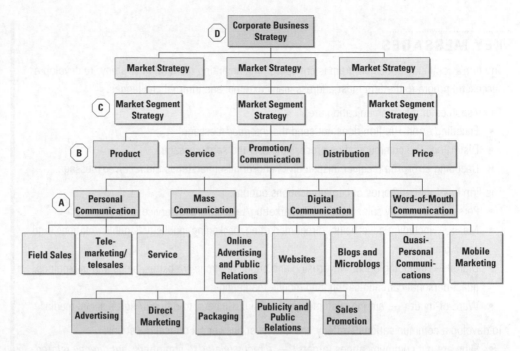

KEY MESSAGES

The firm's communications program is critical for implementing the market strategy. To develop a successful program, the firm must address many external and internal challenges.

Three sources of miscommunication are:

- Encoding error. The firm does not send the *intended* message.
- Distortion. The communication process distorts the *sent* message.
- Decoding error. The receiver misperceives and/or misunderstands the *received* message.

The firm has four categories of communications options:

- Personal — mainly salespeople, telemarketing/telesales, and service personnel
- Mass — including advertising, direct marketing, packaging, publicity & public relations, and sales promotion
- Digital — including online advertising and public relations, websites, blogs and microblogs, quasi-personal communication, and mobile marketing
- Word-of-mouth — among customers/potential customers, traditional/digital social media

To develop a communications strategy, the firm must answer six critical questions:

- Who are our communications targets? — *directly related* to firm offers; *not directly related*
- What are our communications objectives? — vary by target and the firm's market strategy
- What key messages do we want to get across? — vary by customer target — Chapter 16
- What communications tools shall we use? — examine the effectiveness of many options
- What communications budget shall we set? — Chapter 16
- When is the *right* time to communicate? — consider seasonality and other factors

The firm's core challenge is to integrate the various elements of its communications strategy to form a coherent whole. Four types of integration are:

A. Communications tools for all targets in a single market segment.
B. Communications with other marketing implementation variables — product, service, distribution, price.
C. Communications for all targets in several market segments.
D. Communication tools for all targets — market segments, markets, businesses, corporate.

IMPERATIVE 4
Design the Market Offer

CHAPTER 16

MASS AND DIGITAL COMMUNICATION cv1601

To access O-codes, go to **www.ocodes.com**

LEARNING OBJECTIVES

When you have completed this chapter, you will be able to:

* Articulate how advertising works.
* Define and measure advertising objectives.
* Design an advertising campaign.
* Know when to use each of the firm's major mass communication options — advertising, direct marketing, publicity & public relations, and sales promotion.
* Understand various digital communications options — advertising and public relations, websites, blogs, social media, quasi-personal communications, and mobile marketing.
* Evaluate the mass and digital communications mix.

OPENING CASE: MASTERCARD INTERNATIONAL

In the late 1990s, MasterCard (MC), a credit card company owned by member banks, was in trouble. Market share had declined for 10 straight years and competitive pressures from Visa, AmEx, and Discover were intensifying. MC enjoyed the same retail acceptance as Visa, but top-of-mind awareness was 10 percentage points inferior. MC was also losing support from member banks, both domestic and international: In the U.S., MC's share of direct-mail solicitations trailed Visa significantly.

MC conducted an extensive advertising agency review and selected McCann-Erickson (ME). ME concluded that this once-dominant brand had lost emotional relevance with consumers. MC had also lost credibility with critical member banks, and the power to make independent decisions. Worse, not only did the MC brand have different campaigns in almost every international market, Visa and AmEx consistently spent more.

ME's research in the U.S. and key international markets indicated consumers viewed MC as a stodgy, functional, everyday brand, with little aspirational relevance. AmEx was professional,

worldly, and responsible; Visa was sociable, stylish, and on-the-go. By contrast, MC was unassuming, unpretentious, and practical. ME saw its task as shifting MasterCard from an emotionally neutral generic card to a card that consumers felt good about using.

ME's secondary data analysis revealed a shift away from the materialistic and outer-directed consumer culture of the 1980s and early 1990s. Success symbols like wearing designer clothes, shopping at prestigious stores, staying at luxury hotels, owning expensive cars, and using a prestigious credit card had been replaced. The new success symbols were being in control of, and satisfied with, one's life; having a good home and family; and being able to afford what was really important. The vast majority of consumers believed an unpaid credit card balance was "necessary and justified." ME dubbed this emerging mindset as good revolving *and set out to target* good revolvers, *by helping them lead* rich lives. *ME's selling idea was: MasterCard is* The Better Way to Pay for Everything That Matters.

Armed with this insight and direction, ME's three-person creative team — Joyce King Thomas, Jeroen Bours, and Jonathan Cranin — brainstormed extensively for a month. Cranin generated the tag line "Some things money can't buy" in the shower. A couple of weeks later, over Sunday morning coffee and bagels, Thomas and Bours conceived the first advertisement — set at a baseball game featuring some ordinary transactions. In the ad, voice-over actor Billy Crudup intoned, "Two tickets, $28; hot dogs, popcorn and soda, $18; autographed baseball, $45; real conversation with 11-year-old-son, priceless ... there are some things money can't buy. For everything else, there's MasterCard."

ME crafted more than 300 TV commercials, in 50 languages, shown in 108 countries. Globally, ME's work for MasterCard is the largest single campaign ever and won well over 100 creative awards. Most important, the Priceless *campaign delivered impressive results for MasterCard. MasterCard's gross dollar volume increased by well over 250 percent; banks issued more than one billion cards; brand awareness rose significantly; and the gap with Visa narrowed.*

CASE QUESTION

How do you account for MasterCard's success? What other advertising campaigns do you consider memorable? Why?

Advertising is the most visible form of mass communications. Advertising consumes the largest percentage of many FMCG firms marketing budgets and increasingly important for B2B firms. No matter what communications approaches the firm chooses, it must always identify audience targets, set objectives, select specific tools, execute the program, and measure results. In chapter 15 we discussed the principles and strategies that support integrated communications. In this chapter, we focus on how advertising works, but also address other communication options like direct marketing, publicity and public relations (P&PR), and sales promotion. We also dig deeply into digital communication, its unique attributes, and the way marketers use websites, blogs, social media, and mobile marketing.

> *Half the money I spend on advertising is wasted; the trouble is I don't know which half.*
>
> — John Wanamaker[1]

Mass Communications

ADVERTISING FOUNDATIONS

At its essence, advertising is a service. When you pay attention to an advertising message, you receive the functional value of information and sometimes even find it entertaining. Indeed, many of us look forward to Super Bowl advertisements. You may also receive psychological and economic value, but you rarely ever pay for them! From the customer's point of view, TV advertising (and TV) is free, and advertising subsidizes your cost for newspapers and magazines.

But, how does this system really work? Mostly, you (as a customer) receive advertising messages together with some content you desire, like a newspaper article or magazine story or TV show. The advertiser pays the media company to *bundle* its advertising with this content, but it receives nothing *directly* in return. The advertiser receives its value *indirectly*, from the attention of your eyes and ears and, hopefully, your switched-on brain.

As customers, we receive value from highly subsidized (or free) content; advertisers receive value from customer attention to their messages. Hence, customers have immense value to advertisers. Google's high market valuation is based on substantial website traffic and subsequent click-through from Google AdWords and Google+ services to advertiser websites.

In many industries, particularly FMCG, advertising is central to implementing market and communications strategies. (Opening Case — MasterCard.) Table 16.1 shows critical questions for developing an **advertising strategy** and the relevant links to market and communications strategies. Similar questions are instrumental in developing strategy for other mass and digital communications options.

TABLE 16.1

ELEMENTS OF AN ADVERTISING STRATEGY

Element	Question	Link to Market and Communications Strategies
Target audience	Whom are we trying to influence?	Customers in target segments (market strategy)
Advertising objectives	What are we trying to achieve?	Directly related to strategic and operational objectives (market strategy)
Messaging	What content should the target audience receive?	Related to the value proposition (market strategy)
Execution	How shall we communicate the message?	The most effective way to target customers
Media selection and timing	Where and when shall we place our advertising?	Select media to reach target customers at the appropriate time
Advertising budget	How much shall we spend on advertising?	Advertising budget is one element of the entire communications budget
Program evaluation	How shall we test our advertising and measure its effectiveness?	Choose from a variety of measurement methodologies

KEY IDEA

➤ Advertising is critical for both market and communications strategies.

Firms should consider advertising as an *investment*. Today's advertising should achieve short-term results, but may also have long-run impact. Advertising may contribute to building the brand and lead to future customer purchases. Unfortunately, advertising is an expense on the firm's income statement and counts against current year revenues. Hence, many firms underfund advertising.

The Advertising Program

TARGET AUDIENCE: WHOM ARE WE TRYING TO INFLUENCE?

As we learned earlier, a key element in formulating the market strategy is deciding which segments to target. For each target segment, the positioning statement identifies customer targets with whom the firm wishes to communicate. For a *push* strategy, the firm focuses on direct customers; for a *pull* strategy, the firm focuses on indirect customers. The firm must also decide whether to reach decision-makers, influencers, and/or other entities in the purchase decision process. Because advertising funding is limited, the firm must carefully select its **target audience** before making advertising budget allocations.

How Advertising *Works*

Advertising effectiveness is perhaps the most-studied marketing topic.[2] **Hierarchy-of-effects** models are central to understanding how advertising works. Figure 16.1 shows models for high-involvement and low-involvement products.[3] Typically, the ultimate firm goal is to reinforce the brand and encourage *purchase* and *repeat purchase*. Note particularly the intermediate steps between *awareness* and *repeat purchase* in each model. High-involvement processes typically take longer.[4]

FIGURE 16.1

HIERARCHY-OF-EFFECTS ADVERTISING MODELS

High involvement. The customer believes the purchase, like a new automobile, involves financial and/or psychosocial risk. The customer engages in a staged learning process:

- **Awareness.** Learning the product is available for purchase
- **Knowledge.** Understanding product attributes, features, benefits, and values
- **Liking/preference.** Developing favorable/positive feelings about the product
- **Trial.** Testing the product before purchase and use
- **Purchase.** Exchange money or other resources for the product
- **Repeat purchase.** Purchasing the product again. Advertising can reinforce positive feelings that lead to repeat purchase

Low involvement. Customers see little risk and require little pre-purchase knowledge — FMCG categories such as soda or cereal. Because risk is low, the hierarchical process is quite different. Advertising's role is to create high *awareness* and motivate customers to *trial*. If customers like the product, they purchase and repurchase.

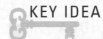

KEY IDEA

➤ Hierarchy-of-effects models for high involvement and low involvement products are central to understanding how advertising works.

Marketing Exercise

Apply a hierarchy-of-effects model to your purchase of a HDTV set.

ADVERTISING OBJECTIVES: WHAT ARE WE TRYING TO ACHIEVE?

Once the firm has validated advertising as the appropriate communications vehicle, it should formulate **advertising objectives**. Two considerations are:

- **Output objectives** — what the firm ultimately wants to achieve, like sales, repeat purchase, market share, and brand loyalty.
- **Intermediate objectives** — relate to hierarchy-of-effects models and include awareness, knowledge, liking/preference, trial, and emotional commitment (to a brand). For a new product launch, the firm may initially focus on *awareness* as the crucial advertising objective. The importance of other intermediate objectives depends on the particular hierarchy-of-effects model governing purchase.

To achieve output objectives, the firm takes many actions, like delivering and servicing products, in addition to advertising. Hence, a failure to achieve an output objective like sales may not be directly related to success or failure of an advertising campaign. By contrast, monitoring well-chosen *intermediate objectives* provides excellent feedback on advertising effectiveness.

MESSAGING: WHAT CONTENT SHOULD THE TARGET AUDIENCE RECEIVE?

The firm's advertising message derives directly from the market strategy — Chapter 9. Look back at that chapter, revisiting the four positioning elements:

Convince	[customer target]
In the context of other alternatives	[competitor targets]
That they will receive these benefits	[value proposition]
Because we have these capabilities/features	[reasons to believe]

The firm's advertising message should follow directly from the positioning statement, with special emphasis on the value proposition. The message should focus upon core benefits and values and reflect unique claims where the firm has a differential advantage. Clear positioning statements provide excellent guidance for creative personnel in advertising agencies to develop effective messages. By contrast, poor positioning often leads to unsatisfactory and/or confusing messages. The messaging must also reflect the amount of time the audience may be exposed to advertisements.

Firms active in multiple countries must decide whether, and to what extent, they should *standardize* messages globally or *localize* them for national/regional markets. If the firm standardizes, it should still seek local input to avoid potential translation problems.

EXECUTION: HOW SHALL WE COMMUNICATE THE MESSAGE?

Execution focuses on the method (style) firms use to turn core messages into effective advertising. This task is daunting and challenging. Columbia colleague, branding guru Schmitt, explains: "Creative output [is] the most visible part of advertising. Although judging creative output may be easy, the creative process is an enigma, more art than science, mysterious and unexplainable. The essence of creativity seems to be a willingness to alternate between divergent and convergent thinking, between brainstorming and analytic reasoning, between pushing the limits and being reasonable and practical. [The result, ideally,] culminates in an illumination — the Big Idea."[5]

KEY IDEA

➤ The firm should set two types of advertising objectives — output and intermediate.

➤ *Output objectives* are what the firm ultimately wants to achieve:
  - Purchase
  - Repeat purchase

➤ *Intermediate objectives* relate to hierarchy-of-effects models and include:
  - Awareness
  - Knowledge
  - Liking (preference)
  - Trial

Marketing Question

Can you think of advertising messages or slogans that would not work globally?

KEY IDEA

➤ Creating advertising is an enigma, more art than science, mysterious, and unexplainable.

In the Opening Case, we saw how a *Big Idea* drove MasterCard's highly successful advertising campaign. Another creative success is Absolut vodka. Figure 16.2 shows typical Absolut ads, beginning with a two-word headline (*tag line*) starting with *Absolut*, then adding carefully chosen words to reinforce the imagery — like Absolut Perfection, Absolut Appeal, Absolut Original — always in the context of the bottle shape. Absolut's campaign, featuring several hundred executions on a single theme, has won many awards for elegance, simplicity, and effectiveness.

FIGURE 16.2

EXAMPLES OF ABSOLUT ADVERTISEMENTS

Advertising executions come in two major forms — *rational* and *emotional*:

RATIONAL APPEALS

Rational appeals focus on people's sense of logic. Five main styles are:

- **Comparative (Attack).** Successful comparative advertising focuses on demonstrating superiority over competition. Small market share firms often compare products to the leader, so as to enter the customer's consideration set like "We try harder" — Avis, Duracell versus Energizer batteries, and multiple executions of the Mac versus PC.[6]

- **Demonstration.** Shows the product in use and focuses on performance. Many B2B communications use **demonstration ads**; they are also common in sales force materials.

- **One-sided and two-sided. One-sided advertising** focuses only on positive product attributes; **two-sided advertising** presents both positive and negative messages.

- **Primacy or recency.** Research shows that items at the beginning of a message — *primacy* — and at the end — *recency* — are more effective than those in the middle.[7] When the audience is less interested in a product, or has an unfavorable prior impression, primacy advertising is generally more effective in gaining attention and/or minimizing objections. When the audience is initially favorable, and disinterest and/or objections need not be overcome, recency advertising generally reinforces a favorable product impression.

- **Refutational.** A special case of two-sided advertising explicitly mentions competitor claims, but then directly refutes them.

Marketing Exercise

Use available resources like print media and YouTube to identify advertisements using each of the rational and emotional appeals discussed. Bring to class.

KEY IDEA

➤ Rational-style advertising includes:

- Comparative
- Demonstration
- One- and two-sided appeals
- Primacy or recency
- Refutational

Marketing Question

Select three of your favorite advertisements. Describe their message styles. Were they *rational* — comparative, demonstration, one- or two-sided appeals, primacy or recency, refutational? Or *emotional* — celebrity endorsement, fear, humor, storytelling? Or a combination of styles?

Marketing Question

Identify an advertisement using a fear appeal. What is the objective and the advertiser's anticipated outcome? Do you think the ad works?

Marketing Question

View Go Daddy's *Censorship Hearing* advertisement (www.godaddy.com). Do you think it is funny? Why or why not? Bring your favorite humorous advertisement to class.

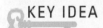

KEY IDEA

➤ Emotional-style advertising includes:
- Celebrity endorsement
- Fear
- Humor
- Storytelling

EMOTIONAL APPEALS

These advertising approaches appeal to emotions. Four main styles are:

- **Celebrity endorsement.** Advertisers often use well-known people to endorse products/brands, especially on TV. A good celebrity/product match creates product awareness and brand credibility. But celebrity endorsement is not a *slam dunk*. To be effective, the audience must attend to the product, not just the celebrity! Further, a celebrity may lose credibility by endorsing too many products, and negative publicity for the celebrity may flow to the product/brand.

- **Fear.** Fear appeals create anxiety; behaving as the advertising suggests removes the anxiety. *Physical danger* is common in insurance advertising; *social disapproval* for personal hygiene products; *monetary loss* for security products and credit cards; and *female insecurities* for cosmetic creams.

- **Humor.** Humor is widespread in advertising but should be used carefully. Humor helps create awareness, sets a positive tone, and enhances memory; but improperly crafted humor may distract from the core message. The result: The audience remembers the ad but not the product/brand, finds it *unfunny*, or worse, may *mis-index* — link the humor to competition.

- **Storytelling.** Storytelling can be a very effective way of appealing to people's emotions. MasterCard's *Priceless* campaign and Nike's *Just Do It* are great storytelling examples.

In practice, many firms combine/blend these pure-form message approaches. Moreover, the firm must understand the context, culture, and language of target customers, especially when venturing abroad. A British firm whose product is great for "knocking you up" might be surprised at its reception in the U.S.!

MEDIA SELECTION AND TIMING: WHERE AND WHEN SHALL WE PLACE OUR ADVERTISING?

In 2012, global advertising spending was $557 billion; U.S. spending was $142 billion.[8] Figure 16.3 shows global spending by major media class. Media choices are expanding; Internet advertising is growing fastest.

FIGURE 16.3

GLOBAL ADVERTISING SPENDING BY MAJOR MEDIA CLASS 2011 ($ BILLIONS)[9]

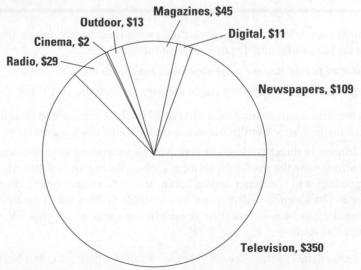

Outdoor, $13
Magazines, $45
Cinema, $2
Digital, $11
Radio, $29
Newspapers, $109
Television, $350

Marketing Exercise

Redraw Figure 16.3 with your forecast of advertising spending 10 years in the future.

To select appropriate media, the firm must answer five related questions:

- **Media objectives.** What should our media strategy accomplish?
- **Type of media.** Which media classes shall we use — print, broadcast, outdoor?

- **Specific media.** Which media vehicles shall we use — *Vanity Fair*, *Survivor*, bus stops?
- **Timing.** When will our advertising appear?
- **Media schedule.** Specifically, where and when shall we place our ads?

MEDIA OBJECTIVES

WHAT SHOULD OUR MEDIA STRATEGY ACCOMPLISH? Key concerns are **reach**, **frequency**, and **impact**:

- **Reach.** Number of target individuals exposed to the advertising at least once.
- **Frequency.** Average number of times a target individual is exposed to the advertising.
- **Reach and frequency.** Reach and frequency calculate **gross rating points (GRPs)**.

Gross rating points (GRPs) = Reach × Frequency

Generally, advertisers trade off reach and frequency. GRP objectives are popular, but may cause problems. For example, to secure 250 GRPs:

- 100 percent of the audience receives, on average, 2.5 exposures.
- 10 percent of the audience receives, on average, 25 exposures.

Many advertisers require a minimum number of exposures; hence, they set GRP objectives subject to a minimum required frequency. The firm should also be concerned about excessive frequency and diminishing returns. Media objectives should relate directly to advertising objectives.

Illustration of Media Objectives

- *Reach* 50 percent of the target audience five times in the next six months — *frequency*.
- Deliver 250 *GRPs* subject to a minimum 70 percent *reach*.

Illustration of Advertising Objectives (AO) and Media Objectives (MO)

AO: Increase repeat purchase of Munchee candy bars from 30 to 50 percent among 10- to 16-year-old boys by end of June.

MO: Deliver 1,500 GRPs, subject to a minimum 60 percent reach.

When the firm uses different media types, duplication is an issue. Suppose the firm decides to advertise on both radio and TV; two relevant measures are:

- **Duplicated reach:** Receive a message from *both* radio and TV.
- **Unduplicated reach:** Receive a single message, *either* radio or TV, but not both.

Sometimes the firm wants to maximize *duplicated reach* by exposure to several media types. Alternatively, the firm may want to maximize *unduplicated reach* regardless of media type.

- **Impact.** Impact is directly related to creativity in generating advertisements — indeed, many *creatives* view the media department's job as boring and routine. But mass media has fragmented and consumer media habits are more varied; hence, the media task is increasingly challenging. Thirty years ago, an FMCG firm could reach 70 percent of women aged 25 to 54 with less than 10 advertising spots on network TV; today it takes more than 100 spots.

Häagen-Dazs successfully launched super-premium ice cream in Britain, using only black-and-white newspaper ads, for just £375,000. This unexpected copy gained significant publicity and the creatives won a major advertising award.

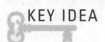

KEY IDEA

➤ Critical media selection and timing decisions:

Media objectives
↓
Type of media
↓
Specific media
↓
Timing
↓
Media schedule

KEY IDEA

➤ Important media objectives include:

- Reach
- Frequency
- Impact

TYPE OF MEDIA

WHICH MEDIA CLASSES SHALL WE USE? A **media class** is a group of closely related media. Media classes differ from one another on dimensions like time availability and intrusiveness. A common category system (with examples) is:

- **Broadcast** — television and radio; exist for short time periods — significantly intrusive.
- **Online** — e-mail, mobile, and web alerts; delivered in real time. Read at leisure — more intrusive than print.
- **Outdoor** — billboards and in-store; long presence — relatively non-intrusive.
- **Print** — newspapers and magazines; read at leisure — relatively non-intrusive.

Table 16.2 shows advantages and disadvantages of selected media classes for advertisers[10]:

TABLE 16.2

ADVANTAGES AND
DISADVANTAGES
OF SELECTED
MEDIA CLASSES

Media Class	Advantages	Disadvantages
Direct mail	High information content High selectivity Opportunities for repeat exposures Reader controls exposure	High cost per contact High level of in-store clutter Long production lead times Poor image (junk mail)
In-store	Customers ready to buy Location specific Many options — special displays, packaging, TV	Difficult to measure impact
Digital	Ability to optimize Ability to remarket Measurement by click-through Multiple options Segmented audiences	Less understood than others Placement sensitivity
Magazines	High information content Longevity Multiple readers (high pass-along) Quality reproduction Segmentation potential	Lack of design flexibility Long lead time for placing advertising Visual only
Newspapers	Ads can be placed in interest sections Can be used for coupons High coverage Low cost Reader controls exposure Short lead time for placement Timely (current ads)	Clutter Low attention-getting capabilities Poor reproduction quality Selective reader exposure Short life
Outdoor	Easily noticed High repetition Location specific	Local restrictions Poor environmental image Short exposure time requires short ad
Radio	Flexible High frequency Local coverage Low cost Low production costs Well-segmented audiences	Audio only Clutter Fleeting message Low attention-getting Low remembering
Television	Attention-getting Favorable image High prestige High reach Impact of sight, sound, and motion Low cost per exposure Mass coverage	Clutter High absolute cost High production costs Long production lead times Low selectivity Short message life

Marketing Question

You are launching an Internet security system for large and small businesses. Identify your communications targets. Identify media classes. Why these?

Figure 16.3 (p. 243) shows that the most-used media classes are direct mail, newspapers, and television, but others may be attractive, especially digital. Some firms base their success on outdoor advertising where unusual placements may be effective: Brut placed print ads at eye level mostly in bar bathrooms; in Beijing, groups of 15 teenagers, wearing identical Ai Jia ("love home") neon-yellow warm-up jackets and matching baseball caps, ride bicycles in formation along set street routes; and Hotels.nl, a Dutch online reservations firm, displayed its corporate logo on waterproof blankets worn by sheep.

SPECIFIC MEDIA

WHICH MEDIA VEHICLES SHALL WE USE? A **media vehicle** is a specific entity in a media class. The *newspaper* media class includes *The New York Times*, *The Boston Globe*, and *The San Francisco Examiner*. The *magazine* media class includes *Good Housekeeping*, *Time*, and *Vanity Fair*. The *television* media class includes *60 Minutes*, *American Idol*, and *Days of Our Lives*. How do you select which vehicle is right for your product or service? Critical issues in choosing media vehicles are audience size, audience type, cost, and nature of the vehicle (in particular whether the advertisement is complementary, like a serious ad on a TV news show).

TIMING

WHEN WILL OUR ADVERTISING APPEAR? The four main **timing patterns** are:

- **Concentration.** Commit all expenditures at one time.
- **Continuous.** A regular periodic advertising pattern.
- **Flighting.** Repeated high advertising levels followed by low (or no) advertising.
- **Pulsing.** Combines continuous and flighting. Pulsing can occur within a media vehicle, within a media class, or across multiple media vehicles and classes.

Generally, advertising experts believe *continuous advertising* is most effective for products purchased throughout the year. *Flighting* and *pulsing* are more effective when demand varies as for seasonal products — cruises and air travel.

MEDIA SCHEDULE

SPECIFICALLY, WHERE AND WHEN SHALL WE PLACE OUR ADS? In selecting its media schedule, the firm tries to optimize media objectives like reach, frequency, and GRPs, subject to a budget constraint. Securing the best media buy in one media class is a complex task. Designing a campaign embracing multiple media classes is even more difficult. Major advertisers use computer models, modified by managerial judgment, to develop optimally effective **media schedules**.

ADVERTISING BUDGET: HOW MUCH SHALL WE SPEND ON ADVERTISING?

The **advertising response function (ARF)** relates advertising spending to advertising objectives like sales. The ARF is crucial for setting the **advertising budget** but its shape is typically not known. The firm faces two questions in deciding its advertising budget:

- **What shape is the ARF?** Figure 16.4 shows alternative ARFs, A and B. Each has some intuitive appeal and research support.[11] Spending implications are different for low and moderate spending.

KEY IDEA

➤ Choice of media vehicle depends on:
- Audience size
- Audience type
- Cost
- Nature of the media vehicle

KEY IDEA

➤ The advertising message must appear in the right place at the right time.

➤ Major timing options are:
- Concentration
- Continuous
- Flighting
- Pulsing

• **Where is the firm currently operating?** If the firm were at I on ARF **A**, it would probably increase spending modestly; if the firm were at II, it would probably hold or reduce spending. At I' on ARF **B**, the firm should increase spending dramatically.

FIGURE 16.4

ALTERNATIVE ADVERTISING RESPONSE FUNCTIONS

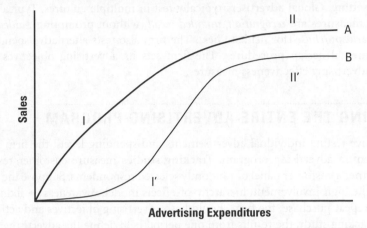

If the firm can answer these two questions, budgeting is simply a matter of marginal analysis: Set the budget where marginal revenue equals marginal cost. Managers estimate sales, or other advertising objectives, at various advertising levels; the models estimate ARFs for different media vehicles and calculate optimal spending levels and media allocations.

OBJECTIVE AND TASK

This *bottom-up* approach focuses on reaching advertising objectives like *achieving 80 percent awareness* by a specified time; then identifies the necessary tasks. The firm can use historical and/or experimental data to estimate the budget for each task, then sums the costs to calculate a total. Because linking advertising spending to advertising objectives is difficult, the objective and task method is not broadly popular. But as pressures grow to justify marketing and advertising expenditures, more firms will likely use this approach, if only to establish *ballpark* estimates.

OTHER BUDGETING METHODOLOGIES

The firms can also use *top-down* methods to calibrate budgets they develop by *objective and task*:

• **Percentage of sales.** The advertising budget is a **percentage of sales (A/S)**; *sales* is current sales, anticipated next-year sales, or some combination.

• **Competitive parity.** The firm bases advertising on competitor actions by using competitor spending as a benchmark.

• **What the firm can afford.** There is no rational basis for this approach. Unfortunately, it is not uncommon.

PROGRAM EVALUATION: HOW SHALL WE TEST OUR ADVERTISING AND MEASURE ITS EFFECTIVENESS?

Now we have answered the who, what, how, where, when, and how much to spend advertising questions, we must evaluate advertising relative to objectives. The firm may test individual advertisements, different levels and types of spending, and/or evaluate the entire advertising program.

Marketing Question

The price of advertising on the U.S. Superbowl is around $3 million for 30 seconds. Is It worth It?

KEY IDEA

➤ The objective and task method should underpin the budgeting process. Rule-of-thumb methods can lead to unsatisfactory results.

TESTING INDIVIDUAL ADVERTISEMENTS AND SPENDING LEVELS

The firm tests ads with target customers, individually or in groups; in a laboratory or experimental field setting. Global advertisers typically test in multiple cultures. Typical **advertising effectiveness measures** are *recognition, unaided recall* (without prompting), *aided recall* (with prompting), and *purchase* (for field studies). The firm also tests alternative spending patterns using experimental design procedures. The firm sets its advertising objectives then selects appropriate advertising effectiveness measures.

EVALUATING THE ENTIRE ADVERTISING PROGRAM

Over and above testing individual advertisements and spending levels, the firm may wish to evaluate an entire advertising program. **Tracking studies** measure customer responses over time, using either a customer panel or randomly selected respondents. Suppose the firm's objectives mirror the high-involvement, hierarchy-of-effects model: Awareness → liking → trial → purchase → repeat purchase; the firm should base advertising objectives and actions on these stages. In a tracking study, the results from one period help define the advertising program for the following period.

THE ADVERTISING AGENCY SYSTEM

Most major U.S. advertisers outsource advertising program development to advertising agencies, but some firms like The Prudential and Ryanair conduct advertising activities in-house. By outsourcing, firms have better access to creative talent and greater flexibility. These firms can demand refreshed creative teams and switch agencies on a few months notice. The firm usually works with three agency groups:

- **Account/relationship managers** — the key agency interface and help craft the strategy;
- **Creative department** — develops advertising messages and executions;
- **Media department** — prepares the media schedule and provides supporting data.[12]

The core agency job is to translate firm market strategy into an advertising message, and execute on that message. Firm and agency personnel should jointly develop a **creative brief** (boxed insert) — a *contract* between firm and agency, particularly with *creatives*. Each messaging initiative should have a creative brief — for advertising, but also for visual aids like displays and sales force materials.

Core Elements of the Creative Brief

Marketing objective. What the firm wants to achieve — output and intermediate objectives.

Assignment. The type of campaign including media type, timing, and approval process.

Customer insight. Informs the creative process — critical insight into target market; identifies rational and emotional factors that drive product purchase/use.

Competitive insight. Informs the creative process — includes barriers to achieving firm objectives.

Target audience. Whom the firm wishes to influence — customer types and segments, includes demographics, psychographics, and current products.

Key benefit. The most important benefit/value the firm wishes to emphasize.

Reasons to believe. Why the target customer should believe firm claims.

Brand identity. How the firm wants the target audience to feel about its product. Should be important to the audience, deliverable by the firm, and unique to the brand.

Mandates. Elements outside the advertiser's control — must or must not be included, like corporate and/or legal requirements advertising must meet.

Measurement. How the firm will know if the campaign has been successful.

KEY IDEA

➤ The firm should test both individual advertisements and the entire advertising program.

➤ Important advertising effectiveness measures are:
- Recognition
- Unaided recall
- Aided recall
- Purchase

KEY IDEA

➤ Evaluating advertising effectiveness is a complex task. The firm must choose among various types of tests and measures.

KEY IDEA

➤ The advertising agency system is in a continuous state of flux.

Marketing Question

Suppose your school, college, or university plans advertising to increase student applications. Develop a creative brief for developing a campaign idea.

Other Mass Communications Options

DIRECT MARKETING

Direct marketing is a fast-growing communications tool embracing many ways of requesting a customer response. Today, direct marketing includes traditional print and broadcast advertising, packaging, package inserts, warranty cards, take-ones, and newer digital options.[13] The direct mail subcategory includes items like brochures, catalogs, and statement inserts. Firms like L.L. Bean, Lands' End, and Lillian Vernon continually develop and refine demographic and product-preference customer databases to fine-tune their product development, product assortments, and communications programs. Advances in technology have greatly impacted direct marketing; from lower bulk postal rates, online shopping, and widespread credit card use. Other factors that continue to grow direct marketing include:

- **Data and analytics.** Using advances in computer and telecommunications technologies, firms can develop, manage, and mine customer databases for more targeted efforts.
- **Delivery systems.** Package delivery firms like FedEx and UPS increasingly offer greater service variety.
- **Demographics and lifestyles.** The growth of dual-income families facing increasing time pressures, especially in developed countries, has reduced available shopping time. Direct marketing is attractive because consumers can shop from home.
- **Digital.** Digital channels allow far greater personalization/customization and immediacy than other direct marketing methods.
- **Product quality.** The generalized increase in product quality has reduced customer risk when buying products remotely.
- **Professionalism.** Direct marketing firms are more professional and sophisticated, especially in segmenting, targeting, and communicating.

Although direct marketing can be more expensive than advertising on a cost per thousand (CPM) basis, it offers several advantages:

- **Ability to identify prospects.** By relating customer profiles to purchase patterns, direct marketers can identify high-quality prospects.
- **Ability to tailor the offer.** Direct marketers know the products customers purchase; hence, they can tailor messages and offers to individuals.
- **Action-oriented customer response.** Advertising programs typically work via an effects hierarchy; purchase often occurs after awareness, knowledge, and liking. By contrast, direct marketing is more action-oriented and typically requests purchase.
- **Better customer knowledge.** Many direct marketing firms have extensive information on customers. But they must be sensitive to privacy concerns and act appropriately.
- **Better measurement.** The firm can test program elements like message, price, incentives, and/or type of direct marketing to assess their impact on sales and adjust accordingly.
- **Flexibility.** The firm can develop some direct marketing campaigns, like e-mail, much more quickly than mass advertising.
- **Predictability.** Because direct marketing typically requests purchase, sales forecasts for direct marketing programs can be fairly accurate. Budgeting for direct marketing is simpler than for advertising.

PUBLICITY AND PUBLIC RELATIONS

Publicity and public relations (P&PR) are closely related; publicity is really a subset of public relations. **Publicity** focuses on securing neutral or favorable short-term media coverage. **Public** relations (PR) is a formal communication process that attempts to builds favorable relationships between the firm and public audiences. PR embraces corporate reputation, crisis management, government relations (lobbying), internal relations, press relations, product publicity, and shareholder relations. P&PR generally relies on intermediaries to transmit messages to target audiences. The advantage for P&PR is that the audience may view the intermediary as impartial, and the firm does not pay for media space and time!

In a classic case, College Saving Bank launched the CollegeSure CD by focusing initial communication efforts on news releases and press conferences. Within one month, more than 300 news stories were written or broadcast. Articles and editorials appeared in all major U.S. newspapers; weekly news magazines like *Time, Newsweek,* and *U.S. News and World Report;* major business magazines; and local newspapers.[14]

Firms also use P&PR and advertising synergistically. Victoria's Secret (VS) spends several million dollars advertising its annual fashion show; the extensive publicity sends millions of visitors to the VS website. For difficult situations in the public eye, P&PR can be negative or positive. *The Social Network* movie caused problems for Facebook because of the unflattering portrait of founder Mark Zuckerberg. When 200 Coke drinkers suffered nausea, headaches, and diarrhea, and several children were hospitalized, observers criticized Coke for "forget[ing] the cardinal rule of crisis management — to act fast, tell the whole truth, and look as if you have nothing to hide." *The Economist* concluded that "Coca-Cola has made a big mess of what should have been a small public-relations problem."[15] By contrast, J&J received considerable praise for its handling the mid-1980s Tylenol poisoning scare. CEO James Burke took charge and J&J focused its concern on customers. J&J temporarily withdrew Tylenol tablets, then relaunched in tamper-free packaging. J&J's actions and related P&PR campaign put senior executives, including Burke, on many U.S. talk shows; they explained J&J's actions and commitment to customers. J&J turned a major debacle into a major coup.

Regardless, P&PR has several drawbacks. The firm selects *friendly* intermediaries like editors, journalists, and media personalities but does not have direct control of the choice of audience. Also, despite the *pitch,* the intermediary may ignore, modify, or shorten the firm's message — or worse, portray the firm inconsistently or even negatively.

SALES PROMOTION

Sales promotion (SP) is a complex blend of communications techniques providing extra customer value, typically for trial to stimulate immediate sales. Sometimes SP has longer-run objectives like increasing awareness. The three main SP types are:

- **Consumer promotion** — manufacturer to consumer
- **Trade promotion** — manufacturer to retailer
- **Retail promotion** — retailer to consumer

Consumer and retail promotions include cash refunds, contests, coupons, deals, games, rebates, point-of-purchase displays, premiums, prizes, samples, and sports sponsorships. *Trade promotions* include advertising and merchandising allowances; contests, deals and prizes; special price deals; *spiffs*[16]; and trade shows. Firms are continually creating new SP techniques. Like other communications methods, before selecting a SP device, the firm should always set clear objectives.

Generally, SP is not a good standalone approach; the firm should tightly integrate SP with other communications. Firms often execute several sales promotions simultaneously, but these should all support (or be supported by) the firm's advertising and/or personal selling efforts. Rarely is SP the central element in the firm's communications strategy, but may be a large portion of the budget.

Marketing Question

In 2010, BP (Gulf oil spill), Goldman Sachs (banking crisis), and Toyota (product quality) each received significant negative publicity. How do you assess their responses? What would you have done differently?

Marketing Exercise

Three African countries — Mozambique, Swaziland, and South Africa — formed the *East3Route* initiative to attract European tourists. *East3Route* has issued an RFP (request for proposal) to develop a P&PR campaign to support the initiative. Prepare a proposal.

Marketing Question

Identify a recent sales promotion. What was the firm's objective? Was the firm successful? Why or why not?

Marketing Question

Why would Minute Maid sponsor a sports stadium? What are the benefits of this promotion? What are drawbacks and risks of this investment?

The firm should always track SP's long-term impact, particularly if SP involves short-term price reductions. Regular discounts may lead to competitive price escalation; or prime customers may accumulate inventory at the promotional price and never return to the *regular* higher price.[17] Further, volume fluctuations from frequent price changes may lead to mismatched production schedules, inventory build-up, and higher costs. Also, multiple SP programs are costly to manage.

Digital Communications[18]

In addition to offering new communications approaches, digital does three things traditional communication methods do not — communicates globally 24/7/365; makes it easy for customers to communicate with the firm; and makes it easy for customers to communicate with each other.

Using digital approaches, the firm can follow customers as they visit websites, blogs, view advertisements, and make purchases. The firm can combine these data sets with bricks-and-mortar purchases and telephone and other interactions to increase sales, enhance customer satisfaction, and strengthen brand image.

ONLINE ADVERTISING AND PUBLIC RELATIONS

As a communications tool, the Internet offers many effective ways for marketers to communicate with customers and attract audiences, each with its own characteristics:

SEARCH

The search function exemplified by Google, Yahoo!, and Bing has two important facets for marketers — **paid search** and **search engine optimization**:

PAID SEARCH. Advertisers pay to appear next to, and be associated with, search results based on keywords. An electronics retailer may pay to appear next to searches for HDTV or digital cameras. Typically, the advertiser pays only when a searcher actually clicks on the advertisement. Advertisers bid for position; higher bids, higher relevance, and higher click-through rates earn higher page listings.[19]

SEARCH ENGINE OPTIMIZATION (SEO). SEO embraces a variety of strategies, tactics, and techniques for increasing the number of website visitors by securing high rankings in search results. To be successful requires understanding the mechanics of search engines — using *spiders* to crawl through websites to determine relevance — and *optimizing* the firm's website by selecting significant keywords. Vertical search focuses on specific topics like hotels (Tripadvisor), automobiles (Edmunds), and jobs (Monster). Advertisers generally pay-per-click, but may pay flat fees for inclusion in directories or affiliate listings.

DISPLAY

Display advertising comprises banner ads on websites. Originally based on a magazine model, banner ads tend to come in standard sizes; hence, they are easy to develop, purchase, track, and measure. The basic banner ad has been standard for many years but new sizes include tall, skyscraper-like placements, medium-rectangle ads, and dynamic peel-away ads that cover web pages. Banner ads direct users to click on the ad to reach the advertiser's website. Firms measure banner advertising effectiveness by click rate or other customer action (like download).

CLASSIFIEDS

Online classifieds are typically text listings for specific types of products and services like automobiles, jobs, real estate, yellow pages, and time-sensitive auctions. Migration of classifieds from offline to online has been swift and devastating for newspapers. The free Craigslist network of local community sites commands a huge audience.

VIDEO

As bandwidth increases, so does Internet video. Firms place videos on their own and affiliate websites, and on branded *channels* in public sites like YouTube. Videos can be advertising focused, or designed for public relations purposes. As more commercial TV-show episodes migrate to the Internet and content providers produce Internet-only programming, the firm's advertising choices will increase dramatically.

E-MAIL

E-mail is inexpensive and measurable. *Outbound* e-mail communication is a popular way for firms to maintain contact with current customers and to prospect for new customers. Retailers like CheapTickets and Netflix regularly send e-mails to stimulate purchase and maintain relationships. Many community-oriented sites and content publishers regularly send e-mail news alerts to keep customers returning and engage their user bases for advertising. To acquire new customers, the firm may buy e-mail lists or develop its own **behavioral targets** based on website visits learned from *cookies*, sales data, or opt-in responses; **spam** filters may reject unsolicited e-mail.

But e-mail is a two-way street. *Inbound* e-mail allows the firm to interact with customers on a personal basis, but it must develop processes to address inbound communications candidly and promptly. Firms like Zappos encourage consumers to tweet or post comments about recent offers, purchases, and other experiences with their products. Others develop automated response systems like frequently asked questions (FAQs) to tier responses and cut costs by minimizing the human responder workforce.

WEBSITES

At a minimum, the firm's website is a form of mass communications (brochureware); it can also enable sales promotion by automating offers for free samples, upgrades, and discounts. Regardless, the website's true potential is its ability to be the anchor for engaging customers and build brand equity. Websites allow firms to generate product awareness, provide product information aligned to user preferences, and explain and demonstrate products. Website design comprises words and pictures and videos, but may also host webinars and podcasts, and offer branded games, free assessments, and mobile apps. Websites often allow customers to register for premier content or information (for later communications) and/or secure access. Customers can interact with the firm by posting responses, downloading content, uploading videos and photos, entering contests, posting reviews and/or recommending products and distribution outlets.

Nestlé builds highly targeted communities. Nespresso is a several-million-person club whose members, like actress Penelope Cruz, "treasure quality coffee as part of the simple moments of pleasure in everyday life." Club Buitoni members (Italian-culture lovers) click on favorite Italian recipes made with Buitoni pasta and may win a trip to Buitoni's testing kitchens in Tuscany.

Marketing Question

Many firms have developed creative approaches using digital communications. What is your favorite example of a digital campaign? Was it successful? Why or why not?

KEY IDEA

➤ Important digital options include:

- Online advertising and public relations
- Websites
- Blogs
- Social media
- Mobile marketing

Marketing Question

Firms are increasingly using blogs for commercial purposes. Search the Internet. Which company blog do you think is most effective? Why? What are the benefits and limitations of blogs?

Most commercial websites use **cookies** to track data on customer activity. Cookies are small text files installed on personal computers, tablets, and mobile devices and are an important component in web-based marketing. Cookies and related identification technologies track user behavior, preferences, and time spent on a particular website. The data gathered allow marketers to target personalized messages to individuals who previously visited its website.

For example, suppose a person searching a website for cameras (presumably with some interest in purchasing) *abandons* the site prior to purchasing. That person will likely receive a camera ad on a subsequent visit. *Remarketing* (or retargeting) occurs when an advertiser, via cookies, automates specific individuals to see dynamic banner ads when visiting related websites. Hence, a person who spent time on the Mattel site may see ads for Mattel products when visiting a website like Amazon or Target. Google Ads work in a similar fashion, *pushing* personalized paid content to users as they search various websites.

Some firms encourage customers to use the Internet for routine tasks like product information search, placing orders, and checking delivery status. Sometimes websites replace communication forms like telephone operators and on-the-road salespeople. Other firms integrate websites within different communication vehicles.

The Internet also benefits many tiny specialty merchants like Germany-based Wurzburger — selling sheet music for accordion players; and Wessex Press — publisher of *Capon's Marketing Framework*. Check out **www.axcesscapon.com**.

BLOGS

Blogs (from web logs) are online platforms that offer opinionated commentary. In most cases, *bloggers* allow readers to interact with them by posting comments on their blogs. Blogs are often highly specialized (celebrities, food, travel, wine); some bloggers have enormous followings and are important opinion leaders. Hence, blogs offer marketers the ability to target specialized audiences.

Technology firms often provide bloggers with advance versions of new products, hoping for favorable comments. Other firms start their own blogs. *Brandweek* reported, "Nike, Dr Pepper, Mazda, SBC, and others have ... found blogging an easy, cheap way to appear hipper and keep customers engaged with the brand." Microsoft lets 1,000 developers set up personal blogs to build relationships.[20] But blogging can backfire if bloggers view it as the invasion by commercial interests into a non-commercial domain.

SOCIAL MEDIA

Social media (SM) are online tools and platforms that allow Internet users to share insights and experiences for business or pleasure, share content (words, pictures, audio, video), entertain each other, offer reviews and opinions, and collaborate. SM communications are very powerful: Customers often find strangers' opinions more credible than paid spokespeople!

Twitter is a microblogging service; users send and read other users' messages — *tweets* — text posts of up to 140 characters displayed on the author's profile page. Users send tweets to friends' lists and subscribe to other authors' tweets. Tweet volume is approaching 200 million daily; 50 percent of *tweeters* claim to follow their favorite brands. Advertising on Twitter includes *Promotional Tweets* — look like regular tweets; *Promotional Trends* — the advertisement appears on top of a list of hot topics on Twitter's home page; and *Promoted Accounts* — Twitter recommendations that users *follow* a particular account's tweets.

THE BRIGHT SIDE OF SOCIAL MEDIA

SM embraces an ever-expanding array of tools including blogs and microblogs, Internet forums and communities, networks, photo and video sharing, podcasts and webinars, and **wikis**. Many firms engage in community building by bringing together users, like HOGs (Harley Owners Group), Cisco developers, and Mac users. These communities offer excellent opportunities to stimulate positive word of mouth, gain awareness, enhance brand image, expand product capabilities, build brand equity, and drive sales. Many firms like EBags use customer feedback for product redesign; other firms engage customers in new product development — Chapter 14. Gardening retailer Burpee asks customers to post product reviews online; very positive reviews lead to immediate sales.

Facebook and LinkedIn are the most well known communities. These sites invite people to post personal information and automate connectivity with friends and professional associates. They also offer robust environments for marketers to establish branded communities where individuals can meet and connect with new people based on shared interests and experiences.

Other communities that bring together like-minded users include *Tripadviser.com* (hotel and vacation destinations), *Inthemotherhood.com* (mothers), and many disease-specific sites. Community members are often attractive targets for coupons, online and offline conversations, product previews, and samples. Many of these sites discourage or ban traditional advertising. Firms will have to design new strategies to build engagement, relationships, and interactive dialog. But communication fundamentals remain the same.

> ### Marketing Question
> As book publishers have embraced electronic publishing (iPad, Kindle, Nook), some are assessing the opportunity to secure additional revenues by placing advertising in both electronic and printed books. As a publishing marketing executive, how would you approach an assignment to investigate this opportunity?

THE DARK SIDE OF SOCIAL MEDIA

Much social media activity by firms aims to create favorable *buzz* about the firm and its brands among customers and other third parties. But SM also enables customer-to-customer (C2C) communications; these can be negative. Defecting customers may encourage network members to defect also.[21] Disenchanted customers can broadcast dissatisfactions widely using websites, blogs and microblogs, and YouTube.

Increasingly, firms are deploying software and training employees to monitor the Internet for negative communications and implement ways to mitigate brand damage. The firm's response to negative communications should depend on the situation. Some general options are:

- Correct misinformation;
- Do not respond but allow loyal customers to address negative issues;
- Use customer comments as a form of marketing research;
- Fix the problem and advise the unhappy customer.

In general, the firm should develop creative approaches to enhance the positives and mitigate the negatives, both by acting directly and by engaging community members to implement its approaches. Measurement is crucial: The many alternative measures include website visits and duration, community membership, blog and microblog followers and mentions, and sales.

> ### Marketing Question
> What is your favorite example of a mobile marketing campaign? Why is this campaign your favorite?

MOBILE MARKETING

Hand-held personal digital assistants (PDAs), smartphones (like the iPhone and Android phones), and tablet computers (like the iPad) free web surfers from personal computers. Digital communications can now occur *on the go* 24/7/365. Although currently small, mobile marketing is the fastest growing advertising channel. Accordingly, mobile marketing will increase considerably in importance as *mobile*-device sales surpass PC sales.

Mobile devices offer new options for marketers:

- **Short message service (SMS)** — short text messages (up to 160 characters) that remain stored until the user opens the mobile device.
- **Multimedia message service (MMS)** — similar to SMS but may include graphics, video clips, and sound files.

Marketers may send unsolicited messages, but response rates are low. For **permission-based** (*opt in*) alternatives, users subscribe to a service like *foursquare*, Groupon, or *shopkick*. They receive advertisements, *coupons of the day*, loyalty points, or other benefits like feedback options, games, mini-dramas, music, polls, quizzes, ringtones, sports, and videos. Future mobile communications will only be limited by designer creativity.

KEY MESSAGES

- Advertising *works* via hierarchy-of-effects models incorporating awareness, knowledge, liking, trial, purchase and repeat purchase as major variables.

- High-involvement and low-involvement products have different hierarchies.

- A well-developed advertising strategy requires answers to seven critical questions:
    - **Target audience**. Whom are we trying to influence?
    - **Advertising objectives**. What are we trying to achieve?
    - **Messaging**. What content should the target audience receive?
    - **Execution**. How shall we communicate the message?
    - **Media selection and timing**. Where and when shall we place our advertising?
    - **Advertising budget**. How much shall we spend on advertising?
    - **Program evaluation**. How shall we test our advertising and measure its effectiveness?

- The core of the advertising message should reflect the positioning statement in the market segment strategy.

- Advertising messages embrace many rational and emotional approaches.

- Key issues for media selection are reach, frequency, and impact.

- The firm should approach the marketing budget from a marginal analysis perspective and limit rule-of-thumb approaches.

- The creative brief is the critical interface between the firm and advertising agency.

- Direct marketing (DM), publicity and public relations (P&PR), and sales promotion (SP) are mass communications approaches that supplement or replace advertising.

- The Internet is fast becoming an important communications medium. Critical areas for marketers to explore include online advertising and public relations, websites, blogs and microblogs, social networking, and mobile marketing.

VIDEOS AND AUDIOS

Advertising	v1602	🎥	Joseph T. Plummer	Columbia Business School
Internet Marketing	v1603	🎥	Jeremy H. Kagan	Columbia Business School
Social Media	v1604	🎥	Peter Propp	
Buzz Marketing	v1605	🎥	Mark Hughes	Buzzmarketing

v1602

v1603

v1604

v1605

IMPERATIVE 4
Design the Market Offer

....

PART B – COMMUNICATING CUSTOMER VALUE

CHAPTER 17

DIRECTING
AND MANAGING
THE FIELD
SALES EFFORT cv1/U1

To access O-codes, go to **www.ocodes.com**

LEARNING OBJECTIVES

When you have completed this chapter, you will be able to:

- Understand marketing's role in the field sales effort.
- Lead a field sales force.
- Implement the six tasks of sales management.
- Develop a sales strategy: Set sales objectives, determine and allocate selling effort, and design sales approaches.
- Design and staff the sales organization to implement the sales strategy.
- Manage critical organizational processes to support sales strategy implementation.
- Integrate market strategy and sales strategy.
- Design a strategic (key) account management program.

OPENING CASE: HONEYWELL BUILDING SOLUTIONS

Honeywell Building Solutions (HBS) provides building automation, security, and fire and life safety solutions and services to public- and private-sector facilities. HBS is also a global leader in energy services, helping organizations conserve energy, optimize building operations, and leverage renewable energy sources. HBS has a storied history as a Honeywell business unit. Chances are that when you adjust your heat or air conditioning at home or in the office, you are using a Honeywell product.

HBS addresses three market segments for commercial buildings:

- **Installation.** *Mostly for new buildings where the decision-making unit frequently includes owners, architects, and mechanical and electrical contractors.*

- **Service.** *Making sure that customer installations and equipment perform optimally.*
- **Energy.** *Retrofitting current buildings to improve energy efficiency. HBS acts as project designer and general contactor, but most work is sub-contracted.*

In 1999, Honeywell merged with AlliedSignal to form Honeywell International Inc. In 2000, United Technologies held merger talks with the new firm, but these broke down when GE attempted to buy Honeywell. The U.S. Justice Department approved the GE acquisition; but in 2001, the European Commission refused and Honeywell continued as an independent firm.

Following months of turmoil, when its employees were preparing for the expected GE acquisition, HBS did not perform well: Sales declined 20 percent annually. In an attempt to save the business, Honeywell's CEO Dave Cote appointed a new leadership team for HBS including a President and VPs of operations, marketing, and sales. Kevin Madden became worldwide VP of sales. Cote gave the team 90 days to develop a turnaround plan, and to "get rid of their ancestors" — the cause of the poor performance.

Madden, a 20-year Honeywell veteran, described the situation he inherited. "Not only were sales declining, internally a victim *mentality was pervasive. Because of the turmoil, 35 to 40 percent of the intellectual capital had left and the business unit was in a tailspin. The entire organizational focus was on productivity and cost, and most sales were to current HBS customers; we were securing a minimal number of new customers. We had dismantled most of the sales teams that focused on the installations of our systems. HBS had outsourced this activity to transaction-oriented partners who had little interest in building deep relationships or delivering complete solutions. Quite frankly, customers had lost confidence in HBS to do an installation and we no longer had any competitive advantage."*

Madden said that energy and many installation projects were make *businesses. Sales reps had to be proactive in getting in front of customers and writing specifications. But that was not happening, for several reasons:*

- *HBS had lost many of its good salespeople.*
- *Current salespeople were generalists; they sold in all three lines of business. Yet the nature of the challenges and the skills required tended to be quite different by market segment.*
- *The first-line sales leaders'* **span of control** *averaged 25 to 1. They were too preoccupied with administrative tasks, and gave little guidance and coaching to salespeople.*

Madden said that the turnaround plan focused on five key areas:

- **Marketing and sales alignment.** *Marketing and sales became tightly integrated. The sales force not only agreed on all new marketing initiatives, but often stimulated new ideas.*
- **Customer coverage model.** *When Madden arrived, the Americas region had 192 generalist salespeople. Seven years later, it had over 400 salespeople, many hired from competitors with the challenge to be part of the build, focused in individual market areas. Many new salespeople displaced outsourced partners as HBS returned to the installation marketplace.*
- **Sales planning.** *The five-stage sales process — HBS' playbook was tightly linked:*
  - **First calls.** *The salesperson figures out the customer's decision-making unit, what needs to be done, and secures agreement to develop a list of requirements.*
  - **Requirements definition.** *The salesperson prepares the list of requirements — technical, financial, legal — and gets the customer to agree.*
  - **Commitment.** *The salesperson identifies HBS resources meeting customer requirements, and gets agreement from the customer.*
  - **Solutions development.** *The salesperson brings in Honeywell engineers to design the installation.*
  - **Final negotiation.** *The customer and HBS sign the contract.*

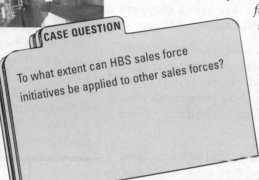

For all jobs over $750,000, HBS conducts an impact review with senior sales executives. The review team focuses on the customer's best competitive alternative and HBS' next move. At these reviews, the team may telephone the customer to check its understanding and probe additional ways to add value. HBS also rigorously qualifies all sales opportunities and only allocates expensive sales support manpower where it believes it can win. HBS rigorously debriefs all wins and losses.

- **Roles and responsibilities.** *HBS reduced first-line sales manager spans from 25 to 1, to an average 10 to 1, to increase salesperson coaching.*
- **Performance management.** *HBS implemented a rigorous performance measurement system and pays for results. Base pay is comparable to competition, but HBS designs incentive compensation and rewards to be among the most lucrative in the industry.*

Madden said an important investment was in a sales force data system. The sales process also functions as a funnel and HBS knows, for example, that a certain number of agreements to prepare a list of requirements will lead to a certain number of contracts. HBS manages the funnel aggressively and salespeople must update their funnels continuously. If 10 days have lapsed without a salesperson updating, Madden communicates with that salesperson.

CASE QUESTION

To what extent can HBS sales force initiatives be applied to other sales forces?

Since the new leadership team took over, sales have turned around; HBS is now a multi-billion-dollar business and a strong member of the Honeywell portfolio. The renewed HBS has beaten the industry's 4- to 5-percentage growth rate every year. Sales growth rates have ranged from 6 percent to 30 percent, doubling the business.

In many firms, the sales force is the only group specifically charged with and compensated for generating sales and securing revenues. Field salespeople efforts are the firm's critical persuasive component. Some sales forces are huge. Several U.S. life insurance firms employ more than 10,000 salespeople; GE, IBM, and Pfizer have 40,000, 50,000, and 35,000 salespeople respectively around the world.

In B2B marketing, the field sales force has always been critical; salespeople typically introduce firm products/services directly to customers. Business customers increasingly want vendors to possess real expertise in their specific industries and/or functions. They expect salespeople to help solve business problems, not just sell widgets. In turn, many B2B vendors have expanded their product lines, and added solutions specialists that help knit together disparate products/services into integrated offers.

By contrast, in B2C marketing, advertising or digital information is often the main communication channel to consumers; the sales force plays a supporting role. But as the retail industry concentrates and a few large retailers or distributors secure significant power, direct B2C field sales efforts are increasing. Some FMCG firms now spend more heavily on direct selling and *relationship management* to wholesalers and retailers than on advertising to consumers! At P&G, more than 400 persons work exclusively with Walmart buyers.

MARKETING'S ROLE IN THE FIELD SALES EFFORT

This book's title is *Capon's Marketing Framework*, so why do we include a chapter on directing and managing the field sales effort? Aren't there enough dedicated books on sales management? Of course there are! But one in nine Americans works in sales. Hence, understanding the role of sales and aligning firm **selling efforts** with marketing is more crucial than ever. Salespeople's actions often *make or break* the market strategy as at SalesCo:

> At SalesCo (disguised name), marketing's job was to develop sales leads. Marketing worked hard but salespeople often did not follow up and leads languished in files. A new management team harvested 3,000 dormant leads and assigned a special group to work them. Within six months, 250 new customers were providing $5 million in new revenues.

As the SalesCo example shows, lead generation can be an area fraught with conflict. Marketing complains about poor follow-up on sales leads; salespeople complain about marketing's limited understanding of customers and competitors, and poor quality leads.

As competition increases, these perceptions damage the firm. Marketing and sales must be on the same team, each performing its own critical functions. We do not pretend this is easy. Marketing and sales often have different perspectives. Marketing tends to have a long-term more strategic view; the sales organization must meet or exceed short-term revenue targets.

Although creative tension is often beneficial for firm performance, badly coordinated or ill-formed sales strategies can lead to distracting internal competition among product managers. A multi-product firm may have several product-market strategies, each product-market strategy comprising several market-segment strategies. The sales strategy must integrate all these market strategies, typically focusing efforts on selling a range of products to a variety of market segments.

> Salespeople at FMCG Co (disguised name) sold the firm's entire product line to retail customers. Some brand managers devised incentive schemes to secure disproportionate sales force effort on their products. These actions caused considerable internal dissension.[1]

Marketing Exercise

Interview a senior marketing executive and ask two core questions:
- What works well in your relationship with the sales force? Why do these things work?
- What works poorly in your relationship with the sales force? Why do these things not work?

FMCG Co's practice is inexcusable in this day and age. As more leading firms adopt strategic (key) account management programs, and customers have more access to data and information, firm-to-customer relationships are evolving. The sales force is increasingly responsible for securing deep understanding of customer needs, proposing actionable solutions, and accessing firm resources to solve customer problems. Leading sales organizations combine people, processes, and technology to optimize sales performance and stay ahead of competition. The recent emergence of mobile, social media, cloud, and big data all have all become technology enablers for sales leaders.

When the sales person is in the driver's seat with a specific customer, marketing must play a supportive role.

In many firms, marketing and sales report to separate VPs. Although members of the same management team, their different approaches, backgrounds, objectives, and philosophies can create separate cultures leading to misaligned plans and execution. Some firms pointedly address this issue by creating a combined position — VP of Sales and Marketing (or Chief Revenue Officer) — to whom both sales and marketing VPs report. Other alignment processes include integrating marketing and sales metrics, sharing revenue and profit targets, and reward systems.

Marketing Exercise

Interview a senior sales executive and ask two core questions:
- What works well in your relationship with marketing? Why do these things work?
- What works poorly in your relationship with marketing? Why do these things not work?

Well-managed firms implement processes that tightly coordinate marketing and sales efforts. They encourage disciplined reporting and communications, create joint assignments, rotate jobs, co-locate marketing and sales personnel, and improve sales force feedback. Marketing develops market plans in good time with significant sales force input; sales executives develop sales strategy in sync with the market planning process. Senior marketing and sales managers meet frequently to hammer out realistic and coordinated marketing and sales objectives and priorities in a spirit of cooperation. Many large firms even appoint sales/marketing coordinators whose job is to build effective senior marketing and sales manager relationships.

KEY IDEA

➤ Effectively managing the sales/marketing interface is critical for achieving sales excellence.

LEADING THE SALES EFFORT[2]

Once planning is in place, put simply, the sales management job is to make salespeople successful. All sales managers, junior and senior, should *lead from the front*, spending time in the field with their salespeople — coaching, inspecting, observing, teaching, and selling. They should empower salespeople to take initiative by fostering a culture of acting like "it's your own business." The most effective sales managers innovate new ways of delivering customer value, help drive entry into attractive markets, and spearhead the evolution of new sales resources, models and sales organizations.

To secure the best results, sales leaders treat human resource expenditures as an investment and view selling as a training ground for general management. The sales force gets *tough love*: Performance expectations are challenging and very clear, but support is plentiful. The most effective sales leaders treat sales people as investments, *advancing the science of sales, and the art of the customer relationship*, by making fact-based decisions, like allocating sales resources — salespeople, strategic (key) account managers, telesales — across customer segments and sales channels. They leverage sophisticated intellectual capital by:

- Supplementing firm products with advisory services to offer customer solutions.
- Building specialist expertise to fashion and develop customer solutions.
- Working with specialists to install and implement customer solutions.

Sales leaders understand viscerally that customer success drives firm success. They create a *risk-taking* culture where failed experiments for delivering customer value are *accepted* and *expected*. They celebrate and reward learning from honest mistakes, but penalize repeated mistakes. They hire and develop people willing to try, fail, and learn. Sales leaders discover and develop best practice by following the *fail or scale* principle.

Perhaps the most critical leadership function is encouraging sales people to *live the mission* — to provide a rationale for the sales job over and above financial rewards. Salespeople who internalize a greater purpose build credibility and trust with customers and develop a powerful differentiator for defeating competitors.

The Tasks of Sales Force Management

To mount an effective selling effort, sales managers must focus on six sales force management tasks. Three tasks address *developing* sales strategy; three deal with *implementing* sales strategy. This chapter discusses the six tasks sequentially but also shows how each task relates to the others.

Developing the sales strategy	Implementing the sales strategy
Task 1: Set and achieve sales objectives.	Task 4: Design the sales organization.
Task 2: Determine and allocate selling effort.	Task 5: Create critical organizational processes.
Task 3: Develop sales approaches.	Task 6: Staff the sales organization.

TASK 1: SET AND ACHIEVE SALES OBJECTIVES

Sales objectives are the firm's desired results. They derive from the strategic focus in the market segment strategy: Retain current sales, increase customer use, attract sales from competitors, and secure new business. Achieving sales objectives is the sales force's central task. The firm makes profits, survives and grows, and enhances shareholder value only by selling products/ services to customers. Achieving sales objectives takes precedence over all other activities like collecting payments, delivering goods, entertaining, and gathering information. Sales objectives turned into specific performance requirements are **sales quotas**.

DEFINING SALES OBJECTIVES

The firm can choose among several sales performance measures. Most firms set sales objectives in terms of volume measures like gross sales revenues (dollars) or gross sales units. But focusing solely on volume can short-change profits, so profitability objectives like **profit contribution** — gross profits less direct sales force costs — are also popular. Well-set objectives specify *how much* and *by when* the sales force must meet targets. We illustrate sales objectives for Essex (fictional firm):

> **Essex, Inc.: Overall Sales Objectives**
>
> In 20xy, sales revenue objectives — $40 million.
>
> In 20xy, gross profit contribution objectives — $14.5 million.

KEY IDEA

➤ Sales objectives are the firm's desired results. Achieving sales objectives is the sales force central task. Sales objectives turned into specific performance requirements are called quotas.

RELATING SALES OBJECTIVES TO MARKETING OBJECTIVES

As noted, integrating market strategy with sales strategy is a difficult problem for many firms. A useful way of driving integration is to rigorously translate marketing objectives into sales objectives. Essex offers three products (I, II, III) to three market segments (A, B, C). Table 17.1 shows several ways to view Essex's sales revenue objectives:

- Overall objectives — $40 million.
- Objectives by market segment: A — $10 million, B — $20 million, C — $10 million.
- Objectives by product: I — $26 million, II — $5 million, III — $9 million.
- Individual cells show objectives by product/market segment. Essex sets revenue objectives for IA, IB, IC, IIB, IIC, IIIA, and IIIB, but zero revenue objectives for IIA and IIIC.

Although each approach to Essex's sales revenue objectives has value, only product/market segment objectives really integrate market and sales strategy perspectives.

KEY IDEA

➤ Sales objectives integrate firm market strategy and sales strategy.

		Product			Totals
		I	II	III	
Market Segment	A	$7	$0	$3	**$10**
	B	$13	$1	$6	**$20**
	C	$6	$4	$0	**$10**
	Totals	**$26**	**$5**	**$9**	**$40**

TABLE 17.1

ESSEX, INC. SALES REVENUE OBJECTIVES BY PRODUCT AND MARKET SEGMENT ($ MILLIONS)

BREAKING DOWN SALES OBJECTIVES

Typically, the sales force breaks down overall sales objectives into **control units** like sales regions, sales districts, and individual sales territories. Senior sales managers gain significant insight by comparing actual sales performance versus sales objectives for individual control units; they see if a particular region, district, or territory is performing well or poorly.

Firms also establish sales objectives in time units like quarterly, monthly, and weekly. **Calendarizing** allows the firm to monitor performance continuously and sets the stage for making course corrections when performance falls short of objectives.[3] Table 17.2 shows Essex's San Francisco district's overall sales revenue objectives by quarter.

TABLE 17.2

ESSEX, INC. AGGREGATE
SALES REVENUE
OBJECTIVES BY
QUARTER — SAN
FRANCISCO DISTRICT'S
WESTERN REGION ($000s)

Quarter 1	Quarter 2	Quarter 3	Quarter 4	Total
$1,100	$1,450	$950	$1,500	**$5,000**

ALTERNATIVE SALES PERFORMANCE MEASURES

Sales and profit-based objectives are the most popular performance measures, but there are many other metrics the firm may consider:

- **Close rate.** The proportion of sales attempts resulting in actual sales.
- **Customer retention.** The proportion of customers from the start of the year who are still customers at the end of the year — the opposite of customer defection (churn). (This measure speaks to customer lifetime value issues — Chapter 2.)
- **Customer satisfaction.** Specific metrics focusing on the customer experience.
- **Market share.** This measure focuses on firm performance versus competitors.
- **Price realization.** The extent to which the firm achieves planned price levels.

The firm should choose sales objectives carefully, based on the nature of the business and its strategic situation.

TASK 2: DETERMINE AND ALLOCATE SELLING EFFORT

The best way to determine and allocate **selling effort** is by examining four interrelated decisions:

- **Sales force size.** How much selling effort should the firm expend in total? In particular, how many salespeople should sell its products?
- **Sales force activities.** What activities should salespeople do? What proportion of total time should salespeople spend actually *selling*?
- **Selling effort allocation.** How should salespeople allocate selling time among firm products and segments?
- **Telesales.** What proportion of overall selling effort should the firm allocate to telesales? What should telesales people do?

SALES FORCE SIZE

For effective selling effort, the firm must have the *right* number of well-trained, motivated salespeople. Managing *headcount* is typically a crucial HR function and sales managers often wage difficult internal battles to optimize sales force size. Figure 17.1 shows an underlying conceptual framework for determining sales force size — the **sales response function**. When selling effort is low, the firm makes few sales. As selling effort increases, sales increase. Ultimately, sales *top out* at a maximum level, even if the firm adds extra salespeople. The firm should continue hiring until the marginal revenue from adding a salesperson equals that salesperson's marginal cost. Many sales managers find this curve intuitively reasonable, but do not know their sales force position. Approaches to the sizing decision are either experimental or analytic.

KEY IDEA

➤ The firm should consider four key issues in determining and allocating selling effort:

- Sales force size
- Sales force activities
- Selling effort allocation
- Telesales

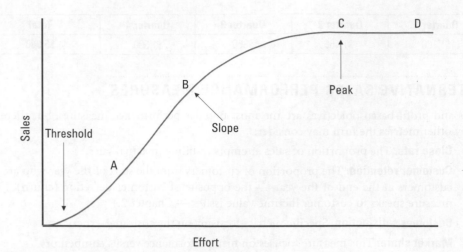

FIGURE 17.1

THE SALES RESPONSE FUNCTION

EXPERIMENTAL METHOD. Sales managers change sales force size and see what happens. Two broad hypotheses follow from Figure 17.1:

- The sales force is too small, perhaps at B.
- The sales force is too large, perhaps at D.

Sales managers should decide what criteria would support/reject each hypothesis. Then they select one or more sales districts/regions for a trial and comparable districts/regions as controls. Sales managers increase/decrease sales force size in the trial geography for a predetermined period. If the experimental data supports hypothesis 1, the firm should add salespeople; if the data support hypothesis 2, the firm should reduce sales force size.

KEY IDEA

➤ The firm should develop a hypothesis about the shape of, and its position on, the sales response function.

ANALYTIC METHOD. The analytic approach has three steps:

1. Total number of selling hours required to achieve sales objectives. Two broad approaches for calculating *required number of selling hours* are *single-factor models* and *portfolio models*:

- **Single-factor models.** The firm classifies current and potential customers into A, B, C, and D categories (I) by a value measure like sales potential (II). Table 17.3 illustrates the single-factor model:

Customer category, I	Sales potential, II	Number of customers, III	Selling time per customer annually, IV	Required selling time annually, III × IV = V
A	>$2M	100 accounts	100 hours	10,000 hours
B	$250K to $2M	250 accounts	50 hours	12,500 hours
C	$10K to $250K	800 accounts	12 hours	9,600 hours
D	<$10K	3,000 accounts	4 hours	12,000 hours
Total				44,100 hours **(VI)**

TABLE 17.3

ILLUSTRATION: SINGLE-FACTOR MODEL FOR CALCULATING REQUIRED SELLING TIME

Single-factor models are simple to use, but may not fully capture the complexity of selling to various customers. Portfolio models can do a better job.

- **Portfolio models.** The firm classifies customers on multiple dimensions. Figure 17.2 uses *customer potential* and firm share of customer business — *customer share*. The firm partitions each dimension into low, medium, and high. The firm then identifies the number of customers in each matrix cell (III); and the required selling time per customer (IV). The analysis proceeds as before.

FIGURE 17.2

PORTFOLIO MODEL FOR DETERMINING REQUIRED SELLING TIME

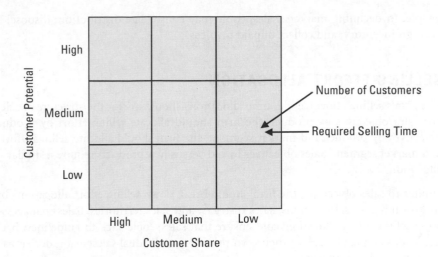

2. Number of available selling hours per salesperson. Salespeople conduct many activities. Sales managers must calculate the time available for selling.

3. Required sales force size. Continuing the Table 17.3 illustration:

  i. Total available salesperson time per annum (hours)
    = (365 days less 104 [weekends] less 30 [holidays/vacations])
    = 231 × 10 hours per day = **2,310 hours**

 ii. Actual selling time per salesperson
    = Total available salesperson time × 30% (assumed)
    = 2,310 × 30% = **693 hours**

iii. Number of salespeople required
    = Total number of selling hours required/Actual selling time per salesperson
    = 44,100/693 = **64 salespeople**

In practice, this calculation provides a *ballpark* estimate for sales force size. The firm should expect some variation from the actual size, but significant variation demands action.

SALES FORCE ACTIVITIES

The main sales force job is to make sales. But claims on salespeople's time include checking credit and inventories, collections, customer service, delivering products, education and training, gathering market intelligence, internal communications, meetings, qualifying sales leads, receiving payments, record-keeping, report writing, sales planning, and travel. In many firms, even the best salespeople spend less than 20 percent of their time face to face with customers trying to make sales.

Firms regularly deploy technology to improve salesperson effectiveness. Most salespeople use cell phones, e-mail, laptop and tablet computers, smartphones, standardized slide show presentations, voice mail, and/or websites. Other devices and applications like *salesforce.com* enable advertising coordination, best practice and knowledge sharing, reseller training and virtual meetings, sales training, technical support, trade show participation, well-designed sales literature, and working models. Cisco's TelePresence reduces travel time by allowing remote face-to-face sales meetings. Sales managers should develop guidelines specifying salesperson time commitment to various activities.

Time allocations differ from one sales territory to another. Salespeople in urban areas need less travel time than those in rural areas, hence greater **face time**. Salesperson activities also evolve. In growth markets, salespeople should make many sales calls to potential customers; they may also forecast product volumes, gather competitive intelligence, and train distributor sales-

---

Marketing Question

If you, a friend, or a colleague have worked in sales, what percentage of time was *face time* with customers? What other activities were part of the job? Were the time allocations good? Why or why not? What were the challenges of increasing face time?

 KEY IDEA

➤ Sales managers should develop guidelines specifying how salespeople should spend their time.

people. In declining markets, salespeople may consolidate distribution; dispose, liquidate, or reassign inventory; and collect unpaid invoices.

SELLING EFFORT ALLOCATION

The firm's selling effort (selling time allocation) should mirror the *structure* of sales objectives. For sales objectives by product, the firm should allocate selling effort by product. For sales objectives by product and market segment, the firm should allocate selling effort by product and market segment. Sales objectives by old versus new products require a similar selling effort allocation.

Similar to sales objectives, the firm should break down selling effort allocations by individual control units — sales regions, sales districts, and sales territories. Sales managers must make these selling effort allocations and ensure that salespeople stick to guidelines. If managers do not lead, salespeople will set their own priorities. Individual salesperson decisions are unlikely to optimize firm performance.

TELESALES

In recent years, many firms have reduced sales costs by adding telesales departments. Telesales functions differ markedly from firm to firm but include lead generation, interfacing with potential customers and current customers, and partnering with the field sales force.

TASK 3: DEVELOP SALES APPROACHES

The value proposition — Chapter 9 — anchors the **sales approach**, and is the central message the salesperson delivers to customers. Because customer needs differ by segment, the firm should offer a different value proposition for each market segment. Hence, salespeople selling multiple products to multiple segments must have multiple sales approaches — one per market segment. Aided by sales managers and product managers, salespeople should develop messages for specific customers and competitive threats. They should:

- Secure insight into specific needs and competitive threats at individual customers.
- Understand the various perspectives of customer decision-makers and influencers.
- Develop sales approaches that address critical customer needs, answer objections, and counter competitor sales approaches.
- Secure support from sales managers and bring in senior executives as necessary.

The traditional sales approach has two major components:

- Tailoring the sales message for different customer targets, and
- Designing a process to explain values and benefits in the firm's offer.

TAILORING THE SALES MESSAGE FOR DIFFERENT CUSTOMER TARGETS

Customer needs and competitive offers drive the sales approach. Sometimes customers are clear about their needs; other times, individual decision-makers and influencers have different perspectives. Salespeople must decide whom to target and how to tailor sales messages for each person. Procurement personnel are typically interested in price, engineers focus on product design, and manufacturing personnel are concerned about production efficiency. The salesperson must orchestrate the sales approach for each customer role (and individual).

KEY IDEA

➤ Selling effort allocation guidelines must mirror the structure of sales objectives.

➤ The firm must break down selling effort allocations by individual control units like sales regions, sales districts, and sales territories.

➤ The firm should allocate selling effort by customer category.

KEY IDEA

➤ The value proposition anchors the sales approach — the central message the salesperson delivers to customers.

KEY IDEA

➤ The firm should tailor the sales message to different customer targets and design a process to explain firm benefits and values.

Enterprise is the largest car rental firm in the U.S. Starting in 1964, Enterprise provided temporary replacement cars for drivers whose cars were being repaired. One key customer target was garage mechanics. Salespeople made morning calls and always carried donuts. This sales approach got garage mechanics' attention very quickly!

In designing the sales approach, salespeople should sharpen competitive focus. Table 17.4 shows firms I, II, and III, each trying to sell to a customer requiring four benefits — A, B, C, and D.

TABLE 17.4

FORMULATING SALES APPROACHES

Customer Benefits	Relative Importance	Firm I		Firm II		Firm III	
		Benefit	Rank	Benefit	Rank	Benefit	Rank
A	1	A	1	A	2	A	3
B	2			B	1		
C	3			C	1	C	2
D	4	D	2			D	1

Marketing Question

Based on Table 17.4 and the boxed insert, what marketing research and product development would you suggest for Firm I? Firm II? Firm III?

Developing the Sales Approach: Sharpening Competitive Focus

- The customer seeks four benefits in importance order: Benefit A > B > C > D.
- The three firms — I, II, III — each offer different benefit packages.
- Each firm performs better on some benefits than on others:
  - Benefit A: All three firms offer — firm I > II > III
  - Benefit B: Only firm II offers
  - Benefit C: Firm II > III; firm I does not offer
  - Benefit D: Firm III > I; firm II does not offer

- **Firm I.** Should focus on the customer's most important benefit — A. Firm I dominates on this benefit but is vulnerable on the other benefits.

- **Firm II.** Dominates firm III on benefits A, B, and C and is inferior only on the least important benefit — D. Hence, firm II's major challenge is from firm I. Firm II's major problem is that firm I ranks best on the most important benefit — A. Further insight and possible sales approaches for firm II are:
  - Competitive ranking on benefit A is incorrect; actually, firm II > I. Firm II should persuade the customer it offers the best benefit A. Firm II then dominates both competitors on the three most important benefits — A, B, and C.
  - Customer benefits are incorrectly ordered; actually, B > A > C > D. By persuading the customer of its error, firm II dominates both competitors on the now most important benefit, B, and also on benefit C.
  - Customer should base its decision on the benefit set. Firm II's offer is superior; it provides all of the most important benefits — A, B, and C.

- **Firm III.** Has little hope of making the sale. Firm III's best sales approaches focus on benefit D and the combination — A, C, and D. More importantly, why is firm III spending time with this customer when its benefits are so inferior?

No firm offers all of the desired benefits, so each is vulnerable to competition.

When Xerox launches a new product or product upgrade, it makes sure that salespeople have in-depth knowledge about competitive products. Xerox provides easy-to-use charts and a professional video showing key strengths and weaknesses versus *face-off* products. Xerox's laboratories create courses for salespeople including hands-on experience with competitive products and techniques to combat competitive threats.

DESIGNING A PROCESS TO EXPLAIN THE FIRM'S BENEFITS

Selling is a process that facilitates customer buying. We learned that a standardized process is undesirable, but sales managers should guide salespeople via coaching, counseling, and well-designed training programs to guide their approaches. Good sales managers break the selling task into discrete easy-to-learn steps like:

- **Call objectives.** Know the desired results from each sales call and at each stage in the buying process. Many salespeople use pre-call planning processes to help set call objectives.

- **Sales interview tone.** Decide how strident or aggressive to be in different situations.

- **Need elicitation.** Develop procedures to elicit customer needs.

- **Presenting product benefits.** Present product benefits in the context of customer needs.

- **Handling objections.** Anticipate customer objections and know how to address them. Objections differ from product to product and from customer to customer.

- **Communications timing and closing the deal.** Communicate in a strategic sequence. For example, do not elicit customer needs after presenting product benefits. Learn how to close a sale and ask for the order. Learn when to accept rejection and move to another customer and learn to better qualify prospects.

> In Bose's retail stores, customers relax and enjoy exquisite sound from a large TV and huge speakers. When the show concludes, the salesperson executes *the reveal*. She removes the *fake* speakers to show baseball-sized Bose speakers.

TASK 4: DESIGN THE SALES ORGANIZATION

Tasks 1, 2, and 3 address *developing* the sales strategy. Tasks 4, 5, and 6 focus on *implementing* the sales strategy, ensuring that the sales force delivers the planned levels and types of selling effort. Task 4 addresses sales organization design; firm choices should reflect strategic realities. For example, if the firm's product line is complex and heterogeneous, perhaps it should have multiple sales forces. Three critical questions are:

- Should firm employees conduct the selling effort? Or should the firm outsource selling?

- How should an employee-based sales force be organized? Or reorganized?

- How should the firm design its sales territories?

SHOULD FIRM EMPLOYEES CONDUCT SELLING EFFORT? OR SHOULD THE FIRM OUTSOURCE SELLING?

Today, many firms outsource functions like call centers, computer systems, financial processes, legal, payroll, production operations, and security. Should the firm outsource selling effort? Three issues are critical to this decision:

- **Control.** Employee-based sales forces are more likely to follow managerial direction. Outsourced agents, brokers, and reps earn commissions; hence, the firm may exercise little control over time and effort, particularly if the outsourcer sells other firm (even competitor) products.

- **Cost.** Employee-based sales forces typically incur substantial fixed costs like salaries, travel and entertainment, sales management, and other overhead, regardless of sales volume. By contrast, third-party sellers on commission are a variable cost: No sales, no costs!

- **Flexibility.** To modify an employee-based sales force takes time in onboarding and equipment. Third-party sellers typically work with strict performance criteria and short-term contracts; hence, relatively easy termination.

KEY IDEA

➤ Selling is a system to facilitate customer buying.

➤ Coaching, counseling, and training can improve the selling process.

Marketing Question

Baby food firm Gerber fired 250 salespeople and sold to grocery store chains via food brokers. In the education market, by contrast, Apple shifted from third-party sellers to an employee-based sales force. Why did these firms move in opposite directions? When is outsourcing the better decision?

Direct sales costs were too high for software firm Altiris so it fired the entire sales force. Altiris partnered with Compaq, Dell, IBM, Microsoft, and others to sell its products. Altiris customized partner relationships, like making communication materials partner-specific. In less than 10 years, Altiris grew from $1 million sales to an acquisition value of $830 million (by Symantec).

KEY IDEA

➤ The firm should implement sales force reorganizations *very carefully.*

Sometimes the balance favors employee-based selling; sometimes it favors outsourcing the selling effort. There is no right or wrong answer. If the firm has insufficient salespeople for a new market entry, third-party sellers can take up the slack. Conversely, long lead times and/or high market share in mature markets with predictable sales may favor employee-based selling.

HOW SHOULD AN EMPLOYEE-BASED SALES FORCE BE ORGANIZED?

Avon's sales organization has a group vice president of sales, three regional vice presidents, seven regional sales directors, 85 division sales managers, and 2,500 district sales managers. In some geographies, district sales managers have several hundred reps. Avon also aligns its sales force ethnically in terms of language and culture.

KEY IDEA

➤ Key sales organization design variables are:

• Degree of centralization/decentralization
• Number of management levels
• Managerial span of control

Three interrelated variables for organizational design are the desired degree of centralization/ decentralization, the number of management levels, and managerial span of control.

Specialization is one of the most important design variables. Should the firm specialize its selling effort? And if so, how?

- **Unspecialized.** Two organization forms are generally considered unspecialized. The firm:
  - Does not place geographic bounds on a salesperson's search for sales opportunities.
  - Organizes territories by geography where salespeople sell all products, to all customers, for all applications, in specified geographic areas.
- **Specialized.** Specialization can take various forms — by product, maintenance/new business, distribution channel, market segment, and/or customer importance or size (strategic accounts). Generally, specialized selling effort leads to higher sales, but selling costs are also higher.

As the firm's environment evolves, so must its market and sales strategies evolve. The sales organization must also evolve but effective implementation is critical:

In May 2000, Xerox fired CEO Rick Thoman after only 13 months on the job. Thoman shifted Xerox's sales organization from a product and geographic focus to an industry focus. Thoman saw the salesperson job as analyzing an entire customer business and identifying the best way to manage complex flows of data, graphics, and images. Thoman believed salespeople's intellectual capital would generalize by industry. But Xerox made the change before salespeople were trained, and did a poor job of switching accounts among salespeople. Xerox *orphaned* previously well-served accounts. Many salespeople left rather than relocate. Competitors hired disgruntled Xerox salespeople.

Apple's shift to an employee-based sales force was also less than stellar:

Apple's CEO Steve Jobs said: "We were very straightforward and told these third-party salespeople that, 'Hey, in four months we're going to switch [the sales force organization] and you're going to be out of a job.' Obviously these folks did everything they could to sell as much as they could by June 30, when we let them go, and did absolutely nothing to build for sales in the July quarter. So when our folks got there, they found there was no pipeline work at all: They had to start from scratch. And, duh, this was during the *peak buying time for schools* [emphasis added]. It was just stupid on our part to do this then, and that was my decision. It was a train wreck, and it was totally my fault."[4]

HOW SHOULD THE FIRM DESIGN SALES TERRITORIES?

Within the sales organization structure, the firm must design (redesign) **sales territories**. Of course, frequent territory design changes are undesirable as they disrupt customer-salesperson relationships. The two key variables are **sales potential** — available sales; and **salesperson workload** — time to complete required activities. Four standard sales territory design steps are:

- **Design by sales potential.** The firm identifies geographically contiguous territories with roughly equal *sales potential.* Some trial territories are geographically larger than others. Equivalent potential territories for Xerox might be a few blocks of midtown Manhattan or several Western states.
- **Calculate workload.** Use sales-effort allocation decisions (Task 2) to determine *workload.* Based on the initial design, in some territories, salespeople may have time left over; in other territories, they may have insufficient time.
- **Adjust initial design for workload.** Make territory design adjustments to optimize sales potential and salesperson workload.
- **Continuous monitoring.** Sales managers must monitor salespeople and their territories and continually adjust.

> ConstructCo's (disguised name) analysis showed that market share by territory ranged from 8 to 50 percent. Also, many high-revenue salespeople had low territory shares. ConstructCo redesigned sales territories to take advantage of untapped potential and added salespeople. Revenue decline turned into revenue growth.

TASK 5: CREATE CRITICAL ORGANIZATIONAL PROCESSES

All sales organizations employ processes like sales planning, pipeline analysis and sales forecasting, evaluation methods, and reward systems to help implement planned selling effort.

SALES PLANNING

The firm should actively engage salespeople in a detailed sales planning process. As discussed earlier, senior sales managers work with regional and district sales managers to decompose overall firm sales objectives into individual control units like sales regions, districts, and territories. They also decide on broad selling effort allocations by product and market segment. In bottom-up planning, salespeople analyze their individual territories, work with district sales managers to agree on territory objectives, and develop sales action plans. Deviating from the sales strategy can cause problems:

> A startup medical device firm, specialized in hemodialysis treatments (blood cleansing for failed kidneys), decided to focus selling effort on major teaching hospitals. The sales approach required salespeople to provide customers with high service levels to ensure proper use. But in implementation, salespeople made sales to more hospitals than they could service. The product was widely misused and the firm suffered serious credibility problems.

PIPELINE ANALYSIS AND SALES FORECASTING

The sales pipeline comprises stages in the selling process as customers move from prospects (potential customers) to buyers. **Pipeline analysis** tracks firm success as customers traverse these stages and is critical for sales forecasting. For example, IBM's pipeline comprises:

- **Discover.** The salesperson believes the customer is intending to buy.
- **Identify.** The customer is interested in working with IBM.

KEY IDEA

➤ Sales territory design should aim for roughly equal:
- Sales potential
- Workload

KEY IDEA

➤ The firm should actively engage salespeople in the sales planning process.

KEY IDEA

➤ A pipeline system continually tracks success at different stages in the selling process. Rigorous pipeline analysis leads to better sales forecasts.

KEY IDEA

➤ Important specialization dimensions for sales organization design are:

• Product
• Maintenance/new business
• Distribution channel
• Market segment
• Customer importance

Marketing Recap

Talk to a salesperson about current and potential customers. Do IBM's six stages in the selling process —

• Discover
• Identify
• Validate
• Qualify
• Conditional agreement
• Business won

— work for them? Don't forget to check if customer expectations were met.

• **Validate.** The customer states a need and buying vision. The customer allows IBM access to project sponsors — customer personnel responsible for the purchase.

• **Qualify.** Project sponsors and an IBM team work on a preliminary solution.

• **Conditional agreement.** Project sponsors conditionally approve IBM's proposed solution.

• **Business won.** The customer and IBM team sign a contract.

• **Customer expectations met.** The customer is satisfied as purchase and installation move forward — and IBM receives payment as scheduled.

A pipeline system tracks success at different stages in the selling process. Rigorous pipeline analysis leads to better sales forecasts.

Many firms use software applications like SAP and *salesforce.com* to track and manage sales pipelines and decide where and when to apply additional selling resources — like securing leads or validating opportunities. These applications have many tools: For salespeople to better analyze customer data; and for sales managers to gain greater insight into sales force performance so they can make appropriate interventions. (Sometimes salespeople resist entering pipeline data, but the firm must make this mandatory.) Table 17.5 illustrates typical pipeline data for a single sales territory.

TABLE 17.5
ILLUSTRATION:
PIPELINE ANALYSIS

	Total Sales Leads Discovered	Opportunities Identified	Opportunities Validated	Opportunities Qualified	Conditional Agreements Made with Customer	Business Won
Territory total	$76 million	$28 million	$17 million	$13 million	$10 million	$8 million
Percentage of total pipeline leads	100%	37%	22%	17%	13%	11%
Percentage success from previous stage	100%	37%	61%	76%	77%	80%

We cannot overstate the importance of good sales forecasting. At a minimum, good forecasts are important for financial budgeting and production planning. Poor forecasting can lead to significant problems:

To meet *explosive demand*, Canadian multinational telecom Nortel Networks (NN) added 9,600 jobs and spent $1.9 billion to boost production. One year later, NN lost $19 billion in a single quarter and eliminated 10,000 jobs.

Cisco vastly overestimated demand by basing forecasts on orders. Cisco did not realize that end users, worried about product shortages, placed orders with several distributors. Cisco sales were less than expected, and inventory swelled.

EVALUATION METHODS

Chapter 22 provides a comprehensive view of monitor-and-control processes. For salespeople, the most critical evaluation measure is sales performance versus sales objectives. Sales managers should also assess both the quantity and quality of selling effort. Are salespeople working hard? Are they working smart?

To assess selling effort, sales managers should use several measures — Table 17.6 — as a single measure can be misleading. Typically, sales managers at every level — district, regional, and national — receive regular data on direct reports and can access selective data deeper in the sales force as needed.

Measure	Value	Limitations
Calls per day	Identifies level of calling effort	Measures quantity of calls, not quality
Calls per account	Identifies level of calling effort	Measures quantity of calls, not quality
Calls per new account	Identifies where time is spent; links to sales strategy	Should be used together with calls per existing account
Calls per existing account	Identifies where time is spent; links to sales strategy	Should be used together with calls per new account

TABLE 17.6

MEASURES FOR ASSESSING A SALESPERSON'S EFFORT

REWARD SYSTEMS

Reward systems are powerful motivators for salespeople. To establish a truly motivating system, salespeople should answer "yes" to the following questions:

- Can I *achieve* my sales objectives?
- Do I *value* the rewards I will earn for meeting my sales objectives?
- Do I believe I will truly *receive* the rewards I earn?
- Is the reward system fair?

Sales reward systems can have several components:

- **Financial compensation.** The firm combines three financial rewards in various ways:
  - **Base salary.** Paid to the salesperson regardless of sales performance (in the short run).
  - **Bonus.** Reward paid for achieving quota — typically a target sales or profit level.
  - **Sales commission.** Variable compensation based on sales or profits. In some industries, like life insurance, salespeople earn no base salary and work strictly on commission.
- **Recognition.** This important reward is relatively inexpensive but can be a powerful motivator. Creative sales managers recognize salespeople for performance like highest revenues, best sales growth, most profitable sales, most new accounts, and/or most lost accounts retrieved. Many sales forces recognize high performers with membership in a President's club, often associated with an annual trip (with spouse) to an exciting destination.
- **Promotions and work assignments.** Promotions and more interesting and responsible job possibilities are highly motivating for some salespeople. Others may not value such advancement or change.

Generally, financial compensation is a salesperson's most important motivator. By developing a fair and consistent compensation plan, the firm drives the behavior it desires.

Every six months, 400–500 customers provide Siebel Systems (an Oracle division) with satisfaction data on its various departments and individual salespeople. These data drive bonuses and commissions. Salespeople do not receive full commissions until one year after a sale, and then only if customer satisfaction scores are up to par.

Marketing Question

Think about jobs you have had. How were you compensated? What types of incentives did the employer provide? What did you find demotivating?

KEY IDEA

➤ The firm's reward system should motivate salesperson behavior. Primary components are:
- Financial incentives
- Recognition
- Promotions and work assignments

➤ The primary ways to pay salespeople are:
- Salary
- Commission
- Bonus

Marketing Question

What are the challenges of consistently motivating a sales team? How would you address these challenges?

KEY IDEA

➤ The firm should develop rigorous systems for the sales force, including:

- Recruiting
- Selecting
- Training
- Coaching
- Retaining
- Replacing

Marketing Question

How would you go about identifying potential candidates for first-line sales manager positions?

KEY IDEA

➤ Strategic account managers are responsible for individual major customer.

KEY IDEA

➤ Successful strategic account management requires critical decisions in:

- Strategy
- Organization structure
- Human resources
- Systems and processes

TASK 6: STAFF THE SALES ORGANIZATION

Salespeople are one of the firm's most important resources. Sales managers must ensure the sales force is fully staffed and all territories are filled, at all times. To achieve this goal, sales managers must plan for natural attrition, dismissal, promotions, and/or transfers. Sales managers should *inventory* salespeople and have their own *pipeline* of candidates ready to move to a territory when one opens up.

Many firms have policies of recruiting salespeople internally; they may create career paths in related departments like sales support or customer service. Others recruit externally, continually interviewing candidates to bring in fresh perspectives and expertise.

The staffing process to hire and prepare effective salespeople involves several steps:

- **Recruiting.** Sizing and defining the pool from which the firm will select salespeople.
- **Selecting.** Using selection criteria to choose salespeople from the recruitment pool.
- **Training.** Ensuring salespeople have the knowledge, skills, and abilities (KSAs) to be effective.
- **Coaching.** Continuous efforts by first-line sales managers to improve selling effectiveness.
- **Retaining.** Maintaining high-performing salespeople.
- **Replacing.** Weeding out and replacing poorly performing salespeople.

KEY/STRATEGIC ACCOUNT MANAGEMENT

Realizing that the 80.20 rule applies to their revenue and profit distributions, many firms implement key/strategic account (SA) programs.[5] These firms identify the most important current and potential customers, then invest in them by providing additional resources and generally lavishing greater attention than on *regular* customers. Winning or losing a strategic account is a significant organizational event. In most SA programs, **strategic account managers** (**SAMs**) are responsible for building and sustaining relationships with individual strategic accounts. Generally, SAMs are responsible for many millions of revenue dollars annually; hence, they work with fewer customers than regular salespeople.

In recent years, domestic SA programs have evolved to managing regional and global accounts.[6] When a strategic account has far-flung operations, local salespeople are often responsible for local relationships. Typically, such salespeople report to a first-line sales manager but also have dotted-line relationships to one or more SAMs (or GAMs).

Successful strategic account programs adopt the *congruence model*, requiring critical decisions in four areas:

- **Strategy.** Includes deciding firm commitment to the strategic account program, overall resource allocation, number of SAs and revenue and profit targets, nominating and selecting criteria for SAs, and types of firm/SA relationships.
- **Organization structure.** Concerned with organizational placement of the SA program, reporting structure, and interfaces with other functions, notably the sales force.
- **Human resources.** Securing the appropriate personnel to be SAMs; includes other classic HR functions like training, retaining, and compensation.
- **Systems and processes.** Methodologies for helping SAMs do their jobs like SA planning systems, customer profitability, benchmarking, and best practice sharing.

KEY MESSAGES

- The marketing/sales interface should be seamless. Successful sales managers are true leaders.

- Effective sales managers must successfully complete six tasks.

- The first three sales management tasks address developing sales strategy:
  - **Task 1.** Set and achieve sales objectives.
  - **Task 2.** Determine and allocate selling effort.
  - **Task 3.** Develop sales approaches.

- The second three tasks focus on implementing the sales strategy:
  - **Task 4.** Design the sales organization.
  - **Task 5.** Create critical organizational processes.
  - **Task 6.** Staff the sales organization.

- Many firms are developing strategic account and/or global programs for their most valuable customers.

VIDEOS AND AUDIOS

Consultative Selling	v1702	Eric Baron	The Baron Group
Sales Force Compensation	v1703	Dave Cichelli	The Alexander Group
Managing Strategic (Key) Accounts	v1704	Hajo Rapp	Siemens AG
Becoming a Strategic Partner	v1705	Gus Maikish	IBM

v1702

v1703

v1704

v1705

IMPERATIVE 4

Design the Market Offer

....

PART C – DELIVERING CUSTOMER VALUE

CHAPTER 18

DISTRIBUTION DECISIONS cv1801

To access O-codes, go to **www.ocodes.com**

LEARNING OBJECTIVES

When you have completed this chapter, you will be able to:

- Understand the nature and function of distribution systems.
- Develop and implement effective distribution strategies.
- Trade off alternative forms of direct and indirect distribution.
- Identify challenges and opportunities in ongoing management of distribution channels.
- Manage power and conflict in distribution systems.

OPENING CASE: CISCO

Cisco is the world's leading supplier of products to power the Internet. A small portion of Cisco's more than $46 billion revenues goes though direct channels, well over 85 percent through 28,000 channel partners in 160 countries. Previously Cisco sold direct to end-user customers, but in the late 1990s shifted its major efforts to three types of intermediaries:

- **Tier 1 partners.** *Systems integrators including global players like Accenture, Oracle, and SAP, but also well-established local partners. Tier 1 partners integrate Cisco products with technology products from other firms to provide end-user customers with complete solutions.*

- **Tier 2 resellers.** *Intermediaries that sell to smaller end-user customers than Tier 1 partners. Reseller sales range from a few thousand to several million dollars; they secure Cisco products from distributors. Distributors hold inventory and provide logistics value to Cisco. Cisco may have thousands of resellers in a particular geography, but only a few distributors.*

- **Service provider partners.** *Mainly telecommunications firms that supply Cisco equipment to their customers. These channel partners may also make customer-service agreements to relieve customers of the management burden of operating Cisco equipment.*

Cisco's sales force works hand-in-hand with channel partners to serve large end-user customers. Salespeople develop end-user customer relationships and make joint sales calls with channel-partner salespeople. Channel partners are responsible for local relationships, developing business solutions, consultancy assistance, product delivery, after-sales support, and financing customer purchases. Cisco develops and monitors joint business plans with channel partners; they provide significant value to Cisco.

Cisco classifies channel partners as Premier, Silver, or Gold, based on partner investment in securing capabilities to provide value to end-user customers.[1] Higher value levels earn greater recognition from customers and greater resources and support from Cisco. This classification does not consider revenues, so some gold accounts are smaller than some premier accounts. Cisco's incentive system considers three performance categories:

- **VIP** — *Developing advanced technological expertise*
- **OIP** — *Seeking out new opportunities and/or new customers*
- **SIP** — *Developing new and innovative solutions*

Cisco encourages channel partners to earn VIP, OIP, and SIP incentives; an individual partner may earn incentives in more than one category. In the mid-2000s, Cisco introduced an innovative structure that placed all emerging-market countries, regardless of geographic location, into an emerging-markets organization. Hence, a country like Saudi Arabia, formerly part of the Europe, Middle East, and Africa (EMEA) region, no longer had to compete for resources with advanced western countries like France and Germany. The emerging-market organization contained channel partners from 140 developing countries around the world. Cisco's tasks in these markets were:

- *Develop sufficient channel partners to have good coverage. Cisco hired country managers and salespeople and identified partners in each country.*

- *Develop replicable channel-partner models by industry vertical to transfer across countries — like tourism, and oil and gas. Partners could be non-traditional — like Schlumberger in oil and gas markets.*

- *Work with country-level policy makers to encourage investment in information technology infrastructure and spur economic growth.*

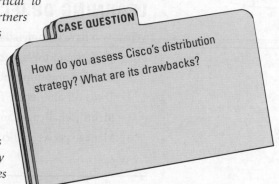

CASE QUESTION

How do you assess Cisco's distribution strategy? What are its drawbacks?

More than 95 percent of emerging-markets revenues go through channel partners (100 percent in many countries); annual growth rates exceed 40 percent. Having successfully established itself in many emerging markets, in 2011, Cisco folded emerging-market countries into a new global organization comprising three geographic regions.

Firm products reach customers through distribution channels. Distribution can be direct from supplier to customer, or it can be highly complex involving many intermediaries. Intermediaries fulfill many different functions and frequently enjoy mutually beneficial relationships with suppliers. But supplier and distributor goals rarely overlap completely; hence, distribution systems are riddled with conflict and power inequalities. FMCG firms like Colgate, Nabisco, and P&G work hard to secure good shelf positions in supermarkets. But they often compete with chains like Albertsons, Royal Ahold, and Walmart who put store brands in the best positions, and want suppliers to reduce prices and pay *slotting fees* for shelf space.

Power inequalities may prevent firms from making distribution innovations. Yet no distribution system lasts forever; new approaches that add value and reduce costs can unseat market leaders. Consider video rental: Traditionally, consumers rented from retail outlets like Blockbuster or Hollywood Movies. But, as we saw earlier, Netflix (Chapter 3 — Opening Case) allows consumers to order movies directly online, initially delivered by mail but now also available as video on demand.

Two Views of Distribution — Broad and Narrow

Inputs like raw materials, sub-assemblies, and assemblies undergo changes in *state*, *physical location*, and/or *time* before the firm delivers a finished product to an end-user customer.[2] The *broad view of distribution* includes all of these changes. For example, consider the delivery of prefabricated steel beams to an Argentinean builder.

- **Raw materials.** Iron ore, coal, and limestone are mined in Australia and separately shipped to an integrated steel manufacturer in Korea.
- **Processing equipment.** Sourced in Germany for use in Korea.
- **Capital**. Bank loans to finance equipment purchasing and working capital for manufacturing based on bank deposits made by Korean citizens.
- **Steel beams.** Manufactured in Korea.
- **Completed steel beams.** Shipped to a distributor in Argentina.
- **Finishing.** The Argentine distributor does minor finishing operations and delivers beams to the building site.

Major changes that these activities embrace include:

- **Change of state.** Iron ore, coal, and limestone into prefabricated steel beams.
- **Change of physical location.** Australian raw materials and German processing equipment shipped to Korea. Completed steel beams shipped to Argentina.
- **Change in time.** This process takes time to accomplish.[3]

Along with most marketers, we adopt a *narrow view of distribution*. We focus on changes in *physical location* and *time* of *finished* products. Marketing also addresses minor *state* changes like final processing and repackaging. Major state changes like turning iron ore, coal, and limestone into steel beams are the concern of manufacturing; procurement secures raw material and capital equipment; and finance secures capital.

Most people understand that firms create value by making *state* changes. Firms also create value by making *physical location* changes and in the *timing* of those changes. The Korean manufacturer creates value by forming steel beams from iron ore, limestone, and coal. But the Argentinean builder receives no value if the beams are in Korea or on a ship; they have value only at the building site. And unless they arrive on time, the entire construction project will stop. Delays may cost millions of dollars.

DISTRIBUTION SYSTEMS AND THEIR EVOLUTION

Table 18.1 identifies and describes intermediaries that facilitate supplier goods and services reaching consumers and/or other end-user customers. A **distribution channel or network** comprises a subset of these entities; the functions they perform and their interrelationships are continually in flux. Changes in customer needs, competitor actions, and environmental forces exert pressure. Leading indicators of impending change include unhappy consumers, end-user customers, and/or suppliers; complacent intermediaries; deteriorating system economics; market coverage gaps; new technology; outdated system interfaces; poor logistics; and unexplored channels.[4]

DISTRIBUTION ENTITY	DESCRIPTION OF DISTRIBUTION ENTITY
Agents, brokers, manufacturers' representatives	These entities have similar functions. Generally, they sell products but do not take title or physically handle goods. They may work for the supplier or the customer, or be impartial between supplier and customer.
Banks and finance firms	Provide financing for customers to aid in purchasing products.
Distributors	Provide promotional support for suppliers, especially for selective or exclusive distribution (discussed later). Often a synonym for wholesaler.
Retailers	Display and sell products to consumers. May operate at a fixed location — bricks-and-mortar stores, as traditional direct marketers, or on the Internet.
Shipping companies	Transport products.
Warehouse operators	Receive and inventory products, arrange product pickup, often break bulk.
Wholesalers	Primarily buy, take title to, store, and physically handle goods in large quantities. Usually break bulk — resell to retailers or industrial businesses.

TABLE 18.1

DEFINITIONS OF SELECTED DISTRIBUTION ENTITIES[*5]

* Developed in part from the American Marketing Association Glossary of Terms

Ultimately, customer needs drive distribution arrangements. Early in the life cycle, products are often unreliable and service needs are high; customers require help to make choices and support to use the new technology. These requirements diminish as customers become more self-sufficient. Customers may no longer require the benefits intermediaries provide, and early market leader distribution strategies become increasingly outdated.

The effectiveness of any distribution system changes over time, but suppliers often have difficulty making adjustments. Suppliers can revise prices overnight and, in the short run, develop new promotions or even add/delete products and services. By contrast, the firm's distribution arrangements often remain unchanged for many years, in part because of end-user customer loyalty to distributors. The average tenure of Caterpillar's 186 dealer relationships worldwide exceeds 50 years!

KEY IDEA

➤ A distribution channel comprises many enterprises, their interrelationships, and the functions they perform.

➤ Distribution system effectiveness changes over time.

➤ Distribution arrangements are longer lasting and more difficult to change than other marketing implementation elements.

Developing a Distribution Strategy

To develop distribution strategy, the firm must make several critical decisions:

- **Distribution functions.** What actions must take place in the distribution channel?
- **Distribution channel: direct or indirect?** Should the firm deal directly with consumers and/or end-user customers? Or should the firm use intermediaries, and if so, which ones?
- **Distribution channel breadth.** How many intermediaries should there be at each distribution level? For example, how many wholesalers and/or retailers? Should there be selectivity or exclusivity?
- **Criteria for selecting and evaluating intermediaries.** How should the firm decide whether a particular intermediary is appropriate for handling its products?

We focus largely on physical goods but distribution is also important for services. Our focal concern is sometimes with manufacturers, sometimes with other entities. Consider Whirlpool and Nike: Whirlpool manufactures kitchen appliances but Nike outsources production.

Marketing Question

Which distribution entities do a good job of providing recorded music to consumers? Why did you select them?

DISTRIBUTION FUNCTIONS

By completing many functions, distribution closes gaps in physical location and time between factory-finished products and consumers/end-user customers. Sometimes the supplier undertakes a particular function; other times intermediaries or end users do so. In a complex distribution channel, some functions, like physical movement, must be done several times.

Increasingly, channel members, especially retailers, work at enhancing the customer buying experience. Product display is critical but at Forum shops in Las Vegas, the experience of Atlantis rising and falling on the hour keeps customers in the store. The Mall of America (Minneapolis) attracts consumers to its 400 retail stores with Camp Snoopy (indoor amusement park) and Underwater World (walk-through aquarium). At Wizards stores (owned by toy manufacturer Hasbro), a game room occupies one-third of retail space. Conversely, Costco and Sam's Club offer minimal services and compete on price.

The firm should align incentives to motivate distribution channel entities to perform required functions. Actions that improve firm sales and profits should also benefit channel members.

DISTRIBUTION CHANNELS: DIRECT OR INDIRECT?

Figure 18.1 shows alternative channel designs for conducting various distribution functions:

- **Direct channels.** Suppliers manage most contact with consumers and end users.
- **Indirect channels.** Intermediaries like distributors, wholesalers, and retailers play a major role in transferring products to consumers and end users. Some indirect channels have a single intermediary; others have multiple intermediaries.

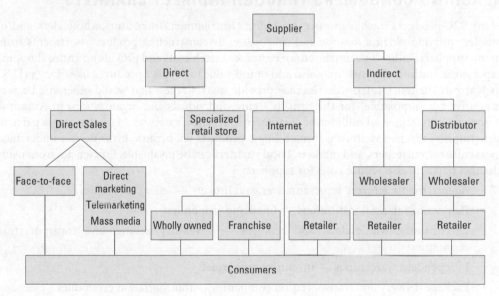

REACHING CONSUMERS THROUGH DIRECT CHANNELS

Direct distribution, combined with database marketing,[6] is a serious alternative to indirect distribution. In B2C, *direct distribution* has several forms:

FACE-TO-FACE DIRECT SALES. Direct customer contact can give suppliers intimate insight into customer needs. In advanced economies, direct selling and distribution costs are often too high for consumer goods. Regardless, Avon, Mary Kay, and Tupperware successfully sell and deliver products direct to consumers. In less-developed countries, lower incomes make personal selling more viable. When Citibank launched credit cards in India, face-to-face sales were quite successful.

DIRECT SALES USING DIRECT MARKETING, MASS MEDIA, AND TELEMARKETING/TELESALES. The firm makes contact with individual consumers; they receive products directly by package delivery from remote locations. The firm may initiate contact to target customer lists via *outbound* communications — firm-to-customer — or the customer may initiate via *inbound* communications — customer-to-firm. Regardless of communications mode, message central-ization gives the firm greater control and cost efficiencies in addressing customers. The high cost of face-to-face selling drives telemarketing/telesales.

INTERNET. The Internet is the fastest-growing *inbound* communications method for many product forms. Customers initiate the buying process at supplier websites. Some firms integrate the Internet with telesales: When a Landsend.com visitor clicks on the *help* icon, a salesperson uses instant messaging to help the potential buyer navigate the site. Internet sites offer lower prices on many products, reduce search costs, and often **disintermediate** wholesalers and bricks-and-mortar retailers.

SPECIALIZED RETAIL DISTRIBUTION. In this channel, the supplier controls product display and the customer experience in retail outlets. Retail outlets are either *wholly owned* by the supplier — Apple, Gap, Body Shop, and Starbucks; or *franchised* to a third party — H&R Block (tax preparation) and 7-Eleven (convenience stores). Many fast-food brands like KFC, McDonald's, and Taco Bell use **franchising**. Typically the franchisor develops the business model and seeks entrepreneurs to invest capital. The franchisee agrees to implement the franchisor's strategy and pays an initiation fee and ongoing fees.

REACHING CONSUMERS THROUGH INDIRECT CHANNELS

Many B2C products reach consumers via *indirect distribution*: Distributors, wholesalers, and/or retailers provide *physical location* and *time* value. By constructing product assortments from many suppliers, indirect channels reduce customer search costs and provide an entire shopping experience. Indirect channels may also add brand value to supplier products, like Macy's (U.S.) or Harrods (Britain). Intermediaries may provide market access that would otherwise be very expensive (or impossible) for the firm to secure. Individuals and organizations in Amazon's Associates program send millions of customers to Amazon's website. Market access is particu-larly important when venturing abroad. Many products fail because firms do not understand local cultures, customers, and markets. Local partners can be invaluable. Efficiencies from using channel partners also reduce costs for suppliers:

- Agents, manufacturers' representatives, and brokers — selling economies
- Banks and financial institutions — financing economies
- Distributors, wholesalers, and retailers — inventory, selling, and transportation economies
- Independent warehouses — inventory economies
- Package delivery and transportation companies — transportation economies

REACHING ORGANIZATIONAL CUSTOMERS

B2B firms also use both direct and indirect distribution to reach organizational customers:

- **Direct distribution.** Firms sell directly to end-user customers through on-the-road sales forces, telemarketing/telesales, direct marketing, and/or the Internet. (Few B2B firms operate retail stores.) Suppliers use various transportation methods to deliver products to customers.
- **Indirect distribution.** Some suppliers reach customers, especially small businesses, through retail stores — like Office Depot and Staples for office supplies. Plumbing, elec-trical, and home building firms purchase from Home Depot and Lowe's. More generally, many firms reach customers via distributors and wholesalers.

Distribution speed is increasingly important as firms use **just-in-time** (**JIT**) manufacturing and inventory systems to increase operating efficiencies. Industrial distributors must provide cus-tomers with complex product assortments in a timely manner. Typically, some requirements are

Marketing Question

Review the websites for L.L. Bean, Lands' End, or a direct marketer of your choice. Phone your firm and order a product. In a couple of days, order another product. What data did the firm request on each occasion? Did the firm remember you from the first order to the second order?

KEY IDEA

➤ Intermediaries offer value-added benefits like providing:

- Product assortments
- Shopping experience
- Market access

Also, they often reduce the costs of conducting various distribution functions.

predictable but others are not. Holding sufficient inventory to satisfy both predictable and unpredictable demand can be very expensive. Volvo partners with FedEx to manage demand fluctuations:

Volvo GM (VGM) Heavy Truck Corporation sells replacement parts via commercial truck dealers; VGM supplies dealers from regional warehouses. Parts inventories in Volvo warehouses were rising, but sometimes dealers could not secure needed parts because of stockouts! VGM worked with FedEx Logistics to set up a warehouse in Memphis (FedEx's hub). Dealers with emergencies call a toll-free number; FedEx ships the required parts and delivers to dealer offices, holds for airport pickup, or drops off at the required site. VGM closed three warehouses, reduced total inventory by 15 percent, and regained much business previously lost to stockouts.[7]

KEY IDEA

➤ **Direct channels**: Suppliers manage contact with consumers and end users.

➤ **Indirect channels**: intermediaries like distributors, wholesalers, and retailers play a major role in transferring products from suppliers to consumers and end users.

DISTRIBUTION CHANNEL BREADTH

Distribution channel breadth refers to the number of channel members the firm uses at a particular distribution level — like wholesalers or retailers. The firm can increase or decrease channel breadth as circumstances dictate.

The firm should also consider different types of distributor. Adding a new distributor type can be important when customers have preferred outlets. In the Pacific Northwest, consumers prefer to shop at *either* marine *or* forest-products distributors depending on their interests; each distributor type relates to specific problems and issues. Many firms use both types of distributor.

Adding new distributor types can be positive or negative. Tupperware halted a 15-year revenue slide by placing booths in shopping malls and selling over the Internet; later Tupperware added distribution in Target stores. With ready product availability, consumers no longer had a reason to go to Tupperware parties. Sales dropped 17 percent, profits 47 percent, and Tupperware's sales force by 25 percent as many "good, solid performers" left. Tupperware stopped distributing at Target; profits doubled.

An average Staples store carries 8,000 office-supply items; an average shopper spends $600–$700 annually. Staples.com offers 200,000 items; an average store *and* catalog shopper spends $1,200–$1,400. Staples installed in-store computer kiosks linked to Staples.com; sales jumped to $2,500 per store *and* catalog shopper. Each of Staples' 1,000 retail outlets now has at least four computer kiosks.

When the firm distributes through multiple channels, channel crossing becomes an issue — customers secure product information and/or try the product in one (or more) channels (showrooming), but purchase from a third channel. The first channel(s) provides free service — only the third channel earns **revenues**.[8] This problem is increasing for traditional channels as Internet commerce grows. The firm benefits from the sale, but some channel partners receive no revenues for their services. In the long run, this practice may lead to channel breakdown.

Firms have three broad **distribution-channel-breadth** options:

INTENSIVE DISTRIBUTION. When customers limit search, products should be easily available. The firm maximizes the number/type of outlets where customers buy. Intensively distributed consumer products include convenience goods like cigarettes and soft drinks. In emerging markets, intensive distribution is a critical strategic thrust for firms like Coca-Cola and P&G.

EXCLUSIVE DISTRIBUTION. When customers are willing to search and travel, the firm should be very careful in selecting outlets. When retailers provide brand equity and positive shopping experiences, a B2C firm may choose a few prestigious outlets.

SELECTIVE DISTRIBUTION. Selective distribution is a compromise between intensive and exclusive distribution. Too many outlets can lead to excessive competition; too few outlets and firm products are difficult to find. Sony and Samsung distribute products selectively, making careful outlet decisions.

Marketing Question

Best Buy discovered that many customers were examining products in its stores, then searching the Internet for better prices and placing orders online. How would you advise Best Buy?

Distribution breadth raises three related **distribution-exclusivity** issues:

- Should suppliers grant distributors geographic exclusivity?
- Should suppliers grant distributors product exclusivity?
- Should suppliers require distributors to be exclusive to its products?

CRITERIA FOR SELECTING AND EVALUATING INTERMEDIARIES

Clear and unambiguous criteria for selecting channel partners favor both suppliers and distributors. The firm should clearly specify the functions and performance standards distributors must meet. Would-be distributors can then fairly assess their capabilities versus supplier requirements.

Both the firm and distributors should recognize their separate obligations before making an agreement. To improve success probabilities, the supplier should ask several questions of potential distributors[9]:

- Does the distributor have adequate market coverage?
- How competent is distributor management?
- How does the distributor rate on aggressiveness, enthusiasm, and taking initiative?
- Is the distributor the appropriate size to do business with us?
- What is the distributor's credit and financial condition?
- What is the distributor's general reputation among suppliers and customers?
- What is the distributor's selling capability? What is its historic sales performance?
- Will the distributor forgo competitive products? Does it welcome the supplier's products?

The answers drive the supplier's decision to accept/reject a potential distributor.

PUTTING IT ALL TOGETHER: THE DISTRIBUTION STRATEGY

Figure 18.2 shows an eight-step method for developing distribution strategy.[10]

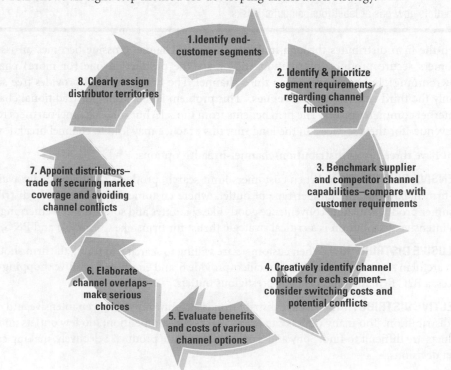

KEY IDEA

➤ Suppliers should select distribution channel(s) that are appropriate for their target segment(s) and perform the required functions.

➤ Providing customer benefits and values, rather than traditional industry practice, should guide supplier distribution choices.

KEY IDEA

➤ Critical distribution strategy decisions include:
- Functions to be performed
- Direct versus indirect channels
- Distribution channel breadth
- Criteria for selecting intermediaries

FIGURE 18.2

A STEP-BY-STEP APPROACH TO DEVELOPING AND IMPLEMENTING DISTRIBUTION STRATEGY

1. Identify end-customer segments
2. Identify & prioritize segment requirements regarding channel functions
3. Benchmark supplier and competitor channel capabilities—compare with customer requirements
4. Creatively identify channel options for each segment—consider switching costs and potential conflicts
5. Evaluate benefits and costs of various channel options
6. Elaborate channel overlaps—make serious choices
7. Appoint distributors—trade off securing market coverage and avoiding channel conflicts
8. Clearly assign distributor territories

MANAGING DISTRIBUTION CHANNELS

Ensuring top performance from distributors day by day can be a significant challenge. We discuss intermediary compliance, power inequalities, conflict, and the emerging-partnership model.

INTERMEDIARY COMPLIANCE

The firm must ensure that channel intermediaries stick to their agreements and implement its market strategies.

When firms compensate intermediaries with standard commissions for all products and customers, they may encounter compliance problems. The firm can better direct distributors by varying commissions by product and customer type. The firm can also tie evaluation and compensation directly to contract requirements like maintaining inventory levels, providing customer service, and ensuring customer satisfaction. Table 18.2 shows a partial list of performance measures for evaluating distributors.

Marketing Question

Have you or a friend or colleague ever been involved in distribution? Which issues posed problems? How did you solve them?

TABLE 18.2

CHANNEL MEMBER PERFORMANCE EVALUATION[11]

KEY IDEA

➤ A well-designed compensation system can help the supplier direct distributor efforts.

Criterion	Frequently Used Operational Performance Measures	
Sales performance	Gross sales Sales by product, market segment Sales growth over time	Actual sales/sales quota Market share Realized prices
Inventory maintenance	Average inventory maintained Inventory/sales ratio	Inventory turnover On-time delivery
Selling capabilities	Total number of salespeople Salespeople assigned to supplier's products	Salespeople assigned by geography Account managers assigned to strategic customers
Information provision	Sales data by customer Information on end-user needs	Information on inventories and returns

The firm should continuously evaluate intermediary performance. But the firm must remember that intermediary relationships are a two-way street. Distributors also evaluate supplier performance. Are the supplier's products selling? Are consumers and/or end-users complaining about supplier products? Are supplier deliveries prompt? Is the supplier easy to do business with?

POWER IN DISTRIBUTION SYSTEMS[12]

KEY IDEA

➤ Power is one channel member's ability to get another channel member to do what it wants it to do.

Power and conflict are endemic in distribution systems. **Power** is one channel member's ability to get another member to act as it wants. Typically, some channel members have more power than others; they also have different objectives. When a supplier is more powerful, it can impose demands. Microsoft sets many conditions for PC manufacturers. Similarly, powerful intermediaries may exert power when they enjoy strong market positions. Walmart pressures suppliers for low prices, takes control of product delivery, and demands adherence to supply-chain guidelines and sustainability initiatives. Over time, power tends to shift from one channel member to another.

Figure 18.3 shows several entities in a distribution system. We explore power relationships among manufacturers/brand owners, distributors/wholesalers, retailers, and end-user customers.

FIGURE 18.3

POWER IN DISTRIBUTION SYSTEMS

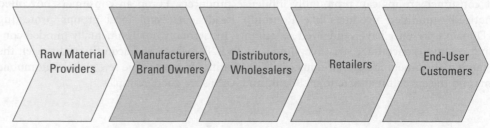

Raw Material Providers — Manufacturers, Brand Owners — Distributors, Wholesalers — Retailers — End-User Customers

MANUFACTURERS/BRAND OWNERS. In the early 20th century, manufacturers grew and increased power over distributors and wholesalers. Manufacturers researched customer needs, designed good products, and reduced costs and prices via mass production. Firms like Budweiser, Campbell's, Coca-Cola, Frito-Lay, Gillette, Kellogg's, Kodak, Levi's, and PepsiCo used consumer advertising to build powerful brands and become *channel captains*. Not all brand owners are manufacturers: Calvin Klein, Nike, and Polo outsource production but carefully manage distribution. Sometimes raw material/ingredient providers like NutraSweet (artificial sweetener) and Intel (chip maker) earn significant distribution power.

DISTRIBUTORS/WHOLESALERS. In the late 19th century, full-line, full-service wholesalers like Alexander T. Stewart and H.B. Claffin (long defunct) were *channel captains*. Wholesalers dominated U.S. consumer goods distribution, linking distant manufacturers with retailers and consumers.[13] Economic changes and growth in manufacturer and retailer power diminished these once-powerful intermediaries, but they still play a major role in many industries. As depicted in the movie *Blood Diamond*, De Beers buys nearly all of the world's raw diamonds and virtually sets diamond prices worldwide. **Value-added resellers (VARs)** are a new type of intermediary, building software modules on other firms' platforms and modifying computer hardware for niche markets. **Systems integrators** like Accenture and Infosys add value by installing/ servicing software and hardware from many vendors and making them work together.

Intermediaries often provide information value. Insurance brokers dominate business insurance by identifying and analyzing business risks and helping firms secure coverage from insurers. Intermediaries provide end-user customers with product choices and reduce the necessary number of supplier relationships. Consider the time you would spend to buy groceries from individual specialists: milk from a farm, produce from various growers, and meat from a butcher. Dairies, grocers, and butchers were once valuable intermediaries, but today supermarkets provide their products in one convenient location.

RETAILERS. Strong retail chains have evolved through industry consolidation. In the U.S., *category killers* like Best Buy, Home Depot, and Toys "R" Us virtually dictate industry direction. Tesco, ASDA, and Sainsbury's dominate British supermarkets; Walmart, Royal Ahold, Kroger, and Safeway also play a similar role in the U.S. National warehouse clubs like Costco and Sam's Club place significant pressure on grocery suppliers. Retailing has trailed many industries in globalization, but Carrefour (France), Walmart (U.S.), and vertically integrated Zara (Spain) have significant global operations.

Major retailers are often price leaders. They use buying power and efficient logistics to drive down costs, but must trade off cost efficiencies from standardized product assortments against more customer-responsive local variations. More sophisticated chains study customer needs and use powerful information technology to tailor assortments and offer consumers customized promotions. Frequently, they force suppliers to make direct payments to secure shelf space — aka **slotting fees**.[14] Data released a few years ago revealed that slotting fees for five major food companies — Campbell's, Coca-Cola, Kellogg's, Kraft, PepsiCo — were 14 percent of sales at retailers that sold their products. Coca-Cola spent $2.6 billion, Kraft $4.6 billion, and PepsiCo $3.4 billion just to optimize product placement on retailer shelves. At Christmas, to enhance its own highly profitable battery sales, Walmart *persuaded* Kodak to stop supplying batteries with its cameras. An important trend is the introduction of smaller stores: Traditional Best Buy stores average 38,750 square feet; Best Buy Mobile stores average 1,420 square feet.

END-USER CUSTOMERS. In B2C markets, individual consumers seldom have significant power, but consumer groups can profoundly influence producers. European consumers boycotted genetically modified products like Roundup Ready corn, and local groups protesting McDonald's presence have vandalized restaurants. In Germany, environmentally minded consumer coalitions encourage strict recycling laws. In B2B, mergers and acquisitions have left the remaining customers in several industries with significant power. The few global automobile firms and the aircraft manufacturers Boeing and Airbus are good examples.

KEY IDEA

➤ Over time, power shifts from one type of channel member to another.

KEY IDEA

➤ Intermediaries add value by reducing the number of relationships a supplier and end-user customer must have.
➤ Intermediaries occupy the nexus between suppliers and end-user customers.

Marketing Question

National retailers must balance the benefits and efficiencies of national purchasing with greater market responsiveness from decentralized buying. How would you advise Macy's?

Marketing Question

Many local retailers make short-term offers at highly discounted prices via Internet firms like Groupon that maintain e-mail subscriber lists. As consultant to a small retailer, would you advise signing up? Why or why not?

KEY IDEA

➤ Distribution channel members have high conflict potential:
  • Operating conflict
  • Strategic conflict

KEY IDEA

➤ Both *upstream suppliers* and *downstream customers* have various ways of initiating strategic conflict.

KEY IDEA

➤ Suppliers and distributors each have various ways to improve power positions.

CONFLICT IN DISTRIBUTION SYSTEMS

Because distribution channel members have multiple organizational relationships, the potential for conflict is high. *Operational conflict* occurs daily due to late shipments, invoice errors, unfulfilled promises, and/or unacceptable product quality. ESPN distributors (cable companies) continually complain about price increases but don't dare stop distributing ESPN. These conflicts are annoying, frustrating, and channel disrupting, so most members try to minimize them. But some firms, **downstream** customers or **upstream** suppliers, take actions that generate *strategic conflict* and *gain advantage*.

STRATEGIC CONFLICTS INITIATED BY DOWNSTREAM CUSTOMERS. Typically we see four types of conflict:

- **End-user customers grow and desire direct-to-supplier relationships.** Many suppliers start out using distributors to reach end-users (especially small businesses). As these customers grow, they believe that distributors provide insufficient value for the margins they receive. End users believe they can secure lower prices from direct supplier relationships.

- **Distributors become large and change the power balance.** When small single-location retailers characterized U.S. automobile retailing, manufacturers like GM, Ford, and Chrysler were very powerful. But the emergence of multiple-location mega-dealers like AutoNation, CarMax, and Potemkin, selling huge volumes from several producers, has shifted the power balance from manufacturers to retailers.

- **Distributors supply private-label products.** In B2C, many supermarkets, department stores, and other retail chains increasingly offer private label products. In B2B, innovative distributors disrupt channel relationships by offering their own branded products in competition with (or instead of) supplier products.

- **New buying influences enter the distribution channel.** In some industries, independent buying groups amass buying power for members. The Independent Grocers Association (IGA) and TruValue have long served small grocery and hardware stores respectively. In hospital supply, Novation and Premier purchase for many small and large hospitals.

STRATEGIC CONFLICTS INITIATED BY UPSTREAM SUPPLIERS. Here we see three types of conflict:

- **To reach end-user customers more efficiently, the supplier goes direct.** Sometimes suppliers believe they can be more effective than distributors. Suppliers bypass distributors and sell direct to end-user customers. Distributors typically resent these initiatives.

  The Internet has enhanced suppliers' ability to sell direct to end-users and hence increased the likelihood of conflict with intermediaries. Some firms place major efforts on Internet sales, but others restrict commercial Internet activity, directing website visitors to distributors so as to avoid conflict.

  Sometimes suppliers go direct in a limited way that minimizes conflict. Hershey, Mars, and Nike (NikeTown) have their own retail stores. Wholesalers and retailers believe these stores enhance supplier brands, so there is little conflict. Mattel sells a wide range of toys and apparel over the Internet, but avoids conflict by never undercutting distributor retail prices and not offering some popular items.

- **For better market penetration, the supplier adds new distributors and/or distributor types.** Suppliers sometimes initiate *horizontal conflict* by adding additional distribution types; current distributors are often unhappy with these initiatives. Hill's Science Diet pet food experimented with a store-within-a-store pet-shop concept in grocery channels, but lost support from pet shops and feed stores.[15]

PLANNING FOR POWER CHANGES

All things equal, the firm is better off having a stronger (versus weaker) power position relative to other channel intermediaries. If the firm initiates strategic conflict, it must assess the likely impact on other channel members and anticipate how they may respond. A strong negative response may hurt the supplier. Regardless, when major U.S. airlines eliminated travel-agent commissions and encouraged passengers to purchase flights at their websites, travel agents had few options and continued to sell airline seats.

THE PARTNERSHIP MODEL

When firms exercise power and generate strategic conflict, the underlying assumption is a *zero-sum game*. If the firm *wins*, another channel member *loses*, and vice versa. The **partnership model** assumes the possibility of a *positive-sum game*. By developing trust and working together, several channel members win; there are no losers.

P&G and Walmart have developed a highly effective distribution partnership. Walmart captures point-of-sale data for P&G products and transmits to P&G in real time using state-of-the-art information systems. By combining these data with seasonal purchasing trends, P&G improves forecast accuracy; gains purchasing, manufacturing, and packaging efficiencies; reduces inventory; and cuts costs. P&G codes products by store destination and places them directly on Walmart trucks at warehouse interchange points (**cross-docking**). Full trucks leave frequently for store-to-store deliveries. P&G and Walmart also use paperless systems for receiving goods and managing payables/receivables.[16]

By developing partnerships, channel members can establish joint strategic goals like cutting costs and reducing supply-chain inventory while limiting stockouts. Better forecasting allows retailers to offer more efficient product sets, conduct more effective promotions, and eliminate heavy discounts on unwanted merchandise. By working with retailers, suppliers can achieve lower production and distribution costs and better use promotional funds.

LEGAL ISSUES IN DISTRIBUTION

Other than pricing, distribution issues are more subject to legal concerns than any other marketing-mix variable. The legality of various distribution practices varies by industry and legal jurisdiction. What is illegal in the U.S. may be normal business practice elsewhere. Many **antitrust** lawsuits focus on distribution. Many violations occur when firms with significant market power take actions that reduce competition. Sometimes offended competitors file lawsuits; other times the federal government initiates legal action — through agencies like the FTC and/or DOJ-ATD. Critical U.S. issues include:

- **Exclusive territories.** Generally, the courts look unfavorably on arrangements that give distributors exclusive territories when this reduces competition.
- **Price discrimination.** The Robinson-Patman Act prohibits suppliers from collusion, and setting different prices for different buyers where this would reduce competition.
- **Resale price maintenance (RPM).** Under RPM, suppliers set *retail* prices. RPM used to be illegal, but a 2007 Supreme Court decision allowed its reestablishment in situations that do not impede competition.
- **Selecting and terminating distributors.** Generally, suppliers are free to select and terminate distributors.

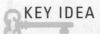

KEY IDEA

➤ The partnership model is an increasingly popular alternative to the power/strategic conflict approach. Channel members jointly set goals and work together for greater efficiency and effectiveness.

Marketing Question

Walmart is well known for driving tough bargains with suppliers to secure low prices. Yet Walmart has a partnership agreement with P&G. Why? Why does P&G partner with Walmart?

KEY IDEA

➤ Distribution laws vary by industry and legal jurisdiction. What is illegal in the U.S. may be normal business practice in other countries.

➤ In the U.S., many antitrust lawsuits involve distribution issues.

- **State and local laws.** Many local laws focus on distribution. Some states tightly regulate alcohol sales — especially type of outlet and opening hours. In some localities, *blue laws* prohibit certain types of store from opening on Sunday.
- **Tying agreements.** Sometimes, strong suppliers force resellers to sell their entire product lines. **Full-line forcing** is illegal if it reduces competition.

KEY MESSAGES

- A broad view of distribution embraces *changes in state, physical location*, and *time*. Marketing generally takes a narrow view — distribution includes *changes in physical location* and *time of finished products*.

- Distribution channels continuously evolve; the firm can gain competitive advantage by innovating its distribution arrangements.

- In developing distribution strategy, the supplier firm must make crucial decisions in four areas:
  - **Distribution functions.** What exactly must be done in the distribution channel?
  - **Distribution channels: direct or indirect?** Should the firm deal directly with consumers and/or end-user customers? Or should the firm use intermediaries? If so, which?
  - **Distribution channel breadth.** How many intermediaries at each distribution level? For example, how many wholesalers and/or retailers? Should there be exclusivity?
  - **Criteria for selecting and evaluating intermediaries.** How should the firm decide whether a particular intermediary is appropriate for handling its products?

- Implementing strategy through distributors can be very challenging. The supplier must clarify each channel member responsibilities, understand potential distributor problems, and take steps to gain compliance.

- Typically some channel members have more power than others, but each has options to improve its position. Distributors/wholesalers, manufacturers/brand owners, retailers, and consumers or end-user customers may each become *channel captains*. Many firms are moving to partnership models where each member gains.

- Operating conflict is endemic in distribution channels but most firms work at reducing it. Strategic conflict is more serious and may lead to significant change in channel relationships.

- The Internet is driving many changes in distribution.

VIDEOS AND AUDIOS

The Future of Retailing   v1802 📺   Mark Cohen   Columbia Business School

v1802

IMPERATIVE 4

Design the Market Offer

....

PART D – GETTING PAID FOR CUSTOMER VALUE

CHAPTER 19

CRITICAL UNDERPINNINGS OF PRICING DECISIONS cv1901

To access O-codes, go to **www.ocodes.com**

LEARNING OBJECTIVES

When you have completed this chapter, you will be able to:

- Discriminate between pricing strategy and pricing tactics.
- Recognize the key role of price in capturing customer value.
- Analyze the role of costs in pricing decisions.
- Incorporate competitor objectives and strategies in determining your prices.
- Relate strategic objectives to your pricing decisions.

OPENING CASE: SOUTHWEST AIRLINES

Southwest Airlines (SWA) is a major U.S. domestic airline. But in 1973, SWA was a puny upstart battling Braniff, a significant national/international carrier (based in Texas). That SWA survived a harrowing period was due in no small part to astute pricing decisions by CEO Lamar Muse.[1]

SWA was formed in the mid-1960s to fly among three major Texas cities — Dallas, Houston, and San Antonio. Flight distances ranged from 190 to 250 miles; flight times were about 45 minutes. Because SWA's proposed routes were within Texas, the Texas Railroad Commission, rather than the Civil Aeronautics Board (CAB), was its regulator. To start flying, SWA fought an extensive legal battle with Braniff and Texas International Airlines (TI) that went to the U.S. Supreme Court; SWA prevailed.

Braniff and TI fares from Dallas were $27 to Houston and $28 to San Antonio. SWA entered at $20 on both routes. Braniff and TI immediately met SWA prices. In November 1971, SWA added San

Antonio–Houston, also $20, and shifted some flights from Houston Intercontinental airport (HI) to the close-in Hobby airport (HH). In late 1972, SWA abandoned HI altogether.

During the next few months, SWA made several pricing moves. In November 1971, SWA experimented with $10 on weekend evening flights; in May 1972, SWA extended the $10 fare to all flights after 9 p.m. Load factors were higher than full-fare flights. In July 1972, facing a deteriorating financial condition, SWA raised its basic fare to $26, increased leg room, and provided free drinks. In one week, TI matched SWA's fares; Braniff followed two days later and increased onboard service.

By the end of July 1972, SWA's market share on the important Dallas-to-Houston route was 40 percent. Braniff's share dropped from 75 to 48 percent and TI's from 25 to 11 percent. But Braniff's passenger load was roughly the same as before SWA's entry. In October 1972, SWA replaced its $10 fares with $13 fares after 8 p.m. on weekdays and all weekend, supported with heavy advertising; traffic increased. SWA was now profitable on Dallas–Houston, but was unprofitable on Dallas–San Antonio where Braniff had four times as many flights. On January 22, 1973, SWA announced a "60-Day Half-Price Sale" from Dallas to San Antonio. Passenger loads increased threefold almost immediately and SWA reached an 85 percent load factor. On February 1, Braniff responded with a 60-day half-price "Get-Acquainted" sale at $13 for all Dallas–HH (but not HI) flights.

Muse said he believed the public should realize that SWA's highly reliable hourly service was worth $26, and that it should be disgusted at Braniff's action. SWA ran double-truck advertisements in Dallas and Houston newspapers with a picture of Muse, a statement — "Nobody's Goin' to Shoot Southwest Airlines Out of the Sky for a Lousy $13" — and all the reasons the public should not let that happen. SWA also printed 50,000 brochures with even stronger language. SWA gave these to all passengers, and off-duty hostesses handed them out at lunch hour in downtown Dallas and Houston.

SWA also offered a premium. It told passengers that the flight was worth $26; SWA would like them to pay $26. But if they felt they had to fly Braniff because of the $13 price, Southwest would also take them for $13. Those who paid the full fare received a gift — a fifth of Chivas Regal or Crown Royal, or a nice leather ice bucket. These items cost SWA around $7 to $8, but each had a retail value of around $13. Businessmen, in particular, put $26 on their expense reports and took a fifth of Chivas Regal home! On April 1, Braniff ended its "Get-Acquainted" sale; SWA also went back to $26. February 1973 was SWA's best month, and in March it made its first profit. SWA has not looked back.

CASE QUESTION

How do you assess Southwest Airlines' pricing actions? How do you assess Braniff's pricing actions? Could similar price actions occur in today's airline industry?

Pricing is critical for earning profits and creating shareholder value. Pricing is also pivotal for entering new markets, introducing new products, and changing firm objectives and/or strategy. Figure 19.1 shows that price decisions have greater profit impact than other profit levers. Reasons include:

- Price affects profit margin since margin equals price *less* cost.
- Price affects unit volume via the demand curve.
- Because price affects volume, it also affects costs via economies of scale.
- Price often affects customer quality and value perceptions.

FIGURE 19.1

HOW PRICING VERSUS OTHER FACTORS AFFECTS PROFITS[2]

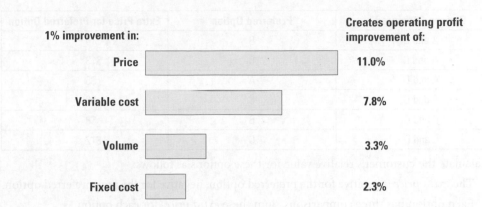

1% improvement in:		Creates operating profit improvement of:
Price		11.0%
Variable cost		7.8%
Volume		3.3%
Fixed cost		2.3%

KEY IDEA

➤ Price has a larger impact on profits than any other lever. Price affects:

• Margins
• Unit volumes
• Costs
• Customer value perceptions (often)

Pricing strategy is the firm's overall approach to setting price. The four critical underpinnings of pricing decisions are: *perceived customer value, costs, competition,* and *strategic objectives.* Too much emphasis on a single element leads to suboptimal pricing, like the destructive, downward pricing spiral that can follow from an excessive focus on competitors. Skilled pricing executives assess all factors before developing pricing strategy.

PERCEIVED CUSTOMER VALUE

KEY IDEA

➤ In setting prices, the firm should consider:

• Perceived customer value
• Costs
• Competition
• Strategic objectives

Excessive focus on a single element leads to suboptimal pricing decisions.

When increased competition brings more customer options, they invariably seek lower prices. As customers turn elsewhere, the firm may believe it has a pricing problem. More likely, it has a **perceived value** problem — the firm delivers insufficient value, or has not established a good price/value relationship. We focus on three value-related issues — creating, measuring, and capturing value; then we turn to a closely associated issue — price sensitivity.

CREATING VALUE

Chapter 9 showed that the value proposition is central to market strategy. The firm creates value in its offer primarily through non-price elements in the marketing mix — Chapters 12–18: product, promotion, distribution, and service.

Price may also create value by contributing to brand image. Products like Bentley, Ferrari, and Rolls-Royce automobiles; Rolex; and Apple's iPod are all perceived as quality brands. Factors outside the firm's control also affect customer value perceptions. On a hot day, you may value a can of Coke at $3 if that is your only option, but if you could also obtain Pepsi and 7-Up, Coke's value would be less.

MEASURING VALUE

KEY IDEA

➤ Critical topics in perceived customer value are:

• Creating value
• Measuring value
• Capturing value

Measuring the value customers perceive in firm and competitor offers is critical. If you don't know **customer value** perceptions, you'll never make good pricing decisions. Some approaches are:

DIRECT VALUE ASSESSMENT. The firm simply asks customers what they would pay for various products. Downward response bias is a concern, but carefully phrased questions can provide helpful data. In launching the original Ford Mustang, Lee Iacocca asked customers to estimate its price. Estimates were much higher than Ford's planned price, so Iacocca knew it would be a winner. The Mustang is the U.S.' best-selling new car ever.

DOLLARMETRIC METHOD. For each pair of options, customers say which they prefer and how much extra they would pay. Summing positive and negative differences reveals the relative value of the options. Table 19.1 shows the responses for four products: A, B, C, and D.

Options Compared	Preferred Option	Extra Price for Preferred Option
A and B	B	$10
A and C	C	$13
A and D	A	$5
B and C	C	$3
B and D	B	$8
C and D	C	$12

TABLE 19.1

ILLUSTRATIVE
DATA FROM THE
DOLLARMETRIC
METHOD

We calculate the customer's relative value for these options as follows:

- The *extra price* is positive for the preferred option, negative for the non-preferred option.
- Each option has three comparisons. Sum these *extra prices* for each option.
- Divide the sums of *extra prices* by three to calculate the average *extra price*.

  The average extra prices customers are prepared to pay for the four options are:

  $A = -10 - 13 + 5 = -18/3 = -6$ $B = 10 - 3 + 8 = 15/3 = +5$
  $C = +13 + 3 + 12 = 28/3 = +9.3$ $D = -5 - 8 - 12 = -25/3 = -8.3$

- Using the least valued option as a base, find the difference between the base and the average *extra price* for each option. This figure is what the customer would pay over the base.

  D is the least valued option so the base is –8.3. The *extra prices* for the other options are:

  $A = (-6) - (-8.3) = \$2.3$ $B = 5 - (-8.3) = \$13.3$ $C = 9.3 - (-8.3) = \$17.6$

PERCEIVED VALUE ANALYSIS. Table 19.2 identifies five steps for measuring an offer's perceived value. Data are best secured directly from customers, but sometimes experienced managers provide *best-guess* data that marketing research can validate.

Step	Description
1. Identify customer-required benefits/values	Identify the key benefits/values customers require — typically 5 to 8 — but exclude price.
2. Weight relative value of benefits/values to customers	Weight each benefit/value by allocating 100 points based on its importance to customers. Weights sum to 100.
3. Rate each offer from the various suppliers	Rate each offer based on how well customers believe it delivers the required benefit/value (1 = poor; 10 = excellent).
4. Develop benefit/value scores	For each offer, form individual benefit/value scores by multiplying the results of step 2 and step 3 for each benefit/value. Benefit/Value score = Weighting × Rating.
5. Develop the perceived value scores	For each offer, sum the individual benefit/value scores.

TABLE 19.2

MEASURING THE
PERCEIVED VALUE
OF AN OFFER

Table 19.3 shows a numerical illustration: A, B, and C represent three different suppliers of easy chairs. Perceived value measures for each option are in bold. (We note prices in the table.) The results and interpretation are:

- **Perceived value.** Supplier B at 820 offers the greatest perceived value, followed by A — 665; and C — 580.
- **Price.** Supplier A has the highest price — $500; followed by B — $450; and C — $300.

Supplier C has the lowest perceived value and the lowest price, but A and B are misordered. Supplier B has the greatest perceived value — 820 versus 665 for supplier A. But supplier A's price is higher — $500 versus $450. Since supplier B provides greater value for a lower price, it should be gaining market share.

Marketing Question

The price for *Capon's Marketing Framework* is 80 percent less than the price of competitor books. How should Wessex Press address a potential concern with price/quality perceptions?

Marketing Question

The prices for *Managing Marketing in the 21st Century* (600 pages) and *Capon's Marketing Framework* (360 pages) are identical. Do you agree with this pricing decision? Why or why not?

TABLE 19.3

ILLUSTRATION:
PERCEIVED VALUE
ANALYSIS FOR
SUPPLIERS OF
EASY CHAIRS

Benefits Required	Relative Importance Weighting	Supplier A Price = $500		Supplier B Price = $450		Supplier C Price = $300	
		Rating (1–10)	Total	Rating (1–10)	Total	Rating (1–10)	Total
Chair design	20	5	100	7	140	6	120
Comfort	30	6	180	8	240	4	120
Fabric quality	15	10	150	9	135	8	120
Fabric design	15	5	75	7	105	4	60
Ease of purchase	20	8	160	10	200	8	160
Grand Total	**100**		**665**		**820**		**580**

ECONOMIC ANALYSIS — ECONOMIC VALUE FOR THE CUSTOMER (EVC). Many B2B firms use EVC — the maximum price customers will pay — to calculate the economic value of new products. EVC analysis depends critically on competitive products in the customer's choice set. EVC helps clarify firm options: Should the firm add more value for a higher price or provide less value for a lower price? Chapter 4, p. 56 shows an EVC calculation.

PRICE EXPERIMENT. The firm offers the test product at different prices in different market areas, like geographic locations. Sales levels at different prices reflect customer value.

CAPTURING VALUE

The firm incurs many costs to develop an offer; it creates value if these costs are less than the value customers perceive. Figure 19.2 shows how price apportions the created value: The firm retains some value; customers receive some value. High prices imply that the firm retains most value; low prices imply that the firm transfers most value to customers.

FIGURE 19.2

PRICING AS
VALUE SHARING

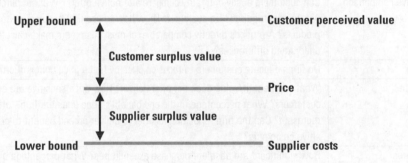

Most firms develop new products, then set prices based on costs or some value estimate using a method like we just discussed. By contrast, Avon starts with the value it wants a new product to deliver to customers, then sets a target price. Avon translates this price into cost parameters that enable it to meet profit targets. Engineering and manufacturing must then design a product/production process that delivers desired customer value within the cost parameters.[3]

KEY IDEA

➤ Price apportions value
— some to the firm,
some to customers.

CUSTOMER PRICE SENSITIVITY

Reducing price a little (increasing customer value a little) may lead to a major increase in customer purchase volume. Other times, customers may only buy more if the price reduction is large (major increase in value). (Equivalent effects hold for price increases.) Sometimes customers are **price sensitive**; other times they are **price insensitive**. Classical microeconomics focuses on price sensitivity at the market level; we also discuss individual price sensitivity.

MARKET-LEVEL PRICE SENSITIVITY. Figure 19.3 shows elastic and inelastic **demand curves**:

- **Price elasticity.** When price goes down a little, volume increases significantly; when price goes up a little, volume decreases significantly. Includes products like many grocery items.
- **Price inelasticity.** Volume does not change much, even with significant price changes.[4] Includes products like critical raw materials, electricity, and heart pacemakers.

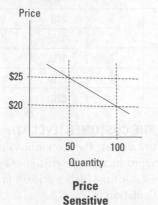

Price
Sensitive

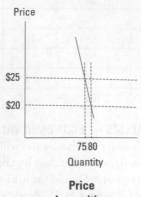

Price
Insensitive

FIGURE 19.3

MARKET DEMAND
CURVES

> ### *Marketing Question*
> How should firm marketing efforts differ between price-elastic versus price-inelastic markets?

INDIVIDUAL CUSTOMER PRICE SENSITIVITY. Markets are rarely homogeneous. Some customers place high value on an offer; other customers value the offer less. Some consumers are price sensitive because disposable income is low and/or they face financial demands. Some business customers are price sensitive because competitors are cutting prices, and profits are under pressure. Customers with full information on alternatives, benefits/values, and prices tend to be more price sensitive than those with less information. Table 19.4 provides a fairly comprehensive list of factors affecting price sensitivity.

Factors	Related Questions
Competitive comparison	Can customers easily and fairly compare alternative offers? Without purchasing? Are experts required? Do customers know how to use firm and competitor products? Are prices directly comparable, or must customers make calculations to understand differences?
Education	Do firms educate customers to focus on price by fierce price competition?
End benefit	What end benefit/value does the offer deliver? How price sensitive are end-user customers? What percentage of the end benefit's price does the firm's offer represent? Can the firm reposition its offer to deliver an end benefit to price-insensitive customers?
Expenditures	How significant are absolute purchase expenditures? What percentage of annual spending, income, or wealth does the purchase represent?
Fairness	How does the current price compare to customer experience with similar products? What do they expect to pay? Is the price justified?
Inventory	Do buyers hold inventory? Do they expect current prices to be temporary?
Non-monetary costs	What effort, time, and/or risk must customers expend to make a purchase?
Perceived substitutes	What competitive offers and prices do customers consider? Can the firm influence customer price expectations via positioning decisions?
Price/quality	Are price and quality related for competitor products?
Shared cost	Do customers pay the full cost? If not, what portion do they pay?
Switching costs	What costs/investments would customers incur if they switched suppliers? Are they locked into current suppliers? For how long? Can the firm encourage switching?
Terms	Are financing options available and clearly communicated?
Unique value	How do customers weigh elements of the firm's offer that influence their decisions? Is the firms' offer differentiated from competitors? Can the firm persuade customers some offer elements are more important than others?

TABLE 19.4

FACTORS AFFECTING
INDIVIDUAL CUSTOMER
PRICE SENSITIVITY

> ### *Marketing Question*
> Are airline tickets, theater tickets, health club memberships, milk, and HIV medication price elastic or price inelastic? How did you decide?

COSTS

Costs are important for setting prices. After all, costs represent one-half of the profit equation: *Profit = sales revenues – costs*. In practice, many firms use costs for setting prices, but often do so inappropriately. Because you must understand these issues, we start with them. Then we show how the firm *should* use costs in pricing decisions.

THE INAPPROPRIATE ROLE FOR COSTS: COST-PLUS PRICING

Cost-plus pricing is a pricing methodology used by most firms, harkening back to our earlier discussion of an *internal* orientation — Chapter 1. Despite its popularity, it is the wrong way to set prices.[5] Cost-plus pricing proceeds simply by identifying product costs, then adding a pre-determined profit margin (mark-up). Table 19.5 shows how this works:

Variable costs	$400,000
Total fixed costs	$300,000
Total costs	$700,000
Standard mark-up: 15% of costs	$105,000
Price	**$805,000**

Advantages of cost-plus pricing are:

- **Profitability.** All sales seem profitable as price must, by definition, be above cost.
- **Simplicity.** If the firm knows its costs, pricing is simple. Anyone can do the math.
- **Defensibility.** Legally acceptable and often required for government and other cost-plus contracts.

Regardless, cost-plus pricing has four main disadvantages:

PROFIT LIMITATIONS. Customer value has no role in price-setting:

- **Prices are too low.** Customers value the offer at more than the cost-plus price — suppose $900,000 in the Table 19.5 example. By setting price at $805,000, the firm forgoes $95,000 profit on each item sold: $900,000 less $805,000 = $95,000.
- **Prices are too high.** Customers value the offer at less than the cost-plus price — suppose $750,000 in the Table 19.5 example. They will not purchase at $805,000. The firm forgoes $50,000 profit on each item it could have sold at $750,000: $750,000 – $700,000 = $50,000.

In both cases, the firm sets prices incorrectly because it has not assessed customer value. Cost-plus pricing leads to over-pricing in price-sensitive markets and under-pricing in price-insensitive markets. Cost-plus pricing also leaves the firm vulnerable to competitors. By estimating firm costs, competitors can predict firm prices.

INAPPROPRIATE TREATMENT OF FIXED COSTS. Firms frequently classify costs as fixed and variable — Table 19.5:

- **Variable costs.** Vary directly with the volume of sales and production. Variable costs usually include raw materials, utilities to power production machines, direct labor, and sales commissions.
- **Fixed costs.** Do not vary with the volume of sales or production, over a reasonable range. Fixed costs include overhead and allocated items like depreciation, rent, salaries, and SG&A (selling, general, and administrative expenses).

As noted, the firm's cost-plus price equals costs plus a predetermined margin.

Cost per unit = *variable* cost per unit plus *fixed* cost per unit

Variable cost per unit is relatively straightforward, but calculating fixed cost per unit is illogical:

1. Fixed cost per unit equals fixed costs divided by number of units sold.
2. But the number of units varies with the price.
3. Hence, to set the price, price is an input to the calculation; this makes no sense!

In practice, many firms arbitrarily assume some sales level to calculate fixed costs per unit.

ARBITRARY OVERHEAD ALLOCATIONS. Suppose a firm has two business units, A and B; A is comfortably profitable but B is not. Corporate may reduce B's overhead allocation and increase A's. B's fixed costs are reduced, but A's are increased. Such financial machinations are typical of firms striving to even out profits across products. But they can be highly demotivating!

MISMATCH WITH MARKET REALITIES. When demand falls, logic suggests the firm should lower prices. Pure cost-plus pricing does not allow such action. As sales fall, and the firm spreads fixed costs over lower volumes, fixed costs per unit increase — and so must price! When demand surges, logic suggests the firm should raise prices. But the firm spreads fixed costs over larger volumes, and fixed costs per unit decrease. And so must price! Variable mark-ups based on demand can partially solve this problem.

APPROPRIATE ROLES FOR COSTS

Cost-plus pricing is the lazy way to set prices. But we should not underestimate the role costs play in price-setting. Costs are important in three critical situations:

BIRTH CONTROL. Costs are particularly important for new product introduction. Typically, a new product must meet or exceed financial criteria like the firm's **hurdle rate** to receive go-ahead approval.[6] The firm bases cash flow estimates on target prices, volumes, and costs. The relevant costs are *fully loaded costs*, meaning they include all incremental costs related to the new product, *including* incremental overhead.

DEATH CONTROL. Costs are also important when the firm is considering dropping a product. The relevant cost is the *marginal cost* — the cost to make and sell one additional unit. Marginal cost includes all variable costs plus some incremental fixed costs,[7] but *excludes* all allocated overhead. The marginal cost is the **floor price**.

PROFIT PLANNING. Birth control and death control are special cases; the major role for costs is profit planning. The firm explores various possible prices and estimates unit volumes and unit costs. The firm uses these data to forecast sales revenues and profits.

COMPETITION

The firm should always consider competitor prices. Basing the firm's price on competitor prices is legal and ensures price parity, but focusing too heavily on competitor pricing strategies has distinct disadvantages:

- *Price parity* with competitors devalues attributes/features and benefits/values, and tends to *commoditize* products. Customers then focus buying decisions on price.
- An *excessive price focus* may lead to losses for everyone, both the firm and competitors.

Generally, the firm should not focus on beating the competitor's *price*. Rather, the firm should beat the competitor's *offer* — product, service, and other marketing-mix elements. The firm should attempt to make offers with greater value per unit price than competitors. *Offer* superiority is crucial, not *price* superiority. Of course, price plays a critical balancing role.

KEY IDEA

➤ In cost-plus pricing, the firm identifies its costs and adds a profit margin.

➤ Cost-plus pricing does not consider customer value.

KEY IDEA

➤ Firms often determine fixed costs per unit arbitrarily by assuming some level of sales or production.

Marketing Question

What would be the implications for Apple and Verizon if they based prices for the iPod and cell phone service, respectively, on cost?

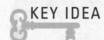

KEY IDEA

➤ Costs have three important price-setting roles:
- Birth control
- Death control
- Profit planning

KEY IDEA

➤ In high fixed cost/ low variable cost oligopolies, competitors often cut prices to gain extra volume. Prices can spiral downward and profits vanish.

HOW WILL COMPETITORS RESPOND TO FIRM PRICE CHANGES?

When making price changes, the firm should always consider likely competitor responses. Although pricing tactics can be quite complicated, basically competitors have three pricing options — *raise*, *hold*, or *lower*. Whether or not firm price moves are successful depends on competitor choices.

Assessing likely competitor response is always important, but is vital in oligopolies with few major competitors, high fixed costs, and low variable costs (as in airlines and many highly capital-intensive industries). When several competitors have poor profits, sometimes one firm cuts price to gain volume and better cover fixed costs. Competitors follow and prices spiral downward. Sometimes firms launch *trial balloons*, strategic pre-announced price intentions to gauge likely competitor response. Warnings and other signals (Chapter 5) may pre-empt competitors, but can raise antitrust issues. Successful and unsuccessful price leadership examples are:

Oligopoly Pricing

Successful price leadership. Coca-Cola raised concentrate price by 7 percent, twice the usual rate. Two weeks later, PepsiCo announced a similar increase.

British Aluminum Company (BACO) competed fiercely against Alcoa and Alcan in the low-growth, barely profitable British aluminum oligopoly. BACO divided the market into three: BACO's long-term contract customers — *ours*; competitors' long-term contract customers — *theirs*; and switchers — *up-for-grabs*. BACO resolved not to lose any *our* business on price. If it did lose, BACO *punished* the competitor by pricing low at one of *theirs*. BACO effectively executed this *tit-for-tat* strategy; Alcoa and Alcan *got the message*.

Unsuccessful price leadership. American Airlines (AA) attempted to change the pricing structure for domestic U.S. airlines. American West, Continental, Delta, Northwest, United, and USAir quickly followed AA's lead. But TWA under-cut AA's prices by 10 to 20 percent, and the attempt failed.

KEY IDEA

➤ Rampant price-cutting is disastrous for all but the low-cost producer.

Marketing Question

Select a product and then search the Internet for different prices. Do the prices vary? Why? If you were to purchase, which supplier would you use? Why?

HOW SHOULD THE FIRM RESPOND TO COMPETITOR PRICE REDUCTIONS?

The firm's response depends on its market position. Generally, strong firms should match price cuts only after exhausting other options. But weak firms with minimal sustainable differential advantage may have to respond right away. Only the low-cost producer wins when price-cutting is rampant; how that firm uses its cost advantage determines other competitors' fates.

Firms with dominant market shares often face severe price competition from small competitors and/or new entrants. These competitors may believe the leader:

- Has not carefully managed costs, and assumes its own costs are lower.
- Does not know individual product costs because of difficulties allocating overhead.
- Will not retaliate directly because it would sacrifice profits on its much larger volume.

Unless demand is *price elastic*, the firm should minimize direct price-cutting responses. The nature of competitive price reductions governs the firm's price and non-price options.

Price options include price retaliation in a different segment, selective price cuts, introducing a lower priced *fighting* brand, and — ultimately — cutting prices across the board. *Non-price options* include signaling to competitors, investing in fixed cost expenditures to reinforce the firm's position, clarifying and reinforcing the price/quality relationship, changing the basis of competition (for example, by bundling), and reducing customers' bargaining power by making pricing opaque. If these actions fail, the firm may have to partially or totally withdraw.

STRATEGIC OBJECTIVES

Choosing strategic objectives is a major component of developing market strategy. The three major options are increase volume and/or market share, maximize profits, and maximize cash flow. Generally, each strategic objective relates to a particular pricing strategy:

MAXIMIZE GROWTH IN VOLUME AND/OR MARKET SHARE. The firm must offer high customer value — a value/price (V/P) ratio superior to competitors. Appropriate conditions are:

- Deep pockets to absorb initially low profit margins
- Desire to deter competitors
- Good ability to cut costs in the future
- Price-elastic market
- Sufficient capacity to fulfill increased demand

Ryanair's price leadership in European air travel and P&G's aggressive price strategy in disposable diapers follow this **penetration-pricing** approach.

MAXIMIZE PROFITABILITY. When the firm's paramount objective is maximizing profits, it provides less value to customers and retains more for itself as profit. Firms use this **skim-pricing** approach when products have patent protection, like pharmaceuticals, or offer high value, like pioneering high technology products. Apple used a skim-pricing strategy for the iPhone. Introduced at $599, Apple reduced price to $399 after just two months. Less than one year later, Apple priced the new iPhone 3G at $199.

> ### Penetration Pricing and Skim Pricing
>
> Here we review *penetration pricing* and *skim pricing*, introduced in Chapter 10. These pricing strategies correspond to different strategic objectives: maximizing growth and/or market share, and maximizing profits, respectively.
>
> **Penetration pricing**. The firm provides significant customer value by setting prices close to costs. Volume increases, unit costs fall, the firm reduces price, and volume increases ... in a virtuous spiral. The firm forgoes high profits today in favor of achieving high volumes and ultimately earning profits from high unit volumes, but low profit margins.
>
> **Skim pricing**. The firm retains value for itself by pricing high. It earns high profit margins, but provides less value to its relatively few customers. The firm reduces prices periodically — sequential skimming, to attract increasing numbers of customers. These customers experience greater value in part because of the original higher-price framing.

MAXIMIZE CASH FLOW. If the firm plans market withdrawal, maximizing cash flow is often a good short-term strategic objective. In Chapter 10, we discuss *harvesting* products as the approach to short-term cash-flow maximization.

KEY MESSAGES

- Pricing is a big deal. Pricing decisions have a major impact on profitability.

- Four critical considerations should enter firm pricing decisions: perceived customer value, costs, competition, and strategic objectives.

  - **Perceived customer value**. The firm must make key decisions about creating, measuring, and capturing value. The firm must understand customer price sensitivity.

  - **Costs**. Many firms use cost inappropriately by implementing cost-plus approaches to setting price. Costs have three proper roles: birth control, death control, and profit planning.

  - **Competition.** Critical firm issues are predicting how competitors will respond to price changes, and deciding how to respond to competitor price reductions. The firm can take a variety of price and non-price actions.

  - **Strategic objectives**. The firm should link strategic objectives — growth in volume and/or market share, maximizing profits, and maximizing cash flow, to pricing actions.

VIDEOS AND AUDIOS

| Pricing | v1902 📹 | Reed Holden | Holden Advisors |

v1902

IMPERATIVE 4

Design the Market Offer

CHAPTER 20

SETTING

PRICES cv2001

To access O-codes, go to **www.ocodes.com**

LEARNING OBJECTIVES

When you have completed this chapter, you will be able to:

- Set price for a new product.
- Change price for an existing product.
- Manage and monitor pricing tactics.
- Use the pricing toolkit and price waterfall concept for price setting.
- Assess several approaches to setting prices.
- Address several pricing issues.
- Design a system for price management.
- Converse about legal and ethical issues in pricing
- Integrate pricing with other marketing implementation elements.

OPENING CASE: ORACLE CORPORATION

Oracle develops, manufactures, distributes, and services databases and middleware software, application software, and hardware systems worldwide. Oracle's 2012 $37.2 billion revenues and back-to-back years of 20 percent-plus net profit margins were a sharp improvement from a decade earlier.

In the late 1990s and early 2000s, Oracle competed strongly with Microsoft and IBM in the small- and medium-size business (SMB) software market. Oracle pursued a clear pricing strategy, placing its list prices online for customers, implying pricing rigidity and fair pricing for all. But in the early 2000s, IBM and Microsoft lowered prices for enterprise databases for SMB customers. Oracle reacted strongly by offering large discounts to close deals. Many customers delayed purchase commitments until the end of the quarter, anticipating that Oracle salespeople would offer heavily discounted prices to make their numbers. As competition between IBM, Oracle, and Microsoft heated up, Oracle adopted price competition as a strategic weapon. But Oracle's pricing actions led to significant margin erosion and did not impede IBM and Microsoft's determination to fight for revenues.

To address decreasing margins, Oracle pursued an aggressive acquisition strategy so as to offer customers a more compelling value proposition. Between 2005 and 2009, Oracle acquired more than 50 software firms. Oracle invested more than $30 billion in this effort.

By pursuing acquisition in the context of a deep understanding of customer needs, Oracle could offer customers very attractive product bundles, and incentivize them to purchase additional software for integration with database software. Oracle's acquisitions also brought an extensive customer base to which it then offered integrated solutions. Oracle secured innovation and revenue growth, and constructed a software ecosystem whose constituent products worked well together.

In addition to offering integrated solutions, Oracle's ecosystem created high customer switching costs and allowed it to ease out of the price war with IBM and Microsoft. Oracle's new strategy even allowed it to raise prices by 20 percent in the 2009 economic slowdown. Oracle became a one-stop shop for many customers, keen to avoid the high financial and organizational costs and risks of migrating databases from one software supplier to another.

Oracle's financial results demonstrated the success of its strategy. Revenues increased from $9.6 billion in 2002 to $37.2 billion in 2012. The stock market reacted favorably: Oracle's stock price increased from $11 in 2003 to $34 in 2013.

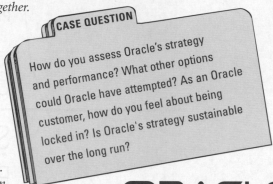

CASE QUESTION

How do you assess Oracle's strategy and performance? What other options could Oracle have attempted? As an Oracle customer, how do you feel about being locked in? Is Oracle's strategy sustainable over the long run?

Using Chapter 19 as background, Chapter 20 shows the mechanics of price setting. The firm should use the four factors we discussed — *perceived customer value, costs, competitors,* and *strategic objectives* — to approach price-setting holistically. The firm starts with perceived customer value, considers costs, then factors in competitors and its strategic objectives.

SETTING PRICE FOR A NEW PRODUCT

Ace (fictional firm) is setting price for a new manufacturing furnace. Ace believes the furnace offers superior value versus competitor Beta. Table 20.1 shows data that Ace collected. Customer startup costs and post-purchase costs are the same for both Ace and Beta. To frame the *right* approach for setting price, we first show improper methods — cost-plus and competitive-equivalence approaches. Then we introduce the correct method:

Beta	Furnace price	$260,000
Ace	Economic value to the customer (EVC)	$360,000
Ace	Direct out-of-pocket cost: variable and fixed	$100,000
Ace	Fully loaded cost, including overhead allocations	$160,000

TABLE 20.1

DATA FOR PRICE-SETTING COLLECTED BY ACE FURNACE

IMPROPER APPROACHES

COST-PLUS PRICING. Since the pricing decision concerns a new product, Ace must consider the fully loaded cost — $160,000. Commonly used mark-ups in the furnace industry are 75 percent and 50 percent. Price options are:

>   75 percent mark-up: Price = $160,000 × 1.75 = **$280,000**

>   50 percent mark-up: Price = $160,000 × 1.5 = **$240,000**

Note that at 75 percent mark-up, Ace's price exceeds Beta's — $280,000 versus $260,000. At 50 percent mark-up, Ace's price is less than Beta's — $240,000 versus $260,000. We do not know which is a *better* price for Ace.

➤ **Setting Price for a New Product**

Incorrect approaches:
- Cost-plus
- Competitive equivalence

Correct approach:
- Determine maximum price
- Determine minimum price
- Set price based on:
  - Strategic objectives
  - Likely competitive response

COMPETITIVE EQUIVALENCE PRICING. Strict competitive equivalence suggests that Ace set a $260,000 price, the same as Beta. But Ace offers considerable extra value. If Ace sets price at $260,000, it should sell lots of furnaces. But does a $260,000 price represent appropriate value-sharing between Ace and its customers? Note: This approach does not consider Beta's response.

THE *RIGHT* WAY TO SET PRICE

Figure 20.1 diagrams the recommended three-step approach:

- **Step 1: Determine the maximum price.** The maximum price is the EVC from Ace's furnace — $360,000.[1] At $360,000, rational customers should be indifferent between furnaces from Ace and Beta. (Of course, customers may believe Ace's furnace poses a greater risk because the new product has no track record — we ignore this factor in the illustration.)

- **Step 2: Determine the minimum price.** The minimum price is Ace's fully loaded cost — $160,000. (Ace earns profit contribution at any price above direct out-of-pocket cost — $100,000, but this is an incorrect figure for the minimum price of a new product.)

- **Step 3: Set the price based on Ace's strategic objectives and Beta's likely competitive response.** From steps 1 and 2, Ace's price should be between $360,000 and $160,000 — the crucial question is where. Ace should consider its strategic objectives and its forecast of Beta's likely response — probably correlated factors. Possible strategic objectives are:

  - **Toehold.** Ace wants a market presence but has little other ambition. Perhaps Ace identified a small high-price segment. Ace sets price around **$320,000**. Sales will be low, but profit margins will be high. Beta is unlikely to respond.

  - **Short-term profit.** Ace has greater ambition than the toehold option, so price is closer to Beta's $260,000. Because Ace offers greater customer value, it may set the price between **$260,000** and, say, **$280,000**. Ace will probably take some volume from Beta — the closer Ace's price to $260,000, the more likely Beta will reduce price. Prices significantly above $260,000 signal Beta that Ace wishes to avoid price competition.

  - **Market share.** Ace is ready to battle Beta for market share. At $260,000 and below, Ace offers customers significant value. Between **$200,000** and **$220,000**, Ace may sell many furnaces with good profit margins. But these prices will encourage a strong response from Beta. Ace must plan how to address Beta's likely actions.

When setting price, Ace should also consider potential customer lifetime value (CLV). Ace should ask several questions. Is this a one-time purchase, or will customers purchase more furnaces? Can Ace sell furnace parts and accessories and/or multi-year service contracts? Can Ace sell complementary products and services? Will customers recommend Ace to others? Responses should influence Ace's price setting decision.

FIGURE 20.1

PRICING ANALYSIS FOR A NEW ITEM OF CAPITAL EQUIPMENT

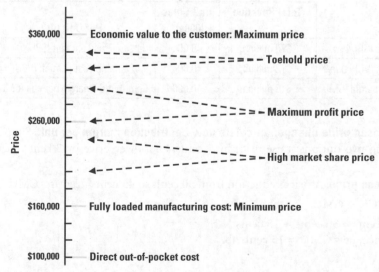

CHANGING THE PRICE OF AN EXISTING PRODUCT

The firm has many reasons to change price. Sometimes external competitive pressures are critical, but other pressures may be internal. Financial managers may want increased profit margins by raising prices. Seeking increased volume, the sales force may lobby for price decreases. Critical questions are:

- Can the firm *increase price* without losing significant volume? How much volume will it lose? Will the incremental profit margin offset the lost volume?

- If the firm *decreases price*, will it gain significant volume? How much volume will it gain? Will the extra volume offset the reduced profit margin?

To answer these questions, the firm must calculate the volume of sales necessary at the proposed price in order to make the same profit it earns at the current price. Figure 20.2 shows a five-step process for considering price changes.

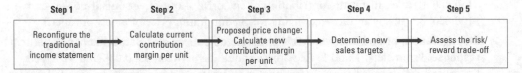

FIGURE 20.2

A PROCESS FOR DETERMINING PRICE CHANGES

Step 1: Reconfigure the traditional income statement. We partition costs into two categories: variable costs and fixed costs[2] — Table 20.2.

Sales Revenues (SR) (40 million lbs. @ 50 cents/lb. selling price [SP])	$20,000
Variable Costs (VC)	$12,000
Contribution Margin (CM)	$ 8,000
Fixed Costs (FC)	$ 6,600
Net Profit before Taxes (NP)	$ 1,400

TABLE 20.2

EXAMPLE: PRODUCT INCOME STATEMENT ($000s)

KEY IDEA

➤ **Changing Price for an Existing Product**

The firm must calculate required sales at the new price to make the same profit as at the current price.

Step 2: Calculate current contribution margin per unit. Contribution margin (CM) is an important concept. CM must cover fixed costs; any remainder is profit. CM equals (is identical to) sales revenues (SR) less variable costs (VC). (Hence, variable costs do not enter future CM calculations.)

Restated: $SR - VC \equiv CM$ On a per-unit basis, $SP - VCU \equiv CMU$

And: $SR \equiv CM + VC$ On a per-unit basis, $SP \equiv CMU + VCU$

Table 20.3 shows that *contribution margin per unit (CMU)* is simply CM on a per-unit basis — similarly for *variable cost per unit (VCU)*:

	Total Revenue	Unit Sales (000s)*	Per Unit (lb.)	
Sales revenue (SR) *less*	$20 million	40,000	Price per unit (SP)	50 cents
Variable costs (VC) *equals*	$12 million	40,000	Variable cost per unit (VCU)	30 cents
Contribution margin (CM)	$ 8 million	40,000	Contribution margin per unit (CMU)	20 cents

* lbs.

TABLE 20.3

CONTRIBUTION MARGIN PER UNIT (CMU) CALCULATION

Step 3: Proposed price change: Calculate new contribution margin per unit. Suppose the firm is considering two options: raise price by 5 cents, and lower price by 5 cents. VCU does not change. But:

- **Decrease price.** A price reduction from 50 cents to 45 cents *decreases* CMU:

    $SP \equiv VCU + CMU$ so that:

       45 cents $\equiv$ 30 cents + 15 cents
       Hence, new CMU = **15 cents/lb.**

- **Increase price.** A price increase from 50 cents to 55 cents *increases* CMU:

  $SP \equiv VCU + CMU$ so that:

  55 cents $\equiv$ 30 cents + 25 cents

  Hence, new CMU = **25 cents/lb.**

Step 4: Determine new sales targets. Determine what sales volumes, at the proposed 45 cents/lb. and 55 cents/lb. prices, are necessary to make the same profit — $1.4 million — as at the old 50-cent/lb. price. These are minimum requirements:

- **Decrease price.** Unit sales volume for $1.4 million profit when price = 45 cents/lb.:

Target sales volume (lbs.)	= (Fixed costs + profit objective)/CMU
	= ($6.6 million + $1.4 million)/15 cents
	= $8 million/15 cents
	= **53.3 million lbs.**
Percent sales volume increase	= (53.3 – 40 million) × 100 /40 million
	= **32.5%**
Target sales revenue ($)	= 53.3 million lbs. × 45 cents/lb.
	= **$24 million**

  If the firm *reduces* price to 45 cents/lb., it must sell **53.3 million pounds** (32.5% increase) to make the same profit as previously.

- **Increase price.** Unit sales volume for $1.4 million profit when price = 55 cents/lb.:

Target sales volume (units)	= (Fixed costs + profit objective)/CMU
	= ($6.6 million + $1.4 million)/25 cents
	= $8 million/25 cents
	= **32 million lbs.**
Percent sales volume decrease	= (32 – 40 million) × 100 /40 million
	= **20%**
Target sales revenue ($)	= 32 million lbs. × 55 cents
	= **$17.6 million**

  If the firm *increases* price to 55 cents/lb., it must sell **32 million pounds** (20% decrease) to make the same profit as previously.

We summarize these results in Table 20.4.

TABLE 20.4

SUMMARY OF PRICING CALCULATIONS

Price	CMU	Target Volume	Sales Volume Percentage change	Target Revenues
50 cents	20 cents	40 million lbs.	—	$20 million
45 cents	15 cents	53.3 million lbs.	+ 32.5%	$24 million
55 cents	25 cents	32 million lbs.	– 20%	$17.6 million

Step 5: Assess the risk/reward trade-off. The results from Step 4 *do not make* the pricing decision. The firm must assess the likelihood it can meet (or exceed) the new volume targets: 53.3 million lbs. @ 45 cents/lb., or 32 million lbs. @ 55 cents/lb. The answer depends, in part, on competitive response. Considering all factors, the firm must decide whether or not to change price and take the chance of meeting or exceeding its volume targets.

TACTICAL PRICING

Tactical pricing is the ongoing stream of pricing decisions the firm makes on a daily basis. Generally, robust strategic pricing drives good tactical pricing, but tactical pricing has a major impact on firm performance. A common misconception is that a product has a single price; in fact, single prices are rare. Table 20.5 shows the **pricing toolkit**, the variety of tools the firm can use to make price adjustments, often for individual customers. Undisciplined use of the toolkit can lead to **price waterfall** problems (next page).

Acceptable currency	Credit terms	Guarantees and warranties	Price stability
Allowances	Discounts	Inventory carrying costs	Slotting fees**
Barter	Company shares	Leasing	Returns
Buy-backs	Freight	List price	Unbundling and bundling
Credit availability		Markdown money*	

 * Agreements by suppliers to make payments to retail customers if products are discounted

** Payments by suppliers to retailers to put products in stores

TABLE 20.5

A SELECTION OF TOOLS IN THE PRICING TOOLKIT

THE PRICING TOOLKIT

Sometimes the firm wants a price change to be highly visible to customers and competitors; other times, the firm wants to keep it secret. Firms often set highly visible list prices (rate cards), but make minimal sales at list price. Rather, list price is the basis for discounts and rebates; actual prices may be 20 or 30 percent off list. The firm can base discounts on many factors like firm/customer relationship, inventory, matching competitors, quantity, selling effort, and timing.

Less visible ways to change price include allowances — for advertising, selling effort, trade-ins, and returns. Credit availability and terms (time to pay and interest rates) can be potent pricing tools, especially during inflation. Freight or shipping charges are important price-changing mechanisms. For CIF (cost, insurance, freight) prices, the supplier pays; for FOB (free on board) prices, the customer pays.[3] The firm can change price by modifying customer inventory arrangements: JIT (just-in-time) systems cut customer inventory holding costs; selling on consignment (pay when used) reduces inventory costs to zero.

Leasing versus purchasing offers customers the ability to reduce capital employed; and product guarantees and warranties reduce prices by protecting customers from repair costs. The firm should recognize that *toolkit* elements are differentially important across customers. For an equivalent price reduction, one customer may prefer a larger discount; another may prefer an advertising allowance. In B2B, the reward system for purchasing staff may be important: Some customers incentivize staff based on price reductions off the invoice price. A cash discount applied when the firm receives the order may be very attractive! Sometimes firms and customers prefer barter and buy-backs to money transactions:

Barter

- British Aerospace earned $20 billion revenues from Saudi Arabia for Tornado fighters, Hawk trainers, and backup services. Most payments were in oil.

- During an Argentine recession, consumers acquired food and clothing, psychological counseling, and dental work, all by barter.

- In Siberia's Altai territory, over 50 percent of economic transactions are bartered; some large firms transact 90 percent of business by barter.

- A Polish organization contracted with Norton to erect a turn-key grinding wheel factory. Part of the payment was a buyback of products made in the plant.[4]

Marketing Question

Identify six specific pricing tools you have observed. Why do you think they were used?

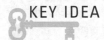

KEY IDEA

➤ Single product prices are rare in the real world.

➤ Pricing actions vary between highly visible and opaque.

The firm can also modify prices by shifting between *unbundling* — pricing items separately (like an à la carte restaurant meal), and *bundling* — each offer has a single price (like a prix-fixe meal). *Mixed bundling* combines bundled and unbundled prices — Chapter 12.

THE POCKET PRICE AND PRICE WATERFALL

Some firms use toolkit items appropriately, but many others have poor systems for tracking use. List price and invoice price are transparent, but other pricing elements are often deeply buried in myriad financial accounts: early payment discounts — interest-expense account; cooperative advertising allowances — promotion and advertising accounts.[5] Hence, these firms do not know their **pocket prices** — the money they actually receive (in their pockets). When firms conduct pocket-price analysis, they are often surprised to find a broad price range, but little rationale. Small-volume customers may receive large discounts; high-volume customers do not. The most aggressive, clever, or persistent customers get the best prices, aka the *squeaky wheel* syndrome. These customers manipulate supplier management systems for extra discounts; firm salespeople often cooperate:

> Knowing Oracle's concern with end-of-quarter results, customers waited for salespeople to offer larger discounts. Oracle booked most sales at the end of the quarter. To address the problem, Oracle started rejecting last-minute deals with large discounts. (See also Opening Case.)

The **price waterfall** — Figure 20.3 — illustrates how pricing toolkit elements cumulate to produce the pocket price. Customers can earn 27.6 percent reductions from four separate discounts (1 to 4) to make the invoice price 72.4 percent of the standard list price. They can also earn 15.3 percent reductions from seven other toolkit items (5 to 11) to make the pocket price 57.1 percent of list price.

1. Wholesaler discount
2. Supply house discount
3. Retailer discount
4. Special promotion
5. Cash discount
6. Factor discount
7. Cooperative advertising
8. Spiffs for retail salespeople
9. Annual volume rebate
10. Insurance
11. Freight

Standard List Price — Invoice Price — Pocket Price

To optimize pricing, the firm must understand the pocket price for each customer and the way these prices developed. This task may not be easy; the firm may have to modify its accounting systems. One firm took several initiatives to address price-waterfall problems:

- Acted aggressively to bring over-discounted customers into line with other customers.
- Delivered specific benefits to profitable customers to increase sales volumes.
- Brought price-setting under control by improving the accounting system.
- Tightened up on discounts and based sales force compensation on the pocket price.

DESIGNING PRICING APPROACHES

Several pricing methods are available:

PRICE DISCRIMINATION AND VARIABLE PRICING

The firm optimizes profits by setting different prices for different customers and segments — some pay more, others pay less. The firm can amplify this effect by designing multiple offers with different values: AmEx offers several personal credit cards — green, gold, platinum, and black — at successively higher prices. The core benefit is identical, but extra services differentiate the offers.

> An 18th-century economist explained the rationale for price discrimination: "It is not because of the few thousand francs which would have to be spent to put a roof over the third-class carriages or to upholster the third-class seats that some company or other has open carriages with wooden benches ... What the company is trying to do is to prevent the passengers who can pay the first-class fare from traveling third-class: it hits the poor, not because it wants to hurt them, but to frighten the rich ... And it is again for the same reason that companies, having proved almost cruel to the third-class passengers and mean to the second-class one, become lavish in dealing with first-class passengers. Having refused the poor what is necessary, they give the rich what is superfluous."[6]

Regardless, the firm may benefit from an inflexible single price. When salespeople have no **price discretion**, aggressive customers cannot negotiate price discounts (Oracle boxed insert, previous page). Also, a single price is simpler to understand and provides a perception of fairness, like CarMax's *no haggle* pricing policy for automobiles.

DYNAMIC PRICING

Dynamic pricing is a special case of **price discrimination** that occurs when demand varies over time. Some prices change *predictably*, like cities setting road and bridge tolls higher during rush hours and/or on weekdays, lower on weekends. Electric utilities, movie theaters, and telecommunications firms price by time of day, and hotels by day and season. Airlines use dynamic pricing continuously and *less predictably* via **yield management** systems, algorithms that adjust fares based on demand and available seat capacity. European discount airlines like easyJet and Ryanair set low fares weeks before the flight, then raise prices as seats fill and flight time approaches.

VARIABLE-RATE VERSUS FLAT-RATE PRICING

Firms selling services can price by use — *variable rate*; or by time period — *flat rate*. Variable prices may earn greater revenues, but flat-rate prices are generally easier (and less costly) to administer. Previously, ski resorts charged for chair lifts by the ride — variable rate; but today, most charge per day, week, or season — flat rate. Commuter rail travelers and season ticket holders for sporting and cultural events pay a flat-rate price per season; others pay by the trip or event. Some firms combine flat rates and usage fees, like cell phone providers.

CUSTOMER-DRIVEN PRICING

In many markets, sellers set a price and buyers accept it or not. In customer-driven pricing, the customer names the price; the firm can accept or not. At Priceline.com, customers can *name their own price* for automobiles, hotel reservations, mortgages, and airplane tickets. If the product is available, customers *must* complete the purchase. Customer-driven pricing has significant potential in services where products cannot be inventoried.

Marketing Exercise

Compare and contrast pricing in 19th-century French railroads with 21st-century passenger air travel.

Marketing Exercise

Next time you fly, ask fellow travelers what fare they paid. What is the basis for the price differences? Be prepared for them — or you — to be disgruntled!

 KEY IDEA

➤ Important approaches to pricing include:

- Price discrimination — variable pricing
- Dynamic pricing
- Variable rate versus flat rate
- Customer-driven pricing
- Auction pricing

AUCTION PRICING

Auction pricing is a form of customer-driven pricing where customers compete with other potential buyers to purchase a product.

ENGLISH AUCTION. Used especially for secondhand items. Prices start low, and potential buyers bid up the price. Auctioneers seek the buyer willing to pay the highest price. eBay and Amazon use an English auction.

VICKREY AUCTION. A *sealed-bid* English auction where the winning bidder pays the price of the second-highest bid. Google uses Vickrey auctions for online advertising.

DUTCH AUCTION. Prices start high; the seller reduces price until a buyer bids.

REVERSE AUCTION. This type of auction is for suppliers. The customer states its requirements; suppliers bid to provide the product. Prices go down and the lowest bidder wins the business.

SETTING THE ACTUAL PRICE

Several issues are important when setting the actual price:

FEES AND SURCHARGES

Many firms use *fees and surcharges* to increase pocket prices, especially in difficult economic times. Banks charge for ATM use and bounced checks; airlines charge fees and surcharges for checked bags, flight changes, fuel, pillows, and preferred seats. Revenues and profits increase, but overly aggressive fees may lead customers to go elsewhere.

PROMOTIONAL PRICING VERSUS STEADY PRICING

In many situations, sales are sensitive to short-term price promotions — Chapter 16. Firms often execute price promotions by comparing the sale price with the regular (or reference) price. In *loss-leader pricing*, retailers deliberately take losses on some products to build customer traffic and sell other products. Despite sales increases, promotions can have negative effects:

- **Brand image.** The promotion negatively affects the brand, especially upscale and luxury brands.
- **Diversion.** Retailers and/or distributors may *divert* the product to non-competing outlets, often in different geographic areas.
- **Hidden costs.** Frequent price promotions can be difficult and costly to administer.
- **Poor forecasting.** Demand exceeds forecast and customers are upset. Hong Kong Disneyland's one-day discounted tickets were not valid on *special days* like Chinese New Year. Chinese New Year was four days in Hong Kong but longer in mainland China. When Chinese New Year was over in Hong Kong but still continued on the mainland, mainlanders flooded into Hong Kong, and Disneyland had to close its gates.
- **Time-shifting.** Customers buy for inventory to avoid paying the full price later.

PSYCHOLOGICAL PRICING

For many customers, the psychological distance from $9.95 to $10.00 is greater than from $10.00 to $10.05; hence, many firms set prices to end with 95 cents.[7]

Louis Vuitton (LV) creates high-priced limited-edition *products of the year;* LV priced the *Theda* bag at $5,550. Said factory director Stephen Fallon, "The aim of the fashion bags isn't to make money, but to make envy." Compared to the *product of the year*, LV's other bags are inexpensive, so they seem like bargains.

PRICING BASES

Most industries have accepted bases for setting prices, typically by individual product, but changing the **price basis** may be a way to secure advantage. Some firms sell individual medical diagnoses rather than diagnostic machines; some software firms price per use rather than by software package. Japan's Viking chain of buffet restaurants sets prices in *yen per minute* to increase customer turns; Zipcar prices by annual membership fee plus a per hour charge versus daily or weekly prices like most car-rental firms. Relatedly, customers pay $79 annually for Amazon Prime, then receive unlimited free two-day shipping and other benefits. In Africa, Asia, and Latin America, fast-growing Millicom International Cellular charges customers per second (versus per minute). Some B2B firms share risk with customers by *gain sharing* — receiving partial payment in customer profits earned with their products; customers pay advertising agencies by results rather than percentage of billings (traditional). Auction firms Christie's and Sotheby's offer customers price guarantees for artwork, but share differences in price above the guarantee (plus sales commissions).

SPECIAL TOPICS IN SETTING PRICES

We examine several special pricing topics:

COMPLEMENTARY PRODUCT PRICING

Complementary products are used together — hot dogs and buns, automobiles and spare parts, vacuum cleaners and bags, printers and cartridges, and movies and popcorn. The firm must make a two-part pricing decision. Gillette is well known for pricing razors low and blades high, but strong differential advantage from recent innovations lets Gillette price each component high.

GRAY MARKET PRICING

Gray markets undercut the firm's strategy. Gray markets develop when the firm sells a similar product in different markets at different prices. Customers purchase the product in a low-price market, then ship for resale to a high-price market — *diversion*. Suppliers can avoid gray markets by reducing price dispersion.

PAY-WHAT-YOU-WANT PRICING

In a pricing innovation, British rock band Radiohead released *In Rainbows* as a digital download; customers chose their own prices! Wessex, publisher of *Capon's Marketing Framework* and other textbooks, similarly offers read-online versions.

KEY IDEA

➤ Special pricing topics include:
- Complementary product pricing
- Gray market pricing
- Pay-what-you-want pricing
- Topsy-turvy pricing
- Transfer pricing

Marketing Question

How do you assess the pay-what-you-think-it's-worth pricing approach for *Capon's Marketing Framework*? As incoming marketing director, what prices would you set for printed and pdf versions of *Capon's Marketing Framework*? Why?

TOPSY-TURVY PRICING

Suppliers and customers exchange value. The firm provides product/service value; the customer provides monetary value via the price. But sometimes the customer provides additional value and the supplier, not the customer, pays the price — *topsy-turvy pricing*. Sports teams typically pay medical practitioners to treat players, but some hospitals and medical practices receive value by calling themselves *official medical providers*. They pay sports teams up to $1.5 million annually to treat players.

TRANSFER PRICING

Firms set *transfer prices* among business units and geographic subsidiaries — a firm in Australia shipping to a sister subsidiary in Italy. Of course, transfer prices affect subsidiary profits and, internationally, firm tariff and tax liabilities.

PRICING MANAGEMENT

Now that you have learned about critical underpinnings of pricing decisions — Chapter 19 — and actually setting prices — Chapter 20, you probably have several questions. How should the firm create a **price management** structure? How should the firm set prices? Who should be responsible? Generally, centralized pricing provides greater control; decentralized pricing offers greater market sensitivity. But decentralized pricing may also have long-run negative effects[8]:

KEY IDEA

➤ The firm should develop pricing policies at high levels in the firm.

➤ Price-setting can be a strategic capability.

- **Information sharing.** Customers talk to each other about prices; those paying higher prices exert pressure for price reductions.
- **Limited perspective.** A local decision-maker like a salesperson is unlikely to consider the potential long-run impact of a local price reduction on the firm's entire customer base.
- **Negotiation.** Customers learn to place end-of-period orders when suppliers are anxious about revenues and may reduce prices. They also learn to play off multiple vendors against one another.

For these reasons, many firms develop pricing policies via a governance process that addresses long-run strategic questions like pricing new products, as well as short-term tactical decisions. These policies set guidelines for addressing multi-person buying decisions like those involving purchasing agents (tend to focus on price), and engineers, operations, and marketing personnel (other concerns).

Some experts argue that price-setting is a strategic capability, comparable to new product development and advertising.[9] Most firms have significant capabilities for creating customer value, but less expertise in measuring and capturing value. Far too often, managers with pricing responsibility do not understand price-volume-profit trade-offs. They lack good analytic skills and rely instead on gut instinct, hearsay, response to competitors, and *rules of thumb*.

The *Marketing University* at pharmaceuticals giant Roche builds pricing knowledge and teaches three areas of pricing capability:

- **Human capital.** Broad pricing knowledge at decision-makers' command.
- **Social capital.** The ability to negotiate agreements on prices among firm decision-makers.
- **Systems capital.** Supports pricing decisions by:
  - Assembling accurate information on customer purchase history, including actual prices paid.
  - Managing price changes.
  - Providing product and customer profitability.

- Quickly responding to requests for price quotations.
- Testing different prices.
- Tracking competitors' prices and discounts.
- Tracking firm prices, discounts, and reasons for different customer discounts.

LEGAL AND ETHICAL ISSUES IN PRICING

Most firms engage professionals to advise on legal implications of pricing decisions; we only scratch the surface. Marketers should have a working knowledge of three broad topics: anti-competitive pricing, dumping, and fairness in consumer pricing[10]:

ANTI-COMPETITIVE PRICING

Several pricing approaches are anticompetitive:

DISCRIMINATORY PRICING. Under the U.S. Robinson-Patman Act, firms cannot sell identical products to different customers at different prices when the effect is to lessen competition or create a monopoly. Defenses against Robinson-Patman are cost-justification and meeting a competitive threat.

PREDATORY PRICING. The U.S. defines **predatory pricing** as pricing below average variable costs, with the intention of putting the competitor out of business. Dominant firms sometimes engage in predatory pricing by temporarily pricing very low to thwart a competitive threat.

PRICE CONSPIRACIES. A firm and competitors overtly collude to fix prices, make implicit agreements to price in parallel, and/or exchange price information. Higher prices and customer harm typically occur. A high-level U.S. businessman, secretly recorded by an FBI whistleblower, summed up the **price-fixing** philosophy: "Our competitors are our friends; our customers are the enemies!" Two senior executives at Archer Daniels Midland (large U.S. agribusiness firm) earned long jail terms.[11]

DUMPING

Some firms **dump** products in foreign markets at less than fair market value, below home market prices, and often below average costs. Dumping prices are often higher than variable costs, so the firm's contribution margin is positive. This practice may be illegal in the receiving country if it causes or threatens material harm to the domestic industry.

FAIRNESS IN CONSUMER PRICING

Two important fairness issues for consumers are:

BAIT AND SWITCH. Retailers advertise a low price product but have only limited availability. The *bait* sells quickly, then retailers offer most customers a higher price product, the *switch*.

DECEPTIVE PRICING. False prices or prices that may confuse or mislead customers are deceptive. If the firm advertises a product, price = $X, but the product cannot function without other critical elements, the $X price is deceptive. (That's why many products carry the disclaimer "batteries not included.") Difficult-to-understand prices and price information in *fine print* may also be deceptive.

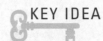

KEY IDEA

➤ Important legal and ethical pricing issues include:

- Anti-competitive pricing, including:
  - Discriminatory pricing
  - Predatory pricing
  - Price conspiracies
- Dumping
- Fairness in consumer pricing, including:
  - Bait and switch
  - Deceptive pricing

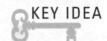

KEY IDEA

➤ Many governments scrutinize prices for illegal activity.

KEY MESSAGES

- To set price for a new product, the firm should start with perceived customer value, consider costs, then factor in competitors and its strategic objectives.

- When contemplating changing price for an existing product, the firm should use a contribution margin approach to assess volumes needed to meet various profit targets.

- The firm may avoid making frequent price changes by implementing a price menu system.

- The firm has many pricing toolkit elements available for setting the actual price.

- Undisciplined use of pricing toolkit elements leads to price waterfall problems. Appropriate systems and pricing discipline can address these problems.

- The firm should consider many issues in designing pricing approaches and setting actual prices.

- To set prices well, the firm must invest in human, systems, and social capital.

- Price-setting is fraught with legal and ethical issues.

Summary questions for making better pricing decisions are in Table 20.6.

TABLE 20.6

SUMMARY QUESTIONS FOR SETTING PRICES

1. What is the pricing objective, as stated in the market strategy?
2. What value do customers place on the firm's product/service?
3. Is there variation in the way in which customers value the firm's product? Search for segments.
4. How price sensitive are customers?
5. How are competitors likely to respond to firm prices?
6. What is the optimal approach to setting prices — variable pricing, dynamic pricing, variable-rate pricing, flat-rate pricing, customer-driven pricing, or auction?
7. What pocket price does the firm receive?
8. What are customers' emotional reactions to prices?
9. How do factors like brand preferences, demand shifts, and seasonality affect price?
10. Which firm customers are profitable to serve?

VIDEOS AND AUDIOS

Segmented Pricing   v2002 📹 Hitendra Wadhwa   Columbia Business School

v2002

IMPERATIVE 5

Secure Support from Other Functions

CHAPTER 21

ENSURING THE FIRM IMPLEMENTS THE MARKET OFFER AS PLANNED cv2101

To access O-codes, go to **www.ocodes.com**

It is amazing what you can accomplish if you do not care who gets the credit.

— Harry S. Truman

LEARNING OBJECTIVES

When you have completed this chapter, you will be able to:

- Understand how several externally oriented firms became successful via functional excellence.
- Recognize the challenges of creating an externally oriented firm.
- Deploy an organizational development model to facilitate becoming externally oriented.
- Explain the pros and cons of traditional and newer approaches of organizing for marketing.
- Appreciate the critical role of systems and processes, and human resources in developing and implementing market strategy.
- Realize the importance of other functions in contributing to marketing as a philosophy.
- Understand the importance of integrating many organizational functions and business units.
- Take steps to ensure your firm maintains an external orientation.

OPENING CASE: BRISTOL-MYERS SQUIBB

Senior executives at Bristol-Myers Squibb (BMS) (multinational pharmaceutical/healthcare) concluded BMS needed greater market focus and greater consistency in marketing processes and application among its therapeutic franchises and across the organization. Senior marketing leaders formulated and implemented a Marketing Excellence *initiative with two main elements: a* marketing system — *a systematic and analytic approach to marketing; and a* talent system — *an approach to career and talent development for all marketers. BMS also implemented a formal development program to educate and train marketers worldwide so as to embed marketing excellence within the culture.*

NEW MARKETING APPROACH. *The primary impact of* Marketing Excellence *was implementation of a specific marketing process across BMS. Previously, brand managers planned in an ad hoc fashion; senior management presentations reflected this individuality.* Marketing Excellence *provided a disciplined, systematic, and analytic approach that gave BMS a philosophy, a consistent framework, and application tools to enable and empower marketers. The new approach facilitated better performance measurement and cross-brand comparisons.*

- **Marketing principles.** *BMS's key focus areas were: customer focus, value and brand creation, and their collective strategic implementation. To illustrate,* principle 1: *"Marketers should* secure *deeper insights into customers and their interactions."* Principle 3: *"BMS should anticipate and out-maneuver competitors' activities."*

- **Brand management choices.** *BMS created a set of choices categorized as strategic, planning, and execution. Strategic choices included: deciding what the market definition is now and will be in the future and how BMS will differentiate the brand. Planning and execution choices included: How to implement the strategic choices by considering customer segmentation and messaging, and specific brand tactics.*

- **Marketing application tools.** *BMS supported each choice with a specific set of tools, guiding questions, and worksheets to assist BMS marketers' thought processes.*

ENHANCE MARKETING COMPETENCE. *To embed* Marketing Excellence *worldwide, BMS marketing executives of all levels attended programs directed and taught by Columbia Business School marketing faculty. BMS marketers developed experience with the principles and choices; BMS developed a unique, innovative, and sustainable training program.*

RESULTS. Marketing Excellence *benefited BMS in three important areas:*

- **Cross-functional integration.** *The new approach encourages cross-functional teamwork and strongly recommends that marketers consult, inform, and align with functions like R&D, market research, and medical affairs.*

- **International operations.** *BMS substantially changed its approach to international operations. BMS placed core positioning decisions for new drugs centrally; local executives cannot change positioning.*

- **Marketing culture.** Marketing Excellence *fostered a strong marketing culture within BMS. Brand managers around the world follow the same process, and vocabulary is common.*

Marketing Excellence *has embedded a sustainable and consistent approach to marketing within BMS; industry experts rate three consecutive product launches among the top 10 in pharmaceuticals.*

CASE QUESTION

How do you assess BMS' *Marketing Excellence* initiative? Do you think the design is applicable to firms in other industries?

In previous chapters, we focused on gaining insight into markets, customers, competitors, the company, and complementers; developing market strategy; and designing implementation programs around product, promotion, distribution, service, and price. People with marketing titles tend to do much, but not all, of this work. By contrast, executing implementation programs involves many people throughout the firm, across a variety of functional areas.

To execute well, the firm must practice the Principle of Integration and seamlessly align various implementation programs with its market strategies. All employees must recognize that customers are central to the firm's success and act accordingly. Vision, mission, and strategy form the superstructure within which they do their jobs; the firm's values underpin its culture. Much of the hard implementation effort relates to organization structure, systems and processes, and human resource practices. Unfortunately, these elements tend to evolve slowly and lag both environmental changes and the firm's market strategies.

Chapter 1 showed that securing appropriate alignment is much easier when the firm has customer-focused values leading to a true external orientation. Chapter 21 presents a model for creating and maintaining an external orientation, including specific action steps. To frame the chapter, we show how several externally oriented firms became successful by achieving excellence in particular functional areas. We should all try to emulate these exemplars.

Marketing Question

When you place an order online, many supplier functions are involved in getting the product to you. Chart out the supplier process.

FUNCTIONAL EXCELLENCE IN SUCCESSFUL EXTERNALLY ORIENTED FIRMS

What does it take to deliver customer value and secure differential advantage? Successful firms deploy various resources and expertise to build core competence. Functional expertise includes customer service, finance, human resources, operations and the supply chain, research and development, and sales. Table 21.1 shows firms that leveraged such expertise into success.[1]

TABLE 21.1

DELIVERING CUSTOMER VALUE AND SECURING DIFFERENTIAL ADVANTAGE VIA FUNCTIONAL EXCELLENCE

Functional Area	Company	Capability	Customer Benefit
Customer Service	Amazon	Collaborative filtering; one-click	Ease purchasing
	Fidelity	24/7/365 availability	Convenience
	Nordstrom	Values and reward system	Attentive personalized service
Finance	GE Capital	Sophisticated financial engineering	Innovative financing to leverage clients' shareholder returns
	Monsanto	Accepts barter payment	Able to purchase without cash
	Praxair	Flexible billing system	Site-based bills to facilitate project management
Human Resources	Google	Employee quality of life	Innovative products/services
	In-N-Out Burger	Training and benefits	Superior service
	Ritz Carlton/ Singapore Airlines	Selection and training	Superior service
Operations and the Supply Chain	Alcoa	Integrated operations and supply chain	Just-in-time delivery
	Dell	Design/build to order	Customization
	FedEx	System ownership	Reliability
	Walmart	Logistics and inventory management	Low prices
Research and Development	3M	Many new technologies	Innovative products
	Apple	Design skills	Aesthetically pleasing, functional, trendy products
	DuPont/Monsanto	Research skills in chemistry	Productivity increases

Marketing Question

Think about your cell phone supplier. With what functions or departments have you had contact — mail, e-mail, retail store, or customer service rep? Did one area provide a good experience? Is this part of the supplier's differential advantage?

CONTINUES ON NEXT PAGE

Functional Area	Company	Capability	Customer Benefit
Sales	Avon	*Avon Lady* sales force	Close personal relationships between buyer and seller
	Direct Line	Direct sales of insurance	Lower prices
	IBM	Global account management program	Partnership relationship with leading technology firm

TABLE 21.1

CONTINUED

> ### *Marketing Question*
> Select three firms from Table 21.1. What investments in resources are they making to maintain their differential advantages?

CUSTOMER SERVICE

We discussed the key dimensions of customer service in Chapter 13. But increased competition has made customer service strategically important to the firm for delivering customer value, securing differential advantage, and attracting, retaining, and growing customers. Yet, in many firms, customer service does not report to marketing. This may not matter when an external orientation is the firm's dominant philosophy and everyone is on the same page. But poor customer service generates significant customer dissatisfaction, especially if expectations are high, and can destroy an otherwise effective market strategy.

Some externally oriented firms differentiate their offers from tough competitors via customer service excellence. Nordstrom (department store) is rightly famous for employees' customer service zeal. Careful employee selection, enlightened management, and supportive incentive systems encourage the *right* behavior. Nordstrom accepts returned goods without question, sometimes from competitor stores!

Mutual fund leader, Fidelity, is a fine example of customer service excellence. Fidelity's key insight was that investors preferred to interact with brokers on their personal schedules, not just when the market was open. Fidelity's innovation was to become the first financial services firm open 24/7/365. Many other factors contributed to Fidelity's leadership, but customer confidence and trust in the Fidelity brand and the customer service convenience it offered were critical. Today, online brokerage competitors offer similar convenience and trading resources, causing Fidelity to lose some ground. Recall our earlier message: Competitors eventually eliminate virtually all advantages. The quest for differential advantage must be central and ongoing.

> ### *Marketing Question*
> Which firm has provided you personally with the best customer service? What was so great about it? How could your selected firm improve its performance?

FINANCE

Clearly, technical financial skills are a key success factor in finance departments, but financial decisions and controls play a critical role in managing the broader operations of any successful firm. Financial engineering is central to marketing major capital goods and services, from aircraft and earth-moving equipment to business systems. Externally oriented firms galvanize their finance and accounting functions; they contribute to the firm's marketing efforts in many ways, like helping to assess and quantify market opportunities.

Getting paid is also a critical part of any firm's business model, but sometimes the firm must be creative. Monsanto provides genetically modified seeds to large growers in many countries. When growers have difficulty in paying cash, Monsanto accepts finished crops in payment (barter); later, Monsanto sells these crops at market prices to realize cash.

Invoicing and billing systems can be a major customer problem, but a good place to seek differential advantage. After all, the bill is one supplier communication that customers always read! Praxair (industrial gases) has many construction customers that work simultaneously on different projects; they must account for costs by site and project. Praxair created a flexible billing system that offers customers this service; they appreciate it.

> ### *Marketing Question*
> Can you think of a firm whose finance operations made doing business with it easier? What specifically did you like? How could the firm improve?

HUMAN RESOURCES

Human resources (HR) is a vital function for any business, but some firms create differential advantage by developing and motivating their workforces to achieve high levels of excellence. Many consulting firms claim HR advantages are the most sustainable since excellence in recruiting, selecting, onboarding, and *talent management* is difficult to copy. GE and IBM are well known for developing successive generations of business leaders and many former GE executives become CEOs of major corporations. Managing human resources is especially important in services firms, where employee/customer interaction is constant and ongoing. Major hotel chains like Four Seasons, Marriott, and Ritz-Carlton place particular emphasis on their employees at every organizational level.

OPERATIONS AND THE SUPPLY CHAIN

Internal operations and **supply chain** management are important areas for the firm to improve its external focus, especially in services where it touches the customer most often. All contemporary approaches to teaching operations start with the firm's strategy, then design systems by working back from the marketplace. The operations system is a great place for the firm to secure differential advantage.[2] Alcoa continuously introduces innovation into its operating processes, including forecasting customer needs, and created advantages unlike other sheet metal providers. Dell started out with a services model, modifying IBM and IBM-compatible PCs, then back-integrated into manufacturing. Michael Dell believed the traditional model — forecast demand, build PCs to meet demand, then persuade customers to buy PCs — was ineffective. Dell created an entirely new business model for building customized computers that customers had already agreed to buy. This demand-driven, direct-to-customer model is very successful, minimizing costs and investment throughout the system.

RESEARCH AND DEVELOPMENT

R&D breakthroughs have given birth to many great firms. 3M, Apple, DuPont, GlaxoSmithKline (GSK), HP, Intel, Medtronics, Monsanto, and Xerox are just a few that achieved and maintained pre-eminence based on technological strengths. When the firm manages its R&D/Marketing interface well, the impact can be dramatic. 3M has a formidable record for innovation combined with successful, even ingenious, marketing. Apple has become one of the U.S.'s most valuable firms based on a culture of continuous innovation. For many years, Macintosh computers have offered elegant design and functionality. More recently, Apple's innovation machine has produced game-changing products like the iPod, iTunes, iPhone, and iPad.

SALES

In Chapter 17, we discussed many aspects of the sales function and showed how innovation in sales can be the key to success. In B2C, several firms have gained differential advantage via new selling efforts or sales channels. Avon sells cosmetics differently from most cosmetics firms. Avon Ladies are independent businesswomen who have close personal relationships with customers. They consult on cosmetics issues, help customers select the most relevant products, and personally deliver orders. Concerning B2B, we learned that firms like IBM and DHL are driving successful growth by innovating with strategic (key) account and global account programs. Better and faster data from CRM systems like SAP and salesforce.com can also provide differential advantage by enabling salespeople to offer customers greater value.

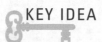

INTEGRATED SYSTEMS

Specific functional areas bring success to externally oriented firms. These firms succeed, not because of a single strong suit, but because they integrate efforts from many functions. Toyota is an outstanding example of high performance based on three integrated systems:

- **Research and development.** Toyota's process begins with extensive research into customer demographics and lifestyle trends. These data feed into Toyota's four research and design studios in Japan (1), U.S. (2), and Europe (1). These studios compete for the best design in a target market.

- **Manufacturing.** Toyota's process is perhaps the world's best-known, most-discussed, and most-praised industrial operation. The Toyota system has spawned many books and is a model of Total Quality Management (TQM). Boeing and Airbus copied the Toyota system.

- **Dealer management and customer service.** Toyota invests heavily in its dealers and customer service. All Toyota's franchised dealers must adhere to a strong set of guidelines; if not, Toyota does not renew agreements. When Toyota introduced the Lexus, it set up a completely independent dealer system. The first Lexus cars had a minor quality problem; for every car, Toyota fixed the problem, filled the gas tank, and returned a clean car. For Lexus' first 10 years, each management employee telephoned four customers per month to gain real-time data on the car and dealer.

Transforming the Organization to Become Externally Oriented

Culture eats strategy for breakfast. — Peter F. Drucker

To achieve success in increasingly competitive markets, the firm must focus resources to deliver customer value and secure differential advantage. In the final analysis, nothing else matters. Continual realignment is difficult, but necessary; some firms do better than others. The most successful firms develop an **external orientation** culture.

Chapter 1 introduced the idea of organizational orientations; we described the external orientation and various **internal orientations**. Firms with internal orientations focus on various internal functional needs, and are often excessively regimented and rule-based. But the externally oriented firm looks outward, focusing on customers, competitors, and broader environmental variables. This firm knows that current products and processes are the key reasons for past and present success. But the firm also knows that the external environment is always changing and that it must make internal changes in organization structure, systems and processes, and human resources to adjust to new market realities. Rather than fearing change, the externally oriented firm knows that change is inevitable. The externally oriented firm welcomes change as a challenge and understands new opportunities are the firm's *lifeblood*.

It's one thing to recognize the value of an external orientation; it's quite another to change the organization from the *status quo*. Some successful corporate leaders believe instilling an external orientation is a critical part of their job and institute *change-management* processes to accomplish the task. Intel owes its success to addressing environmental discontinuities, like legal and regulatory issues, and competitive challenges. When asked about his most important achievement, former CEO Andy Grove said: "It's that I've played a significant part in developing the work environment and culture at the company and with the directors."[3]

We demonstrate how to develop an external orientation. Figure 21.1 shows the standard inverted-pyramid used by externally oriented firms like SAS and Nordstrom. This framework places customers at the top of the pyramid and reinforces their critical role in firm success.

KEY IDEA

➤ Any model/framework for developing an external orientation must focus on customers.

KEY IDEA

➤ An EO framework comprises:

Values
↓
Vision, Mission, Strategy
↓
Organizing the Firm's Efforts
↓
Systems and Processes
↓
Managing Human Resources

FIGURE 21.1

A FRAMEWORK
FOR DEVELOPING
AN EXTERNAL
ORIENTATION (EO)

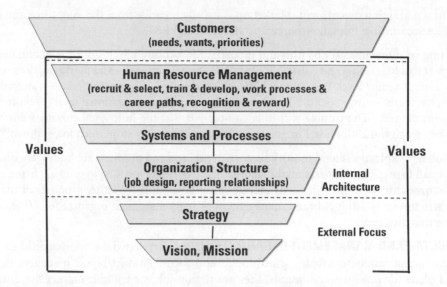

*Marketing
Question*

Select two of your favorite
firms; identify their values.
Are these firms living up to
their values? If not, where
are they failing? What is the
marketing significance of
communicating these
values?

KEY IDEA

➤ Well-thought-through
vision, mission, and
strategy are critical for
developing an external
orientation.

KEY IDEA

➤ Organizational values
are a common set of
beliefs that guide the
behavior of the firm's
members. They are
often integral to firm
success.

➤ Values statements are
worthwhile only if the
entire firm embraces
them.

VALUES, VISION, MISSION, STRATEGY

Many firms use a values statement emphasizing a customer-focused culture to reinforce placing customers at the top of the pyramid. **Values** are a common set of beliefs that guide the behavior of all organization members, in all functions. Some values are *hard*, easily measured like profitability and market share; other values are *soft*, like customer pre-eminence, integrity, respect for others, and trust.

Beginning with a values statement emphasizing the pre-eminence of customers, all other framework elements must reflect and reinforce firm commitment to an external orientation. Many organizational transformations start at the bottom of the pyramid, developing (or reworking) external elements discussed in Chapter 7:

- **Vision.** A description of the firm's ideal future state — an impressionistic picture of what the future should be. Good vision statements set a broad direction — they should inspire employees for the long run. A good vision statement is not too broad, nor is it too specific nor easily achievable.

- **Mission.** Guides the firm's search for market opportunities more directly. A well-developed mission keeps the firm focused in a limited arena where success is likely.

- **Strategy.** The firm's game plan for the market, pointing the way to firm actions. The market strategy specifies what the firm is trying to achieve, which segments it will target for effort, and how it will position itself in those segments.

ORGANIZING THE FIRM'S MARKETING EFFORTS

To execute its market strategy, the firm must design the marketing organization's **internal architecture**. Some traditional structures still have great value, but contemporary approaches are breaking new ground.[4]

TRADITIONAL ORGANIZATIONAL MODELS

FUNCTIONAL MARKETING ORGANIZATION. The firm places activities like advertising and promotion, distribution, marketing administration, marketing research, and new product development in a marketing department. Marketing is usually separate from the sales force and functions like accounting, human resources, production, and R&D.

Reporting relationships vary by firm and industry. Most commonly, heads of sales and marketing report to a Marketing and Sales SVP. One variant is separate sales and marketing VPs reporting to a more senior level. But conflict between marketing — long-term focus — and sales — short-term focus — may result; it is only resolvable at high organizational level (C-Suite). One CEO commented: "The trouble with this company is that the functional elevators don't stop until they reach the 20th floor. I'm going to make sure that they stop much lower down!"

Functional organizations tend to work best when markets and products are homogeneous (like many small firms). Sometimes, functional organizations linger too long in growing firms. As the firm becomes more complex, it needs specialized responsibility for either products or markets. Firms structured as product/brand management or market segment organizations (below) try to solve this problem.

PRODUCT/BRAND MANAGEMENT ORGANIZATION. P&G developed the original product management organization to provide a product/brand focus. Product/brand managers develop market plans for products and brands; they are responsible for volume, market share, and/or profits, but do not control all inputs. In many FMCG firms, product/brand managers compete for resources like promotional dollars and sales force time. Sometimes firms view internal brand-manager competition as healthy because it spurs extra effort, but it may undermine a coherent product-line strategy. This organization structure has two significant problems: potentially destructive internal brand manager competition (as noted) and brand manager turnover. Each can lead to long-time in coherence and a disjointed long-run strategy.

CATEGORY MANAGEMENT ORGANIZATION. This approach attempts to address problems with the product/brand management organization, in part by leveraging success from strong brands to weaker brands. The *category management* organization directs multiple brands in a complementary manner. P&G category manager for laundry products is responsible for Tide, Downy, Gain, Cheer, Bounce, Febreze, Dryel, and Ivory.

> **New Meaning to Category Management**
>
> Increasing retailer power in FMCG has given a new meaning to *category management.* Major supermarkets now manage operations on a category-by-category basis. Sophisticated data analysis allows for more granular determination of individual product profitability — by region, state, city, and even individual store. Retailers add new products and brands only if they help achieve category goals.
>
> In the U.S., some retailers outsource product category management to suppliers. Retailers charge the chosen supplier with increasing category revenues and profits. Mostly (but not always) the retailer appoints the market-leading supplier as *category captain.* This supplier gains privileged access to retail sales data for all category suppliers, including competitors. Appointments are typically for several years.

MARKET SEGMENT ORGANIZATION. The market segment organization is more externally focused than the preceding options; managers are responsible for individual market segments. The market segment organization may overlie other marketing and sales functions. Typically, the rest of the firm is functionally organized.

COMBINED PRODUCT/BRAND MANAGEMENT AND MARKET SEGMENT ORGANIZATION. Product/brand and market segment organizations each omit a crucial dimension: In product/brand organizations, no one is specifically responsible for market segments; in the market segment organization, no one is specifically responsible for individual products/ brands. Figure 21.2 shows how a synthetic fibers firm incorporated both dimensions. Segment managers were responsible for end-use markets like household textiles, apparel, and industrial

KEY IDEA

➤ A variety of traditional and newer organizational firms are available for organizing marketing efforts.

KEY IDEA

➤ *Traditional* marketing organizations include:

- Functional
- Product/brand management
- Category management
- Market segment
- Combined product/ brand management and market segment

products. Product managers were responsible for individual product lines like nylon, polyester, and new fibers.

FIGURE 21.2

COMBINED
PRODUCT/BRAND
MANAGEMENT-
MARKET SEGMENT
ORGANIZATION

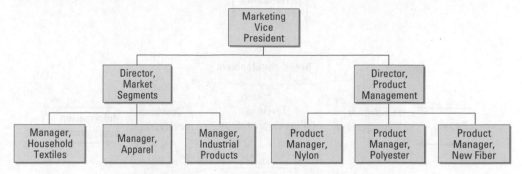

FIGURE 21.2

COMBINED
PRODUCT/BRAND
MANAGEMENT-
MARKET SEGMENT
ORGANIZATION

NEWER NON-TRADITIONAL ORGANIZATIONAL MODELS

INCLUSION ORGANIZATION. Figure 21.3 shows the newer inclusion organization; the firm groups many activities under marketing. British Airways (BA) adopted this approach; BA recognized that Operations controlled two critical customer requirements — safety and schedule reliability. BA restructured so that Operations reported to Marketing; indeed, 80 percent of employees reported through Marketing. The *inclusion organization* may work well in service businesses, where marketing and operations are difficult to distinguish, but is not appropriate for all firms.

FIGURE 21.3

THE INCLUSION
ORGANIZATION

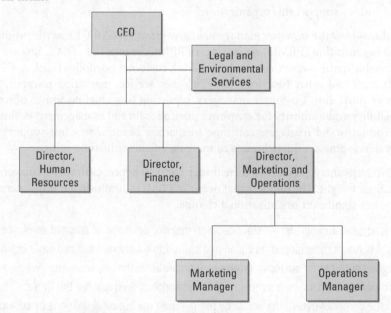

BUSINESS PROCESS ORGANIZATION. One outgrowth of the re-engineering movement was some firms' attempts to organize around *business processes.*[5] The firm retains a classic functional structure, but much organizational output results from cross-functional teams. Figure 21.4 shows how a British-based Unilever subsidiary reorganized on this basis. Marketing's major responsibilities are brand development, innovation, and related strategic tasks. The sales force conducts operational marketing tasks like trade promotions.

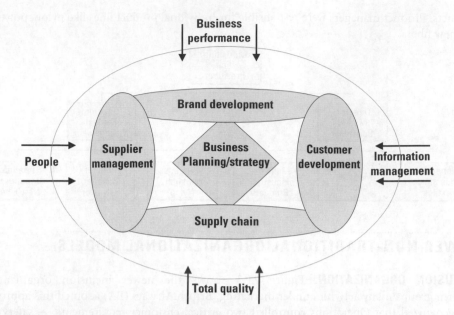

FIGURE 21.4

THE BUSINESS PROCESS
ORGANIZATION —
EXAMPLE FROM A
UNILEVER SUBSIDIARY

CUSTOMER-MANAGEMENT ORGANIZATION. This organization focuses specifically on customers. We expect this organizational form to become more popular as firms become increasingly aware of the customer lifetime value (CLV) concept and the importance of customer retention — Chapter 2. CRM systems that allow firms to identify customers by name, buying patterns, and history support this organization.[6]

Figure 21.5 shows how the *customer management organization (CMO)* turns the product/ brand management organization (PBMO) on its side. In PBMO, brands (B1 ... B4 ... Bn) are pillars; all other functional activities serve the brands. In CMO, customer portfolios (CP1 ... CP4 ... CPn) are pillars; brands and other functions like customer service, marketing research, and R&D serve customer portfolios. Customer managers, reporting to a chief customer officer (CCO), have responsibility and authority for customer portfolios; brand management is almost a staff function.[7] Product/brand managers continue to manage brand assets, but support customer managers by developing products/brands to increase customer lifetime value.

A specific CMO advantage is increased customer contact; hence, customer managers gain significant customer insight. The blinders that occur in PBMOs diminish, but implementing CMO typically requires significant organizational change:

> Microsoft faced several problems — slow decision-making, defection of talented employees, and increasingly tough competition. Microsoft redeveloped its vision and shifted to a customer-focused organization. Individual organizational units became responsible for customer groups — corporate customers, knowledge workers, home PC buyers, game players, software developers, web surfers, and cybershoppers. Said founder Bill Gates: "The new structure puts the customer at the center of everything we do by reorganizing our business divisions by customer segment rather than along product lines."[8]

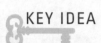

KEY IDEA

➤ *Newer* marketing organizations include:

- Inclusion
- Business process
- Customer management

Marketing Question

As a current or potential customer, how do you think Microsoft classifies you? Call the customer service department or go to Microsoft's website to find out.

FIGURE 21.5

THE TRANSITION FROM BRAND MANAGEMENT TO CUSTOMER MANAGEMENT

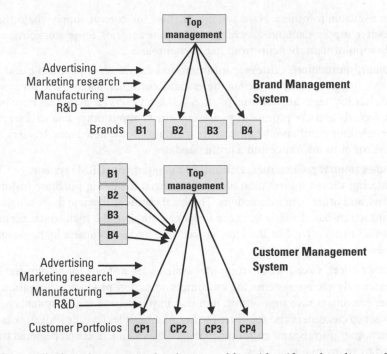

KEY IDEA

➤ The firm's organizational structure should support an integrated marketing approach.

More B2C firms will adopt the CMO as they become able to identify and understand individual customers. Most B2B firms already identify customers; hence, customer management is becoming more widespread via strategic (key) account management programs; firms with global customers are developing global account programs.

The firm may implement CMO at the corporate level or in individual business units, but there are trade-offs. At corporate, customer management may be ineffective because account managers do not have deep understanding across the firm's many businesses. Focus at the business level only, and the firm may be unable to develop an integrated corporate-wide offer:

> Lucent's (now Alcatel-Lucent) business-unit organization pushed authority and responsibility deep in the firm. But getting business units to cooperate was difficult. Several businesses developed variations of the *softswitch* telecommunications product.[9] One customer said that he was "confused on what Lucent is actually offering, because I've heard different descriptions of the same solution from different Lucent teams."[10]

SYSTEMS AND PROCESSES

All organizations use systems and processes to produce organizational outputs; we can array them along a continuum. One pole embraces *hard systems*. Hard systems typically require capital equipment and are often computer-based, like automatic teller machines, Internet portals, and auction sites. At the other pole are human-resource-intensive *soft systems*, like retail customer service desks. Many customer interactions involve a combination of hard and soft systems. Although they are getting better every day, all customer-facing systems can be improved.

KEY IDEA

➤ Systems and processes help produce organizational outputs and provide consistency to customers.

HARD SYSTEMS. Hard systems improve operational efficiency and reduce costs. But they can also contribute to creating an external orientation, improve marketing effectiveness, optimize sales force efforts, and help secure differential advantage. Perhaps the most popular hard systems in major firms are enterprise resource planning (ERP). ERP software contains customer-focused modules and attempts to integrate data from many departments and functions across the firm. ERP uses a single computer platform serving each department's needs and makes information available to others. Hard systems are also the core of supply-chain management, leading to better supply/demand matching, reduced inventories, fewer stockouts, and reduced customer disappointment. Benefits from hard systems are:

- **Customer information.** Customer information is more readily available and widely distributed; hence, employees better understand customer needs. At insurance firms like USAA, hard systems are essential to success. USAA's service associates have full access to client records and are prompted to ask customers about other financial services. A customer telephone call about homeowner insurance for a new home triggers a change of address for auto insurance and a profile update.

- **Customer intimacy.** Customer relationship management (CRM) systems — Chapter 2 — provide significant information about customers, including purchase histories, buying patterns, and other firm interactions. These data sources alleviate the soul-less anonymity of transaction-based markets. Large firms can emulate the high-touch personal service that small firms offer, like the local grocer who knew customers by name and built his business on that basis.

- **Customer effort.** User-friendly computer systems are not just for employees. Many firms use externally facing systems for customers to access product information and order online; customers save time, effort, and risk in purchasing. These systems help the firm get closer to customers and reinforce the brand. Examples include FedEx package tracking and customer portals, and customer-managed check-in kiosks and personal travel portals offered by many major airlines.

> At Dell's website, customers design computers to meet their needs, place orders, and pay. Dell builds the product to order and delivers it promptly. Apple, HP, and IBM have emulated Dell's ordering and production systems.

SOFT SYSTEMS. People-based soft systems can also help the firm become more externally oriented. Consider the planning process. Good planning is externally driven: Planning commences by emphasizing insight into the market, customers, competitors, complementers, and the environment in general. Well-developed situation analyses, based on the precepts in Chapters 3, 4, and 5, can force an external orientation and help deliver solid planning assumptions for developing market strategy. Firms that build market strategy using the Chapter 9 framework become more externally focused. Try it yourself: Use *The Virgin Marketer* (companion volume) to develop a market strategy for an organization of your choice.

Good planning is collaborative-participative, and involves cross-functional involvement at multiple management levels. Planning brings people across the firm face-to-face with external realities. Outputs from market planning set firm direction; they also play a critical role in driving an external orientation via monitor and control processes — Chapter 22. A good planning system produces measures that encourage organizational members to look beyond their narrow silos.

MAKING FIRM SYSTEMS AND PROCESSES THE BEST THEY CAN BE. More important than any individual system are methodologies for evolving and integrating systems and processes to drive an external orientation:

- **Best practice transfer.** For any process, some business units, departments, or functions are probably more effective than others. Unfortunately lateral communication within firms is generally poor: Underperforming units may know little about their more effective cousins. A **best practice** system helps identify and transmit superior expertise, knowledge, and processes across the firm. Multi-business, multi-national firms offer rich terrain for identifying best practices. Samsung's system communicates hundreds of best practice examples company-wide. An extensive annual evaluation process identifies the *best of the best*; the winners personally receive awards from Samsung's CEO.

Starbucks shares best practices among U.S. operations and international partners. Founder and CEO Howard Schultz opines, "In some cases the international partners are better than we are, and they're teaching us some things. At our first global conference, 30 countries were represented. We had a mini controlled Starbucks trade show where each country set up a booth to show its best practice."[11]

Some firms assign specific employees as *thought leaders* to identify and promote best practices throughout the organization. At Intel, the *data czar* identifies best-known methods and places them in a knowledge repository. Bain employees write up each consultancy project as a *knowledge module*; these are stored electronically so employees don't *reinvent the wheel* when they encounter similar challenges. Any firm's market success or failure is an opportunity to identify best practices and barriers to best practices. Some firms institutionalize this process by analyzing every customer *win* and *loss*.

Disseminating best practices, expertise, and knowledge across the firm can be a major challenge. Contemporary methods include specially tagged databases for easy search, and collaborative *communities of practice* where experts share information. Other options include regular e-mail communications, *virtual meeting technology* for spur-of-the-moment knowledge-sharing, and meetings designed to break down barriers and facilitate transfer. Other ways to encourage internal communications are physical organization of workspaces and frequent personnel transfer from one organizational unit to another.

- **Benchmarking.** Best practices frequently occur in other firms. **Benchmarking** competitors, customers, suppliers, and firms in other industries, like Xerox's *best-in-class* concept, can improve firm processes.[12] Global fast-food firm Yum! Brands (KFC, Pizza Hut, Taco Bell) identified internal best practice and benchmarked its fierce rival McDonald's. Yum! identified three improvement areas — more healthy food, greater drink variety, and menus matched to time of day. Target implemented *Horizontal Councils* in each merchandising and functional area. Council members meet regularly to share best and worst practices, but senior managers always ask them: "What did you find out from other firms about this?" They must have answers to these questions! The Columbia Initiative in Global Account Management enabled 3M, Citibank, Deloitte & Touche, HP, Lucent, Milliken, Saatchi and Saatchi, and Square D-Schneider to benchmark one another's global account management programs.

- **Re-engineering.** The **re-engineering** approach examines fundamental assumptions about firm systems and processes and seeks alternative approaches for redesign and improvement. Many organizational processes have a long history, but changes in customers, competitors, technology, and other environmental factors may make them obsolete. The critical question is: Can a new process reduce costs and/or increase customer value? The Internet has driven change in many business processes, like supplier-customer relationships where online communication has superseded telephone calls and faxes for purchase orders, invoices, and shipping notices. Most successful firms have made major commitments to process-based re-engineering:

Marketing Question

Identify a specific customer service process — like buying a product in a store. Visit several establishments to examine their processes. What improvement suggestions do you have?

IBM Credit's (IBMC) process for financing major computer system sales traditionally involved several steps: A salesperson provided purchase and customer data to a *logger*; the logger created a file and sent it onward; credit specialist — conduct credit check; business practices — request changes in standard loan covenants; pricer — decide the interest rate; administrator — develop formal quote, sent overnight to the salesperson for presentation to the client.

To deliver a quote averaged six days, but sometimes took two weeks. Salespeople could not access application status, and anxious customers switched to competitors. IBMC researched actual work time per application — average, 90 minutes! The file spent much time at in- and out-boxes. IBMC's new *deal structurers* averaged four hours for 90 percent of requests; specialists did the rest. Today, customers input data online; credit scoring, agreeing on terms and conditions, setting the interest rate and payment terms, and sending out contracts takes a few minutes.[13]

MANAGING HUMAN RESOURCES

Many firms trying to become more externally oriented believe the simple mantra — *Happy employees make happy customers.* **Human resource management (HRM)** conducts activities like recruiting, selecting, training, measuring and rewarding, career developing, and talent managing, providing many opportunities for the firm to emphasize the importance of an organization-wide external focus. An external orientation should follow from hiring the *right* people, supporting high performance, and developing and managing career transitions effectively.

Workforce measurement systems should be tightly linked to reward systems. When customer focused measures drive incentive compensation, the external orientation effort has real teeth. Managers are often skeptical about basing take-home pay on survey findings, but Microsoft and Xerox each report excellent results using customer satisfaction measures. Good survey design, rigorously tested items, and competent and independent data collectors reduce skepticism. At Bloomberg, every employee, including the janitor and the person who stocks the kitchen, receives incentive compensation based on terminal sales. *Equity equivalence certificates* get everyone's attention; they know Bloomberg's core objective is to sell terminals.

Sustaining an External Orientation

Many industry leaders have stumbled badly and lost their pre-eminent positions. Why? The stories are strikingly similar: The firm originally gained industry leadership by delivering customer value and securing differential advantage. The firm developed and focused resources, core competencies, and expertise toward this goal. The firm was externally oriented ... but then things changed. Past success began to hold the firm back; it could not sustain an external orientation and adjust to the new reality. We can find old and new leaders in many industries: air freight (Emery — FedEx), automobiles (General Motors — Toyota), home video (Blockbuster — Netflix), imaging systems (Xerox — Canon), and PCs (IBM, Dell — Lenovo). The original leader had superior technology, scale economies, substantial buying power, and well-established brands. But the new leader introduced a new business model, technology, and/or product design.

Getting everything right is difficult, and a chain is only as strong as its weakest link. For perfect integration of the market offer, the firm should execute every *moment of truth* flawlessly. The firm must not merely satisfy customers, it should delight them. Poor performance on some dimensions can overwhelm world-class performance on others.

Sustaining an external orientation is a little easier if the firm understands its challenges:

- **Accounting systems.** The firm must produce data in a form that supports an external perspective. Despite advances in business intelligence and analytics, many firms measure profits only by product; they should also assess profits by customer and/or customer group.

- **Bureaucracy.** As firms grow, departmentalization and task specialization are efficient ways to complete repetitive tasks. But rules and behaviors, reinforced by day-to-day work pressures, become embedded in the organization. As customers, we have all dealt with employees who tell us, "That's not my department" or "You'll have to talk to XYZ about that." Firms must complete day-by-day tasks, but they must also build the agility to serve customers well, and introducing sensing mechanisms to identify and address market opportunities.

- **Centralization versus decentralization.** Centralizing and standardizing can have great value, especially for cost reduction. But excessive centralization leads to standardized actions, rather than customer *responsiveness*. Key decision-makers are distant from the customer; those with detailed market, customer, and competitor insight play less significant decision-making roles. But excessive decentralization can leave the organization

KEY IDEA

➤ Hiring experienced marketers, including those at the highest levels, can play a major role in developing an external orientation.

➤ Marketing education helps marketers learn new behaviors that can instill an external perspective.

KEY IDEA

➤ If the firm hires the *right* people and develops and manages them appropriately, an external orientation should follow.

Marketing Question

What firms should have customer-focused training for employees? What sort of training do you think they should have?

Marketing Question

How do you assess your college, school, or university on its degree of external orientation? Are some parts more externally focused than others? If yes, what accounts for these differences?

without a clear focus. Deciding which activities are better centralized and which are better decentralized (closer to the customer) is a critical firm challenge.

- **Excessive focus on organizational efficiency.** Many firms work extremely hard to reduce costs by improving organizational efficiency. They use techniques like *Six Sigma* to make continuous incremental improvements in processes — operations and customer service. An organizational culture dominated by *Six Sigma* can become internally focused and less innovative, and drive out behavior addressing external changes.

- **Functional divisions.** Firms develop specialized functions to increase expertise in key areas. But specialization can lead to silo thinking and divisiveness among specialties. Functional heads must recognize the importance of cross-functional cooperation.

- **Functional view of marketing.** The firm must distinguish between marketing as a *philosophy* and marketing as a *department*. The firm that delegates all marketing problems to a marketing department will neither create nor deliver fully integrated offers. Achieving integration demands coordination among many different functional departments.

- **Internal politics.** The CEO and/or business head must actively support institutionalizing an external orientation and frequently communicate this support. If not, some functions will be suspicious of customer-focused initiatives. Jockeying for power and position occurs in all firms; leaders must not allow political concerns to override customer centricity.

- **Inward-oriented marketing departments.** Marketing departments are sometimes their own worst enemies. They implement a not-invented-here (NIH) syndrome that quashes *foreign* ideas and initiatives to *protect their turf*. This problem tends to be most serious in firms with good reputations for marketing expertise, where the marketing department has great political power.

- **Misaligned incentives.** People in organizations do what is *inspected* of them, not what is *expected* of them! They behave in ways that earn rewards. Conflicting and function-specific performance objectives and rewards make it difficult to integrate across functions. The result is often internal conflict and division.

- **Social fabric of institutions.** Firm employees know each other and interact daily. Customers, competitors, and suppliers are occasional *intruders* who interrupt daily life! How often have employees ignored you, the customer, as they chat together, seemingly oblivious of your presence?

For long-run success, the firm must be responsive yet dynamic, learning but not forgetting, understanding of human resources yet demanding of high performance, customer-sensitive yet competitive, and shareholder-value-creating but not short-sighted. In the 1980s and 1990s, Jack Welch lifted performance at an already highly regarded GE to an entirely new level. In one of his more famous exhortations, he stated, "I want managers who manage with their face to the customer and their backside to the CEO!" Jeff Bezos, founder of famed dotcom Amazon describes himself and his organization as "customer obsessed!" And at IBM, customer-focused Lou Gerstner restored the fallen computer giant to its former glory with a *services* vision. Leadership counts! Leaders must spread an external orientation throughout the firm.

KEY MESSAGES

- For long-run success, the firm must develop and sustain an external orientation.

- Firms with an external orientation often build success on functional excellence — customer service, finance, human resources, operations and the supply chain, research and development, and sales.

- The model for developing an external orientation contains external elements — vision, mission, and strategy; and internal architectural elements — organization structure, systems and processes, and HRM practices. Customer-focused values help achieve the necessary alignment.

- The firm can achieve an external orientation only if employees in various functional areas do their jobs with a keen understanding that customers are central to firm success.

- Most action in developing an external orientation rests in the firm's internal architecture.

- Sustaining an external orientation can be very difficult. Past and current firm success contains the seeds of future failure. Inability to adapt leads many previously successful firms to fail.

- The firm must beware of several impediments to sustaining an external orientation: accounting systems, bureaucracy, centralization versus decentralization, excessive focus on organizational efficiency, functional divisions, functional view of marketing, internal politics, inward-oriented marketing departments, misaligned incentives, and the social fabric of institutions.

VIDEOS AND AUDIOS

Developing the Marketing Organization	v2102 📹	Samuel Moed	Bristol-Myers Squibb
Marketing at GE	v2103 📹	Steve Liquori	GE
Leading the Marketing Organization	v2104 📹	William Klepper	Columbia Business School
Marketing Imperative 5	a2101 🎧		

v2102

v2103

v2104

a2101

IMPERATIVE 6

Monitor and Control

CHAPTER 22

MONITORING AND CONTROLLING FIRM PERFORMANCE AND FUNCTIONING cv2201

To access O-codes, go to **www.ocodes.com**

LEARNING OBJECTIVES

When you have completed this chapter, you will be able to:

- Describe critical elements in the monitor-and-control process.
- Implement key principles of the monitor-and-control process.
- Measure input, intermediate, and output variables.
- Monitor and control firm performance versus objectives.
- Monitor and control firm functioning.
- Understand and recognize success factors.

OPENING CASE: SONY ELECTRONICS

Ron Boire, then President of Sony Electronics Sales, talked about Sony's careful focus on well-chosen measures and how it uses them to secure the behavior it requires. "Sony is really driven by the concept of, 'If you can't measure it, you can't do it.' Sometimes that's straightforward; sometimes it's very complicated.[1] *Interactions that Sony salespeople have with our retail trade channel customers are a good example.*

"With national customers like Best Buy, Sears, Target, and Walmart, we used to do classic sales compensation. Each salesperson had a sales budget, and we measured salespeople performance against budget. If you had a budget target of $1 million for a product category, and you sold at $1.1 million, you did a great job and you made a good bonus. Regardless of what was stuck in the barn at the end of the month or the end of the year. Regardless of whether or not they could pay for it. Regardless of whether you delivered it to them on time.

"Today, we base up to 70 percent of our inventory management/asset management group's compensation, and 50 percent of our salespeople's compensation, on customer scorecards. We agree on metrics individually with each national and strategic customer. Most focus on simple things like on-time delivery, percent in-stock, forecast accuracy, and gross margin return on inventory [GMROI] — the key retail performance metric. To set these metrics we ask each customer: 'What's important to you? What are your targets? What are your strategic concerns?' Depending on their size, we track retailers either monthly or weekly. And our salespeople are bonus compensated twice a year based on their customer scorecards.

"When you change the basis of people's paychecks, it really is remarkable how fast they change their behavior. We've seen a tremendous shift in the behavior of the organization, and a very positive reaction from the marketplace. It's revolutionary in consumer electronics for a salesperson to say, 'No, I won't take your purchase order, because you have too much inventory.' Everybody talks about aligning with your customers, but if you're paying your salespeople to stuff the box you can't be aligned — it's impossible."

Sony wants to know customer profitability. Boire continued, *"We measure customer profitability from a contribution margin perspective. Once you get past that sell-in mentality, you can focus on simple measurements like contribution margin; incremental contribution margin is the best ongoing measure of a marketing relationship with our trade channel customers. Marketing holds the P&Ls on these major customer accounts, but the only thing we load in are direct costs attributable to that customer; we include the sales team and all its funding, but we take nothing from headquarters. We look at the contribution margin in dollars per customer; we project mid-range contributions some years ahead, and we calculate a net present value [NPV] with a conservative termination value.*

"Sometimes we have one or two customers that are in financial difficulties. And we ask, what's the contribution margin of this customer? If they go away, the fixed cost at headquarters doesn't go away. But there may be $30 million in contribution margin that goes away. The contribution dollars and the NPV give you the measures to say, 'What should we invest in this customer to try to help them stay healthy?' To help one customer, we hired outside consultants to go in as a crisis management team. And the at-risk number in our minds is this annual contribution margin. If we invest up to that point and the customer turns the corner, we're not going to claim sole credit for saving them, but we certainly didn't help them go down, right? On a day-to-day basis, this grounds management as to the relative value of any customer. Because we can say, 'You know what? The net present value of this customer is $600 million. That's what this relationship is worth.'"

> **CASE QUESTION**
>
> Compare and contrast Sony's old measurement-and-control system with its new system. Suppose a firm with which you are familiar made this sort of change. What implementation problems would you anticipate? How would you deal with them?

KEY PRINCIPLES OF MONITOR-AND-CONTROL PROCESSES

You have likely heard this popular management saying: *"If you can't measure it, you can't manage it."* People in organizations tend to do what is *inspected* of them, not what is *expected* of them. Hence, good monitor-and-control processes are critical for ensuring that people do what they are supposed to do, so the *right* actions lead to the *right* results. *Monitoring* focuses on measuring how well the firm is doing in various business aspects. *Control* is concerned with making changes or adjustments so the firm does better. Monitor-and-control processes are the most powerful means of changing individual behavior and enhancing long-term results.[2] Chapter 22 focuses on two complementary areas: firm performance and firm functioning:

- **Firm performance.** *Is the firm achieving planned results?* Planned results are the **standards** against which the firm measures actual results. All things equal, if actual results meet or exceed standards, performance is satisfactory and the firm continues to operate as planned. If actual results are below standards, the firm should modify its actions.[3]

> *Marketing Question*
>
> Consider your personal objectives and strategy: Have you thought through these rigorously? Are you achieving your planned objectives? Are you functioning well in trying to achieve your objectives?

• **Firm functioning.** To achieve desired results, the firm allocates resources and takes actions. *Is the firm functioning well?* For greater insight, we drill down into three aspects:
  • **Implementation.** Did the firm implement planned actions?
  • **Strategy.** Is the firm's market strategy well conceived and on target?
  • **Managerial processes.** Are the firm's managerial processes the best they can be?

Monitor and control should not occur as managerial whim; the firm should build a monitor-and-control philosophy into its DNA. This is not simple; it may take considerable time and effort to assemble the infrastructure for an effective system. Measurement is crucial; in this chapter we discuss many types of measures. But the best-designed measures have no impact unless the firm also implements a process for developing standards and assessing results against those standards. Effective monitor-and-control processes rest on five core principles:

• Focus on market levers and develop alternative plans.
• Implement steering control rather than post-action control.
• Use the right performance measures at the right organizational levels.
• Model the relationship between input, intermediate, and output measures.
• Tie compensation to performance.

FOCUS ON MARKET LEVERS AND DEVELOP ALTERNATIVE PLANS

Market levers flow from the firm's market strategy and implementation plans; they include actions like introducing new products, increasing/decreasing advertising, adding/replacing salespeople, and enhancing training. The firm allocates resources and takes actions to achieve planned performance. The firm's actual performance versus standards tell if firm resource allocations and actions were successful. Monitor-and-control efforts should focus on market levers. If actual results fall below standards, the firm should be ready with alternative plans.

Historically, Samsung focused on low-price, high-volume products so production managers could optimize capacity utilization. Samsung's new monitor-and-control system measures market price position and encourages sales of higher-price products.

IMPLEMENT STEERING CONTROL RATHER THAN POST-ACTION CONTROL

Steering control and *post-action control* are different **monitor-and-control approaches.** Firms using post-action control wait a pre-set time period, then compare actual results against standards. If results are unsatisfactory, they take corrective action. Firms exercising post-action control typically develop annual marketing plans and set standards by quarter. By contrast, steering control is dynamic, continuous, and anticipatory. Firms using steering control set standards for measures like sales, market share, and profit, then calendarize by month, week, or even day. These firms set control limits for performance and continually compare actual results against standards. Because they also track leading indicators, these firms are more market responsive.

Historically, Gillette consolidated sales every quarter; now these figures are available daily. Cisco can close its books in a single day by converting 50 different ledgers in a single global system. Managers can view revenues, margins, backlog, expenses, and other data by region, business unit, channel, and account manager daily and take appropriate actions. At Zara's Spanish headquarters, sales managers sit at terminals monitoring sales at every store around the world, thus enabling twice-per-week restocking.

USE THE RIGHT PERFORMANCE MEASURES AT THE RIGHT ORGANIZATIONAL LEVELS

If possible, the firm's monitor-and-control process should use objective measures like sales, market share, and profits. When less concrete measures like customer satisfaction are appropriate, the firm should use validated scales.[4] Regardless, the firm should use the *right* measures.

The firm should measure performance at multiple organizational levels, like corporate, geographic region, business unit, market segment, marketing function, customer, sales region, sales district, and/or sales territory. Alcoa measures profitability by market sector, business, and customer and, in its aerospace division, by airplane program.[5] Organizational position should largely drive the data employees receive. Senior managers do not typically require performance variances by salesperson, but they should have the ability to do deep dives. Salespeople do not need to know performance variances of peers in other sales regions. But as the **iceberg principle** — Figure 22.1 — suggests, many problems may lie beneath the surface. Good performance in a unit or sub-unit can *hide* poor performance elsewhere. To improve overall performance, the firm must isolate problem areas.

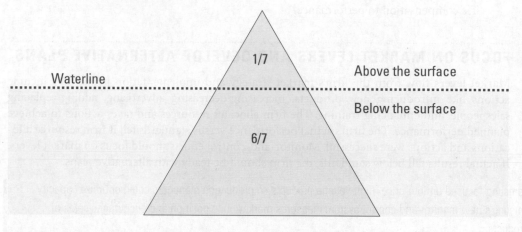

Waterline

1/7

Above the surface

Below the surface

6/7

MODEL THE RELATIONSHIP BETWEEN INPUT, INTERMEDIATE, AND OUTPUT MEASURES

Monitor-and-control systems must distinguish between cause and effect to gain insight. Suppose we observe that advertising spending increases and sales also increase. One interpretation is that advertising was effective: Increased advertising spending led to increased sales. The alternative interpretation is that increased sales led to an increase in advertising spending: The advertising budget is a fixed percentage of sales! To ensure the firm makes valid inferences, it must distinguish among:

- **Input measures** — actions the firm takes.
- **Intermediate measures** — customer actions or changes in their state of mind.
- **Output measures** — performance variables like sales and profits.

Figure 22.2 shows the flow chart of input measures leading to intermediate measures; in turn, intermediate measures lead to output measures in a cause-and-effect relationship. Market levers provide the input measures; inputs affect intermediate steps that must occur before customers purchase products and provide the firm with outputs. Generally, collecting data on input and output measures is relatively easy; securing data on intermediate measures is often more resource-intensive.

KEY IDEA

➤ The firm should use objective measures for monitor-and-control purposes; if scales are appropriate, these should be validated.

FIGURE 22.1

THE ICEBERG PRINCIPLE

KEY IDEA

➤ The firm should measure performance at multiple organizational levels.

➤ Good performance in a unit or sub-unit can hide poor performance elsewhere. The firm must isolate problem areas.

KEY IDEA

➤ Critical control variables are:

Input measures
↓
Intermediate measures
↓
Output measures

The firm must have confidence in the presumed relationships between inputs and intermediates and between intermediates and outputs.[6] To illustrate, when the firm takes advertising and sales force actions, input, intermediate, and output measures may be as follows:

- **Input measures.** Financial resources spent on advertising, number of sales calls per day
- **Intermediate measures:**
  - **Customer actions.** Number of customers agreeing to a product trial, number of customers placing deposits for future purchases.
  - **Customer mental states.** Product awareness, associations, attitudes, product interest, intention to purchase.
- **Output measures.** Sales, market share, profits.

Output measures are *lagging indicators* — *rearview mirror* — what has happened. Intermediate and input measures are *leading indicators* — *dashboards* — what should happen.[7]

TIE COMPENSATION TO PERFORMANCE

The performance-to-compensation linkage is the final but critical piece of the monitor-and-control puzzle. Developing the performance-to-compensation linkage is not easy. When compensation design is poor, employees optimize individual performance and compensation but, as we saw in the Opening Case, may harm the firm.

CRITICAL ELEMENTS OF THE MONITOR-AND-CONTROL PROCESS

Figure 22.3 shows nine repeatable yet distinct stages for any monitor-and-control process[8]:

1. **Identify the process to control.** Clarify the control system's focus.
2. **Decide and define measures.** Options include input, intermediate, and/or output variables.
3. **Develop a measurement system.** Figure out a system to collect, integrate, and analyze relevant data and distribute results.
4. **Set standards.** Decide which standards to apply for each measure. Generally, standards flow from action programs related to the market strategy.
5. **Measure results.** Using the measurement system from step 3, collect, integrate, analyze, and distribute results.
6. **Compare results against standards.** Compare results — step 5, against standards — step 4, to identify *performance gaps* and variances.
7. **Understand and communicate performance gaps.** Communicate data and interpretation of performance gaps to executives responsible for taking action. Some gaps will be positive; others will be negative.
8. **Generate and evaluate alternatives.** Executives identify alternative corrective actions to close negative gaps. Large positive gaps may require higher performance standards.
9. **Select alternative and take action.** Executives select a course of action, then develop and implement an action plan.

Monitor-and-control processes are not one-time events. After completing the nine stages, the firm should confirm that stages 1, 2, and 3 are well developed. Then, completing step 9 leads directly to step 4 — confirm or reset standards. The firm optimizes motivated behavior when standards are moderately challenging; standards that are too easy or too difficult reduce motivation.[9]

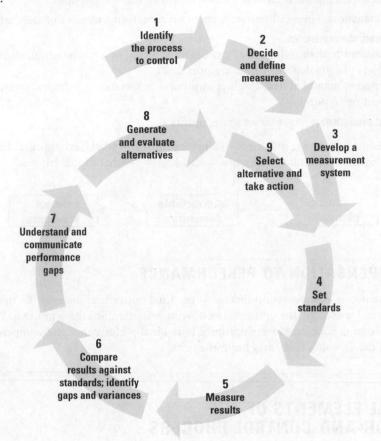

FIGURE 22.3

THE MONITOR-AND-CONTROL PROCESS

Monitoring and Controlling Firm Performance

What performance should the firm monitor and control? The Figure 22.3 framework — *input → intermediate → output* — helps answer this question. We address this topic in reverse order.[10]

OUTPUT MEASURES

Recall that *output measures* are the *final* results the firm wants to achieve. These measures can be *hard* — objectively assessed; or *soft* — like rating scales requiring more interpretation. Let's look carefully at the various types of measures the firm can assess.

INTERNAL HARD MEASURES — SALES VOLUME

Sales volume includes sales units, sales revenues, and their growth rates. Overall measures are important, but breaking these down to identify components provides greater insight. Two alternative revenue breakdowns are:

REVENUE PREDICTABILITY. We may classify revenue in three ways:

- **Continuous.** Revenue the firm expects to receive on a regular week-by-week or month-by-month basis.
- **Periodic.** Sales are infrequent but can be forecast, like capital equipment sales or seasonal goods.
- **Episodic.** Occur because of unanticipated events and cannot be forecast, like building materials sales following a hurricane.

PENETRATION VERSUS GROWTH. Many firms want to distinguish between sales based on current business — *penetration* — and sales from new business — *growth.* Retail organizations gain deeper insight by partitioning sales into *same-store* (penetration) and *new-store* (growth).

ISSUES WITH SALES MEASURES. We consider three topics:

- **Different sales volume measures.** At a minimum, the firm should measure both sales units and sales revenues. Both measures are necessary to distinguish between revenue growth based on sales units and revenue growth based on price increases.
- **Sales quality.** Some firms focus on specific types of sales. General Mills measures sales of products meeting certain nutritional targets and sets goals on that basis.
- **Accuracy and consistency of sales volume measures.** The firm must ensure sales units and sales revenue measures are accurate, and consistently derived from period to period.

INTERNAL HARD MEASURES — PRODUCT PROFITABILITY

Achieving good sales volume performance is important, but management is generally more interested in profits. Unfortunately, the most common profit measure — *bottom-line profit* — may not be terribly useful for assessing marketing effectiveness. Failure to meet profit targets may result from lack of promised resources or *unfair* corporate overhead allocations. The firm should focus on measures that exclude allocations — like **profit contribution** and **direct product profit**.

PROFIT CONTRIBUTION equals sales revenues less variable costs. To earn positive net profits, profit contribution must exceed fixed costs.

DIRECT PRODUCT PROFIT assesses profit performance after taking into account fixed costs. The firm separates fixed costs into two parts: costs *directly related* to the product (would disappear if the product were dropped) — *direct fixed costs*; and *allocated* costs — *indirect fixed costs* (would remain). Direct product profit equals profit contribution less direct fixed costs.[11]

PROFIT RETURN MEASURES. Some firms prefer *profit return measures* to absolute measures. Two popular measures are *return on sales (ROS)* and *return on investment (ROI).*

INTERNAL HARD MEASURES — CUSTOMER PROFITABILITY

Most firms have systems to measure product profitability; some are rudimentary, others are highly sophisticated. By contrast, relatively few firms measure their profits from customers. Yet customers provide firm revenues and are its core assets. Hence, the firm should understand the profitability dynamics of individual customers, market segments, and distribution channels.

To summarize: Sales volume and profit measures provide good data on firm performance, but lack an external benchmark. Market-based measures address this issue.

EXTERNAL HARD MEASURES — MARKET SHARE

Market share compares firm performance directly with competitors and is the most common *market-based* measure. The firm should measure market share in both units and revenues. When price exceeds the average market price, revenue share exceeds unit share (and vice versa). **Market occupancy ratio** measures the breadth of the firm's market activity. Table 22.1 shows several market-based measures.

Measure	Calculation	Information Provided
Market share (MS) (%)	Firm sales/sales of all competitors	Market position versus all competitors
Relative market share (RMS) (%)	Firm sales/sales of major competitor(s)	Market position versus the firm's major competitor(s)
Market occupancy ratio (MOR) (%)	Number of firm customers/ Total number of customers	Fraction of potential customers with which the firm does business

SOFT MEASURES

The firm should regularly take its customers' pulse. Customer satisfaction and attitudes are widely employed *soft* output measures. Soft measures help track how customers are responding to the firm and competitors. Because many soft measures are tied to hard measures, like customer satisfaction to sales, they can be valuable intermediate measures.[12]

Net Promoter Score (NPS) is a widely used soft measure, derived from a single question measured on a 0 to 10 scale:

> "How likely is it that you would recommend XXXX to a friend or colleague?"
> 0 = not at all likely; 5 = neutral; 10 = extremely likely.

Net Promoter Score = percentage of customers scoring 9 or 10 (promoters) minus percentage of customers scoring 0 to 6 (detractors).

Firms using NPS also probe for the reasons behind the score.

INTERMEDIATE MEASURES

The firm takes actions — *inputs* — to improve *outputs. Intermediate* measures sit between inputs and outputs. Success on intermediate measures does not guarantee output performance. But the firm only achieves good output performance by securing good intermediate performance. Intermediate measures have two characteristics:

- **Input effect.** The firm's marketing effort must affect the intermediate measure.
- **Output effect.** The intermediate measure must influence another intermediate measure and/or an important output measure(s).

The distributor of inexpensive Fleischmann's gin developed a new retail distribution strategy; shelve products next to high-quality Gordon's and Gilbey's. The theory: Consumers would reach Gordon's and Gilbey's displays, see less expensive Fleischmann bottles, then select Fleischmann's. The key intermediate measure: number of stores accepting Fleischmann's shelf placement.

The best intermediate measures are leading indicators of output performance; they should result from a tested customer purchase model: inputs → intermediates → outputs. Intermediate measures are particularly important in long-cycle sales processes, like major capital goods. Many months or even years may pass between an initial customer contact and the actual sale. Many firms manage sales pipelines — Chapter 17 — using intermediate measures.[13]

Monitoring and Controlling Firm Functioning

In a well-developed monitor-and-control system, input measures are closely and explicitly linked to intermediate measures. In turn, intermediate measures are closely and explicitly related to output measures.

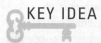
INPUT MEASURES

Input measure performance depends on three aspects of firm functioning:

- **Implementation control.** Did the firm implement planned actions?
- **Strategy control.** Is the firm's market strategy well conceived and on target?
- **Managerial process control.** Are firm processes the best they can be?

IMPLEMENTATION CONTROL

The firm's market strategy spawns many implementation programs; these programs generate action plans in marketing-mix areas like product, service, promotion, distribution, and price. The market strategy may also generate action plans in functional areas like engineering, operations, R&D, and technical service. Marketing and other functional managers are typically responsible for ensuring these action plans are executed. Table 22.2 illustrates possible input measures for the sales force.

TABLE 22.2

POSSIBLE INPUT MEASURES — SALES FORCE

Measure	Measure Focus
Implementation of sales planning system	Ensure sales force plans time allocations
New product knowledge training	Ensure sales force is competent to sell new products
Sales calls per day	Ensure sales force is working hard
Sales calls on new accounts	Ensure sales force spends time with target accounts
Sales territories vacant	Ensure sales managers plan for attrition
Total expenses	Manage sales force discretionary costs

STRATEGY CONTROL

Strategy control answers the question: *Is the firm's market strategy well conceived and on target?* The firm typically sets strategy for the medium or long run; it should not overreact to poor output performance by making hasty changes. For strategy control, post-action control is generally superior to steering control.

Figure 22.4 shows how to integrate strategy control and implementation control to isolate causes of firm output performance.[14] Performance is good in Cell A, but less so in the other cells:

MARKET STRATEGY GOOD/IMPLEMENTATION GOOD (CELL A). A well-developed and well-implemented strategy should drive good output performance. The firm must monitor customers, competitors, and the general environment to ensure the strategy remains on track.

MARKET STRATEGY GOOD/IMPLEMENTATION POOR (CELL B). Poor implementation of a good strategy will probably lead to poor output performance. Sometimes an especially robust strategy can survive poor implementation, but this is unusual. Cole National (CN) targeted hardware and other small stores for key-making machines and key blanks; CN succeeded despite poor sales force execution. The firm should focus on improving execution.

MARKET STRATEGY POOR/IMPLEMENTATION GOOD (CELL C). Rarely does excellent implementation overcome a poor strategy. If the firm fails to provide customer value, successfully implementing other marketing elements will not compensate. Some years ago, Frito-Lay failed with a new cookie despite legendary sales force implementation.

MARKET STRATEGY POOR/IMPLEMENTATION POOR (CELL D). Output performance is likely disastrous. The firm's challenge is to isolate the cause: poor strategy or poor implementation?

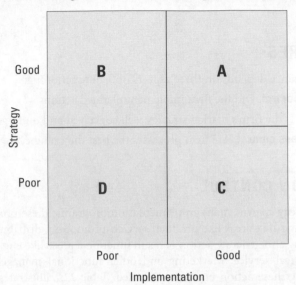

FIGURE 22.4

INTEGRATING
STRATEGY AND
IMPLEMENTATION
CONTROL

This framework explicitly recognizes that good output performance requires both good strategy *and* good implementation. Poor output performance has many authors; the challenge for management is isolating the cause. Deep analysis across many aspects of the business may be necessary. No matter where the firm isolates problems — strategy or implementation — some things must change. For example, advertising is relatively easy to change. Conversely, distribution arrangements are more difficult to alter due to logistical, contractual, and interpersonal relationships.[15]

MANAGERIAL PROCESS CONTROL

Are the firm's processes the best they can be? We addressed this question in Chapter 21. Here, we examine the *marketing audit* which focuses explicitly on improving marketing functioning.[16]

THE MARKETING AUDIT. The **marketing audit** is a comprehensive process for evaluating firm marketing practices embracing market strategy, systems, activities, and organization. To ensure confidences are kept and findings are unbiased, outsiders typically conduct the audit. A useful auditing framework has six parts, each spawning several questions[17]:

- **Marketing environment.** What changes are occurring at customers, competitors, complementers, and suppliers? What PESTLE trends affect the industry? How do these changes and trends affect the firm? What are the performance implications?

- **Market objectives and strategy.** Are the firm's market objectives and strategy realistic given the environment and firm strengths? Do managers understand the objectives and strategy?

- **Marketing implementation.** How do firm offers compare to competitor offers in terms of product, service, promotion, distribution, and price? Does the firm's marketing mix implement the market strategy? Are they mutually consistent?

- **Marketing organization.** Are job roles and responsibilities clear and consistent? Is recruiting, hiring, training, and development on track? Is senior management engaged with major customers? Do measurement and reward systems motivate performance?

KEY IDEA

➤ Strategy control:
Is the firm's market
strategy well conceived
and on target?

➤ Post-action approaches
are generally superior
for strategy control.

KEY IDEA

➤ Distinguishing
between strategy
and implementation
problems is crucial.

KEY IDEA

➤ Managerial process
control: Are the firm's
processes the best they
can be?

KEY IDEA

➤ The marketing audit is a
comprehensive process
for evaluating the firm's
marketing practices.

- **Marketing systems.** How effective are firm marketing systems, like brand monitoring, competitor intelligence, customer database design, pipeline management, and tapping into social media?
- **Marketing productivity.** How profitable are the firm's products, customers, and segments? Should resource allocation be modified?

Marketing audits can be a very effective diagnostic tool.

THE BALANCED SCORECARD

KEY IDEA

➤ The balanced score-card reflects a steering control philosophy, balancing input, inter-mediate, and output marketing measures.

The **balanced scorecard** is an increasingly widespread approach for monitoring and controlling firm performance and firm functioning. The balanced scorecard seeks a middle ground between using too few measures and too many. Each extreme leads to problems:

TOO FEW MEASURES. Managers may *game* the system to optimize performance on those measures, especially if they drive compensation. Such behavior may cause unintended consequences. When short-term profit is the only standard, performing well is very easy: Just cut back on advertising and R&D for a couple of quarters. Of course, such actions hurt the firm in the long run. Previously, U.S. airlines competed on shorter flight times; when on-time performance data became widely available, airlines lengthened advertised flight times and improved *on-time* performance!

Marketing Question

In your educational institution, each instructor has his or her own way of measuring student performance. Can you suggest a balanced-scorecard framework that all instructors could use to measure student performance?

TOO MANY MEASURES. Multiple measures cause problems if they are unclear or conflicting. Employees have difficulty discerning required behavior and may focus efforts on actions that do not further firm goals.[18] Many firms address these problems via the balanced scorecard.[19] Well-balanced scorecards reflect a steering control philosophy by *balancing* input, intermediate, and output measures. Perhaps the most commonly used measures for balanced scorecards are:

- **Market share** — hard output measure
- **Customer satisfaction relative to competition** — soft output measure
- **Customer retention versus industry averages** — hard output measure
- **Investment as a percentage of sales** — hard input measure
- **Employee attitudes and retention** (especially customer-facing employees) — soft and hard input measures

Many balanced scorecards focus on four measurement categories — financial, customer, internal business processes, and learning and growth. Table 22.3 shows candidate measures for a global account management program.

TABLE 22.3

CANDIDATE VARIABLES FOR A BALANCED SCORECARD APPROACH TO MEASURING THE GLOBAL ACCOUNT PROGRAM

Financial	Internal Business Process
• Year-on-year revenue and profit growth • Sales expense as a percentage of revenues	• Percentage of customers with long-term contracts • Percentage of customers with *solutions* contracts • Process improvements from collaboration — summary billing, product development
Customer	**Learning and Growth**
• Customer satisfaction and loyalty • Access to customer at the C-level — CEO, CFO, CIO, and COO	• Number of best practices adopters • Improved management practices

The firm should closely align scorecards for different functional areas and managerial levels — like brand and category managers, and district, regional, and national sales managers. Carefully designed and aligned sets of measures improve firm chances of securing high performance.

KEY MESSAGES

The purpose of monitor-and-control systems is to improve firm performance. Four key principles are:

- Focus on market levers and develop alternative plans.
- Implement steering control rather than post-action control.
- Use the right performance measures at the right organizational levels.
- Model the relationship between input, intermediate, and output measures.

Critical stages in developing a monitor-and-control process are:

- Identify the process to control
- Decide and define measures
- Develop a measurement system
- Set standards
- Measure results
- Compare results against standards; identify gaps and variances
- Understand and communicate performance gaps
- Generate and evaluate alternatives
- Select alternative and take action

The firm should monitor and control three sorts of measures:

- Output measures — final results the firm wants to achieve; can be *hard* or *soft.*
- Intermediate measures — sit between input and output measures, affect other intermediate measures and/or output measures.
- Input measures — concerned with firm functioning, explicitly linked to intermediate measures. Input measures concern three types of control:
  - Implementation control
  - Strategy control
  - Managerial process control
- The balanced scorecard typically embraces input, intermediate, and output measures.

VIDEOS AND AUDIOS

Monitor and Control	v2202 📹	Alan Fortier	Fortier & Associates
Monitor and Control	v2203 📹	Ron Boire	Toys R Us
Marketing Imperative 6	a2201 🎧		

v2202

v2203

a2201

SECTION V
SPECIAL
MARKETING TOPICS cvs5

SECTION V — SPECIAL MARKETING TOPICS — COMPRISES A SINGLE CHAPTER. Chapter 23 focuses on a topic appearing in various places throughout *Capon's Marketing Framework* — International, Regional, and Global Marketing. Globalization is one of the major trends facing practically all firms in practically all industries today. Chapter 23 helps firms decide whether or not to enter foreign markets, which foreign markets to enter, and which entry options to choose. Further, the chapter discusses designing, implementing, and organizing for international, regional, and global marketing.

Capon's Marketing Framework

SECTION I: MARKETING AND THE FIRM

CHAPTER 1
Introduction to Managing Marketing

CHAPTER 2
The Value of Customers

SECTION II: FUNDAMENTAL INSIGHTS FOR STRATEGIC MARKETING

CHAPTER 3
Market Insight

CHAPTER 4
Customer Insight

CHAPTER 5
Insight about Competitors, Company, and Complementers

CHAPTER 6
Marketing Research

TRANSITION TO STRATEGIC MARKETING

SECTION III: STRATEGIC MARKETING

IMPERATIVE 1
Determine and Recommend Which Markets to Address

CHAPTER 7
Identifying and Choosing Opportunities

IMPERATIVE 2
Identify and Target Market Segments

CHAPTER 8
Market Segmentation and Targeting

IMPERATIVE 3
Set Strategic Direction and Positioning

CHAPTER 9
Market Strategy – Integrating Firm Efforts for Marketing Success

CHAPTER 10
Managing through the Life Cycle

CHAPTER 11
Managing Brands

SECTION IV: IMPLEMENTING THE MARKET STRATEGY

IMPERATIVE 4
Design the Market Offer

PART A: PROVIDING CUSTOMER VALUE

PART B: COMMUNICATING CUSTOMER VALUE

PART C: DELIVERING CUSTOMER VALUE

PART D: GETTING PAID FOR CUSTOMER VALUE

CHAPTER 12
Managing the Product Line

CHAPTER 15
Integrated Marketing Communications

CHAPTER 18
Distribution Decisions

CHAPTER 19
Critical Underpinnings of Pricing Decisions

CHAPTER 13
Managing Services and Customer Service

CHAPTER 16
Mass and Digital Communication

CHAPTER 20
Setting Prices

CHAPTER 14
Developing New Products

CHAPTER 17
Directing and Managing the Field Sales Effort

IMPERATIVE 5
Secure Support from Other Functions

CHAPTER 21
Ensuring the Firm Implements the Market Offer as Planned

IMPERATIVE 6
Monitor and Control

CHAPTER 22
Monitoring and Controlling Firm Functioning and Performance

SECTION V: SPECIAL MARKETING TOPICS

CHAPTER 23
International, Regional, and Global Marketing

CHAPTER 23

INTERNATIONAL, REGIONAL, AND GLOBAL MARKETING

LEARNING OBJECTIVES

When you have completed this chapter, you will be able to:

- Assess alternative foreign markets and decide which to enter.
- Become familiar with economic and political issues and governmental organizations relevant for entering foreign markets.
- Understand the options for entering foreign markets.
- Develop market strategy for approaching global markets.
- Segment global markets and develop global branding strategies.
- Implement international and global market strategies.
- Develop the *right* organization for managing the firm's activities in foreign markets.
- Manage global customers.

OPENING CASE: DHL

DHL (Dalsey, Hillblom, and Lynn) was founded in 1969 as a document courier in the Asia-Pacific region several years before Federal Express (now FedEx).[1] During the next 30 years, DHL expanded throughout Asia Pacific, Europe, and the Americas. In 2002, Deutsche Post (DP) acquired DHL. Subsequently, DP acquired more than 100 firms in related fields, including Danzas-AEI (Europe's largest freight forwarder) and leading domestic parcel firms in Britain, France, Spain, and the Benelux countries. (In 2008, DHL withdrew from the U.S. domestic market.) By 2009, DHL had annual revenues approaching $100 billion and employed 285,000 people worldwide.

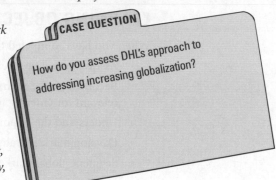

DHL serves the express delivery and logistics business segments for its parent DP. DHL's express service links 120,000 destinations in more than 220 countries and territories. DHL provides delivery services from a network of 5,000 offices with a fleet of more than 70,000 vehicles and 400 aircraft. DHL maintains 3.5 million square meters of warehouse space at over 1,000 distribution centers and provides freight forwarding, logistics, and supply-chain-management services.

DHL's vision states: "Customers trust DHL as the preferred global express and logistics partner, leading the industry in terms of quality, profitability, and market share. DHL enhances the business of our customers by offering highest quality express and logistics solutions based on strong local expertise combined with the most extensive global network presence."

To serve customers, DHL's four major brands (businesses) have profit and loss responsibility:

- *DHL Express: same-day, time-definite, day-definite express delivery services*
- *DHL Supply Chain CIS: contract logistics and industry solutions — supply-chain management, warehousing, distribution, value-added services, logistics outsourcing, and lead logistics supplier*
- *Global Forwarding Freight Air Freight and Ocean Freight Services: air freight, ocean freight, industrial projects, and customer program management*
- *Global Forwarding Freight Road and Rail Freight: flexible and customized road and inter-modal transport network*

DHL customers comprise three tiers. Tier 1 — top 100 customers, managed by Global Customer Solutions (GCS) globally. Tier 2 — other multinational customers, managed by individual business units globally. Tier 3 — thousands of local customers, managed by individual business units locally.

Global Customer Solutions. *DHL organizes GCS by nine industry sectors (Aerospace; Automotive; Chemical; Consulting; Fashion; Industrial, Engineering, and Manufacturing; Life Sciences; Retail; and Technology). Each Tier 1 customer has a dedicated global customer manager (GCM) who reports into one of the industry sectors. GCMs are responsible for global revenues and profits at their customers. They enjoy three types of support:*

- *Local Key Account Managers (KAMs). Individual KAMs work for one of the brands in a specific country but are assigned to GCMs on a dotted-line basis.*
- *Regional Customer Managers (RCMs). RCMs are responsible for certain areas of the world — Asia Pacific; Europe, Middle East, Africa; and the Americas. They report to the GCMs but have more direct everyday contact with KAMs.*
- *Staff Support. Various types including program management, supply-chain consultants, pricing, information technology, tender management, and legal/risk expertise.*

CASE QUESTION

How do you assess DHL's approach to addressing increasing globalization?

The world is being flattened. I didn't start it and you can't stop it, except at great cost to human development and your own future. But we can manage it, for better or worse.

— Thomas L. Friedman[2]

Opportunities for firms to engage in *international and global marketing* are large and growing.[3] Since the 1950s, inter-country trade has increased dramatically — Figure 23.1. One trend is critical: Individual firms increasingly seek opportunities beyond their domestic markets. The purpose of this chapter is to help you think through critical issues for approaching foreign markets.

Note that Chapter 23's title is deliberate — international, regional, and global marketing. One size does not fit all. Some firms engage in *global marketing* by entering many foreign markets in different continents; some focus on specific geographic regions — *regional marketing*; and others on just a few foreign countries — *international marketing.* But venturing into unfamiliar territory is not for everyone; many firms prefer to focus on their domestic markets.

In this chapter you will learn to assess international markets, develop market strategy, implement market offers, and manage the marketing process anywhere in the world.

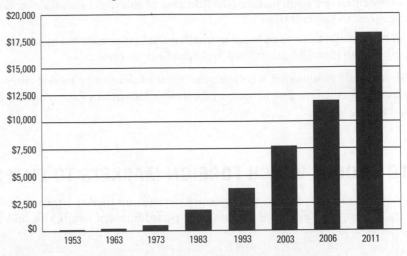

FIGURE 23.1

GLOBAL MERCHANDISE TRADE ($ BILLIONS)[4]

Source: World Trade Association

Chapter 23 focuses on key marketing issues for expanding geographically. We draw on the marketing imperatives, principles, and philosophy from previous chapters as we ask and answer several questions:

- Should the firm engage in marketing outside its domestic borders?
- How should the firm choose which foreign markets to enter?
- What foreign-market-entry options are available?
- What market strategy should the firm choose for foreign markets?
- What global market strategy issues must the firm address, and how should it do so?
- How should the firm organize for global markets?
- How should the firm address global customers?

SHOULD YOU ENTER FOREIGN MARKETS?

Historically, large firms were more likely to venture abroad than medium-size and small firms. Firms like Citibank, Ford, General Motors, Heinz, IBM, Nestlé, Shell, Unilever, and many others have operated overseas for decades.[5] Today, firms of all sizes contemplate taking the plunge.

Generally, firms go abroad for a variety of different reasons:

- **Diversify risk.** Domestic firms spread risk by seeking revenues in countries with different local and regional business cycles.
- **Follow customers.** When an important customer enters a foreign market, the firm may have little choice but to follow, like Toyota's suppliers.
- **Gain knowledge.** Foreign market entry may be the best way to enhance firm intellectual capital, especially if the industry's most demanding customers are abroad.
- **Growth opportunities.** Revenue and profit opportunities may seem greater abroad than at home. An attractive opportunity may arrive randomly, like an unsolicited request for firm products from a foreign market, or result from a broad search process.

- **Keep competitors honest.** Sometimes a foreign competitor subsidizes entry in the firm's domestic market with profits earned at home. To *keep it honest*, the firm may enter the aggressor's home market.
- **Reduce costs.** Sometimes firms drive success from low-cost operations that allow low prices. By entering foreign markets, the firm may be able to enhance scale economies and secure access to low-cost labor.
- **Small home market.** For firms based in small countries, going abroad may be the only reasonable way to grow like many Swiss and Scandinavian firms.

The firm should only go abroad if it believes that profits from foreign market entry outweigh the risks. Conversely, the firm should not hesitate to withdraw from a foreign market(s) if entry is unprofitable.

HOW TO CHOOSE WHICH FOREIGN MARKETS TO ENTER

Just like domestic markets, foreign market entry depends on market attractiveness and the firm's ability to compete. Key considerations are expected financial return, risk, and timing of profit flows.

FOREIGN MARKET ATTRACTIVENESS

To assess what makes a foreign market attractive, we adapt the PESTLE framework — Chapter 3. PESTLE factors affect market attractiveness in different ways. For international markets, we examine several dimensions that factor heavily in assessing market attractiveness: economic, political, legal/regulatory, and sociocultural and geographic distance.

ECONOMIC, POLITICAL, AND LEGAL/REGULATORY

Economic. The crucial economic issue is the current and potential market size for firm products and services. A critical determinant is often country wealth: Wealthier countries' greater spending power implies larger markets for many products and services, but some firms target low-income consumers and societies. The most important wealth measures are **gross domestic product (GDP)** and *GDP per capita*.[6]

GDP is the annual market value of all final goods and services made within a country's borders. For intercountry comparisons, economists typically convert local-currency GDP into U.S. dollars using one of two approaches — *current currency exchange rate (nominal)* or *purchasing power parity (PPP)*. Economists often prefer PPP because it better indicates living standards in less-developed countries.

In less-developed countries, the population exceeding certain thresholds may be better market potential measures for some products than GDP per capita. At US$1,000 per year, family diets shift from vegetables to meat; at US$10,000 per year, people purchase automobiles.

Political. Many countries develop governmental and institutional processes to benefit local firms. Some give exporters financing and tax advantages; others impose tariffs and quotas on imported goods. Governments may use administrative procedures like inspections, delayed approvals, and the courts to restrict foreign firms' products.

International marketers sometimes adapt systems and processes to address disadvantageous decisions by foreign governments. Many firms avoid high tariffs on finished products by importing parts for local assembly — like the Segway personal transporter. Regulation is often a critical entry variable. Many French entrepreneurs start businesses in Britain because the regulatory environment is friendlier. Corruption is a serious problem in many countries.

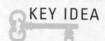

KEY IDEA

➤ Considerations in assessing foreign market attractiveness include:

- Economic, political, and legal/regulatory issues:
  - Domestic
  - International
- Sociocultural and geograhic distance

Marketing Question

In Kenya, sugar was sold in 50 and 100 kg bags for both industrial and consumer markets. Trade liberalization and common market protocols led to severe price competition from imported sugar. How should Kensug Inc. (disguised name), a major Kenyan sugar producer, address this challenge?

Marketing Question

Segway is considering entry into Asia. Which countries should Segway enter? Why? What additional data would you require to appropriately advise Segway?

Increasingly, firms with international aspirations are targeting emerging markets, especially **BRICI** — Brazil, Russia, India, China, and Indonesia. As these economies grow, large numbers of consumers who previously lived at subsistence levels become able to afford higher-value products.[7]

Legal/Regulatory. Several major global organizations have missions to enhance foreign-market attractiveness by securing intercountry agreements to increase trade and investment:

- **International Monetary Fund (IMF).** With 188 member countries, the *IMF* works to foster global monetary cooperation, secure financial stability, facilitate international trade, promote high employment and sustainable economic growth, and reduce poverty.
- **World Bank (WB).** 188 member countries own the *WB*, providing financial and technical assistance to developing countries.[8]
- **World Trade Organization (WTO).** The *WTO* succeeded the General Agreement on Tariffs and Trade (*GATT*). Now with 153 member countries, the WTO addresses a broad scope of international agreements to liberalize trade via trade rules and dispute resolutions.

Relatedly, many governments cooperate in investigating and prosecuting bribery.

Regional organizations. Several regional organizations focus on increasing member-country trade and reducing administrative barriers to investment. You have likely heard of the most important groups:

- **European Union (EU).** The EU's 28 member countries comprise an economic and political union of 500 million people generating 30 percent of global world product. People, goods, services, and capital move freely and all EU countries apply a common external tariff. Most EU countries use the euro, but Great Britain and Denmark do not.
- **NAFTA.** A trade agreement among Canada, Mexico, and the U.S., NAFTA focuses almost exclusively on trade and investment.
- **Mercosur.** Mercosur has four members — Brazil, Argentina, Paraguay, and Uruguay — and several associate members. Like NAFTA, Mercosur is a free-trade zone.
- **ASEAN.** ASEAN is a 10-member group promoting economic growth and cultural development in Southeast Asia. All are also members of AFTA, a free-trade area dedicated to reducing tariffs among members.

In addition, many countries form bilateral trade agreements, like Australia with New Zealand and the U.S. with Peru.

When contemplating foreign market entry, the firm should understand the type and scope of the target country's international relationships, and predict how these may evolve.

SOCIOCULTURAL AND GEOGRAPHIC DISTANCE

Sociocultural. Countries often differ from each other on multiple dimensions — language, religion, values and attitudes, education, social organization, technical and material, politics, law, and aesthetics.[9] *Sociocultural distance* varies widely from one country pair to another. Low sociocultural distance — common cultural dimensions — between the home and target countries implies reduced firm risk. High sociocultural distance can lead to failure despite other promising factors. When sociocultural distance is high, the firm may improve its chances of success by hiring people and organizations from the target country and seeking common ground among various sociocultural imperatives.

Firms can get in trouble with seemingly straightforward dimensions like language. Because translation mistakes are easy to make, leading firms work with established language services.

Geographic. *Geographic distance* concerns the ease/difficulty of transporting people and goods and communications between the home and target country. Technology and the physical envi-

---

KEY IDEA

➤ Important global organizations impacting international trade include:

- International Monetary Fund (IMF)
- World Bank (WB)
- World Trade Organization (WTO)

Marketing Question

Your firm manufactures inexpensive consumer goods. Management has asked you to identify the most attractive countries to enter taking regional organizations into account. How would you proceed?

ronment are also key issues. In addition to physical distance, important factors include presence/absence of physical land borders, separation by land/water, time zones, transportation and communication alternatives, topography, and climate.

BALANCING COUNTRY ATTRACTIVENESS FACTORS

When assessing foreign market attractiveness, the firm must consider various economic, political, legal/regulatory, sociocultural, and geographic issues.[10] In general, positive economic, political, legal/regulatory factors and low sociocultural and geographic distance imply attractive opportunities, but typically the firm must balance positives and negatives. Table 23.1 illustrates a simple approach to securing an attractiveness score for several individual countries.

Criteria	Importance Weight (I)	Great Britain Rating (RA) (1 to 10 scale)	Australia Rating (RB) (1 to 10 scale)	Mexico Rating (RC) (1 to 10 scale)	Great Britain I × RA	Australia I × RB	Mexico I × RC
1 Market size	30	8	3	5	240	90	150
2 Growth potential	20	5	7	8	100	140	160
3 Communications ease	10	10	10	3	100	100	30
4 Travel ease	10	5	2	9	50	20	90
5 Currency stability	10	7	7	4	70	70	40
6 Firm learning	10	3	3	8	30	30	80
7 Degree of corruption	10	8	8	5	80	80	50
	100				670	530	600

TABLE 23.1

ASSESSING COUNTRY ATTRACTIVENESS — ILLUSTRATION FOR A U.S. FIRM

ASSESSING THE FIRM'S ABILITY TO COMPETE

What are the firm's chances of attracting, retaining, and growing customers in the face of current and potential competitors, in a proposed foreign market? A new market entrant may secure differential advantage on the basis of technological expertise or brand strength, but also from an ability to execute projects and political and networking skills.

The firm should pay very close attention to strong domestic competitors and other foreign entrants. Generally, local firms are effective in catering to local tastes, use local resources efficiently, and know how to address local obstacles. In less-developed countries, local competitors often enjoy low labor costs and technological parity with the firm.[11]

Increasingly, firms from less-developed countries are making significant inroads in mature advanced-economy markets. A foreign entrant may serve an unfilled market need for a basic low-price product, then later add higher-value, higher-priced products. In the 1980s, Japanese automobile firms secured high market shares in many developed countries using this approach.

KEY IDEA

➤ Regardless of foreign market attractiveness, before entry, the firm should assess its ability to compete.

OPTIONS FOR ENTERING FOREIGN MARKETS

A firm with regional or global ambitions may have already entered many foreign markets and have significant international experience. By contrast, a domestic firm going abroad for the first time starts from scratch. In either case, the firm must consider its options: how many foreign markets to enter, how quickly, and in what order. Increased number of entries expand the firm's opportunities and permit better fixed-cost amortization; but they may also require more resources and open the firm to greater risk.

KEY IDEA

➤ When entering foreign markets, the firm can choose among several *passive* and *active* entry modes.

Speed of entry involves several trade-offs. Simultaneous or fast-sequential entries earn profits more quickly, preempt competition, and erect entry barriers. Taking it more slowly is less risky and allows the firm to learn so that later entries may be more effective. When the firm makes sequential entries, order is important. Several *passive* and *active* entry modes are available for the firm:

PASSIVE ENTRY

These approaches allow the firm to leverage another firm's skills and resources for market entry. This organization does all or most of the work; hence, the firm has little control over marketing and sales efforts. Risk and financial return are lower than for active entry. Two of the most common passive enty modes are:

KEY IDEA

➤ Major options for *passive* entry into foreign markets are:

• Exporting
• Licensing

EXPORTING

The firm exports products but outsources most in-country activities in foreign markets by simply responding to orders. The firm may also decide which foreign markets to address, then appointing local sales agents and/or distributors to conduct marketing and sales efforts.

LICENSING

The firm has an asset — like product or process technology (patent or trade secret), brand name, or trademark — with value in foreign markets. The firm (licensor) agrees that another firm (licensee) can use the asset commercially; in return, the licensee typically pays *minimum* royalties (right to use the asset) and/or *earned* royalties (based on sales or profits) to the licensor. **Brand licensing** is very common in B2C, particularly for movies and sports-related merchandise and toys. In B2B markets, international licensing agreements are largely technology based. The licensor must always consider possible risk in damage to brand equity.

Marketing Question

Tasks Everyday <*www.taskseveryday.com*>, based in Mumbai, India, offers virtual assistants for small, midsize, and large businesses and busy professionals. Tasks Everyday has a ready supply of university-educated graduate assistants and is seeking rapid expansion. What actions would you advise Tasks Everyday to take?

ACTIVE ENTRY

In these approaches, the firm plays an active role in marketing and sales, but with greater profit potential and higher risk. The firm should be especially careful in projecting from domestic experience but can reduce uncertainty via marketing research, though this may be difficult in emerging markets. We discuss three broad *active-entry* approaches:

IMPORTING

Traditional. Products enter foreign markets as imports from the firm's home country and/or third countries. The firm actively participates in marketing and selling products via traveling home-based sales representatives, and local salespeople and/or distributors. These firms may supply raw materials, parts, or finished products. Some firms even outsource production, then import goods into target countries. Have you heard of Foxcom? If you own an Apple iPod or iPhone, Sony Playstation, Dell PC, or some other electronic product, Foxcom probably made it.

Facilitated by the Internet. The Internet and the growth in air-courier transportation have changed the game for many firms, helping them identify and serve customers in many foreign markets. The firm sells products online; buyers pay for products and shipping by credit card. Even better, the firm can *export* any digital product without traditional import arrangements. Wessex offers all of its products as pdf e-books; customers pay by credit card and can *import* to any geography.

KEY IDEA

➤ Major options for *active* entry into foreign markets are:

• Importing
• Local production
• Franchising

LOCAL PRODUCTION

For success in many country markets, local presence is at least desirable and may be necessary. The firm has several options for producing products locally:

ACQUISITION

The firm acquires a firm/business unit in the foreign market. Marketing, sales, distribution, operations, and other functions are already in place. The firm leverages local management and customer relationships.

GREENFIELD

In a *greenfield* **project**, the firm constructs local facilities from scratch. Factors driving this option include high tariff barriers, high transportation costs, local content rules, and wanting to be close to customers. Some firms enter foreign markets via imports and build local marketing and sales organizations. When revenues reach a threshold, they switch to local production. Trade liberalization, transportation cost reductions, and outsourcing have reduced greenfield's attraction but it remains popular.

JOINT VENTURE

A joint venture with a local partner helps the firm reduce political, legal/regulatory, and socio-cultural risks, but degree of ownership can be a critical issue. Some governments require foreign entrants to have domestic partners, and may limit percentage ownership. Overall, results from international joint ventures are mixed; problems arise when investment requirements and results differ from expectations, partner objectives change, and parent-firm problems negatively affect the joint venture.

Local production requires host-country investment but strengthens local institutional and customer ties. The firm becomes part of the host country's administrative and cultural fabric as supplier, customer, employer, and taxpayer. Challenges for firms producing in foreign markets are exposure to local labor laws, safety and security, and currency and expropriation risk. Increasingly, firms are shifting operations to low-wage countries or outsourcing to third parties. Many U.S. service firms place call centers in India, Malaysia, Pakistan, and African English-speaking countries. Some firms site production to gain marketing and sales advantage.

FRANCHISING

As we discussed for domestic markets — Chapter 18 — **franchising** is a popular foreign-entry mode when the firm's value proposition requires local production and/or delivery. Fast food is the most prevalent example, with brands like Burger King, KFC, McDonalds, Pizza Hut, Subway, and Wendy's expanding into many foreign markets. The franchisee invests in local operations, directs local marketing and sales, and pays fees to the franchisor.

Because many franchisees are local entrepreneurs, market entry can be fast and profitable. Regardless, independent franchisees can be difficult to deal with, and failure or inconsistency may negatively affect the brand. Sometimes franchisors allow local market variation to better address local needs: KFC offers egg sandwiches for breakfast in Japan, the Chickpea Burger in India, and the *Twister* in Australia.

Marketing Question

On the opening day of the 2008 baseball season, the Boston Red Sox beat the Oakland Athletics by six to five. But they did not play in Massachusetts or California; the game was in Japan. Develop an international marketing strategy for Major League Baseball.

KEY IDEA

➤ Firms that set up production operations in a foreign country may choose among:

- Acquisition
- Greenfield
- Joint venture

➤ Sometimes host countries insist that foreign firms form joint ventures with local firms.

STRATEGIES FOR INTERNATIONAL, REGIONAL, AND GLOBAL MARKETING

Globalization is driving increased numbers of firms to expand outside their home countries. They must decide on the scope of their foreign activities, then make serious strategic international and global marketing and investment decisions. The basis for these decisions should be the six marketing imperatives at the heart of *Capon's Marketing Framework*. Specifically, they must make decisions about objectives, and consider segmentation and branding decisions.

SCOPE

Firms engage in *international marketing* when they decide to expand outside their domestic markets. They engage in *global marketing* when they expand into multiple countries. The distinction involves the *scope* of their efforts: how many and which foreign markets to address, and the challenges they face in each — Figure 23.2:

FIGURE 23.2

APPROACHES
TO ADDRESSING
FOREIGN MARKETS

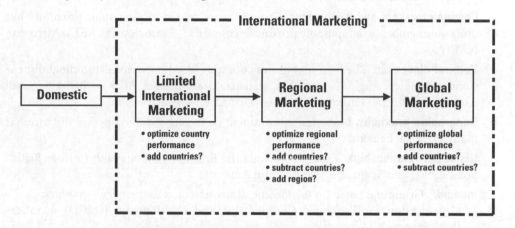

KEY IDEA

➤ When firms expand internationally, they often follow a trajectory of:
  • Limited international marketing
  • Regional marketing
  • Global marketing

LIMITED INTERNATIONAL MARKETING

Typical exemplars are firms that enter a few geographically proximate countries, like U.S. firms in Canada, Mexico, and/or Caribbean countries. State Farm (insurance) and Alaska Airlines are good examples.

REGIONAL MARKETING

These experienced international marketers focus their efforts on a relatively large group of countries, typically but not always within a single continent or geographic area — like Europe, Latin America, or portions of the Asia-Pacific region. Many airlines focus on geographically proximate countries, like Ryanair and easyJet (Europe) and Air Asia.

GLOBAL MARKETING

Like regional marketers, global marketers have extensive international experience, but set their sights more broadly, seeking opportunities globally. The typical global marketer has multicountry presence in several continents, and faces the challenge of optimizing performance across different regions and countries.

Both regional and global marketers are serious about foreign markets, carefully selecting which markets to address. Each firm must continually manage and adjust its country portfolio via vigilant assessment and performance measurement. Sometimes the firm *fills out* geographic scope by adding countries; other times it may withdraw — some country markets may be less attractive than they appeared before entry.

Marketing Question

You have been appointed Tata Motors' Marketing Vice President for North America. Your immediate task is to launch the *Nano*, a four-door, four-passenger vehicle that sells in India for about $2,200. What will be the core elements in your three-year launch plan? Make sure you ask and answer critical strategic questions.

OBJECTIVES

The firm should consider objectives at two levels: international business overall, and selectively by region and country. In general, relevant measures are similar to those for domestic markets — revenues, profits, and market share — Chapter 22.

SEGMENTING MULTIPLE COUNTRY MARKETS

International and global marketers should answer two critical questions:

- How should we form segments for developing international market strategy?
- How should we decide which segments to address?

SEGMENTATION BY GROUPING COUNTRIES

This approach examines markets by country groupings:

- **Common markets and trade zones.** Groupings are related to geographic proximity but omit nonmember geographically proximate countries.[12] Examples: EU, AFTA, Mercosur, NAFTA.
- **Cultural closeness.** The firm may group countries based on various attitudinal dimensions. Examples: Anglo — Australia, Canada, Great Britain; Arab — Bahrain, Saudi Arabia, United Arab Emirates; Nordic — Denmark, Norway, Sweden.
- **Geographic proximity.** Grouping by continent or region; reduced physical distance has many logistical benefits.
- **Historical relationships.** Examples include the British Commonwealth (former British possessions) and Spain and Spanish Latin America.
- **Income.**[13] Groupings based on the income dimension of consumer demographics:
  - **Organisation for Economic Co-operation and Development (OECD) members (high income):** 34 countries — includes Australia, Italy, U.S.
  - **Other high income:** 39 countries — includes Andorra, Israel, United Arab Emirates
  - **Upper middle income:** 46 countries — includes Algeria, Lithuania, Venezuela
  - **Lower middle income:** 55 countries — includes Albania, Kosovo, West Bank and Gaza
  - **Low income:** 43 countries — includes Afghanistan, Madagascar, Zimbabwe
- **Language.** These groupings comprise elements of geographic proximity and historical relationships but focus specifically on language, like English- or Spanish-speaking countries.
- **Specific purpose.** Examples include OPEC (oil production) and NATO (defense).

ACROSS-COUNTRY SEGMENTATION

The firm may form market segments regardless of geographic location by focusing on customer attributes:

- **Demographic characteristics.** Traditional demographic variables alone or in combination — Chapter 8 — can form segments. B2C attributes include age, education, gender, income, and religion. B2B attributes include firm size, growth, industry, and profitability.
- **Values.** Roper Starch Worldwide identified six global B2C segments based on core values:
  - **Strivers.** Place greater emphasis on material and professional goals than other groups
  - **Devouts.** Tradition and duty very important
  - **Altruists.** Interested in social issues and society welfare
  - **Intimates.** Value close personal family relationships
  - **Fun seekers.** Frequent restaurants, bars, and movies
  - **Creatives.** Strong interest in education, knowledge, and technology

KEY IDEA

➤ Many firms form segments by grouping countries. Geographic proximity is the most common method but other approaches may be more useful.

KEY IDEA

➤ Some firms develop international segments by grouping countries; other firms form segments that cross country boundaries.

Marketing Question

Over many years, Toyota earned an enviable record for high-quality products. But in 2009, Toyota was forced to recall over seven million automobiles because of unintended acceleration. What actions would you suggest that Toyota take to repair the damage to its brand image?

KEY IDEA

➤ Alternative approaches to international marketing include:

- Global — focus on consistency and efficiency across multiple countries
- Local — focus on serving specific customer needs in individual countries
- *Glocal* — marries global and local via global market strategy and local implementation

Marketing Question

In the aftermath of WWII, Western customers viewed Japanese goods as cheap and poor quality; today, many customers have positive associations with Japanese products. How would you advise a Russian firm seeking to export to the U.S.?

BRANDING IN GLOBAL MARKETS

The firm's first branding choice is between *local* and *global*. When the firm provides the same or similar products in multiple countries, should it offer a single brand — *global branding* — or multiple *local brands*? The branding decision follows directly from the firm's segmentation choices. Arguments for a global branding approach include:

- **Cross-border travel.** Increased travel drives demand as consumers seek out their favorite brands while traveling. Beverages and hotels are two good examples.
- **Growth.** The firm may be able to leverage brand equity in new geographic markets.
- **Homogeneity of customer tastes across countries.** Global media and global product availability shape consumer tastes for global brands like H&M (Sweden) and Zara (Spain).
- **Increased global media reach and lower costs.** Television — like Star TV (Asia), CNN, ESPN, BBCWorld News — and the Internet cross country borders to reach multinational audiences.

Global brands offer specific advantages:

- **Aspirational values.** Global brands deliver aspirational values for products like cosmetics and sports drinks by associating them with global events — Olympic Games and World Cup.
- **Brand image.** A global brand promotes a consistent brand image.
- **Best practice.** Global branding eases best-practice transfer across geographies.
- **Competitive advantage.** Global brands often signify quality and innovation.
- **Global appeal.** Some brands like BMW, Rolls-Royce, and Marlboro have global appeal from many years of international exposure.
- **Human capital.** A global brand can help recruit and retain better people worldwide. Ernst & Young, IBM, and Seimens invest heavily in using their brands for global recruiting.

Firms that adopt global branding make branding decisions at corporate headquarters.[14] Global branding does not imply identical implementation programs across countries. Differing national tastes often drive product design variations; MTV is a global brand with local and regional adaptations. Pricing should reflect what local customers can pay; promotional activities should be appropriate for the market, and the firm should base distribution on local options. *Think global, act local — glocal —* is a mantra that guides many firms.

In practice, global firms have global, regional, and local brands. Coca-Cola offers 500 brands in 200 countries: Four brands are global — Classic Coca-Cola/Coca-Cola, Diet Coke/Coke Light, Sprite, and Fanta. Many soft drink brands — fruit juice, bottled water, and sports drinks — are only available regionally, sometimes only in a single country. Local bottlers support these brands as they often outsell global brands.

COUNTRY OF ORIGIN

Our final area of strategy assessment is country of origin (COO): The firm's origin may add to (or subtract from) firm brands in forming customer attitudes and intentions and securing purchase.[15] Three possible effects are[16]:

- **Cognitive.** COO signals product quality but can be positive or negative by product. German engineering and French wine — positive; French cars and computers — negative.
- **Affective.** COO has symbolic and emotional meaning for customers and confers attributes like authenticity, exoticness, and status. Many second-generation Italian-American women are strongly attached to Italian products, especially food-related — *Italy* has a strong emotional and symbolic connotation for these consumers.

- **Normative.** Customers view purchasing from certain countries as being the *right* thing to do — domestic products to help the national economy[17] or products from a developing country to help alleviate poverty; or the *wrong* thing to do — British consumers avoiding Argentine beef during the Falklands/Malvinas war.

IMPLEMENTING INTERNATIONAL, REGIONAL, AND GLOBAL MARKET STRATEGIES

The core challenge for international and global marketers is balancing the efficiency benefits of centralized corporate control versus addressing local market needs. Core problems are:

- **Excessive control.** The firm makes most decisions at corporate. Local managers must sell standard products, at standard prices, using standard communications and distribution systems. Lack of flexibility in meeting customer needs causes problems.

- **Excessive flexibility.** The firm offers a core product in multiple countries but allows country managers to make most other decisions. The firm gains few benefits from being a multinational firm. Country-specific approaches may also cause problems when individual customers purchase in several countries.

Today, most serious international and global marketers try to balance control and flexibility benefits. These firms typically set market strategy centrally, but allow significant discretion for local implementation. For marketing mix implementation decisions, we assume the firm has set market strategy centrally but provides significant autonomy to meet local needs.

PRODUCT

The degree of product standardization is the critical *product* decision for international, regional, and global marketers. Product standardization across national markets reduces costs and may allow the firm to offer lower prices. Conversely, standardization ignores local requirements and makes it easier for **gray markets** to form by shipping a standard product across national borders. Alternatively, the firm may develop a core product appropriate for many foreign markets but allow local variations.

COMMUNICATIONS

Firms expanding internationally may have to adapt communications and messaging approaches to local conditions. In Brazil, Nestlé's barge, *Nestlé Até Voce a Bordo* (*Nestlé Takes You on Board*), travels the Amazon to showcase Nestlé products to river-port inhabitants. Citibank launched credit cards in India using door-to-door salespeople — an unthinkable practice in developed economies.

Language differences across countries imply different communications approaches. But the firm must be careful about translations and context: Poor translations can cause problems and a simple phrase often means something different in different countries. Also, in low-literacy countries, the firm should emphasize visuals, including graphs and diagrams, rather than words.

> Exxon gains globalization benefits while localizing its message. Typically, Exxon develops TV advertising campaigns with expensive visuals, but uses multiple groups of local actors to tailor these campaigns to local markets.

Communications are also critical in face-to-face situations. Different negotiating styles are more or less successful in different cultures. *Individualistic* cultures like the U.S. favor direct *to-*

Marketing Question

Successful Spanish restaurant chain 100 Montaditos (inexpensive sandwiches and beer) entered the U.S. with a goal of opening 4,000 outlets in five years, via a combination of company-owned and franchised stores. Do you think 100 Montaditos will be successful? Why or why not? How would you advise 100 Montaditos?

the-point approaches; *collectivist* cultures like China favor an emphasis on developing personal relationships. Further, English is fast becoming the lingua franca of international business.

DISTRIBUTION

The firm's distribution efforts should be appropriate to the local market. In China, Gucci and Louis Vuitton prosper with large stores that offer wide product variety with prices as low as a few hundred dollars — attracting luxury entrants and gift buyers. By contrast, Tiffany has done less well with small stores and limited high-end product selection. Distribution systems common in developed countries may not be available in foreign markets, so creativity is critical. In Russia, P&G secured distribution to 80 percent of the population by funding 32 regional distributors and 68 subdistributors. In Eastern Europe, P&G's *McVan* model provides significant competitive advantage by funding distributors to secure information technology, training, vans, and working capital.

PRICE

The basic framework for setting prices — Chapters 19 and 20 — applies equally well in global markets. Regardless, the firm should pay particular attention to gearing prices to target market segment(s) in specific countries. Firms may successfully offer mass-market products at similar prices in several developed countries. But in less-developed countries, similar product/price combinations may only address wealthy elites. To reach broader customer segments with the same product, the firm may have to reduce prices.

When exporting products, the firm must consider gray markets, and also ensure it does not run afoul of *antidumping* regulations. **Dumping** occurs when the firm exports goods to a foreign country below its home market price or production cost. Typically, governments initiate antidumping investigations to protect local industries.

When the firm targets multinational B2B customers, price differences by country are a special problem. Historically, many firms set markedly different prices for similar products in different countries. These differential prices did not pose a serious problem when multinationals made procurement decisions locally. Today, many multinationals use global procurement systems. They do not understand why they should pay widely different prices from country to country and thus pressure suppliers for price equivalence around the world.

Transfer pricing is a special issue for international marketers. Transfer prices are internal to the firm — between one subsidiary and another. Generally, firms set high transfer prices when exporting from low tax-rate countries (low transfer prices when exporting from high tax-rate countries). Taxes are lower, but high transfer prices may lead to increased import duties.

ORGANIZING FOR INTERNATIONAL, REGIONAL, AND GLOBAL MARKETS

Thus far we have discussed how to analyze options, design strategy, and select implementation approaches to successfully compete in foreign markets. In this last section, we address critical organizational decisions that can make or break the firm's international, regional, and global initiatives. Many international efforts begin with export departments and international divisions; but as we see in Figure 23.3, these evolve to more advanced forms where segmentation plays an important role in organizational design.[18]

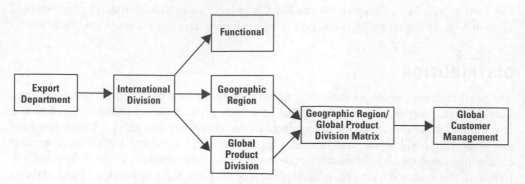

FIGURE 23.3

ORGANIZATIONAL
APPROACHES TO
INTERNATIONAL,
REGIONAL, AND
GLOBAL MARKETS

Typically an *export department* at the firm's head office directs initial firm efforts in foreign markets. This department interfaces with agents and brokers, and develops intellectual capital about international marketing and sales. As foreign sales increase, the firm replaces its export department with an international division; usually with country managers reporting to the international division head.[19] Export departments and international divisions are appropriate organizational devices when the firm has limited entry in foreign markets.

As more advanced organizational forms become appropriate, the firm often place individual countries into *geographic regions*; country managers have P&L responsibility. Advantages of the geographic-region organization over the international division are:

- Allows the firm to integrate functions across countries, within regions
- Avoids duplication costs
- Offers greater ability to manage performance across several countries

The geographic-region organization is most appropriate when customer needs are *heterogeneous* across countries and firm offers differ markedly. By contrast, when customer needs are *homogeneous* and the firm offers little product variety, the second axis in Figure 23.4 comes into play and the firm organizes by *global product division*. The global-product-division structure is popular among FMCG firms with large product lines. Headquarters allows for regional and/or country organizations to have sales and distribution responsibility, but often provides regions with standardized advertising programs for adaptation to local markets. The firm manages P&L globally by product; hence, making product changes globally is relatively straightforward.

The geographic-region organization emphasizes customer diversity in national markets, whereas global-product-division organizations emphasize consistency, efficiency, and cost reduction. Sometimes firms choose a *geographic-region/product division matrix* approach to balance both geographic and product concerns.

In the *functional structure*, all reporting lines are directly to corporate; the firm makes all major decisions in one location. For many years, Toyota was very successful with a functional structure. But the Toyota organization was unresponsive to local-U.S.-dealer complaints about unintended acceleration in its automobiles prior to the 2009 recall crisis.

Finally, when firms expand operations to multiple countries they often evolve their procurement operations to better enable global contracts, manage global supplier relationships, secure better prices, and optimize customer service. Global procurement is often more effective and efficient than sourcing locally. Hence, B2B suppliers must develop organization structures that interface effectively with their global customers. In a *global customer management* structure, *customer* becomes a major organizational design axis — Figure 23.4. The center piece of a global customer management organization is the **global account manager** (**GAM**). GAMs have full customer responsibility, but balancing customer priorities with product-division and geographic imperatives is often difficult.

KEY IDEA

➤ As firms increase participation in foreign markets, they typically evolve their organizational structures.

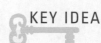

KEY IDEA

➤ Firms operating in many countries often develop matrix organizations where the two major axes are product and geography.

FIGURE 23.4

**ORGANIZATIONAL
DESIGN DIMENSIONS
FOR GLOBAL MARKETING**

KEY IDEA

➤ Many B2B firms adopt
global customer man-
agement organizations
to address multinational
customers.

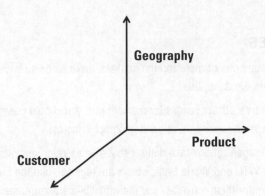

KEY MESSAGES

- Before your firm enters one or more foreign markets, make sure you have a good answer to the question — why are we doing this?

- In assessing a country's attractiveness for market entry, you should consider economic, political, legal/regulatory, sociocultural, and geographic factors.

- Many international organizations take actions that affect foreign markets. Some organizations are global, like the WTO and World Bank; others are regional, like the EU, NAFTA, and ASEAN. The firm should monitor their activities, and individual bilateral agreements between countries.

- Passive entry strategies for entering foreign markets include exporting and licensing.

- Active entry strategies for entering foreign markets include importing — traditional and Internet-facilitated; local production — greenfield, acquisition, joint venture, and franchising.

- Many firms follow a strategy of progressive commitment to international markets via limited commitment to international marketing, regional marketing, then global marketing.

- When firms address the global market they may segment by country group or identify across-country segments.

- Many factors are driving firms to develop global marketing strategies.

- Many firms offering products globally also provide products for specific regions and countries.

- A *glocal* approach combines global strategy and local implementation.

- International and global marketers may choose among a variety of organizational forms.

VIDEOS AND AUDIOS

Global Marketing   v2302 📹   Spencer Pingel   Colgate-Palmolive

v2302

CONCLUDING
COMMENT

MANY READERS OF *CAPON'S MARKETING FRAMEWORK* HAVE NO DOUBT VISITED Las Vegas, Reno, Monte Carlo, Macau, or some other similar location. If not, you are no doubt familiar with the way gambling establishments work. You may win a lot of money, or you may lose a lot of money, but the gambling house always wins. And even if you do win, the odds are stacked against you, and you will almost certainly lose over the long run as the laws of probability govern your performance. Essentially, you play games of chance and if you attempt to change the odds by counting cards or by some other means, you will be ejected.

In business, you are also gamblers. You make bets on markets, market segments, and products. Sometimes you win big; other times you may lose big. In many respects you are just like the patrons of gambling establishments. But there is one big difference: You have the ability to shift the odds in your favor. That's what *Capon's Marketing Framework* is all about — shifting the odds. Two matters are crucial: data, information, and insight; and frameworks to help organize your thinking and your approaches. In *Capon's Marketing Framework*, we show you how to secure data, information, and insight; and we provide many useful frameworks. You now have the ability to improve your chances of success. Good luck!

ENDNOTES

CHAPTER 1

1 Based in part on an interview with Howard Schultz; N. Capon, *The Marketing Mavens*, New York: Crown Business, 2007.

2 In *CFO* magazine. Also R. Martin, "The Age of Customer Capitalism," *Harvard Business Review*, 88 (January–February 2010), pp. 58–65.

3 IBM's earnings were: 1990 — $6.02 billion; 1991 — $2.82 billion; 1992 — ($4.96 billion); and 1993 — ($8.10 billion). L.V. Gerstner, *Who Says Elephants Can't Dance?* New York, Harper Business, 2002.

4 P.F. Drucker, *The Practice of Management*, New York, Harper and Row, 1954, pp. 37–38.

5 P.F. Drucker, *Management: Tasks, Responsibilities, Practices*, New York, Harper & Row, 1973, p. 63.

6 Personal communication from David Haines, former Director of Global Branding, Vodafone.

7 Gerstner, *op. cit.*, p. 72.

8 *Ibid*, p. 189.

9 This term is taken from military usage.

10 J.C. Narver and S.F. Slater, "The Effect of a Market Orientation on Business Profitability," *Journal of Marketing*, 54 (October 1990), pp. 20–35. Kohli and Jaworski place more emphasis on using market intelligence and less on environmental understanding: A.K. Kohli and B.J. Jaworski, "Market Orientation: The Construct, Research Propositions and Management Implications," *Journal of Marketing*, 54 (April 1990), pp. 1–18; B.J. Jaworski and A.K. Kohli, "Market Orientation: Antecedents and Consequences," *Journal of Marketing*, 57 (July 1993), pp. 53–70. Also B. Shapiro, "What the Hell Is 'Market-Oriented'?," *Harvard Business Review*, 67 (November–December 1989), pp. 119–225, and R. Deshpandé, *Developing a Market Orientation*, Thousand Oaks, CA: Sage, 1999.

11 A.J. Slywotsky and B.P. Shapiro, "Leveraging to Beat the Odds: The New Marketing Mind-Set," *Harvard Business Review*, 71 (September–October 1993), pp. 97–107. Rahm Emmanuel, President Obama's first chief of staff, captured this perspective cogently by paraphrasing Niccolò Machiavelli (*The Prince*): "You never want a serious crisis to go to waste."

12 "As Antidote to Slowdown, Intel Will Spend, Not Cut," *The New York Times*, February 28, 2001.

13 "Don't Cut Back on Innovation," *Fortune*, April 22, 2009, p. 69.

14 "Wachovia Bank and Trust Company," in N. Capon, *The Marketing of Financial Services*, Englewood Cliffs, NJ: Prentice Hall, 1992.

15 Personal communication from Pat Kelly, former Senior Vice President Worldwide Marketing, Pfizer Pharmaceuticals.

16 K. Simmonds, "Removing the Chains from Product Strategy," *Journal of Management Studies*, 5 (1968), pp. 29–40.

17 "A Cheerleader, for a Company in a Midlife Funk," *The New York Times*, June 23, 2002.

18 J. Collins, *Good to Great: Why Some Companies Make the Leap ... and Others Don't*, New York: Collins, 2001. Also J.R. Williams, "How Sustainable Is Your Competitive Advantage?," *California Management Review*, 34 (Spring 1992), pp. 29–52; P. Ghemawat, "Sustainable Advantage," *Harvard Business Review*, 64 (September–October 1986), pp. 53–94.

19 Personal communication from Michael Francis, former Senior Vice President of Marketing, Target Stores.

CHAPTER 2

1 L. Selden and G. Colvin, *Angel Customers & Demon Customers*, New York: Portfolio, 2003; used by permission.

2 This chapter benefited considerably from discussions with colleagues Sunil Gupta and Don Lehmann: S. Gupta, D.R. Lehmann, and J. Ames Stuart, "Valuing Customers," *Journal of Marketing Research*, 41 (February 2004), pp. 7–19; S. Gupta and D.R. Lehmann, "Customers as Assets," *Journal of Interactive Marketing*, 17 (Winter 2003), pp. 9–24; and S. Gupta and D.R. Lehmann, *Managing Customers as Investments*, Philadelphia, PA: Wharton, 2004.

3 The firm applies the sum of net margins across all customers to its fixed costs to identify overall gross margin. Net margin equals gross margin less specific costs for retaining customers.

4 Deciding if a customer has defected is not simple. Amazon, eBay, and L.L. Bean treat customers who haven't purchased within the prior year as having defected. This judgment varies with the purchase cycle.

5 Strictly speaking, the margin-multiple formula applies to a series of terms summed to infinity. Hence, we avoid arbitrary assumptions about actual customer lifetime. Assuming reasonable values for retention rate (r) and discount rate (d), after a few years the impact of all terms is very small. You can check this out for yourself.

6 F.F. Reicheld, *The Loyalty Effect*, Boston, MA: Harvard Business School Press, 1996, p. 51.

7 Reicheld, *op. cit,* p. 36. Also F.F. Reicheld, *Loyalty Rules*, Boston, MA: Harvard Business School Press, 2001; B.J. Pine II, D. Peppers, and M. Rogers, "Do You Want to Keep Your Customers Forever?," *Harvard Business Review*, 73 (March–April 1995), pp. 103–154; R.C. Blattberg and J. Deighton, "Manage Marketing by the Customer Equity Test," *Harvard Business Review*, 74 (July–August 1996), pp. 136–144; R.C. Blattberg, G. Getz, and J.S. Thomas, *Customer Equity*, Boston, MA: Harvard Business School Press, 2001; and R.T. Rust, V.A. Zeithaml, and K.N. Lemon, *Driving Customer Equity*, New York: Free Press, 2000.

8 Steady state market shares are independent of starting positions. Jane's and Joe's initial division of the 1,000 customers does not affect the long run.

9 Personal communication from Dave Goudge, former senior vice president for marketing, Boise Office Solutions (now OfficeMax).

10 Advances in CRM systems (below) like *www.salesforce.com* have eased this problem somewhat.

11 For this discussion, overhead comprises costs not directly assigned to customers, like long-run R&D and corporate assessments for advertising, legal services, and government relations.

12 V. Mittal, M. Sarkees, and F. Murshed, "The Right Way to Manage Unprofitable Customers," *Harvard Business Review*, 86 (April 2008), pp. 95–101, suggest a *reassess, educate, renegotiate, migrate* process with customers prior to termination.

13 The fast growth of blogs and Twitter is raising this concern to new levels.

14 These customer types and non-payers (deadbeats) are *jaycustomers*: C. Lovelock and J. Wirtz, *Service Marketing: People, Technology, Strategy* (7th ed.), Upper Saddle River, NJ: Prentice-Hall, 2011.

15 I. Gordon, *Relationship Marketing: New Strategies, Techniques and Technologies to Win the Customers You Want and Keep Them Forever*, Ontario: Wiley, 1998, p. 9. Also R. Winer, "A Framework of Customer Relationship Management," *California Management Review*, 43 (2001), pp. 89–105.

16 M. Ebner, A. Hu, D. Levitt, and J. McCrory, "How to Rescue CRM," *The McKinsey Quarterly*, 4 (2002), pp. 49–57; also D.K. Rigby, F.F. Reicheld, and P. Schefter, "Avoid the Four Perils of CRM," *Harvard Business Review*, 80 (February 2002), pp. 101–109.

17 Peter Heffring, former President CRM Division, Teradata, 2002.

18 R. Glazer, "Strategy and Structure in Information-Intensive Markets: The Relationship between Marketing and IT," *Journal of Market-Focused Management*, 2, (1997), pp. 65–81.

CHAPTER 3

1 T. Levitt, "Marketing Myopia," *Harvard Business Review*, 53 (September–October 1975), pp. 26 *et seq.*

2 R.K. Srivastava, M.I. Alpert, and A.D. Shocker, "A Customer-Oriented Approach for Determining Market Structures," *Journal of Marketing*, 48 (Spring 1984), pp. 32–45.

3 Some use *product category* instead of *product class; product sub-category* instead of *product form.*

4 Since B2C market demand drives B2B market demand, we focus on key indicators of B2C market size.

5 Migration data from the United Nations.

6 United Nations Population Database from *The Economist*. Estimates of population percentages over age 65 in 2050 are Italy and Spain — 70 percent, Germany — 57 percent, France — 53 percent, Sweden and Britain — 49 percent, and Ireland — 48 percent.

7 E.M. Rogers, *Diffusion of Innovations* (5th ed.), New York: Free Press, 2003. We address this topic in Chapter 12.

8 R.W. Olshavsky, "Time and the Rate of Adoption of Innovations," *Journal of Consumer Research*, 6 (March 1980), pp. 425–428; W. Qualls, R. W. Olshavsky, and R.E. Michaels, "Shortening of the PLC–An Empirical Test," *Journal of Marketing*, 45 (Fall 1981), pp. 76–80.

9 M. E. Porter, *Competitor Strategy: Techniques for Analyzing Industries and Competitors*, New York: Free Press, 1980. B. Greenwald and J. Kahn, *Competition Demystified*, New York: Portfolio, 2005, builds on Porter's model but focuses attention on barriers to entry.

10 C. Zook with J. Allen, *Profit from the Core: Growth Strategy in an Era of Turbulence*, Boston, MA: Harvard Business School Press, 2001, pp. 26–28.

11 R.M. Kanter, "Collaborative Advantage: The Art of Alliances," *Harvard Business Review*, 72 (July–August 1994), pp. 96–108.

12 In pyramid sales forces, salespeople earn commissions from direct sales. They also earn *overrides* on sales of salespeople they recruit. They may also earn overrides on sales from their recruits' recruits, and so on.

13 Some firms address large commodity price swings by *hedging* purchases. Some multinationals, like Caterpillar, strive to match production and sales by country to avoid currency swing problems.

14 K. Harrigan, *Strategies for Vertical Integration*, Lexington, MA: Lexington Books, 1983.

15 H. Simon, *Hidden Champions: Lessons from 500 of the World's Best Unknown Companies*, Boston, MA: Harvard Business School Press, 1996; also *Hidden Champions of the Twenty-First Century: The Success Strategies of Unknown World Market Leaders*, New York: Springer-Science+Business Media, 2009.

16 This section draws on P. Fitzroy, A. Ghobadian, and J.M. Hulbert, *Strategic Management: The Challenge of Creating Value*, London: Routledge, 2012.

17 *The New Shorter Oxford English Dictionary*, Oxford: Clarendon, 1993.

18 *Baby Boomers* — 77 million persons born in the U.S. between 1946 and 1964; *Generation X* — 50 million persons born between 1965 and 1976; *Generation Y* (echo boomers, millennium generation) — 77 million persons born between 1977 and 1995.

19 C. M. Christensen, *The Innovator's Dilemma: When New Technologies Cause Great Firms to Fail*, Boston, MA: Harvard Business School Press, 1997.

20 L. Downes and C. Mui, *Unleashing the Killer App: Digital Strategies for Market Dominance*, Boston, MA: Harvard Business School Press, 1998, pp. xix, 243. George Washington University Forecast of Emerging Tech-

nologies identified several future technologies and dates: 2005 — fuel-cell-powered cars introduced; 2008 — virtual assistants common and genetically modified food widely accepted; 2010 — smart robots in homes and factories; 2012 — children genetically designed; 2030 — average life span 100 years; 2050 — humans travel to nearby star systems. See also The World Future Society.

21 D. A. Beck, J. N. Fraser, A. C. Reuter-Domenech, and P. Sidebottom, "Personal Financial Services Goes Global," *The McKinsey Quarterly*, 3 1999, pp. 39–47.

22 K. O'Neill Packard and F. Reinhardt, "What Every Executive Needs to Know About Global Warming," *Harvard Business Review*, 78 (July–August 2000), pp. 129–135.

CHAPTER 4

1 T.V. Bonoma, "Major Sales: Who Really Does the Buying?," *Harvard Business Review*, 60 (May–June 1982), pp. 111–120.

2 Personal communication from Dale Hayes, former Vice President Brand Management and Customer Communications, UPS.

3 In addition to *communicating* value, the communications process may also *create* value.

4 A. Maslow, *Motivation and Personality*, New York: Harper, 1954. Maslow's framework raises the question, discussed extensively by Freud: Are all needs fully conscious?

5 R. Friedmann, "Psychological Meaning of Products: Identification and Marketing Applications," *Psychology and Marketing*, 3 (Spring 1986), pp. 1–15.

6 J.L. Forbis and N.T. Mehta, "Value-Based Strategies for Industrial Products," *Business Horizons*, 24 (1981), pp. 32–42.

7 This calculation does not include savings from avoiding costs to repair cotton-based conveyor belts, nor downtime costs of more frequently replacing cotton conveyor belts.

8 B. Schmitt, *Experiential Marketing: How to Get Customers to Sense, Feel, Think, Act and Relate to Your Company and Brands*: New York: Free Press, 1999; and B. Schmitt, "Experience Marketing: Concepts, Frameworks, and Consumer Insights," *Foundations and Trends in Marketing*, 5 (2010), pp. 55–112, for a review. Also B.J. Pine II and J.H. Gilmore, "Welcome to the Experience Economy," *Harvard Business Review*, 76 (July–August 1998), pp. 97–105.

9 H. Stern, "The Significance of Impulse Buying Today," *Journal of Marketing*, 26 (April 1962) pp. 59–62.

10 This section relies heavily on I. Simonson, "Get Closer to Your Customers by Understanding How They Make Choices," *California Management Review*, (Summer 1993), pp. 74–84.

11 I. Simonson and A. Tversky, "Choice in Context: Tradeoff Contrast and Extremeness Aversion," *Journal of Marketing Research*, 29 (1992), pp. 281–295; also R. Kivetz, O. Netzer, and V. Srinivasan, "Alternative Models for Capturing the Compromise Effect," *Journal of Marketing Research*, 41 (August 2004), pp, 237–257, and G.E. Smith and T.T. Nagle, "Frames of Reference and Buyers' Perception of Price and Value," *California Management Review*, 38 (1995), pp. 98–116.

12 R. Dhar and I. Simonson, "The Effect of the Focus of Comparison on Consumer Preferences," *Journal of Marketing Research*, 29 (November 1992), pp. 430–440.

13 T. Levitt, "After the Sale Is Over," *Harvard Business Review*, 61 (September–October 1983), pp. 87–93.

14 E. Hall, *The Silent Language*, Garden City, NY: Anchor, 1973.

15 500 companies produce more than 2,000 kretek brands.

16 W. Chan Kim and R. Mauborgne, *Blue Ocean Strategy*, Boston, MA: Harvard Business School Press, 2005, pp. 71–74.

17 Chapter 3 discussed broad environmental influences — globalization, industry concentration, and increased competition. This section is based on N. Capon, *Key Account Management and Planning*, New York: The Free Press, 2001, and N. Capon, D. Potter, and F. Schindler, *Managing Global Accounts*, Bronxville, NY: Wessex, 2008.

CHAPTER 5

1 Based on material from Boeing and Airbus websites and Wikipedia.

2 *Groupthink* refers to drawing conclusions based on the shared, and poorly examined, assumptions of group members: Wikipedia; I.L. Janis, *Groupthink: Psychological Studies of Policy Decisions and Fiascoes* (2nd ed.), Boston: Wadsworth, 1972.

3 L.M. Fuld, *The Secret Language of Competitive Intelligence*, New York: Crown Business, 2006, pp. 40–41. For a good example of gaining insight from a competitor's production process, pp. 123–134.

4 Based on L. Fahey, *Outwitting, Outmaneuvering and Outperforming Competitors*, New York: Wiley, 1999, Table 5.3, p. 133, by permission.

5 For a good description of a war game, see Fuld 2006, *op. cit.*, pp. 69–118.

6 Based on a competitor analysis framework in Fahey, *op. cit.*, by permission.

7 The firm should conduct this analysis with a more general objective including opportunities and threats: SWOT — strengths, weaknesses, opportunities, threats.

8 To reinforce this point, around 500 B.C., Chinese warrior Sun Tzu said: "All men see the tactics whereby I conquer, but none see the strategy out of which victory evolved." *The Art of War*, Wikipedia; Oxford; Oxford University Press, 1963.

9 Reproduced from Fahey, *op. cit.*, Table 4.1, p. 90, by permission.

10 This section based on Fahey, *op. cit.*, Chapter 16, by permission.

11 For an excellent discussion of signaling, see Fahey, *op. cit.*, Chapter 4.

12 This section based in part on A. Brandenburger and B.J. Nalebuff, *Co-opetition*, New York: Doubleday, 1996. Broadly, complementarity includes relationships by which the firm secures needed resources. Formal agreements include co-branding; joint production, marketing, and distribution; joint ventures; R&D partnerships; and supply agreements; but formality is not a requirement for complementarity.

13 A major exception is Southwest Airlines — it has no interline agreements.

CHAPTER 6

1 Note: *Data* is a plural word; *datum* is singular.

2 Case material from Client Insight, LLC, Boston.

3 Personal communication.

4 Personal communication.

5 Personal communication from Michael Francis, former Executive Vice President of Marketing, Target Stores.

6 For a good review, J. Manyika, M. Chui, B. Brown, J. Bughin, R. Dobbs, C. Roxburgh, and A. Hung Byers, "Big Data: The Next Frontier for Innovation, Competition, and Productivity," *McKinsey Global Institute*, May 2011.

7 A. McAfee and E. Brynjolfsson, "Big Data: The Management Revolution," *Harvard Business Review*, 90 (October 2012), pp. 60–67.

8 S. Madden, "How Companies Like Amazon Use Big Data To Make You Love Them," *fastcodesign.com*, 2013.

9 A.C. Micu, K. Dedeker, I. Lewis, O. Netzer, J. Plummer, and J. Rubinson, "The Shape of Marketing Research in 2021," *Journal of Advertising Research* (March 2011), pp. 1–9.

10 Attributed to Yogi Berra, baseball player and manager — New York Yankees and New York Mets.

11 F. Gouillart and F. Sturdivant, "Spend a Day in the Life of Your Customers," *Harvard Business Review*, 72 (January–February 1994), pp. 116–125.

12 Ordinal scales measure rank order; interview scales measure differences among scale points; ration scales possess a non-arbitrary zero value.

13 Numbers of brands/comparisons are: 3 brands/3 comparisons; 4 brands/ 6 comparisons; 5 brands/10 comparisons; 6 brands/15 comparisons; 7 brands/21 comparisons; etc.

14 Panel members may be subject to the Hawthorne effect. Because someone is observing, they behave differently.

15 D.T. Campbell and J.C. Stanley, *Experimental and Quasi-Experimental Designs for Research*, New York: Houghton Mifflin, 1963.

16 J. Surowiecki, *The Wisdom of Crowds*, New York: Doubleday, 2004.

17 Attributed to Yogi Berra, *op. cit.*

18 For information on multiple regression analysis, see any good marketing research textbook.

CHAPTER 7

1 Response to a question asked by R. Rumelt (1998). D. Lovallo and L.T. Mendonca, "Strategy's Strategist: An Interview with Richard Rumelt," *The McKinsey Quarterly*, August 2007.

2 C. Zook with J. Allen, *Profit from the Core*, Boston, MA: Harvard Business School, 2001; C. Zook, *Beyond the Core*, Boston, MA: Harvard Business School, 2004; and C. Zook, *Unstoppable*, Boston, MA: Harvard Business School, 2007. For a shortened version of the 2007 book: C. Zook, "Finding Your Next Core Business," *Harvard Business Review*, 85 (April 2007), pp. 66–75.

3 O. Gadiesh and J.M. Gilbert, "Profit Pools: A Fresh Look at Strategy," *Harvard Business Review*, 76 (May–June 1998), pp. 139–147.

4 In May 1961, President John Kennedy developed a vision for NASA. "Achieving the goal, before this decade is out, of landing a man on the moon and returning him safely to Earth."

5 J.C. Collins and J.I. Porras, "Building Your Company's Vision," *Harvard Business Review*, 74 (September–October 1996), pp. 65–77.

6 J.B. Quinn, *The Intelligent Enterprise: A New Paradigm*, New York: Free Press, 1992.

7 This insight underlay the famous article: T. Levitt, "Marketing Myopia," *Harvard Business Review*, 53 (September–October 1975), pp. 26 *et seq.*

8 Based in part on H.I. Ansoff and J.M. Stewart, "Strategies for a Technologically-Based Business," *Harvard Business Review*, 45 (November–December 1967), pp. 71–83.

9 T. Levitt, *Marketing for Business Growth*, New York: McGraw-Hill, 1974.

10 G.J. Tellis and P.N. Golder, *Will and Vision: How Latecomers Grow to Dominate Markets*, New York: McGraw-Hill, 2006.

11 Tellis and Golder, *op. cit.*

12 *We've Got Rhythm! Medtronic Corporation's Cardiac Pacemaker Business*, 9-698-004, Harvard Business School.

13 Chapter 12 describes systematic methods for incorporating such market factors into an evaluation scheme. For definitions of terms — the glossary and any good finance textbook.

14 T. Kuczmarski, *Managing New Products* (3rd ed.), Englewood Cliffs, NJ: Prentice Hall, 2000.

15 The seminal article: C.K. Prahalad and G. Hamel, "Core Competence of the Corporation," *Harvard Business Review*, 68 (May–June 1990), pp. 79–91. K.P. Coyne, S.J.D. Hall, and P.G. Clifford, "Is Your Core Competence a Mirage?," *The McKinsey Quarterly*, 1 (1997), pp. 40–54, proposes a formal definition: "A core competence is a combination of complementary skills and knowledge bases embedded in a group or team that results in the ability to execute one or more critical processes to a world-class standard" (p. 43). Also P. Leinwand and C. Mainardi, "The Coherence Premium," *Harvard Business Review*, 88 (June 2010), pp. 86–92.

16 Ansoff, *op. cit.*; M. Goold and A. Campbell, "Desperately Seeking Synergy," *Harvard Business Review*, 76 (September–October 1998), pp. 131–143.

17 N. Capon and R. Glazer, "Marketing and Technology: A Strategic Co-Alignment," *Journal of Marketing*, 51 (July 1987), pp. 1–14. Pharmaceutical giant Merck focuses largely on internal development but has had problems with product failure.

18 N. Capon, J. U. Farley, and J. Hulbert, *Corporate Strategic Planning*, New York: Columbia University Press, 1988; and N. Capon, J.U. Farley, and S. Hoenig, *Toward an Integrative Explanation of Corporate Financial Performance*, Norwell, MA: Kluwer Academic Publishers, 1997.

19 L.V. Gerstner, Jr., *Who Says Elephants Can't Dance*, New York: HarperBusiness, 2003, p. 222. Gerstner adds that IBM often accelerated technology development through highly focused acquisitions.

20 M.A. Hayward and D.C. Hambrick, "Explaining the Premiums Paid for Large Acquisitions: Evidence of CEO Hubris," *Administrative Science Quarterly*, 42 (1997), pp. 103–127.

21 M. Bradley, A. Desai, and E.H. Kim, "Synergistic Gains from Acquisitions and Their Division between the Stockholders of Target and Acquiring Firms," *Journal of Financial Economics*, 21 (1988), pp. 3–40; E. Berkovitch and M.P. Narayanan, "Motives for Take-overs: An Empirical Investigation," *Journal of Financial and Quantitative Analysis*, 28 (1993), pp. 347–362; M.L. Sirower, *The Synergy Trap: How Companies Lose the Acquisition Game*, New York: Free Press, 1997.

22 Capon, Farley, and Hoenig, *op. cit.*

23 W.H. Bergquist, *Building Strategic Relationships: How to Extend Your Organization's Reach through Partnerships, Alliances and Joint Ventures*, San Francisco, CA: Jossey-Bass, 1995.

CHAPTER 8

1 Ideally, segments are mutually exclusive and collectively exhaustive.

2 "Taxonomy at the Pump: Mobil's Five Types of Gasoline Buyers," *The Wall Street Journal*, January 30, 1995.

3 "Mirabella Told Summer Issue to Be Its Last," *The New York Times*, April 28, 2000.

4 D.K. Rigby and V. Vishwanath, "Localization: The Revolution in Consumer Markets," *Harvard Business Review*, 84 (April 2006), pp. 82–92.

5 B.J. Pine II, B. Victor, and A.C. Boyton, "Making Mass Customization Work," *Harvard Business Review*, 71 (September–October 1993), pp.

108–119; B.J. Pine II, D. Peppers, and M. Rogers, "Do You Want to Keep Your Customers Forever?," *Harvard Business Review*, 73 (March– April 1995), pp. 103–114; and E. Feitzinger and H.L. Lee, "Mass Customization at Hewlett-Packard: The Power of Postponement," *Harvard Business Review*, 75 (January–February 1997), pp. 116– 121.

6 A.J. Slywotzky, "The Age of the Choiceboard," *Harvard Business Review*, 78 (January–February 2000), pp. 40–41.

7 M.J.A. Berry and G. Linoff, *Data Mining Techniques for Marketing, Sales and Customer Support*, New York: Wiley, 1997.

8 *TESCO PLC: Getting to the Top ... Staying at the Top?* 599-037-1BW, European Case Clearing House. Tesco's loyalty card comes in gold, silver, and bronze tiers, reflecting customer profitability. G.S. Linoff and M.J.A. Berry, *Data Mining Techniques: For Marketing, Sales, and Customer Relationship Management*. Indianapolis, IN: Wiley, 2011.

9 H. Simon, *Hidden Champions: Lessons from 500 of the World's Best Unknown Companies*, Boston, MA: Harvard Business School Press, 1996; also *Hidden Champions of the Twenty-First Century: The Success Strategies of Unknown World Market Leaders*, New York: Springer-Science+ Business Media, 2009.

10 "Wish I'd Thought of That!" *Fortune*, May 15, 2000.

CHAPTER 9

1 Personal communication.

2 Note: *market strategy*, not *marketing strategy*. Many functional areas, not just marketing, should help develop and implement the strategy.

3 To ensure the firm seriously considers competition, re label *Market Strategy* as *Competitive Market Strategy*.

4 R.D. Buzzell, B.T. Gale, and R.G.M. Sultan, "Market Share — a Key to Profitability," *Harvard Business Review*, 53 (January–February 1975), pp. 97–106, was the first paper in a stream of research on the relationship between market share and profitability. In general, the relationship is positive, but may break down at high market share levels.

5 The strategic-focus-alternatives tree is loosely based on the famous DuPont formula; Wikipedia.

6 End-user customers are individuals, family, or formal organizations.

7 H. Evans, *They Made America*, New York: Little Brown, 2004, pp. 391–392.

8 P. M. Nattermann, "Best Practice Does Not Equal Best Strategy," *The McKinsey Quarterly*, August 18, 2004.

9 Thanks to Mary Murphy, Impact Planning Group, for this acronym.

10 A. Ries, J. Trout, and P. Kotler, *Positioning: The Battle for Your Mind*, New York: McGraw-Hill, 2000.

11 Robert Christian, formerly of Impact Planning Group, Old Greenwich, CT, developed this structure.

12 Developed by the author from published data.

13 With these capabilities, Cemex saves on fuel, maintenance, and payroll, and uses 35 percent fewer trucks. Cemex secures higher prices by delivering a perishable item within minutes of receiving an order. Customers use the Internet to place orders, secure delivery information, and check payment records.

CHAPTER 10

1 A separate but related issue: At what stage should the firm enter the market? We address this question in Chapter 7.

2 Entry barriers retard firm market *entry*; exit barriers retard firm market *exit*. The general term for inhibiting firm movement is *mobility barriers*. For entry barriers: T.S. Gruca and D. Sudharshan, "A Framework for Entry Deterrence Strategy: The Competitive Environment, Choices, and Consequences," *Journal of Marketing*, 59 (July 1995), pp. 44– 55; and B. Greenwald and J. Kahn, *Competition Demystified: A Radically Simplified Approach to Business Strategy*, New York: Portfolio Hardcover, 2005.

3 Many marketing textbooks address penetration and skim pricing in the pricing chapter. We believe the fundamental issues these strategies represent make them appropriate for Chapter 10.

4 G.S. Carpenter and K. Nakamoto, "Consumer Preference Formation and Pioneering Advantage," *Journal of Marketing Research*, 26 (August 1989), pp. 285–298. Research supporting the success of pioneering firms includes: G. Urban, T. Carter, S. Gaskin, and Z. Mucha, "Market Share Rewards to Pioneering Brands: An Empirical Analysis and Strategic Implications," *Management Science*, 32 (June 1986), pp. 645–659; and M. Song, C.A. DiBenedetto, and Y. L. Zhao, "Pioneering Advantages in Manufacturing and Service Industries: Empirical Evidence from Nine Countries," *Strategic Management Journal*, 20 (1999), pp. 811–836.

5 J. Dean, "Pricing Policies for New Products," *Harvard Business Review*, 28 (November–December 1950), pp. 28–36.

6 Personal communication from former senior Nokia marketing executive Richard Geruson.

7 R. Buaron, "New Game Strategies," *The McKinsey Quarterly* (Spring 1981), pp. 24–30.

8 G. Stalk Jr., D.K. Pecaut, and B. Burnett, "Breaking Compromises, Breakaway Growth," *Harvard Business Review*, 74 (September–October 1996), pp. 131–139; and Y. Moon, "Break Free from the Product Life Cycle," *Harvard Business Review*, 83 (May 2005), pp. 77–94.

9 Price elasticity = percentage change in quantity demanded divided by percentage change in price = $dQ/Q \div dP/P$.

10 For interesting approaches to securing growth in mature markets: W.C. Kim and R. Mauborgne, "Creating New Market Space," *Harvard Business Review*, 77 (January–February 1999), pp. 83–93; and *Blue Ocean Strategy*, Boston, MA: Harvard Business School, 2005 (same authors).

11 Managers often confuse *harvesting* with *milking*. Milking focuses on securing resources for use elsewhere in the firm — *the cow must be fed so the milk continues to flow*. Harvesting implies a decision to exit, sooner or later.

12 K. Harrigan, "Strategies for Declining Industries," *Journal of Business Strategy*, 1 (Fall 1980), pp. 20–34. Of course, in the decline stage, the investment can be quite low if the firm has mostly depreciated its capital equipment.

CHAPTER 11

1 J. Sampson, "Brand Valuation: Today and Tomorrow," Chapter 20 in *Brand Valuation*, R. Perrier and P. Stobart (eds.), London: Premier Books, 1997.

2 Adapted from B.H. Schmitt and D. Rogers, "SAP: Building a Leading Technology Brand," Center on Global Brand Leadership, Columbia Business School, and personal communication from Marty Homlish. In 2011, Homlish joined HP as executive vice president and chief marketing officer.

3 S. King, *Developing New Brands*, London: J. Walter Thompson Co. Ltd., 1984.

4 American Marketing Association, from K.L. Keller, *Strategic Brand Management*, Upper Saddle River, NJ: Prentice-Hall, 2003, Chapter 1.

5 J. M. Hulbert, N. Capon, and N. Piercy, *Total Integrated Marketing: Breaking the Bounds of the Function*, New York: Free Press, 2003.

6 B.H. Schmitt, *Experiential Marketing*, New York: Free Press, 1999; and *Customer Experience Management*, Hoboken, NJ: Wiley, 2003.

7 www.virgin.com

8 A. Muniz, Jr. and T.C. O'Guinn, "Brand Community," *Journal of Consumer Research*, 27 (March 2001), pp. 412–432. S. Fournier and L. Lee, "Getting Brand Communities Right," *Harvard Business Review*, 87 (April 2009), pp. 105-110.

9 Thanks to David James, Henley Management College.

10 J. Aaker, "Dimensions of Brand Personality," *Journal of Marketing Research*, 34 (August 1997), pp. 334–356. Based on data from 1,000 U.S. respondents: 60 well-known brands and 114 personality traits.

11 E. Joachimsthaler and D.A. Aaker, "Building Brands without Mass Media," *Harvard Business Review*, 75 (January–February 1997), pp. 3–10.

12 D.A. Aaker, *Managing Brand Equity*, New York: Free Press, 1991, p. 15; *Building Strong Brands*, New York: Free Press, 1995; and *Brand Leadership* (with E. Joachimsthaler), New York: Free Press, 2000.

13 Norio Ohga, Chairman and CEO, Sony, quoted in *Fortune*, June 12, 1995.

14 "Big Blue," *Fortune*, April 14, 1997.

15 P. Berthon, J.M. Hulbert, and L.F. Pitt, "Brand Management Prognostications," *Sloan Management Review*, 40 (Winter 1999), pp. 53–65.

16 M.E. Barth, M.B. Clement, G. Foster, and R. Kasznik, "Brand Values and Capital Market Valuation," *Review of Accounting Studies*, 3 (1998), pp. 41–68.

17 D.A. Ailawadi, D.R. Lehmann, and S.A. Neslin, "Revenue Premium as an Outcome Measure of Brand Equity," *Journal of Marketing*, 67 (October 2003), pp. 1–17.

18 The cost to create a successful mid-size B2C brand is about $100 million. At a 15 percent success rate, brand value = $670 million (100/0.15).

19 Developed from G. Gordon, A. di Benedetto, and R. Calantone, "Brand Equity as an Evolutionary Process," *The Journal of Brand Management*, 2 (1994), pp. 47–56.

20 "Bringing a Corporate Brand to Life Using the Principles of Experiential Marketing," Presentation by C.P. Lange and S. Tollefson at True Love or One-Night Stand?: Conference on Brand Relationships and Experiences. Columbia Business School, May 29-30, 2001.

21 K.L. Keller, "Conceptualizing, Measuring, and Managing Customer-Based Brand Equity," *Journal of Marketing*, 57 (January 1993), pp. 1– 22; and "The Brand Report Card," *Harvard Business Review*, 78 (January–February 2000), pp. 147–157.

22 Aaker, 1991, *op. cit.*

23 S. K. Reddy, S. L. Holak, and S. Bhat, "To Extend or Not to Extend: Success Determinants of Line Extensions," *Journal of Marketing Research*, 31 (May 1994), pp. 243–262.

24 D.A. Aaker and K.L. Keller, "Consumer Evaluation of Brand Extensions," *Journal of Marketing*, 54 (January 1990), pp. 27–41; S.M. Broniarczyk and J.W. Alba, "The Importance of the Brand in Brand Extension," *Journal of Marketing Research*, 31 (May 1994), pp. 214–228; S.J. Milberg, C.W. Park, and M.S. McCarthy, "Managing Negative Feedback Effects Associated With Brand Extensions: The Impact of Alternative Branding Strategies," *Journal of Consumer Psychology*, 6 (1997), pp. 119–140; D.R. John, B. Loken, and C. Joiner, "The Negative Impact of Extensions: Can Flagship Products Be Diluted?," *Journal of Marketing*, 62 (January 1998), pp. 19–32; and V. Swaminathan, R.J. Fox, and S.K. Reddy, "The Impact of Brand Extension Introduction on Choice," *Journal of Marketing*, 65 (October 2001), pp. 1–15.

25 Personal communication from David Haines, former Director of Global Branding, Vodafone.

CHAPTER 12

1 We use *product* to include both physical products and intangible services.

2 Portfolio approaches are appropriate for resource allocation at both the business unit and corporate levels.

3 For a detailed treatment of financial analysis techniques: J.C. Van Horne and J.M. Wachowicz, Jr., *Fundamentals of Financial Management* (13th ed.), Englewood Cliffs, NJ: Prentice Hall, 2008.

4 Most firms try to maximize shareholder value by improving return on shareholder equity (ROE). They often use return-on-investment (ROI) as a proxy for ROE, N. Capon, J.U. Farley, and J. Hulbert, *Corporate Strategic Planning*, New York: Columbia University Press, 1988.

5 A simple principle underlies discounting — the future value of $1 is less than today's value of $1.

6 Stern Stewart trademarked EVA; J. M. Stern, J. S. Shiely, and I. Ross, *The EVA Challenge*, New York: Wiley, 2001.

7 Portfolio analysis helps set priorities among market segments — Chapter 8.

8 P. Haspeslagh, "Portfolio Planning: Uses and Limits," *Harvard Business Review*, 60 (January–February 1982), pp. 58–74.

9 The visual appearance of portfolio matrices — 2×2, 3×3 — is arbitrary. Regardless, by placing products in the matrix, the firm can assess potential return and risk and gain insight into strategic options. "A picture is worth 1,000 words" captures much of portfolio models' appeal — senior managers can assess the firm's products in two simple dimensions.

10 Aka the stoplight matrix — three green (invest) cells, three red (don't invest) cells, and three amber (be careful) cells.

11 R. Vernon, "Gone Are the Cash Cows of Yesteryear," *Harvard Business Review*, 58 (November–December 1980), pp. 150–155.

12 Note we define the x-axis as low to high, different from the growth-share matrix.

13 A.J. Slywotzky and D.J. Morrison, *The Profit Zone*, New York: Times Business, 1997.

14 C. Shapiro and H.R. Varian, *Information Rules*, Boston, MA: Harvard Business School Press, 1999.

15 R.F. Maruca, "Is Your Brand at Risk?," *Harvard Business Review*, 77 (November–December 1999), pp. 22, 25. For a case study on counterfeiting: P.F. Nunes and N.P. Mulani, "Can Knockoffs Knock Out Your Business?", *Harvard Business Review*, 86 (October 2008), pp. 41–50. Commercial brand protection services are proliferating.

CHAPTER 13

1 From *The Economist*.

2 C.H. Lovelock and J. Wirtz, *Services Marketing* (7th ed.), Upper Saddle River, NJ: Prentice Hall, 2011; C.H. Lovelock, *Product Plus: How Product + Service = Competitive Advantage*, New York: McGraw-Hill, 1994. Government statistics typically count manufacturers' in-house activities as value-added manufacturing. Identical outsourced activity is mostly counted as a service. This statistical quirk has helped fuel reported service growth.

3 B.G. Auguste, E.P. Harmon, and V. Pandit, "The Right Service Strategies for Product Companies," *The McKinsey Quarterly*, 1 (2006), pp. 41– 51.

4 J. Carlzon, *Moments of Truth*, Cambridge, MA: Ballinger, 1987.

5 C.W.L. Hart, "The Power of Unconditional Service Guarantees," *Harvard Business Review*, 66 (July–August 1988), pp. 54–62.

6 P. Kotler and S.J. Levy, "Demarketing, Yes, Demarketing," *Harvard Business Review*, 49 (November–December 1971), pp. 74–80.

7 E.W. Anderson, C. Fornell, and S.K. Mazvancheryl, "Customer Satisfaction and Shareholder Value," *Journal of Marketing*, 68 (October 2004), pp. 172–186; L. Askoy, B. Cooil, C. Groening, T.L. Keiningham, and A. Yalçin, "The Long-Term Stock Market Valuation of Customer Satisfaction," *Journal of Marketing*, 72 (July 2008), pp. 105–122.

8 *Not* perceived quality alone. A. Parasuraman, V.A. Zeithaml, and L.L Berry, "A Conceptual Model of Service Quality and Its Implications for Future Research," *Journal of Marketing*, (Fall 1985), pp. 41–50, and V.A. Zeithaml, A. Parasuraman, and L.L. Berry, *Delivering Quality Service: Balancing Customer Expectations and Perceptions*, Free Press, 1990. Some expectations' models include a *tolerance zone*: Service quality below expectations but still acceptable.

9 V.A. Zeithaml, L.L. Berry, and A. Parasuraman, "The Behavioral Consequences of Service Quality," *Journal of Marketing*, 60 (April 1996), pp. 31–46.

10 Technical Assistance Research Program (TARP), Consumer Complaint Handling in America: An Update Study, Parts I and II, Washington, DC: TARP and U.S. Office of Consumer Affairs, April 1986.

11 Lovelock and Wirtz, *op. cit.*

12 H. Takeuchi and J.A. Quelch, "Quality Is More than Making a Good Product," *Harvard Business Review*, 61 (July–August 1983), pp. 139–145. We can decompose extended purchase decisions into finer-grained pre-purchase customer service.

13 M.M. Lele and U.S. Karmarkar, "Good Product Support Is Smart Marketing," *Harvard Business Review*, 61 (November–December 1983), pp. 124–132; I.C. MacMillan and R.G. McGrath, "Discovering New Points of Differentiation," *Harvard Business Review*, 75 (July–August 1997), pp. 133–145.

14 R.G. Bundschuh and T.M. Dezvane, "How to Make After-Sales Services Pay Off," *The McKinsey Quarterly*, 4 (2003), pp. 116–127.

15 T. Baumgartner, R.H. John, and T. Nauclér, "Transforming Sales and Service," *The McKinsey Quarterly*, 4 (2005), pp. 81–91.

16 B. Donaldson and T. O'Toole, *Strategic Market Relationships: From Strategy to Implementation*, Chichester, UK: Wiley, 2002.

17 *Xerox Corporation: The Customer Satisfaction Program*, 9-591-055, Harvard Business School.

18 F.F. Reicheld and W.E Sasser Jr., "Zero Defections: Quality Comes to Services," *Harvard Business Review*, 68 (September–October 1990), pp. 105–111.

CHAPTER 14

1 Based on material provided by Client Insight (CI), LLC, Boston, MA. CI principals work extensively with Thomson businesses.

2 P.F. Drucker, *The Practice of Management*, New York: Harper and Row, 1956, pp. 65–67.

3 R. Foster and S. Kaplan, *Creative Destruction: Why Companies That Are Built to Last Underperform the Market — and How to Successfully Transform Them*, New York: Currency/Doubleday, 2001.

4 C.M. Christensen, *The Innovator's Dilemma: When New Technologies Cause Great Firms to Fail*, Boston, MA: Harvard Business School Press, 1997; New York: Harper Business Essentials, 2004.

5 From Booz Allen and Hamilton — improved performance relates to attention to core competence and focused innovation. Also W. Riggs and E. von Hippel, "The Impact of Scientific and Commercial Values on the Sources of Scientific Instrument Innovation," *Research Policy* 23 (July 1994), pp. 459-469.

6 E. von Hippel, S. Thomke, and M. Sonnack, "Creating Breakthroughs at 3M," *Harvard Business Review*, 77 (September–October 1999), pp. 47–57, at p. 54, and E. von Hippel, *Democratizing Innovation*, Cambridge, MA: MIT Press, 2005. Free download at *http://web.mit.edu/evhippel/www/*. The author was a lead user for gas phase chromatography.

7 Based in part on *www.mindtools.com*; also J. Goldenberg, *Creativity in Product Innovation*, Cambridge, UK: Cambridge University Press, 2002.

8 E. De Bono, *Six Thinking Hats: An Essential Approach to Business Management from the Creator of Lateral Thinking*, Boston, MA: Little Brown, 1985.

9 W.H. Davidow and B. Uttal, *Total Customer Service: The Ultimate Weapon*, New York: Harper & Row, 1989.

10 D.K. Sobek II, J.K. Liker, and A.C. Ward, "Another Look at How Toyota Integrates Product Development," *Harvard Business Review*, 76 (July–August 1998), pp. 36–49.

11 Quotation and boxed insert: Personal communication from Ron Boire, former President Consumer Sales Company, Sony Electronics.

12 E.M. Rogers, *Diffusion of Innovations* (5th ed.), New York: Free Press, 2003; E. Ofek and O. Toubia, "Marketing and Innovation Management: An Integrated Perspective," *Foundations and Trends in Marketing*, 4 (2009), pp. 77–128.

13 Size percentages, based on standard deviations from the mean, have not been empirically validated.

14 G.A. Moore, *Crossing the Chasm — Marketing & Selling High-Tech Products to Mainstream Customers*, New York: HarperBusiness, 2002.

CHAPTER 15

1 G.E. Belch and M.A. Belch, *Advertising and Promotion: An Integrated Marketing Communications Perspective* (9th ed.), Homewood, IL: McGraw-Hill/Irwin, 2011.

2 J. Hulbert and N. Capon, "Interpersonal Communication in Marketing: An Overview," *Journal of Marketing Research*, 9 (February 1972), pp. 27–34.

3 D. Peppers and M. Rogers, *The One-to-One Future: Building Relationships One Customer at a Time*, New York: Currency Doubleday, 1993.

4 *Buzz marketing* focuses on getting people talking about the firm's products. *Guerilla marketing* is a subset of buzz marketing that typically uses stunts. Buzz marketing relies on the six buttons of buzz — taboo (sex, lies, bathroom humor), unusual, outrageous, hilarious, remarkable, and secrets (kept and revealed) — to get people talking. Five popular types of media story enhance *buzz* — David & Goliath, unusual and outrageous, controversy, celebrities, and what's currently hot in the media; M. Hughes, *Buzz Marketing*, New York: Portfolio, 2005. BzzAgent and Buzzador use social networking to pair consumers wth products and give them Internet tools to share opinions.

CHAPTER 16

1 Founder of Wanamaker department store, Philadelphia, 1875. Statement also attributed to Lord Leverhume, founder of Unilever.

2 H.E. Krugman, "What Makes Advertising Effective?," *Harvard Business Review*, 53 (March–April 1975), pp. 96–103, is the classic advertising effectiveness article.

3 For a fine discussion of hierarchy-of-effects models: G.E. Belch and M.A. Belch, *Advertising and Promotion: An Integrated Marketing and Communications Perspective* (8th ed.), Homewood, IL: McGraw-Hill/Irwin, 2011.

4 D. Vakratsas and T. Ambler, "How Advertising Works: What Do We Really Know?," *Journal of Marketing*, 63 (January 1999), pp. 26–43.

5 B.H. Schmitt, "Advertising and Mass Communications," in N. Capon (Ed.), Section 7, *Marketing*, in AMA Management Handbook (3rd ed.), J. Hampton (Ed.), AMACOM, 1994, 2-108 – 2-115, p. 2-112. Creativity is different from impact. Advertising campaigns may earn creativity awards yet fail to achieve objectives.

6 Some countries ban comparative advertising. B. Buchanan and D. Goldman, "Us vs. Them: The Minefield of Comparative Ads," *Harvard Business Review*, 67 (May–June 1989), pp. 38–50, reviews the legal status. For *deceptive advertising*: G.V. Johar, "Consumer Involvement and Deception from Implied Advertising Claims," *Journal of Marketing Research*, 32 (August 1995), pp. 267–279.

7 H.E. Krugman, "On Application of Learning Theory to TV Copy Testing," *Public Opinion Quarterly*, 26 (1962), pp. 626–639.

8 Global — Nielsen; U.S. — Kantar Media.

9 Source: Nielsen. Advertising expenditure breakdown by geographic area ($billions): North America — 172; Western Europe — 108; Asia/Pacific — 140; Central/Eastern Europe — 27; Latin America — 38; Middle East/North Africa — 4; rest of world — 12: Source: ZenithOptimedia. Note: ZenithOptima's total global advertising figure is $501 billion, roughly 10 percent less than Nielsen. Various sources offer conflicting numbers on advertising spending.

10 Belch and Belch, *op. cit.*

11 J.A. Simon and J. Arndt, "The Shape of the Advertising Response Function," *Journal of Advertising Research*, 20 (1980), pp. 11–28; P.B. Luchsinger, V.S. Mullen, and P.T. Jannuzzo, "How Many Advertising Dollars Are Enough," *Media Decisions*, 12 (1977), p. 59. Also D.A. Aaker and J.M. Carman, "Are You Overadvertising?," *Journal of Advertising Research*, 22 (1982), pp. 57–70; and G. Assmus, J.U. Farley, and D.R. Lehmann, "How Advertising Affects Sales: Meta Analysis of Econometric Results," *Journal of Marketing Research*, 21 (1984), pp. 65–74.

12 A recent trend for advertising agencies is to form separate departments focused on social media and analytics. In some agencies, project managers coordinate internal matters, then interface with account/relationship managers.

13 For a synopsis: M. Kalter and E. Stearns, "Direct Marketing," in N. Capon (Ed.), Section 2, Marketing, in *AMA Management Handbook* (3rd ed.), J. Hampton (Ed.), New York: AMACOM, 1994, 2-116 – 2-121.

14 *College Savings Bank (A) and (B)* in N. Capon, *The Marketing of Financial Services: A Book of Cases*, Englewood Cliffs, NJ: Prentice Hall, 1992, pp. 93–121.

15 "Bad for You," *The Economist*, June 19, 1999. Two bottling-system failures emerged: "bad" carbon dioxide at one plant and fungicide contamination from wooden pallets at another.

16 *Spiffs* are direct cash payments from a firm to customer salespeople, contingent on sales success.

17 C.F. Mela, S. Gupta, and D.R. Lehmann, "The Long-Term Impact of Promotion and Advertising on Consumer Brand Choice," *Journal of Marketing Research*, 34 (May 1997), pp. 248–261. M. Tsiros and D.M. Hardesty, "Ending a Price Promotion: Retracting It in One Step or Phasing It Out Gradually," *Journal of Marketing*, 74 (January 2010), pp 49–64 shows that *steading decreasing discounting* (SDD) is more effective than returning to the pre-discounted price in one step.

18 Thanks to Jeremy Kagan, Lyn Maize, Peter Propp, and Judy Strauss for assistance in preparing this section.

19 Click fraud is an ongoing problem for paid search — the paid-search advertising network simulates clicks on the ads it features. Of course, all major search engines work hard to detect and combat click fraud. A second problem is inflated measures from search engine robots and other automated software.

20 "Blogs: Fad or Marketing Medium of the Future?," *Brandweek*, November 24, 2004.

21 I. Nitzan and S.B. Libal, "Social Effects on Customer Retention," *Journal of Marketing*, 75 (November 2011), pp. 24–38.

CHAPTER 17

1 U.S. Bureau of Labor Statistics

2 Material sourced from N. Capon and G. Tubridy, *Sales Eats First*, Bronxville, NY: Wessex, 2011.

3 Calendarization is especially important when sales patterns are seasonal.

4 "Steve Jobs: The Graying Prince of a Shrinking Kingdom," *Fortune*, May 14, 2001.

5 *Key* and *strategic* are interchangeable. Generally, European use is *key*; U.S. use is *strategic*. Firms making excessive price concessions to large customers may find smaller customers are more profitable.

6 N. Capon, D. Potter, and F. Schindler, *Managing Global Accounts* (2nd ed.), Bronxville, NY: Wessex, 2008.

CHAPTER 18

1 From interviews with Cisco executives and data from V.K. Rangan, *Transforming Your Go-To-Market Strategy*, Boston, MA: Harvard Business School Press, 2006.

2 An end-user customer is where the product loses its identity; both consumers and firms can be end-user customers. Consumer advertising may push end-user customers down the channel. Previously, end-user customers for microprocessors were PC manufacturers; *intel inside* turned consumers into end-user customers. Sometimes we use *end user* instead of *end-user customer*.

3 The broad view includes *concentration* and *dispersion*. Inputs are concentrated in Korea, and prefabricated steel beams are dispersed to Argentina. Relatedly, natural resources are randomly distributed — *meaningless heterogeneity*; customers require disparate resource bundles — *meaningful heterogeneity*. All distribution systems transform *meaningless heterogeneity* into *meaningful heterogeneity*. For example, a New York restaurant serves patrons a delicious salad of California lettuce, Mexican tomatoes, and Arizona carrots.

4 C.B. Bucklin, S.P. DeFalco, J.R. DeVincentis, and J.P. Levis III, "Are You Tough Enough to Manage Your Channels?," *The McKinsey Quarterly*, (1996), pp. 105–114.

5 *Distribution* encompasses all these functions — **logistics** is about getting the product from A to B.

6 Chapter 2 — customer relationship management.

7 J.A. Narus and J.C. Anderson, "Rethinking Distribution," *Harvard Business Review*, 74 (July–August 1996), pp. 112–120.

8 P.F. Nunes and F.V. Cespedes, "The Customer Has Escaped," *Harvard Business Review*, 81 (November 2003), pp. 96–105. In response to *show-rooming*, in 2012 Target stopped distributing Amazon's Kindle.

9 From Pegram, *Selecting and Evaluating Distributors*, reproduced in B. Rosenbloom, *Marketing Channels: A Management View* (8th ed.), Stamford, CT: Cengage Learning, 2013.

10 L.W. Stern and F.D. Sturdivant, "Customer-Driven Distribution Systems," *Harvard Business Review*, 65 (July–August 1987), pp. 34– 41; V.K. Rangan, A.J. Menzes, and E. Maier, "Channel Selection for New Industrial Products: A Framework, Method and Application," *Journal of Marketing*, 56 (July 1992), pp. 69–82; V.K. Rangan, *Designing Channels of Distribution*, Boston, MA: Harvard Business School, 1994, 9-594-116; J.M. Hulbert, *Marketing: A Strategic Perspective*, Katonah, NY: Impact Publishing, 1985; E. Anderson, G.S. Day, and V.K. Rangan, "Strategic Channel Design," *Sloan Management Review*, (Summer 1997), pp. 59–69.

11 Reproduced with permission from Rosenbloom, *op. cit.*

12 This section benefited from D. Ford, L.E. Gadde, H. Hakansson, A. Lundgren, I. Snehota, P. Turnbull, and D. Wilson, *Managing Business Relationships*, Chichester, UK: Wiley, 1988.

13 A.P. Chandler, Jr., *The Visible Hand: The Managerial Revolution in American Business*, Cambridge, MA: Harvard University Press, 1977.

14 A 2002 Financial Accounting Standards Board (FASB) rule required that manufacturers restate 2001 revenues by subtracting incentive payments from reported sales. This one-time event revealed these payments.

15 C.B. Bucklin, P.A. Thomas-Graham, and E.A. Webster, "Channel Conflict: When Is It Dangerous?," *The McKinsey Quarterly*, (1997), pp. 36–43.

16 G. Stalk, P. Evans, and L.E. Shulman, "Competing on Capabilities: The New Rules of Corporate Strategy," *Harvard Business Review*, 70 (March–April 1992), pp. 57–69.

CHAPTER 19

1 Personal communication from Lamar Muse. Also J.H. Gittell, *The Southwest Airlines Way*, New York: McGraw Hill, 2003, and *Southwest Airlines (A)*, 9-575-060, Harvard Business School.

2 Based on 2,463 companies in the Compustat database; M.V. Marn and R.L. Rosiello, "Managing Price, Gaining Profit," *Harvard Business Review*, 70 (September–October 1992), pp. 84–94. More recently, percentage reductions in operating profit from a 1 percent price decrease were: food and drug stores — 23.7 percent; airlines — 12.9 percent; computers and office equipment — 11 percent; tobacco — 4.9 percent; semiconductors — 3.9 percent; and diversified financial — 2.4 percent, *Fortune*, May 14, 2001. Fortier & Associates report similar findings for a 2 percent improvement: price — 20 percent; variable costs — 11 percent; volume — 9 percent; fixed costs — 7 percent.

3 P.C. Browne, N. Capon, T.S. Harris, H.N. Mantel, C.A. Newland, and A.H. Walsh, *The Ratemaking Process for the United States Postal Service*, New York: Institute of Public Administration, 1991. Also R. Cooper and R. Slagmulder, "Develop Profitable New Products with Target Costing," *Sloan Management Review*, 40 (Summer 1999), pp. 23–33.

4 **Positive sloping** demand curves are relatively rare — volume increases as price increases! They occur with luxury products like perfumes and fragrances. Price conveys information about product and/or service quality.

5 E. Shim and E.F. Sudit, "How Manufacturers Price Products," *Management Accounting*, (February 1995), pp. 37–39 report that more than 80 percent of U.S. manufacturers use cost-plus pricing — 7 percent use *fully allocated costs*.

6 The hurdle rate is the minimum return for a new investment. Typically hurdle rate is tied to the firm's cost of capital.

7 For example, if the firm adds fixed capacity or a new shift.

CHAPTER 20

1 We omit time value of money issues to simplify the illustration.

2 Traditional income statements partitions are cost of goods sold (COGS) and all other costs — mostly marketing and SG&A. Table 20.2 gathers variable costs and fixed costs from these traditional categories:
   - *Variable costs* — raw materials, direct labor, electricity (for production), freight, and sales commissions.
   - *Fixed costs* — indirect labor, manufacturing overhead, and depreciation; also advertising, field sales (salary, expenses), and product and marketing management.
We assume variable costs per unit and fixed costs are constant over the volume range we consider.

3 For more on these terms, see *http://www.investopedia.com/terms/f/fob.asp* and *http://www.investopedia.com/terms/c/cif.asp*.

4 *Norton Company*, 9-581-046, Harvard Business School.

5 M.V. Marn and R.L. Rosiello, "Managing Price, Gaining Profit," *Harvard Business Review*, 70 (September–October 1992), pp. 84–94.

6 From R.B. Ekelund, "Price Discrimination and Product Differentiation in Economic Theory: An Early Analysis," *Quarterly Journal of Economics*, 84 (1970), pp. 268–278. Question: Is this analysis applicable to contemporary airline travel?

7 E. Anderson and D. Simester, "Mind Your Pricing Cuts," *Harvard Business Review*, 81 (September 2003), pp. 97–103.

8 J. Zale and W. Wise, "Pricing When Sales Slow," *The Professional Pricing Society Journal*, 10 (3rd Quarter 2001), pp. 1–9.

9 S. Dutta, M. Bergen, D. Levy, M. Ritson, and M. Zbaracki, "Pricing as a Strategic Capability," *Sloan Management Review*, 43 (Spring 2002), pp. 61 66; and S. Dutta, M. Zbaracki, and M. Bergen, "Pricing Process as a Capability: A Resource-Based Perspective," *Strategic Management Journal*, 24 (2003), pp. 615–630. Also *Organizing for Pricing*, Perspectives, Boston Consulting Group, 2002.

10 For a fuller discussion and bibliography: G.W. Ortmeyer, "Ethical Issues in Pricing," in N.C. Smith and J.A. Quelch, *Ethics in Marketing*, New York: McGraw Hill, 1993, Chapter 5.1. If unsure about pricing actions, consult a knowledgeable attorney.

11 K. Eichenwald, *The Informant*, New York: Broadway, 2000.

CHAPTER 21

1 J. M. Hulbert, N. Capon, and N. Piercy, *Total Integrated Marketing: Breaking the Bounds of the Function*, NY: Free Press, 2003.

2 B.F. Shapiro, "Can Marketing and Manufacturing Coexist?," *Harvard Business Review*, 55 (September–October 1977), pp. 104–112.

3 J. Garten, "Andy Grove Made the Elephant Dance," *BusinessWeek*, April 11, 2005, p. 26.

4 R.S. Achrol, "Evolution of the Marketing Organization," *Journal of Marketing*, 55 (October 1991), pp. 77–93. J.P. Workman Jr., C. Homburg, and K. Gruner, "Marketing Organization: An Integrative Framework of Dimensions and Determinants," *Journal of Marketing*, 62 (July 1998), pp. 21–41; L.P. Katsanis, "Some Effects of Changes in Brand Management Systems: Issues and Implications," *International Marketing Review*, 16 (1999), pp. 518–532. C. Homburg. J.P. Workman Jr., and O. Jensen, "Fundamental Changes in Marketing Organization: The Movement Toward a Customer-Focused Structure, *Journal of the Academy of Marketing Science*, 28 (2000), pp. 459– 478.

5 M. Hammer and J. Champy, *Reengineering the Corporation: A Manifesto for Business Revolution*, New York: Nicholas Brealy, 1993.

6 R.C. Blattberg and J. Deighton, "Interactive Marketing: Exploiting the Age of Addressability," *Sloan Management Review*, 33 (Fall 1991), pp. 5–14; D. Peppers and M. Rogers, *The One-to-One Future: Building Relationships One Customer at a Time*, New York: Century Doubleday, 1993.

7 This thinking has influenced terminology in Blattberg and Deighton, *op. cit.* and Peppers and Rogers, *op. cit.* Wachovia Bank (merger of First Union and Wachovia) has long managed retail customers like this. N. Capon, "Wachovia Bank and Trust Company," *The Marketing of Financial Services*, Englewood Cliffs, NJ: Prentice Hall, 1992.

8 "Visionary-in-Chief," *BusinessWeek*, May 17, 1999.

9 A communications switch programmable by outsiders.

10 "The Genesis of a Giant's Stumble," *The New York Times*, January 21, 2001. In 2006, Lucent merged with Alcatel.

11 Personal communication from Howard Schultz.

12 R.C. Camp, *Benchmarking: The Search for Industry Best Practices that Lead to Superior Performance*, Milwaukee, WI: American Society for Quality, 1989.

13 Hammer and Champy, *op. cit.* Business processes often cut across existing functional departments. Internal *political opposition* to change may be widespread, contributing to the failure of many well-intended re-engineering projects.

CHAPTER 22

1 Personal communication from Ron Boire.

2 The reward system should reinforce appropriate behavior if performance meets or exceeds standards; it should change behavior if performance fails to reach standards. Former Columbia professor J.O. Whitney identifies several inappropriate behaviors leading to poor performance: vacillation, paralysis, bravado, intransigence, impatience, hand-wringing, breast-beating, rage, withdrawal, and flight!

3 Note the use of *performance* in this chapter. Suppose the performance measure is sales dollars; actual sales were $12 million versus a standard of $10 million. Performance refers to the variance between actual sales and the standard, in this case a positive $2 million (12–10). Performance does *not* refer to the actual sales, $12 million.

4 For a comprehensive set of performance measures: P.W. Faris, N.T. Bendle, P.E. Pfeifer, and D.J. Reibstein, *Marketing Metrics: 50+ Metrics Every Executive Should Master*, Upper Saddle River, NJ: Pearson, 2006.

5 Said Dick Melville, Vice Chairman Alcoa's Aerospace Market Sector Lead Team, "If you want to push a button and say, 'What does the entire Alcoa profit look like on a Canadaire CRJ-70?' or 'What is the profitability of all of our castings in the new Pratt & Whitney jet engine?' we can tell you." Personal communication.

6 D. Bowman and H. Gatignon, "Market Response and Marketing Mix Models: Trends and Research Opportunities," *Foundations and Trends in Marketing*, 4 (2009), pp. 129–207.

7 P. Lapoint, *Marketing by The Dashboard Light*, New York: Association of National Advertisers, 2005.

8 W. Edwards Deming is widely credited as the founder of the Quality movement. The famous Japanese quality prize is named after Deming. An anecdote: In the early 1990s, the author attended a small meeting of Columbia faculty with then 90-year-old Deming. During the conversation, some of us were surprised to hear Deming say, "... when I turned around Japan. ..." Then we thought about it. He actually did! The following system elaborates the Deming Cycle:
   Plan. Design/revise business process components to improve results.
   Do. Implement the plan and measure performance.
   Check. Assess measurements; report results to decision makers.
   Act. Decide on changes needed to improve the process.

9 R. Simons, *Levers of Control*, Boston, MA: Harvard Business School Press, 1994.

10 Note that this framework is equally effective for overall performance, and for sub-elements like advertising, innovation, and sales force.

11 After subtracting indirect fixed costs from direct product profit, the residual is bottom-line profit.

12 E.W. Anderson, C.G. Fornell, and D.R. Lehmann, "Customer Satisfaction, Market Share, and Profitability," *Journal of Marketing*, 58 (July 1994), pp. 53–66. Brand health checks (Chapter 11) fall into this category.

13 As digital media has increased in importance, many web-based intermediate measures have been developed, like *hits*, *page views*, and *unique visitors*.

14 T.V. Bonoma, "Making Your Strategy Work," *Harvard Business Review*, 62 (March–April 1984), pp. 68–78.

15 T.V. Bonoma, "Market Success Can Breed 'Marketing Inertia'," *Harvard Business Review*, 59 (September–October 1981), pp. 115–121.

16 Former Columbia Business School professor Abe Shuchman, mentor to the author, was one of the first writers on the marketing audit. A. Shuchman, "The Marketing Audit: Its Nature, Purposes and Problems," Management Report No. 32, *Analyzing and Improving Marketing Performance*, New York: American Management Association, 1959.

17 W.H. Rodgers, G.A. Osborne, and P. Kotler, "Auditing the Marketing Function," in N. Capon, (Ed.), Section 7, *Marketing*, in AMA Management Handbook (3rd ed.), J. Hampton, (Ed.), AMACOM, 1994. This section is heavily based on this material. Also P. Kotler, W.T. Gregor, and W.H. Rodgers III, "The Marketing Audit Comes of Age," *Sloan Management Review*, 30 (Winter 1989), pp. 49–62.

18 Other performance measurement problems include only comparing against internal referents like prior years' performance. A. Likierman, "The Five Traps of Performance Measurement," *Harvard Business Review*, 87 (October 2009), pp. 96–101.

19 Kaplan and Norton, *op. cit.* For a more thorough and recent treatment: R.S. Kaplan and D.P. Norton, *Strategy Maps: Converting Intangible Assets into Tangible Outcomes*, Boston, MA: Harvard Business School Press, 2004.

CHAPTER 23

1 For DHL's founding and biography of the *H* (Larry Lee Hillblom): J.D. Scurlock, *King Larry: The Life and Ruins of a Billionaire Genius*, New York: Simon & Schuster, 2012.

2 T.L. Friedman, *The World is Flat: A Brief History of the Twenty-First Century* (expanded edition), New York: Farrar, Strauss & Giroux, 2006.

3 Source: World Trade Organization: International Trade Statistics 2007.

4 For a thoughtful analysis of globalization: T.L. Friedman, *op. cit.*

5 W.J. Henisz and B.A. Zelner, "The Hidden Risks in Emerging Markets," *Harvard Business Review*, 88 (April 2010), pp. 2–8.

6 GDP per capita source: Wikipedia, from The World Bank.

7 Goldman Sachs originally coined the term BRIC; it also identified the *Next 11 (N11)* — Bangladesh, Egypt, Indonesia, Iran, Korea, Mexico, Nigeria, Pakistan, Philippines, Turkey, and Vietnam, poised to rival the G7 — Canada, France, Germany, Great Britain, Italy, Japan, United Kingdom, and United States (adding Russia formed the G8), in economic influence in the 21st century. In 2010, Indonesia received a promotion: *BRIC* became *BRICI*.

8 Additionally, leaders of the world's wealthiest countries meet annually to discuss global economic issues. The G8 comprises the following countries:

	Population (millions)	GDP per capita (US $billions)
Canada	32	29.3
France	60	26.0
Germany	82	26.2
Great Britain	60	25.5
Italy	58	25.1
Japan	127	28.7
Russia	145	9.7
U.S.	290	36.3

A.K. Vaidya, Ed., *Globalization: Encyclopedia of Trade, Labor, and Politics*, 2006, p. 600. The G20 is an outgrowth of the G8 and comprises 19 nations plus the EU — 85 percent of global GDP, 80 percent of global trade, and two thirds world population. Member countries are Argentina, Australia, Brazil, Canada, China, France, Germany, Great Britain, India, Indonesia, Italy, Japan, Mexico, Russia, Saudi Arabia, South Africa, Korea, Turkey, and the U.S.

9 G. Hofstede, *Culture's Consequences: Comparing Values, Behaviors, Institutions and Organizations Across Nations* (2nd ed.), Thousand Oaks, CA.: Sage, 2001. An alternative framework embraces seven dimensions: *Universalism* versus *particularism*, *collectivism* versus *individualism*, *affective* versus *neutral* relationships, *specificity* versus *diffuseness*, *achievement* versus *ascription*, *orientation toward time*, and *internal* versus *external control*; F. Trompenaars, "Resolving International Conflict," *Business Strategy Review*, 7 (1996), pp. 51–68.

10 Adapted from the CAGE framework in P. Ghemawat, *Redefining Global Strategy: Crossing Borders in a World Where Differences Still Matter*, Boston, MA: Harvard Business School Press, 2007.

11 A.K. Bhattacharya and D.C. Michael, "How Local Companies Keep Multinationals at Bay," *Harvard Business Review*, 86 (March 2008), pp. 85–95.

12 Several European countries like Iceland, Lichtenstein, Norway, and Switzerland are not members of the EU.

13 Source: The World Bank.

14 M. Schultz and M.J. Hatch, "The Cycles of Corporate Branding: The Case of the LEGO Company," *California Management Review*, 46 (Fall 2003), pp. 6–26.

15 P. Kotler and D. Gertner, "Country as Brand, Product, and Beyond: A Place Marketing and Brand Marketing Perspective," *Brand Management*, 9 (April 2002), pp. 249–261; and N. Papadopoulos and L. Heslop, "Country Equity and Country Branding: Problems and Opportunities," *Brand Management*, 9 (April 2002), pp. 294–314.

16 P.W.J. Verlegh and J.-B. E.M. Steenkamp, "A Review and Meta-Analysis of Country of Origin Research," *Journal of Economic Psychology*, 20 (1999), pp. 521–546.

17 Likely driven by ethnocentrism: T.A. Shimp and S. Sharma, "Consumer Ethnocentrism: Construction and Validation of the CETSCALE," *Journal of Marketing Research*, 24 (August 1987), pp. 220–289.

18 N. Capon, J.U. Farley, and J. Hulbert, *Corporate Strategic Planning*, New York: Columbia University Press, 1988, for empirical data concerning organization structure for international business.

19 G. Ghislanzoni, R. Penttinen, and D. Turnbull, "The Multi-local Challenge: Managing Cross-Border Functions," *The McKinsey Quarterly*, 2008.

QUESTIONS

FOR STUDY &

DISCUSSION

Can you answer the questions implied by
each chapter's learning objectives? Check!

CHAPTER 1

1. Select a well-known FMCG firm. From its financial statements, identify the book value of its assets. Also identify the firm's market value based on its stock price. Is there a difference? What accounts for this difference? Do these findings change the way you think about marketing's role in delivering value?

2. Does your school approach the market for new students in a systematic way? How could it use the six marketing imperatives to improve its efforts?

3. Why did Kmart decline? Which marketing principle(s) did it neglect? What would you have done differently? How do you assess Kmart's merger with Sears? Compare Kmart's performance with Target's — what accounts for the performance differences?

CHAPTER 2

1. A cable company spends on average $600 to acquire a customer. Annual maintenance costs per customer — $45; record-keeping and billing costs — $30 per customer per annum. Price of a basic service package — $30 per month. Typically, 40 percent of customers buy a premium package — $50 per month; 10 percent buy the super-premium package — $80 per month. Over time, 80 percent of customers remain with the company from one year to the next.

   • What is the average CLV for all customers?

   • What is the CLV of a super-premium customer?

2. Chapter 11 introduces *brand equity*. Skip forward and read the section on pp. 174–176. What is the relationship between CLV and brand equity?

3. Which firms do a good job of retaining and growing current customers, while simultaneously acquiring new customers? What has made these firms successful?

CHAPTER 3

1. For many years, Kodak has been a leading U.S. company. Use the five-forces model to assess the industry forces Kodak faces.

2. American Airlines (AA) is a major U.S. carrier. Use the five-forces and PESTLE models to scope out the various external forces AA faces.

3. Identify and classify environmental pressures that Walmart faces. Why does Walmart face these pressures? How do you assess Walmart's performance in addressing them?

CHAPTER 4

1. a. Airbus developed the A380, a jet aircraft with more than 500 seats. Other than the airlines, what organizations should Airbus consider as macro-customers? Why did you select them?
   b. Suppose your job was to sell a fleet of A380s to Singapore Airlines. Who would you target for effort? What issues would you focus on for each of these targets?

2. Many teenagers have smartphones. Use the feature/benefit/value ladder to identify the benefits and values that smartphones deliver. Suppose you were advising Nokia on new products — what benefits and values could smartphones offer teenagers that they are currently not receiving? How would these benefits and values differ for adults?

3. a. Suppose you are going to take a two-week vacation when you graduate. How will you decide on your destination? Use the five-stage purchase-decision process to structure your answer.
   b. Based on your answer to 3a, what marketing program would you suggest for a vacation company targeting graduating students like you?

CHAPTER 5

1. Evidence suggests that large companies sometimes dismiss competitive threats. Do you believe this is true? Why or why not? How could you ensure that a successful large company retains a competitive outlook?

2. Many observers believe that competition between Microsoft and Google will increase. Microsoft has a large lead in operating systems, office suites, and browsers; Google leads in search. Identify one or two colleagues to act as Google's top managers; identify one or two colleagues to act as Microsoft's top managers. First, the Google team develops a market strategy for Google; the Microsoft team develops a market strategy for Microsoft. The two teams exchange strategies. Second, the Google team develops a market strategy to counteract Microsoft's strategy, and vice versa. How did you define the field of competition? What did you learn from this competitive-gaming exercise? (Feel free to substitute Facebook for Microsoft.)

3. In the hair-coloring market, L'Oreal competes with Clairol; in the men's shaving market, Gillette competes with Schick. Suppose you work for Clairol — use the competitor assessment analysis to evaluate L'Oreal and identify its strategic options. Or suppose you work for Gillette — use the competitor assessment analysis to evaluate Schick and identify its strategic options.

CHAPTER 6

1. Suppose you are product manager for a pharmaceutical firm hoping to launch a new drug to treat schizophrenia. Identify the types of people from whom you would secure marketing research data and the sorts of data you would seek.

2. As marketing director for a hotel chain, responsible for an observational technique to learn about customer needs and to provide data to individual hotels, you receive the following report from your San Francisco property. "Last night, one of our regular customers, Mr. Jackson, arrived to check in with a female companion. The desk clerk used the information system to greet the couple: 'Welcome back, Mr. and Mrs. Jackson, it's good to see you at the hotel again.' Apparently, the woman was not Mrs. Jackson, and Mr. Jackson had not told his companion he was married. The woman was furious with Mr. Jackson; Mr. Jackson was furious with us; they both stormed out of the hotel." How would this incident affect your observational program?

3. You are consulting for a local restaurant with strong brand recognition and loyalty that has many weekend customers; yet from Monday through Thursday, business is slow. Design a questionnaire to understand consumer behavior, lifestyle, and eating habits on weekdays. Your objective is to identify and address marketing opportunities during the week.

CHAPTER 7

1. Google raised large sums of money by going public and making a secondary equity offering. From publicly available data — using Google's search feature — develop a *strategy for growth* for Google. What should be Google's vision, mission, growth path, and timing of entry? Identify growth options for Google. Define and set standards for measuring Google's success.

2. From your knowledge of business, identify current-day examples of pioneer, follow-the-leader, segmenter, and me-too entry strategies.

3. Founded in 1998, by 2012, eBay had merchandising volume of about $70 billion and profits approaching $2 billion. What accounts for eBay's success? How should eBay ensure continued growth and profits?

CHAPTER 8

1. Suppose your firm decides to address the human pain-relief market. How would you segment this market? What market segments can you identify? Can you identify both coarse- and fine-grained segments — market segments and customer segments?

2. Describe a segment of the higher education market that includes you. Appraise this segment in terms of the criteria for *good* segments — differentiated, identifiable, accessible, appropriate size, measurable, and stable.

3. Visit retail outlets for Banana Republic, The Gap, and Old Navy. Observe customers and products. What do you infer about owner Gap Inc.'s segmentation and targeting?

CHAPTER 9

1. Apple's iPod is one of the 21st century's most successful consumer products. Using the framework in this chapter, describe Apple's market strategy for the iPod.

2. The National Basketball Association (NBA) has slumped, whereas the National Football League (NFL) is very successful. Why? How would you turn around the NBA?

3. Historically, several competitive battles stand out: Adidas vs. Nike, Bloomberg vs. Thomson-Reuters, Boeing vs. Airbus, Coke vs. Pepsi, GM vs. Ford, Google+ vs. Facebook, Intel vs. AMD, Microsoft vs. Google, Oracle vs. SAP, Sears vs. Montgomery Ward. Compare and contrast two or more rivalries that interest you. What can you learn about market strategy?

CHAPTER 10

1. Identify the product life-cycle stage for each product. Why did you choose those stages?

Cell phones	Digital cameras	Movies on VHS tapes	Index mutual funds
Desktop PCs	Music on compact discs	Vacation travel	Books on tape

2. Suppose you are the newly appointed marketing VP for the Segway Human Transporter. Identify feasible strategic options. Be prepared to support your choices.

3. Installations of U.S. payphones are decreasing by several percentage points each year — payphone calls are also decreasing. How would you advise an independent payphone firm?

CHAPTER 11

1. Your text quotes a leading advertising executive as saying: "A successful brand is timeless." Do you agree or disagree? Should the statement be modified in the context of young consumers valuing change, innovation, and unique choice? Support your answer with current examples.

2. Select a well-known brand and track its brand history. How have brand identity and brand image evolved? Did the brand owner attempt to change brand identity to keep the brand contemporary? Or was the brand owner trying to broaden the market?

3. Identify an example of poor brand architecture and be prepared to explain your assessment. The example could include multi-branding versus umbrella branding, unwise brand extensions or attempts at broadening (leveraging), brand migration, strategic alliances, and aging brands.

CHAPTER 12

1. Review cereal product lines at your local supermarket. How do you assess General Mills, Kellogg's, and Quaker? What are their strategies? What recommendations can you offer them?

2. The president of Sony Electronics put the problem this way: "If we're selling a $200 DVD player, we may want to give away Sony DVD software. But that's not in the best interest of Sony Pictures. And Sony Music may want to sell a Springsteen box set for $80 with a coupon that says, 'Get $20 off your Sony CD Player.' Why would Sony Electronics want to do that?" How would you advise the president of Sony Electronics? How would you advise the president of Sony Corporation?[1]

3. Some service providers bundle services — amusement parks and ski hills provide unlimited use for a single price. Others unbundle services, like restaurants with a la carte menus. Prepare guidelines for a service provider making bundling/unbundling decisions.

CHAPTER 13

1. Use the SERVQUAL scale to assess service quality for some aspect of your school or college, like the admission process or a finance class. How does your institution rate on tangibles, reliability, responsiveness, assurance, and empathy?

2. Select a local restaurant or bar. How could this institution improve customer service and enhance customer loyalty? What advice would you give the proprietor?

3. Many airlines are roundly criticized for poor customer service. Chart out your interactions with the airline on your most recent trip, from the time you decided to take the flight until you exited your destination airport. Identify the various touch-points. At each touch-point where service was poor, develop a system to improve customer service.

---

1 Personal communication from Ron Boire.

CHAPTER 14

1. Customer dissatisfaction is an opportunity for firms to learn. When were you dissatisfied with a purchase experience? Why? What new product or service ideas would you suggest?

2. Suppose that, on graduation, you accept a position as new product director for a medium-size firm with a poor new product innovation record. The CEO has set a three-year goal for 20 percent of sales to come from new products. What actions will you take in your first 100 days?

3. Apple has been successful with its G4 series of desktop and laptop computers and with the iPod, iTunes, iPhone, and iPad. But Apple withdrew the Newton and G4 Cube computer (now in New York's Museum of Modern Art). How do you assess Apple's new product performance? How does your assessment reconcile with Apple's profit performance?

CHAPTER 15

1. Identify a personal communication that you sent but the receiver did not receive as intended. Was this an encoding, distortion, or decoding problem? How could you improve the communication?

2. Many firms have shareholder-relations departments. What do these departments do? Compare and contrast their activities to the advertising department in a business unit.

3. Sketch out an integrated communications program for Samsung's newest cell phone, or for a product that interests you, or this book — *Capon's Marketing Framework.*

CHAPTER 16

1. Suppose GM is about to launch a new car powered by fuel cells — suggested retail price about $30,000. Mileage is 80 mpg city, 100 mpg highway. Use the table below to develop a consumer advertising campaign.

Advertising Element	Question
Target audience	Whom are we trying to influence?
Advertising objectives	What are we trying to achieve?
Messaging	What content should the target audience receive?
Execution	How shall we communicate the message?
Media selection and timing	Where and when shall we place our advertising?
Advertising budget	How much shall we spend on advertising?
Program evaluation	How shall we test our advertising and measure its effectiveness?

2. Message execution includes rational styles — comparative, demonstration, one-sided and two-sided appeals, primacy, recency, and refutational; and emotional styles — celebrity endorsement, fear, humor, and storytelling. Bring to class an example of each advertising style. Is the advertisement effective? Why or why not?

3. Identify a direct marketing campaign to which you responded. Why did you respond to that one yet ignore so many others?

CHAPTER 17

1. Which of the six sales management tasks are the most important? Why? Interview a sales manager to develop your answer.

2. Aco (disguised names) sells adhesives for a high-end printing application. Printfirm is a major customer, but its specifications are difficult to meet. Historically, Aco was Printfirm's sole supplier, but Bco has started to supply Printfirm with similar adhesives. Aco believes Bco is a low-cost producer that sometimes cuts corners. Last year, Aco's plant flooded and closed for one week. Aco halted all deliveries and Printfirm is adamant that it wants a second supplier. Aco's top management has set a goal of retaining 80 percent of Printfirm's business. How would you advise Aco's sales and marketing managers?

3. PrdCo's (fictional firm) recent sales growth has mirrored the industry — the incoming CEO is demanding improved performance. She wants to implement forced ranking evaluation like Jack Welch introduced at GE. In the sales force, 20 percent would be rated superior, 70 percent average, and 10 percent inferior. Inferior salespeople would be fired. PrdCo's salesforce comprises a national sales manager (NSM), three regional sales managers (RSM), 12 district managers (DSM), and 110 salespeople. Assume you are the NSM; how do you respond to the CEO's ideas?

CHAPTER 18

1. Your friend operates a highly successful loose-meat sandwich restaurant (regional specialty) in his hometown in Iowa. He wants to expand nationally. What are his options and the pros and cons? How would you advise him to proceed? Why? What pitfalls should he look out for?

2. Alasdair MacLean wanted a high-speed bicycle. He gathered information about several bicycles from a department store. He test-rode several models at a local bicycle store. Then he purchased his favorite model from the manufacturer's website. Several major department stores and a trade association of local bicycle stores have complained about this kind of customer behavior to BikeCo, a leading bicycle manufacturer. How would you advise BikeCo?

3. U.S.-based Detha (disguised names) produces wire harnesses to protect electric wires in automobiles. Detha sells to a distributor; the distributor sells to CarSup, a Tier 1 supplier to U.S. auto firms. Also, Detel, one of Detha's sister businesses, sells significant quantities of electric wire direct to CarSup. Last year, Detha's sales to the distributor dropped by 20 percent. Detha discovered that auto firms were demanding local supply in various geographic areas globally. CarSup was enforcing compliance; 40 percent of requirements were now sourced in Asia, hence the drop in Detha's business. How should Detha proceed?

CHAPTER 19

1. Merck priced prescription hair-growth drug Propecia at $50 per month's supply. Over-the-counter competitor Rogaine (topical liquid) was about $30 per month. Merck's drug for enlarged prostate, Proscar, has the same active ingredient — finasteride — as Propecia. Merck's price for 30 Proscar tablets was $70 — one Proscar tablet equals five daily doses of Propecia. Some physicians write Proscar prescriptions for balding men, who slice the pills into five parts. Hence, they pay about $14 per month ($70/5) for hair-loss treatment, versus $50 for Propecia. Merck defends Propecia's price premium by citing research costs including clinical trials — $450 million. Most insurance policies cover Proscar, but not Propecia. The makers of Rogaine launched an $80 million advertising campaign for extra-strength Rogaine, applied twice daily. An Italian website offers Proscar tablets for U.S. delivery at $63 per 36 tablets. Suggest actions for:

   • Merck's director of marketing.
   • The compliance director for a national HMO.
   • Rogaine's marketing director.

2. Large competitors frequently have cost structures with a high proportion of fixed costs. Why? What pricing alternatives would you recommend to one of their small competitors? Why?

3. In 1958, Kaplan, Dirlam, and Lanzillotti showed that cost-plus pricing was the most common pricing method. In 1995, Shim and Sudit found essentially the same result. This chapter argues that cost-plus pricing is deeply flawed. Why does this apparent incongruity exist? What should firms do about it?

CHAPTER 20

1. A British entrepreneur is testing variable prices for movies. Do you think he will succeed? Why or why not?

2. Select a product in which you are interested. What price would you set? Why? Does your recommended price differ from the current price? Why?

3. How would you go about setting price for a subscription-based online specialized news site, an automobile repair shop, and an accounting service?

CHAPTER 21

1. Identify three firms that do a great job of being externally oriented — what makes you think they really are externally oriented?

2. Think about a time when you decided you would no longer be a customer of a business or other organization. Why did you quit? How could the organization have acted for you to have stayed? How would the organization have to change for you to become a customer again?

3. What markets does your school or college address? How does your school or college organize to address these markets? Is the organization structure appropriate? How would you change it?

CHAPTER 22

1. Use the input → intermediate → output framework to identify alternative measures for the marketing executive responsible for Apple's iPad. Using these measures, develop a balanced scorecard to assess executive performance. Alternatively, complete this task for a product in which you are interested, or this book — *Capon's Marketing Framework*.

2. Many managers are distrustful of *soft* performance measures like customer satisfaction. How would you convince managers that *soft* measures have value?

3. How can a marketing audit enhance brand value? What do you expect to learn from the audit process?

CHAPTER 23

1. Wessex Inc. has secured a manuscript entitled *The Song of Hiroshima* by Atsuhiro Ozaki. Ozaki was working at a radio station in Hiroshima on August 6, 1945, the day the atom bomb dropped. *The Song of Hiroshima* is a personal account of his experience on that day and the following few days. How would you advise Wessex to proceed with publishing the book?

2. As the CEO of a successful budget-hotel firm in the U.S., you have decided to expand operations to Spanish-speaking Central and South America. In the U.S., all hotels are company run but you are willing to contemplate a franchise business model. Either way, there are significant entry costs for any new foreign market and you must choose the countries very carefully. How would you go about developing an ordered list of countries by market attractiveness? Pick half a dozen countries to test your approach.

3. To solve an unexpected vacancy, Citibank has suddenly promoted you from a regional sales manager position in the midwest U.S. to become global account manager (GAM) for an important Citibank customer, German electrical giant Siemens. You will be based in Siemens' headquarters in Munich, Germany. On Monday morning you are due to meet with your new boss, the global account director, for the first time. Prepare a list of questions that you would like him to answer.

GLOSSARY

80:20 rule. 80 percent of a firm's revenues come from 20 percent of its customers. An extension is the **80:20:120 rule** — these 20 percent of customers earn the firm 120 percent of its profits.

20:80 rule. This rule follows directly from the 80:20 rule: 20 percent of a firm's revenues come from 80 percent of its customers. An extension is the **20:80:20 rule** — these 80 percent of customers are responsible for reducing the firm's profits by 20 percent.

ACCORD. An acronym for factors that affect the speed of new product adoption: **A**dvantage, **C**ompatibility, **C**omplexity, **O**bservability, **R**isk, and **D**ivisibility.

Acquisition. A firm purchases another firm or business.

Acquisition cost (AC). The cost of attracting a new customer to the firm.

Adoption categories. Describe consumer behavior in adopting innovations — innovators, early adopters, early majority, late majority, and laggards.

Advertising. Paid communications directed at a mass audience.

Advertising agency. A third-party organization to which many firms outsource the development and execution of their advertising.

Advertising budget. The monetary amount to be spent on advertising. Approaches to budget setting are:
   Objective and task. A *bottom-up* approach focusing on advertising objectives and the tasks to be accomplished.
   Percentage of sales. A rule-of-thumb approach that sets the budget as a percentage of sales: current sales, anticipated next-year sales, or some combination.
   Competitive parity. An approach that bases the budget on competitors' spending.

Advertising effectiveness measures. Used to test advertising effectiveness. Options include:
   Recognition. Advertising that respondents recognize.
   Aided recall. Advertising that respondents remember with prompting.
   Unaided recall. Advertising that respondents remember without prompting.

Advertising objectives. What the firm is trying to achieve with its advertising:

    Intermediate objectives relate to the hierarchy-of-effects models and include awareness, knowledge, liking or preference, trial, and emotional commitment (to a brand).

    Output objectives. What the firm ultimately wants to achieve, like sales, repeat purchase, market share, and brand loyalty.

Advertising response function (ARF). Relates advertising spending to an objective like sales.

Advertising strategy. Specifies how the firm will spend resources to achieve advertising objectives and includes decisions about target audience, advertising objectives, messaging, execution, media selections and timing, advertising budget, and program evaluation.

Alliances. Formal economic relationships between the firm and other entities (partners) — suppliers, customers, and distributors.

Alpha test. A new product test within the firm by company employees.

Angel investors. Wealthy individuals who provide funding for new business ventures at a very early stage. Angel investors typically invest before venture capitalists.

Antitrust. U.S. laws that prohibit actions to reduce competition.

Auction pricing. A product's price resulting from competition among potential buyers:

    Dutch auction. Prices start high; the seller reduces price until a buyer bids.

    English auction. Prices start low and potential buyers bid up the price.

    Reverse auction. The buyer states product requirements; suppliers bid to provide the product, and prices go down.

    Vickrey auction. A form of **sealed-bid** English auction where the winning bidder pays the price of the second-highest bid.

B2B — Business-to-business. This acronym generally describes marketing where customers are other organizations — business, public, and not-for-profit.

B2C — Business-to-consumer. This acronym generally describes marketing where customers are consumers.

Backward integration. A customer undertakes activities currently performed by its suppliers.

Bait and switch. Retailers advertise a low price for a product with limited availability. The *bait* sells quickly. Retailers offer most customers a higher-priced product — the *switch*.

Balanced scorecard. A performance measurement system that balances input, intermediary, and output variables.

BDI. See brand development index.

Behavioral targeting. An Internet-based technique that uses information collected from a users online activity to present (on a website visit) or send by e-mail specific messages to motivate purchase or other goals.

Benchmarking. The practice of securing best practices from outside the firm at other organizations.

Benefits and values, categories of:

    Economic. Result from financial considerations of purchasing a product or service.

    Functional. Follow from the product's design.

    Psychological. Satisfy customer needs like status, affiliation, reassurance, risk, and security.

    Search. Customers can gain good information before they purchase.

    Use. Customers do not know the value at the time of purchase.

    Credence. Customers do not know the value until long after the purchase.

Best practice transfer. An approach to identifying and transmitting superior processes across the firm.

Beta test. A new product test by cooperating customers.

Big data. Collections of large and complex data sets that offer the possibility of gaining insight.

Blog. An Internet vehicle for individuals to offer opinions and receive feedback from others.

Brand. The traditional definition is: *a name, term, sign, symbol, or design (or letter, number, or character), or a combination of them intended to identify the goods and services of one seller or group of sellers and to differentiate them from competition.* A more customer-focused definition is: *a collection of perceptions and associations that customers hold about a product, a service, or a company. This collection embodies values that create meaning for customers that represent a promise of the experience customers expect when they have contact with the brand.*

Brand architecture. The organizing structure for the firm's brand portfolio.

Brand associations. The meanings the brand has for customers.

Brand awareness. The extent to which customers know that the brand exists.

Brand broadening/leveraging. A branding approach for extending an existing brand into a new product form/class.

Brand coherence. The extent of agreement between brand identity and the experience a customer has with the brand.

Brand development index (BDI). A U.S.-based measure of brand strength used in B2C. BDI in a specific geographic area is percentage of brand sales divided by percentage of the U.S. population, converted to a percentage.

Brand equity. The classic definition is: *a set of brand assets and liabilities linked to a brand, its name, and symbol that add to (or subtract from) the value provided by a product or service to a firm and/or that firm's customers.* There are two types of brand equity:

> **Customer brand equity** is the value customers receive from a brand, less the value they receive from a generic product. Customer brand equity comprises value received before purchase — **pre-purchase equity**, and value received after purchase — **post-purchase equity**.

> **Firm brand equity** derives directly from customer brand equity when the firm secures in its customers brand awareness, positive attitudes, high perceived quality, positive word-of-mouth, intentions to purchase, purchase, brand loyalty, positive brand image and associations (or brand personality), and satisfaction.

Brand health check. A way of measuring the overall health of the brand.

Brand identity. What the firm wants the brand to mean to customers, including brand personality and the brand promise.

Brand image. The overall meaning that the brand has to customers.

Brand licensing. The practice of making agreements with third-party organizations to attach the brand to their products.

Brand loyalty. The extent to which customers are predisposed to make repeat purchases of the brand.

Brand management. The practice of developing and/or sustaining brand identity by designing and executing marketing actions.

Brand migration. The process of transferring the equity in a brand being retired to a surviving brand.

Brand personality. A set of enduring and distinct human characteristics associated with a brand.

Brand positioning. The process by which the firm attempts to align brand image with brand identity.

Brand resilience. The ability of a brand to recover from negative information.

Brand revitalization. An approach designed to rejuvenate under-performing brands.

Brand valuation. The process of putting a monetary value on brand equity, typically firm brand equity (FBE).

Branding. The attachment of a symbol to a product, service, and/or organization that uniquely identifies the supplier and/or owner. The symbol may consist of words, a concept, or an auditory or visual signal.

Breakeven analysis. The approach for calculating the breakeven point.

Breakeven point (BE). The level of sales required to cover fixed costs.

Bundling. The firm sells a product and sets a price only in combination with other products and/or services. **Unbundling.** The firm sells products and sets prices for each item individually. **Mixed bundling.** The firm offers its products as part of a bundle, but also individually.

Business-case analysis. Assesses the financial viability of a project, including various risk factors.

Business model. The way the firm creates value, generates revenues, and incurs costs.

Business strengths. Capabilities, competences, and resources the firm needs to be successful.

Buzz marketing. A communications approach designed to secure positive word of mouth — *buzz* — about the firm's products.

Calendarize. Partitioning sales objectives by time period like quarter, month, or week.

Candidate descriptor variables — segmentation variables. Used to identify segments; typically fall into one of four categories: geography, demography, behavioral, and socio-psychological.

Capabilities, resources, competences. Three related terms that embrace several factors the firm can use as the basis for securing differential advantage. Often called business strengths.

Category development index (CDI). A U.S.-based measure of category strength used in B2C. CDI in a specific geographic area is percentage of category sales divided by percentage of U.S. population, converted to a percentage.

CDI. See category development index.

Chasm. The transition between making sales to innovating and early-adopting customers, and to the mainstream market. Products failing to **cross the chasm** do not realize their potential.

Co-branding. An approach to branding typically involving cooperation between two brands from different firms.

Commercialization. The final step in bringing a new product to market.

Communication process. The activities involved in sending and receiving information.

Communications tipping point. The level above which communications generate customer resentment.

Competitor assessment analysis. A way of mapping customer needs, required benefits, and values, with the required resources, to assess the competitive position of various suppliers.

Competitive data:
　　Level of. The organizational level for collecting data — corporate, business unit, market, and market segment.
　　Type of. The sorts of quantitative and qualitative data the firm can collect.
　　Secondary. Data that have been collected for another purpose.
　　Primary. Data that require a focused acquisition effort.

Competitive intelligence department. An organizational unit that collects, analyzes, and distributes competitive information.

Competitive intelligence system. A process to collect, analyze, and distribute competitive information.

Competitor. Any organization whose products and services provide similar or superior benefits and values to the same customers that the firm seeks to attract and retain. They may be:
　　Current. Competitors that the firm faces *today*.
　　Potential. Competitors that the firm may face *tomorrow*.
　　Direct. Offer similar benefits with similar products, technologies, or business models.
　　Indirect. Offer similar benefits with alternative products, technologies, or business models.

Competitor target. The organizational entity against which the firm decides to compete.

Complementary products. Products that are used together like razors and razor blades, vacuum cleaners and bags, and printers and toner cartridges.

Complementer. Any organization like independents and competitors whose actions can affect the firm's sales.

Concentrated market. A market with few substantial competitors.

Concept definition. See product concept.

Contribution margin (CM). Sales revenues less variable costs, and:

> **Contribution margin per unit (CMU).** Contribution margin stated on a per-unit basis.
>
> **Contribution margin rate (CMR).** Contribution stated per monetary unit of sales revenues.

Control, types of:

> **Firm functioning.** Asks the question, "Is the firm functioning well?" Three sub-areas are:
>
> > **Implementation.** Did the firm implement its planned actions?
> >
> > **Strategy.** Is the firm's market strategy well conceived and on target?
> >
> > **Managerial process.** Are the firm's managerial processes the best they can be?
>
> **Performance control.** Did the firm achieve its desired results?
>
> **Post-action.** The firm waits until a pre-set time, then compares actual results against standards.
>
> **Steering.** A dynamic, continuous, and anticipatory system. The firm sets control limits for performance standards and compares results against standards on an ongoing basis.

Control unit. An element of the sales force for monitoring and controlling sales activities and performance, like a sales region, sales district, or sales territory.

Cookie. A piece of text stored by a user's web browser for identification and authentication.

Cooperation with competitors:

> **Back-office.** Competitors work together in non-customer-facing activities to reduce costs and improve efficiency for all firms.
>
> **Marketplace or front-office.** Competitors work together to better satisfy customer needs like developing a new technology standard.

Core product. The central element in the firm's offer of a physical product, like an automobile.

Core service. The central element in the firm's service offer, like overnight package delivery.

Cost of capital. The financial return the firm must earn to recover its capital outlay. The cost of capital is a weighted average of the firm's cost of equity and debt. In evaluating investment opportunities, the firm discounts expected future cash flows at its cost of capital.

Cost per 1000 (CPM). A measure of the advertising cost. CPM = Absolute Cost of Advertising Space x 1000/Circulation.

Costs, types of:

> **Direct.** Occur because a particular product, organizational unit, or activity exists or is being contemplated. Can be identified with, or directly linked to, a product, sales territory, or function. Include all variable costs and at least some fixed costs.
>
> **Direct fixed costs.** Costs directly related to the product. These costs do not vary directly with the number of units sold, but are associated with individual products.
>
> **Fixed.** Do not vary with the volume of sales or production over a reasonable range. Usually comprise overhead items like managerial salaries, depreciation, and selling, general, and administrative expenses (SG&A).
>
> **Fully loaded.** Incremental costs plus overhead charges.
>
> **Indirect.** Relate to several products, organizational units, or activities. Cannot be identified with a single product, sales territory, or activity. Are always fixed costs.
>
> **Marginal.** The cost to make and sell one additional unit. Includes all variable costs and some incremental fixed costs, but *excludes* overhead charges.
>
> **Variable.** Vary directly with the volume of sales and production. Increase as volume increases and decrease as volume decreases.

Counterfeiting. Illegal copying of a firm's products.

Creative brief. A *contract* between the firm and its advertising agency that provides parameters and information for translating the firm's market strategy into an advertising message.

Cross-docking. The logistics practice of unloading materials from an incoming truck/railroad car and reloading directly onto outbound trucks/rail cars, with minimal (or zero) storage.

Cross-selling. Selling different products to a customer who has already purchased from the firm.

Customer. Any person or organization in the channel of distribution or decision (other than competitors) whose actions can affect the purchase of the firm's products and services. Categories of customers include:

  Current (today). The firm does business with these customers today.

  Potential (tomorrow). The firm hopes to do business with these customers in the future.

  Direct. Exchange money or other resources with the firm for its products.

  Indirect. Secure the firm's products from intermediaries like manufacturers or distributors.

  Macro-level. Organizational units like manufacturers, wholesalers, retailers, government entities, and families.

  Micro-level. Individuals with influence or decision-making authority within the macro-level customer.

Customer experience. A state, condition, or event that consciously affects a customer.

Customer insight. A deep and unique understanding of customers' needs and required benefits and values.

Customer lifetime. The estimated length of time a firm's customer will remain a customer.

Customer lifetime value (LTV). The economic value to the firm from a customer over the lifetime of its relationship. LTV is the discounted future stream of profits the customer generates.

Customer needs. A basis for identifying market segments.

Customer needs, types of:

  Latent. The customer is not consciously aware of these needs.

  Recognized. The customer is consciously aware of these needs; they may be **expressed** to others, or **non-expressed**.

Customer profitability. The profit the firm earns from an individual customer or group of customers.

Customer relationship management (CRM). The ongoing process of identifying and creating new value with individual customers and sharing these benefits over a lifetime of association with them.

Customer segment. A finer-grained group of customers than a market segment. Within a market segment, the firm might identify several customer segments.

Customer service. Any act, performance, or information that enhances the firm's core product or service.

Customer service strategy. An approach to delivering customer service based on understanding customers' needs for customer service.

Customer target. Individuals and/organizations that the firm tries to make its customers.

Customer value. The utility a customer receives from purchasing the firm's product or service. Value is a higher-level construct embracing several benefits the product offers.

Customer value, methods of assessing:

  Dollarmetric method. A method for assessing customer value. For several pairs of alternatives, the customer states which alternative she prefers and how much extra she would pay.

  Direct value assessment. The firm simply asks customers what they would pay for various products.

  Economic value for the customer (EVC). The price the customer pays for a competitive product, plus the net additional value the firm's product provides. EVC is an upper bound for price.

  Perceived value analysis. The firm secures data directly from customers, but sometimes experienced managers provide *best-guess* data that can be validated later by marketing research.

  Price experiment. The firm offers the test product at different prices in different market areas, like geographic locations.

Data mining. A quantitative approach to gain insight into customers' purchasing behavior as the basis for making specialized offers.

Data warehouse. A place to store data on an individual customer's characteristics and purchase transactions.

Decision-making process (DMP). The individual stages that members of the decision-making unit complete in making a purchase.

Decision-making unit (DMU). The individuals involved in a purchase decision.

Defection rate (1–r). The rate at which the firm loses customers from one time period to the next (also called *churn*). Sometimes calculated as a probability. The opposite of retention rate.

Demand curve. A graph of the relationship between price and volume showing price sensitivity.

Demarketing. Firm efforts to reduce demand, typically because of a supply/demand imbalance.

Demonstration ad. Shows the product in use and focuses on its performance.

Development. The process of turning a product concept into an actual product.

Digital communication. The electronic transmission of digitally encoded information.

Direct marketing. A communications tool embracing many ways of requesting a direct customer response. Includes traditional print and broadcast advertising as well as newer digital options like e-mail and the Internet.

Direct product profit. Assesses profit performance after taking into account the fixed costs the product incurs.

Discount rate (d). The rate at which the firm discounts future earnings so as to calculate customer lifetime value. The discount factor is typically set equal to the firm's cost of capital.

Disintermediation. The removal of a layer in a distribution system.

Distribution channel or Distribution. Encompasses the entities, interrelationships, and functions that members perform, so that the supplier's products reach customers.

Distribution channel breadth. The number of members at a particular level in the channel system:
    Exclusive. A distribution strategy that focuses on a few well-chosen outlets.
    Intensive. A distribution strategy that maximizes the number of outlets.
    Selective. A sort of compromise between intensive and exclusive distribution.

Distribution conflict:
    Operational. Focuses on day-to-day issues like late shipments, invoicing errors, unfulfilled sales-person promises, unacceptable product quality, supplier attempts to load channels, and price and margin disputes.
    Strategic. May change the relationships among distribution channel members.

Distribution exclusivity:
    Geographic. The supplier gives the distributor a monopoly on selling products in its territory.
    Product. The supplier gives the distributor exclusivity to sell a group of products.
    Supplier. The intermediary agrees to distribute only the supplier's products.

Distribution functions. The activities that the distribution channel must perform. Concerned with the physical product, information, and/or ownership.

Distribution, method:
    Direct. The supplier supplies products directly to consumers and end users.
    Indirect. Intermediaries like distributors, wholesalers, and retailers play a major role in transferring products to consumers and end users.

Distribution, view of:
    Broad view. Encompasses changes in *state*, *physical location*, and *time*.
    Narrow view. Encompasses mainly changes in *physical location* and *time*.

Diversion. The practice of purchasing the firm's products ostensibly for sale to one set of customers, then reselling (diverting) those products to a different set of customers. Typically, the firm's strategy is negatively affected.

Divest. Selling a business to another firm.

Dollarmetric method. A method for estimating the monetary value of customer brand equity.

Downstream. The firm's customers and its customers' customers, etc.

Dumping. Selling products in foreign markets below home market prices at "less than fair market value" and often below average costs.

Dynamic pricing. A special case of price discrimination where the price varies over time.

Economic value for the customer (EVC). The price the customer pays for a competitive product, plus the net additional value the firm's product provides. EVC is an upper bound for price.

Endorsed brand. The firm uses one firm brand to support — endorse — another.

Entry barrier. Something that forestalls or slows a firm's entry into a market.

Environmental influences. Factors external to the consumer that affect decision-making, embracing culture, social class, other people, family, and the situation.

Ethnographic research. An observational research technique derived from anthropology.

Exchange. The firm and its customers exchange value. Through its products and services, the firm offers value to customers. Customers typically offer value to the firm via their financial resources. If the firm and customer each accept the value offered by the other, an exchange occurs.

Executional style. The way the firm turns the core message into effective advertising:
  Rational-style advertising appeals to people's sense of logic.
  Emotional-style advertising appeals to the emotions.

Expectations disconfirmation. A key feature of the SERVQUAL model. Customer satisfaction is the *difference* between expected quality and perceived quality.

Experience curve. An empirical relationship between unit product cost and the firm's experience in making and distributing the product.

Experiment. A research approach where the researcher manipulates one or more independent variables to assess the impact on a dependent variable.

External orientation. A firm with this orientation focuses on customers, competitors, complementers, and factors in the external environment that could affect its future health.

Face time. The time a salesperson spends face-to-face with customers.

Family or masterbrand. The brand for a group of closely related products serving a similar function.

Feature or attribute. A characteristic, function, or property of the seller's offer.

Feature/benefit/value ladder. A hierarchy that joins the product's features with the benefits and values those features deliver to customers.

Features of services:
  Divisibility. A feature of services emphasizing that they often comprise a sequence of activities.
  Inseparability. A feature of services emphasizing that production and consumption occur simultaneously.
  Intangibility. A feature of services emphasizing that they have no physical presence. They cannot be touched, driven, flown, worn, kicked, batted, squashed, or sat upon.
  Perishability. A feature of services relating to *inseparability*. Services cannot be inventoried.
  Variability. A feature of services emphasizing a lack of consistency because of human involve-.ment in service delivery.

Financial analysis approaches. Methods for making resource decisions.
  Economic profit or economic value added (EVA). The firm's annual profit less an explicit charge for capital.
  Internal rate of return (IRR). A method of evaluating investment opportunities using future cash flows. IRR is the discount rate that equalizes cash inflows and cash outflows.
  Net present value (NPV). A method of evaluating investment opportunities using future cash flows. **NPV** is the monetary value from discounting cash flows at a predetermined rate, typically the firm's cost of capital.
  Payback. Payback is the forecast time to pay back the investment. In general, shorter paybacks are better than longer paybacks.
  Return on investment (ROI). ROI calculations project future accounting data. They compare the product's forecast rate of return with a target (or *hurdle*) rate.

Financial analysis perspective. Making resource allocations based on financial analysis.

Firewall brands. Brands that defend the firm's profitable products, sometimes termed *fighting brands.*

First-mover advantage. An advantage gained simply by being first. The firm may earn a leading reputation for quality.and/or gain superior market knowledge.

Five-forces model. A set of forces impinging on the firm:
> **Current direct competitors.** Satisfy customer needs by offering similar benefits with similar products, technology, or business models.
> **New direct entrants.** Offer similar products, but were not previously competitors.
> **Indirect competitors.** Satisfy similar customer needs by offering alternative products, technologies, or business models.
> **Suppliers.** Provide the firm's inputs.
> **Buyers.** Purchase the firm's products.

Floor price. The price below which a firm should never sell a product, typically the marginal cost.

Flower of customer service. Eight elements of customer service: safekeeping, order-taking, information, consultation, billing, payment, exceptions, and hospitality.

Focus group. A small number of people, typically eight to 12, assembled by a marketing researcher to secure insight into customers' needs and motivations.

Follower. A firm that enters after the pioneer has created a new market.

Forecasts, types of:
> **Market.** The predicted market-level sales in a future time period.
> **Sales.** The firm's predicted sales in a future time period:
>> **Bottom-up.** A forecast that starts with customer-by-customer forecasts.
>> **Synthetic.** A forecast that combines top-down and bottom-up forecasts.
>> **Top-down.** A forecast that starts with a market-size forecast.

Forward integration. A supplier undertakes activities currently performed by its customers.

Fragmented market. A market with many competitors.

Franchising. A distribution strategy in which the franchisor develops a business model. Franchisees agree to implement the franchisor's model and typically pay an initiation fee and ongoing fees.

Full-line forcing. See tying agreements.

Global account manager (GAM). A person responsible for the firm's most important global customers.

Global branding. A branding approach that uses a common brand around the world.

***Good* market segments.** Segments that satisfy five criteria: differentiated, identifiable, stable, appropriate size, and accessible.

Gray markets. A reseller offers the firm's product in a market at a price lower than the firm's price in that market.

Gross domestic product (GDP). A measure of the nation's economy based on its production of goods and services.

Gross profit. Sales revenues less cost of goods sold.

Gross rating points (GRPs) Combines reach and frequency. GRP = Reach × Frequency.

Growth path. Describes the route the firm or business unit takes to achieve its growth objectives. Nine individual approaches reduce to four basic options:
> **Market growth.** Engage related and new customers with existing products.
> **Market penetration.** Focus on existing products in existing markets.
> **Product and market diversification.** Bring new products to new customers.
> **Product growth.** Bring related and new products to existing customers.

Growth-share matrix. BCG's portfolio analysis system; dimensions are forecast long-run market growth rate and relative market share. Product types in the growth-share matrix are:

    Cash cows. High market shares in low growth markets; should generate cash.

    Dogs. Low market shares in low growth markets; many *dog* products have poor financial performance, but some are respectable.

    Stars. High market shares in high growth markets; comparatively rare. Many *stars* consume significant cash, but should create generous returns later.

    Problem children, question marks, lottery tickets, or wildcats. Low market shares in high growth markets. Need a lot of investment and are high risk.

Guerilla marketing. Word-of-mouth communication stimulated by the firm.

Harvest. The firm seeks short-term cash flow at the expense of sales and market share.

Hierarchy-of-effects models. Describes how advertising works for different types of products:

    High-involvement products. The purchase involves financial and/or psychosocial risks.

    Low-involvement products. The purchase involves little risk.

Hierarchy of needs. Developed by psychologist Maslow; needs are in five groups, ordered low to high — physiological, safety and security, social, ego, and self-actualization.

Hospitable market. A market that is attractive to the firm.

Human resource management (HRM). Processes for managing people including recruiting, selecting, training and development, work processes, talent management and career paths, and recognition and reward.

Hurdle rate. A minimum return that any investment opportunity must exceed.

Iceberg principle. An analogy to the iceberg whereby good aggregate performance in a unit or subunit can *hide* poor performance elsewhere in the same unit.

Idea library. A storage medium for ideas that were suggested and/or discussed but not used.

Imitation. Copying a competitor's strategy; often used in early-growth markets to surpass leaders.

Implementation (of growth strategy). Alternative approaches for the firm to achieve its objectives:

    Acquisition. The firm acquires another firm or a business unit.

    Equity investment. The firm takes an ownership position.

    Insourcing. The firm undertakes activities currently done by others.

    Internal development. The firm develops the opportunity in-house.

    Licensing and technology purchase. The firm secures access to technology developed by others. License — the original firm maintains ownership. Technology purchase — the firm gains ownership.

    Outsourcing. The firm secures other firms to undertake activities it previously conducted in-house so it can focus on higher return opportunities.

    Strategic alliance. Two firms join together to develop a stronger combined entity.

Implementation programs. Alternative approaches for the firm to achieve its objectives. In the context of market strategy, these include the marketing mix and other functional programs.

Independent inventors. Innovators working independently outside any corporate umbrella.

Indicators, types of:

    Leading. Help managers assess if they are on track to achieve planned results.

    Lagging. Measure what has already occurred.

Inhospitable market. A market that is unattractive to the firm.

Initial public offering (IPO). A company's first sale of stock to the public. Venture capitalists often sell equity stakes in an IPO.

Innovation. Endowing human and material resources with new and greater wealth-producing capacity.

Innovation, types of:

    Disruptive innovations. Developed from a new technology offering new and very different value propositions, initially for new applications and a limited number of new-to-the-market customers.

    Sustaining innovations. An innovation that improves the performance of established products along dimensions valued by mainstream customers.

Insight. Securing understanding of strengths and weaknesses in order to gain strategic perspectives. Three important types are:

    Competitive insight is the ability to describe, evaluate, project, and manage competitors.

    Company insight is the firm's understanding of itself — its advantages and disadvantages compared to the competition.

    Complementer insight is insight into any organization whose actions affect the firm's sales.

Integrated marketing communications. The integration of the firm's various communications efforts, using various tools, for various communications targets.

Internal architecture. The firm's organizational structure, systems and processes, and HRM practices.

Internal orientation. A firm with this orientation looks inward. It focuses on internal functions like finance, operations, sales, and technology (R&D), rather than external factors.

Intra-firm competition. A type of competition where different firm units compete with each other.

IPO. See initial public offering.

Just-in-time (JIT). An approach to reducing inventory by making raw materials and parts deliveries shortly before use in the production line.

Kenneling. The practice of purchasing low-share businesses in low growth markets and placing them together. The acquirer typically makes profits by rationalizing operations to achieve lower costs.

Kill point. A point where the firm must decide to proceed or drop the project.

Lead users. Organizations and individuals who think up, and may even prototype, new products.

Leapfrog. A way of surpassing the market leader by developing innovative and superior products, and/or entering emerging market segments; often used in early growth markets.

Leveraged buyout (LBO). Formation of a new firm when an existing firm spins off a business to a group of investors and/or management — a management buyout (MBO).

Life cycles. A common means for describing the evolution of markets and products. Product class and product form life cycles are typically partitioned into several stages:

    Introduction. The period from product launch until sales take off and grow at an accelerating rate. Total sales during introduction are generally low.

    Early growth. The period from sales take-off until the growth rate begins to slow.

    Late growth. Sales are still growing, but the rate of growth is slowing.

    Maturity. The sales growth rate ranges from flat to growth in gross national product (GNP).

    Decline. Overall sales decrease year by year.

Liquidate. Closing down a business and selling its assets.

Lock-in. The situation when customers are committed to buying from the firm. Lock-in customers have high **switching costs**.

Loyalty programs. Methods that firms use to enhance customer retention.

    Hard rewards. Denominated in dollars and cents, or translatable points.

    Soft rewards. Include toll-free information numbers, restaurant seating, theater ticket availability, hotel room and airline seat upgrades.

    Probabilistic rewards. The customer wins a large reward, or zero.

    Deterministic rewards. The customer accumulates points, then collects the reward.

Maintenance expenses. Expenses specifically designed to enhance customer retention.

Margin. Embraces many specific definitions based on revenues less costs.

Margin multiple. A quick way to calculate LTV if customer margin, customer retention rate, and discount rate are constant from time period to time period. LTV equals customer margin multiplied by the margin multiple.

Market. Customers — people and organizations — who require goods and services to satisfy their needs. Customers must have sufficient purchasing power and a willingness to pay for the products that suppliers offer.

Market-factor testing. A process for exploring the effect of one or more marketing-mix elements on expected sales. Typically performed in a simulated environment.

Market insight. The understanding firms secure about future market changes that lead to an appreciation of opportunities and threats.

Market levers. The actions the firm takes to achieve its performance standards.

Market occupancy ratio. A performance measure defined as the ratio of firm's number of customers to the total number of customers.

Market offer. The package of benefits and values the firm offers to customers.

Market-segment attractiveness. How attractive a segment is to the firm. An individual segment may be differentially attractive to different firms.

Market segmentation. A conceptual and analytic process for grouping actual and potential customers into market segments.

Market share. The most common market-based performance measure; compares the firm's sales units or revenues directly with competitors.

Market strategy. The firm's game plan for addressing the market.

Market structure. The market, products serving the market, and suppliers offering these products.

Market tinkering. An approach to new product development in which a firm makes minor modifications to its current products.

Marketing. There are several related meanings:

> **Philosophy.** Marketing as a guiding philosophy for the entire organization embraces an external orientation. It recognizes that revenues from customers are the critical source of cash flows.

> **Imperatives.** Marketing as six imperatives describes the specifics of the marketing job. These are the *must dos* of marketing.

> **Principles.** The firm must apply four marketing principles to do the marketing job well. They act as guidelines for making good marketing decisions based on the six imperatives.

> **American Marketing Association (AMA).** The AMA periodically redefines *marketing*. The 2004 definition stated, "Marketing is an organizational function and a set of processes for creating, communicating, and delivering value to customers and for managing customer relationships in ways that benefit the organization and its stakeholders." In 2007, the definition became, "Marketing is the activity, set of institutions, and processes for creating, communicating, delivering, and exchanging offerings that have value for customers, clients, partners, and society at large."

Marketing audit. A comprehensive process for evaluating the firm's marketing practices.

Marketing mix. The traditional description of the tools marketers use to construct an offer. They are often called the 4Ps—**p**roduct, **p**lace (distribution), **p**romotion, and **p**rice. Today, **s**ervice is often treated separately to form 4Ps and an **S**.

Marketing myopia. The tendency for firms to have such an overly narrow view of their market that they miss opportunities and/or fail to recognize threats.

Marketing principles. Guidelines for making good marketing decisions:

> **Selectivity and concentration.** Because resources are scarce, the firm should be selective in its choice of market and market segment. It should concentrate its resources against its chosen targets.

> **Customer value.** Success in target market segments depends on the firm's ability to provide customers with value.

Differential advantage. To be profitable, the firm must provide a net benefit, or cluster of benefits, to a sizable group of customers, that they value and are willing to pay for, but cannot get, or believe they cannot get, elsewhere. Competition eventually erodes away any differential advantage—the firm must continually renew its differential advantage.

Integration. The firm must carefully integrate and coordinate all elements in the design and execution of its market strategy. Integration includes elements of the marketing mix and the activities of all functions that play a role in delivering promised benefits.

Marketing research, types of:

Primary. The firm collects data for the specific purpose of the study.

Secondary. Based on data that has already been collected for another purpose.

Qualitative. A flexible and versatile approach comprising several techniques that is not concerned with numbers. Often used for exploratory studies.

Quantitative. A research approach that uses numerical data to test hypotheses.

Marketing research process. A rigorous methodology for improving the probability that investments in marketing research will produce actionable insights.

Mass communication. Communications intended to reach a large audience via mass media.

Mass customization. Related to segments-of-one. The firm customizes its products to individual requirements on a large scale.

Mass-market brand. A brand the firm targets at the mass market.

Means/ends tree. A diagrammatic method for outlining, assessing, and choosing among various alternatives.

Measures, types of:

Input. Focus on actions taken by the firm — leading indicators.

Intermediate. Focus on actions that customers take — leading indicators.

Output. Focus on performance variables like sales and profits — lagging indicators.

Hard. Objectively measured like sales volume, profit, and market performance.

Soft. Rating scale measures like customer satisfaction or attitudes.

Media class. A group of closely related media — newspapers, TV, and billboards are each media classes.

Media objectives. What the firm wants to accomplish with its media strategy:

Frequency. The average number of times a targeted individual is exposed to the advertising.

Impact. The effect of an advertising message on the target audience: Impact results from a combination of frequency, reach, and creativity.

Reach. The number of targeted individuals exposed to the advertising message at least once.

Duplicated reach. The portion of the target audience exposed to the advertising message from multiple media sources.

Unduplicated reach. The portion of the target audience exposed to the advertising message from a single source.

Media schedule. The placement and timing of advertisements for the advertising program.

Media vehicle. A specific exemplar of a media class — *The New York Times* and *60 Minutes* are each media vehicles.

Merger. Two firms join together to form a new entity.

Miscommunication. Misperception and/or misunderstanding by a *receiver* of a message the *sender* intended to send. Problems may occur in:

Encoding. Translating and interpreting the intended message into the actual sent message.

Distortion. Receiving a different message from the message that was sent.

Decoding. Misperceiving and/or misunderstanding the received message because of selective attention, distortion, and/or retention.

Mission. Guides the firm's search for opportunity so it can focus on a limited number of areas where it is likely to be successful.

Modularity. A design approach in which the firm uses common components (modules) to produce a broad product line.

Moment of truth. An interaction between a service customer and service personnel.

Monitor-and-control system. A process for measuring whether the firm's actions, individually and collectively, are consistent with its plan. Forms the basis for making adjustments.

Monolithic brand. The brand for a group of products fulfilling many different functions. A **corporate brand** — for the firm as a whole — is a special case of a monolithic brand.

Multi-branding. A brand architecture approach in which the firm uses multiple brands for its entries in various product classes.

Multifactor matrix. A portfolio analysis system that helps the firm decide which segments to target by assessing the attractiveness of market segments and the extent to which the firm possesses the business strengths to succeed.

Negative complementarity. The negative effect on sales of one product caused by customer dissatisfaction with another product.

Negative working capital. Working capital equals current assets minus current liabilities. Negative working capital implies that the firm's suppliers and/or customers are financing its operations.

Net Promoter Score (NPS). Widely used measure of customer satisfaction derived from a single question measured on a 0 to 10 scale: "How likely is it that you would recommend XXXX to a friend or colleague?"

New idea processes. Methods for generating new ideas:
  Structured thinking. Logical ways to create new product ideas.
  Unstructured thinking. A family of approaches that attempt to *break the mold* and develop totally new ideas by thinking *outside the box*.

Noncompete agreement. An employee agrees not to work for a direct competitor for a specified period of time after he or she leaves the company.

Nondisclosure agreement (NDA). Aka a confidentiality agreement; a contract promising to protect confidential data disclosed during employment or other business transaction.[1]

One-on-one interviews. A marketing research approach conducted by interviewing respondents individually.

One-sided advertising. Advertising that focuses only on the product's positive attributes.

Opportunity costs. Costs incurred by not taking a course of action. They are not out-of-pocket costs but represent forgone profits due to inaction.

Organization structures, types of:
  Business process. An outgrowth of re-engineering movement, the firm organizes around business processes.
  Category management. An evolutionary development of a product/brand management structure in which the firm manages multiple brands in a complementary manner.
  Combined product/brand management/market segment. Combines a product/brand focus with a market segment focus.
  Customer management. An organization focused specifically on customers.
  Functional marketing. The firm places activities like marketing research, distribution, advertising and promotion, marketing administration, and new product development in a marketing department. Other major functional areas are likewise in separate departments.
  Inclusion. The firm groups many activities together under marketing.
  Market segment. Managers are responsible for individual market segments.
  Traditional product/brand management. Product and brand managers develop market plans for their products and brands. They are responsible for volume, share, and/or profit — they compete for resources like advertising dollars and sales force time.

---

1 Definitions of noncompete and nondisclosure from *Everyday Law for Everyday People*, <www.nolo.com>.

Organizational orientations, types of:

   External. A firm with this orientation focuses on customers, competitors, complementers, and factors in the external environment that could affect its future health.

   Internal. A firm with this orientation looks inward. It focuses on internal functions like finance, operations, sales, and technology (R&D), rather than external factors.

   Financial. This firm is *run by the numbers* with scant regard for strategic issues. It avoids expenses with long-term payoff like R&D and marketing, in favor of increasing short-term profits. It often minimizes capital investment.

   Operations. This firm's culture revolves around operational efficiency; there is typically a shared belief that cost reduction and volume maximization will ensure success. The firm does not have a deep understanding of customers' needs.

   Sales. Maximizing short-term sales volume is the over-arching goal. This firm often cuts prices to secure orders, but does little forward planning. As markets evolve, broadly acceptable new products are not available.

   Technological (R&D). "Have technology, will travel—our technology will sell itself." This firm is often technologically sophisticated but rarely understands marketing and makes new product decisions with little or no customer input.

Outsourcing. When the firm engages a supplier to conduct an activity previously done inhouse.

Packaging communication. Communication delivered by the package containing the product.

Paid search. Online advertisers pay to appear next to and be associated with search results based on keywords. For example, an electronics retailer might pay to appear next to searches for HDTVs.

Panel. A group of respondents who agree to provide data over time.

Partnership model. An approach to distribution channel members that involves building cooperation and trust.

Penetration pricing. A long-run low-price strategy to grow a market and secure high market share.

Perceived customer value. The value the customer believes the firm is delivering.

Performance objectives. Describe the business results the firm hopes to achieve. A performance objective has two components:

   Strategic. The qualitative and directional results the firm wants to achieve. Strategic objectives typically fall into three categories: growth and market share, profitability, and cash flow.

   Operational. Quantitative statements of business results the firm hopes to achieve that relate directly to the strategic objectives. How much is required and by when.

Personal communication. Face-to-face communications with targeted individuals or groups.

PESTLE model. An acronym for identifying the environmental forces acting on an industry — Political, Economic, Sociocultural, Technological, Legal, and Environmental (Physical).

Pioneer. A firm that creates new markets and is the first, or among the first, with a new product form.

Pipeline analysis. A method for tracking the firm's performance at different selling process stages.

Pocket price. The amount of money the firm actually receives — in its pocket.

Portfolio analysis. A method of evaluating investment opportunities that arrays the firm's products in two dimensions.

Portfolio approach. Individual products play different roles in the firm's portfolio. Some products generate growth and market share, some products earn profits, and some deliver cash flow.

Positioning. The heart of the market strategy that should create a unique and favorable image in the minds of target customers. Positioning requires four key decisions: select customer targets, frame competitor targets, design the value proposition, and articulate the reasons to believe.

Potentials, types of:

   Market. The maximum market-level sales that the firm expects in a future time period.

   Sales. The maximum sales that the firm could achieve in a future time period.

Power. The ability of one channel member to get another to do what it wants it to do.

Predatory pricing. Pricing below cost with the intent to eliminate a competitor.

Pre-emptive. Acting before competitors.

Preliminary screening. The first stage for eliminating new product ideas.

Price bases. The ways in which a firm can set prices such as by individual product, by use, or by results.

Price discretion. The firm's ability to use several pricing approaches. Firms that offer high value but also have low costs enjoy the most price discretion.

Price discrimination. Setting different prices for the same product to different segments or customers.

Price management. Organizing the firm to make its strategic and tactical pricing decisions.

Price sensitivity. Degree of change in volume related to change in price:
> **Price-elastic market.** Volume *increases/decreases* significantly as price *decreases/increases*.
> **Price-inelastic market.** Volume is *relatively insensitive* to price changes.

Price setting, types of:
> **Competitive-driven pricing.** Pricing based on competitors' prices.
> **Cost-plus pricing.** Setting price by identifying costs and adding a *satisfactory* profit margin.
> **Customer-driven pricing.** Customers name the prices they are prepared to pay. If the product is available, they must complete the purchase.
> **Deceptive pricing.** False prices and prices that might confuse or mislead customers.
> **Fees and surcharges.** Extra charges such as bank fees for ATM use or airline fees for checked bags.
> **Flat-rate pricing.** Pricing for a fixed time period. **Variable-rate pricing.** Pricing by use.
> **Loss-leader pricing.** Retailers deliberately take losses to build customer traffic.
> **Psychological pricing.** A common retail practice of pricing just below a *benchmark* number, like $9.95 or $9.99 versus $10.00.
> **Topsy-turvy pricing.** The supplier receives additional value from a customer so that suppliers pay a price, rather than customers.
> **Transfer pricing.** A price set for transactions among a firm's business units.
> **Variable pricing.** Setting different prices for different customers/segments.

Price skimming. A strategy of setting high prices even though costs are falling. Often used in the early stages of the product life cycle.

Price waterfall. The reduction, by discounts and allowances, from list price to pocket price.

Pricing, and transportation:
> **CIF (carriage, insurance, freight).** The supplier pays the cost, insurance, and freight.
> **FOB (free on board).** The customer pays freight, insurance, and other charges.

Pricing strategy. The firm's overall approach to setting prices; should be based on four considerations — perceived customer value, costs, competition, and strategic objectives:
> **Penetration pricing.** The firm sets prices close to costs as it seeks growth and market share.
> **Skim pricing.** The firm keeps prices high to secure high margins.

Pricing toolkit. A set of pricing tactics for the firm to change a product's price.

Product. Sometimes *product* refers to the core offer, both *physical products* and *services*. We use this shorthand in much of the book. But tangible physical products can be touched, worn, kicked, or sat upon; a service cannot.

Product, types of:
> **Product class.** A set of products offered by competing suppliers that serve a set of customer needs in a roughly similar manner.
> **Product form.** A group of products offered by competing suppliers that are more closely similar in the way they meet customer needs than products in a product class.
> **Product item.** A uniquely identified product offered by the firm.
> **Product line.** A group of related products offered by the firm.

Product cannibalization. Sales of the firm's lower margin product decrease sales of a higher margin product.

Product complementarity. Relationships among the firm's products. **Positive complementarity** occurs when one product helps another; **negative complementarity** when one product hurts another.

Product concept. A description of a product idea that details the benefits and values the product should deliver to customers.

Product portfolio. Describes the set of products that the firm or business unit offers.

Product portfolio imbalance. The firm's products are misbalanced between resource generating and resource consuming. In the growth/share matrix, this imbalance refers to cash flows.

Product proliferation. The firm offers a large number of products. Often viewed as undesirable, but can act as a barrier against competitive entry. Sometimes confused with market segmentation.

Profit contribution. The extent to which the product's sales revenues exceed variable costs.

Publicity. Communication for which the firm does not pay, typically via the press.

Public relations (PR). Communication that embraces publicity but is broader — includes other ways of managing the firm's image to gain favorable responses.

Pull. A communications approach that focuses on indirect customers.

Push. A communications approach that focuses on direct customers.

Quasi-personal communication (QPC). Interaction and feedback without human involvement, usually via artificial intelligence software.

Reasons to believe. Claims that support the firm's value proposition. Should provide compelling evidence to make the firm's claims believable.

Recommendation systems. Software that enables a firm to make personal recommendations to customers based on their prior purchases or browsing behavior on the Internet, or personal or social characteristics.

Re-engineering. Examines fundamental assumptions about the way the firm conducts its activities. Seeks alternative approaches for redesigning and improving the firm's processes.

Reference groups. Individuals and groups that influence customers in their decision-making:
    Primary. Include family members and organizational work groups.
    Secondary. Include club and church members and professional organizations.
    Aspirational. Those to which the customer would like to belong.

Relative market share (RMS). A dimensionless ratio used in the growth-share matrix; the firm's market share divided by the nearest competitor's market share.

Resale price maintenance (RPM). A distribution practice where suppliers set the prices at which retailers can sell their products. Following a 2007 Supreme Court decision, RPM is legal in the U.S., but is illegal in many other countries.

Retention rate (r). The rate at which the firm retains customers from one time period to the next. Sometimes calculated as a probability. The opposite of defection rate.

Reward system. The way to compensate salespeople for their efforts and performance. Includes elements like financial compensation, recognition, and promotions and work assignments.

Sales approach. The essential message that the salesperson delivers to customers.

Sales force management tasks. Six related jobs that sales managers must complete to be effective.
    Task 1. Set and achieve sales objectives.
    Task 2. Determine and allocate selling effort.
    Task 3. Develop sales approaches.
    Task 4. Design the sales organization.
    Task 5. Create critical organizational processes.
    Task 6. Staff the sales organization.

Sales forecast. The firm's predicted sales in a future time period:
  Bottom-up. A forecast that starts with customer-by-customer forecasts.
  Top-down. A forecast that starts with a market-size forecast.

Sales objectives. The firm's desired results — typically stated in terms of sales revenues, sales units, or profit contribution.

Sales potential. The maximum sales that the firm could achieve in a future time period.

Sales promotion (SP). Activities providing extra customer value, often for immediate sales. Includes:

  Trade shows. Products displayed to large numbers of customers at one time.

  Product placement. Products placed in movies and TV shows.

Sales quotas. Sales objectives stated in terms of specific performance requirements.

Sales response function. The relationship between selling effort and sales results.

Sales territory. A set of customers or geographic area assigned to an individual salesperson.

Salesperson workload. The effort a salesperson must expend to complete assigned activities; a key variable for designing sales territories.

Scanner data. Purchase data collected electronically at point of sale, typically from bar codes (product/service identifiers).

Scenario. A descriptive narrative of how the future may evolve for a plausible option.

Screening criteria. Aids for evaluating and selecting opportunities. Important screening criteria are:
  Objectives. What does the firm seek to achieve by investing in the opportunity?
  Compatibility (or fit). Can the firm successfully address the opportunity?
  Core competence. Can the firm use its core competencies or gain new core competencies?
  Synergy. Can the firm use existing resources and earn greater returns than a standalone entry?
  Contribution to the venture portfolio. Does the opportunity add positively to the set of opportunities the firm is pursuing?

Search engine optimization. An element of search marketing strategy whose goal is to move the firm's website link as high up the ranking list as possible.

Secondary market. Resale of a product or service. Most financial markets are secondary markets.

Segment-of-one. The firm addresses customers individually by developing customized offers.

Selling effort. The demands of the sales job. Methods to estimate required selling effort include:
  Single-factor model. Uses a simple classification of customer importance.
  Portfolio model. A more complex approach for estimating required selling effort.

Sentiment analysis. The analysis of text to determine its polarity. Used by firms to examine comments about their brands in social media.

Service. Any act or performance that one party can offer another that is essentially intangible and does not result in the ownership of anything. Anything that cannot be dropped on your foot.

Service equipment. Physical products needed to perform the service.

Service facilities. Where the firm produces the service. These facilities can be:
  Offstage. Out of the customers' sight.
  Onstage. Where customers experience deeds, performances, or efforts.

Service guarantee. A promise about the service experience that includes elements of value if the firm does not keep its promise.

Service personnel. People who provide the service.

Service quality. The extent to which the firm's service performance exceeds customers' expectations.

SERVQUAL. A popular model and measurement device for service quality based on several *gaps*.

Shadow system. Securing competitive information by having executives *shadow* specific competitors.

Shareholder value. The total value to shareholders—market capitalization—is measured by the market price of the firm's shares times the number of shares outstanding. Increasing shareholder value has become a mantra for many firms.

Shareholder-value perspective. Management's job is to maximize returns for shareholders. The shareholder-value perspective is prevalent in many capitalist countries—particularly in the U.S.

Signal. Information the firm sends to competitors, hoping they will process the information and act accordingly.

Six Sigma. A data-driven methodology for eliminating defects in any process.

SKU. See stock-keeping unit.

Slotting fees. Payments that suppliers make to retailers for providing shelf space for their products.

SMART goals. Goals that are **s**pecific, **m**easurable, **a**chievable, **r**ealistic, and **t**imely.

Social media. Online tools and platforms that allow Internet users to collaborate on content, share insights and experiences, and connect for business or pleasure. Involves multimedia and includes blogs, wikis, photo and video sharing, forums, and networks for meeting like-minded people.

Spam. Unsolicited and unwanted e-mail messages.

Span of control. The ratio of subordinates to supervisors. For example, a sales manager supervising 10 salespeople would be a span of 10-to-1.

Special relationships. Informal economic relationships between the firm and other entities such as government agencies, political parties, and public interest groups, as well as suppliers and customers.

Stage-gate approach. A systematic process for condensing a large number of ideas to a few products the firm can successfully launch. After each **stage**, the idea or project must pass through a **gate** (meet or exceed a standard) to continue. Each gate is a **kill point** where the firm must decide whether to proceed or drop the project.

Standalone brand. An individual brand with no apparent relationship to any other firm brand.

Standards. The firm's planned results; criteria against which the firm measures its performance.

Stock-keeping unit (sku). A unique identifier assigned to a specific product or service.

Strategic account manager (SAM). A person responsible for the firm's most important customers.

Strategic (or key) accounts. Customers that provide the highest levels of current and/or potential sales and profits.

Strategic alliance. A cooperative arrangement that pools the strengths of individual partner firms. Strategic alliances range in formality from a new joint-venture firm to temporary, informal arrangements.

Strategic focus. Selected from a tree of alternatives and states broadly how the firm will achieve its performance objectives.

Strategic options. A variety of alternatives, each requiring significant investment, among which the firm must choose.

Strategic sourcing. A discipline of specially designed systems and processes for reducing the costs of purchased materials and services.

Strategy for growth. A set of frameworks that helps the firm decide which businesses to be in and which businesses not to be in. Includes vision, mission, growth path, and timing of entry.

Supply chain. A coordinated system of organizations, people, activities, information, and resources that move a product or service, physically or virtually, from supplier to customer.

Survey. A common technique for securing data by asking respondents questions.

Switching costs. The costs that a customer must incur to switch from one supplier to another. Customers with high switching costs experience **lock-in**.

Synergy. Occurs when the combined effect of two or more elements is greater than the sum of their separate effects — **positive synergy**. If the combined effect is less than the sum of the separate effects, there is **negative synergy**.

Systems, types of:

    Hard. Based on information technology.

    Soft. Based on employees.

Systems integrators. Firms that install, service, and integrate software from many vendors.

Tactical pricing. The ongoing stream of pricing decisions the firm makes on a daily basis.

Target audience. The audience that the firm is trying to reach with its advertising.

Targeting. Deciding the market segments against which the firm should concentrate its resources.

Technology, types of:
> **Disruptive technology.** A new technology offering new and very different value propositions, initially for new applications and a limited number of new-to-the-market customers.
> **Sustaining technology.** A new technology that improves the performance of established products along dimensions valued by mainstream customers.

Telemarketing/Telesales. Communication by telephone, usually viewed as a subset of personal communication:
> **Inbound.** Initiated by the customer.
> **Outbound.** Initiated by the firm.

Test marketing. Tests a full-scale product launch on a limited basis.

Timing of entry. Denotes alternative entry stages in the product form life cycle:
> **Pioneer.** Creates new markets.
> **Follow-the-leader.** Enters markets when they are growing rapidly.
> **Segmenter.** Enters in the late-growth stage by matching offers to emerging customer needs.
> **Me-too.** Enters mature markets.

Timing pattern. When the advertising will appear. The major options are:
> **Continuous.** A regular periodic advertising pattern.
> **Flighting.** Repeated high advertising levels followed by low (or no) advertising.
> **Pulsing.** Continuous and flighting advertising combined, within a single media vehicle or class or across multiple media vehicles and classes.

Tracking study. A method of securing research data. In a tracking study, aka a longitudinal study, a panel of individuals agrees to provide responses periodically over time.

Two-sided advertising. Presents both pro and con messages for a product as a way of gaining credibility.

Tying agreements. Strong suppliers *force* resellers to sell their entire product line. This practice is illegal in the U.S. if it reduces competition.

Umbrella branding. A brand architecture approach in which the firm uses a monolithic brand for several products, like a corporate brand.

Upstream. The firm's suppliers and its suppliers' suppliers, etc.

Value-added resellers (VARs). Firms that build additional software modules onto other firms' platforms and modify hardware for niche markets.

Value proposition. The heart of positioning that provides a convincing answer to a deceptively simple question: Why should target customers prefer the firm's offer to competitors' offers?

Values, types of. A common set of beliefs that guide the behavior of the firm's employees. Values can be:
> **Hard,** like profitability and market share.
> **Soft,** like integrity, respect for others, trust, and customer pre-eminence.

Venture capitalists. Individuals and firms that provide funds for new early-stage businesses.

Venture portfolio. The set of opportunities the firm decides to pursue.

Viral marketing. Marketing techniques that use pre-existing social networks to convey marketing messages.

Vision. A description of an ideal future state; an impressionistic picture of what the future should be:
> **Corporate vision.** Focuses on the firm
> **Business-unit vision.** Focuses on the business.

Wiki. A website that allows user to easily create and edit interlinked websites. Uses include creating collaborative websites, powering community websites, and for knowledge management systems.

Winback. Securing sales from a customer that previously defected.

Word-of-mouth (WOM) communication. Communication between and among current and potential customers.

Yield management. Continuous price adjustments based on demand and available capacity.

IMAGE CREDITS

CHAPTER 1

4 Cup courtesy of Starbucks

CHAPTER 2

18 Courtesy of Royal Bank of Canada

21 Reprinted by permission from F.F. Reicheld, *The Loyalty Effect*, Boston, MA: Harvard Business School, 1996, p. 51.

CHAPTER 3

40 Reprinted by permission from M.E. Porter, *Competitive Strategy: Techniques for Analyzing Industries and Competitors*, New York: Free Press, 1980.

CHAPTER 4

50 Logo used by permission of Inter IKEA Systems B.V.

CHAPTER 5

66 Courtesy of Boeing and Airbus

CHAPTER 6

84 Reprinted by permission of Thomson Corporation.

CHAPTER 7

106 Courtesy of Zipcar

CHAPTER 8

120 Logos courtesy of Marriott International

CHAPTER 9

136 Courtesy of Mayo Clinic

CHAPTER 10

152 all Courtesy of Ryanair

CHAPTER 11

140 SAP is the trademark or registered trademark of SAP AG in Germany and several other countries and is used by permission of SAP AG.

171 l Pepsi and the Pepsi Globe design are registered trademarks of Pepsico. Used by permission.

171 lm Dunkin' Brands Inc.

171 rm Poland Spring Water, Division of Nestlé Waters North America

171 r © Miller Brewing. Used by permission.

174 l FedEx service marks used by permission.

174 lm Courtesy of GE

174 rm Courty of IBM

174 r Courtesy of Caterpillar Inc.

CHAPTER 12

188 all Reprinted by permission of Procter & Gamble

CHAPTER 13

200 all Courtesy of Celebrity Cruises

207 V.A. Zeithaml, L.L. Berry, and A. Parasuraman, "The Behavioral Consequences of Service Quality," *Journal of Marketing*, 60 (April 1996), pp. 31-46. Reprinted by permission of American Marketing Association.

209 Courtesy of Christopher Lovelock

CHAPTER 14

214 Logo reprinted by permission of Thomson Corporation

225 Reprinted by permission from G.A. Moore, *Crossing the Chasm*, New York: HarperCollins, p. 12. © 1991 by G.A. Moore and Levine Greenberg Literary Agency.

CHAPTER 15

228 Courtesy of California Milk Advisory Board

CHAPTER 16

238 Courtesy MasterCard

242 l Under permission by V&S Vin & Spirit AB. ABSOLUT®VODKA. ABSOLUT COUNTRY OF SWEDEN VODKA & LOGO, ABSOLUT, ABSOLUT BOTTLE DESIGN AND ABSOLUT CALLIGRAPHY ARE TRADEMARKS OWNED BY V&S VIN & SPIRIT AB. © 1998 V&S Vin & Spirit AB. Photograph by Steve Bronstein.

242 r Under permission by V&S Vin & Spirit AB. ABSOLUT®VODKA. ABSOLUT COUNTRY OF SWEDEN VODKA & LOGO, ABSOLUT, ABSOLUT BOTTLE DESIGN AND ABSOLUT CALLIGRAPHY ARE TRADEMARKS OWNED BY V&S VIN & SPIRIT AB. © 1995 V&S Vin & Spirit AB.

CHAPTER 17

259 Permission by Honeywell Business Solutions

CHAPTER 18

276 Courtesy of Cisco

CHAPTER 19

290 Courtesy of Southwest Airlines

CHAPTER 20

302 Courtesy of Oracle Corporation

CHAPTER 21

316 Courtesy of Sony Electronics

CHAPTER 22

332 Courtesy of Bristol-Myers Squibb

CHAPTER 23

346 Courtesy of DHL

INDEX

SUBJECT INDEX

Locators beginning with "G" indicate terms defined in the glossary.